AF522562

[In]Complete Justice? The Supreme Court at 75

Critical Reflections

Edited by

S Muralidhar

[In]Complete Justice?
The Supreme Court at 75

Critical Reflections

Edited by

S Muralidhar

Assisted by
Ninni Susan Thomas
Maitreya Subramanium

JUGGERNAUT BOOKS
C-I-128, First Floor, Sangam Vihar, Near Holi Chowk,
New Delhi 110080, India

First published by Juggernaut Books 2025

10 9 8 7 6 5 4 3

P-ISBN: 9789353452926
E-ISBN: 9789353458690

The views and opinions expressed in this book are the authors' own. The facts contained herein were reported to be true as on the date of publication by the editor to the publishers of the book, and the publishers are not in any way liable for their accuracy or veracity.

Typeset in Adobe Caslon Pro by R. Ajith Kumar, Noida

Printed at Thomson Press India Ltd

The Editor's royalties from the sale of this book will be contributed to Vanavil Trust, which supports the education and empowerment of women and children from Tamil Nadu's Nomadic Tribes.

Contents

Part II: The Court and Criminal Law: Practice and Procedure

Part III: The Court and Equality

Part IV: The Court and Substantive Laws

Table of Abbreviations

Additional Solicitors General for India	ASG
Advocate-on-Record	AOR
Aligarh Muslim University	AMU
All-India Trade Union Congress	AITUC
Alternative Dispute Resolution	ADR
Annual Confidential Reports	ACRs
Artificial Intelligence	AI
Attorney General for India	AG
Bar Council of India	BCI
Bharat Sanchar Nigam Limited	BSNL
Bharatiya Janata Party	BJP
Bharatiya Nagarik Suraksha Sanhita, 2023	BNSS
Bharatiya Nyaya Sanhita, 2023	BNS
Brain Electrical Activation Profile	BEAP
Case Information System	CIS
Central Bureau of Investigation	CBI
Code of Civil Procedure/Central Project Co-ordinator	CPC
Central Vigilance Commission	CVC
Centrally Empowered Committee	CEC
Centrally Sponsored Scheme	CSS
Centre for Development of Advanced Computing	C-DAC
Chief Justice	CJ
Chief Justice of India	CJI

Chief Minister	CM
Child Welfare Committee	CWC
Code of Civil Procedure, 1908	CPC
Code of Criminal Procedure, 1973	CrPC
Committee on the Elimination of Discrimination Against Women	CEDAW
Common Law Admission Test	CLAT
Common Service Centre	CSC
Constitution Benches	CBs
Crime and Criminal Tracking Networks and Systems	CCTNS
Curriculum Development Centre	CDC
Data Protection and Privacy Act, 2023	DPDP Act
Dental Council of India	DCI
Department of Justice	DoJ
Designing Innovative Solutions for Holistic Access to Justice	DISHA
Digital Supreme Court Reports	Digi SCR
Directive Principles of State Policy	DPSP
Director General of Police	DGP
Directorate of Enforcement	ED
District Child Protection Unit	DCPU
District Committees for the Protection of Child Rights	DCPCR
District Court Digitization Centres	DCDCs
District Legal Services Authority	DLSA
Double Tax Avoidance Convention, 1983	DTAC
Double Taxation Avoidance Agreement	DTAA
Economically Weaker Sections	EWS
Eco-Sensitive Zones	ESW
e-High Court Reports	e-HCR
Election Commission of India	ECI

Electronic Case Management Tools	ECMT
Environmental Impact Assessment	EIA
Exclusive POCSO	e-POCSO
Expert Appraisal Committee	EAC
Fact Check Unit	FCU
Fast and Secured Transmission of Electronic Records	FASTER
Fast Track Courts	FTCs
Fast Track Special Courts	FTSCs
First Information Report	FIR
Free and Open Source Software	FOSS
Free, Prior and Informed Consent	FPIC
General Agreement on Tariffs and Trade	GATT
Goan People's Party	GPP
Government Electronic Market	GeM
Government of India	GoI
Gujarat Control of Terrorism and Organised Crimes Act, 2015	GujCTOCA
High Court Collegium	HCC
High Court	HC
Hindu Undivided Family	HUF
Increasing Diversity by Increasing Access	IDIA
India International University of Legal Education and Research	IIULER
Indian Law Institute	ILI
Indian National Congress	INC
Indian Penal Code, 1860	IPC
In-House Procedure	IHP
Intelligence Bureau	IB
Internal Complaints Committees	ICC
International Covenant on Civil and Political Rights	ICCPR

International Labour Organization	ILO
Internet of Things	IoT
Inter-Operable Criminal Justice System	ICJS
Inter-State Migrant Workers Act, 1979	ISMW Act
Janata Party	JP
Judicial Appointments Commission	JAC
Judicial Service Centres/Judicial Service Commission	JSC
Juvenile Justice Committees	JJCs
Labour Appellate Tribunal	LAT
Law Commission of India	LCI
Leader of the Opposition	LoP
Legal Services Authorities	LSAs
Legal Services Authorities Act	LSAA
Liberalization, Privatization and Globalization	LPG
Life Insurance Corporation of India	LIC
Litigation Management System	LMS
Local Area Network	LAN
Machine Learning	ML
Maha Vikas Aghadi	MVA
Maharashtrawadi Gomantak Party	MGP
Maoist Community Centre	MCC
Medical Council of India	MCI
Members of Legislative Assemblies	MLAs
Members of Parliament	MPs
Memorandum of Procedure	MoP
Minimum Support Price	MSP
Ministry of Electronics and Information Technology	MeitY
Ministry of Environment and Forests	MoEF
Most Favoured Nation	MFN
National Commission of Farmers	NCF

National Company Law Tribunal	NCLT
National Core	NC
National Council of Applied Economic Research	NCAER
National Court Management Systems	NCMS
National Democratic Alliance	NDA
National Eligibility cum Entrance Test	NEET
National Green Tribunal	NGT
National Human Rights Commission	NHRC
National Informatics Centre	NIC
National Informatics Centre Network	NICNET
National Judicial Academy	NJA
National Judicial Appointments Commission	NJAC
National Judicial Digital Grid	NJDG
National Knowledge Network	NKN
National Law School's Admission Test	NLSAT
National Law School of India University	NLSIU
National Law University	NLU
National Legal Services Authority	NALSA
National Security Act, 1980	NSA
National Service and Tracking of Electronic Processes	NSTEP
Nationalist Congress Party	NCP
Non-Miscellaneous Day	NMD
Organization for Economic Co-operation and Development	OECD
Other Backward Classes	OBCs
People's Union for Democratic Rights	PUDR
Persons with Disabilities	PwDs
Prime Minister	PM
Progressive Democratic Front	PDF
Provincial Armed Constabulary	PAC
Public Interest Litigation	PIL

Public Private Partnership	PPP
Rarest of Rare test	R-R test
Research and Analysis Wing	R&AW
Right to Information	RTI
Royal Commission of Labour	RCL
Scheduled Castes	SCs
Scheduled Tribes	STs
Shiv Sena Legislature Party	SSLP
Social Action Litigation	SAL
Social Justice Bench	SJB
Solicitor General of India	SG
Special Investigation Team	SIT
Special Leave Petition	SLP
State Judicial Academies	SJAs
State List	List II
State Pollution Control Board	SPCB
State-Wide Area Network	SWAN
Strategic Litigation Against Public Participation	SLAPP
Structured Query Language	SQL
Supreme Court Bar Association	SCBA
Supreme Court Collegium	SCC
Supreme Court Legal Services Committee	SCLSC
Supreme Court of India	SCI
Supreme Court Reporter	e-SCR
Tata Consulting Services	TCS
Tax Deduction at Source	TDS
Telugu Desam Party	TDP
The Great Indian Bustard	GIB
Union List	List I
Union Minister of Law and Justice	MLJ

Union Ministry of Home Affairs	MHA
Union Public Service Commission	UPSC
United Kingdom	UK
United States	US
University Grants Commission	UGC
Vice-Chancellor	VC
Virtual Private Network	VPN
Visual Basic	VB
Vulnerable Witnesses Deposition Centres	VWDC
World Trade Organization	WTO

About the Authors

Amit George is an Advocate practicing before the High Court of Delhi and the Supreme Court of India, and frequently appears before various arbitral tribunals in domestic and international arbitrations. He read law at NALSAR, Hyderabad, and went on to earn an LL.M. (with merit) from the University of London International Programmes, with a specialization in International Dispute Resolution and a Ph.D. in law from the National Law University (NLU), Delhi. He is the author of the book titled *Minority Rights in a Cosmopolitan World*, and frequently contributes opinion pieces and articles on contemporary legal issues.

Justice Ajit Prakash Shah was a judge of the Bombay High Court from December 1992 to November 2005. He was the Chief Justice of the Madras High Court from November 2005 to May 2008 and the Delhi High Court from May 2008 to February 2010. Thereafter, he served as the founding Chairperson of the Broadcasting Content Complaints Council from 2011 to November 2013 and Chairperson of the Law Commission of India from November 2013 to August 2015.

Arvind P Datar began his practice in the High Court of Madras in 1980. He was designated as a Senior Advocate in 2000. He has argued several landmark cases of constitutional importance in the Supreme Court of India. He is the author of several treatises on indirect taxes, direct taxes and constitutional law. He is also a qualified cost and works accountant.

Professor Faizan Mustafa graduated in law from the Aligarh Muslim University (AMU) and taught law there for many years. He was the Vice-Chancellor of the National Law University, Orissa, and The National Academy of Legal Studies and Research, Hyderabad. From 2023 onwards, he has been the Vice-Chancellor of Chanakya National Law University, Patna. He is a prolific writer and author of several books including *Conversion: Constitutional and Legal Implications*.

Gautam Bhatia is a practicing lawyer. He was awarded a doctorate by the University of Oxford in 2021. He is the author of several authoritative legal texts as well as science fiction. His books include *Offend, Shock or Disturb: Free Speech Under the Indian Constitution*, *Unsealed Covers: A Decade of the Constitution, the Courts and the State* and more recently, *The Indian Constitution: A Conversation with Power*. He hosts a blog on constitutional law titled 'Constitutional Law and Philosophy'.

Justice Gautam Patel was a lawyer of the Bombay High Court, specializing in environmental law and commercial, corporate and civil litigation. He was a judge of that High Court from 2013 to April 2024. He is one of the contributors to an edited collection titled *On Citizenship*.

Gopal Subramanium was designated as Senior Advocate by the Supreme Court of India at the young age of 35, and served as the Additional Solicitor General of India from 2005 to 2009, and as Solicitor General of India from 2009 to 2011. He was also the Chairperson of the Bar Council of India from 2010 to 2011. He is a highly regarded legal professional who is in active practice both in India as well as the United Kingdom.

Indira Jaising commenced her law practice in the High Court of Bombay in 1964. She is a Senior Advocate practising before the Supreme Court of India for over five decades. She was the Additional Solicitor General for India between 2009 and 2014. In 2008, she was elected as a representative of India to the United Nations's Committee on the Elimination of Discrimination Against Women (CEDAW). She is the founder of the *Lawyers Collective*, an organization of lawyers rendering legal services and handling a variety of social action litigation. She is the co-founder, along with Anand Grover, of *The Leaflet*, an online law magazine.

Justice K Chandru was a lawyer who practised law predominantly in the areas of human rights and labour law in the High Court of Madras. He was designated as a Senior Advocate in 1996 and later served as a judge of that High Court from July 2006 to 2013. Thereafter, he has been the one-person commission to examine the issues of caste violence in Tamil Nadu's schools and the state of juvenile homes, special homes and places of safety. He is the author of a number of books, including *Listen to My Case! When Women Approach the Courts of Tamil Nadu*.

Professor Kamala Sankaran currently teaches at the National Law School of India University, Bengaluru. She has previously taught at the Faculty of Law, University of Delhi, and at the Jamia Milia Islamia. She has served as the Vice-Chancellor, Tamil Nadu National Law University, Tiruchirappalli, and as Research Professor, Indian Law Institute, New Delhi. She has researched and published in the areas of constitutional law, international labour standards and the regulation of work.

Justice Madan Lokur was a judge of the High Court of Delhi, and the Chief Justice of the High Courts of Guwahati and (undivided) Andhra Pradesh. He was a judge of the Supreme Court of India from June 2012 to December 2018. Thereafter, he was a judge in the Supreme Court of the Republic of Fiji for two terms and has recently been appointed Chairperson of the United Nations Internal Justice Council.

Meenakshi Arora commenced her practice in 1985, topped the exam to qualify as an Advocate-on-Record at the Supreme Court of India in 1989, and was designated as Senior Advocate in 2013 by the Supreme Court of India.

Professor Mohan Gopal graduated from the Faculty of Law, University of Delhi, and holds a doctorate in law and LL.M. from Harvard Law School. He served at the Asian Development Bank as Chief Counsel at the World Bank, and is a former Vice-Chancellor of the National Law School of India University, Bangalore. He was also the Director of the National Judicial Academy and a founder chair (2012 to 2019) of the National Court Management Systems Committee instituted by the Supreme Court of India.

Nitya Ramakrishnan is a Senior Advocate. Besides articles and essays on diverse subjects, she is also the author of the book *In Custody: Law, Impunity, and Prisoner Abuse in South Asia*, published by SAGE Law.

P Sainath is a highly regarded journalist who has worked in print media for several decades writing exclusively on rural India. He runs an organization known as People's Archive of Rural India. He is a recipient of several awards including the 2007 Ramon Magsaysay Award for Journalism Literature and Creative Communications Arts. He is the author of the classic *Everybody Loves a Good Drought*, and more recently, *The Last Heroes: Foot Soldiers of Indian Freedom*.

Raju Ramachandran practices in the Supreme Court of India as a Senior Advocate, and has been a lawyer for four decades. He was the Additional Solicitor General from 2002 to 2004, and is the author of several books including *Professional Ethics for Lawyers* and *I've Been Around for Some Time – Analyses, Reflections and Reminiscences.*

Rebecca Mammen John mainly practices in the area of criminal law. She commenced her practice in the Delhi High Court in 1988 and was designated as a Senior Advocate in 2013. She is a prolific writer and speaker.

Rohan J Alva is an arguing counsel practising before the Supreme Court of India and the High Court of Delhi. He is a prolific writer on issues primarily in the field of constitutional law. He is the author of *Liberty After Freedom: A History of Article 21, Due Process and the Constitution of India* and *A Constitution to Keep: Sedition and Free Speech in Modern India.*

Justice S Muralidhar enrolled as an Advocate in Chennai in 1984 and shifted his law practice to New Delhi in 1987. He was an Advocate-on-Record in the Supreme Court of India till his elevation as a Judge of the High Court of Delhi in May 2006. He was Chief Justice of the High Court of Orissa from January 2021 till his retirement in August 2023. He has authored a book titled *Law Poverty and Legal Aid: Access to Criminal Justice.* He was awarded a PhD by the University of Delhi in 2002.

Justice S Ravindra Bhat practised before the Supreme Court of India as an Advocate-on-Record till his elevation as a judge of the High Court of Delhi in 2004. He served as Chief Justice of the High Court of Rajasthan, and subsequently, as a judge of the Supreme Court of India between September 2019 and October 2023. He is the Chair of Comparative Constitutional Law Studies at the M.K. Nambyar SAARC Law Centre for Advanced Legal Studies at the NALSAR University of Law, Hyderabad.

Sriram Panchu is a Senior Advocate practising before the High Court of Madras and the Supreme Court of India. He was designated as a Senior Advocate in 1996. He is among the pioneers of the mediation movement in India and is the author of *Settle for More: The Why, How and When of Mediation.*

Suhrith Parthasarathy practises before both the High Court of Madras and the Supreme Court of India, having enrolled in 2008. He also holds a degree in journalism from Columbia University Graduate School of Journalism, and is a regular contributor on legal issues to various newspapers and journals.

Professor Upendra Baxi is among the foremost legal scholars in India and has taught law at the University of Delhi for over three decades. He was its Vice-Chancellor from 1990 to 1994. He is an Emeritus Professor of Law at the Universities of Warwick and Delhi, and has taught at Sydney University, Duke University, American University (Washington School of Law), New York Law School and Toronto University, among others. He is the author of several authoritative texts including *The Crisis of the Indian Legal System*, *The Indian Supreme Court and Politics* and *Towards a Sociology of Indian Law*. Four volumes of his writings titled *Law, Justice, Society: Selected Works of Upendra Baxi* as well as a monograph on his personal life and engagements with the law titled *Of Law and Life: Upendra Baxi in Conversation with Arvind Narrain, Lawrence Liang, Sitharamam Kakarala, and Sruti Chaganti* have recently been published.

Usha Ramanathan works on the jurisprudence of law, poverty and rights. She researches, writes and speaks on issues such as the nature of law, the Bhopal Gas Disaster, mass displacement, eminent domain, manual scavenging and civil liberties including the death penalty, beggary, criminal law, custodial institutions, the environment and the judicial process. She has been tracking and engaging with the Indian national ID project. She has also written and debated extensively on technology and the human conditions of freedom and liberty.

Vrinda Grover commenced her law practice in Delhi's trial courts and the Delhi High Court in 1989. She is an active practitioner in the Supreme Court of India and the various High Courts across the country. She was awarded an LL.M. by the NYU School of Law, and was conferred an honorary doctorate by the School of Oriental and African Studies, London, in 2018. She currently serves as a Commissioner on the Independent International Commission of Inquiry on Ukraine, set up by the Human Rights Council of the United Nations. She is the author of an authoritative report on the trial of the 1984 anti-Sikh riots cases.

Cartoon © Adhwaryu. Reproduced with permission.

Introduction

S MURALIDHAR

The imposing structure of the Supreme Court of India (SCI) stands on a triangular piece of land in the heart of New Delhi. Shaped to resemble a balance with two scales when viewed from above, this triangular plot has Bhagwan Das Road at its base, Tilak Marg on the left axial and Mathura Road on the right. Since 1958, when the Court moved to this location, it has expanded from being an eight-judge institution to one that has thirty-four judges, including the Chief Justice of India (CJI).[1]

The first sitting of the Court was held on 28 January 1950, two days after the Constitution of India became operational. During the period of seventy-five years of its existence, its workload has expanded from around 690 pending cases in 1950 to over 81,735 pending cases as of 31 May 2025.[2]

Arguably the biggest apex judicial body in the world in terms of judge strength and workload, the SCI never sits *en banc*.[3] It usually sits in Benches of two or three judges each.[4] On an average, over the past five years, around 37,000 cases have been instituted annually and around 35,000 cases disposed of.

1 The strength has been increased on seven occasions. The strengths have been: eight judges in 1950, eleven in 1956, fourteen in 1960, eighteen in 1978, twenty-six in 1986, thirty-one in 2009 and thirty-four in 2019.

2 Of the total caseload of around 81,735 cases, nearly half, i.e., 41297 cases, comprised SLPs filed under Article 136 of the Constitution against just about any order of a high court (HC), even interlocutory orders and even of statutory tribunals. There are as many as 12,136 unregistered SLPs, i.e., those with diary numbers but with defects remaining to be cured. These figures have been taken from the data available on the National Judicial Data Grid as on 31 May 2025.

3 The largest Bench of the SCI thus far has been the one that decided the *Kesavananda Bharati* case, which had thirteen judges, including the then CJI, SM Sikri. It is stated that a Bench of the same strength was set up to review the judgment when AN Ray J was the CJI; see TR Andhyarujina, *The Kesavananda Bharati Case: The Untold Story of Struggle for Supremacy by the Supreme Court and Parliament* (Universal Law Publishing 2011) 94. Barring this one instance, the maximum Bench strength has been eleven.

4 This creates its own set of problems since under the principle of *stare decisis*, the order or decision of a three-judge Bench is usually binding on a two-judge Bench. As a result, there are a large number of three-judge Bench matters pending in the SCI (till 31 May 2025, there were 1,146 such cases).

With the prospect of increased filings in the years to come being a near certainty, no other body at the highest level in the judicial hierarchy in a country has a more arduous and daunting task on its hands.

Headed by the Secretary General of the SCI, the administrative side, which comprises ministerial staff, has also expanded to 3,770 persons at present.[5] The physical infrastructure has grown over seventy-five years by the addition of courtrooms, buildings, lawyers' chambers and most recently, a multi-storied state-of-the-art annexe for the offices of the SCI on the other side of Mathura Road, connected to the main building through a tunnel.[6] The number of lawyers practising before it has increased to 22,734.[7] Technology has facilitated online filing in the SCI.[8] Post the COVID-19 pandemic, hybrid hearings – with some or all lawyers involved in a case appearing online – are routine.[9]

These are the most obvious tangible changes that are immediately apparent. However, the more intangible changes are in the nature of litigation, the types of cases, manner of presentation of cases by lawyers, the time devoted by the Court to the consideration of a case depending on the stage at which it is, variance in the approaches of the judges to issues and in the ability to cope with the tremendous pressures brought upon it as the 'third pillar' of

---

5 This would include the drivers, peons, court masters, stenographers, registrars, assistant registrars and perhaps even the law researchers. Each judge of the SCI can have up to four law researchers, who are chosen through a rigorous process of written tests and interviews.

6 While the main building has 4 separate blocks of 134 lawyer chambers (named after Senior Advocates AK Sen, RK Garg, GL Sanghi and RK Jain) across the Bhagwan Das Road, there are the MC Setalvad and CK Daphthary chamber blocks with 172 and 72 chambers, respectively. In 2022, along with the inauguration of the new administrative block of the SCI, across Mathura Road, a separate D-Block of 263 lawyer chambers (along with 68 cubicles) was also inaugurated. A metro line runs behind the rear of the Court. The metro station there has been renamed as 'Supreme Court'. In October 2024, the foundation stone for a new building within the SCI complex was laid.

7 Although the SCBA directory lists out 'outstation' advocates as well, it may still not accurately reflect the number of lawyers actively practicing before the SCI. It is not unusual for a HC lawyer outside Delhi to make a day visit to argue cases before the SCI. There are around 3,500 Advocates-on-Record (AoRs).

8 The e-filing system commenced in the year 2020, but is yet to be embraced in full measure by the lawyers. Each Bench of the SCI has digital devices placed on the dais on which the judges can read documents and reported judgments while the case is in progress. The bookmarked copies of every case listed before the Court is made available to the lawyers involved on the website of the SCI. Judges can also bring their own laptops to the dais. Since some of the judges are not comfortable with soft copies yet, lawyers tend to file the hard copies in addition.

9 Not all of the Benches of the SCI have been welcoming of this change. It is, therefore, not unusual for lawyers to appear physically before certain Benches (as a strategy).

democracy.[10] The analysis of these intangible changes can help us understand if the SCI has been able to deliver on the constitutional promise of equal justice.

It is trite that the institution has played a significant role in shaping the legal and political landscape while having a lasting impact on lives of individuals and artificial persons, including the State and corporate entities. Consistent with the need to preserve institutional memory and guard against institutional amnesia, there has to be a constant endeavour to document, analyse and critically evaluate the functioning of the SCI.[11] For an institution controlled by time in every aspect of its functioning, it is not unusual for legal scholars to review the performance of the SCI over periods of time, say yearly, decennially, twenty-five, fifty or seventy-five years.[12] With the advent of online legal news platforms, the manner of reporting on the happenings in the courts as well has undergone a dramatic shift.[13]

How does one view the SCI, which has, while undergoing changes in its composition and functioning, also been the driving force of changes in other organs of the State? What has been its performance on the parameters of

---

[10] Regular practitioners before the SCI for over four decades vouch for the fact that much of the working hours of the SCI are now taken up by the fresh cases and 'after-notice' cases that are yet to be formally admitted and that very little time available to deal with the regular 'final hearing' of already admitted appeals. It is therefore not unusual that there are a sizable number of appeals of the '10+ years' category. See Nick Robinson, 'A Quantitative Analysis of the Indian Supreme Court's Workload' *J Empirical Legal Stud* (2012) <https://ssrn.com/abstract=2189181> accessed 28 December 2024; Aparna Chandra, Sital Kalantry and William HJ Hubbard, *Court on Trial: A Data-Driven Account of the Supreme Court of India* (Penguin Random House India 2023).

[11] To commemorate the fiftieth year, a museum of curated artefacts was launched. This is permanently housed in the campus of the SCI at its rear. Taking a cue from the practice adopted by the US SC, in the year 2011, the SCI commissioned 'restatements of the law' on specific topics including parliamentary privilege, PIL. During the tenure of CJI TS Thakur, the SCI brought out in 2014 a publication titled *Courts of India: Past to Present* containing a detailed exposition of the history of the judiciary in India, which has since been translated and digitally republished in thirteen regional languages. The SCI also has a separate research wing, Centre for Research and Planning, which periodically publishes research material. In 2024, it published reports titled 'Prisons in India' and 'Handbook Concerning Persons With Disabilities'.

[12] Beginning 2005, the SCI has been publishing an annual report, available on its website. On the occasion of the fiftieth year, the SCI brought out an official publication of commemorative essays titled *Supreme But Not Infallible*, edited by BN Kirpal, Ashok Desai, Gopal Subramanium, Rajeev Dhavan, Raju Ramachandran and published by OUP in 2000. The Indian Law Institute also published a book titled *Fifty Years of the Supreme Court of India: Its Grasp and Reach* (Oxford University Press 2000). For the seventy-fifth year, a book titled *Justice for the Nation: Reflections on 75 Years of the Supreme Court of India* was launched by the SCI in 2024 at a function held at the Rashtrapati Bhavan.

[13] Two of the prominent online legal journals closely followed by the legal community, namely, *LiveLaw* and *BarandBench*, are able to deploy various technological tools of the social media to deliver legal news in real time. Live-tweeting from courts has also now become a regular phenomenon.

accountability, transparency and answerability to the people and the law? Has it always been able to maintain the balance between judicial activism and the demands of accountability for the exercise of judicial power? How consistent has the Court been? Given the quick overturning of its verdicts of its larger Benches, is the Court undermining its position as 'final arbiter' of disputes? By the reluctance shown in applying the general principles in its decisions to particular cases where it matters, is it becoming a Court defined by its contradictions? How far has the Court succeeded in being a counter-majoritarian institution that succeeds in keeping in check majoritarian and State excesses? On the administrative side, what have been the significant changes in the functioning of the office of the CJI and the *inter se* controls over the other courts in the judiciary? How has the SCI responded to the demand of interpreting the Constitution *per se* and specific laws in particular areas, in light of the overarching tapestry of desired constitutional values of liberty, equality, fraternity and dignity? What has been the response and role of the Bar in shaping the trajectory and course of the development of law? How has the institution adapted to technology in its functioning and what is the vision for the future?

II

This book, through the voices and thoughts of former judges, active practitioners, academics, law researchers and a journalist, attempts to answer some of these questions in the form of essays and interviews. These have been written, over eighteen months, preceded by discussions between the individual authors and the editor. The book's ambitions are modest. It does not offer either a comprehensive or an exhaustive analysis of the topics listed. Constraints of space have led to the exclusion of some of the areas of the Court's work like human rights, disability rights, sexual minorities, property law, rent control law, service law, corporate law, banking law, contempt of court, election law, consumer protection laws, right to information, inter-state river water disputes, suits between states and between states and the centre, family law including cross-border child abduction, and niche areas like intellectual property rights, insolvency, competition, telecom, and electricity.[14]

---

[14] To a regular practitioner, it is plainly discernible that some of these specific areas – for instance, corporate insolvency or even bails under the Prevention of Money Laundering Act, 2002 – with high litigating capacity, now occupy a disproportionate amount of the Court's time even while other more pressing

The SCI's extensive use of its powers under Article 142 of the Constitution to do 'complete justice' could well justify a whole tome.[15]

The idea, nevertheless, is to provide the reader with the views of those actively engaging with and studying the functioning of the SCI: not only on what the Court has achieved in positive terms but an informed critique of where it may have failed to advance the constitutional project of preserving and enforcing democratic freedoms. The essays reflect on the challenges before the institution, its preparedness to face them and generally how its working may be improved. They also seek to ask whether, over seventy-five years, the SCI has taken measures that would make it more accessible and transparent in terms of both its judicial and administrative functioning.

The book is divided into parts. Part I of the book looks at the SCI and its actors. AP Shah and Madan Lokur JJ approach the issues concerning the appointments made of and by judges of the SCI from different perspectives. While Shah J explains the background leading to the evolution of the 'Collegium system' and its failures to achieve the objective behind the dramatic shift in the process in 1993, Lokur J, having been for many years part of the Collegium at the High Courts (HCs) of Delhi, Guwahati and Andhra Pradesh, and for more than two years in the Supreme Court Collegium, brings an 'insider's' perspective. The two essays complement each other and give the reader a rounded view of the working of the Collegium system. They reveal that the problem with getting the 'right' individuals appointed to the SCI and the HCs has not been made easier post the *Second Judges*, case in 1993 or the *Third Judges*, case in 1997. Both essays together give the reader a rather comprehensive analysis of the judgment in the *Fourth Judges*, case that struck down in 2018 the constitutional amendment to establish a National Judicial Appointments Commission (NJAC).

Senior Advocate Raju Ramachandran weighs in next with an incisive analysis of the processes involved in the impeachment and ultimate removal of

issues arising in the remaining areas are vying for the Court's attention. An assessment of the 'judicial impact' of new enactments or changes in the existing ones on the workload of the SCI requires to be studied in depth.

[15] One egregious instance of the use of this 'all encompassing power' under Article 142 is the direction issued in *L Chandrakumar v. Union of India* (1997) 3 SCC 261 that a party aggrieved by the decision of an administrative tribunal should, before directly approaching the SCI under Article 136, challenge it before a HC in a writ petition under Article 226 of the Constitution, which will then be heard by a Bench of not less than two judges. Even today, no such provision exists in the Administrative Tribunals Act 1985, under which these tribunals function.

judges of constitutional courts, and why every attempt thus far has failed. Usha Ramanathan reflects on the vexed issue of delays in the judicial system generally and its effect in specific instances. She illustrates this by analysing a few of the significant decisions in particular areas, like the challenge to the scheme of electoral bonds, the challenge to the legislation passed as a Money Bill seeking to legitimize the unique identity scheme, the crumbling of the criminal law administration and the litany of judicial blunders in the aftermath of the Bhopal gas disaster.

Ravindra Bhat J offers an insider's perspective of issues faced, by the judiciary at all levels, on the administrative side. These include managing physical infrastructure, finances, staff and officers and caseloads. The essay also analyzes the reasons for many of these challenges continuing over seven decades of the functioning of courts in independent India. In Rohan Alva's essay on Constitution Benches, he examines how matters get referred to Constitution Benches and what have been the trends in their decision-making in particular areas over the past seventy-five years.

Before the commencement of Part II we have an interview with Professor Upendra Baxi on the topic of public interest litigation (PIL). India's leading legal academic insists on terming it as social action litigation (SAL) and tells us why. Drawing on his vast experience as a close observer of the SCI for over six decades, Baxi reveals how a few individual judges played a decisive role in the evolution and shape of the PIL jurisdiction, which has come now to stay as an important component of the SCI's functioning. Baxi does not share the pessimism of those who are critical of the Court overstepping its limits by using the PIL jurisdiction to indulge in what they term as unbridled judicial activism.[16]

Part II has three important contributions on the SCI and criminal law. The first is by Senior Advocate Rebecca Mammen John. She explains how, over the years, there has been a systematic dilution of the rigours of the Criminal

---

[16] A much-discussed work in this regard is Anuj Bhuwania's book *Courting the People: Public Interest Litigation in Post-Emergency India*, which Prof. Baxi also responds to during his interview. The number of instances where the SCI or a HC in the PIL jurisdiction take up *suo motu* or otherwise an issue that the Court has with the government (which has remained unresolved on the administrative side) would make for an interesting study. For instance, the issue of the working conditions of the district judiciary (*All India Judges Association v. Union of India*) and finding more space for the expansion of HCs (*In Re: Heritage Building of the Bombay High Court and Allotment of Additional Lands for the High Court* SMW (C) No 5/2024.)

Procedure Code through the decisions of the SCI, resulting in arbitrary exercise of police powers and their resultant immunity from prosecution. This, in turn, has encouraged the enactment of harsh criminal laws and procedures that are inconsistent with the constitutional guarantees of the right to life and liberty. This sets the background for the next essay by Senior Advocate Nitya Ramakrishnan, which focuses on extraordinary criminal laws that have been persisted with by free India since the inception of the Constitution of India despite their obvious failures in achieving their avowed objectives. Ramakrishnan explains why draconian criminal laws result in low conviction rates with harsh and disproportionate punishments; they delegitimize the rule of law that is premised on the constitutional guarantees of equality and non-discrimination in the administration of criminal justice.[17] Vrinda Grover, a lawyer with four decades of practice, focusing on criminal law at all levels of the judiciary, reflects on sentencing. She explains how despite the SCI's judgements on the specific exercise to be undertaken by trial judges before awarding a severe sentence, it still does not get implemented in practical terms. She reminds us that judges often get dictated by their emotions and the need for approval from the dominant voice in society. She highlights the inconsistencies in the approaches to sentencing that renders the exercise arbitrary and unpredictable.

Part III on the SCI and equality begins with an essay by Professor Faizan Mustafa, which examines a range of judgments delivered by the SCI on the right of minorities to worship and administer institutions of their choice. He analyses the recent verdict concerning the minority character of the Aligarh Muslim University. The next essay is by Professor Mohan Gopal on caste and the SCI. He is pointedly critical of the major premise underlying its verdicts on what constitutes the tenets of Hindu religion and its consequent verdicts in the area of reservations for Other Backward Classes (OBCs), Scheduled Castes (SCs) and Scheduled Tribes (STs) in educational institutions and government employment. His particular criticism is of the SCI conflating *jaati* and *varna*, adopting a Brahmanical perspective and attempting to co-opt into the Hindu fold the vast array of *jaatis*, thereby negativing their distinct identities. The next essay is by the eminent journalist P Sainath, who is able to tell us, from a reporter's perspective, the highs and lows of the decisions of

[17] These essays underscore the need for a separate exhaustive treatment of the 'hard issues' of custodial violence, encounter killings, forced and mass disappearances, mass crimes, and immunity and impunity by both State and non-State actors.

the SCI, touching on issues concerning rural India and the concomitant issue of law and poverty. For those interested in learning how a vast majority of the people view the SCI, Sainath's is an important voice that cannot afford to be ignored.[18] Part III ends with an interview with Senior Advocate Indira Jaising. It covers a wide range of topics including issues of gender discrimination and systemic challenges faced by women lawyers. As a leading practitioner in the areas of labour and constitutional law, with a vast experience of nearly six decades, Jaising offers valuable insights into the backstories, preparation and presentation of some of the important cases handled by her.

Part IV has a cluster of essays on various aspects of a sampling of substantive laws. Each of the authors – K Chandru J on labour law, Gautam Patel J on environmental law, Senior Advocate Arvind P Datar on taxation laws, Gautam Bhatia on media freedom, Suhrith Parthasarathy on the anti-defection law, and Amit George on arbitration law – bring fresh perspectives to the analyses of SCI decisions in these areas. These could be viewed as snapshots, but their informed critique is thought-provoking for the serious law researcher. These essays also show us discernible shifts in the trend of the different Benches of the SCI over the years. They also tell us that judges are political actors who make definitive choices, conscious of the impact they are likely to have on the parties before the Court.

The Bar and law students are the focus of Part V. It begins with a background note on the SCI Bar, followed by an interview with Meenakshi Arora, who, before being designated as a Senior Advocate, was an Advocate-on-Record (AOR) in the SCI. She has useful insights into the working of the Bar in the SCI in general and the AOR system in particular. Drawing on his extensive law practice of over four decades at the Bar in a wide range of areas, Senior Advocate Gopal Subramanium pens sketches of some of the prominent legal practitioners who dominated the Bar in the SCI over the period of seven decades. Having been a part of the Bar and having watched it at close quarters, there is an authenticity and unavoidable subjectivity to Gopal's voice.

Law students are an important component of the legal system, as it is from among them that litigating lawyers and judges ultimately emerge. The quality

---

18 For a subaltern perspective of a court's functioning and verdicts, Peter Irons' *A People's History of the Supreme Court* (Penguin Books 1999, inspired by historian Howard Zinn's classic treatise with a similar title) could be referred to. Legal historian Rohit De's *A People's Constitution* (Princeton University Press 2018) is another contribution in a similar vein.

of the Bar mirrors the quality of legal education, a point that comes through in the essay by Professor Kamala Sankaran who has taught and written extensively on constitutional and labour law for over four decades. She tells us about the role of the SCI and its judges, apart from the Bar Council of India, in shaping the course of legal education in the country.

The last part begins with an essay on digitalizing the courts by the Editor. Having been a part of the Information Technology Committee of the Delhi HC for years and being among the first judges to hold a paperless court, the Editor is well-placed to discuss the evolution of the process of digitization of the courts and their functioning through the vision documents for three phases, ending with 2028, put out by the e-Committee of the SCI. The book ends with an interview with Sriram Panchu, a Senior Advocate, with nearly five decades of experience. He shares with us his thoughts on what he hopes the SCI might be twenty-five years hence.

For long now, cartoonists have contributed to the public discourse through their incisive and insightful work. This is vividly portrayed by the seventeen illustrations the reader will find at various places in this book. Some have been commissioned and others reproduced with permission. Arguably, they mirror the public perception of the institution in its various roles.

III

An objective analysis of the SCI would necessitate acknowledging its highs and lows over the last seventy-five years. The attempt here is not to exhaustively list out the instances, but to mention a few critical ones. Many legal scholars share the view that an early 'low' was the 1950 verdict of the SCI in the *AK Gopalan* case.[19] By a 5:1 majority,[20] the SCI declined to strike down as unconstitutional a draconian preventive detention statute.[21] The perception of the SCI in its early years as being 'conservative' remained unaltered, notwithstanding its verdict in the *Romesh Thappar* case striking down the ban by the Government

19 For instance, see KG Kannabiran, *Wages of Impunity: Power, Justice and Human Rights* (Orient Longman 2004) 36.

20 The much-celebrated dissent of Fazl Ali J was, nearly sixty-seven years later, acknowledged by the SCI itself, in *KS Puttaswamy (Privacy-9J) v. Union of India 7* (2017) 10 SCC 1, as laying down the correct legal position.

21 Preventive Detention Act 1950.

of Madras of a magazine run by a card-carrying communist.[22] This perception would be corrected much later in 1970 by the verdict (6:1) of a seven-judge Bench in the *Bank Nationalisation* case.[23] The 'due process' reading of the rights under Article 21 of the Constitution was authoritatively restated in the 1978 verdict in the *Maneka Gandhi* case.[24] The SCI then held that a conjoint reading of Articles 14, 19 and 21 made it mandatory for the elements of both substantive and procedural due process requirements to be satisfied by administrative decisions and legislative enactments.

Another definitive low point was the 4:1 verdict in 1976 of the Constitution Bench in *ADM Jabalpur v. Shiv Kant Shukla*,[25] which upheld the validity of the draconian Maintenance of Internal Security Act, 1976, and the imposition of Emergency in June 1975.[26] It would take over four decades for the SCI to formally acknowledge, in *KS Puttaswamy (Privacy-9J) v. Union of India*, that the said verdict was a mistake and 'should never have been' rendered.[27] The launch of the PIL jurisdiction, which purportedly took the Court closer to the people, commenced in 1979 and was viewed by many a legal scholar as an 'atonement' for not striking down the Emergency Proclamation that denied people access to constitutional courts for justice.[28]

---

[22] *Romesh Thappar v. State of Madras* 1950 AIR SC 124. See also, *Brij Bhushan v. The State of Delhi* 1950 AIR SC 129 and *Pandit MSM Sharma v. Shri Sri Krishna Sinha* 1959 AIR SC 395.

[23] *RC Cooper v. Union of India* (1970) 1 SCC 248, the sole dissenter being AN Ray J, who, as a result of the 'first supercession' engineered by the Indira Gandhi government in 1973, became a CJI.

[24] (1978) 1 SCC 248. While the majority verdict of the seven-judge Bench was delivered by PN Bhagwati J, separate opinions were authored by CJI MH Beg, YV Chandrachud and VR Krishna Iyer JJ.

[25] The sole dissenter was HR Khanna J, and this triggered the 'second supercession', with MH Beg J (who was junior to him) being appointed as CJI instead of him.

[26] During the heated exchanges in the courtroom in the hearing of this case, the then Attorney General for India, Niren De, is reported to have answered in the affirmative the question posed by the SCI whether there would be no remedy of approaching a HC if a police shot someone in plain daylight, 'A Story About a Law Officer and the Violence in His Arguments' (*The Wire*, 1 June 2020) <https://thewire.in/law/adm-jabalpur-emergency-niren-de-tushar-mehta> accessed 2 January 2025; Another unfortunate decision rendered during this time was *Union of India v. Bhanudas Krishna Gawde*, with MH Beg J observing that a HC's jurisdiction under Article 226 is curtailed during an Emergency if the purpose of the proceeding is to uphold the fundamental right to personal freedom, even if that includes deciding whether a rule made under laws allowing preventive detention is constitutional.

[27] *KS Puttaswamy (Privacy-9J)* (n 20). DY Chandrachud J, authoring the majority opinion, had this to say of the 1976 verdict, in which his father YV Chandrachud J was part of the majority: 'The judgments rendered by all the four Judges constituting the majority in ADM, Jabalpur are seriously flawed. Life and personal liberty are inalienable to human existence. These rights are, as recognised in *Kesavananda Bharati*, primordial rights.'

[28] In his interview in this book, Professor Baxi agrees with this proposition.

Among the low points of the 1980s was the verdict in the *First Judges'* case, in which the SCI declined to alter the *status quo* which gave the executive the dominant hand in the matter of appointment of judges to the HC and the SCI. Given that there were two instances – first in 1973 and then in 1976 – in which the appointed CJI superseded junior colleagues, the decision in the *First Judges'* case disappointed many a constitutional scholar.[29] The 1980s also witnessed the SCI putting its stamp of approval on the now infamous settlement of claims of the Bhopal gas disaster victims for a paltry USD 470 million USD while insulating the UCC and its Indian counterpart UCIL from future claims, civil or criminal.[30] This low point could hardly be rectified by its 1991 verdict in which it revived the criminal liability but declined to reopen the settlement of civil claims.[31] The attempt by the Union of India to reopen the settlement by a curative petition failed in 2023.[32]

The verdict in 1993 in the *SR Bommai* case delegitimized the casual use of the powers under Article 356 of the Constitution to impose President's Rule in states where the opposition was in power.[33] This high point was preceded by

---

[29] 'The majority decision may have been constitutionally correct, but it was definitely not in accordance with the constitutional convention.', Fali S Nariman, *Before Memory Fades: An Autobiography* (Hay House 2010) 392; 'The judgment will be known in future less for its erudition though there has been learned discussion relating to some aspects of the problem but more for its declaration of policy in the significant and sensitive area of structuring of the higher judiciary.', Govind Das, *Supreme Court in Quest of Identity* (Chaitanya Publishing House 1974) 143; 'And what is more, the executive got a thumping endorsement of a wide-ranging power of transfer. If reason is to hold sway, Justice Desai's analysis cogently showing that no consideration of public interest can be invoked to sustain Chief Justice Singh's transfer has to be accepted. But the majority held otherwise. In other words, a petition designed to support the independence of the judiciary has effectively undermined it. Whatever real safeguards *Sankalchand* created have been destroyed by the Judges' case! A historic contribution by the leaders of the Indian Bar to the preservation of their meaning of the independence of the judiciary.', Upendra Baxi, *Courage, Craft and Contention: The Indian Supreme Court in the Eighties* (N.M. Tripathi 1985) 53.

[30] *Union Carbide Corporation v. Union of India* (1989) 1 SCC 674. See also, the Introduction by Prof. Upendra Baxi in *Valiant Victims and Lethal Litigation: The Bhopal Case* (Indian Law Institute 1990). See also, Upendra Baxi, *Inconvenient Forum and Convenient Catastrophe: The Bhopal Case* (Indian Law Institute 1986), and *Mass Disasters and Multinational Liability: The Bhopal Case* (Indian Law Institute 1986).

[31] *Union Carbide Corporation v. Union of India* (1991) 4 SCC 584.

[32] See Usha Ramanathan's essay in this book.

[33] The majority opinion written by SR Pandian J drew from a Pakistan SC decision in *Federation of Pakistan v. Saifullah Khan* to mandate the tabling in the Parliament for its approval within six months of the executive order imposing President's Rule. Apart from the fact that the number of instances of use of this power dropped sharply thereafter, every attempt to use it has met with failure, See, for instance, *Rameshwar Prasad v. Union of India* (2006) 2 SCC 1 (Bihar) and *Harish Chandra Singh Rawat v. Union of India* 2016 AIR CC 2455 (Uttarakhand). Ultimately, the Central Government withdrew the proclamation of President's Rule in the State of Uttarakhand on 11 May 2016.

the low point in December 1992 when the SCI failed to pass orders to prevent the congregation of *kar sevak*s in Ayodhya and the resultant demolition of the Babri Masjid on 6 December, which then triggered large-scale communal violence across the country.[34] History will view this failure as a grave inaction by the SCI to protect the values of freedom, liberty and fraternity enshrined in the Constitution.[35] 1993 was also the year in which the verdict in *Kartar Singh* was delivered, upholding the validity of the draconian Terrorist and Disruptive Activities Act, 1985.[36] This low point would be repeated in 2003, when the successor statute was also upheld.[37] The environmental law verdicts in the *MC Mehta* case as well as other cases in the decades of the 1980s and 1990s, which made the polluter pays and the precautionary principle as part of Indian law, were high points.[38]

The progressive verdict of the Delhi HC in 2009 in the *Naz Foundation* case,[39] reading down Section 377 IPC and making it inapplicable to consensual sex between adults in a private space, was reversed by two judges of the SCI, four years later, in *Suresh Kaushal*.[40] This verdict that set the clock back was soon followed by the progressive judgment of another two-judge Bench in 2014 in *NALSA v. Union of India*, recognizing the rights of transgender persons to full personhood.[41] *Naz* was resurrected in 2017 and affirmed by a nine-judge

[34] The two-judge Bench of MN Venkatachaliah and GN Ray JJ opted to remain assured by the false undertaking given by the Uttar Pradesh government, headed by Kalyan Singh, communicated by its lawyer KK Venugopal, senior advocate, that the structure would be safe. Much later, shortly before his retirement, MN Venkatachaliah CJI headed the Bench that punished Kalyan Singh to a 'token' imprisonment of a day for this gross contempt of court; *Mohd. Aslam v. Union of India* (1994) 6 SCC 442.

[35] The criminal act catalysed the enactment of the Places of Worship Act 1991, which was forcefully validated by the authorless verdict of the five-judge Bench in *M Siddiq (D) Thr Lrs v. Mahant Suresh Das* (2020) 1 SCC 1, which incidentally acknowledged that the demolition was a 'serious violation of the rule of law'. This has not prevented concerted attempts at undermining the very objective of this legislation, with multifarious claims of mosques being built over the debris of demolished temples being made before various courts. This was temporarily halted by the SCI by its order dated 12 December 2024 in *Ashwini Kumar Upadhyay v. Union of India*, WP(C) 1246/2020, as it now considers the validity of the statute.

[36] This is also discussed in the essay by Nitya Ramakrishnan in this book.

[37] The challenge to the validity of the Prevention of Terrorism Act, 2002, was negatived in *People's Union for Civil Liberties v. Union of India* (2004) 9 SCC 580.

[38] For a critical evaluation, see the essay by Gautam Patel in this book.

[39] *Naz Foundation v. Government of NCT of Delhi* (2009) 111 DRJ 1 (DB).

[40] *Suresh Kumar Koushal v. Naz Foundation* (2014) 1 SCC 1. Interestingly, this was pronounced twenty-one months after the orders were reserved, on the day of retirement of GS Singhvi J.

[41] *National Legal Services Authority v. Union of India* (2014) 5 SCC 438.

Bench in *KS Puttaswamy (Privacy-9J)*, which carved out a right to privacy as a fundamental right relatable to Article 21 of the Constitution.[42] This was certainly high as far as the SCI was concerned but was followed the very next year by the decision in *KS Puttaswamy (Aadhaar-5J) v. Union of India*[43] in which, by a 4:1 majority, the SCI upheld the legislation that instituted the Unique Identification Authority of India and made the possession of a unique identity number by a person mandatory for a range of services, including banking, taxation and telephone connection.[44] This decision was a definite low.[45]

The simmering discontent within the SCI over the CJI exercising the master-of-the-roster prerogative of allocating cases to be heard by particular Benches came to a head in 2018 when Dipak Misra took over as CJI. In three cases decided that year, the SCI reiterated that this power of the CJI could not be delegated to the next senior-most even when the question arising for decision in a case involves the CJI.[46] The issue blew out in the open when in an unprecedented move, four of the senior-most judges of the SCI held a press conference in the forenoon of 12 January 2018.[47] The judges felt that

---

42 *KS Puttaswamy* (n 20). The privacy verdict made the decriminalization of consensual same-sex in private spaces relatively simple for the five-judge Bench in *Navtej Johar v. Union of India* (2018) 10 SCC 1, where the Petitioners faced no resistance by the Union of India and also benefitted by the total absence of the religious groups that had mounted a spirited defense in *Naz*.

43 (2019) 1 SCC 1.

44 The powerful sole dissent of DY Chandrachud J highlights the glaring illegality involved in the Parliament passing the UIDAI Act as a Money Bill, which, as an issue, is still pending before a larger Bench of the SCI.

45 The devastating effects of exclusion from state welfare of disturbingly large tracts of the Indian population now stands well documented. See, 'How Mandatory Aadhaar Authentication Leads to Exclusion of the Marginalised from PDS' (*Frontline*, 23 March 2024) <https://frontline.thehindu.com/social-issues/mandatory-aadhaar-authentication-leads-to-exclusion-of-the-marginalised-from-pds/article67983558.ece> accessed 29 December 2024. See also the essay by Usha Ramanathan in this book.

46 In *Campaign for Judicial Accountability and Reforms v. Union of India* (2018) 1 SCC 196 as well as *Shanti Bhushan v. Supreme Court of India* (2018) 8 SCC 396, the role of the CJI as master of the roster was reiterated. In *Asoke Pande v. Supreme Court of India* (2018) 5 SCC 31, along with reiterating this position, the SCI rejected the suggestion that Constitution Benches should necessarily include the three senior-most judges and observed that every judge appointed to the SCI was qualified to hear every case filed and that 'To hold otherwise, would be to cast a reflection on the competence and ability of other Judges to deal with all cases assigned by the CJI notwithstanding the fact that they have fulfilled the qualifications mandated by the Constitution for appointment to the office.'

47 'Cases Having Far-reaching Consequences for the Nation and Judiciary assigned to Benches without any Rationale. This Must Be Guarded Against At All Costs: Senior Judges' (*LiveLaw*, 12 January 2018) <https://www.livelaw.in/cases-having-far-reaching-consequences-for-the-nation-and-judiciary assigned-to-benches-without-any-rationalethis-must-be-guarded-against-at-all-costs-senior-judges/> accessed 29 December 2024.

they had 'no other choice but communicate to the nation to please take care of this institution.'[48] Even thereafter, this issue has refused to die down.[49] Not much has been written about the CJI's tasks on the administrative side, which if studied carefully, might underscore the impact that one individual can have on the functioning of not only judicial institutions but even tribunals[50] and educational institutions.[51]

The authorless unanimous verdict by a five-judge Bench in 2019, upholding the claim of the Hindu group that the birthplace of Lord Ram was at the very spot where the demolished Babri Masjid stood, was perplexing for its utter lack of any legal basis.[52] Even more strange was its direction to create a trust to build the Ram Mandir temple in the entire disputed land and form a Board of Trustees within three months, a relief that no one had sought.[53] The same year witnessed a grave allegation of sexual harassment made by an employee of the SCI against the CJI, which triggered an unprecedented special *suo motu* sitting on a Saturday morning to consider imaginary threats

---

[48] Chelameswar J, said they did not want 'any wise men to say 20 years later that Justices Chelameswar, Ranjan Gogoi, Lokur and Kurian sold their souls and did not take care of the interests of this illustrious institution.' See: 'Four SC judges air differences with CJI Misra' (*The Hindu*, 13 January 2018). Ironically, one of those judges who went on to become the next CJI, did an irreparable disservice to the institution by presiding over a Bench on a Saturday morning on 20 April 2019 to address 'threats to the independence of the judiciary' and bad-mouthing his lady staffer who had accused him of sexual harassment. For a more detailed account refer to the essay by Raju Ramachandran in this book.

[49] 'It should not be left to one person to select four or five judges for a Bench, says former Supreme Court judge Kurian Joseph' (*The Hindu*, 24 February 2024).

[50] As at present, the CJI has to give a nod to the proposals by the central government for appointment of the former judges of the SCI to various tribunals and commissions which has the inevitable effect of altering the interpersonal relationships between an incumbent CJI and the retiring judge. This also holds true of orders that might be passed on the judicial side on appointing former judges of the SCI as arbitrators in international commercial arbitration.

[51] The CJI is the Chancellor to a number of national law universities and has a definite say in constituting search committees and in the appointments of Vice-Chancellors in these universities. The CJI is also the Patron-in-Chief to the National Judicial Academy and in that capacity, oversees and indirectly controls all aspects of its functioning.

[52] It also had an unsigned appendix which, too, was authorless. The photograph in the public domain of the five judges of the Bench 'celebrating' it in a five-star hotel badly dented the public perception of the Court as an impartial arbiter of complex issues having religious and political overtones. For an incisive analysis of the verdict, see Suhrith Parthasarathy, Gautam Bhatia, 'Peace Bought By an Unequal Compromise' (*The Hindu*, 14 April 2021), Faizan Mustafa, Aymen Mohammed, 'Ayodhya Judgment Is a Setback to Evidence Law' (*The Indian Express*, 10 November 2019).

[53] The Prime Minister of India laid the foundation stone for the temple at an elaborate *bhoomipuja* on 5 August 2020 and inaugurated it with great fanfare on 22 January 2024. On the other hand, the other direction issued by the SC that a mosque should come up in the land given to the Muslim community elsewhere in Ayodhya is yet to be implemented.

to the independence of the judiciary.[54] The Bench was presided over by the CJI against whom the complaint was made! He proceeded to proclaim his innocence and the malice of the complainant from the high Bench, with his two colleagues in silent agreement.[55] Many would wonder if a lower point than this could have been reached by the SCI.[56] The criticism provided by some towards the SCI allowing itself to be dominated by a powerful executive during this phase stood vindicated by the post-retirement nomination to the Rajya Sabha of the former CJI who presided over the Bench that delivered the *Ayodhya* verdict,[57] the appointment as Governor of Andhra Pradesh of a judge who presided over a Bench that upheld the demonetization of 500- and 1,000-rupee notes,[58] appointment as Lok Pal of the judge who presided over the Benches that upheld the provisions of the Prevention of Money Laundering Act[59] and the denial of bail in a case under the Unlawful Activities (Prevention) Act.[60]

---

54 The one-man committee of AK Patnaik J, constituted by the SCI, submitted a report on this aspect but the matter was closed without the report having been made public. See, 'SC Refuses to Disclose Probe Report into "Conspiracy" against Former CJI Ranjan Gogoi' (*Scroll.in*, 18 March 2021) <https://scroll.in/latest/989874/sc-refuses-to-disclose-probe-report-into-conspiracy-against-former-cji-ranjan-gogoi> accessed 24 February 2025.

55 The other two judges on the Bench were Arun Mishra and Sanjiv Khanna JJ. Khanna J had joined the Court less than three months ago. Even more astonishing was the fact that when the order passed on that date was uploaded, it did not reflect the presence of CJI Gogoi.

56 The hearing took place on 20 April 2019. The then AG KK Venugopal, SG Tushar Mehta, SCBA President Rakesh Khanna were physically present and tacitly agreed with whatever was said. The manner of handling of the complaint also left much to be desired. See, Madan Lokur, 'A One-Sided Justice' (*The Indian Express*, 20 May 2019) <https://indianexpress.com/article/opinion/columns/justice-ranjan-gogoi-sexual-harrassment-case-clean-chit-supreme-court-5741244/?pfrom=HP> accessed 24 February 2025.

57 When repeatedly questioned during a TV interview on whether this was acceptable to his judicial conscience, Gogoi remained unfazed. See interview with Arnab Goswami at: <https://www.youtube.com/watch?v=oyO6K0MN8N0> accessed 24 February 2025.

58 Abdul Nazeer, who presided over the Bench, was appointed Governor of Andhra Pradesh by the President of India in February 2023.

59 *Vijay Madanlal Choudhary v. Union of India* 2022 INSC 757, delivered by a three-judge Bench comprising AM Khanwilkar, Dinesh Maheshwari and CT Ravikumar JJ.

60 *NIA v. Zahoor Ahmad Shah Watali* 2019 INSC 456, delivered by a two judge Bench comprising AM Khanwilkar and Ajay Rastogi JJ. The verdict in *Watali* was diluted in the subsequent cases which have been discussed in the essay by Nitya Ramakrishnan in this book.

IV

There are many 'what if' moments in the seventy-five year history of the SCI. For instance, what if VR Krishna Iyer J had not on 24 June 1975 stayed the judgment of the Allahabad HC setting aside the election of the sitting Prime Minister Indira Gandhi? Would it then have avoided the imposition of the infamous Emergency two days later?

What if the SCI had upheld that invalidation of her election by dismissing Mrs Gandhi's appeal in *Indira Nehru Gandhi v. Raj Narain*,[61] even while it struck down the constitutional amendment that sought to insulate from judicial challenge the elections to the office of the President, Vice President and Prime Minister? What if the SCI had ordered a complete ban on the congregation of *kar sevak*s in Ayodhya? Would that have prevented the demolition of the Babri Masjid and all that followed?

What if the SCI had declined to put its seal of approval on 14 February 1989 of the unjust settlement of the claims of the Bhopal gas disaster victims for a paltry USD 470 million?[62] Would that have rendered fairer justice and strengthened the law on corporate criminal liability? What if the SCI had accepted the challenge to the inking of the Rafale deal on the basis of the file notings presented to it by the petitioners?[63] What if the SCI had ordered the registration of a criminal case in the Birla-Sahara diaries case?[64]

What if the powerful dissents of Fazl Ali J in *AK Gopalan*, Subbarao J in *Kharak Singh*,[65] Khanna J in *ADM Jabalpur*, Venkatachaliah J in *AR Antulay*,[66] Bharucha J in *Narmada*,[67] Dharmadhikari J in *ND Jayal*,[68] DY Chandrachud J in *Puttaswamy (Aadhaar-5J)*[69] and *Bhima Koregaon*[70] and Nagarathna J in the demonetization case[71] were, in fact, the verdicts of the Court? The list could

---

61 *Indira Nehru Gandhi v. Raj Narain* 1975 INSC 272.

62 *Union Carbide Corporation* (n 30).

63 *Manohar Lal Sharma v. Narendra Damodardas Modi* 2019 3 SCC 25. The petitions seeking review of the verdict were dismissed in *Yashwant Sinha v. CBI* 2019 6 SCC 1.

64 *Common Cause v. Union of India* WP (C) No 505/2015, order dated 11 January 2017.

65 *Kharak Singh v. State of Uttar Pradesh* AIR 1963 SC 1295.

66 *AR Antulay v. RS Nayak* 1988 2 SCC 602.

67 *Narmada Bachao Andolan v. Union of India* 2000 10 SCC 664.

68 *ND Jayal v. Union of India* 2004 9 SCC 362.

69 *KS Puttaswamy (Aadhaar-5J) v. Union of India* 2019 1 SCC 1.

70 *Romila Thapar v. Union of India* 2018 10 SCC 753.

71 *Vivek Narayan Sharma v. Union of India* 2023 3 SCC 1.

be endless,[72] but it shows that the SCI has, during the seven decades of its functioning – and many a time deliberately – shaped the political and legal history and thereby, the destiny, of this country.

If this book triggers dissent, debate and even perhaps disapproval, then it would have served its purpose. It would reassure us as argumentative Indians that we could still hope to be a democracy governed by the Rule of Law.

[72] Suhrith's essay in this book points to how the delay in dealing with the Shiv Sena defection case has defeated justice. Likewise, the delay in taking up the challenge to demonetization, the repeal of Article 370 of the Constitution and the electoral bonds case has resulted in the Court knowingly presenting itself with an unalterable *fait accompli*. See also, the essay by Usha Ramanathan in this book.

Part I

The Court and Its Actors

Cartoon © SanitaryPanels.

Judicial Appointments

AJIT PRAKASH SHAH

Any attempt at understanding judicial appointments in India today, whether to the Supreme Court of India (SCI) or to the High Courts (HCs), in the absence of a historical and developmental context would be inadequate. Therefore, it is useful to first examine how and why we came to appoint our judges in a particular way.

India has a rich constitutional history. One could argue that the starting point for a discussion on judicial appointments in modern India should be the Government of India Act of 1935, which established the Federal Court of India. Perhaps it might be more fitting to begin with the Constituent Assembly debates that led to the drafting of the Constitution of India where the blueprint for India's present judicial architecture was laid down.

Constituent Assembly on Judicial Appointments

The framers had been given an unenviable task. The complexity of the endeavour meant that greater attention was paid to some aspects of the Constitution than others. The judiciary was among those that invited much intensity of discussion.

Granville Austin, in his book *The Indian Constitution,* says, 'The members of the Constituent Assembly brought to the framing of the judicial provisions of the Constitution an idealism equalled only by that shown towards the fundamental rights.'[1] The driving force behind the Constitution was inarguably the need to set right historical inequalities and rectify the absence of civil liberties. But these guiding principles and ideals would be illusory without a robust institutional setup to ensure their fulfilment. It was no surprise then that a great deal of time and energy was spent by the Constituent Assembly

1 Granville Austin, *The Indian Constitution: Cornerstone of a Nation* (Clarendon Press 1966) 164.

on how the judiciary would remain independent, for judicial independence was indispensable to a court's ability to deliver the quality and kind of justice envisioned in the Constitution itself. In other words, as Austin put it, '[i]f the beacon of the judiciary was to remain bright, the courts must be above reproach, free from coercion and from political influence.'[2]

To achieve this end, it followed that the judiciary had to be fiercely protected from political influence and interference. Consequently, the Constituent Assembly spent considerable time on questions such as the tenure of judges, and their salaries, allowances and retirement ages. To a contemporary observer, this detailing might appear excessively elaborate, but the exercise was clearly required to shield the judiciary from external – particularly political – influence.

In matters of appointment process, though the Constituent Assembly relied on multiple sources, it was greatly influenced by the *Sapru Committee Report*,[3] which predated the constitutional framing exercise.[4] Among various legal and governance questions it tackled, the Report recommended a consultative process where the judges of the SCI would be appointed by the 'Head of the State' in consultation with the CJI. Judges of the HCs would be appointed in consultation additionally with the CJ of that HC.[5]

Indeed, the extent to which there was to be any consultation between the judiciary and 'outsiders' was dwelt upon greatly. George H Gadbois Jr points out that this 'was the subject of more debate and greater attention than any other of the twenty-four articles concerning the Supreme Court', the 'aim of the framers . . . [being] to remove or guard against every possible danger of political considerations, political pressures or political patronage in the process of appointing judges.'[6] Therefore, in order to keep the judiciary independent and unassailable, the participation of the executive or legislature in the appointment process had to be kept to a minimum.

Dr BR Ambedkar was particularly cognisant of the alternative ways in which appointments could be carried out, for example, as in the United Kingdom

---

[2] ibid 164–165.

[3] TB Sapru, *The Constitutional Proposals of the Sapru Committee/Sapru Committee Report* (Padma Publications 1945).

[4] While the principal remit of the Sapru Committee was to examine communal issues and rights of minorities, the report offered much useful guidance for the future of the Constitution itself.

[5] Sapru (n 3) xi-xii.

[6] George H Gadbois Jr, *Supreme Court of India: The Beginnings* (Oxford University Press 2017) ch 3.

where appointments are made by the executive without any limitation, or as in the United States where appointments to judicial office are to be made only with the concurrence of the Senate.[7] On appointments, he concluded that the 'middle course' that had been proposed in the draft article in the Constitution saying that there should be a consultation with persons well-qualified to give proper advice, was appropriate. On the question of concurrence of the CJI, although he noted that he was a 'very eminent person', it was not safe to allow him to veto the appointment of judges. He observed, 'But after all the Chief Justice is a man with all the failings, all the sentiments and all the prejudices which we as common people have; and I think, to allow the Chief Justice practically a veto upon the appointment of judges is really to transfer the authority to the Chief Justice which we are not prepared to vest in the President or the Government of the day. I therefore, think that is also a dangerous proposition.'[8]

Clearly, Dr Ambedkar was of the view that a consultative process of appointment was necessary to avoid any spheres of influence getting created on either side of the balance. These debates eventually led to Articles 124 (2) and 217 (1) for appointments of judges to the SCI and HCs, respectively. Article 124 (2) provides that every SCI judge will be appointed by the President 'after consultation' with such judges of the SCI and HCs 'as the President may deem necessary for that purpose', and that for the 'appointment of a Judge other than the Chief Justice, the Chief Justice of India shall always be consulted'.[9] Similarly, Article 217 (1) states that every HC judge would be appointed by the President, in consultation with the CJI, the CJ of the concerned HC and the Governor of the state.[10] Consultation, therefore, was embedded into the constitutional provisions, making it an integral part of the appointment process.

To explain this process better, it is necessary to bear in mind that appointment by the President is not to be taken literally – the President is expected to act in accordance with the advice of the government, comprising the Prime Minister and the Cabinet or the Council of Ministers. Additionally, while Article 124 (2) requires that the CJI must always be 'consulted', it does not

7 Constituent Assembly Debates, 24 May 1949, vol 8, para 8.90.157 <www.constitutionofindia.net/debates/24-may-1949/> accessed 11 February 2025.

8 ibid para 8.90.158–8.90.158.

9 Constitution of India 1950, art 124 (2).

10 ibid art 217 (1).

require that the CJI must also 'concur'. In other words, the CJI need not necessarily agree with the eventual decision. Indeed, at the time of drafting the Constitution, there was some debate on whether concurrence ought to be inserted as a constitutional requirement, but this was not accepted by the Constituent Assembly.[11]

Early History of Judicial Appointments

To the credit of the Executive of the day, Prime Minister Jawaharlal Nehru remained very respectful of the independence of the judiciary, maintaining that India deserved 'first-rate' judges,[12] and not subservient courts.[13] Perhaps it was his personal involvement in the nation-building process that made him committed to ensuring that the ideals imagined by the Constituent Assembly were realized. Nehru's stance led to a situation where the CJIs in his time had a virtual veto in judicial appointments, even though his concurrence was not a requirement. It meant that political influence was not really of concern. But, according to Austin, other kinds of influences crept into the appointment process, such as influences from linguistic, religious, caste or regional groups, or even from families and clans – these were the kinds of 'extraneous influences' people were more concerned about at the time.[14] Arguably, it was in response to this that the Law Commission of India (LCI), in its 14th Report, recommended that judicial appointments to the higher courts had to be on merit alone, without reference to communal and regional considerations.[15]

While the provisions of the Constitution dealt with appointment of judges generally, the appointment of the CJI was more a matter of convention than rule, the convention being that of seniority. But this convention also meant

---

[11] See, for example, comments by Dr BR Ambedkar, B Pocker, and Mahboob Ali Baig, Constituent Assembly Debates, 24 May 1949, vol 8.

[12] ibid para 8.90.115.

[13] Granville Austin, *Working a Democratic Constitution: The Indian Experience* (Oxford University Press 1999) 124. For another point of view, see MC Chagla, *Roses in December: An Autobiography* (Bharatiya Vidya Bhavan 2016) 171. It discusses the instance of Nehru, on the suggestion of the then Attorney General for India MC Setalvad, attempting to appoint MC Chagla as the next CJI after CJI Kania's demise without following the seniority convention. It was only after all the judges of the SCI threatened to resign if the seniority convention was not followed that Patanjali Sastri J was appointed as the CJI.

[14] ibid 125.

[15] Law Commission of India, 'Fourteenth Report on the Reform of Judicial Administration' (vol 1, 1958) 34 <https://cdnbbsr.s3waas.gov.in/s3ca0daec69b5adc880fb464895726dbdf/uploads/2022/08/2022080514.pdf> accessed 11 February 2025.

shorter tenures and, by corollary, unstable leadership. The LCI took note of this in its 14th Report, expressing concerns that in a short span of eight years, India had already had five CJIs. It recommended that, ideally, tenures of CJIs should be at least five to seven years, which meant that seniority should not be the sole criterion for appointment to the office of CJI, and that merit and judicial and administrative talent could also be considered.[16] Short tenures were rightly identified as a challenge, because if India desired a strong judiciary, it needed a strong leader at its helm who remained in a leadership position for a meaningful duration of time; a mere few months as CJI would never achieve that end. Gadbois, too, while acknowledging that the seniority convention was useful because it kept out political interference, said that the inevitable consequence of shorter tenures meant that no individual judge was able to truly exhibit their leadership skills (as he noted, ideally, a CJI would be 'a competent administrator, a shrewd judge of men and personalities and a towering personality himself').[17] Relying on seniority alone meant that individuals were not being selected for other characteristics, and competence in leadership was a matter left entirely to chance. Nevertheless, the seniority convention regarding the appointment of the CJI remained unchanged – in the early years, at least.

Rules and conventions aside, it is not as though that the Constitution was able to create a theoretical framework that would operate seamlessly in the practical world. Indeed, there were some controversies in the Nehru era, even if relatively minor compared with what occurred in later decades.[18]

One issue that was of great concern was the threat of transfers of HC judges. Article 222 (1) of the Constitution empowers the President to transfer a judge from one HC to another after consultation with the CJI,[19] implying that transfers of HC judges are subject to Executive discretion, and thus, could be effected if the government was dissatisfied with, say, a judicial pronouncement by a particular judge. The judiciary made things less clear by transferring judges of its own accord on disciplinary grounds.[20] Some conventions and policies came to be developed to counter the concerns around transfers,[21] such

---

16 ibid 38–39.

17 Gadbois, *Supreme Court of India* (n 6) ch 3.

18 Austin, *Working a Democratic Constitution* (n 13) 125–135.

19 Constitution of India 1950, art 222 (1)

20 Austin, *Working a Democratic Constitution* (n 13) 136.

21 ibid 135–136.

as, not transferring judges without their consent; but the threat remained, and was abused most prominently by the government under Prime Minister Indira Gandhi.[22]

The Quiet Before the Storm

In the first twenty years of its existence, the SCI sailed along relatively smoothly. CJI M Hidayatullah, who held office between 1968 and 1970, was perhaps the most influential of CJIs that the SCI had in that era. His tenure was followed by a thirty-five day tenure of JC Shah as CJI; and arguably, the decline of the authority of the CJI started thereafter, under the leadership of SM Sikri, who became the CJI in January 1971. Soon after his appointment, Indira Gandhi's Congress (I) party returned to power with a convincing majority. Multiple cases, either already decided or ongoing, involving weighty constitutional matters around the time (*Golak Nath*,[23] the Bank Nationalisation,[24] Privy Purses[25] and *Kesavananda Bharati*[26]) meant that the judiciary and its role in governance was a focal subject of electoral interest perhaps for the first time in Indian democratic history. In all these cases, the SCI had either curtailed government powers or otherwise decided against the government.[27] The renewed and re-appointed 1971 Indira Gandhi Government believed that its victory was an endorsement of a stronger executive. This was also when the phrase 'committed judges' came into currency,[28] referring to judges with an inclination to support the policies and political direction of the government.

---

22 Apoorva Mandhani, 'Can Judiciary Stand Up to All-Powerful Executive? How Judges Did It During Emergency' (*The Print*, 15 July 2022) <https://theprint.in/india/governance/can-judiciary-stand-up-to-all-powerful-executive-how-judges-did-it-during-emergency/1027493/> accessed 12 February 2025.

23 *C Golaknath v. State of Punjab* AIR 1967 SC 1643

24 *Rustom Cavasjee Cooper v. Union of India* AIR 1970 SC 564.

25 *HH Maharajadhiraja Madhav Rao Jivaji Rao Scindia Bahadur of Gwalior v. Union of India* AIR 1971 SC 530.

26 *His Holiness Kesavananda Bharati Sripadagalvaru v. State of Kerala* 1973 4 SCC 225.

27 It is notable that in all of these cases, with the exception of *Golak Nath*, one judge – AN Ray J – had remained consistently in the minority, choosing to favour the government.

28 The concept of a 'committed judiciary' is attributed to politician M Kumaramangalam, who was the Minister of Steel in the Indira Gandhi Government, according to which the government would consider not only 'judicial integrity' but also the 'philosophy and outlook' of judges. See M Kumaramangalam, *Judicial Appointments: Analysis of the Recent Controversy Over the Appointment of the Chief Justice of India* (Oxford & IBH 1973), as cited in BD Dua, 'A Study in Executive-Judicial Conflict: The Indian Case' (1983) 23 No 4 *Asian Survey* 463; George Gadbois speculates that this may be an incorrect attribution. See GH Gadbois Jr, *Judges of the Supreme Court of India: 1950–89* (Oxford University Press 2011) 152.

Consequently, the new government started to push for the names of those it wanted in the SCI. This shifted the power centre in matters of appointments, away from the virtual veto that the CJI had enjoyed in the Nehru-era. Initially, the dominant Executive chose judges less for their ideological preferences and more based on considerations of friendships and patronage,[29] to the extent that it was not 'court-packing' in the conventional sense of the term. The idea of a 'committed' judge, with explicitly articulated ideological leanings, reached its apogee in the selection of the next CJI, that is, AN Ray J, who followed Sikri J, in 1973.

The seniority convention followed in the appointment of the CJI since 1950 was abandoned abruptly with the appointment of Ray J, who was promoted over three other judges immediately senior to him (the three superseded judges submitted their resignations). The next CJI, too, was appointed by supersession – MH Beg J came to office instead of HR Khanna J, the latter having been penalized for his courageous dissent against the government in the *ADM Jabalpur*[30] case.

The First Judges' Case (1981)

An all-powerful Executive with a stated agenda of 'court-packing' meant that the Damoclean sword of transfers (Article 222 (1)[31] discussed earlier) was no longer a mere threat. In 1976, at the height of the Emergency, sixteen judges of various HCs were transferred without their consent. Coincidentally, these judges had also decided cases against the government – the transfers were clearly intended to be punitive, driven by political factors.[32] One individual, Sankal Chand Himatlal Sheth J, transferred from the Gujarat HC to the Andhra Pradesh HC, challenged his transfer before the SCI. Although he abided by the transfer order eventually, the decision in his case laid down that arbitrary transfers would compromise the judiciary's ability to function without fear or favour. Two key observations were made: first, as noted by Krishna Iyer J in his opinion, 'consultation .... in Art. 222 (1) must be real,

[29] Gadbois, *Judges of the Supreme Court of India* (n 28) 163.

[30] *ADM Jabalpur v. Shivkant Shukla* AIR 1976 SC 1207.

[31] Constitution of India 1950, art 222 (1).

[32] C Jaffrelot and P Anil, 'Ambivalent to the Core: How the Judiciary Capitulated – or Resisted – During the Emergency' (*Scroll.in*, 8 February 2021) <https://scroll.in/article/986204/ambivalent-to-the-core-how-the-judiciary-capitulated-or-resisted-during-the-emergency> accessed 12 February 2025.

substantial and effective consultation'; and second, that there is a 'high legal risk of invalidation of any Presidential order made in the teeth of the Chief Justice's objection'.[33]

By the time the decision in Sheth J's case was delivered, the Emergency had been lifted and the Janata Government had assumed office. It appointed HR Khanna J as Chairperson of the 8th LCI which prepared the 80th Report on 'The Method of Appointment of Judges', recommending that SCI judges should be of the highest calibre and that the CJI ought to consult the three senior-most judges of the court before making any recommendations to the President for appointment of judges.[34] Although the Report does not use the specific term 'collegium', arguably, the seeds for it were sown.

But the Janata Government did not last long. Indira Gandhi returned to power at the Centre, and the balance between the executive and the judiciary shifted once again. Law Minister Shiv Shankar said that the judiciary was 'a vestige of British imperialism and it should be reorganised', to justify shutting down special courts and making untoward transfers and appointments.[35] Much criticism of the government's actions followed, amidst concerns that the executive was out to undermine judicial independence.

These developments set the stage for the first major confrontation between the executive and the judiciary in *SP Gupta v. Union of India*,[36] which came to be known as the '*First Judges*' case', dealing with various questions on the independence of the judiciary. In summary, the SCI held that the term 'consultation' did not amount to 'concurrence' and that the CJI's opinion in appointment decisions had no primacy. It also said that, in appointing HC judges, the President had to consult with the CJI, the CJ of the HC and the Governor of the State; but the President could take an independent decision if the other three functionaries disagreed. In this regard, the Executive became the more powerful institution. One leading newspaper, *The Statesman*, said

[33] *Union of India v. Sankal Chand Himatlal Sheth* 1977 AIR SC 2328; The Bench comprised of YV Chandrachud, PN Bhagwati, VR Krishna Iyer, NL Untwalia and Syed Murtaza Fazal Ali JJ.

[34] Law Commission of India, 'Eightieth Report on the Method of Appointment of Judges' (1979) <https://cdnbbsr.s3waas.gov.in/s3ca0daec69b5adc880fb464895726dbdf/uploads/2022/08/20220805100-2.pdf> accessed 12 February 2025; The report, however, was released by the successor LCI.

[35] Austin, *Working a Democratic Constitution* (n 13) 516–519.

[36] 1981 Supp SCC 87; The Bench comprised of PN Bhagwati, AC Gupta, Syed M Fazal Ali, VD Tulzapurkar, DA Desai, RS Pathak and ES Venkataramiah JJ; Although there were nine issues formulated, the Court was unanimous on the point of 'consultation' not meaning 'concurrence'.

that the Law Minister's original proposals 'were born in original sin', and that the decision had 'handed over to the government, on a platter as it were, the final powers in judicial appointments', with the government now 'relentlessly' trying to change the judiciary.[37] Fali S Nariman later referred to this decision as a 'disaster' for judicial independence.[38] Indeed, the general view was that it had struck a blow to judicial independence altogether.

The Second Judges' Case (1993)

The next major confrontation between the judiciary and the executive on appointments came over a decade later. By now, things were quite different: Indira Gandhi was no longer around, the Rajiv Gandhi-led Congress leadership, after being accused of packing the court with 'sycophant judges',[39] had also ended, and India had begun to be governed by a series of coalition governments.

It was not just a differently-charged political atmosphere. The LCI, in its 121st report in 1987, expressed concern that a 'parochial, regional or narrow outlook … [was] becoming discernible in the judiciary', discussed a collegium mechanism, and proposed the constitution of a 'National Judicial Service Commission' to deal with judicial appointments.[40] A 'crisis of credibility' took hold in the judiciary after corruption charges against several Bombay HC judges surfaced;[41] and concerns were expressed that standards in the judiciary had 'deteriorated', with those judges being appointed who were 'willing to be "influenced" by lavish parties and whisky bottles'.[42] Also, for the first time, a sitting SCI judge – V Ramaswami J – was accused of corruption; an impeachment motion against him was moved in the Parliament but failed to

---

37 Austin, *Working a Democratic Constitution* (n 13) 516–519.

38 Fali S Nariman, 'A Case I Won. But Which I Would Prefer to Have Lost' in S Paul (ed), *Choosing Hammurabi: Debates on Judicial Appointments* (Oxford University Press 2013) 29–43.

39 P Chawla, 'Flouted Guidelines' (*India Today*, 15 June 1985) <http://prabhuchawla.com/data/pdf/1479799074_6_15_1985_appointment__flouted_guidelines.pdf> accessed 12 February 2025.

40 Law Commission of India, 'One Hundred Twenty-First Report on a New Forum for Judicial Appointments' (1987) <https://cdnbbsr.s3waas.gov.in/s3ca0daec69b5adc880fb464895726dbdf/uploads/2022/08/2022080849-1.pdf.>

41 Sabyasachi Mukharji CJI, as quoted in R Chengappa, 'There Are No Set Rules for Hearing Appeals: CJI Sabyasachi Mukharji' (*India Today*, 15 July 1990) <https://www.indiatoday.in/magazine/special-report/story/19900715-there-are-no-set-rules-for-hearing-appeals-cji-sabyasachi-mukharji-813625-1990-07-144> accessed 12 February 2025.

42 *Vishwanath v. ES Venkataramiah* (1990) 92 BomLR 270.

obtain the requisite two-thirds majority in the Lok Sabha to proceed, and Ramaswami J eventually retired a year later.[43] In this background, in October 1993, a nine-judge Constitution Bench of the SCI heard *Supreme Court Advocates-on-Record Association v. Union of India*,[44] also known as the '*Second Judges'* case'.

Here, the SCI, by a 7:2 majority, reversed its decision in the *First Judges'* case, holding that the CJI had primacy in appointment – that 'consultation' meant 'concurrence' – and formally created a Collegium system for the appointment of judges. However, when appointing HC judges, the SCI held that the CJI did not have a veto over the opinion of the CJ of a HC, and the President was not bound to act on the opinion of the CJI in these matters. In other words, the Court held that 'consultation' amounted to 'concurrence', but *not always*. While the Court emphasised on seniority as a criterion for appointments, it said that factors such as regional representation, caste and merit ought to be considered as well. But no clarity was offered on how these factors were to be balanced against each other. There was also scant regard paid to the selection of factors themselves (e.g., gender and minorities barely received mention) or whether they were representative of society as a whole. Nevertheless, this decision was clearly an assertion by the judiciary of its own authority, and an attempt to retain control and regain relevance in judicial appointments.

Unsurprisingly, this decision received much criticism. Not long after its issuance, noted jurist and scholar Sir Robin Cooke, in his article titled 'Making the Angels Weep' (a slant reference to JS Verma J quoting from *Measure for Measure* in his opinion), offered an insightful critique. He pointed out that the words 'consultation' and 'concurrence', in ordinary contexts, had quite different meanings. He said that the Constituent Assembly had discussed amendments 'specifically requiring the *concurrence* of the Chief Justice of India for high judicial appointments . . . But they were defeated', and that despite the clearly expressed legislative intent to reject 'concurrence', it was puzzling as to 'how in less than half a century, "consultation" . . . has been transmuted into concurrence'. He also noted that the decision failed to make a convincing

43 'Number of Times Impeachment Proceedings Were Initiated Against a SC or HC Judge' (*Supreme Court Observer*, 28 March 2018) <www.scobserver.in/journal/number-of-times-impeachment-proceedings-were-initiated-against-a-supreme-court-or-high-court-judge/> accessed 12 February 2025.

44 *Supreme Court Advocates-on-Record Association v. Union of India* AIR 1994 SC 268; The Bench comprised S Ratnavel Pandian, AM Ahmadi, Kuldip Singh, JS Verma, MM Punchhi, Yogeshwar Dayal, GN Ray, AS Anand and SP Bharucha JJ (with Ahmadi and Punchhi JJ dissenting).

case for conflating these two terms, and that the reasons listed by JS Verma J in arriving at the conclusion were completely inadequate to 'change the meaning of [consultation] to concurrence'.[45]

Many years after the decision, the lawyer Fali S Nariman, who had appeared for the Supreme Court Advocates-on-Record Association, wrote an essay, tellingly titled 'A Case I Won: But Which I Would Prefer to Have Lost'.[46] He said that, contrary to the majority view that a contextual and purposive construction of the Constitution was preferred to a literal one, 'the interpretation of Article 124 (and Article 217) . . . was neither contextual nor purposive. There was nothing in the language of the constitutional provision or in the debates in the Constituent Assembly that indicated that the founders ever contemplated that judges were to be entrusted with the power to select judges.' The Collegium created by this decision was, many years later, also criticised by Krishna Iyer J, as 'a curious creation with no backing under the Constitution', acerbically adding, 'the collegium on its own makes the selection. There is no structure to hear the public in the process of selection. No principle is laid down, no investigation is made, and a sort of anarchy prevails.'[47]

The Third Judges' Case (1998)

The President, perhaps to avoid having to accept the then CJI's recommendations for appointments,[48] tactically made a reference under Article 143,[49] listing questions that were essentially related to the CJI's duty as it was understood, to consult other judges on judicial appointments or transfers, as well as a clarification on whether recommendations of the CJI that did not comply with such consultation processes were binding on the government. Note

---

45 Robin Cooke, 'Making the Angels Weep' (1994) *New Zealand Law Journal* 361–364, <https://ssrn.com/abstract=2488322> accessed 12 February 2025.

46 Nariman, 'A Case I Won' (n 38).

47 VK Krishna Iyer, 'Judicial Appointments and Disappointments' (*The Hindu*, 18 August 2012) <https://www.thehindu.com/opinion/lead/judicial-appointments-disappointments/article3785898.ece4> accessed 12 February 2025.

48 Nariman, 'A Case I Won' (n 38); See also, Robin Cooke, 'Where Angels Fear to Tread' (1998) *Victoria University of Wellington Legal Research Paper Series* <https://ssrn.com/abstract=2398661> accessed 12 February 2025; MM Punchhi J was the CJI at the time.

49 Article 143 (1) of the Constitution of India, 1950, enables the President to consult the SCI on a question of law or fact that is of public importance and it is expedient to obtain the opinion of the SCI upon it.

that the government did not seek a review of the older decision,[50] but the SCI volunteered a review unilaterally. The Attorney General for India, Soli Sorabjee, in fact, had stated that the Union of India shall accept and treat as binding the answers of the Court to the questions set out in the reference. The nine-judge Bench of the SCI unanimously reaffirmed the earlier decision in what is known as the '*Third Judges'* case'.[51]

While making clear once again that 'consultation' meant 'concurrence', the decision expanded the Collegium to five members, now comprising the CJI and the next four senior-most judges. Fali S Nariman later perspicaciously noted that there was nothing 'special' about the five senior-most SCI judges, that mere seniority did not always equate to 'superiority of wisdom or competence', and that this 'closed circuit network of five judges' should be 'disbanded'.[52] The decision clarified that the consultation was to be made with the Collegium as a whole and not just the CJI, and acknowledged that judges of outstanding merit could also be appointed, notwithstanding seniority.

Much criticism followed this judgment too, including, once again, by Sir Cooke, who implied that 'fools rush in' in his drolly-titled critique 'Where Angels Fear to Tread'.[53] His view was that the decision expressed no juridical reasoning, and was, at best, 'a promulgation of policy' – the decision did not discuss how five judges in the Collegium would improve on the existing three in matters of either preserving judicial independence or ensuring non-arbitrariness. The meat of the issue, that is, the *method* of appointment, remained unexamined – the Collegium had no office, no institutional staff or framework, no mechanism to gather data and no criteria for selection. The system design was *ad hoc* and a black box.

With this decision, the judiciary firmly and effectively excluded the primacy of the Executive in the appointment process and empowered judges to have the final say in the appointment of judges of the constitutional courts. In doing so, Dr Ambedkar's apprehensions of the dangerous consequences of giving powers of appointment to an individual CJI were conveniently forgotten.

---

50 Cooke, 'Where Angels Fear to Tread' (n 48).

51 *Re Special Reference 1 of 1998* AIR 1999 SC 1; The Bench comprised SP Bharucha, MK Mukherjee, SB Majmudar, Sujata V Manohar, GT Nanavati, S Saghir Ahmad, K Venkataswami, BN Kirpal and GB Pattanaik JJ.

52 Nariman, 'A Case I Won' (n 38).

53 Cooke, 'Where Angels Fear to Tread' (n 48).

The National Judicial Appointments Commission and the Fourth Judges' *Case (2015)*

Two decades on, the era of weak coalitions ended with the coming to power of the Narendra Modi-led National Democratic Alliance (NDA) Government at the centre. Being a strong Executive, it mooted an NJAC for India.

Commissions for the appointment of judges exist in many parts of the world. They are intended to keep the judicial system independent and free from political interference, improve the quality of appointments and bring transparency and accountability to the appointment process. In the judicial appointment commissions in Canada,[54] South Africa[55] and the United Kingdom,[56] the executive also has a role in the functioning of the commission, along with the presence of the civil society.

In India, too, the idea of a Commission for the appointment of judges was not new: the LCI's 80th report[57] had proposed a concept along these lines; Bhagwati J had mooted such a body in the *First Judges'* case; the LCI's 121st report[58] had also recommended a Commission that the Constitution (67th Amendment) Bill of 1990[59] had tried to push for but could not because the Prime Minister had resigned;[60] the Constitution (98th Amendment) Bill of 2003 also sought to introduce a Commission, but lapsed because the Lok Sabha was dissolved in 2004;[61] and the Constitution (120th Amendment) Bill, 2013 accompanied by a draft legislation creating a Judicial Appointments Commission,[62] also eventually lapsed. Finally, the NDA Government took initiative and succeeded in seeing through the Constitution (99th Amendment)

---

54 'Home' (Office of the Commissioner for Federal Judicial Affairs Canada) <www.fja-cmf.gc.ca/home-accueil/index-eng.html> accessed 12 February 2025.

55 'About the JSC' (South Africa Judicial Service Commission) <www.judiciary.org.za/index.php/judicial-service-commission/about-the-jsc> accessed 12 February 2025.

56 'About Us' (UK Judicial Appointments Commission) <https://judicialappointments.gov.uk/> accessed 12 February 2025.

57 Law Commission of India, 'Eightieth Report' (n 34).

58 Law Commission of India, 'One Hundred Twenty-First Report' (n 40).

59 Advisory Panel on Strengthening of the Institutions of Parliamentary Democracy, 'Consultation Paper on Superior Judiciary' (2001) para. 8.18 <https://legalaffairs.gov.in/sites/default/files/(XII)Superior%20Judiciary.pdf> accessed 12 February 2025.

60 Nariman, 'A Case I Won' (n 38).

61 V Venkatesan, 'A Flawed Mechanism' (*Frontline*, 6 June 2003) <https://frontline.thehindu.com/the-nation/article30217285.ece> accessed 12 February 2025.

62 Nariman, 'A Case I Won' (n 38).

Bill and the accompanying NJAC Act in 2014. By these statutes, the NJAC was constituted, consisting of the CJI as Chairperson, and five other members, that is, the two next senior-most judges of the SCI, the Law Minister, and two eminent persons (who would be nominated by a committee of the Prime Minister, the CJI and the Leader of Opposition in the Lok Sabha). The NJAC would make decisions on appointments by a special majority, and two negative votes against a candidate would amount to that candidate's rejection. But the constitutionality of this arrangement came under judicial scrutiny very quickly, leading to the '*Fourth Judges*' case',[63] sometimes also referred to as the '*NJAC Judgment*'.

By a majority of 4:1, the SCI struck down the NJAC Act for being unconstitutional and the Constitution (99th Amendment) Act for being violative of judicial independence, which, in turn, was part of the basic structure of the Constitution that could not be amended. However, there was no attempt to define judicial independence itself. JS Khehar J, in his majority opinion, decided that judicial 'primacy' was a key component of judicial 'independence', offering no further explanation. By corollary, according to the decision, as the NJAC did not allow for judicial primacy to be preserved, it was violative of the basic structure doctrine. Besides lacking explanation, the Court's reliance on the *Second Judges*' case to demonstrate that primacy of the CJI was a part of judicial independence was also entirely incorrect. The *Second Judges*' case nowhere made such a declaration.

Problematically, the majority view also misinterpreted Dr Ambedkar's views in the Constituent Assembly to assume that he meant judicial primacy was to be maintained. A plain reading of Dr Ambedkar's comments, relevant portions of which are referenced earlier, show that the members of the Constituent Assembly wanted a well-balanced system of judicial appointments, where neither the Executive nor the judiciary would be all-powerful; it was never intended to remove the primacy of the Executive from the appointments process.

If the basic structure doctrine were to be taken to a logical conclusion, the doctrine of checks and balances also comes into play, as that too is an integral part of the basic structure. Following this, the role of eminent persons, as representatives of the common people, becomes an accountability mechanism

---

63 *Supreme Court Advocates-on-Record Association v. Union of India* (2016) 5 SCC 1; The Bench comprised JS Khehar, Jasti Chelameswar, Madan Lokur, Kurian Joseph and AK Goel JJ.

in the appointments process, and therefore a necessary requirement. Even if, as articulated by Madan B Lokur J in his opinion,[64] the concern was more with the veto granted to such eminent persons, instead of invalidating the NJAC in its entirety by concluding that their mere presence was violative of the basic structure – surely the Court could have read down the provision pertaining to the role of eminent persons.

Finally, what stood out particularly was that Kurian Joseph J openly acknowledged that 'the present Collegium system lacks transparency, accountability and objectivity' and 'very serious allegations and many a time not unfounded too, have been raised that its approach has been highly subjective.' Yet, the same judge joined the majority, striking down the NJAC law and restoring the Collegium, without really offering an alternative to the problematic Collegium system itself.

Chelameswar J was the sole dissenter in the case. He held that the Collegium system was the 'product of an interpretative gloss on the text of Articles 124 and 217',[65] and that it 'may not be the best to establish and nurture an independent and efficient judiciary'. The dissent also negated the argument that the primacy of the CJI is part of the basic structure of the Constitution. Instead, the dissent states that the basic feature is the 'non-investiture of absolute power in the President to choose and appoint judges of constitutional courts.'[66]

The State of Appointments After the NJAC Decision

As events transpired, after the NJAC decision, the SCI Collegium did not manage to regain the authority it once had in appointments. Multiple instances – and rejections – of recommendations made by it for appointments, promotions and transfers of judges, reveal the denuded powers of the Collegium. Keen observers will note that there is a pattern to how interactions between the Collegium and the government have been taking place lately: the Collegium makes an internal decision on selection or promotion or transfer, and sends its recommendations to the Executive, but the Executive takes no action for months or even years, or rejects the recommendations on flimsy grounds

64 ibid [884] (Lokur J).

65 ibid [1178] (Chelameswar J).

66 ibid [1213] (Chelameswar J).

without providing any substantial basis. As a result, the cycle of appointments has to start all over again. The grounds cited by the Executive for rejection or reconsideration are usually unreasonable, sometimes even bordering on the absurd. The recommendation for elevating KM Joseph J to the SCI was kept in abeyance for six months, ostensibly because the executive wanted a bouquet of names to choose from and the collegium had sent up only one – that of Joseph J. Many believed that Joseph J's name was held back because a Bench headed by him had earlier quashed President's Rule imposed by the Centre in Uttarakhand.[67] The Collegium recommendation to elevate a practising lawyer, Saurabh Kirpal, was returned because the government had relied upon two letters from the Research and Analysis Wing (R&AW), which disclosed that Kirpal was openly gay and had a foreign partner. Despite repeated reiteration by the SCI Collegium, the government has not cleared the file.[68] Similarly, the file recommending another legal practitioner, Somasekhar Sundaresan, was sent back by the Executive, with a recorded opinion that he aired his views on social media on matters that were *sub judice*, but reconsidered its position and appointed him to the Bombay HC ten months after the file was first sent to it.[69]

Then, there are also inexcusable delays in the Executive clearing the Collegium's nominations for the SCI as well as the HCs. The appointments of Indu Malhotra J to the SCI (which took three months from recommendation to approval), and of Wasim S Nargal J to the Jammu & Kashmir HC (which took more than five years!), are just a few examples of lawyers in practice being kept in uncertainty until the Executive deigned them appointment-worthy.[70]

Another affront to the Collegium system is the Executive's interference in altering the seniority amongst judges who are to be sworn in. On 10 January 2018, the Collegium had recommended KM Joseph J to be elevated to the SCI. On 16 July 2018, the Collegium had reiterated its recommendation. Later, on the same day, the Collegium had separately recommended Indira Banerjee and

---

67 'Finally, Order's Out: Justice K M Joseph in Supreme Court' (*The Indian Express*, 4 August 2018).

68 Resolution of the Collegium, Supreme Court of India (18 January 2023) <https://main.sci.gov.in/pdf/Collegium/19012023_105547.pdf> accessed 12 February 2025

69 Ashish Tripathi, '10 Months After Collegium's Reiteration, Centre Clears Appointment of Sundaresan as Add'l Bombay HC Judge' (*Deccan Herald*, 23 November 2023); It does not appear that the notes on file discuss factors integral to being a judge, such as competence, integrity, merit or legal soundness.

70 Madan B Lokur, 'Supreme Court Collegium Is Now Nothing More Than a Post Office with a Fancy Pin Code' (*The Wire*, 16 June 2022) <https://thewire.in/law/supreme-court-collegium-judges-appointment-centre-pick-and-choose> accessed 12 February 2025.

Vineet Saran JJ. This meant that the Collegium intended for Joseph J to be the senior-most of the three. However, on the day of the swearing-in, it became apparent that the Executive had altered this position. Joseph J was the third to be sworn in and thus became junior to both Banerjee and Saran JJ. This resulted in the delayed entry of Joseph J into the SCI Collegium.

Such consistent treatment of Collegium recommendations and the frequency of them being either rejected or returned for reconsideration imply that this is strategic positioning on the part of the Executive. In each such instance, it appears to be keen to emphatically assert its dominance over the judiciary.

To be fair, the Collegium is also partly responsible for contributing to the decision paralysis on judicial appointments. Different Collegiums, even with some of its members continuing, take different positions on the same set of names, causing much confusion. Two examples suffice. The SCI Collegium signed a resolution elevating Rajendra Menon and Pradeep Nandrajog JJ to the SCI. But after the retirement of one of the Collegium members, that is, MB Lokur J, these names were dropped and some others proposed by the same Collegium.[71] The Bombay HC Collegium in 2021 under the brief thirty-nine-day tenure of CJ BP Dharmadhikari recommended the names of twenty-two people for appointment. However, this list was objected to by two sitting SCI judges who were consultees, being originally from the Bombay HC.[72] They expressed concerns on the hasty manner in which these names had been selected, ignoring criteria such as integrity, diversity or even age. Despite the objections, the Collegium sent the names to the government. Subsequently, the government returned the file, by which time, the CJI who had forwarded the list had retired, and the Collegium was reconstituted under the new CJI. The list was returned for reconsideration to the HC Collegium, where also a new judge had taken over as CJ, which revoked the names of all those recommended originally.[73] These situations are hardly unique. They stem from a systemic malaise in the Collegium system – there are no criteria for the appointment of judges that a collegium must adhere to. Obviously, this means that recommendations are entirely subjective, and

---

[71] Seema Chishti, 'Disquiet in Section of Court over Way in Which Collegium Changed Judge Choices for SC' (*The Indian Express*, 15 January 2019). See also, the essay in this book by Madan Lokur.

[72] Dhananjay Mahapatra, 'Collegium returns 18 names to the Bombay High Court' (*The Times of India*, 8 September 2021).

[73] Dhananjay Mahapatra, 'SC Judges Red-Flag Bombay HC Names for 22 New Judges' (*The Times of India*, 25 February 2021).

whims, biases, favourites, all creep in. Ultimately, it becomes a case of 'you show me the person and I will show you the rule', where different rules are employed for different people depending on who those people might be.

Take the case of Akil Kureshi J for instance. The government refused to accept the Collegium's recommendation to appoint Kureshi J (of the Gujarat HC), as CJ of the Madhya Pradesh HC, reportedly because he had passed multiple orders against the government, including an order to remand a high political functionary in a case of an extra-judicial killing. Later, Kureshi J's name was also not cleared for elevation to the SCI by its Collegium, due to internal disagreements (insisting on the elevation, Rohinton F Nariman J vetoed all names being discussed by the Collegium for the next two years, thus indicating that it was the others in the Collegium, that is, the CJI and other members, who disapproved of Kureshi J).[74]

Appointments by High Court Collegiums

In discussions around judicial appointments, most attention is paid to the way in which judges are appointed to the SCI. Relatively less attention is devoted to studying how judges are appointed to the HCs. Arguably, the HC Collegium is an important link in the entire chain of judicial appointments in India because it is the originator of the names of those who may be part of the pool for ultimate elevation to the SCI. It is effectively a stepping stone for SCI judges, although, of course, there are exceptions in the case of direct appointments to the SCI.

Most judges of the SCI, barring those who are direct appointees, come from one HC or the other. Their association with their parent HCs continues into their tenure as SCI judges as well. When the SCI Collegium discusses prospective candidates for appointment from specific HCs, it will invariably consult judges originally from that HC, if there are any, sitting in the SCI, who are considered 'consultee judges'. Sometimes, members of the Collegium and the 'consultee judges' from the specific HCs concerned become unofficial power centres, directly interfering in the selection of the HC judges. Invariably, an HC is likely to have a CJ from another state

---

[74] Aryushi Saraogi and Aarathi Ganesan, 'Justice Akil Kureshi Retires Without Elevation to the Supreme Court' (*Supreme Court Observer*, 10 March 2022) <https://www.scobserver.in/journal/justice-akil-kureshi-retires-without-elevation-to-the-supreme-court/> accessed 12 February 2025.

who might aspire to be elevated to the SCI. Thus, the HC CJ could be under pressure to quietly acquiesce to the choice of the consultee judge and sometimes even a member of the SCI Collegium. This ends up perpetuating a culture of subservience and sycophancy in the judiciary. The Collegium system has altered – unfortunately, to the detriment of the HCs – the relationships between judges of the HCs and the SCI. The prestige that was once associated with being a HC judge has now lost its sheen. It is a cause for concern that HC judges appear to be over eager to please a consultee judge or members of the SCI Collegium, believing that it will support their future prospects.

Some, like Ruma Pal J, have long maintained that the process by which a judge is appointed to a superior court is 'one of the best kept secrets in the country'. She adverts to this 'excessive degree of secrecy', resulting in there being usually no information or discussion on the abilities or suitability of potential candidates.[75] Consequently, appointments rest on subjective assessments based on anecdotal revelations, personal friendships, obligatory relationships and even trade-offs between the members of the Collegium or between the Collegium and the executive. Having any 'selection criteria' for identifying and appointing judges has no meaning in this entire process.

In his opinion that formed part of the SCI's decision on the contempt proceedings against CS Karnan J, Jasti Chelameswar J expressed concern over how an individual with such a personality could be appointed as a HC judge. He wrote that the case highlighted 'the need to revisit the process of selection and appointment of judges to the constitutional courts, for that matter any member of the judiciary at all levels'. He acknowledged that 'there [was] a failure to make an assessment of the personality of [Karnan J] at the time of recommending his name for elevation,' and said that there is an 'unquestionable' need for a suitable and appropriate mechanism to assess the personality of a candidate under consideration for appointment to a constitutional court.[76] We may recall that Chelameswar J dissented in the *Fourth Judges'* case and held the 99th Amendment and the NJAC Act to be constitutionally valid.

The original intent of the members of the Constituent Assembly to have impartial and apolitical appointment processes and judges appears to have

75 Ruma Pal, 'An Independent Judiciary' (2011) 75(9) *The Radical Humanist* 6–15; Lecture delivered at V.M. Tarkunde Memorial Lecture in IIC, New Delhi on 10 November 2011.

76 *Re Hon'ble Mr Justice C S Karnan* (2017) 2 SCC 756 [78] (Chelameswar J).

been thrown to the wind because of the way in which the Collegium system has evolved.

The Damoclean Sword of High Court Transfers

The process of intra-HC transfers has its own issues, separate from that of appointment. Often, HC judges are treated like bureaucrats or government servants, who are transferred at the whims of their overlords. Besides being demeaning to the office of a judge, abrupt and unreasonable transfers fail to recognize that judicial work is very closely tied to jurisdiction and local expertise. Sometimes, on examining the reasons given by collegiums for transfers, one comes across the phrase 'in the public interest', implying indirectly that the transfer was perhaps made on disciplinary grounds. Such transfers arguably do more harm than good, and it does not help that the Executive weighs in with its own views on transfers.

Transfers are also sometimes outright punitive against judges who issue adverse decisions against the incumbent government. One example is the transfer of Rajiv Shakdher J, who was moved from the Delhi HC to the Madras HC, reportedly because he had issued an order against the government's censure of an international non-governmental organisation.[77] Similarly, S Muralidhar J was transferred from the Delhi HC to the Punjab and Haryana HC and transferred again to be made CJ of the HC of Orissa but was not elevated to the SCI.[78]

Besides sheer arbitrariness and the absence of any clearly stated policy on transfers, the manner in which some judges are shunted around the country has a chilling effect on the dispensation of justice itself – for judges will be doubly careful about deciding matters that may be regarded as unfavourable by the government lest they invite unwanted, unjustified and unpredictable transfers.

---

77 Sohini Ghosh, 'Outgoing Delhi High Court Judge on Past Transfer: "No Consent"' (*The Indian Express*, 25 September 2024).

78 Fali S Nariman, Madan B Lokur and Sriram Panchu, 'A Question for the Collegium: Why Was Justice Muralidhar Not Brought to the Supreme Court' (*The Indian Express*, 19 April 2023).

The Diversity Debate

Nobody will deny that a diverse judiciary is desirable, with its relationship with the legitimacy of decision-making and the quality of justice, as well as its reflection of equality of opportunity for all in accessing the upper echelons of the judiciary.[79] CJI DY Chandrachud, making a case for diversity, has said, 'people will start trusting the judiciary only when they see a reflection of themselves in the people who dispense justice.'[80] However, a diversity study of the SCI in 2023, and its Collegium appointments, reveal 'a startling lack of representation of religious minorities, women and marginalised communities.'[81] Diversity is not a concern merely of the SCI, but also of the HCs – data suggests that only seventeen per cent of judges appointed to HCs between 2018 and 2023 belong to SCs, STs or OBCs[82] and the representation of women judges in the HCs and SCI is around thirteen per cent.[83]

When diversity is considered, it must go beyond mere regional representation and embrace gender, class, caste and religion as well. Nevertheless, a criterion of minimum merit must be followed, and diversity must not be pursued as a goal at the cost of merit. India has had many fine judges from minority communities, and many fine women judges as well, who have been left at HCs but not appointed to the SCI; many practising lawyers from such groups have also been ignored in appointments to the HCs from the Bar. This is, of course, slowly changing. However, it is a harsh truth that class consciousness still prevails in many states, and the idea of diversity remains merely theoretical in many parts of the country. Biases are inbuilt into our society and culture, which manifest in judicial appointments as well; this needs to change urgently, and an intentional policy of affirmative action (while balancing for merit) needs to be implemented.

---

79 E Rackley, 'A Short History of Judicial Diversity' (2023) 76(1) *Current Legal Problems* 265.

80 Utkarsh Anand, 'Collegium Aims for a Diverse Bench, to Make SC "People-Centric": CJI Chandrachud' (*The Hindustan Times*, 23 August 2023).

81 Leena Gita Reghunath and Sushovan Patnaik, 'Supreme Court Review 2023: The Diversity Problem Remained Unaddressed' (*Supreme Court Observer*, 4 January 2024) <https://www.scobserver.in/journal/supreme-court-review-2023-the-diversity-problem-remained-unaddressed> accessed 12 February 2025.

82 'Of 650 HC Judges Appointed Since 2018, Nearly 17 Pc Belong to SC, ST, OBC Categories: Govt' (*The Hindustan Times*, 14 December 2023).

83 Government of India, Ministry of Law and Justice (*Lok Sabha Unstarred Question 598*, 7 December 2023) <https://sansad.in/getFile/annex/262/AU598.pdf?source=pqars> accessed 12 February 2025.

Thinking Afresh About Judicial Appointments

There is no doubt that India needs an organized system with a predictable, transparent, accountable method of operations that would facilitate the appointment of judges in the SCI and HCs. In such a system, while a majority of judges could retain control over the appointments process, the processes and policies followed in the method of selection and appointment of candidates need to evolve significantly.

There are obligations and commitments aplenty that India has signed up to internationally that require transparent and clear procedures in the selection and appointment of judges. The guidance note issued by the United Nations Human Rights Committee on Article 14 of the International Covenant on Civil and Political Rights provides that 'States should take specific measures guaranteeing the independence of the judiciary, protecting judges from any form of political influence in their decision-making through the constitution or adoption of laws establishing clear procedures and objective criteria for the appointment, remuneration, tenure, promotion, suspension and dismissal of the members of the judiciary and disciplinary sanctions taken against them.'[84]

The *Beijing Statement of Principles on the Independence of Judiciary in the LAWASIA region*,[85] more commonly referred to as just the *Beijing Statement*, provides detailed commitments adopted by the Sixth Conference of Chief Justices of Asia and the Pacific, including on judicial appointments. Collectively these instruments, commentaries and guidances, emphasize that the selection and appointment process of judges should be independent from the Executive and be composed not only of judges and members of the legal profession. They underscore that transparent procedures should be followed, preferably through clearly defined and formalized systems.

This international guidance on transparency and appointments is useful, particularly because the understanding of transparency in the Collegium system today is limited to making public the resolutions of Collegium meetings. It is a truth not openly acknowledged that the present assessment

---

84 UN Human Rights Committee, 'General Comment No. 32, Article 14: Right to Equality before Courts and Tribunals and to a Fair Trial' (23 August 2007) CCPR/C/GC/32.

85 Law Association of Asia and the Pacific, *Beijing Statement of Principles on the Independence of Judiciary in the LAWASIA Region* (1995) Sixth Conference of the Chief Justices <https://www.icj.org/wp-content/uploads/2014/10/Beijing-Statement.pdf> accessed 12 February 2025; This was amended at the Seventh Conference of Chief Justices, Manila, 28 August 1997.

procedure of prospective candidates, which involves seeking inputs from the Intelligence Bureau on the candidate's antecedents, is unsatisfactory.

The judiciary must also acknowledge and accept the fact that the current stalemate with the Executive is a product of the Collegium system itself. The judiciary has chosen to create a system – the Collegium – that is designed to be not accountable; and this unaccountable system is foisted upon other organs of the State. Previously, the other organs, specifically the Executive, did not attempt to resist or interfere with the Collegium's process because they were relatively weaker and operated as coalitions and were more concerned with ensuring their own survival. But now that India has had a stronger Executive for a considerably lengthy period, it is inevitable that a strong Executive will wish to assert its power, particularly over the judiciary. This is a clear shortcoming of the Collegium system.

In this regard, in the *Second Judges'* case, the Constitution Bench essentially expressed the view that if you place the Executive outside the appointments process, all problems relating to political influence in appointments would be resolved; and somehow, magically and automatically, accountability, transparency and all desirable measures of checks and balances would be achieved. Although the SCI's model might have been designed to deny the Executive primacy in the appointments, the last decade has witnessed a strong Executive finding other ways to exert its primacy.

This circuitous manner of the government attempting to influence a process from which they are excluded lends itself to greater unpredictability, loss of transparency and one-upmanship between the judiciary and the Executive. Instead, it may be prudent to institutionalize the involvement of the Executive, such that their seat and the table is assured, with their role clearly defined and thus limited. Furthermore, as Chelameswar J noted in the *Fourth Judges'* case, civil society representation in judicial appointments could foster 'transparency, commitment, and participation of the ultimate stakeholders – the People'.[86]

There is evidence of this approach being effective, albeit in jurisdictions that may be dissimilar from ours in certain material aspects. If one looks at other common law jurisdictions, we have the Constitutional Reform Act, 2005 (CRA) in the United Kingdom, which establishes a Judicial Appointments Commission (JAC), an independent body of fifteen members including

86 *Supreme Court Advocates-on-Record Association* (n 63) [1212] (Chelameswar J).

laypersons, legal professionals and judges. The JAC recommends candidates for vacancies in the judiciary, whereas special panels handle senior appointments. Interestingly, the CRA removed the traditional power of the Lord Chancellor to make selections, substantially in consultation with the serving judiciary and others, but did not remove the Lord Chancellor's role completely. In relation to each vacancy, the Lord Chancellor may accept the JAC's selection, require the JAC to reconsider its selection, or reject it. For SCI appointments, there is a five-member Commission that includes representatives from the JAC, the Scottish and Northern Irish appointment bodies, and at least 1 layperson. The CRA mandates appointments based on merit and requires the selection process to promote diversity. The Parliament plays no direct role in appointments, but the Lord Chancellor remains accountable to it, ensuring the process balances independence with oversight.[87]

Likewise, in South Africa, we have a Judicial Service Commission (JSC), which has a diverse composition that includes laypersons apart from representatives of the judiciary and the South African parliament. Prior to the JSC, South Africa's system of appointment of judges was based on the principle of parliamentary supremacy, with the President being vested with the sole authority to appoint judges with the only input coming from the senior judge of the court to which the new appointment was being made.[88] This bears a striking resemblance to Article 124 (2), prior to its interpretation in the *Judges'* cases. Eventually, as it is now the situation in India, this method of appointment created controversy due to its lack of transparency and absence of representation of members of civil society and the legal fraternity. The JSC was created to break away from this practice. Today, for appointing constitutional court judges, the JSC compiles a list of nominees with three more names than the required vacancies and submits it to the President. The President, after consulting the CJ and party leaders in the National Assembly, selects judges from this list or requests further nominees if any are deemed unsuitable.[89]

---

[87] Constitution Committee, *Twenty-Fifth Report on Judicial Appointments* (HL 2010-12, 272) 8.

[88] Alsion Tilley and Zikhona Ndlebe, 'Judicial Appointments in South Africa' (2021) 10(3) *British Journal of American Legal Studies* 457 <www.researchgate.net/publication/360675596_Judical_Appointments_in_South_Africa > accessed 12 February 2025.

[89] Constitution of the Republic of South Africa 1996, sec 174 (1)–(8); For other courts, the president appoints judges based on the JSC's advice, ensuring all appointments consider merit, the judiciary's demographic representation and judicial independence.

The Future of Judicial Appointments

There is no doubt that one of the most pressing questions we are faced with today, as observers and participants of the Indian judicial system, is whether the appointments process we presently have is the most appropriate, efficient or best functioning system that we could have arrived at. Is this system desirable? Must we continue with this? Should we strive to look for better alternatives? What are the possibilities? The 14th Report of the LCI[90] asked that we must staff our courts with first rate, best possible judges; but surely, we must ask whether we are in fact getting such judges with the present system. These are iterative questions that must be asked every now and then, because circumstances change, and conditions and individuals and ideologies evolve, all of which impact how systems function.

All this leaves one to speculate on where the future of the appointments process lies. We need a formalized system with appropriate transparency and accountability measures. Given the spectacular failure of the government's attempts to push through the NJAC, we are unlikely to see a judicial appointments commission in any form.

However, we must also acknowledge that the current system cannot be pursued any longer, or we will be burdened with all kinds of attendant problems. The tussle between the Executive and the judiciary, for example, has left Indian courts with vacancies galore, which only serve to exacerbate the situation of pending cases. The political class, especially, must think about this, and all stakeholders must be brought together to arrive at a reasonable and workable arrangement that prevents the situation from getting worse. It would seem that the present arrangement, where the Executive is kept out as per the *Judges'* cases, works very well for the Executive itself – for, even from the outside, it can pick and choose whom to appoint, stall recommendations and operate with a virtual veto on selections. The very idea of a collegium where the Executive should not interfere, which was the original intent behind its creation, has been reversed in present-day India.

There is no magic bullet that will solve the many, many problems that the Indian judiciary and the judicial appointments process is currently undergoing. It requires untangling multiple spheres of influence, dismantling deep-seated

[90] Law Commission of India, 'Fourteenth Report' (n 15).

power centres, and ultimately, acknowledging with brutal honesty that the Indian system has limitations that need to be overcome, and that things are not all rosy and perfect. When all of that happens, we might have a brighter future ahead.

The Working of the Collegium

MADAN LOKUR

The appointment of judges to the SCI and the HCs across the country has been a subject of discussion over the years. The *First Judges'* case[1] gave primacy to the Government of India (GoI) in the appointment of judges of the HCs and the SCI.[2] This had its problems, which need not be discussed presently. In *Subhash Sharma v. Union of India,*[3] a three-judge Bench of the SCI referred the issue of primacy in the appointment of judges to the HCs and the SCI to a nine-judge Bench. In the *Second Judges'* case,[4] by a majority of 7:2, it was held that prior consultation with the Chief Justice of India (CJI) as head of the judiciary is mandatory. The word 'consultation' in Article 124 (3) of the Constitution of India was read to mean 'concurrence'. However, the CJI was required to form his opinion (for the appointment of judges to the HCs) after taking the views of a Collegium consisting of 'two senior-most Judges of the Supreme Court and the senior-most Supreme Court Judge who comes from the State'.[5] The Collegium for appointment of judges to the SCI consisted of the CJI and the two senior-most judges of the SCI.

---

1 *SP Gupta v. Union of India* (1981) Supp SCC 87; This was a Bench composed of PN Bhagwati, AC Gupta, S Murtaza Fazal Ali, VD Tulzapurkar, DA Desai, RS Pathak, ES Venkataramiah JJ.

2 For a detailed discussion, see AP Shah's essay in this book.

3 1991 Supp (1) SCC 574.

4 *Supreme Court Advocates-on-Record Association v. Union of India* (1993) 4 SCC 441; This was a Bench composed of S Ratnavel Pandian, AM Ahmadi, Kuldip Singh, JS Verma, MM Punchhi, Yogeshwar Dayal, GN Ray and SP Bharucha JJ. The majority opinion (7:2) was delivered by JS Verma J and the dissenting opinion by AM Ahmadi and MM Punchhi JJ. This larger Bench considered, among others, two questions relevant to this discussion: one, regarding the primacy of the CJI in the matter of appointment of judges of the HCs and the SCI, and the other, the reconsideration of the majority opinion in the *First Judges'* case. For a detailed exposition see Shah's essay in this book.

5 *Second Judges'* case (n 4) 676; Similarly, for the appointment of a judge of the HC, it was directed that the process should commence with the recommendation of the CJ of the HC. It was further directed that, 'He must ascertain the views of the two senior-most Judges of the High Court and incorporate the same in his recommendation. The [CJI] while examining the recommendation must take into account the views of two senior-most Judges of the Supreme Court and also the opinion of the senior Judge conversant with the affairs of the concerned High Court.'

The composition of the Collegium, both at the level of the HCs and the SCI underwent a modification in the *Third Judges'* case.[6] A nine-judge Bench now unanimously ruled that the Collegium for the appointment of judges of the SCI and to transfer a CJ or puisne judge of a HC would stand expanded to include four senior-most *puisne* judges of the SCI, apart from the CJI. For appointments to the HC, the recommendation was required to be made by the CJI in consultation with the two senior-most *puisne* judges of the SCI.[7]

The MoP for Appointment of Judges and Chief Justices

The conclusions of all the decisions rendered by the SCI on the subject of appointment of judges were distilled in a document dated 30 June 1999 prepared by the Ministry of Law, Justice and Company Affairs called the Memorandum of Procedure (MoP) for appointment of judges and CJs. The steps outlined in the MoP, relevant to the present context are[8]:

Step 1: The CJ of the concerned HC has the responsibility of communicating, to the Chief Minister of the state concerned, the names of persons to be selected for appointment. Details are furnished to the Chief Minister in terms of the format appended to the Memorandum. Additionally, if the Chief Minister desires to recommend name(s) of person(s) for such appointment, he or she must forward the same to the CJ for their consideration.

Step 3: Copies of recommendations made by the CJ of the HC to the Chief Minister of the concerned state, are required to be endorsed to the Union Minister of Law and Justice (MLJ), the Governor of the concerned state and the CJI.

---

6 *Special Reference No 1 of 1998* (1998) 7 SCC 739; This was an Advisory Opinion given by the SCI on questions of law referred by the President to the SCI. The Bench comprised SP Bharucha, MK Mukherjee, SB Majmudar, Sujata V Manohar, GT Nanavati, S Saghir Ahmad, K Venkataswami, BN Kirpal and GB Pattanaik JJ.

7 *Third Judges'* case (n 6) [30]; On consultation with the two senior-most puisne judges of the SCI, it was made clear that, 'The requirement of consultation by the Chief Justice of India with his colleagues who are likely to be conversant with the affairs of the concerned High Court does not refer only to those Judges who have that High Court as a parent High Court. It does not exclude Judges who have occupied the office of a Judge or Chief Justice of that High Court on transfer.'

8 These steps have been summarized in the judgment of the SCI in *Supreme Court Advocates-on-Record Association v. Union of India* (2016) 5 SCC 1 (*Fourth Judges'* case); The Bench comprised JS Khehar, Jasti Chelameswar, Madan Lokur, Kurian Joseph and AK Goel JJ; Chelameswar J was the sole dissenter. Steps two, four and six are not immediately relevant for the topic discussed here and therefore, have not been set out. In a welcome move, the SCI on 5 May 2025, uploaded on its website details showing the process of appointment of judges both to the HCs as well as the SCI.

Step 5: The MLJ would, on his own, consider the recommendations placed before him in the light of the reports, as may be available to the government in respect of the persons under consideration. The recommended persons would be subject to scrutiny at the hands of the Intelligence Bureau (IB), through the Union Ministry of Home Affairs (MHA). The IB would opine on the integrity of the individuals under consideration.

Step 7: Based on the material made available, and additionally the views of judges of the SCI (who are conversant with the affairs of the concerned HC), obtained in writing, the CJI, in consultation with the Supreme Court Collegium (SCC), would forward the recommendation to the MLJ.

Step 8: The MLJ would then place the said recommendation before the Prime Minister, who would examine the entire matter in consultation with the MLJ and advise the President.

The MoP was in operation for more than a decade until the Parliament amended the Constitution[9] and created a body for the appointment of judges called the NJAC.[10] In the *Fourth Judges'* case, the Constitution (99th Amendment) Act, 2014 creating the NJAC was struck down, by a 4:1 majority, on the ground that it violated the basic structure of the Constitution.[11]

Importantly, during the submissions in the *Fourth Judges'* case, grievances were expressed about the 'functioning in practice' of the Collegium system of appointments. In my concurring opinion, I had asked for a consequence hearing to be held for 'steps to be taken in the future to streamline the process and procedure of appointment of Judges, to make it more responsive to the needs of the people, to make it more transparent and in tune with societal needs, and more particularly, to avoid a fifth Judges case!'[12] In its operative

---

9 Constitution (99th Amendment) Act 2014.

10 While the concept of the NJAC (or a similar body) was in the pipeline even earlier, it came to fruition only in April 2015.

11 *Fourth Judges'* case (n 8); In his dissenting opinion, Chelameswar J was critical of the working of the collegium system and referenced Fali S Nariman, in which Nariman, criticizing the collegium, said 'I would suggest that the closed circuit network of five Judges should be disbanded'. See *Fourth Judges'* case (n 8) [1207.8] (Chelameswar J). See also, Fali S Nariman, *Before Memory Fades: An Autobiography* (Hay House India 2010) 400; Kurian Joseph J, who joined the majority, echoed the concerns of Chelameswar J of the current collegium system lacking transparency, accountability and objectivity, See *Fourth Judges'* case (n 8) [990] (Joseph J); Kurian Joseph J later said that he regretted his decision and voiced misgivings on the working of the Collegium system. See 'Former Supreme Court Judge Kurian Joseph Regrets his Decision Quashing National Judicial Appointments Commission' (*The Hindu*, 1 January 2020).

12 *Fourth Judges'* case (n 8) [969] (Lokur J).

order, the Court directed listing of the case on 3 November 2015 'to consider introduction of appropriate measures, if any, for an improved working of the "Collegium System".'[13]

The Department of Justice (DoJ) placed a public notice on its website inviting suggestions, and in response, about 11,500 pages of views were received. These were considered by a two-member committee of Ms Pinky Anand, Additional Solicitor General, and Mr Arvind Datar, Senior Advocate, who presented a compilation to the Court. After conducting hearings on two consecutive dates, the Court pronounced a unanimous order on 16 December 2015 requiring the GoI to finalize the MoP and supplement it in consultation with the CJI. The CJI and the four senior-most *puisne* judges of the SCI held deliberations and suggested incorporating in the MoP an 'eligibility criteria' – measures that would ensure 'transparency in the appointment process', establishment of a 'secretariat for each High Court and the Supreme Court' and prescribe its functions, duties and responsibilities. It was also suggested that the MoP would provide for 'an appropriate mechanism and procedure for dealing with complaints against anyone who is being considered for appointment as a judge.' Interaction between the Collegium and a 'recommendee' was also considered for inclusion in the MoP.[14]

The revised MoP was then finalized and approved by the CJI and sent to the DoJ for implementation as the basic document for appointment of judges of the HCs and the SCI.[15] Surprisingly, it transpires that the DoJ had a rethink on some aspects of the revised MoP, and a letter was sent either to the CJI or to the Secretary General of the SCI in this regard.[16] As far as I recall, three suggestions were given by the DoJ – one being inclusion of a representative of the government in the SCC, and another incorporating the authority of the government to reject the recommendation of the SCC on grounds of national

[13] ibid [1239].

[14] ibid [1256.1]–[1256.5].

[15] GoI, Ministry of Law and Justice (*Rajya Sabha Unstarred Question No. 906*, 9 February 2023) <https://sansad.in/getFile/annex/259/AU906.pdf?source=pqars> accessed 25 February 2025.

[16] ibid; Per the MLJ, 'Thereafter, the Supreme Court in a judgment dated 04.07.2017 in a Suo-Motu Contempt proceedings against a Judge of Calcutta High Court brought out the system's failure of not providing an appropriate procedure for making assessment of the personality of the contemnor at the time of recommending his name for elevation as High Court Judge inter-alia highlighting the need to revisit the process of selection and appointment of Judges to the Constitutional Courts. The views of the Government on the relevant points were conveyed to Supreme Court of India vide letter dated 11.07.2017.'

security. The 'national security' ground is quite amazing. Does the government seriously believe that the SCC consisting of the CJI, and the four senior-most judges of the SCI would recommend the appointment of a person as a judge of the HC or the SCI if that person is a threat to national security? Presumably, the letter was placed before the CJI, but for some unknown reason, he took no action on the letter, with the result that, as on date, though the revised MoP is operational without the three suggestions of the government, the Executive believes it has not been finalized and it is not bound by it.[17]

High Court Collegium

Composition

The High Court Collegium (HCC) consists of the CJ of the HC, who is invariably a judge transferred from another HC,[18] and two senior-most puisne judges, commonly referred to as J1 and J2, are likely to have either practised in the HC or have been judicial officers of the state and are, therefore, more familiar with the working of the HC and the district courts as well as the requirements of the judiciary in the state.[19] Occasionally, though not infrequently, J1 or J2 or both are from a different parent HC; their familiarity or unfamiliarity with the justice delivery system in the state matches with that of the CJ.[20] This might delay the process of making recommendations. There have been instances when the SCC would transfer a judge from one HC to another with the intention of that judge succeeding as the CJ of the transferor

---

[17] This was also noted in *The Advocates Association Bengaluru v. Barun Mitra*, Conmt. Pet. (C) No. 867/2021 I TP (C) 2419/2019, order dated 8 December 2022 (SK Kaul, AS Oka and Vikram Nath JJ).

[18] The reason for this is that a resolution was passed in the conference of Chief Ministers and CJs way back in the 1980s that the CJ of a HC will be from a different HC. An exception is that if the senior-most judge of that HC has less than a year remaining to retire, such judge can be made the CJ of that very HC. For instance, in May 2023 and February 2023, RP Dhanuka and Sonia Gokani JJ were made CJs of their own parent HCs, i.e., the Bombay and Gujarat HCs respectively, and on 29 September 2024, Manmohan J, who was to retire on 20 December 2024, was made the CJ of the Delhi HC. He was, two weeks prior to the said retirement date, on 5 December 2024, sworn in as a judge of the SCI.

[19] It is not necessary to go into the reasons for this resolution, which does not now seem to be available in the public domain, but the reasons for the resolution are no longer valid particularly after the Collegium system became operational. In my view, the CJ of a HC should not be from a different parent HC but should be a judge of the same court.

[20] During 2018, when DP Maheswari J, whose parent HC was the HC of Rajasthan, was the CJ of the HC of Karnataka, his J1 and J2 were Raghavendra Chavan and Vineet Kothari JJ, who too were from Rajasthan.

HC in a few months or so, to minimize unfamiliarity with the state's justice delivery system. It may be of interest to know that, at any point in time, the number of vacancies in all the HCs across the country hovers between thirty per cent and forty per cent.[21]

Working

While there have not been any complaints about the working of the HCC, I am of the opinion that, depending upon the size of the state and the HC, the HCC should consist of five judges. However, relatively smaller states such as Sikkim, Tripura, and some of the north-eastern states have a small judiciary and very few HC judges.[22] In such states, the HCC of three can continue.

The reason for the suggested change is that, in large states, such as Uttar Pradesh, Madhya Pradesh and Maharashtra, it is not easy for the HCC to identify potential candidates for appointment as HC judges. For example, the Bar Council of Maharashtra and Goa claims to have a membership of over 215,000 lawyers, and there are over 2,400 judicial officers across both states. All of them are not eligible for appointment as HC judges since the Constitution of India provides that an HC judge should have been a practising advocate in an HC or a judicial officer for at least ten years. Even so, if only one per cent of this vast body of lawyers and judicial officers qualify for appointment as HC judges, it still leaves the HCC to find the best and the brightest from among more than 2,000 lawyers and 24 judicial officers. This is a difficult task for a variety of reasons.

It is not possible for the HCC to actually know such a large number of lawyers. Then, there may also be some practitioners, mainly in the district courts, who infrequently appear in cases in the HC. In a city-state like Delhi, it is easy to identify such lawyers and in fact some of them have actually been appointed as HC judges, but this is practically not possible in large states.

---

[21] As of 1 February 2025, against the sanctioned strength of 1122 the working strength is 755. See 'Vacancy Position as on 01.02.2025' (Department of Justice, 1 February 2025) <https://cdnbbsr.s3waas.gov.in/s35d6646aad9bcc0be55b2c82f69750387/uploads/2025/02/202502032012564006.pdf> accessed 25 February 2025.

[22] The Bench strength corresponds to the overall pendency of cases in the HCs in the north-eastern states. On a lighter note, it is not unusual for the Bar in these HCs to protest if there is a quick disposal of cases as that might result in the reduction of the sanctioned strength or perhaps the Bench altogether.

In my opinion, to make the selection process for HC judges more meaningful, the HCC should be expanded to five judges, and if necessary to seven judges, depending upon the state and the HC concerned.

The appointment of a CJ from outside the state is, in my opinion, not a good idea. It takes time for the CJ to become familiar with the practice and procedure of the HC and the district courts. I recall, on being appointed CJ of the Gauhati HC, it took me quite some time to familiarize myself with the working of the HC, which had seven Benches, one in each of the north-eastern states.[23]

Consultation by the High Court Collegium

There is a general belief that the HCC cannot consult or should not consult anybody else while making its recommendations. Judgments of the SCI do not prevent the HCC from obtaining inputs from persons within and outside the legal fraternity. I have met reporters from newspapers who have spent decades reporting on court proceedings and they have considerable knowledge of the calibre and potential of lawyers and judicial officers, and their suitability for being appointed as HC judges. As is often said, 'They also serve who only stand and wait.' These reporters can advise the CJ on the legal acumen of a person and also about the character, integrity and behaviour of a lawyer in the court and sometimes outside the court premises. There is, therefore, value in the HCC informally getting feedback or inputs from civil society.

To ensure that a recommendation for appointment is not turned down for reasons other than relatable to merit, it would also be appropriate for the HCC to obtain additional inputs from the local intelligence authorities. As per the procedure presently followed, after a recommendation is made by the HCC, the state government occasionally obtains inputs from the local intelligence authorities. This is then communicated to the GoI but not to the HCC. If an adverse input is received by the state government, it would not only embarrass the person recommended at a later stage but would also place the HCC in not a very good light. To avoid such a situation, I see absolutely no harm in –

[23] This was during the period between 24 June 2010 and 14 November 2011 when the separate HCs of Tripura, Manipur and Meghalaya were yet to be established. At present, apart from these three HCs, the HC of Gauhati has additional Benches in Kohima in Nagaland, Itanagar in Arunachal Pradesh and Aizawl in Mizoram.

in fact would actually suggest – the HCC obtaining feedback from the state intelligence sources before making a recommendation.

I would strongly recommend that the HCC should make efforts to obtain the views of as many persons as possible, including the local police and intelligence authorities, before recommending a person for appointment as an HC judge, so that the recommendations made are of the best and most meritorious lawyers and judicial officers.

Secretariat

In Andhra Pradesh, when it came to be known that, as the CJ, I had initiated the process of making recommendations for appointment of HC judges, I came across a somewhat strange practice. Lawyers began submitting applications with their *curriculum vitae* to the CJ's secretariat for being considered for appointment. Frankly, I found this practice a bit strange, but soon realised that, as far as the lawyers were concerned, how else would the CJ from a different parent HC know of their existence. This brought home the fact that not only was it difficult to identify competent and meritorious lawyers for appointment as HC judges but how difficult it is for an 'outsider' CJ to carry out the exercise of identification. Added to this is the receipt of anonymous complaints received by the Secretariat protesting against the consideration of a potential candidate. This adds a different dimension to the task of the HCC. This birthed, in my mind, the idea of a Secretariat to assist the HCC in the matter of appointment of judges.

Whether or not the CJ of the HC or J1 and J2 have a different parent HC, I am firmly of the view that every HC must establish a Secretariat to assist in the selection of candidates for recommendation as HC judges.

The functions and responsibilities of the Secretariat may be many, but two of them are extremely important. First, the Secretariat must maintain a record of the performance of every judicial officer in the state. This can include a variety of factors, including judgments written, participation in activities, such as programs and conferences relating to issues of law, complaints received (if any) and so on.

As it currently stands, every HC has a judge in charge of a district known as an administrative judge or a guardian judge or some other nomenclature.

This HC judge is expected to be in the nature of a mentor for all judicial officers in the district. The mentorship system is not always taken seriously for a variety of reasons. Sometimes there is not enough time to build up a relationship, sometimes work pressures make it difficult for the administrative judge to visit the district and attend to issues that may arise, and sometimes the responsibilities of an administrative judge change from one district to another because of the retirement of a judge or the transfer of a judge, or for some other such reason. Therefore, the inputs that the HCC may receive from an administrative judge may not necessarily be accurate or complete thereby depriving the HCC of valuable information. The Secretariat, working full-time, will not suffer from any such handicap and can always provide all necessary inputs not only to the HCC but also to the administrative judge.

Second, the Secretariat can also keep a track of judgments in which advocates have appeared. The nature and significance of the cases in which advocates appear, the frequency of their appearance can assist, to some extent, the HCC (particularly if it consists of judges from a different parent HC) in knowing who the prominent advocates are and who could, at some point in time be considered for appointment as HC judges. The idea is not to keep a surveillance on lawyers or to maintain a dossier on them but to be sufficiently informed so that discussions in the HCC meetings are meaningful. In all respects, therefore, the Secretariat has considerable value.

Functioning: Anecdotes

Deliberations of the HCC are dependent upon the CJ. The CJ decides when the Collegium should meet; the CJ initiates consideration of lawyers and judicial officers for appointment as judges of the HC – the CJ has the final word in the HCC. Almost twenty years ago, it was anecdotally narrated, that a CJ of the Punjab and Haryana HC unilaterally recommended some lawyers for appointment as judges. This was a unilateral recommendation in the sense that J1 and J2 (both of that HC) disagreed with the CJ (from a different parent HC) and voiced their opinion in writing. The CJ's recommendation was considered by the SCC and accepted.

There is an identical anecdote of a somewhat recent vintage concerning the HC of Telangana. It is not known whether the recommendation went through, but J1 and J2 were transferred out of the HC fairly soon. These developments, if true, are disconcerting to say the least, for they place J1 and J2 not as equals in the HCC but as judges whose opinion is of little consequence. Fairly recently, the SCC returned a recommendation made by the Himachal Pradesh HCC for reconsideration. The recommendation was reconsidered by the CJ and sent to the SCI, who did not agree with the procedure adopted and again returned the recommendation to be reconsidered by the HCC.[24] Perhaps, increasing the membership of the HCC may bring some certainty in the process. There is also a phenomenon said to be prevailing: 'one from your list, one from mine', when no consensus is arrived at by the HCC. This undermines the very purpose of constituting the HCC in the first place.

The Collegium system has also altered power dynamics, where the consultee judge in the SCI, particularly if such judge is either in the five-judge or three-judge SCC, becomes a key player. It is now believed that the CJ of the HC gets the list of proposed names informally cleared by the consultee judge or judges in the SCI even before the HCC sits down to finalize the list.

A custom that has evolved over the years is that the Acting CJ of the HC should not make any recommendations for appointment. Frankly, I do not see the purpose or value of such a custom. Surely, the HCC with an Acting CJ can be trusted to make the best possible recommendation. The custom has a rather detrimental effect on the functioning of the HC particularly when the acting CJ has been in their position for several months, as in the case of Manmohan J of the Delhi HC. No meeting of the HCC could be held for over ten months, and judges of the HC retired in the meanwhile and their vacancy could not be filled. This obviously serves no useful purpose, as far as the HC is concerned. Also, when a CJ has a very short tenure (a frequent occurrence these days), they are in no position to get the HCC to recommend names. Recently, RP Dhanuka was the CJ of the Bombay HC for just 3 days and Sonia Gokani the CJ of the Gujarat HC for ten days. Shakdher J had a tenure as CJ of Himachal Pradesh HC of less than a month.

My experience is that the discussions in the HCC have always been cordial – aside from the two instances mentioned above, I did not encounter any problem during deliberations in the HCC. Disagreements are bound to take place, and it is eventually for the CJ to take a call on whether to drop the

---

[24] *Chirag Bhanu Singh v. High Court of Himanchal Pradesh* (2024) 9 SCC 41.

candidature of a particular lawyer or a judicial officer, or to persist with it. But that is only to be expected when free and frank discussions take place.

Minutes of the Discussion

The minutes of the meeting of the HCC need to be carefully prepared, giving full details of the discussions that have taken place. Presently, the minutes only reflect the names of the persons recommended and nothing more. They do not reflect whether a particular lawyer or a judicial officer has been considered but not recommended, and the reasons therefore. Since the minutes of the meeting are confidential, recording reasons will not adversely impact anybody's reputation. On the contrary, it will be useful information for future meetings of the HCC. The minutes also do not reflect why a person has been recommended. It may not be possible for the HCC to give a comparative assessment, but certainly the reasons for recommending a particular person must be recorded, for this will be of assistance to the SCC as well.[25]

It is theoretically possible that a lawyer or a judicial officer is undeservedly overlooked, but at a later stage, some other HCC might find that person suitable for being recommended. There is value in reconsideration, but there is also a disadvantage depending on whether the decision of the HCC is coloured or not. For example, judicial officers are sometimes superseded by their juniors for no apparent reason. This leads to considerable speculation and rumour-mongering, adversely impacting the reputation of the superseded judicial officer. A few months later, the judicial officer may be recommended for appointment by the same HCC or the succeeding HCC. The superseded judicial officer then becomes junior in the HC seniority to his erstwhile colleague of several years. What purpose does the supersession serve? Is it to satisfy the whims and fancies of the HCC, or is there a more important reason?

In a scenario such as the one illustrated above, the Secretariat can play a role as a key source for the HCC and SCC in the decision-making process.

By the way, I was informed by a former CJ of Fiji (where I worked at the time of writing) that a recording of the deliberations of the judicial commission that

[25] See the concurring opinion of DY Chandrachud J in *Central Public Information Officer, Supreme Court of India v. Subhash Chandra Agarwal* (2020) 5 SCC 481 [321].

recommends appointment of judges is archived. A proposal was also made to videograph the meetings, but that was not accepted.

My recommendation is that the HCC should minute its discussions meticulously. It should record reasons for the recommendations made and place it in the public domain.

Recommendations of the High Court Collegium

The material before the SCC consists of the recommendation given by the HCC (without any reasons or further information) and a note prepared by the DoJ summarizing the 'case' for consideration. As far as I recall, the report of the local intelligence unit is not included in the material before the SCC. Interestingly, there are no known instances in the recent past where a state government has objected to a proposed name. For instance, although Victoria Gowri J was the erstwhile Secretary of the Mahila Morcha (women's wing) of a national political party, the state government (of a rival political party) did not raise any objection.

The material from the state is processed in the DoJ, which makes a requisition, perhaps through the MHA to the IB for inputs on the person recommended by the HCC for appointment. The report, along with the material received from the state government, is placed before the SCC. Now, I believe, the primary material is accompanied by an opinion of the DoJ. The entire material is then compiled by the Registry of the SCI and placed before the SCC. I am told that at present the Secretariat of the CJI prepares this compilation.

The time factor, between the date when the recommendation is made by the HCC and the date when the recommendation is placed for the SCC, is crucial. When two lawyers were recommended for appointment to the Gauhati HC in 2010, the entire process, including obtaining the views of the Chief Minister and the Governor of seven states and the SCC, was over in a matter of a couple of months. Now, it can take any amount of time, and for reasons that are not at all clear. Recently, the HCC of the Delhi HC recommended five lawyers for appointment as judges. Recommendations were made by the HCC on 23 October 2023 and the recommendations were considered by the SCC on 21 August 2024 after an inexplicable lapse of almost ten months and thereafter on 29 August 2024.[26] This is inexcusable. There is no way of knowing what caused this delay and whether the delay was caused by the Executive or by the SCI. The resolution of the SCC states that it had first recommended three lawyers and thereafter one for appointment as judges. One can only conclude that the recommendation regarding the fifth was not accepted. The SCI had two consultee judges, but only one was consulted. The other judge had been the CJ of the Delhi HC and had recommended, under his signature, five lawyers for appointment as judges. In my opinion, that judge ought to have been consulted, and the SCC would have had a far better understanding of the reasons for recommendation made by the HCC. If the other two lawyers were not worthy of being recommended, why did the former CJ of the Delhi HC recommend them; and if they were worthy of being appointed judges, in the view of the HCC, what is it that tilted the scales against them in the SCC? This is not to suggest that reasons for not accepting the recommendation of the HCC need to be disclosed by the SCC. What is suggested is that the SCC must consult the CJ of the HC making the recommendation whether that CJ is a judge of the SCI or not. There is absolutely no harm in such consultation, but it would certainly give the SCC a much better insight into why the recommendations were made.

Mysteriously, the SCC met again a few days later and recommended one of the two lawyers who was earlier not recommended.[27] It is not known what caused the reconsideration and, importantly, whether the delayed recommendation would affect the seniority of the fourth lawyer – in a given case, it could. The fate of the fifth lawyer is not known at the time of writing, but presumably, the recommendation of the HCC was not accepted. At the time of writing, two out of the three lawyers recommended on 21 August 2024 and the lawyer recommended on 29 August 2024 have been appointed.

It must be appreciated that the recommendations made by the HCC are not and never have been a closely guarded secret. Everybody in the Bar of the HC gets to know the recommendations within a few days. Anybody who believes to the contrary needs to wake up and keep their ears open. I am reminded

[26] Resolution of the Collegium, Supreme Court of India (21 August 2024) <https://cdnbbsr.s3waas.gov.in/s3ec0490f1f4972d133619a60c30f3559e/uploads/2024/08/2024082184.pdf> accessed 25 February 2025; Resolution of the Collegium, Supreme Court of India (29 August 2024) <https://cdnbbsr.s3waas.gov.in/s3ec0490f1f4972d133619a60c30f3559e/uploads/2024/08/2024082956.pdf> accessed 25 February 2025.

[27] ibid.

of having read somewhere that a former Attorney General for India told the Constitution Bench of the SCI, during a hearing, that nothing in Delhi was a secret, except the deliberations in the Cabinet, and those too come to be known after half-an-hour.

On the impact of seniority of judges, it will be of interest to know that, on 19 January 2024, and later, on 19 April 2024, the HCC of the Bombay HC recommended the names of nine advocates for appointment as judges of that HC. The SCC accepted the recommendations on 24 September 2024. However, only five of these advocates have been appointed as mentioned in the notification of 23 October 2024 issued by the DoJ. Arbitrary decisions such as these are disturbing.

The SCC has converted itself into a body without any teeth. Only three cases need to be highlighted in this context. First is the well-known case of Saurabh Kirpal, an eminent lawyer in Delhi, who was recommended by the HCC for appointment to the Delhi HC sometime in October 2017.[28] It is believed that the government is averse to his appointment because he is gay. That can hardly be a reason for the government not taking a decision on his appointment. This issue was taken up in the SCI by a Bench presided over by Sanjay Kishan Kaul J but, unfortunately, when the questioning by the Bench became 'hot', the CJI withdrew the case from his Bench, and there has been no progress thereafter. If the SCC finds itself unable to have its recommendations implemented by the government of the day, it says a lot both about the SCC and the government.[29]

The second case is that of Aditya Sondhi, an eminent lawyer from Bengaluru, who was recommended for appointment to the Karnataka HC by the SCC on 4 February 2021.[30] Since the recommendation was not implemented by the Executive, he withdrew his consent on 4 February 2022, for appointment as a judge of the Karnataka HC. The SCC did not formally follow up on the recommendation for his appointment for one year.

---

[28] Resolution of the Collegium, Supreme Court of India (18 January 2023) <https://main.sci.gov.in/pdf/Collegium/19012023_105547.pdf> accessed 22 October 2024.

[29] Recently, four more names of lawyers were reiterated for appointment as HC judges, which are pending with the Department of Justice; 'No Forward Movement on 4 Names Reiterated by Collegium Headed by Justice Chandrachud' (*The Times of India*, 3 November 2024) <https://timesofindia.indiatimes.com/india/no-forward-movement-on-4-names-reiterated-by-collegium-headed-by-justice-chandrachud/articleshow/114909106.cms> accessed 25 February 2025.

[30] Resolution of the Collegium, Supreme Court of India (4 February 2021) <https://cdnbbsr.s3waas.gov.in/s3ec0490f1f4972d133619a60c30f3559e/documents/collegium/05022021_062520.pdf> accessed 21 October 2024.

The third case is that of Akil Kureshi J, who was recommended for appointment as the CJ of the Madhya Pradesh HC, which has fifty-three judges. But, if anecdotal evidence is to be believed there was resistance to the recommendation from the Executive, the reasons being quite apparent to the discerning many in the legal fraternity. The SCC recalled its recommendation and then recommended his appointment as CJ of the Tripura HC, which has five judges. The Executive accepted this recommendation and acted on it. The government achieved its purpose of putting down Kureshi J, an upright and outstanding judge of the Gujarat HC – a judge of great character and great integrity. The unsavoury episode made it more than obvious that the Government of India would ensure that he is never appointed to the SCI. It is the people of India who have suffered these losses. It may be mentioned that Akil Kureshi J was later appointed CJ of the Rajasthan HC, which has fifty judges.

My suggestions, therefore, at the intermediate step are several. First, the names of persons recommended by the HCC for appointment as judges of the HC should be placed on the website of the Court for information. That the recommendations made by the HCC are a secret is a myth.

Second, the resolution of the HCC should contain reasons why a lawyer or a judicial officer is recommended for appointment. The reasons need not be published on the website of the HC but should be communicated to the SCC, since it will definitely be of some value to the SCC.[31]

Third, the timelines at all levels must be placed on the website of the DoJ and the SCI. Therefore, it must be disclosed when the HCC made its recommendation, the date when the Chief Minister and Governor of the State recorded their opinion and sent it to the DoJ, the date when the DoJ communicated the entire material to the SCI, the date when the SCC considered the recommendation made by the HCC, and finally the date of notification of the appointment. If there is delay at some stage, it will be known and can be obviated in public interest.[32]

---

[31] On 5 May 2025, the SCI uploaded on its website detailed information explaining the entire process of appointments to the HCs and the SCI, including, the factors considered in evaluating the suitability of a candidate for such an appointment. See, Press Release of the Supreme Court dated 5 May 2025 < https://cdnbbsr.s3waas.gov.in/s3ec0490f1f4972d133619a60c30f3559e/uploads/2025/05/2025050520.pdf> < https://cdnbbsr.s3waas.gov.in/s3ec0490f1f4972d133619a60c30f3559e/uploads/2025/05/2025050587.pdf> accessed 8 May 2025.

[32] Since 5 May 2025, the SCI's website contains information on the time taken for the recommendations

Deliberations in the Supreme Court Collegium

Depending on the agenda for deliberation, the SCC consists of the CJI and the two senior-most judges or four senior-most judges. Consideration of the HCC recommendations is done by the SCC comprising the CJI and two judges. All other deliberations are done by the SCC comprising the CJI and four judges.[33] So, how does the SCC actually function in the selection process?

First of all, it must be clear that although there could *be* and *are* disagreements within the SCC, the deliberations are by and large cordial. There have been problems in the recent past. For example, when Chelameswar J decided not to attend the meetings of the SCC, or when, a couple of years later, Rohinton Nariman J also decided not to participate. During these periods, no meeting of the SCC could be held. In another instance, DY Chandrachud J held court till 9 p.m. on a day when a meeting of the SCC was scheduled and kept the CJI and three other judges waiting, till the CJI decided to call off the meeting.[34]

It must be assumed that recommendations made by the HCC are after due deliberations and only after receiving inputs from all those whom the HCC consults. This assumption is basic, and the SCC accords due consideration to the recommendations. However, in terms of the MoP, the SCC invites the views of consultee judges.

Another reason why the assumption is basic is that the HCC is fully conversant with the competence, character and integrity of the lawyer or a judicial officer recommended for appointment. If there is some doubt, it is

---

made by the SCC to the Central Government for appointments between 9 November 2022 and 5 May 2025 for appointments to the HCs and the time taken for those recommendations to result in notifications of appointments. A detailed analysis of this information will reveal that in some cases, there is hardly any time lag, whereas in some others, it can be even beyond two years. See, Press Release of the Supreme Court dated 5 May 2025 <https://cdnbbsr.s3waas.gov.in/s3ec0490f1f4972d133619a60c30f3559e/uploads/2025/05/2025050618.pdf> accessed 8 May 2025.

[33] Rarely, the sixth member of the SCC is the very next potential CJI, for instance Sanjiv Khanna was a member from 9 November 2022 to 15 May 2023. See, K Parameshwar and A Sregurupriya, 'A Six-Member Collegium Under Justice DY Chandrachud?' (*BarandBench*, 17 September 2022) <https://www.barandbench.com/columns/a-six-member-collegium-under-justice-dy-chandrachud> accessed 25 February 2025.

[34] Joyston D'Souza, 'Discord in the Collegium Provides Rare Insight on Member Deliberations - Supreme Court Observer' (*Supreme Court Observer*, 9 October 2023)<https://www.scobserver.in/journal/discord-in-the-collegium-provides-rare-insight-on-member-deliberations/> accessed 25 February 2025; Resolution of the Collegium, Supreme Court of India (9 October 2022) <https://cdnbbsr.s3waas.gov.in/s3ec0490f1f4972d133619a60c30f3559e/documents/collegium/10102022_055250.pdf> accessed 25 February 2025.

unlikely that the HCC would recommend that person for appointment. But, as mentioned above, the views of consultee judges are obtained by the CJI. Frankly, with the passage of time, a consultee judge may not be up to date with the calibre of the lawyers and judicial officers recommended for appointment. In such a situation, the opinion of the consultee judge hardly adds any value to the deliberations. It is difficult to say how much weight is accorded to the opinion of the consultee judge.[35]

It is imperative for the SCC to have an interaction with the person considered for appointment on the recommendation of the HCC. By and large, judges in the SCC would probably not have met the recommended lawyer or judicial officer. Should the case for appointment be considered only on the basis of file notings? For an important constitutional position, where the law is to be solemnly interpreted for the entire state, I am of the view that a decision should not be taken by the SCC only on the basis of file notings and without actually having a conversation, however brief, with the person recommended for appointment. This interaction is not only to familiarize the SCC with the person concerned (the recommendee) but also to provide any clarification, if required, or clear any doubt in the mind of any of the judges in the SCC or a consultee judge. This practice was initiated by the SCC on my suggestion when Ranjan Gogoi was the CJI. The perception went around that it was an interview, but it was always only a familiarization interaction.

In a strange incident, many years ago, a lawyer from Delhi was recommended for appointment to the HC. Since his college days, he was jocularly nicknamed 'Boozer' even though he was and is a teetotaller. The recommendation was turned down because his nickname gave a faulty impression to the GoI and the SCC. I believe a brief conversation between the SCC and the CJ of the HC, or the lawyer would have cleared up any doubts. Such are the dangers of the SCC working in a silo. However, the good news is that he was eventually appointed as a judge, though several years later.

The SCC ought to be more open and communicative, both with every lawyer or judicial officer recommended by the HCC and the CJ of the concerned

[35] It is believed that an eminent lawyer was recommended for appointment by the HCC of the Madras HC. However, the recommendation was not accepted by the SCC even though four consultee judges were in favour of the recommendation while one consultee judge is believed to have given an adverse opinion. The SCC should have, in my opinion, had a collective discussion with all consultee judges in the matter; but they did not do so, thereby depriving the Madras HC of the services of an eminent lawyer.

HC, whether that CJ continues in that position or has become a judge of the SCI. The SCC must not only apply its mind to every recommendation but also delve into the mind of the HCC to appreciate the reasons for the recommendation in case they are not explicitly stated in the resolution of the HCC.

Requesting the High Court Collegium to Reconsider Recommendations

Sometimes, the SCC returns a recommendation made by the HCC for its reconsideration. In my view, the SCC ought to take a decision one way or the other in consultation with the CJ of the concerned HC. The entire appointment process takes considerable time, and to send the recommendation back for reconsideration makes little sense. To make matters worse, the SCC does not assign any reasons for reconsideration. This places the HCC in an unenviable position, for it has to try and decipher the mind of the SCC. I have had that experience in the Andhra Pradesh HC and had to consult judges of the HC to try and read the mind of the SCC when it sent back two recommendations for reconsideration. Fortunately, the HCC reconsidered the recommendation from every possible angle (only on a guess) and eventually both lawyers were appointed as judges.

MoP's Requirements

It is very important for the SCC (and also for the HCC) to follow the requirements of the MoP. One of the requirements is that the person recommended (usually a lawyer) should be forty-five years of age when the recommendation is made. This requirement has been unfailingly observed at least since the *Fourth Judges'* case. The importance of this requirement was recently taken note of by the SCC while considering a recommendee for appointment to the Delhi HC, as mentioned in the resolution of the SCC of 21 August 2024. The SCC noted in its resolution, 'As far as the observation regarding age of the candidate is concerned, we are of the view that the candidate fulfils the threshold age criterion of forty-five years as on the date of recommendation by the Collegium of the High Court.'[36] In the recent past,

---

36 Resolution of the Collegium, Supreme Court of India (21 August 2024) <https://cdnbbsr.s3waas.gov.in/s3ec0490f1f4972d133619a60c30f3559e/uploads/2024/08/2024082184.pdf> accessed 25 February 2025.

some HCCs sought to circumvent this requirement by stating that by the time the case of the recommendee is considered, he or she would be forty-five years of age. Such recommendations were not accepted by the SCC.

But in many earlier cases, neither the HCC and the SCC, nor the Executive, adhered to this requirement in the MoP. For example, Dipak Misra (17 January 1996), SA Bobde (29 March 2000), NV Ramana (27 June 2000), DY Chandrachud (29 March 2000), AM Khanwilkar (29 March 2000), SK Kaul (3 May 2001) and Dipankar Datta (22 June 2006) JJ were appointed as judges of the HC even though they were not yet forty-five years of age but in their early 40s. More recently, a lawyer in the Madhya Pradesh HC was recommended for appointment when he was forty-four years old.[37] He happened to be closely related to a judge, who at the time when the recommendation was accepted by the SCC, was J3 in the SCI.[38] The resolution of the SCC passed on 10 May 2019 cryptically remarks, 'As far as age factor of Shri [xxx] is concerned, the Collegium is fully satisfied with the justification given by the High Court Collegium while recommending his name.'[39] He was sworn in seventeen days later. What was the justification? Will this case set a precedent? If so, what would be the binding nature of the MoP?

As noted, there have been instances when recommendations have been made by the HCC on the postulate that the lawyer will be forty-five years old by the time the case is processed and appointment made. The SCC has not accepted such recommendations yet seems to have forgotten about it when the Madhya Pradesh lawyer's recommendation was taken up for consideration.

The requirement that a candidate has a minimum threshold income, has its own set of problems. While it is relatively easy for lawyers in Delhi, Mumbai, Chennai, Bengaluru and Kolkata to meet the income limit, the fees commanded by lawyers in smaller jurisdictions, such as Sikkim and some of the states in the north-east, and perhaps some other states, is less than the clerkage paid by senior lawyers in some metropolitan cities. The SCC will need to tweak this requirement so that there is some semblance of equality

---

37 The website of the Madhya Pradesh HC discloses his date of birth to be 17 July 1974.

38 Resolution of the Collegium, Supreme Court of India (10 May 2019) <https://cdnbbsr.s3waas.gov.in/s3ec0490f1f4972d133619a60c30f3559e/documents/collegium/5._2019.05.10-5_advs.-m.p..pdf> accessed 25 February 2025.

39 ibid.

and deserving lawyers in other states are equally well represented. There was an instance when some lawyers from Kerala filed revised returns of income only to meet the income criterion. While there is nothing wrong with this, it gave the impression that the income was jacked up only on advice received so that an income below the threshold would not disentitle them from appointment. These lawyers participated in an interaction with the SCC, and after having satisfactorily removed the doubts, they were recommended for appointment by the SCC. This is the value of the interaction.

Transfer of High Court Judges

There is something to be said about transparency in the functioning of the SCC. On one occasion, I got the distinct impression that the CJI was advised by the Executive to effect a transfer – that of Muralidhar J out of Delhi HC for a judgment he had delivered. In my view, that certainly cannot be a ground for transfer; and so I expressed my disagreement with the proposal, and the CJI readily accepted my view. It appears that after my retirement from the SCI, the transfer issue was raised again. But the new entrant to the SCC, Sikri J, held the same view, and he too opposed the proposed transfer. After the retirement of Sikri J, Muralidhar J was arbitrarily transferred out of the Delhi HC to the Punjab and Haryana HC.

On the other hand, a judge of the Delhi HC who was recommended for transfer by the SCC was not transferred despite the CJI expressing his displeasure in Court at the failure of the Executive to act on the recommendation of the SCC consisting of the CJI and four senior-most judges of the SCI. These events indicate that the Executive could ultimately prevail over an SCC in the matter of the transfer of judges.

The transfer of a judge from one HC to another is, in my opinion, a meaningless exercise. Transfer orders are made 'for the better administration of justice'. It is difficult to appreciate how the administration of justice is served by transferring a judge from one HC to another. The subtext seems to suggest that the transfer is usually recommended as a 'disciplinary' measure, perhaps for some alleged misdemeanour or on the basis of some judgment not to the liking of the Executive or the SCC. In my view, if a judge is not good enough to be retained in the parent HC, transferring him to some other HC is an injustice to that HC. There was an occasion when the Gauhati

High Court Bar Association objected to the proposed transfer of an allegedly 'tainted' judge to that HC. The Bar Association felt that the Gauhati HC could not be treated as a second-rate HC intended to accommodate an allegedly tainted judge. The proposed transfer did not fructify.

If a judge is unfit to remain as a judge in the parent HC, an enquiry should be held against the judge and, if necessary, impeachment proceedings should be initiated; or, if the allegation is not particularly serious, the judge could be counselled by the CJ of the HC, or if necessary, by the CJI. A judge of the Delhi HC in the year 2003, against whom there were some rather serious allegations, was called by the CJI and persuaded to put in his papers. That is the right course of action to adopt. Transfer of a judge is not the best course of action to adopt.

Executive Interference

There is, now, increasing interference by the Executive in the matter of appointment of judges. The worst form of interference is the GoI not taking any decision on a recommendation made by the HCC and accepting the the SCC, thereby stalling appointment of judges arbitrarily and without reason. This is a direct 'attack' on the independence of the judiciary. There are several such instances, and three of them have been adverted to above; there are many more and all of them are of the last ten years or so. Another kind of interference, very serious, is alleged in a recent article published in the *Caravan* magazine, wherein it is stated that of the seventeen names recommended by the SCC for appointment to the SCI during the tenure of CJI Chandrachud, eight were strongly urged by the government, six were the SCC's own choices and three were a consensus between the GoI and the Collegium.[40]

---

40 Saurav Das, 'Performative Justice: The Equivocations of DY Chandrachud' (*The Caravan*, 5 November 2024) <https://caravanmagazine.in/law/equivocations-of-chandrachud> accessed 25 February 2025. The information regarding appointments to the HCs now available on the website of the SCI (n 31) also gives valuable information on how many of the proposals made by the SCC to the Central Government between 9 November 2022 (when CJI DY Chandrachud took over) and 5 May 2025 for appointment to the HCs, did not in fact go through.

Supreme Court Collegium

Appointments

Appointments to the SCI are recommended by a Collegium in the SCI consisting of the CJI and the four senior-most judges. Ordinarily, one of the four senior-most judges is in the line of seniority to be the CJI, but if that is not the case, the next senior-most judge in the line of seniority to be the CJI becomes a member of the SCC.

Article 124 of the Constitution of India requires that the qualification for appointment as a judge of the SCI is that the person should have been a HC judge for at least five years, a HC advocate for at least ten years or is, in the opinion of the President, a distinguished jurist. In the past, almost all judges of the SCI had been judges of the HC. In the initial phase, few lawyers were directly appointed as judges of the SCI under Article 124 of the Constitution.[41] However, in quite a radical move, the SCC has, since 2014, recommended a handful of lawyers for appointment as judges of the SCI.[42] This has not been without its share of animated discussion in the legal fraternity. One view has been that the SCC was not right in overlooking CJs and judges of the HCs for appointment despite their experience and expertise of over a decade as eminent judges.[43]

One such recommendation concerned the appointment of Gopal Subramanium, an eminent Senior Advocate and former Solicitor General of India. The GoI failed to act positively on a recommendation by the SCC made under Article 124 of the Constitution. By humming and hawing on the recommendation, Gopal Subramanium was effectively humiliated by the GoI with the result that he withdrew the consent he had given to the SCC for his appointment. Unfortunately, having tasted blood in this case, the task of the Executive in gaining an upper hand in the appointment of judges to the SCI (and to the HCs) became easy. The Executive realized that if it insisted that a particular person should not be appointed as a judge, it could have its way. The recent past has seen inaction for as long as eight months on the appointment

---

41 SM Sikri (1964), SC Roy (1971), Kuldip Singh (1988), Santosh Hegde (1999) JJ.

42 Rohinton Nariman (2014), CJI UU Lalit (2014), L Nageswara Rao (2016), Indu Malhotra (2018), P S Narasimha (2021) and KV Vishwanathan (2023) JJ.

43 Abhinav Chandrachud, 'From Bar to Bench' (*Frontline Magazine*, 11 June 2024) <https://frontline.thehindu.com/the-nation/from-bar-to-bench/article6100666.ece> accessed 25 February 2025.

of Dipankar Datta J, then CJ of the Bombay HC, to the SCI. On the other hand, some appointments have been made to the SCI within four days of the recommendation of the SCC.[44]

For appointment of judges to the SCI, there is no process of formal consultation between the SCC and other judges of the SCI. It is only one evening after the resolution of the SCC is signed that some judges come to know of the resolution. Also, for appointment of someone directly from the Bar, there is no concept of a 'consultee' judge. In other words, unless such direct appointee gets into the SCC, he or she will not formally be involved in the appointment process.

Role of CJI

Like the CJ of an HC, as far as the SCC is concerned, CJI decides when the SCC should meet and the agenda for the meeting, whether it is for appointment of judges of the HC, or for transfer of judges from one HC to another, or for appointment of the CJ of the HC or judges of the SCI. Nothing beyond that.

There was an occasion when the CJI was of the view that his opinion in the matter of recommending judges for appointment to the HC and the SCI was final, regardless of the opinion of other judges in the SCC. This led the President of India to seek the opinion of the SCI on a question of law of public importance under Article 143 of the Constitution of India. This was the *Third Judges'* case.[45] One of the questions in the Presidential reference concerned the authority of the CJI to act in the matter of recommendation of judges to the SCI and the HCs. The SCI opined that, 'The Chief Justice of India must make a recommendation to appoint a Judge of the Supreme Court and to transfer a Chief Justice or puisne Judge of a High Court in consultation with the four senior most puisne Judges of the Supreme Court. Insofar as the appointment to the High Court is concerned, the recommendation must be made in consultation with the two senior most puisne judges of the Supreme Court.'[46] This practice has been followed ever since.

[44] The recommendations of the SCC for the appointments of Sudhanshu Dhulia and JB Pardiwala JJ were made on 5 May 2022 and they were sworn in on 9 May 2022. Likewise, Prashant Mishra and K V Viswanathan JJ were recommended on 16 May 2023 and sworn in on 19 May 2023.

[45] *Third Judges'* case (n 6).

[46] ibid [44].

A question that arises is whether the CJI can withhold a resolution of the SCC or ensure that it is otherwise not acted upon. There is no answer to this question that arose in December 2018 when the SCC recommended two CJs, Pradeep Nandrajog from Rajasthan HC and Rajendra Menon from Delhi HC, for appointment as judges of the SCI. After due deliberations, a decision was taken and a resolution prepared and signed by all in the SCC, of which I was a member. But for some unknown reason, the resolution was not forwarded by the CJI to the GoI. Subsequently, I retired as a judge of the SCI, and Arun Mishra J became a member of the SCC. The SCC had a meeting convened by the CJI soon thereafter, and it passed a somewhat strange resolution on 10 January 2019, the relevant extract of which is reproduced below:

> Against the sanctioned strength of 31 Judges, the Supreme Court of India is presently functioning with 26 Judges, leaving 05 clear vacancies . . .
>
> . . . The then Collegium on 12th December, 2018 took certain decisions. However, the required consultation could not be undertaken and completed as the winter vacation of the Court intervened. By the time the Court re-opened, the composition of the Collegium underwent a change. After extensive deliberations on 5th/6th January, 2019, the newly constituted Collegium deemed it appropriate to have a fresh look at the matter and also to consider the proposals in the light of the additional material that became available.
>
> In terms of the above, this Collegium unanimously resolves to fill up, for the present, two of the five existing vacancies of Judges in the Supreme Court. The Collegium has discussed names of Chief Justices as well as senior puisne Judges of all High Courts, eligible for elevation to the Supreme Court. The Collegium is of the considered view that at present the following persons are more deserving and suitable in all respects than other Chief Justices and senior puisne Judges of High Courts, for being appointed as Judges of the Supreme Court of India . . .[47]

The resolution does not specify the 'required consultation' that could not be

---

[47] Resolution of the Collegium, Supreme Court of India (10 January 2019) <https://cdnbbsr.s3waas.gov.in/s3ec0490f1f4972d133619a60c30f3559e/documents/collegium/1._2019.01.10-resolution-sc_appointment.pdf> accessed 25 February 2025.

undertaken and completed, nor is it clear whether appointment of judges to the SCI was of less importance than the winter vacation of the SCI. The 'additional material' that became available to the SCC was not specified. Was there any additional material? I doubt it. The result of the January resolution was that the December resolution was simply not acted upon without being withdrawn, and another CJ of a HC and one judge were recommended for appointment to the SCI, overlooking more than twenty CJs and a host of judges while still leaving three clear vacancies in the SCI. This is perhaps the only instance of its kind – most unfortunate, and hopefully, one which will not be repeated.

General Observations and Suggestions

The HCC and the SCC (whether of three judges or five judges) are expected to function in a most cordial manner, after all they are colleagues in the court and reasonable persons. There is usually no rancour if disagreement is voiced and, to the extent possible, all decisions are taken unanimously. This is not to say that there has never been any rancour or dissent, as discussed above, but the CJ is expected to be a part of the majority. This was made clear in the *Third Judges'* case. Notwithstanding this, there is anecdotal evidence of a recommendation made by the HCC in which the CJ was a minority, yet the recommendation went through, as mentioned above. The only possibility of confirming rumours, stories and anecdotes relating to the functioning of the HCC and the SCC is by making the relevant files available to researchers for inspection. Transparency demands that a time limit be specified for keeping the files confidential, say ten or fifteen years.

Discussions in the HCC and the SCC are expected to be free and frank, but a lot depends on the CJ. There is anecdotal evidence of some instances when there has been an informal communication between the CJ and the Executive. In my opinion, if the communication is open, it is perfectly alright, for example, as in the case of the Chief Minister of a State recommending a lawyer for appointment as a judge of the HC.[48] The problem arises if the communication is secretive, for then, other members of the Collegium are

[48] The MoP for appointment of HC judges states, '[I]f the Chief Minister desires to recommend the name of any person he should forward the same to the Chief Justice for his consideration.'; 'Memorandum of Procedure of Appointment of High Court Judges' (*Department of Justice*, 11 August 2021) <https://doj.gov.in/memorandum-of-procedure-of-appointment-of-high-court-judges/> accessed 25 February 2025.

unaware of what has transpired between the CJ and the Executive. This is extremely unhealthy and should be eschewed if the independence of the judiciary is to be maintained.

There have been two instances in the SCI when a judge in the SCC declined to participate in the deliberations of the SCC.[49] In my opinion, these instances clearly show that there have been occasions when the SCC has acted arbitrarily. Why would the SCC do that?

No doubt, there is criticism of the Collegium system of appointment of judges. It is said that India is the only country where judges appoint judges, and there are allegations of nepotism. It should be clear that judges do not appoint judges. They collectively only make a recommendation to the government and it is the President of India who makes the appointment. The Constitution says so in Article 124: 'Every Judge of the Supreme Court shall be appointed by the President by warrant under his hand and seal after consultation with such of the Judges of the Supreme Court and of the High Courts in the States as the President may deem necessary for the purpose ….'.

There is an inherent system of checks and balances laid out in the MoP. It is a matter of common knowledge that in many an instance, recommendations made by the SCC for appointment to the HC have not been accepted by the GoI without assigning any reason. Under such circumstances, it cannot be said that judges appoint judges. On the contrary, recent developments, some of which have been discussed above, suggest that the trump cards are held by the GoI, which is gradually eroding the independence of the judiciary. The expectation is that trump cards should be with the SCC. But, they are not.

Another problem is that, of late, not only the GoI but in some cases the SCC has been arbitrary in its decision-making. The MoP requires that on examining the recommendation of the SCC, the Executive can return

[49] 'Justice Chelameswar Opts Out of Collegium' (*The Hindu*, 2 September 2016) <https://www.thehindu.com/news/national/Justice-Chelameswar-opts-out-of-collegium/article60525786.ece> accessed 25 February 2025; 'Justice Chelameswar Says Collegium Meetings Follow No Principles of Law' (*LiveLaw*, 28 August 2017) <https://www.livelaw.in/justice-chelameswar-says-collegium-meetings-follow-no-principles-law/> accessed 25 February 2025; Joyston D'Souza, 'The Consequences of Absence: Justice Chandrachud and the Collegium' (*Supreme Court Observer*, 9 October 2023) <https://www.scobserver.in/journal/the-consequences-of-absence-justice-chandrachud-and-the-collegium/> accessed 25 February 2025; Additionally, it is not known whether CJI Kabir recused when his younger sister was being recommended to the HC at the age of fifty-nine from the bar. See Atul Dev, 'In Sua Cause: What the Judiciary has Done to Itself' (*The Caravan*, 1 July 2019) <https://caravanmagazine.in/law/what-judiciary-done-itself> accessed 25 February 2025.

the recommendation for reconsideration by the SCC. This is somewhat odd because all the inputs of the GoI are before the SCC even prior to the commencement of its deliberations. However, one should be prepared to accept that every decision of the SCC is not necessarily the correct decision, and the Executive can, in a given case, be expected to send back the recommendation to the SCC for reconsideration. Fair enough. But, the MoP provides that, after reconsideration, should the SCC reiterate its recommendation, the GoI must accept it. After all, the process has to end at some point of time. Unfortunately, the GoI does not think so, with the result that there have been instances when the recommendation has been returned to the SCC for reconsideration on two occasions, and in one case, on three occasions. Even after reiterations by the SCC, the GoI has not accepted the recommendations, which are said to be in cold storage. This is extremely unhealthy; and unfortunately, it is always the SCC that blinks, for it cannot appoint judges but only make recommendations. In the long run, this will have an extremely adverse impact on the independence of the judiciary, a pillar of democracy, which already seems to be a bit shaky.

There is also a view that the NJAC, with some tweaking and changes, is the most appropriate system or method of appointment of judges. It cannot be said so with certainty, particularly since the Executive is increasingly playing a dominant role in the appointment of judges. Considering the manner in which recommendations of the SCC are treated by the GoI, what is the guarantee that a recommendation made by the NJAC, tweaked or otherwise, will be acceptable to the government of the day?

As far as the present dispensation is concerned, one point of view is that the government was unhappy when the NJAC was declared unconstitutional. While this is speculation, the facts may never really be known, but subsequent events have shown that the GoI is the dominant player in the matter of appointment of judges and holds all the trump cards. Perhaps a non-confrontationist approach of the GoI will augur best for the independence of the judiciary, for the people of our country and for democracy.

Cartoon © Pencilashan. Reproduced with permission.

Removing and 'Disciplining' of Judges

RAJU RAMACHANDRAN*

Judges are required to be independent and accountable. The ideals of judicial accountability and judicial independence may sometimes appear to exist in tension with each other. One can easily imagine a legal system leaning too far in one direction or the other – either by making it very difficult to hold judges accountable for their actions, or where accountability tools become susceptible to misuse and thus threaten independence. Sophisticated mechanisms are required in order to balance these two ideals on a case-to-case basis. Success in developing such a mechanism could even be seen to dissolve the tension between the two ideals, such that the accountability tools serve to weed out errant judges and deter other judges from behaving in a manner that would impact the image of the judiciary as an institution.

The Indian Constitution sketches out an outline of the mechanism to be used in seeking to hold judges accountable for misconduct. As the Supreme Court (SCI) has observed, the constitutional provisions concerning removal of judges in India 'seek to achieve a judicious blend of the political and judicial processes'.[1] Through judicial pronouncements, however, the Indian judiciary has incrementally expanded the judicial element, raising serious questions over whether the blend (to be achieved through the provisions of the Constitution) continues to be judicious. Notably, the expanded role of the judiciary, and especially of the CJI, includes both judicial and administrative exercises that are undertaken in ways that either substitute or delay the more transparent processes envisaged under the Constitution. The structure of this essay is as follows: the first part briefly discusses the pre-constitutional position regarding removal of judges and provides an overview of the mechanisms for addressing

* The author wishes to thank Mythili Vijay Kumar Thallam and Vikram Aditya Narayan, Advocates, for their invaluable assistance.

1 *Sub-Committee on Judicial Accountability v. Union of India* (1991) 4 SCC 699 [44].

judicial misconduct under the Constitution and the Judges (Inquiry) Act, 1968. The second part examines the cases and legal principles that emerged following the allegations raised against V Ramaswami J of the SCI. The third part analyses the case-by-case development of extra-constitutional mechanisms to pursue accountability for judicial misconduct. The fourth part reflects on the inconsistencies in the use of accountability mechanisms in two broad categories of misconduct: corruption and sexual harassment. The fifth part looks at the rise in serious allegations being levelled against CJIs, and how the manner in which they have been dealt with does not inspire trust.

Procedure for Removal of Judges in India

Before the Government of India (GoI) Act, 1935 judges of HCs in India held office at the 'pleasure' of His or Her Majesty, which meant that they could be dismissed at the will of the Crown, that is, without assigning any reason. After the GoI Act, HC judges held office until the age of sixty and could only be removed 'on the ground of misbehaviour or of infirmity of mind or body'.[2] The position under the Indian Constitution is somewhat similar. Removal of members of the higher judiciary in India today is governed by Article 124 (4), the Judges (Inquiry) Act, 1968[3] read with the Judges (Inquiry) Rules, 1969 framed under the Act. While Article 124 (4) of the Constitution provides for an affirmative vote of not less than two-thirds of the members of Parliament for removal of a judge,[4] the Judges (Inquiry) Act creates a more elaborate procedure under which, if a motion for removal is admitted in either House of the Parliament, a three-member committee is constituted to investigate the

---

[2] Government of India Act 1935, s 220 (2) (b); SP Sinha J, a judge of the Allahabad HC, was the only judge removed under the GoI Act. The Government of United Provinces moved a petition against the judge listing five charges. The inquiry lasted three weeks and involved the judge cross-examining the deponent who filed affidavits in support of the charges against the judge. All of the evidence was on record and the proceedings took place *on camera* before the Federal Court. Two instances of misbehaviour were held to have been proved against the judge, and an order of removal was passed by the Governor-General as per the Court's recommendation.

[3] Constitution of India 1950, art 124 (5); Enacted as per the requirements of Article 124 (5) of the Constitution.

[4] 'A Judge of the Supreme Court shall not be removed from his office except by an order of the President passed after an address by each House of the Parliament supported by a majority of the total membership of that House and by a majority of not less than two-thirds of the members of that House present and voting has been presented to the President in the same session for such removal on the ground of proved misbehaviour or incapacity;' Constitution of India 1950, art 124 (5).

charges.[5] This committee, which has the power to set its own procedure,[6] is then required to frame definite charges for investigation and prepare a report to be submitted to the Speaker or to both the Speaker and the Chairman.[7] If the committee does not return a finding of guilt on misbehaviour or incapacity on the part of the judge, the process ends.[8] It is only when the committee finds the judge guilty that the Parliament takes up the report for discussion in the House.[9]

The V Ramaswami Case

The impeachment motion against V Ramaswami J and the political climate around it resulted in the judiciary examining its own role in the constitutional mechanism under Article 124. The SCI, in a series of decisions, had the opportunity to examine the impeachment process at different stages for the first time. In this section, we will see how the developments during this time laid the foundation for the law that came to govern judicial misconduct, and how this is inextricably linked to the expansion of the CJI's administrative powers. Whereas in 1990, the CJI said that he had no legal or moral right over a fellow judge of the SCI accused of wrongdoing, in the present times, the mere satisfaction of the CJI is sufficient to close proceedings under an in-house inquiry into a judge. Writing in 1991, a former judge of the SCI, vehemently criticized the efficacy of the mechanisms in place for holding judges accountable for their actions in the following words: 'The escalating misconduct of judges has often gone unpunished because the law of judicial accountability is still in its infancy.'[10] This essay examines how the foundation for holding judges accountable came about.

---

[5] Judges (Inquiry) Act 1968, s 3 (2) which says that the Committee would consist of 1 member chosen from among the CJ and other judges of the SCI, 1 member from among the CJs of the HCs and 1 member who is a distinguished jurist; Judges (Inquiry) Act, *1968*, Section 3 (1) which says that if the removal motion is moved in Lok Sabha, it must be signed by at least 100 members, whereas if it is moved in Rajya Sabha it must be signed by at least 50 members.

[6] ibid, s 4(1).

[7] ibid, s 4(2).

[8] ibid, s 6(1).

[9] ibid, s 6(2).

[10] VR Krishna Iyer, 'Judicial Accountability to the Community: A Democratic Necessity' (27 July 1991) 26 *The Economic and Political Weekly* 1808 at 1814.

Ramaswami J was sworn in as a judge of the SCI in 1989, after holding office as the CJ of the Punjab and Haryana HC. In the middle of 1990, newspapers began carrying reports of his lavish spending during his tenure in Chandigarh. After this, the Supreme Court Bar Association passed a resolution calling for Ramaswami J's impeachment and requested the CJI to withdraw work from him. On 20 July 1990, the then CJI, Sabyasachi Mukherjee, took the unprecedented step of reading out a statement to the Bar, where he acknowledged that he had no right or authority to inquire into the conduct of a sitting judge, but nevertheless requested Ramaswami J to desist from judicial work. Ramaswami J applied for a six-week leave shortly after this. Meanwhile, the CJI constituted an internal inquiry committee consisting of BC Ray, Jagannatha Shetty and Venkatachaliah JJ, who eventually gave Ramaswami J a clean chit.[11]

Meanwhile 108 Members of Parliament (MPs) of the 9th Lok Sabha, across party lines, submitted a motion of impeachment against Ramaswami J. Fourteen charges were cited. These included purchasing furniture and other articles vastly excessive of the requirements of an official residence and misuse of official vehicles and machinery. On the last day of the VP Singh Government, the Speaker, Rabi Ray, constituted a committee under Section 3 of the Judges Inquiry Act, comprising PB Sawant J of the SCI; PD Desai J, CJ of the Bombay HC; and O Chinappa Reddy, retired judge of the SCI, to look into the charges against Ramaswami J.[12] After the elections, the minority Congress Government under PV Narasimha Rao was sworn in. The Union Government was of the opinion that the tenure of the Sawant Committee had ended because the motion of impeachment had lapsed. It was the challenge to this decision that gave the SCI the first opportunity to examine the procedure under Article 124.

In *Sub-Committee for Judicial Accountability v. Union of India*, writ petitions were filed challenging the Government's decision that the impeachment motion had lapsed. The SCI negated the government's decision and allowed the Sawant Committee to continue. In order to justify judicial review of what was until then viewed as an exclusive parliamentary process, the SCI reasoned that the process of removal of a judge under Articles 124 (4) and (5)

[11] Sanjoy Ghose, 'Carpets, Bedsheets, Towels and Intrigue: The Story of Justice v. Ramaswami's Impeachment' (*The Wire*, 22 July 2020) <https://thewire.in/law/justice-v-ramaswami-impeachment-lok-sabha-kapil-sibal-supreme-court> accessed 13 February 2025.

[12] ibid.

was one that was both judicial and political. It reasoned that while the ultimate authority remained with the Parliament, if the Committee recorded a finding of guilt, the process of removal had to continue. Significantly, for the first time, the administrative powers of the CJI's office were recognized. The judgment held that while the entire process was governed only by Articles 124 (4) and (5), the CJI could advise the judge to 'abstain from discharging judicial functions during the pendency of the inquiry'.[13] It was further held that the judge would abide by the advice of the CJI, and it was emphasized that this was in the realm of judicial propriety and not a matter of legal authority.

While the Sawant Committee was in the process of carrying on its inquiry, two petitions were filed, one by M Krishnaswami, a well-wisher of Ramaswami J, and another by his wife, Sarojini Ramaswami, challenging the legality of the Committee as well as requesting a copy of the Report before it was presented to the Speaker, so as not to deprive the accused judge of his right to hearing. The first petition was dismissed for a lack of *locus standi*;[14] and in the second petition the SCI held, after a lengthy discussion, that the report of the Inquiry Committee did not violate any right of the accused and therefore the accused was not entitled to a copy of its Report[15] and that 'misbehaviour' could only be proved once the Parliament adopted the motion against the judge. It was further held that judicial review would be available to the judge only after an order of removal was issued by the President of India.[16]

The Sawant Committee framed fourteen charges against V Ramaswami J, predominantly pertaining to abuse of power and authority in order to purchase a long list of items in his official capacity for non-official use.[17] Apart from choosing not to file a written statement of defence, Ramaswami J wrote a series of letters to the Committee questioning its legality and made various

---

[13] *Sub-Committee on Judicial Accountability v. Union of India* (1991) 4 SCC 699 [10]. Bench comprised of BC Ray, LM Sharma, MN Venkatachaliah, JS Verma and SC Agrawal JJ.

[14] *Krishna Swami v. Union of India* (1992) 4 SCC 605. Bench comprised of JS Verma, NM Kasliwal, K Ramaswamy, K Jayachandra Reddy and SC Agrawal JJ.

[15] *Sarojini Ramaswami v. Union of India* (1992) 4 SCC 506. Bench comprised of JS Verma, NM Kasliwal, K Ramaswamy, K Jayachandra Reddy and SC Agrawal JJ.

[16] ibid [80].

[17] Sawant Committee Report 2, 37–54, 69 (On file with author); The complete list of items found at the residence of V Ramaswami J is detailed by the Sawant Committee in its report. A copy of the charges and the documents placed before the committee detailing the charges were served to V Ramaswami J and the proceedings were held in camera, though on the condition that no part of them would be 'divulged or published in any manner'.

allegations against its members.[18] In his second letter dated 24 January 1992, he categorically stated, 'I do not intend to submit to your jurisdiction.'[19] The Committee declared that it had no option but to proceed *ex parte*,[20] but further clarified that it would follow the principles of the Indian Evidence Act, 1872 and the principles of natural justice.[21]

The Committee was clear that the proceedings were quasi-criminal in nature, and that therefore charges must be proved beyond reasonable doubt.[22] The Sawant Committee Report, which came out on 20 July 1992 held V Ramaswami J guilty of 'wilful and gross misuse of office, purposeful and persistent negligence in the discharge of duties, moral turpitude by using public funds for private purposes' and for undermining the faith of the public in the judiciary.[23] However, the motion for impeachment in the Lok Sabha, on 10 May 1993, had 196 votes in favour, which fell short of the required two-third majority.[24] The vote failed largely due to the 205 MPs belonging to the Congress (I) party abstaining from voting. Sawant J, in an interview, called the impeachment process 'impractical, cumbersome and heavily dependent on politicians'.[25]

At this stage, the author would like to share a personal reminiscence of the proceedings in the Ramaswami case before the Sawant Committee, where he was counsel for the Committee. Senior counsel FS Nariman and Rajendra Singh, an ace criminal lawyer from Jabalpur, assisted the Committee. It was projected as a North–South issue with the Bar in Tamil Nadu feeling that a judge from South India was being victimized for what was perceived to be a minor transgression. And similarly, members of the Supreme Court Bar who

---

[18] *Sawant Committee Report* 1, 13.

[19] ibid; In this regard, the *Sawant Committee Report* 1, 14 observes that, as a judge of the SCI, V Ramaswami J ought to have realized that 'it was improper for him to address letters to the Tribunal constituted to enquire into his conduct.'

[20] ibid 16.

[21] ibid; It is worth noting that while analysing Ramaswami J's refusal to participate, the Committee also found that '[t]he Judge against whom an inquiry is being held is under a constitutional obligation to co-operate with the inquiring authority and not to raise petty-fogging [sic]objections to obstruct the inquiry in which case an adverse inference may be legitimately drawn against him.'

[22] ibid 60–61.

[23] ibid 8.

[24] ibid. A significant aspect of these proceedings in the Parliament was the spirited defence that V Ramaswami J presented through Kapil Sibal, Senior Advocate.

[25] Nagendar Sharma and Satya Prakash, 'Who's Afraid of Impeachment?' (*The Hindustan Times*, 11 September 2008).

were from South India felt the same. Ramaswami J did not participate in the proceedings but appeared through proxies. Interestingly, JS Khehar, then an Advocate from Chandigarh, who ultimately became CJI, was the lawyer appearing for an organization supporting Ramaswami J.

Extra-Constitutional Mechanisms for Judicial Accountability

In addition to the impeachment route available under the Indian Constitution, a range of extra-constitutional mechanisms have been recognized and developed in order to hold judges accountable for their actions. Notably, these mechanisms have been developed through different sources, including the SCI acting as a judicial body, the SCI acting in its administrative capacity and the CJI generally discharging the special responsibility cast upon him. The fourth extra-constitutional mechanism dealt with under this heading, namely, punishment transfers, concerns a power recognized under Article 222 of the Constitution – but one that was not originally conceived as a power meant to redress judicial misconduct. Under all these mechanisms, the view taken by the CJI plays a prominent role in determining whether and how inquiries proceed.

Prevention of Corruption Act – K Veeraswami Case (1991)

The case of *K Veeraswami v. Union of India*[26] is significant as one of the first cases identifying an additional mechanism for holding judges accountable – specifically in the context of corruption. K Veeraswami J became a judge of the Madras HC in 1960; and in 1976, he became the CJ of the HC. In March 1976, a first information report (FIR) was registered against him under the Prevention of Corruption Act, 1947 (PC Act) before the Special Judge, Madras.[27] Upon being informed of the FIR being registered, Veeraswami went on leave, and retired upon attaining the age of superannuation one month later. When the Special Judge issued process for his appearance in Court, Veeraswami did not appear and instead filed a petition before the HC under Section 482 of the Code of Criminal Procedure (CrPC) seeking quashing of the criminal proceedings – wherein the main argument advanced

[26] *K Veeraswami v. Union of India* (1991) 3 SCC 655.

[27] The FIR was registered on the basis of claims that K Veeraswami had amassed an amount of Rs 6.4 lakhs while discharging judicial functions between 1960 and 1976, and that these assets were said to be disproportionate to his known sources of income.

was that judges belonging to the higher judiciary did not come within the purview of the PC Act. A Full Bench of the HC ruled against him, as did the SCI on appeal.

The SCI, by a majority of 4:1, held that members of the higher judiciary were indeed subject to the PC Act, particularly in light of the fact 'that a single dishonest judge not only dishonours himself and disgraces his office but jeopardizes the integrity of the entire judicial system'.[28] However, noting the responsibility of the CJI to ensure the 'integrity and impartiality of the judiciary',[29] the Court directed that no criminal case shall be registered against a judge of the HC, a CJ of a HC or a judge of the SCI unless the CJI is consulted in the matter. It also directed that similar consultation would be required at the stage of examining whether to grant sanction for prosecution, and it clarified that the sanctioning authority under Section 6 of the PC Act would be the President.[30] Pertinently, the Court held that a judge ought to 'voluntarily withdraw from judicial work and await the outcome of criminal prosecution'.[31] If judges were sentenced in a criminal case, they ought to resign unless they obtain a stay order on the conviction and sentence.[32]

It is also worth noting the dissent by JS Verma J, where he declared that bringing members of the higher judiciary under the PC Act would be 'an exercise to fit a square peg in a round hole when the two were never intended to match.'[33] This view puts judges of the higher judiciary in an unjustifiably exalted position by suggesting that they are not meant to be held accountable by the same mechanism that applies to other public servants. This view is inconsistent with the foundations of a constitutional republic. Lastly, in this case, the question of withdrawing judicial work was not a live issue, as Veeraswami J had already retired before the adjudication of the case. However, this continued to be an important issue in cases concerning judicial accountability, as discussed below.

---

[28] *K Veeraswami v. Union of India* (n 26) [79]. Bench comprised BC Ray, K Jagannatha Shetty, LM Sharma, MN Venkatachaliah JJ in the majority and JS Verma J dissenting.

[29] ibid [60].

[30] ibid [61].

[31] ibid [53].

[32] ibid.

[33] ibid [129].

Withdrawal of Judicial Work

The V Ramaswami judgments laid down many fundamental principles that continue to shape the law on judicial accountability. An influential dimension of that case was CJI Sabyasachi Mukharji's position on the discharge of judicial work by V Ramaswami once allegations were raised against him. As mentioned earlier in this essay, CJI Sabyasachi Mukharji took the bold move of issuing a statement to the Bar indicating that propriety required a request be made to V Ramaswami J to desist from discharging judicial work. This would save both him and the institution from embarrassment while an inquiry was pending. Ultimately, the issue of withdrawing judicial work was partially formalized through the issuance of the In-House Procedure (IHP) conceived of by the Court in 1995.

The power of the CJI to withdraw judicial work has been raised in other contexts as well. For instance, in 2016, CJI Thakur stated that he may be constrained to seek the withdrawal of judicial work from Valmiki Mehta J of the Delhi HC and MR Shah J of the Gujarat HC in light of them using their political influence to ensure that the government does not act on the Collegium resolution and issue orders for their transfer.[34] Significantly, MR Shah J, who in August 2018 as CJ of the Patna HC, publicly described the Prime Minister as a 'model and hero,'[35] was elevated to the SCI in November 2018.

In-House Procedure

The background to the decision in *C Ravichandran Iyer v. Justice AM Bhattacharjee,*[36] were the allegations of misconduct against the then CJ of Bombay HC, AM Bhattacharjee. He was alleged to have entered into a book publishing deal for an amount of 80,000 USD as a pay off for certain judgments. The Bar sought his resignation. Ravichandran Iyer, a lawyer, filed

[34] 'Will Withdraw Judicial Work from MR Shah, Valmiki Mehta JJ., CJI Thakur Warns Centre', (*BarandBench*, 13 August 2016) <https://www.barandbench.com/news/will-withdraw-judicial-work-mr-shah-valmiki-mehta-jj-cji-thakur-warns-centre> accessed 21 February 2025.

[35] Manu Sebastian, 'Justice MR Shah: A PM Modi Admirer, Known for Pro-Executive Stance in Civil Liberty Issues' (*LiveLaw*, 16 May 2023) <https://www.livelaw.in/articles/justice-mr-shah-supreme-court-legacy-pm-modi-fundamental-rights-228785> accessed 13 July 2024.

[36] *C Ravichandran Iyer v. Justice AM Bhattacharjee* (1995) 5 SCC 457. Bench comprised of K Ramaswamy, BL Hansaria JJ.

a PIL to restrain the Bar from coercing the CJ to resign. He also sought investigation into the allegations by the CBI.

The SCI noted that the judiciary ought to evolve mechanisms for 'self-regulation', for dealing with instances that are not serious enough to trigger the impeachment process. However, it was necessary to undertake an inquiry to 'ensure that judges do not abuse the trust the society has in them.'[37] This would involve vesting discretionary power in an HC CJ who may act in consultation with the CJI where the complaint pertained to an HC judge. If it concerned an SCI judge, such discretionary power would vest in the CJI.[38] The striking feature of the SCI's emphasis on the need for a self-regulation mechanism to address possible instances of judicial misconduct is its resemblance to its judicial decisions expanding its own authority, and especially that of the CJI, with respect to the appointment of judges. At both levels, the Court appears to be driven by a discomfort with the idea of external actors evaluating judges (or potential judges).

On the administrative side the SCI addressed the issue of judicial misconduct in 1997, when it issued a *Restatement of Values of Judicial Life*.[39] These were a set of 'illustrative' guidelines concerning the distance that judges must keep from the public, and emphasizing that 'there should be no act or omission by [them] which is unbecoming of the high office' of a judge.' A more comprehensive version of the IHP was issued by the SCI in 1999.[40] The CJI now had the power to constitute a three-member committee of judges to carry out an inquiry. However, this was only where the CJI was, after examining the response of the judge complained against, not convinced that the allegations were frivolous. In the event there was substance in the complaint, requiring initiation of proceedings, the CJI was required to advise the concerned judge

---

[37] ibid [35].

[38] ibid [40]; The Court expressed its concern with the possibility of frivolous complaints arising against judges and observed that a self-regulation mechanism would guard against this. The Court found that 'this procedure would not only facilitate nipping in the bud the conduct of a Judge leading to loss of public confidence in the courts and sustain public faith in the efficacy of the rule of law and respect for the judiciary, but would also avoid needless embarrassment of contempt proceedings against the office-bearers of the Bar Association and group libel against all concerned.'

[39] *Restatement of Values of Judicial Life* (Full Court Meeting, Supreme Court of India, 7 May 1997) <https://main.sci.gov.in/pdf/Notice/02112020_090821.pdf> accessed 12 February 2025.

[40] *Report of the Committee on In-House Procedure* (Full Court Meeting, Supreme Court of India, 15 December 1999) <https://main.sci.gov.in/pdf/cir/2014-12-31_1420006239.pdf> accessed 15 July 2024.

to resign or seek voluntary retirement. The IHP acknowledges the possibility of a judge refusing to follow such advice. In that circumstance, the CJI would advise the CJ of the concerned HC not to allocate any judicial work to the concerned judge.

It is noteworthy that the need for the IHP was justified by the Court on the ground that a judge should be examined by his or her peers rather than any 'outside agency'.[41] The Court suggests that this is necessary to safeguard judges from 'vilification by false and frivolous complaints'.[42] This tension in the Court's judicial position and its administrative position suggest that the extra-constitutional accountability mechanisms developed by the Court are not necessarily fully thought through. Perhaps, the greatest indication of the incomplete nature of these accountability mechanisms is the IHP's silence on situations where allegations are raised against the CJI. This gap has become particularly glaring in recent years, with several successive CJI terms being shrouded in controversy due to allegations of misconduct.

An analysis of the emergence of the IHP would be incomplete without also mentioning the case of *Indira Jaising v. Supreme Court of India*[43] – the first case where the SCI followed the IHP. This case concerned 'the Mysore sex scandal'[44] – where allegations were raised against three judges of the Karnataka HC (among others) for running a prostitution racket in a resort in Mysore. After receiving a report from the CJ of the Karnataka HC, the CJI (GB Pattanaik) invoked the IHP to constitute a Committee consisting of two HC CJs and a judge of the Orissa HC to conduct a deeper probe into the sex scandal. After the Committee submitted a report to the CJI finding that there was no proof of the allegations raised, Indira Jaising, a senior lawyer, filed a PIL seeking publication of this Inquiry Report and further seeking a direction 'to any professional and independent investigating agency having expertise to conduct a thorough investigation into the said incident'.[45] The SCI, in a strikingly short judgment, unequivocally declared that the Report

41 ibid.

42 ibid.

43 *Indira Jaising v. Supreme Court of India* (2003) 5 SCC 494. Bench comprised of S Rajendra Babu, GP Mathur JJ

44 This is how the incident came to be referred to by the media which reported on it in November and December 2002.

45 *Indira Jaising v. Supreme Court of India* (n 43) [1].

could not be made public, observing that the Report is only for the CJI and that publishing it 'will only lead to more harm than good to the institution'.[46] Reaffirming its previously expressed concern over the involvement of outside agencies, the Court further refused to direct an external investigation, finding that the petitioner could pursue the issue only through the impeachment route – if so desired.

In a recent development, the Supreme Court adopted a different approach while dealing with allegations of corruption against a judge of the Delhi High Court – Yashwant Varma J. In the context of a search that apparently revealed large quantities of cash kept in an outhouse of Varma J's bungalow, the Supreme Court issued a press release annexing a Report submitted by the CJ of the HC of Delhi as well as the response of Yashwant Varma J.[47] It also declared that it had constituted a three-member Committee to conduct an inquiry into the allegations against Varma J. While it may be premature to comment extensively on this instance at this stage, this instance is significant because it is for the first time that in a context like this the Supreme Court has made a report public – that too of the video of burnt remains of currency notes and pictures of the outhouse that was searched.[48]

Punishment Transfers

The use of the device transfers of HC judges as a means of punishing judges holding the executive to account or for other reasons has been discussed extensively in the earlier essays in this book.[49] A few other instances are noted in this essay.

---

[46] ibid [3].

[47] Press Release by the Supreme Court of India, 22 March 2025 <https://cdnbbsr.s3waas.gov.in/s3ec0490f1f4972d133619a60c30f3559e/uploads/2025/03/2025032266.pdf> accessed 5 April 2025.

[48] 'Supreme Court Publishes Video & Pictures on Cash at Justice Yashwant Varma's Premises; Makes Report of Delhi HC CJ Public' (*LiveLaw*, 23 March 2025) <https://www.livelaw.in/top-stories/breaking-supreme-court-publishes-video-pictures-on-cash-at-justice-yashwant-varmas-house-makes-report-of-delhi-hc-cj-public-287222> accessed 5 April 2025. Recently, the three-member committee formed by the SCI to probe into the allegations submitted its report to the CJI on 4 March 2025. See, Press Release by the Supreme Court of India, 5 March 2025 < https://www.sci.gov.in/press-release-dated-may-5-2025/> accessed 7 May 2025.

[49] See, essays by AP Shah and Madan Lokur in this book.

In 2017, Jayant Patel J was transferred to Karnataka HC from Gujarat HC, where he was the Acting CJ, and then was further transferred to Allahabad.[50] Patel J resigned following the recommendation to transfer him to Allahabad. Other examples include BK Roy J's transfers (Punjab to Gauhati HC, and Gauhati to Sikkim HC) and Sanjib Banerjee J's transfer (Madras to Meghalaya HC).[51] It is widely believed that both judges were supposedly punished for threatening to disclose information about the corrupt practices of other colleagues.[52]

While these instances involve judges who were sought to be 'disciplined' for upholding constitutional ideals and adhering to the rule of law,[53] the other instances where the Collegium recommends the transfer of judges whose serious misconduct is seen to be equally damaging to the judiciary as an institution.[54] Thus, transfers in the context of serious allegations of misconduct constitute a violation of basic principles of rule of law and equality, in addition to being contrary to the legal principles laid down by the SCI.

---

[50] Both transfers were recommended just as Patel J was about to become the senior-most judge in these HCs, reinforcing the general impression that he was being punished for ordering a CBI investigation in the controversial fake encounter case of Ishrat Jahan during the Gujarat riots.

[51] Akshaya Mukul, 'SC Collegium Confirms Gauhati CJ's Transfer' (*The Times of India*, 12 September 2005) <https://timesofindia.indiatimes.com/india/sc-collegium-confirms-gauhati-cjs-transfer/articleshow/1228667.cms> accessed 16 July 2024; Umang Poddar, 'Why a Judge's Transfer from Madras to Meghalaya Has Raised Concerns about Judicial Independence' (*Scroll.in*, 17 November 2021) <https://scroll.in/article/1010635/why-a-judges-transfer-from-madras-to-meghalaya-has-raised-concerns-about-judicial-independence> accessed 16 July 2024.

[52] Sanjib Banerjee in an interview said this in as many words. See 'Reporting corrupt judges who had friends in high places to CJI resulted in my transfer: Justice Sanjib Banerjee [Part I]' (*BarandBench*, 16 March 2024) <https://www.barandbench.com/interviews/justice-sanjib-banerjee-part-i> accessed 23 March 2025.

[53] Often, punishment postings have been stereotypically made to the Northeast, and Bar Associations of Northeastern HCs have protested, saying that their Courts are not a dumping ground. While in *Union of India v. SH Sheth* (1977) 4 SCC 193, the SCI held that transfer orders must only be passed in 'public interest', it is inconceivable that the transfer of a judge who may actually be guilty of misconduct could ever be in public interest. Recently, while the Allahabad High Court Bar Association vehemently protested against the repatriation of Yashwant Varma J from the High Court of Delhi, angrily stating that they are not a 'trash bin' for tainted judges, the Calcutta Bar Association did likewise against the transfer of Dinesh Kumar Sharma J emphasizing that the Court cannot be treated like a 'dumping ground'. See Ishita Mishra, 'We Are Not "Trash Bin", Says Allahabad HC Bar Association on Proposed Delhi HC Judge Transfer' (*The Hindu*, 21 March 2025); Tanusree Bose, '"Calcutta High Court Is Not the Dumping Ground for Tainted Judges": HC Lawyers' Bodies (*The Indian Express*, 1 April 2025).

[54] One instance could be that of the transfer of Karnan J from the Madras HC to the Calcutta HC when he began interfering on the judicial side with orders of the CJ on the administrative side and even with judicial orders of Division Benches.

Inconsistency in Dealing with Judicial Misconduct

Among the various kinds of judicial misconduct that have come to light in India, the most common involve allegations of corruption and sexual harassment. In addition to these two, there have also been several instances involving allegations of judges abusing their office and of making statements and committing actions indicative of caste prejudices. While these are no doubt extremely serious kinds of misconduct, this section of the essay focuses on how different mechanisms have been triggered in the context of corruption and sexual harassment allegations.

Corruption

Although corruption allegations are perhaps the most prominent kind of allegations of misconduct, it may be noted at the outset that this issue is closely related to the question of the extent of information about judges that is available to the public. Despite repeated declarations by the judiciary concerning the need for judges to declare their assets, especially when it is in 'public interest', one finds that the adherence to this norm of voluntary declaration is both irregular across time and inconsistent across HCs.[55] Despite this substantial preliminary hurdle in identifying instances of corruption, there have been several incidents where allegations of corruption have been raised against judges of the higher judiciary – as the cases of CJs K Veeraswami and AM Bhattacharjee demonstrate.[56] This section is concerned with how these allegations have been dealt with, once raised.

Two instances involve invocation of the parliamentary process laid down under the Constitution and the Judges (Inquiry) Act. In 2009, several Senior Advocates raised allegations that PD Dinakaran, the then CJ of the Karnataka HC, had amassed assets disproportionate to his income and had engaged in land encroachment in the State of Tamil Nadu.[57] The allegations were

---

[55] According to a news report from January 2024, less than twelve per cent of the HC judges in the country had declared their assets. This suggests that the idea of voluntary declaration may be an unsuitable and ineffective approach to pursue the ideal of judicial accountability. Soibam Rocky Singh, 'Only 13 of 42 Delhi High Court Judges Have Declared Their Assets' (*The Hindu,* 20 January 2024). Recently, in terms of a resolution passed on 1 April 2025, 21 out of the 33 judges of the SCI declared their assets (as of 7 May 2025). See, Assets of Judges < https://www.sci.gov.in/assets-of-judges/> accessed 7 May 2025.

[56] See subheading 'In-House Procedure' of this essay.

[57] These allegations were raised publicly by senior members of the bar after the Collegium had recommended Dinakaran's name for elevation to the SCI.

confirmed through two reports prepared by the Collector of Tiruvallur, after which the Supreme Court Collegium (SCC) dropped Dinakaran's name for elevation. Subsequently, the Chairman of the Rajya Sabha admitted a motion for his removal and constituted a Committee to prepare an inquiry report. In December 2009, the CJI (KG Balakrishnan) advised HC CJ Dinakaran to go on leave, pending the inquiry proceedings. Upon his refusal, the SCC recommended Dinakaran's transfer to the Sikkim HC as CJ.[58] He ultimately resigned in July 2011, just as the Inquiry Committee was close to submitting its report. He subsequently sought to withdraw his resignation, though this request was then denied.

The other instance was of Soumitra Sen J, a judge of the Calcutta HC. It was alleged that when Sen was an Advocate practising before the Calcutta HC, he had misappropriated large sums of money that he had obtained in his capacity as a court-appointed Receiver. He was alleged to have further misrepresented facts with respect to these sums. The Rajya Sabha Chairman admitted a motion for removing Sen J. In March 2009, he constituted a Committee which in its Inquiry Report submitted in September 2010, found Sen J guilty of misbehaviour. It noted his lack of cooperation during the inquiry process. In August 2011, the Rajya Sabha passed the impeachment motion against Sen J by 189 votes against seventeen. However, Sen J resigned in September 2011, immediately before the impeachment motion was to be taken up in the Lok Sabha.

The Dinakaran and Sen episodes affirm the argument that perhaps the parliamentary process for impeachment is in need of revision. The slow completion of the process means that the seeds of doubt concerning judicial integrity linger over the judiciary for long periods of time. The only beneficiary of this long-drawn process is the judge accused of misconduct, who may even continue to perform judicial work since that is governed by judicial propriety rather than legal principles.[59] In several other instances, corruption allegations against judges have resulted in action being taken as per the IHP, or under the Prevention of Corruption Act, or both consecutively.[60]

---

58 As discussed in the subheading 'Punishment Transfers' of this essay, he took up judicial work as CJ of the Sikkim HC even though the inquiry proceedings were still pending.

59 Perhaps, even more surprising is that despite the existence of evidence concerning the corruption allegations against these two judges, they continued to receive the retirement benefits available to any ordinary judge.

60 In 2003, Shameet Mukherjee of the Delhi HC was arrested by the CBI for his alleged role in a multi-crore land scam involving the Delhi Development Authority. Subsequently, once sanction was granted under

In 2017, allegations of corruption were raised against SN Shukla J, a sitting judge of the Allahabad HC. After a Committee constituted under the IHP found Shukla to be guilty of misconduct, the CJI (Dipak Misra) wrote to the President's Secretariat recommending that proceedings for his removal should be initiated. Despite the report of the committee constituted under the IHP, no notice of motion for impeachment was ever brought in the Parliament. Following the IHP, the CJI also advised Shukla J to seek voluntary retirement – which he refused. Subsequently, the CJI requested the CJ of the Allahabad HC to withdraw judicial work from him. Shukla J ultimately retired in 2020, after 2.5 years of not being allotted judicial work.[61] After Shukla J retired in 2020, the CBI charge-sheeted him in 2021.

The lack of uniformity in the mechanisms used to hold judges accountable for corruption throws doubt over the notion developed by the SCI in *C Ravichandran Iyer* that the IHP was necessitated in order for the judiciary to conduct self-regulation in relatively minor instances of misconduct. There appears to be no clear standard to identify the kinds of misconduct that fall short of meriting the impeachment process.

---

the PC Act and proceedings commenced under the Act, Mukherjee J resigned. In 2008, allegations of corruption arose against Nirmal Yadav J of the Punjab and Haryana HC, after a bag containing Rs 15 lakhs was mistakenly delivered at the residence of another judge of the same Court – Nirmaljit Kaur J. The CJI constituted a three-member committee as per the IHP, which, upon investigation, drew an inference that the money was indeed sent for Nirmal Yadav J. Following this, judicial work was withdrawn from her, and the CBI began an investigation into the incident, after consulting the CJI. The matter dragged on for many years. It took over seven years for the CBI to even frame charges against Yadav J, after which hearings were repeatedly adjourned, and the pronouncement of the final verdict of the CBI court was even stayed by the Punjab and Haryana HC in 2023. See Namit Saxena, 'The Cash at Judge's Door Case: A Chronological Revisit' (*BarandBench*, 6 November 2021) < https://www.barandbench.com/columns/the-cash-at-judges-door-case-a-chronological-revisit> accessed 15 July 2024. A Special CBI Court in Chandigarh finally acquitted Yadav J in March 2025. The Court doubted the credibility of the prosecution's main witness, found that the evidence relied on by the CBI was unreliable and even went to the extent of finding that the CBI had 'fabricated evidence'. See Aiman Chisti, '"CBI Fabricated Evidence": Reasons Why Chandigarh Court Acquitted Justice Nirmal Yadav In Corruption Case' (*LiveLaw*, 2 April 2025) <https://www.livelaw.in/news-updates/cbi-court-acquitted-justice-nirmal-yadav-2008-corruption-case-explained-288233> accessed 3 April 2025.

[61] After his retirement, the CBI charge-sheeted him in 2021. In 2023, it filed an FIR against him for amassing assets disproportionate to his known sources of income. In the recent instance of Yashwant Varma J, the CJI advised both the CJ of Delhi HC and later, CJ of the Allahabad HC not to allocate work to Varma J, pending the completion of the IHP.

Sexual Harassment

Justice Arun Madan

In 2002, a female doctor accused Arun Madan J, a judge of the Rajasthan HC, of soliciting sexual favours from her in exchange for a lenient judgment in a case pending against her. A committee of three CJs formed by the then CJI, GB Pattanaik, found against Madan J. However, since the panel had also indicated other allegations of corruption against him, no action was taken at that point. Before the inquiry committee could announce its findings, Madan J resigned. He did not face any further punitive action.[62]

Justice AK Ganguly

In 2013, a student from a law school levelled charges of sexual harassment via a blog post against AK Ganguly J, a retired SCI judge who was then the Chairman of the West Bengal Human Rights Commission. The CJI took *suo motu* cognizance and constituted a three-judge committee of RM Lodha, HL Dattu and Ranjana Prakash Desai JJ. The complainant was called to depose before the panel and to give a detailed account of what had transpired.[63] The Committee found that a *prima facie* case of sexual harassment was made out against the judge. However, it cited lack of jurisdiction as a reason for not taking action since Ganguly J had already retired when the alleged assault took place.[64] Ganguly J then wrote a letter to the CJI decrying the IHC, denying the allegations against him. He contended that the inquiry was not endorsed by a Full Court resolution.[65] Thereafter, CJI P Sathasivam released a statement reiterating that no further action would be taken against Ganguly J as he had already retired. The statement also said that the Full Court, in its meeting on

---

62 'A Judge's Exit' (*The Frontline*, 10 April 2003) <https://frontline.thehindu.com/other/article30216504 ece> accessed 11 July 2024.

63 Jayant Sriram, 'Alleged Sexual Misconduct Puts Retired SC Judge AK Ganguly, a Star of the Judiciary, on the Defensive' (*India Today*, 5 December 2013, <https://www.indiatoday.in/magazine/nation/story/20131216-justice-ak-ganguly-sexual-misconduct-law-student-wbhrc-768962-2013-12-05> accessed 13 July 2024.

64 A Vaidyanathan, 'Justice Ganguly's Unique Defence of Sexual Harassment Charges against Him' (*NDTV*, 19 December 2013, <https://www.ndtv.com/india-news/justice-gangulys-unique-defence-of-sexual-harassment-charges-against-him-545083> accessed 12 July 2024.

65 TNN, 'Law Intern Hits Back at Justice AK Ganguly, Gives Point-By-Point Rebuttal to His Letter' (*The Times of India*, 24 December 2013).

5 December 2013, had decided that the SCI administration would not entertain any further complaints against Ganguly J.[66]

Justice Swatanter Kumar

In 2013, Swatanter Kumar J, by then a retired judge of the SCI was accused by a young student intern of making 'unwelcome physical contact and sexual advances'[67] while she interned with him in 2011. The intern was hemmed in by the lack of a formal mechanism to make a complaint earlier, but decided to bring this to the attention of the SCI formally after the events of the AK Ganguly case were made public.[68] On 5 December 2013, in response to the complaint, a notice went up on the SCI website that representations made against former judges of the SCI would not be entertained.[69] Thus, in a departure from the approach adopted, in the case of Ganguly J where the SCI immediately instituted an in-house inquiry, in the case of Kumar J the above notice closed the door for the intern to get relief from the administrative side of the SCI.[70]

In January 2014, the intern filed a PIL challenging the Full Court resolution which dismissed her complaint. She prayed for an institutional mechanism to be set up to 'enquire into the complaints of SH against all judicial officers, sitting or retired judges, whether while holding office or not'. She further contended that since Kumar J was a sitting judge at the time of the incident,

---

[66] A few weeks after this, on 3 January 2014, the Union Cabinet approved a presidential reference to the SCI for a statutory inquiry into the charges of sexual harassment. Days later on 9 January 2014, Ganguly J, who had steadfastly refused to resign since the allegations had come to light, resigned as chairman of the West Bengal Human Rights Commission, by his own admission to 'obviate further controversy'. PTI, 'Justice Ganguly's Conduct Is of Sexual Nature: SC Panel,' (*Deccan Herald*, 5 December 2013); 'Justice Ganguly Refuses to Resign,' (*Deccan Herald*, 10 December 2013); Soudhriti Bhabani, 'Law Intern Sexual Harassment Case: I Am Resigning to Save My Dignity, Says Justice Ganguly' (*India Today*, 7 January 2014) <https://www.indiatoday.in/india/story/justice-ganguly-resignation-i-am-resigning-to-save-my-dignity-175951-2014-01-07> accessed 13 July 2024.

[67] 'India Court to Hear Sex Case against Ex-Judge' (*Al Jazeera*, 13 January 2014) <https://www.aljazeera.com/news/2014/1/13/india-court-to-hear-sex-case-against-ex-judge> accessed 18 July 2024.

[68] 'Former SC Judge Swatanter Kumar Named in Sexual Harassment Case' *Mangalore Today*, <https://www.mangaloretoday.com/headlines/Former-SC-judge-Swatanter-Kumar-named-in-sexual-harassment-case.html> accessed 12 July 2024. Swatanter Kumar J was the Chairperson of the National Green Tribunal at this time.

[69] PTI, 'Intern Moves SC for Inquiry Against Justice Swatanter Kumar' (*Rediff.com*, 13 January 2014) <https://www.rediff.com/news/report/intern-moves-sc-for-inquiry-against-justice-swatanter-kumar/20140113.htm> accessed 13 July 2024.

[70] ibid.

the SCI was duty-bound to look into the allegations as per the *Vishaka* guidelines.[71] The petition was admitted for hearing and notice was issued to Kumar J. In his counter-affidavit, Kumar J strongly refuted the charge of sexual harassment as being 'malicious'.

A few days later, Kumar J filed a civil suit against the law intern and media organizations for defamation in the Delhi HC. He alleged a 'trial by media' and demanded Rs 5 crores as damages. The HC issued an interim injunction restraining the media from publishing details of the case and from publishing any photographs of Kumar J while reporting on the case. While Kumar J was represented by nine Senior Advocates at the first hearing, the intern was unrepresented.[72] The 'offending content' was ordered to be removed from the internet and electronic media within 24 hours.[73]

Later, in 2014 itself, the intern applied to the SCI for transfer of the defamation case to Bangalore, stating that she had 'absolutely no chance of equal or near equal legal representation in Delhi.'[74] The said petition was kept pending for nine years. An order dated 24 March 2023 revealed that the defamation suit in the HC had been settled by a private agreement whose details were kept confidential. The Court ordered that the parties would abide by the terms of the agreement and further ordered that all the pleadings, documents and all parts of the record of the suit in the Delhi HC would be kept in a sealed cover. The SCI further ordered that the injunction order passed by the Delhi HC, which restrained the media and the intern, was confirmed and made absolute.[75]

---

71 ibid.

72 Kian Ganz, 'Delhi HC Permits "Fair" Reporting on Swatanter Kumar Sex Harass Allegations (But No More Pictures for Arnab) After 11 Seniors' Full-Court Press' (*Legally India*, 17 January 2014) <https://www.legallyindia.com/the-bench-and-the-bar/swatanter-kumar-defamation-interim-injunction-20140117-4249> accessed 13 July 2024.

73 '"Sexual Harassment" Case: HC Puts Curbs on Media' (*The Indian Express*, 17 January 2014) <https://indianexpress.com/article/india/india-others/hc-imposes-curbs-on-media-reporting-allegations-against-ex-sc-judge/> accessed 12 July 2024; While the stay was to last only until the next hearing on 24 February 2014, it continued indefinitely.

74 Kian Ganz, '#InternJudge Files SC Transfer Petition vs Swatanter Kumar: Won't Get Fair Trial in Delhi HC, Senior Counsel Refuse to Act as Suit 'Engineered' in Favour of Ex-Judge' (*Legally India*, 14 May 2014) <https://www.legallyindia.com/the-bench-and-the-bar/internjudge-transfer-petition-swatanter-kumar-20140514-4712> accessed 18 July 2024.

75 'In Sexual Harassment Case against Former Judge, SC Asks If Transfer Plea Is Necessary' (*Scroll.in*, 9 January 2023) <https://scroll.in/latest/1041499/in-sexual-harassment-case-against-former-judge-sc-asks-if-transfer-plea-is-necessary> accessed 18 July 2024.

Justice SK Gangele

A former Additional District and Sessions judge in Gwalior accused SK Gangele J of the Madhya Pradesh HC of repeatedly sexually harassing her. She claimed that because she resisted his advances, she was transferred mid-season to Sidhi, a remote, 'Naxal-affected' location. Her representations to extend her time in Gwalior by eight months since her daughter had board examinations, she alleged, were rejected at Gangele J's behest.[76] Following this, she resigned from service.[77] A committee was set up by the Madhya Pradesh HC to look into the matter. However, accepting the Complainants' challenge to its constitution and procedure, the SCI quashed the inquiry.[78] The SCI thereafter constituted a 3-member committee comprising Chandrachud J (then CJ of the Allahabad HC), G Rohini J (CJ of the Delhi HC) and Ajay Rastogi J of the Rajasthan HC. This Committee held that there was not sufficient evidence to prove the charge.

In the meanwhile, the Rajya Sabha permitted a motion to impeach on three grounds of misconduct: a) sexual harassment, b) victimization of the junior judge and c) misusing his official position. This motion was spearheaded by Sharad Yadav of the JDU, and supported by MPs across parties.[79] A panel of R Banumathi, Manjula Chellur JJ and Senior Advocate KK Venugopal was constituted by the Rajya Sabha under Section 3 of the Judges (Inquiry) Act. The Committee found that the charges were 'not proved' and had termed Gangele J's conduct to be a part of routine district administration/exercise of supervisory power by the HC. While the Committee highlighted the seriousness of the allegations and their impact on the judiciary as a whole, they also emphasized that charges which may result in impeachment required a higher standard of proof.[80] They termed Gangele J's conduct 'improper'

---

[76] Ananthakrishnan G, 'Explained: Case of Madhya Pradesh Judicial Officer Who Accused HC Judge' (*The Indian Express*, 11 February 2022).

[77] ibid.

[78] ibid.

[79] Aditya AK, 'Rajya Sabha Committee: No Sexual Harassment Charges Proven Against MP High Court Judge' (*BarandBench*, 15 December 2017) <https://www.barandbench.com/news/rajya-sabha-sexual-harassment-judge> accessed 17 July 2024.

[80] ibid.

but not as misbehaviour, as read under Article 124 (4) with Article 217.[81] Upon retirement, the SCI designated Gangele J as a Senior Advocate in December 2021.[82] By a separate order in February 2022, the SCI directed the reinstatement of the complainant in the Madhya Pradesh higher judicial service.[83]

Allegations Against Chief Justices of India

JS Khehar (2017)

In February 2017, Dangwimsai Pul, widow of Khaliko Pul (briefly the Chief Minister [CM] of Arunachal Pradesh), approached the then CJI, JS Khehar, seeking permission to file criminal cases against two SCI judges accused of bribery in her husband's suicide note, including Khehar J himself. In December 2015, the Governor had advanced the Assembly session, causing CM Nabam Tuki to lose majority. Khaliko Pul, now backed by BJP and rebel Congress MLAs, became CM in 2016.[84] Nabam Rebia[85] and Bamang Felix challenged the Assembly's premature convening before the SCI. In July 2016, a Constitution Bench including Khehar J declared the Governor's order unconstitutional and reinstated Tuki.[86] Khaliko Pul died by suicide shortly after, leaving behind a suicide note accusing Khehar and Dipak Misra JJ of

[81] 'Woman Judge Sexually Harassed by Madhya Pradesh High Court's Justice Gangele Files for Reinstatement' (*The Leaflet*, 23 July 2018) <https://theleaflet.in/woman-judge-sexually-harassed-by-madhya-pradesh-high-courts-justice-gangele-files-for-reinstatement/> accessed 13 July 2024. See Indira Jaising's interview in this book.

[82] Srishti Ojha, 'Breaking: Supreme Court Designates 7 Retired HC CJs/Judges and 18 Lawyers as Senior Advocates' (*LiveLaw*, 11 December 2021) <https://www.livelaw.in/top-stories/breaking-supreme-court-designates-7-retired-hc-cjsjudges-and-18-lawyers-as-senior-advocates-187427> accessed 13 July 2024.

[83] Prachi Bhardwaj, 'Harassed, Transferred, Left with No Choice but to Resign: Read How This MP District Judge Won Half the Battle in Alleged Sexual Harassment Case as SC Orders Her Reinstatement' (*SCC Online*, 11 February 2022) <https://www.scconline.com/blog/post/2022/02/11/harassed-transferred-left-with-no-choice-but-to-resign-read-how-this-mp-district-judge-won-half-the-battle-in-alleged-sexual-harassment-case-as-sc-orders-her-reinstatement/> accessed 12 July 2024.

[84] Prasanta Mazumdar, 'President's Rule Lifted, Kalikho Pul Is New Arunachal CM' (*The New Indian Express*, 20 February 2020).

[85] Former Speaker, Arunachal Pradesh Legislative Assembly.

[86] 'President's Rule Quashed in Arunachal: SC Has Saved This Country, Says Ex-CM Tuki' (*The Indian Express*, 13 July 2016).

soliciting bribes through their respective sons.[87] The note did not include evidence to support the claims, and official records show Misra had daughters, not sons.[88]

Dangwimsai's application to the CJI to investigate the judges referenced the *K Veeraswami* case, as per which judges of the HC and SCI can be probed for corruption only with the prior permission of the CJI or any other suitable judge when the CJI himself was implicated. She accordingly requested that CJI Khehar place the matter before an appropriate judge, so that permission to file a criminal case could be granted by them without a conflict of interest arising.[89] Instead, Khehar J converted the letter into a writ petition and listed it before a Bench of AK Goel and UU Lalit JJ, thereby turning an administrative issue into a judicial case.[90] After a charged hearing where the lawyer for the petitioner raised these points,[91] Dangwimsai withdrew the writ petition. Permitting her to withdraw the matter, the Bench declared that the cause of action raised in writing to the CJI had ended.[92]

Dipak Misra (2018)

Dipak Misra became the first CJI to face an impeachment motion, ironically marking a period where the power of the CJI was strengthened and cemented through case law. His tenure also saw a public rebellion by other SCI judges over the CJI's unchecked power.

The issue of 'master of the roster' became a focal point of debate soon after Misra took over as CJI. The Constitution Bench judgment in *Campaign for Judicial*

---

87 Atul Dev, 'Balancing Act: Chief Justice Khehar and the Tussle between the Executive and the Judiciary' (*The Caravan*, 01 June 2017) <https://caravanmagazine.in/reportage/chief-justice-khehar-executive-judiciary> accessed 13 July 2024.

88 Harish V Nair, 'Delhi HC Chief Justice Declares Assets on Website' (*The Hindustan Times*, 29 December 2010).

89 Chandan Nandy, 'Kalikho Pul's Widow Lands CJI Khehar in a Tricky Position' (*The Quint*, 17 February 2017) <https://www.thequint.com/news/politics/arunachal-pradesh-cm-kalikho-pul-widow-lands-cji-khehar-in-uncomfortable-position#read-more> accessed 11 July 2024.

90 This also raises an issue of the CJI's prerogative as 'master of the roster' and whether even on the administrative side, when there is a complaint against the CJI, it should be placed before the next senior-most judge for being dealt with.

91 Dhananjay Mahapatra and Amit Anand Choudhary, 'Kalikho Pul's Widow Withdraws Letter after Allegations' (*The Times of India*, 23 February 2017).

92 'SC Allows Pul's Wife to Withdraw Letter' (*Deccan Herald*, 23 February 2017).

Accountability and Reforms v. Union of India reiterated that the CJI 'alone has the prerogative to constitute the benches of the court and allocate cases to the benches so constituted' – that is, that even in cases where allegations involve the CJI himself, he would decide who would hear those cases.[93]

Soon after, the suspicious death of Judge BH Loya on 1 December 2014 came to light. Loya was the presiding judge over a special CBI court which was dealing with the extrajudicial killing of Sohrabuddin Sheikh by the police in Gujarat in 2005 where the main accused was Amit Shah. Amit Shah was the Minister of State for the State of Gujarat in 2005. By the time of the death of Judge Loya, he was a member of the Gujarat Legislative Assembly and also the National President of the BJP, the party ruling at the Centre. Although his death was recorded as due to a heart attack, his family raised concerns over the veracity of this based on the condition of his body when it was handed over.[94] While two petitions regarding the suspicious death of Loya were pending before the Bombay HC, a third petition was filed before the SCI. CJI Misra transferred the other two petitions to the SCI and then led the three-judge Bench that dismissed the plea for further investigation raised in all petitions.[95]

Following this, four senior judges held a press conference criticizing the SCI's administration, declaring that the administration in the Apex Court was 'not in order' and accusing Misra of assigning sensitive cases selectively.[96] In April 2018, seven opposition parties moved a notice to the Chairman of the Rajya Sabha to impeach CJI Misra, citing five charges, including the handling of the Prasad Education Trust case and abuse of his power as CJI by sending sensitive matters to particular Benches.[97] However, Vice-President Venkaiah Naidu rejected the 'Notice of Motion' with great dispatch, stating that it lacked

93 *Campaign for Judicial Accountability and Reforms v. Union of India* (2018) 1 SCC 196 [6].

94 Niranjan Takle, 'A Family Breaks Its Silence: Shocking Details Emerge in Death of Judge Presiding over Sohrabuddin Trial' (*The Caravan*, 20 November 2017) <https://caravanmagazine.in/vantage/shocking-details-emerge-in-death-of-judge-presiding-over-sohrabuddin-trial-family-breaks-silence> accessed 12 July 2024.

95 The review petition against the judgment in *Tehseen Poonawalla v. Union of India* (2018) 6 SCC 72 was dismissed in *Bandhuraj Sambhaji Lone v. Union of India* 2018 SCC OnLine SC 776.

96 'Supreme Court Crisis: All Not Okay, Democracy at Stake, Say Four Senior-Most Judges' (*Business Line*, 12 January 2018).

97 'Full Text: Opposition Lists Five Charges against CJI Dipak Misra as It Moves Impeachment Motion' (*Scroll.in*, 20 April 2018) <https://scroll.in/latest/876340/full-text-opposition-lists-five-charges-against-cji-dipak-misra-as-it-moves-impeachment-motion> accessed 11 July 2024.

evidence and was an internal SCI matter. The Vice-President stated that it was 'judicial convention' that the CJI was the master of the roster, and said that no one could direct the CJI in the matter of assignment of Benches.[98] He also criticized the opposition for discussing the charges publicly, calling it 'unparliamentary' and against propriety.[99]

Ranjan Gogoi (2019)

On 19 April 2019, a former junior court officer alleged that she was sexually harassed and subsequently victimized by CJI Ranjan Gogoi.[100] The staffer alleged that the incident had taken place on 10 and 11 October 2018 at the residence office of CJI Gogoi, after which she was transferred thrice in three weeks and then issued a show cause notice over a work matter. Without giving her a chance to reply, an administrative panel of the SCI dismissed her from service. In March 2019, a criminal case was filed against her. Further, her husband and brother-in-law, both of whom worked for the Delhi Police, also found themselves suspended.[101]

CJI Gogoi responded to the allegations by initiating *suo motu* proceedings over the allegations, forming a Bench with Arun Mishra and Sanjiv Khanna JJ.[102] In this hearing, CJI Gogoi attacked the complainant, suggesting a conspiracy against the judiciary. The Bench warned the media against undesirable reporting – though CJI Gogoi's signature was absent from the order. This hearing violated judicial principles as CJI Gogoi became a judge in his own case. Later, in an interview, he called this a 'mistake'.[103]

---

98 'Full Text: Venkaiah Naidu Rejects Impeachment Motion against CJI Dipak Misra, Says "Parliamentary Rules Have Been Disregarded"' (*Firstpost*, 23 April 2018) <https://www.firstpost.com/india/full-text-venkaiah-naidu-rejects-impeachment-motion-against-cji-dipak-misra-says-parliamentary-rules-have-been-disregarded-4442251.html> accessed 11 July 2024.

99 ibid.

100 Ananthakrishnan G, 'SC Reinstates Woman Employee Who Levelled Charges at Ex-CJI' (*The Indian Express*, 22 January 2020).

101 ibid.

102 Geffrey Gettleman, 'India's Chief Justice Is Accused of Sexual Harassment' (*The New York Times*, 20 April 2019) <https://www.nytimes.com/2019/04/20/world/asia/india-chief-justice-sexual-harassment.html> accessed 12 July 2024.

103 Bhadra Sinha, '"Was a Mistake": Ex-CJI Gogoi on Being on Bench Hearing Sexual Harassment Case Against Him' (*The Print*, 8 December 2021) <https://theprint.in/judiciary/was-a-mistake-ex-cji-gogoi-on-being-on-bench-hearing-sexual-harassment-case-against-him/778735/> accessed 11 July 2024.

Following this, CJI Gogoi formed an in-house inquiry panel, comprising SA Bobde, Indira Banerjee and Indu Malhotra JJ. The complainant withdrew after being denied legal representation and other procedural rights.[104] On 6 May 2019, the panel cleared CJI Gogoi of the allegations without making the report public. Banerjee J later revealed in an interview that she had wanted to make the details of the inquiry public since that would clear doubts about the procedure. However, citing the judgment in *Indira Jaising v. Supreme Court of India*, the SCI Registry said the report was not liable to be made public.[105]

In January 2020, a couple of months after CJI Gogoi's retirement, the complainant and her husband were reinstated in their jobs, and the criminal case against her was closed.[106] Four months after retiring, CJI Gogoi was nominated to the Rajya Sabha, drawing widespread criticism.[107]

NV Ramana (2020)

The last case in this section is also the most striking one since it involved, for the first time, accusations against a future CJI by a sitting CM. In October 2020, Jagan Mohan Reddy, then CM of Andhra Pradesh, wrote a letter to the then CJI, SA Bobde, accusing NV Ramana J (next in line to become the CJI) of political bias and corruption.[108] The main allegations were that Ramana J's two daughters were beneficiaries of questionable transfers of land in the proposed capital city of Andhra Pradesh, and that Ramana J was 'influencing the course of administration of justice in the State', claiming that matters

---

104 A Vaidyanathan, '"Have Right to the Report": Woman Who Complained against Chief Justice' (*NDTV*, 7 May 2019) <https://www.ndtv.com/india-news/woman-who-accused-chief-justice-of-india-ranjan-gogoi-of-sexual-harassment-writes-to-supreme-court-p-2034264> accessed 13 July 2024.

105 Debayan Roy, '[Exclusive] Report on Former CJI Gogoi Should Have Been Made Public, Would Have Cleared the Air: Justice Indira Banerjee [Part II]' (*BarandBench*, 28 September, 2022) <https://www.barandbench.com/interviews/litigation-interviews/exclusive-report-on-former-cji-gogoi-should-have-been-made-public-would-have-cleared-the-air-justice-indira-banerjee-part-ii> accessed 13 July 2024.

106 Ananthakrishnan G, 'SC Reinstates Woman Employee' (n 100).

107 'In Unprecedented Move, Modi Government Sends Former CJI Ranjan Gogoi to Rajya Sabha' (*The Wire*, 16 March 2020) < https://thewire.in/law/cji-ranjan-gogoi-rajya-sabha-nomination> accessed 13 July 2024.

108 YS Jagan Mohan Reddy, *Letter to Chief Justice of India SA Bobde* (6 October 2020) https://www.scribd.com/document/479516374/Andhra-CM-Jagan-Mohan-Reddy-letter-to-Chief-Justice-of-India-S-A-Bobde accessed 12 July 2024.

pertaining to Telugu Desam Party (TDP) leaders would only be assigned to certain judges.[109]

The public release of this letter prompted strong reactions. The Delhi High Court Bar Association condemned the letter, calling it an attempt to undermine judicial independence.[110] Several PILs were filed against Reddy, accusing him of making politically motivated and baseless allegations against Ramana J.[111] Petitioners highlighted that the letter was released shortly after a CBI court resumed hearings into Reddy's own disproportionate assets case, which had been fast-tracked by Ramana J's orders.[112] An article in *The Telegraph* raised suspicions about the timing of the letter, pointing out that it was dated 6 October 2020 – the same day Reddy met with Prime Minister Narendra Modi.[113] This led to speculation that the letter was part of a larger conflict between the Executive and the judiciary. The matter reached a quiet conclusion in March 2021, where a two-line announcement was posted on the SCI website stating that following an inquiry the allegations were dismissed.[114]

Conclusion

This analysis of the provisions of law and judicial pronouncements on judicial accountability for misconduct tracks the incremental increase in the judiciary's role in addressing instances of misconduct vis-a-vis the role of the Houses of the Parliament. Within this broader trajectory, it is striking to note the wide discretionary power vested in the hands of one individual – the CJI. While the Indian judiciary has innovatively developed a variety of redressal mechanisms for judicial misconduct, there appears to be little certainty over which

---

[109] The letter then refers to an annexure where these judgments were reproduced, but the annexure is not available publicly.

[110] Delhi High Court Bar Association, *Resolution* <https://www.livelaw.in/pdf_upload/pdf_upload-382832.pdf> accessed 13 July 2024.

[111] 'Jagan Reddy vs Justice Ramana: SC Rejects Pleas on Action against Andhra Pradesh Chief Minister' (*Scroll.in*, 1 December 2020) <https://scroll.in/latest/980020/jagan-reddy-vs-justice-ramana-sc-rejects-pleas-on-action-andhra-pradesh-chief-minister> accessed 4 July 2024.

[112] Ananthakrishnan G, 'After Jagan Reddy Letter to CJI: Need Free Judiciary, It Is for a Judge to Withstand Pressure, Says Justice Ramana' (*The Indian Express*, 19 October 2020).

[113] R Balaji, 'More to Jagan Mohan Reddy's Letter "Than Meets the Eye"' (*The Telegraph*, 12 October 2020).

[114] 'Supreme Court Dismisses Jagan's Complaint against Justice N.V. Ramana' (*The Wire*, 24 March 2021) <https://thewire.in/law/justice-n-v-ramana-to-succeed-chief-justice-of-india-bobde-on-april-24> accessed 3 July 2024.

mechanisms would be triggered in which specific circumstances. Further, there appears to be no clear standard to determine what amounts to serious misbehaviour warranting the commencement of impeachment proceedings. Instead, this depends heavily on the context, and on the views taken by a wide range of actors, including the CJI, the CJ of the concerned HC, the local Bar, the Supreme Court Bar and CBI officials.

While in *C Ravichandran Iyer*, the SCI expressed concern over members of the Bar raising frivolous allegations against judges, the instances covered in this essay suggest that a vocal and persistent Bar in fact might be one of the more effective modes of holding judges accountable and having them resign from the Bench.[115] The convoluted and even opaque nature of the self-regulation mechanism evolved by the judiciary creates a flawed incentive structure, where members of the Bar may legitimately feel that the integrity and credibility of the judiciary could be safeguarded more swiftly by increasing the pressure on a judge to resign instead of waiting for a particular CJ of a HC or the CJI to address the allegations.

Strikingly, the IHP developed by the Court does not appear to function along the lines of the justifications advanced for it. Rather than operating as a mechanism to hold judges accountable for 'minor' forms of misconduct, the IHP is predominantly used as an additional stage to be completed prior to other mechanisms of accountability being pursued. It appears to simply add a layer of inquiry before further investigation is carried out, either by a committee constituted under the Judges Inquiry Act or by the CBI. While the Court initially justified the IHP as a necessary mode of 'self-regulation',[116] this mechanism appears to work in favour of judges accused of misconduct by granting them more time before other proceedings are initiated.

It is worth noting here that all the processes developed by the judiciary are time-consuming, which also means that allegations have lingered over the judiciary for long periods of time. While in some cases, the adverse impact of these allegations is arguably addressed by findings in favour of

[115] As can be seen from the instance concerning Vijay Bahaguna of the Bombay HC. Though, after resigning, Bahuguna ultimately joined the Congress party, ran for elections and even became the Chief Minister of Uttarakhand; Olav Albuquerque, 'Legal Eagle: Calcutta Judge's Joining BJP Fuels Charge of Biased Verdicts' (*The Free Press Journal*, 7 March 2024) <https://www.freepressjournal.in/analysis/legal-eagle-calcutta-judges-joining-bjp-fuels-charge-of-biased-verdicts> accessed 3 July 2024.

[116] See subheading 'In-House Procedure' of this essay.

the judge concerned, more often than not the judge resigns towards the end of the proceedings initiated against them. Due to the delay built into this mechanism, doubts over the integrity and credibility of members of the higher judiciary trickle deep into civil society discourse before being redressed.

Scholars have expressed discontentment with the existing processes. Some have argued that 'it is virtually impossible to impeach judges of the SC or High Court' since the procedure 'is aligned completely in favour of the judges',[117] while others have suggested that the existing mechanisms have 'hopelessly failed to discipline judges'.[118] In 2005, the Law Commission of India (LCI) submitted a Report taking note of the various deficiencies in the existing redressal mechanisms for judicial misconduct, and proposed the enactment of a substantially modified law to govern inquiry into judicial misconduct. The Bill annexed to this LCI Report envisaged the establishment of a 'National Judicial Council' consisting of several specified judges to conduct investigations into complaints of misconduct. Prepared almost twenty years ago, this Report does not focus on the possibility of allegations being raised against the CJI – an issue that has risen in prominence in more recent years. However, the Report does emphasize the need for clarity and certainty in the process of investigating allegations of misconduct.[119]

In 2010, the Judicial Standards and Accountability Bill was introduced in the Parliament, stipulating standards to be followed by judges and proposing the establishment of an Oversight Board and a Complaints Scrutiny Panel. This Bill, with its comprehensive framework for handling and deciding complaints against judges, held promise of lending substance to the ideal of judicial accountability in the Indian context. Unfortunately, despite being passed in the Lok Sabha after a detailed Standing Committee Report, the Bill lapsed in the Rajya Sabha. Given the grave instances of judicial misconduct that have arisen in the past three decades, the failure of attempts to increase judicial accountability is deeply disappointing. Unless efficacious avenues exist to

---

[117] Sanjay Jain and Saranya Mishra, 'Scandalizing the Judiciary: An Analysis of the Uneven Response of the Supreme Court of India to Sexual Harassment Allegations Against Judges' (2020) 18(2) *International Journal of Constitutional Law* 568.

[118] Bhairav Acharya, 'A Legal Vacuum Enabled Justice Karnan's Bad Behaviour' (*The Wire*, 4 May 2017) <https://thewire.in/law/legal-vacuum-justice-karnan> accessed 17 July 2024.

[119] Government of India, Ministry of Law and Justice (*Press Note - Law Commission's recommendations on the Judges' (Inquiry) Bill, 2005*, 29 March 2006) <https://pib.gov.in/newsite/erelcontent.aspx?relid=16863> accessed 21 February 2025.

investigate these departures from the 'Values of Judicial Life',[120] and judges lacking integrity are held accountable for their actions, these instances will continue to have a greatly damaging impact on the image and credibility of judicial institutions.

[120] *Restatement of Values of Judicial Life* (n 39).

Cartoon © Satish Acharya. Reproduced with permission.

Judicial Delay and Pragmatism

USHA RAMANATHAN

Anxiety about delay in the judicial system is at least a hundred years old. In 1923, the Civil Justice Committee was set up to enquire into ways 'to provide for more speedy, economical and satisfactory dispatch' of matters transacted in courts and their execution. The first witness to testify before the committee began his paper with this assertion, and with no fear of contradiction:[1] 'That there is delay, in some cases very great delay, in the disposal of suits and appeals, will be readily conceded.'

Examined by the Committee on 29 July 1924, the Chairman is recorded as asking the witness:

Chairman: I see you say in your paper[2] that no change which does not otherwise strongly commend itself as just should be made merely in the hope that it might conduce to speedy disposal of cases ... I understand you do not believe in making any amendment that would be unjust merely for purposes of expediting disposal.

A: Certainly.[3]

Since then, delay has been the preoccupation of the judicial mind incessantly.[4]

---

1 Civil Justice Committee, Report of the Civil Justice Committee 1924–25, Written Statement of TR Venkatarama Sastri, Appendix No 2, vol III, 5.

2 ibid 8.

3 Civil Justice Committee, Report of the Civil Justice Committee 1924–25, Appendix No 2, Oral Evidence of TR Venkatarama Sastri, vol III, 5, 13 (examined 29 July 1924).

4 See, for instance, Law Commission of India, 14th Report (1958); 27th Report (1964); 54th Report (1973), 58th Report (1974), 77th Report (1979); 124th Report (1988); 245th Report (2014); Judicial Reforms Committee of the State of West Bengal (1949); U.P. Law Reforms Committee (1950–51); High Court Arrears Committee Report (1972); PN Bhagwati J, Law Day Speech, 26 November 1985, (1986) 1 SCC (J) 1, 3; PN Bhagwati J, Law Day Speech, 26 November 1986, (1987) 1 SCC (J) 46, 48; *Imtiyaz Ahmad v. State of Uttar Pradesh* (2012) 2 SCC 688; *Rojer Mathew v. South Indian Bank Ltd*

The problem of numbers – of the paucity of judges, of cases filed and disposed as well as low rates of conviction – and of procedure and infrastructure, have been raised in report after report. Answers have been sought in more courts, tribunals, more judges, increased budgets, improved infrastructure, scientific case management, Lok Adalat, mediation, arbitration, judicial impact assessment when laws are enacted, judicial academies to train judges and, more recently, the use of technology. Judicial outrage and incredulity at those consigned to prison and then forgotten has, on occasion, excited the imagination of the Court. Yet, more often, it is the strain on institutions – courts and prisons – that has had the court looking for ways to manage – and recover from – situations that could threaten the legitimacy of the system.

In all this, there is one matter that has been treated with delicate reserve: the changes that have been wrought to the Constitution by the delay, and the responses to delay, over the years. This concern has now exploded into public debate.

The significance of delay in deciding matters that have an immediate and far-reaching bearing on democracy, liberty, citizenship, the making of laws, the government's expanding power and shrinking fundamental rights of the people has provoked public comment and raised public anxiety about the part the court may play in restraining state power.

Electoral Bonds and Democracy

The damage caused by delay erupted in 2017 in the matter of 'electoral bonds'.[5] This was an idea introduced in the Finance Act 2017, to be devised as a scheme by the Central Government, and scheduled banks would be required to issue electoral bonds to purchasers who would then donate them to political parties. The changes that were made to the law on political funding took away the legal requirement of disclosure or reporting of contributions to political parties to the Election Commission (ECI) if the donations were in the nature

---

(2020) 6 SCC 1, 88 [10]–[13].

5 Section 135 of the Finance Act 2017, inserting sub-section (3) to Section 31 of the Reserve Bank of India Act 1934 by which the Central Government may authorize any scheduled bank to issue electoral bond. 'Electoral bond' would mean 'a bond issued by any scheduled bank under the scheme as may be notified by the Central Government.' Section 11 of the Finance Act 2017 amended Section 13A of the Income Tax Act 1961 to exempt political parties receiving monies as electoral bond to maintain records of such contributions.

of electoral bonds.[6] Where, earlier, foreign companies could not fund political parties in elections, and companies that could contribute had a ceiling on how much they could donate to political parties, along with a requirement of disclosure, the Finance Acts of 2016 and 2017 changed even that. Companies were no longer required to disclose the details of their contributions. The ceiling on corporate contributions was removed and opacity was introduced into a process which needed more transparency.

Soon after the scheme was announced on 2 January 2018, a number of petitions were filed in the SCI, challenging the scheme and asking for a stay of the electoral bond scheme. The court did not stay the scheme. In March 2019, the ECI, in its affidavit to the court, said that the electoral bond scheme would hamper transparency, and the amendments made to the law, namely, the Foreign Contribution Regulation Act 2010 (as amended in the Finance Act 2016) 'would allow unchecked foreign funding of political parties in India which could lead to Indian policies being influenced by foreign companies.'[7]

On 12 April 2019, the SCI said that 'the rival contentions give rise to weighty issues which have a tremendous bearing on the sanctity of the electoral process in the country.'[8] Yet, it took close to another five years before the court decided the case and struck down the electoral bond scheme as unconstitutional.[9] By then, there had been twenty-eight elections to state assemblies, and one national election. Also, while the court spoke of disclosure of contributors and the parties that encashed the bond, it allowed the monies collected thus far to remain with the parties. The figures speak volumes. The 'unconstitutional' scheme generated Rs 16,518.11 crores between March 2018 and January 2024.[10] The ruling Bharatiya Janata Party (BJP) collected nearly fifty per cent, or Rs 6565 crore. The Congress received a contribution of Rs 1,123 crores, however, the figures show that, as the years passed, the share of the Congress

---

6 Finance Act 2017, s 137 (amending the proviso to s 29C(1) of the Representation of the People Act 1951).

7 Counter-affidavit on behalf of Election Commission of India (Respondent No.3) in the matter of *Association of Democratic Rights v. Union of India* Writ Petition (Civil) 880 of 2017 dated 25 March 2019 at p. 15 para 8.2 and p.20 para 10.1

8 Gauri Kashyap, 'A Complete Timeline of the Electoral Bond Scheme' (Supreme Court Observer, 14 May 2024) <https://www.scobserver.in/journal/a-complete-timeline-of-the-electoral-bond-scheme/> accessed 13 April 2025.

9 *Association for Democratic Reforms v. Union of India* (2024) 5 SCC 1.

10 'Electoral Bonds: BJP took home lion's share of Rs 16,000 crore political funding' (*The Economic Times*, 17 February 2017).

decreased. Almost fifty per cent of the amount contributed as electoral bonds was from corporates. The damage this delay has done to democracy is incalculable and incontestable. Constitutional reckoning may reveal the extent of the damage this delay has caused to the polity.

Pegasus and Surveillance

In 2019, Facebook (now called Meta) took the NSO Group, an Israeli cybersecurity firm, to court, alleging that the firm had deployed Pegasus, a spyware, to spy on WhatsApp users.[11] The names of forty Indians were on the list of those whose phones had been potentially compromised.[12] In July 2021, a report surfaced, alleging that 50,000 journalists, the political opposition and others had been targeted by the spyware, with many Indian names among them. NSO Group claimed that they sold the spyware only to governments, and only to help in the fight against crime and terrorism. The Indians in this list included editors of news portals, journalists, judges and a minister. The Pegasus controversy reached the SCI in July 2021.[13] On 27 October 2021, the SCI set up a committee to investigate the allegations.[14] The committee handed its report to the court in July 2022, in which it did find malware on five devices, but they could go no further because, as the technical committee reported to the court, the government would not cooperate.[15] The report was placed in a sealed cover. This case is in limbo as the dire warnings of the court about an Orwellian state recedes into the mists of institutional memory.[16] Three years in hibernation, it is now 2025, and there are some signs of stirring.[17]

---

11 Rachel Sandler, 'Facebook Sues Israeli Firm NSO Group for Hacking WhatsApp Messages of Journalists, Human Rights Workers' (*Forbes*, 29 October 2019) <https://www.forbes.com/sites/rachelsandler/2019/10/29/facebook-sues-israeli-firm-nso-group-for-hacking-whatsapp-messages-of-journalists-human-rights-workers/> accessed 13 April 2025.

12 'Pegasus spyware used to "snoop" on Indian journalists, activists' (*The Hindu*, 21 July 2011).

13 *Manohar Lal Sharma v. Union of India*, WP(Crl.) 314/2021.

14 *Manohar Lal Sharma v. Union of India* (2023) 11 SCC 401.

15 G Ananthakrishnan, 'No Evidence, Govt Didn't Cooperate: SC panel on Pegasus' (*The Indian Express*, 26 August 2022).

16 In the meantime, a US court has held the NSO Group liable for intrusive spying, Soumyarendra Barik, 'Pegasus: 300 of 1,400 Users from India, Why Ruling May Re-open Tapping Debate' (*The Indian Express*, 23 December 2024) <https://indianexpress.com/article/business/whatsapp-pegasus-ruling-us-india-9737575/> accessed 14 April 2025.

17 'Supreme Court lists Pegasus Case for Hearing on April 22' (*The Hindu*, 7 March 2025).

Meanwhile, on 20 December 2024, a district court in the Northern District of California held the NSO Group liable for targeting 1,400 Whatsapp user devices with its spyware.[18]

Equal Citizenship

The Citizenship Amendment Act (CAA) was passed by Parliament in December 2019. Soon after, petitions began to be filed against the law's exclusion of Muslims from those entitled to Indian citizenship. The Constitution was brought into existence against the backdrop of the Partition of the country and the riots that tore communities apart. It is one of the fascinating facets of the times that the first election was held in 1951–1952, when citizenship was still in a state of flux. It was to be 1955 before Parliament got around to making a law on citizenship, as was the expectation in Article 11 of the Constitution. The upheavals in the subcontinent continued, with uncertainties around citizenship, till one aspect found its resolution in the Assam Accord and the introduction of Section 6A in the Citizenship Act (the constitutional validity of Section 6A was raised in 2009 and resolved in *In Re: Section 6A of the Citizenship Act 1955* in 2024.[19]) Till 1986, every person born in India was entitled to citizenship. In 1986, the Act was amended and, in a change of considerable significance, the right to citizenship of every person born in India was subject to at least one of their parents being a citizen of India. In 2003, the Citizenship Act was amended again, this time prescribing that if either parent was an 'illegal migrant', they would be excluded from citizenship. By the time the Act was amended in December 2019, experience with the National Population Register (NPR) had raised fear and dread of exclusion and the loss of citizenship.[20] So, in 2019, when the Citizenship Act was amended, with Muslims glaringly missing from the list, it was a cause for deep disquiet.

---

[18] *WhatsApp Inc. v. NSO Group Technologies Ltd.*, No. 19-cv-07123-PJH (ND Cal Dec. 20, 2024) <https://www.documentcloud.org/documents/25467209-gov/> accessed 14 April 2025.

[19] *In Re: Section 6A of the Citizenship Act 1955* 2024 INSC 789.

[20] See, 'Background to In Re: Section 6A of the Citizenship Act 1955' (*Supreme Court Observer*) https://www.scobserver.in/cases/assam-public-works-v-union-of-india-assams-national-register-of-citizens-background/. See also, Abhishek Saha, *No Land's People: The Untold Story of Assam's NRC Crisis* (HarperCollins 2021); Alok Prasanna Kumar, 'More Executive-Minded than the Executive: The Supreme Court's Role in the Implementation of the NRC' (2019) 31(2) National Law School of India Review 203–210.

There were protests against the amendment across the country. The apprehension about what this would do to citizenship was palpable and articulated. A stream of petitions reached the court, displaying an urgency before the law which was leaving out Muslims was put into practice. The constitutionality of the amendment is yet to be heard and decided.

In the meantime, rules have been made[21] and citizenship certificates have begun to be given to those the law deems eligible, which, of course, does not include Muslims.[22] The only decision with a bearing on the CAA has, sadly, been one where the court ordered the dispersal of people from a protest site, Shaheen Bagh,[23] which had had an inspirational role in the protests. 'The erstwhile mode and manner of dissent against colonial rule cannot be equated with dissent in a self- ruled democracy,' the court said, adding: 'Democracy and dissent go hand in hand, but then the demonstrations expressing dissent have to be in designated places alone. The present case was not even one of protests taking place in an undesignated area, but was a blockage of a public way which caused grave inconvenience to commuters. We cannot accept the plea of the applicants that an indeterminable number of people can assemble whenever they choose to protest.' Opinions vary on whether the protesters were blocking the public way or if 'the administration (has) been excessive in the traffic blocks and diversions, and is it deliberate?'[24] While the voice on the street was muted by the judgment, the voice from the courtroom on the constitutionality of the CAA is still to be heard.

Money Bills and the Elusive 'Only'

There has been deep disquiet at the passage of laws as Money Bills, circumventing the parliamentary process of deliberation, debate and a vote in both houses of the Parliament. Money Bills, a device that the Constitution

---

[21] Citizenship (Amendment) Rules 2024.

[22] Munish Chandra Pandey, 'First Citizenship Certificates Handed Out to 14 People under CAA' (*India Today*, 15 May 2024.

[23] *Amit Sahni (Shaheen Bagh, In Re:) v. State* (2020) 10 SCC 439.

[24] See, for instance, Sanket Upadhyay, 'Shaheen Bagh Protest Blockades Excessive and Deliberate? A Ground Report', (NDTV, 14 February 2020) <https://www.ndtv.com/india-news/shaheen-bagh-protest-blockades-excessive-and-deliberate-a-ground-report-2179998> accessed 14 April 2025; Vijeyta Lalwani, 'The Road That Opened Near Shaheen Bagh Had Been Blocked by Delhi Police, Not Protesters' (*Scroll.in*, 24 February 2024) <https://scroll.in/article/954072/the-road-that-opened-near-shaheen-bagh-had-been-blocked-by-delhi-police> accessed 14 April 2025.

imbeds in Article 110 only so that the business of the government does not stop, shrink the relevance of the Rajya Sabha in making law. It does not need a vivid imagination to see the perils this represents.

In 2016, the Aadhaar (Targeted Delivery of Financial and Other Subsidies, Benefits and Services) Act was passed as a Money Bill. It is not quite possible to take seriously the idea that this could be characterized as a Money Bill. For one, a previous version of this law, the National Identification Authority of India Bill 2010, had been introduced in the Rajya Sabha in December 2010. The 42nd Report of the Standing Committee on Finance (2011–2012) was submitted to the Lok Sabha Secretariat in December 2011. The Committee 'categorically' found the proposed law unacceptable, and urged the government to 'reconsider and review the UID scheme as also the proposals contained in the Bill in all its ramifications and bring forth a fresh legislation before Parliament'.[25] On 3 March 2016, the government withdrew the 2010 Bill from the Rajya Sabha, and then introduced the Aadhaar Bill in the Lok Sabha as a Money Bill!

Article 110 of the Constitution is unambiguous that a Bill 'shall be deemed to be a Money Bill if it contains *only* provisions' dealing with the matters set out in the article which are only about moneys collected, expended and managed by the government. The majority judgment in the challenge to the UID scheme and law[26] elided over the meaning of the word 'only' in Article 110, and offered in explanation that Section 7 is the 'main purpose' and 'core provision' of the Aadhaar Act,[27] which is 'to ensure that ... subsidies, benefits and services' are delivered, and for which expenditure would be incurred from the Consolidated Fund of India, and that 'this provision satisfies the conditions of Article 110 of the Constitution'.[28] The other provisions of the Act, the majority said, 'are incidental in nature which have been made in [*sic*] the proper working of the Act.'[29] There was a glaring incongruency in Section 57 of the Act by which:

---

[25] 42nd Report of the Parliamentary Standing Committee on Finance (2011-12), The National Identification Authority of India 2010 35 [13]. The UID scheme involved assigning a twelve-digit unique identification (UID) number (termed as 'Aadhar') to all the residents of India.

[26] *KS Puttaswamy (Aadhaar-5J) v. Union of India* (2019) 1 SCC 1.

[27] ibid 497 [515.2], [515.4]. The judgment drew on the doctrine of pith and substance. DY Chandrachud J, in his dissenting opinion, observed that that doctrine, which applied to legislative entries, would not apply to Money Bills.

[28] ibid 497 [515.4].

[29] ibid 497 [515.5].

> any state, any body corporate or person' could use the 'aadhaar number for establishing the identity of an individual for any purpose pursuant to any law 'or any contract to this effect'. The majority read down and read into parts of this provision[30] and said: 'In any case, a part of Section 57 has already been declared unconstitutional', and 'we, thus, hold that the Aadhaar Act is validly passed as a 'Money Bill'.[31]

A little over a year later, a coordinate Bench of five judges in *Rojer Mathew v. South Indian Bank Ltd*[32] said: 'In the context of Article 110(1) of the Constitution, use of the word "only" in relation to sub-clauses (a) to (f) pose an interesting albeit difficult question which was not examined and answered by the majority judgment in *KS Puttaswamy*.'

Rojer Mathew was a challenge to the Finance Act 2017. In Part XIV of the 2017 Act, a number of legislations were amended concerning the 'qualifications, appointment, term of office, salaries and allowances, resignation, removal and the other terms and conditions of service' of those appointed to tribunals. These included, for instance, tribunals established under the National Green Tribunal Act 2010, the SEBI Act 1992, the Cinematograph Act 1952 and the Consumer Protection Act 1986. The Court had to decide questions raised about delegating these tasks to the Central Government, but was stalled in disposing of the matter in its entirety because the question of the passage of such a law as a Money Bill had to be resolved. The Finance Act 2017 had been passed as a Money Bill, and the *KS Puttaswamy* judgment 'did not substantially discuss the effect of the word "only" in Article 110 (1) and offer little guidance on the repercussions of a finding when some of the provisions of an enactment passed as a "Money Bill" do not conform to Article 110 (1) (a) to (g).... Without expressing a firm and final opinion', the Court referred to a 'potential conflict' between the five-judge Bench that decided *KS Puttaswamy* and the five judges who were dealing with *Rojer Mathew*. The Court then referred it to the CJI to constitute a larger Bench to hear and decide this matter of the Money Bill. That was on 13 November 2019. Four years from the judgment, nine years since the Aadhaar Act 2016 and eight years after

---

30 The words 'for any purpose' were 'read down to mean that such purpose has to be backed by law', and be subject to judicial review. 'Any contract to this effect' was held as failing the proportionality test and, so, unconstitutional.

31 *KS Puttaswamy (Aadhaar-5J)* (n 26) [515.5].

32 *Rojer Mathew v. South Indian Bank Ltd.* (2020) 6 SCC 1 [111].

the Finance Act 2017 was passed as a Money Bill, the case is pending. If the Aadhaar Act is found to have been wrongly passed as a Money Bill, what then?

These are not idle musings. They arise from a recollection of what happened even as the UID scheme and the Aadhaar Act 2016 were taken to court. Enrolment in the UID scheme was initially said to be voluntary. That changed from the fading days of 2012,[33] when there were announcements that, come the new year, the UID would be mandatory for a range of services attached to everyday life, illustratively LPG subsidy,[34] services in Delhi's Revenue Department,[35] income certificates mandatory for establishing eligibility in the economically weaker section (EWS) category and UID mandatory for income certificates.[36]

A wide array of petitioners challenging the UID scheme, including the mandating of enrolment, resulted in the SCI directing, in September 2013, that 'no person should suffer for not getting the aadhaar card in spite of the fact that some authority had issued a circular making it mandatory.'[37] In October 2013, there was a plea from the UIDAI and departments of the government,[38] asking the court to reconsider its order. On 26 November 2013, the court turned down this plea and directed that its order to not

---

33 The first attempt to make it mandatory was by a circular dated 13 October 2011 making enrolment for a UID a precondition for receiving LPG cylinders. The Parliamentary Standing Committee of Finance, in its 42nd Report, rejected the Bill and the scheme. Nothing further happened till the fading months of 2012 when advertisements began to appear informing the public that enrolment for a UID would soon be mandatory for a range of services – including LPG.

34 Jyoti Mukul, 'Aadhaar Compliance Made Mandatory for LPG Subsidy' (*Business Standard*, 15 May 2013).

35 An office order was passed making the UID number mandatory for registration of marriage. Government of NCT of Delhi, Revenue Department, 'Order F(10)6/CCSDivCom/Hqrs/5130-5131' (20 December 2012). This was accompanied by a 'Notice'. See, NOTICE: (from a photograph taken on 28 December 2012 at the Delhi Revenue Department): 'All the parties presenting the document in this office are requested to mention the Aadhaar Number in every document, if available, and it shall be compulsory w.e.f 01.01.2013.....' See also, Neelam Pandey, 'Keep Your UID Cards Ready to Get Married, Buy House' (*The Hindustan Times*, 28 November 2012).

36 'An income certificate is mandatory to apply for an EWS seat .... Those who do not have an Aadhaar number are in a fix.... An income certificate, according to the government, cannot be issued without an Aadhaar number': Pallavi Polanki, 'Delhi Admissions: How Aadhaar Has Put EWS Candidates in a Spot' (*Firstpost*, January 3, 2013) <https://www.firstpost.com/india/delhi-admissions-how-aadhaar-has-put-ews-candidates-in-a-spot-576456.html> accessed 13 April 2025

37 *KS Puttaswamy v. Union of India* WP (C) No 494/2012, interim order dated 23 September 2013.

38 *KS Puttaswamy v. Union of India* WP (C) No 594 of 2012; affidavits submitted by the Ministry of Finance and the Ministry of Petroleum and Natural Gas, Oil Marketing Companies and the UIDAI in October 2013.

make the UID mandatory was to continue.[39] On 24 March 2014, the Court emphasized again:[40] 'More so, no person shall be deprived of any service for want of Aadhaar number in case he/she is otherwise eligible/entitled. All the authorities are directed to modify their forms/circulars/likes so as to not compulsorily require the Aadhaar number in order to meet the requirement of the interim order passed by this Court forthwith.' And, again, on 16 March 2015:[41] 'It is brought to our notice that in certain quarters, Aadhaar identification is being insisted upon by the various authorities. We expect that both the Union of India and States and all their functionaries should adhere to the order passed by this Court on 23rd September, 2013.'

In hearings that culminated in a significant order on 11 August 2015, the Attorney General made an explosive claim: the people of this country do not have a right to privacy, and that two decisions from a time when fundamental rights jurisprudence was still being expanded – *MP Sharma v. Satish Chandra*[42] and *Kharak Singh v. State of Uttar Pradesh*[43] – held the field. This put the case back on the ice block till the privacy question could be resolved, and that would need nine judges – a difficult ask, given the creaking arrears haunting the court. When a nine-judge Bench did give its decision in August 2017,[44] they found neither judgment standing in the way of the right to privacy. By then, another two years had passed. In the early months of 2017, the government had made the UID mandatory in bank accounts threatened with accounts getting frozen, mobile phone verification or the pain of having the connection cut off, filing tax returns[45] and hundreds of notifications were issued wherever people were entitled to state support. So, a person with disability, a person doing manual scavenging or a woman 'rescued' from prostitution, for instance, would all have to part with their UID numbers to receive state assistance. Businesses had

---

[39] *KS Puttaswamy* (n 37) order dated 26 November 2013.

[40] *Unique Identification Authority of India v. CBI* (2017) 7 SCC 157.

[41] KS Puttaswamy (n 37) order dated 16 March 2015. A recorded instance of how this played out on the ground, see, Ankita Anand and Nachiket Udupa, 'How to Get Married Without an Aadhaar Number' (*The Caravan Vantage*, 8 May 2015) <https://caravanmagazine.in/vantage/how-get-married-without-aadhaar-number> accessed 14 April 2025.

[42] AIR 1954 SC 300.

[43] AIR 1963 SC 1295.

[44] *KS Puttaswamy (Privacy-9J.) v. Union of India* (2017) 10 SCC 1.

[45] This, too, was enacted in the Finance Act 2017.

begun to be built around the UID number.[46] This was delay compounded by flagrant violations of court orders, which the Court was quick to recognize,[47] during which the numbers on the database of those enrolled had, according to the records of the UIDAI, reached almost the entire population.[48] A *fait accompli* established with delay as ally.

The question refuses to go away: What will be the effect of delay on the Court's willingness to strike down a law years after the damage has been done? Will it matter that the system has been put in place assisted by a law that is unconstitutional, by deliberately ignoring court orders, and, as in the case of UID, where that which has been foretold in petitions including exclusion, surveillance, convergence, datafication of people has come to pass?

States of Exception and Personal Liberty

The decline of liberty has been a challenge to the legitimacy of the criminal justice system. Judicial exhortation that 'the basic rule of our criminal system is bail, not jail'[49] has not checked the long periods of pre-trial incarceration, especially the detention under laws such as the Unlawful Activities Prevention Act 1967 and the Prevention of Money Laundering Act 2002. The incarceration of human rights and student activists has done little to redeem the reputation of the law. Stan Swamy, whose medical bail was denied, died while still in custody and has become a metaphor for a fatally tardy judiciary.[50] There are the years in prison of the BK-16, referring to the sixteen persons[51] who were held there for several years (starting from 2018), with neither bail nor the hope for an early trial; and young activist Mahesh Raut, who continues to be kept in jail because the SCI stayed a 2023 order of the Bombay High Court (HC) giving

---

[46] Intervention petition dated 11 January 2018 of the Digital Lenders Association in *KS Puttaswamy (Aadhaar) v. Union of India* WP (C) 494 of 2012.

[47] See also the orders of the SCI in the *KS Puttaswamy (Aadhaar/Privacy-3J.) v. Union of India*, (2015) 8 SCC 735 and *All Bengal Minority Students Council v. Union of India* WP (C) No 686/2016, order dated 14 September 2016.

[48] Derrly D'Silva, Zuzana Filková, Frank Packer and Siddharth Tiwari, The design of digital financial infrastructure: Lessons from India, BIS Papers No 106 (Bank for International Settlements, December 2019) 18.

[49] *Arnab Manoranjan Goswami v. State of Maharashtra* (2021) 2 SCC 427 [70].

[50] Alpa Shah, *The Incarcerations: BK16 and the Search for Democracy in India* (HarperCollins Publishers, 2024).

[51] Including Stan Swamy.

him bail, and has not gotten back to the case since.[52] The detention of Umar Khalid since 2020, a student activist who has challenged both being kept in prison as also the law under which he is being held,[53] awaits resolution.[54]

Among many questions raised about these extraordinary laws, the exception claimed by government agencies such as the Enforcement Directorate and the Serious Fraud Investigation Office – that the Criminal Procedure Code does not apply to them[55] – is one significant basis for challenging the constitutionality of these laws. A judgment upholding extraordinary powers to the executive under the PMLA in 2022[56] was quickly brought back for reconsideration.[57] In doing this, the Court was recognizing the disturbing implications of powers of arrest and investigation without the protection of a procedural law that conforms to the promise of Article 21. It awaits determination. It is difficult not to ask what value liberty? What check on executive power?

On 4 August 2023, the Minister of Law and Justice acknowledged that 2615 habeas corpus petitions had been filed in the courts between 2019 and 2023.[58]

---

[52] He had been given interim bail for eighteen days to do his law exams. He was to step back into prison on 30 January 2025. 'Elgar Parishad accused granted interim bail to appear for law exams' (*India Today*, 10 January 2025). The arrests under an extraordinary law, the UAPA, provoked 'five illustrious persons in their own field', as the Court described them, to speak to the Court about the arrested and the threat their arrests held out to free speech and freedom from fear. The Court, with one voice dissenting, refused to intervene in *Romila Thapar v. Union of India*, (2018) 10 SCC 753. Years later, the questions remain. It has inspired a book, Alpa Shah, *The Incarcerations: BK16 and the Search for Democracy in India* (n 50).

[53] *Umar Khalid v. Union of India* WP (Crl.) 513 of 2023. This was tagged along with a petition challenging his rejection of bail by the Delhi HC in *Umar Khalid v. State of NCT of Delhi* CRL A 2826/2023. The appeal was dismissed as withdrawn by an order dated 14 February 2024 by a Bench comprising Bela Trivedi and Pankaj Mithal JJ.

[54] Bail applications of Umar Khalid are tracked here in "Umar Khalid Bail Application Tracker' (*Supreme Court Observer*, 14 February 2024) <https://www.scobserver.in/journal/umar-khalid-bail-application-tracker/> accessed 13 April 2025.

[55] For an engrossing account of how Article 22 entered the Constitution, see Rohan J Alva, *Liberty After Freedom: A History of Article 21, Due Process and the Constitution of India* (HarperCollins Publishers, 2022). The story this book tells is also an explanation for the amount of work that remained for the Court to do in ensuring personal liberty.

[56] *Vijay Madanlal Choudhary v. Union of India* (2023) 12 SCC 1.

[57] *Karti P Chidambaram v. Enforcement Directorate* Review Petition (Crl.) No 219 of 2022. This petition also raised the issue of the amendments to the PMLA being enacted as a Money Bill.

[58] Government of India, Ministry of Law and Justice, Department of Legal Affairs, 'Response to Lok Sabha Unstarred Question No. 2725 on Habeas Corpus Petitions in Courts' (4 August 2023) <https://legalaffairs.gov.in/sites/default/files/AU2725.pdf> accessed 8 April 2025.

As reported in 2020,[59] sixty-one per cent of the cases till then had either been 'dismissed' or 'settled' after the court was informed by the government that the petitions had turned 'infructuous' because the detention order under Public Safety Act (under which they were held) had already been revoked. 'Infructuous' – a strange word meaning that the use is over and that there is nothing further to be achieved through persistence. It says nowhere what that use was. Note, too, that it was either dismissed or settled; there was no conviction and no fault found. Yet, years were spent with people being put away, till it became infructuous.

Liberty and Pragmatism

Hussainara Khatoon[60] rocked the SCI after two news reports in the *Indian Express*, dated 8 and 9 January 1979, reached the Court as a petition in public interest. Undertrial prisoners named in the report had been in jail for five, seven and nine years, and some for more than ten years, 'without their trial having begun'. The report was 'most distressing' and 'sufficient to stir the conscience and disturb the equanimity of any socially motivated lawyer or judge.' They were in jail 'not because they are guilty, but because they are too poor to afford bail and the courts have no time to try them.'[61] The offences with which they were charged were often 'trivial, which, even if proved, would not warrant punishment for more than a few months … and yet (they have been) deprived of their freedom for periods ranging from 3 to 10 years' without trial having commenced.[62] In a recorded instance, a prisoner had remained an undertrial for eight and a half years, having been put away for an offence with a maximum sentence of two years.

There were women and children in 'protective custody', held in jails not because they were suspected to have committed an offence but because they were victims of offences, or they were witnesses. They were directed to be released immediately and be taken to 'welfare or rescue homes (to) be kept

[59] Kaunain Sheriff M, Bashaarat Masood and Naveed Iqbal, 'J&K: Most Habeas Corpus Cases Dragged on as Court Slammed Govt on Due Process' (*The Indian Express*, 4 August 2020).

[60] *Hussainara Khatoon (I) v. State of Bihar* (1980) 1 SCC 81. This was closely followed by *Kadra Pahadiya v. State of Bihar* (1981) 3 SCC 671 which reinforced the emerging acknowledgment that the problem was systemic, not episodic. The response would have to meet deep rooted problems.

[61] ibid 84 [2].

[62] ibid 83-84 [1].

there and properly looked after', while the state government was castigated for providing the explanation that a welfare home had been shut down and thus the women were being kept in jail.[63]

The legitimacy of the criminal justice system was being severely tested, and, in a series of orders, the Court toiled away at finding ways by which this scandalous situation could be allayed.[64]

The Court set on record the state's policy decision to withdraw cases of an 'ordinary nature',[65] to immediately drop cases under Section 109 of the Criminal Procedure Code 1973,[66] and release all persons with leprosy or prisoners suffering from infectious diseases – where the prisoner had already spent at least six months in jail. So, too, 'all cases under the Indian Penal Code and local and special laws *in which the accused is confined in jail for periods exceeding the maximum period of imprisonment possible for which he could be sentenced if convicted*.'[67] And all cases pending investigation by the police where the prisoners had been in jail for more than two years.[68] Prisoners were to be released on personal bond and not be kept in prison only because they were unable to furnish bail or produce sureties.[69]

This last deserves a pause. Having acknowledged this crippling effect of poverty on personal liberty, the concurring judgment leaves the law maker with this thought:[70]

> The CrPC has no explicit provision to enable the release of an undertrial prisoner on his own bond without sureties and without any monetary obligation.... The deprivation of liberty for the reason of financial poverty only is ... incongruous ... [O]ur law-makers would take an important step

---

[63] *Hussainara Khatoon (III) v. Home Secy., State of Bihar*, (1980) 1 SCC 93, 96 [2].

[64] *Hussainara Khatoon (I)* (n 60); *Hussainara Khatoon (II) v. Home Secy., State of Bihar* (1980) 1 SCC 91; *Hussainara Khatoon (III)* (n 63); *Hussainara Khatoon (IV) v. Home Secy., State of Bihar* (1980) 1 SCC 98; *Hussainara Khatoon (V) v. Home Secy., State of Bihar* (1980) 1 SCC 108; *Hussainara Khatoon (VI) v. Home Secy., State of Bihar* (1980) 1 SCC 115.

[65] *Hussainara Khatoon (II)* (n 64) [1(a)].

[66] Pertaining to 'security for good behaviour from suspected persons'.

[67] *Hussainara Khatoon (II)* (n 64) 92.

[68] ibid.

[69] *Hussainara Khatoon (I)* (n 60) 89 [5].

[70] *Hussainara Khatoon (I)* (n 60) 91 [11].

in defence of individual liberty if appropriate provision was made in the statute for non-financial release.

It was only in 2005 that the law recognizing indigence as a reason why undertrials stayed in jail even when they had been given bail was introduced.[71] The wheels of the law certainly grind slowly.[72]

Hussainara Khatoon set off judicial disquisition on speedy trial[73] and legal aid[74] as fundamental rights. In years to come, these themes were to recur with a frequency that, unfortunately, spoke of the intractability of the problem of delay. In *Hussainara Khatoon*[75] and *Kadra Pahadiya*, the shock of what the Court was seeing kept the focus of its orders on liberty. The rigidity of the system that resulted in large numbers of people in poverty being incarcerated for years had to be immediately addressed. As the enormity of the moment settled into the everyday, the responses acquired other shades of concern, too.

The Committee for Implementing Legal Aid Schemes (CILAS) was established in 1980, and the Legal Services Authorities Act was passed in 1987.[76] There have been many attempts to find ways to ensure speedy trial.[77]

'Docket explosion', overcrowding of prisons and low rates of conviction have dogged the system; courts have asked for timely appointment of judges and improved infrastructure, including courtrooms, libraries, staff, housing and, more recently, technology. There was hope that tribunals would lighten the burden of the court.[78] Alternative dispute resolution (ADR – mediation,

---

[71] Code of Criminal Procedure 1973, s 436 (as amended by Act 25 of 2005, effective 23 June 2006).

[72] Then, it comes to a halt. Which is why, over forty years later, we read Mukesh Rawat, 'Poor, Young and Illiterate: Why Most Indian Prisoners Fight Long Lonely Battles for Justice' (*India Today*, 5 April 2022).

[73] *AR Antulay v. RS Nayak* (1992) 1 SCC 225; *Sheela Barse v. Union of India* (1986) 3 SCC 632; *Raj Deo Sharma v. State of Bihar* (1998) 7 SCC 507; *P Ramachandra Rao v. State of Karnataka* (2002) 4 SCC 578.

[74] *Suk Das v. Union Territory of Arunachal Pradesh*, (1986) 2 SCC 401; *Manubhai Pragaji Vashi v. State of Maharashtra*, 1988 SCC OnLine Bom 256; *Khatri v. State of Bihar* (1981) 1 SCC 627. See also, *MH Hoskote v. State of Maharashtra* (1978) 3 SCC 544.

[75] *Hussainara Khatoon (I)* (n 60).

[76] It came into force in 1995, delayed by disquiet about the closing of the distance between the judiciary and the executive. S Muralidhar, *Law, Poverty and Legal Aid: Access to Criminal Justice* (Lexis Nexis Butterworths 2004).

[77] *AR Antulay* (n 73); *Sheela Barse v. Union of India* (1986) 3 SCC 632; *Raj Deo Sharma* (n 73); *P Ramachandra Rao* (n 73).

[78] Law Commission of India (2017) 272nd Report on *Assessment of Statutory Frameworks for Tribunals in India; Gujarat Urja Vikas Nigam Ltd. v. Essar Power Ltd.* (2016) 9 SCC 103, 128-133 [29-45].

arbitration, *Lok Adalat*) have been built into the law, and enforced with a will; while mediation has been a help to the system and to the litigant where it has been deployed, arbitration has been beset with delay and cost. *Lok Adalat*, with its underlying logic that a case that goes to trial is uncertain of result; expensive and uncertain in its outcome, nudges litigants to settle rather than wait for justice, making virtue out of the court's necessity. There have been experiments with closing cases that take too long to come to trial.[79] However, unease at letting people get away with crime because of the failings of the system, and the fear that this could be abused by those who find ways to game the system, has found its wisdom in shelving the thought.

Tragically for the indigent caught in the web of delay, the focus soon shifted to delay generally, with cases of corruption capturing the attention of the Court.[80] By 1995, even a *Hussainara Khatoon*[81] Court was saying:

> While there can be no doubt that undertrial prisoners should not languish in jails on account of refusal to enlarge them on bail for want of their capacity to furnish bail with monetary obligations, these are matters which have to be dealt with on a case-by-case basis ... Sympathy for the undertrials who are in jail for long terms on account of pendency of cases has to be balanced having regard to the impact of crime...

Long periods of pretrial incarceration have been accepted as inevitable.[82] In an emerging trend, acknowledging the inevitability of delay, convicted persons have been allowed bail when, by the court's admission, their appeals

---

[79] *Hussainara Khatoon(II)* (n 64) 93; *Common Cause v. Union of India* (1996) 4 SCC 33; Raj Deo (n 73) 516.

[80] *AR Antulay* (n 73); *Raj Deo Sharma* (n 73); *P Ramachandra Rao* (n 73). These seem to have helped very little, as see, PTI, 'Direction Sought from SC for Speedy Disposal of Nearly 5,000 Cases against Lawmakers' (*The Economic Times*, 9 February 2025).

[81] *Hussainara Khatoon (VII) v. Home Secretary, Bihar* (1995) 5 SCC 326, 328 [2].

[82] Section 436A CrPC as amended in 2005, the maximum period of detention of an undertrial prisoner was to be half the maximum period of imprisonment provided by law for the offence with which they are charged, but not extending to offences punishable with death. A decade after this amendment was made, the court was having to ask for the provision to be effectuated, in *Bhim Singh v. Union of India* (2015) 13 SCC 605. The formula had been set in a precedent in 1994, in the context of large number of undertrial prisoners in jail for offences under the Narcotics and Psychotropic Substances Act 1985, in *Supreme Court Legal Services Committee v. Union of India* (1994) 6 SCC 731.

are 'not likely to be heard in the near future'.[83] The drastic – and disastrous – state policy of incentivizing to increase the speed and rate of disposal of capital cases had to be brought to a screeching (interim) halt by the SCI.[84]

In the midst of this overwhelm, the Court turned its gaze from the plight of the indigent to institutional pragmatism, when *Kadra Pahadiya*[85] reappeared in 1997. The Court released a statement about what is clogging up the system: 'If the load of petty crime is taken out of regular courts, those courts would have time to deal with more serious crimes rather than have their time consumed by such petty cases.'[86]

There are at least two discernible fallouts of this thinking. One, the introduction of plea bargaining into the law of criminal procedure. Two, jail *adalats* or special courts set up within the prison complex to deal with petty cases where the person in detention is given an assurance of early release if they confess to the charge made against them.

Plea Bargaining

Since the 1960s, the SCI has disapproved of plea bargaining as being contrary to public policy. The cases where plea bargaining was in issue before the Court were, for instance, in matters of cheating,[87] food adulteration,[88]

---

[83] *Daryab Singh v. State of Uttar Pradesh* SLP (Cri) 4178 of 2021, order dated 17 September 2021, where the appeal in the HC against conviction was pending since 2007 and the appellant had been in prison 'for more than 15 years'. See also, *Abhay Jaiswal v. State of Madhya Pradesh* SLP (Cri.) 14421/2024, order dated 3 December 2024; *Nanhe Lal Verma v. State of Madhya Pradesh* Cri A 4763/2024, order dated 25 November 2024; *Vipul v. State of Uttar Pradesh* 2022 SCC OnLine SC 1686.

[84] *Irfan v. State of Madhya Pradesh* 2022 SCC OnLine SC 1053. The Court asked that the case be changed from being a matter in the case of an appellant to being a 'suo motu writ petition', a matter that the Court considered it needed to take over: Also see, PTI, 'Madhya Pradesh's policy to reward public prosecutors for successfully arguing death penalty cases comes under SC scanner' (*The Economic Times*, 23 April 2022).

[85] *Kadra Pahadiya v. State of Bihar* (1997) 4 SCC 287.

[86] ibid [26].

[87] *Madanlal Ram Chandra Daga v. State of Maharashtra* (1968) 3 SCR 34.

[88] *Murlidhar Meghraj Loya v. State of Maharashtra* (1976) 3 SCC 684; *Ganeshmal Jashraj v. Government of Gujarat* (1980) 1 SCC 363; *Kasambhai Abdulrehmanbhai Sheikh v. State of Gujarat* (1980) 3 SCC 120.

causing death by negligence,[89] culpable homicide.[90] In each case, the court rejected the practice of plea bargaining. In a significant setting out of the Court's objection, it was said:

> It is to our mind contrary to public policy to allow a conviction to be recorded against an accused by inducing him to confess to a plea of guilty on an allurement being held out to him that if he enters a plea of guilty, he will be let off very lightly. Such a procedure would be clearly unreasonable, unfair and unjust and would be violative of the new activist dimension of Article 21 of the Constitution....it might induce an innocent accused to plead guilty to suffer a light and inconsequential punishment rather than go through a long and arduous criminal trial .... There is no doubt in our mind that the conviction of an accused based on a plea of guilty entered by him as a result of plea-bargaining with the prosecution and the Magistrate must be held to be unconstitutional and illegal.[91]

As the years bent the criminal justice system under the weight of arrears and overcrowding in prisons, plea bargaining was argued into the law.[92] The judgments of the SCI had to be overcome. The 142nd Report of the Law Commission of India reasoned that the 'observations' of the SCI '*should be understood in the context of plea bargaining entered in an informal way without legal sanction.*'[93] The Court's judgment that it is unconstitutional was gingerly side-stepped. And, fourteen years later, in 2005, the Criminal Procedure Code was amended to introduce plea bargaining.[94]

Plea bargaining allowed the Court to shrink procedure. It cast the responsibility on the judge to control the proceedings and do their bit in bringing cases to a close. It dispensed with the requirement of a lawyer for

---

[89] Indian Penal Code 1860, s 304A. The case is that of *Thippaswamy v. State of Karnataka* (1983)1 SCC 194.

[90] *State of Uttar Pradesh v. Chandrika* (1999) 6 SCC 120.

[91] *Kasambhai Abdulrehmanbhai Sheikh v. State of Gujarat* (n 88) [4].

[92] See, for instance, Law Commission of India, Concessional Treatment for Offenders Who on Their Own Initiative Choose to Plead Guilty Without Any Bargaining (142nd Report, 1991); Law Commission of India, The Code of Criminal Procedure, 1973 (154th Report, 1996) ch 13; Law Commission of India, Law Relating to Arrest (177th Report, 2001) ch 9; Malimath Committee, Report of the Committee on Reforms of Criminal Justice System (2003).

[93] Law Commission of India, 142nd Report on Concessional Treatment for Offenders who on their own Initiative Choose to Plead Guilty (1991) 17 [6.14] (emphasis in original).

[94] Criminal Procedure Code 1973, ch XXII A, ss 265A–265L.

the accused.[95] It dealt only with cases that provided a maximum sentence of seven years, that is, the more minor offences, where it may not be farfetched to say that those drawn into the arms of the law are generally from those without any clout or legal assistance. There would be no appeal. This is legal pragmatism taking the place of the elements of fair trial, including the right to be represented by a lawyer and the judge as a disinterested participant who still had the task of reducing the number of cases pending.[96]

Jail Adalat

Jail adalat was an experiment that was a prelude to the insertion of plea bargaining into the law. It was introduced through a letter written by CJI AS Anand to the Chief Justices (CJs) of all HCs.[97] The letter spoke of the 'very large number of prisoners suffer(ing) prolonged incarceration even in petty criminal matters merely for the reason that they are not in a position, even in bailable offences, to furnish bail bonds and get released on bail....merely on account of the fact that they happen to be poor and underprivileged.' He suggested, for the consideration of the CJs, that every Chief Metropolitan Magistrate or Chief Judicial Magistrate may 'take up the cases of those undertrial prisoners who are involved in petty offences and are keen to confess to their guilt. "Legal aid counsel" may be deputed in jails to help such prisoners .... Thereafter, if the prisoner voluntarily pleads guilty', he may be punished according to law. If they 'change their mind', their cases may be sent back to court. The result was jail adalats.

In Tihar Jail, the jail adalat was held on the third Saturday of every month. I was at four sittings of the jail adalat in 2002, on 16 February, 16 March, 20 April and 18 May.[98] These excerpts from my notes are to illustrate the nature

---

95 Criminal Procedure Code 1973, s 265C (as amended by the Code of Criminal Procedure (Amendment) Act 2005).

96 The build-up to the 2005 amendment puts the onus on the judge to work at reducing pendency. It is then significant that, seventeen years after its introduction into the law, a court was to bemoan that plea bargaining has lain 'dormant and used seldom by courts', Vipul (n 83).

97 Letter from CJI AS Anand to the CJs of all HCs (29 November 1999), reproduced in Commonwealth Human Rights Initiative, Liberty at the Cost of Innocence: A Report on Jail Adalats in India (2009) 56–57; Letter from Justice AS Anand, Chairperson of the NHRC to all CJs of the HCs (1 July 2003), reproduced in Commonwealth Human Rights Initiative, Liberty at the Cost of Innocence: A Report on Jail Adalats in India (2009) 29.

98 In Commonwealth Human Rights Initiative, Liberty at the Cost of Innocence (n 97) 18, one of the 'Limitations' the research team faced was that 'despite requests, we were not allowed access to these

of the proceedings. On 16 February 2002, forty-nine cases were taken up, and the roster completed in about three hours. The prisoners picked up were accused of pickpocketing, stealing a manhole cover, stealing a suitcase from a train, being found in possession of a knife, having no ticket while being on the platform (either stealing a suitcase or lurking around with an intention to steal), being found with more liquor than permitted and being involved in drunken brawls. Many of them were from the under-21 jail, Jail No. 5. The common features were that they were young, accused of petty crimes and all of them had to have been in prison for at least two months in order to be eligible for this procedure. It was evident that they had been tutored to admit that they were guilty and that only an admission of guilt could get them out of prison, else they would be sent back to prison to await regular trial and there was no saying when that would be. Many of them were '*angoota chaap*', and affixed their left thumb impressions to the document that would spell their release – and they plainly had no idea what they were signing. They did not understand, either, that having a conviction recorded against them would have consequences if they were arrested another time.

When the proceedings were completed, I realized that the lawyers who I had thought were the prosecution, were, in fact, legal-aid counsel. At the hearing on 20 April, when the Magistrate asked the legal-aid lawyer to say anything they may want to say in the case, the lawyer said (and this is a close paraphrase): 'We are here to do the duty that they be represented by lawyers,' and 'you know and I know why we are doing this', and 'we know they do it out of *majboori*, better they are let off after admitting guilt.'

A closer understanding of what transpires in these proceedings requires a separate essay, and this is merely a cursory sketch, with many details left unwritten. Watching the proceedings, it becomes clear that criminal law is often used as a means of social control, to control those who live on the edge of legality not because they are inherently criminal, but because of their poverty. The vulnerability added by solutions to burdened courts, crowded prisons and low rate of conviction becomes hard to deny. It is difficult not to ask: Is the remedy worse than the problem for those already at risk because

adalats'. It is not clear on what grounds these court proceedings could be closed off to those wishing to attend. There was a certain discomfort when I attended, but I was allowed in after some questioning. It must be said, though, there was no one else attending on the days I was there, raising questions about the accessibility and openness of these courts.

of their precarity, both societal and economic? This procedure cries out for a fundamental rights audit.

Mass Industrial Disaster: The Tragedy of Bhopal

The stunting of the law on mass industrial disaster begins with the Settlement-Order in the case of the Bhopal Gas Disaster, and the defeat held in the words: 'Law's delays are, indeed, proverbial.'[99]

The case that reached the SCI in 1988 was an appeal by the Union Carbide Corporation (UCC), challenging an order of the Madhya Pradesh HC for an interim relief of Rs 250 crore. Having scoured the documents that had been placed before it, the HC held that there was 'more than prima facie established that it was the ... UCC that had real control over the enterprise.'[100]

Upon a detailed consideration of the voluminous documents filed with the court, the judge was clear that the order to pay interim compensation was 'not ....without reference to the merits of the case as held by the trial court but is a payment as damages under the substantive law of torts on the basis of more than prima face case having been made out ...'.[101] The judge recorded that the estimated approximate value of the total claims presented by the government 'would exceed Rs.3,900 crores (US $ 3 billion) if the case was tried to judgement through all the stages.'[102]

Fifteen years after the judgment, Fali Nariman, who had led the case in the Court for UCC, had this to say about the HC judgment: 'Looking back, I find that judgement does afford as good a rationale as any I can see, absent enacted law, for relieving hardship caused to litigants in a mass tort action – they have to wait for years in a three-tier system before they can establish or obtain a final executable decree for damages.'[103]

---

99 *Union Carbide Corporation v. Union of India* (1989) 3 SCC 38 [8].

100 *Union Carbide Corporation v. Union of India*, 1988 SCC OnLine MP 41 [14.03.05] reproduced in Upendra Baxi and Amita Dhanda (eds), *Valiant Victims and Lethal Litigation: The Bhopal Case* (Indian Law Institute, 1990) 338 [380].

101 *Union Carbide Corporation* (n 100) [17.01.02].

102 ibid [2.01.01].

103 Fali S Nariman, 'Some reflections' (2004) 544 Seminar <https://www.india-seminar.com/2004/544/544%20fali%20s.%20nariman.htm> accessed 21 April 2025. A response to this piece was later given by Prof. Upendra Baxi. Upendra Baxi, 'Communication: Open letters to Fali Nariman' (2006) 546 Seminar <https://india-seminar.com/semframe.html> accessed 21 April 2025. A response from Fali Nariman was carried in the same edition. Fali S Nariman, *Before Memory Fades* (Hay House 2012) 218-19.

Why did the SCI turn away from the HC judgment? Why did it consider a sum of USD 470 million for settling all matters – civil and criminal, or of any nature whatsoever (past, present and future) – against the UCC, UCIL, UCE and anyone else connected with the Bhopal Gas Disaster, to be adequate?[104]

'The basic consideration motivating the conclusion of the settlement was the compelling need for urgent relief,' the Court said, while not explaining why interim relief would not serve the purpose. 'Even after four years of litigation, the basic questions of the fundamentals of the law as to liability of the UCC and the quantum of damages are yet being debated.' But neither had the registration of victims been done,[105] which meant that at the time of the settlement, the extent of harm was still based on assumptions, and compensation was based on back-of-the- envelope calculations.[106]

'It has been the unfortunate bane of the judicial process that even ordinary cases, where evidence consists of a few documents and the oral testimony of a few witnesses, require some years to realise the fruits of litigation. This is so even in cases of great and unquestionable urgency such as fatal accident actions brought by the dependants. These are hard realities.' Settlement talks had been on since the matter was in Judge Keenan's court,[107] and a *prima facie* examination of the material before the Court 'having regard to all the circumstances, including the prospect of delays inherent in the judicial process in India…'[108]

The haste in concluding the proceedings arising from the Bhopal Gas Disaster was to have consequences. The Bhopal Claims Act 1985, under which the Central Government had taken over the litigation, had been challenged and was lying unattended when the settlement order was passed. The case was resurrected when victim groups protested that not only had the constitutionality of the Act not been decided before the settlement was endorsed, but they had not been heard or consulted. The Claims Act court

[104] *Union Carbide Corporation v. Union of India* (1989) 1 SCC 674; *Union Carbide* (n 99).

[105] *Union Carbide Corporation* (n 100) [17.01.02] reproduced in Upendra Baxi, Amita Dhanda, Valiant Victims (n 100) [383].

[106] *Union Carbide Corporation* (n 99).

[107] For Judge Keenan's role in the various cases around the Bhopal Gas Disaster and contamination of the site, see Jayant K Krishnan, 'Bhopal in the Federal Courts: How Indian Victims Fail to Get Justice' (2020) 72(3) *Rutgers University Law Review* 705.

[108] The HC had indicated that the claims relating to death and injury had still not been registered. *Union Carbide Corporation* (n 100) [17.01.02].

agreed with the victims – it believed that it would have been best if the case challenging the Claims Act had been decided first, and that they should indeed have been a part of deciding whether, or how, to settle. However, the Court said that, 'One hesitates in matters of this type, where larger consequences follow one way or the other to pull asunder what others have put together.'[109] So, 'while no man or no man's right should be affected without an opportunity to ventilate his views,' the Court would rely on 'sufficient opportunity' in the 'review' proceedings that had been instituted to uphold the settlement. 'To do a great right after all,' the Court said, 'it is permissible sometimes "to do a little wrong".... in the facts and circumstances of the case, this is one of those rare occasions.'[110]

When the settlement order was reviewed, the Court grudgingly agreed to revive the criminal cases, even as it held that it was not without the power and jurisdiction to withdraw the cases to itself and end the prosecution. It said: 'whether on merits, there were justified grounds to quash is a different matter.' So saying, the Court set aside 'the quashing and termination of the criminal proceedings.'[111]

The precipitate closure to the cases arising from the Bhopal Gas Disaster has meant it retarded, indefinitely, the emergence of a jurisprudence on hazardous technologies deployed for profit, especially by multinational companies. The 'pernicious potentialities ... and fundamental issues of technology option', 'hazardous industrial adventurism' and 'whether the citizens of the country are assured the protection of a legal system which could be said to be adequate' were acknowledgement 'of a particular concern', but they were put aside for another day.[112]

Absolute liability, enterprise liability and enhanced liability for hazardous or inherently dangerous activities had been introduced into the law by the Court in the *Oleum Gas Leak* case.[113] However, these rules were cast into the

---

[109] *Charan Lal Sahu v. Union of India* (1990) 1 SCC 613 [121].

[110] ibid [124].

[111] It is a question how the 'settlement' survived the prising out the part on the termination of criminal proceedings. If it was a settlement that had acquired the status of an order of the Court, was the Court, when it was dealing with the case in 2023, right in saying that: 'Either a settlement is valid or it is to be set aside in cases where it is vitiated by fraud.' *Union of India v. Union Carbide Corporation* 2023 SCC Online SC 264 [47]. Can a court, then, change the terms of the settlement without it ceasing to be a settlement?

[112] *Union Carbide Corporation* (n 99) [32].

[113] *MC Mehta v. Shri Ram Foods and Fertiliser Industries* AIR 1987 SC 965.

shadows in the *Bhopal* case while referring to 'a mere hint' from the UCC about these principles being altered with only UCC in mind and to cause it disadvantage. The compulsion of immediate relief could not, in the Court's opinion, 'wait till these questions, vital though they be, are resolved'.[114]

The Bhopal Gas Disaster litigation has had to bear the consequences of haste amidst apprehensions of delay and overwhelm. 'The credibility of the judiciary,' the Court said, 'is as important as the alleviation of the suffering of the victims, great as these were. We hope these adjudications will restore that credibility.'[115] It went on to state that 'the matter concerns the interests of a large number of victims of a mass disaster, but the case equally concerns the credibility of public confidence in, the judicial process.'[116]

Again, in 2023, when victims' groups were before the Court, seeking an order to revise the compensation that was in the settlement, the Court said:

> Providing closure to a *lis* is also a very important aspect. This is more so in the context of the scenario faced by the Indian judiciary, where delay is inevitable. This concern would be further amplified in respect of a tort claim such as the present one - if evidence were to be led for each claimant ... The money was needed in the immediate aftermath of the tragedy and not after three decades.[117]

Forty years after the Bhopal Gas Disaster, the effect on the affected population has grown into a wider array of problems, with intergenerational impact. The state has been remiss in ways that even the Court has had to acknowledge.[118]

And yet... time, judicial anxiety about being overwhelmed and institutional fatigue have created a disconnect between the experience of a mass industrial disaster on the ground and constitutional promises.

---

[114] The judge in the HC had no such doubts. See *Union Carbide* (n 100) [12.02.19].

[115] *Charan Lal Sahu* (n 109) [128].

[116] *Union Carbide Corporation* (n 99) [38].

[117] *Union Carbide Corporation* (n 111) [49]. This petition had been filed in 2010 and decided in 2023.

[118] ibid [46]. The state was to have taken out insurance policies, in case the settlement amount proved inadequate. 'Surprisingly, we are informed that no such insurance policy was taken out. This is gross negligence on part of the Union of India...'

These are but fragments from judicial records and current affairs, yet these anecdotes represent a disturbing relationship between the people, the Court and the Constitution. Foregrounding fundamental rights over judicial pragmatism could, possibly, be the necessary first step to getting out of the situation in which the system is mired.

Cartoon © Satish Acharya. Reproduced with permission.

The Supreme Court and Its Constitution Benches

ROHAN J ALVA

The SCI is often referred to as a polyvocal court due to its institutional structure, where the judges typically sit in smaller Benches of two or three to hear the majority of cases. As a result, the Court's decisions do not always speak in a unified voice. This division reflects the diversity of legal thought and interpretation within the Court.[1] The very architecture of the Court also mirrors this distinction, with multiple courtrooms catering to different judges. However, there exists a category of cases that demand a more authoritative voice; cases of great constitutional significance, which are heard by larger Benches.

At the heart of this institutional structure lies Article 145 of the Constitution, which provides the legal framework for the functioning of the SCI. While Article 145 (1) grants the Court the power to regulate its own practice and procedure, Article 145 (2) specifically empowers the Court to determine how many judges should sit together to hear a case. However, the Constitution envisages certain cases to be of such national importance that they require more than the usual panel. These cases may involve substantial questions of law that relate to the true meaning of the Constitution itself, or they may be matters referred to the Court by the President of India under Article 143. Such cases are heard by Constitution Benches (CBs), comprising five or more judges, as mandated by Article 145 (3). This provision ensures that matters of constitutional interpretation are adjudicated with utmost authority and precision, recognizing the significance of judicial involvement in defining the Constitution's meaning.

---

[1] Nick Robinson, 'Structure Matters: The Impact of Court Structure on the Indian and US Supreme Courts' (2013) 61(1) *American Journal of Comparative Law* 173.

Judgments of CBs hold a unique place in India's legal landscape. They provide clarity on critical constitutional issues and represent the highest form of judicial authority in the country. However, the method of adjudication in these Benches is not always straightforward, and their decisions can be marked by complexities and evolving jurisprudence. The outcomes of CB cases can vary over time, influenced by shifts in the Court's interpretation of constitutional doctrine and the ebb and flow of legal principles.

This essay explores the various dimensions of CB judgments. The first section of the essay traces the constitutional history of Article 145, examining its evolution and the reasoning behind the formation of larger Benches. The second discusses the method of adjudication in CB cases, and under what circumstances CBs are assembled, while the third identifies key trends in CB judgments. The fourth section delves into the phases of CB judgments, analysing how these decisions evolve and the shifts in their reasoning. The fifth section explores the ebb and flow of CB judgments and highlights certain issues in opinion writing and Bench composition. The sixth examines legislative pushback in response to CB rulings, considering the dynamic interaction between the judiciary and the legislature. The seventh section discusses dissents in CB judgments, shedding light on the divergent views within the Court and their impact on legal discourse. Finally, the epilogue suggests reforms to improve clarity and accessibility of CB judgments.

Constitutional History of Article 145(3)

The first ever draft of the Constitution which was to be worked on by the Constituent Assembly, was drawn up by the Constitutional Adviser, Sir BN Rau. When he presented the Draft Constitution in October 1947, a provision such as present-day Article 145 (3) had not been proposed.

In Section 87 of the Draft, Rau proposed the setting up of a Supreme Court for India.[2] The provision pertaining to Supreme Court Rules was proposed by Rau, in Section 102. Section 102 (2) empowered the SCI to frame rules to determine how the Benches of the SCI are to be constituted. However, this provision stipulated that any Bench that is constituted must comprise at least

---

[2] B Shiva Rao, *The Framing of India's Constitution: Select Documents*, vol 3 (Indian Institute of Public Administration 1967) 36–37.

three judges.[3] Rau, however, in the proviso to Section 102, proposed that for a Presidential Reference, when the SCI is advising the President who has sought the Court's opinion on an issue of public importance, all the judges of the Court must be part of the Bench. In other words, the SCI must sit *en banc*.

After having prepared the Draft Constitution, Rau travelled the world seeking to better understand how India's Constitution could be refined. When he travelled to the United States (US) in November 1947, Rau met Felix Frankfurter J, a judge of the US Supreme Court. As Rau reported to the Constituent Assembly, Frankfurter J was emphatic about the point that the SCI ought not to encourage the practice of the judges sitting separately. This was for the reason that all the judges of the apex Court, 'should share the responsibility for every decision of the court'.[4]

Rau's proposals were deliberated upon by the Drafting Committee under the chairmanship of Dr BR Ambedkar.[5] Eventually, in the Draft Constitution presented to the Constituent Assembly on 21 February 1948,[6] Draft Article 121 enumerated the Supreme Court Rules[7] where Clause (2) was similar to present-day Article 145 (3). On the issue of whether the SCI should have *en banc* hearings, it was clear from an appended starred footnote to the article, that the Drafting Committee had considered the proposition. The Drafting Committee was of the opinion that while it may not be practically feasible for the SCI to hear all the cases *en banc*, the SCI should have *en banc* hearings for cases that, 'involve questions of interpretation of the Constitution and those which are referred to the Supreme Court for opinion by the President'.[8] The Committee also left a window open for the Parliament to decide the other types of cases that could be heard *en banc*.

---

[3] ibid 41–42.

[4] ibid 219; Rau recorded Frankfurter J's advice in the following words:

> 'Again, Justice Frankfurter was very emphatic that any jurisdiction, exercisable by the Supreme Court, should be exercised by the full court. His view is that the highest court of appeal in the land should not sit in divisions. Every judge, except of course such judges as may be disqualified by personal interest or otherwise from hearing particular cases, should share the responsibility for every decision of the court.'

[5] B Shiva Rao (n 2) 316; Minutes of the Drafting Committee meeting dated 30 August 1947.

[6] ibid 509–677.

[7] ibid 561.

[8] ibid 561–62.

However, when Draft Article 121 was taken up for debate by the Constituent Assembly on 6 June 1949, the proposals concerning *en banc* hearings were not seriously pursued. Rather the focus was on Clause 2 (a), which corresponds to the proviso to Article 145 (3) today.[9] This provision was introduced in the Assembly on 6 June 1949 by an amendment motion by Sir Alladi Krishnaswami Ayyar, as a measure to save 'judicial time'.[10] In his view, a case need not be referred to a Bench of five judges merely because a party had raised a constitutional point.[11] The Bench hearing a regular appeal must first form an opinion that the case could not be resolved without addressing the constitutional question. If the matter could be decided by the regular Bench itself, there would be no need for a referral. In other words, only if a 'real question of constitutional law has arisen' should the matter travel to a five-judge Bench.[12] On the same day, the Assembly adopted Draft Article 121 with some amendments, including those suggested by Ayyar.[13] In the Constitution, Draft Article 121 became Article 145.

In the Emergency years, like many other provisions of the Constitution, Article 145 underwent an amendment and a new system of CBs was introduced. By way of Section 25 of the 42nd Amendment to the Constitution, a new Article 144-A was introduced. The first part of this Article stipulated that when the SCI was to adjudicate any case that involved the constitutional validity of a law made either by the Parliament or by a State Legislature, then such a case had to be heard by seven judges. For the purposes of Article 144-A, seven judges had to hear the constitutional challenge even though the case did not particularly raise a substantial question of law regarding constitutional interpretation.

The second part of Article 144-A required that any decision by such a Bench, to declare the law constitutionally invalid, should have the majority support of at least two-thirds of the judges on the Bench. This scheme was in contrast to Article 145 (5), which stipulates that all the cases are to be decided by a simple majority. Further, to ensure the supremacy of Article 144-A, Section 26 of the 42nd Amendment sought to amend Article 145 (3) to the extent that it was now made subject to the provision of Article 144-A.

---

9 Constituent Assembly Debates, 6 June 1949, vol 8, 644.

10 ibid.

11 ibid.

12 ibid.

13 ibid 650.

However, Article 144-A was short-lived. It was undone by the 43rd Amendment to the Constitution. Section 5 of the 43rd Amendment simply omitted Article 144-A, and Section 6 of the 43rd Amendment restored Article 145 (3) to its original form.

Article 145 (3): The Method of Adjudication

One of the earliest controversies that the interpretation of Article 145 involved was on the method by which the SCI ought to adjudicate cases involving the interpretation of the Constitution. In 1955, a CB of five judges in the case of *Rao Shiva Bahadur Singh v. The State of Vindhya Pradesh*[14] was seized of this issue.

The case seemingly raised issues of the interpretation of Articles 14 and 20 in the context of a criminal conviction and was adjudicated by a CB of five judges, under Article 145 (3). After the constitutional issues were answered, the case was transferred to a Division Bench in the SCI. The appellant's primary grievance was that a two-stage process of adjudication was not envisaged by Article 145 (3) where one part of the case is heard by a CB, and the other part by a Division Bench.[15] As such, the CB was required to decide the case on merits as well.

The judgment by SR Das J (as he then was) for the majority, understood Article 145 (3) as granting complete discretion to the Court to determine how it ought to adjudicate a case before it. Relying on the proviso to Article 145 (3), Das J reasoned that there is nothing repugnant about a case being split into different stages for the purposes of effective disposal. A case which is referred to a CB for determination of questions of law can always be returned to the regular Bench for a decision on the merits.[16] As Das J saw it, 'no argument can be founded or any supposed general rule of indivisibility of a case for the purpose of its hearing and decision.'[17]

Fundamentally then, whether a case is directly heard by a CB, or whether the case reached a CB by way of a reference or by way of the method prescribed in the proviso to Article 145 (3) did not impact the discretion of the CB to

14 *Rao Shiva Bahadur Singh v. The State of Vindhya Pradesh* (1955) 2 SCR 206.

15 ibid 208–13.

16 ibid 213–215.

17 ibid 216; DD Basu, *Commentary on the Constitution of India* (8th edn, vol 5, Lexis Nexis 2009) 6031–32.

decide how it chooses to deal with the issues involved.

As such, CBs may assemble in a few ways. Traditionally, references to CBs are made after a case initially comes up before a smaller Bench. Consider the judgment of the SCI in *Association for Democratic Reforms v. Union of India* (*Electoral Bonds'* case). The petition challenging the Electoral Bond Scheme was filed some time in 2017. In October 2023, a three-judge Bench referred the case for adjudication by a CB, '[i]n view of the importance of the issue which is raised and having due regard to the provisions of Article 145 (3) of the Constitution . . .'[18] It was in this manner that the *Electoral Bonds'* case was heard and decided by a CB of five judges.[19] Likewise, in respect of the same-sex marriage litigation which culminated in the judgment by a CB of five judges,[20] the case was referred to a CB under Article 145 (3), in view of the 'broader context of the petitions before this Court and the inter relationship between the statutory regime and constitutional rights . . . '[21] Another illustration is the Original Suit filed in 2024 by the State of Kerala against the Union of India in the SCI. In hearing this original suit, a Division Bench opined that the case turned on Article 293 of the Constitution. Since Article 293 had, in the opinion of the Division Bench, not yet been 'subject to any authoritative interpretation'[22] by the SCI, the case was referred for adjudication by a CB since authoritative interpretation was paramount for resolving the controversy raised in the Original Suit.[23] A reference may also be made in the manner discussed above, which is under the proviso to Article 145 (3), where a judicial determination by a CB becomes necessary before the case is decided on merits.

However, a CB does not assemble only to answer substantial questions of law which pertain to the interpretation of the Constitution.[24] A third situation in which a CB may assemble, is when the President of India makes a reference

---

[18] *Association for Democratic Reforms v. Union of India Writ Petition* (Civil) No 880 of 2017, order dated 16 October 2023).

[19] *Association for Democratic Reforms v. Union of India* (2024) 5 SCC 1.

[20] *Supriyo v. Union of India* 2023 INSC 920.

[21] *Supriyo @ Supriya Chakraborty v. Union of India* Writ Petition (Civil) No 1011 of 2022, order dated 13 March 2023.

[22] *State of Kerala v. Union of India* 2024 INSC 253 [8].

[23] ibid [9].

[24] See Shrutanjaya Bhardwaj, 'Constituting CBes of the Supreme Court: An Analysis' (*BarandBench*, 28 September 2019) <https://www.barandbench.com/columns/constituting-constitution-benches-of-the-supreme-court-an-analysis> accessed 25 February 2025. (Outlining the situations in which CBs assemble, which include situations in which there is a conflict of opinion between three-judge Bench judgments, and when later judgments question the correctness of an earlier judgment).

to the SCI. Under Article 143, the President may seek the SCI's opinion on questions of law or fact deemed of significant 'public importance'. Such questions are referred to the Court, which, following a hearing, provides its opinion. Article 145 (3) requires a CB of at least five judges to assemble to answer a Presidential Reference.

A fourth situation in which a CB may assemble is when the case relates to an election petition, challenging the election of the President and Vice-President. Under Section 14 of the Presidential and Vice-Presidential Elections Act, 1952, only the SCI has jurisdiction to try such election petitions, and the SCI is authorized to design rules (under Article 145) for the trial of such petitions. Order XLVI of the Supreme Court Rules 2013, contains the rules governing such election petitions. Under Rule 22, every such election petition filed in the SCI has to be tried by a CB of at least five judges.[25]

A fifth situation in which a case may travel to a CB is when a smaller Bench doubts the correctness of the judgment delivered by another Bench of coordinate strength, that is, comprised of the same number of judges as the Bench which has doubted its judgment. Thus, when a three-judge Bench of the SCI doubted the judgment of another three-judge Bench, in relation to the applicability of the Group of Companies doctrine in arbitration law, the issue travelled to a CB of five judges, in search of finality and an authoritative judgment.[26]

A sixth situation in which a CB assembles is when there is inconsistency between previous judgments on a particular legal issue. The inconsistency in the law, in turn, demands that a larger Bench resolve the conflict in the law. Thus, when a two-judge Bench judgment of the SCI does not take into proper account a judgment of a three-judge Bench (which is binding on the smaller Bench), a CB of five judges is constituted to decide and state the correct position of the law.[27]

Apart from this, there have also been situations in which CBs have decided ordinary cases pertaining to civil and commercial law that do not involve any substantial questions of law. For instance, a glance at the judgments delivered

[25] Supreme Court Rules 2013, Ord XLVI, r 22: 'Every petition calling in question an election shall be posted before and be heard and disposed of by a Bench of the Court consisting of not less than Five Judges.'

[26] *Cox and Kings Ltd v. SAP India Pvt Ltd* 2023 INSC 1051.

[27] *Pratap Singh v. State of Jharkhand* (2005) 3 SCC 551.

by the SCI in the first year of its existence shows that cases which pertained to, for instance, excise duties[28] and limitation law[29] were heard by a CB of five judges, even though, the cases did not raise any significant issue on the interpretation of the Constitution.

Trends in Constitution Benches

A two-volume study of all the CB judgments from 1950–2015 by Govind Goel, reveals interesting statistical insights into the working of CBs.[30] Of all the decades, the period from 1960–1970 was the time when the maximum number of CB judgments were delivered (44.94 per cent). If one were to pinpoint the most bountiful year for CB judgments, it would be 1962 – a total of 175 CB judgments were delivered in that year.[31]

Furthermore, between 1950 and 2015, 2,139 judgments were delivered by five-judge Benches; 48 judgments by six-judge Benches; 83 judgments by seven-judge Benches; 3 judgments by eight-judge Benches; 15 judgments by nine-judge Benches; 8 judgments by eleven-judge Benches; and only 1 judgment by a thirteen-judge Bench. Of all the CB judgments over the years, an overwhelming 93.11 per cent of them have been delivered by five-judge Benches.[32] There have also been instances where Benches have assembled in even numbers, for instance, as a Bench of eight in *MP Sharma v. Satish Chandra*[33] or as a Bench of six in *Kulathil Mammu v. State of Kerala.*[34]

In terms of variance in the opinions, 1,855 were unanimous judgments, while 326 judgments contained a dissenting judgment and 116 judgments had concurring opinions. The decade from 1980–1989 witnessed proportionally, the greatest number of dissenting judgments being delivered – in 22 out of 119 CB judgments. On the other hand, 1990–1999 had the least number of dissents – 3 dissenting judgments out of a total of 154 CB judgments.[35]

---

[28] *Ram Krishna Ramnath Agarwal of Kamptee v. Secretary, Municipal Committee, Kamptee* 1950 SCR 15.

[29] *Bhawanipore Banking Corporation, Ltd v. Gouri Shankar Sharma* 1950 SCR 25.

[30] Govind Goel, *Statement of Indian Law: Supreme Court of India Through Its CB Decisions Since 1950* (Thomson Reuters 2016).

[31] Goel (n 30) vol 2, 2008–09.

[32] ibid 2010.

[33] (1954) 1 SCC 385.

[34] AIR 1966 SC 1614.

[35] Goel (n 31) 2015.

The CJI, by convention and practice, constitutes the Benches to decide which judge will be a part of the CB. In terms of the CJI presiding over Benches, CJI BP Sinha presided over the greatest number of Benches – 304 CBs. He is followed by CJI PB Gajendragadkar who presided over 233 Benches, and CJI SR Das who presided over 154 Benches.[36] Remarkably, CJI K Subba Rao, who was CJI for just about ten months, presided over sixty CBs.[37]

These are the broad statistics, but they can also reveal some patterns. A study by Professor Nick Robinson and a team of experts, in a detailed study of CB judgments, sought to understand the many issues associated with CBs.[38]

One concern was about the decline in numbers. In the beginning of the twenty-first century, on average, about nine CBs heard cases. Yet, about four decades prior to this, there were approximately nearly a hundred CBs that had assembled.[39] Strikingly, as the strength of the SCI judges increased through the years, there was a decline in the total number of CB decisions.[40]

This is a common grievance. As Goel also notes, the most prolific years for CBs (1950–1969) were when the total number of judges reached its peak at fourteen judges. An increase in the number of judges sitting on the Court, conversely, witnessed a steady decline in CBs assembling.[41] There may be an answer to this grievance. It is that, perhaps, the most momentous constitutional issues were decided or settled in the first few decades of the Court's existence. Although there was an increase in the number of judges who were appointed to the Court, there may not have been a burgeoning need to resolve issues that involved substantial questions as to the interpretation of the Constitution.

Indeed, the total number of cases that are awaiting adjudication by a CB, as of July 2024, stood at fifty. There are thirty-five cases pending adjudication by a five-judge Bench; eight cases pending adjudication by a seven-judge Bench; and seven cases pending adjudication by a nine-judge Bench. These were the numbers provided by the Law Minister on 26 July 2024 in reply to an unstarred question in the Parliament on the issues awaiting a judgment by

36 ibid 2023.

37 ibid 2024.

38 Nick Robinson et al, 'Interpreting the Constitution: Supreme Court CBes Since Independence' (2011) 46(9) Economic & Political Weekly 27–31; This study surveyed CB judgments from 1950–2009.

39 ibid 27.

40 ibid 27–28.

41 Goel (n 31) 2008–2009.

a CB.[42] One area of particular concern is the time taken to decide CB cases. By the turn of the twenty-first century, a large segment of cases took over eight years to be resolved.[43]

Constitution Bench Judgments: A Life in Four Phases

The fact that a CB assembles to interpret the Constitution is in itself a momentous occasion. But the real test of a judgment by a CB is to appreciate its true impact on the working of the Constitution. A measure of continuity is represented by the fact that out of the over two thousand judgments that have been delivered, only a small percentage of judgments by CBs have been overruled by subsequent CBs of larger Bench strengths.[44]

Although, by and large, CB judgments enjoy continuity in terms of being relatively undisturbed, intervention by larger Benches at a later point in time is necessitated to accord a progressive vision to constitutional interpretation. For instance, in *AK Gopalan v. State of Madras*,[45] a CB of five judges was of the view that the fundamental rights enumerated in Part III of the Constitution could not be taken to be interrelated. More specifically, in the context of Article 21 of the Constitution, the Court held that the right to life and personal liberty did not guarantee any form of due process protection. Twenty-eight years later, in *Maneka Gandhi v. Union of India*,[46] a CB of seven judges decidedly departed from the *Gopalan* formulation to declare that fundamental rights were indeed interrelated and that Article 21 offered robust protection for life and personal liberty.[47]

The *Gopalan* to *Maneka Gandhi* jurisprudential transformation also illustrates the life journey of a CB decision. It can be understood in four phases.

---

42 'Unstarred Question No. 863 by K. Radhakrishnan' (Government of India, Ministry of Law & Justice, Department of Justice, 26 July 2024) <https://www.livelaw.in/pdf_upload/pending-cases-sc-551815.pdf> accessed 25 February 2025. Since this time, out of the pending cases mentioned in this answer, the Supreme Court has decided and pronounced judgments in three nine-judge Bench cases, two seven-judge Bench cases and nine five-judge Bench cases.

43 ibid 30–31.

44 Goel (n 30) vol. 1, Preface.

45 1950 SCR 88.

46 (1978) 1 SCC 248.

47 Rohan J Alva, *Liberty After Freedom: A History of Article 21, Due Process and the Constitution of India* (HarperCollins 2022) 244–60.

Phase I is the pronouncement of the CB judgment itself. Thus, when the decision in *Gopalan* was delivered, it was to be taken as an authoritative interpretation of the philosophical foundations that informed the spirit of fundamental rights. MK Nambyar, who was arguing the case, emphasized on the importance of reading fundamental rights in an interrelated manner. But this line of argument was not accepted by the Court.[48]

Phase II is the period that follows after the judgment has been delivered. After the judgment in *Gopalan* was pronounced, it remained relatively undisturbed, in that it was not seriously interrogated by later decisions. For instance, in 1955, a CB in *State of Bombay v. Bhanji Munji*[49] found no particular problem with the *Gopalan* formulation that fundamental rights were not interrelated.

Phase III may be characterized as witnessing a transformation in the Court's viewpoint, in that a judgment's correctness that has held the field for some time is now questioned. In 1970, a CB of eleven judges in *RC Cooper v. Union of India*,[50] while deciding the validity of the bank nationalization scheme of the Union Government, categorically doubted the correctness of the judgment in *Gopalan*[51] and ultimately came to hold that there is a degree of inter-connectedness between fundamental rights.[52] The judgment in *Cooper* was then seized upon by the seven-judge Bench in *Maneka Gandhi* to elevate the importance of taking a holistic view of fundamental rights, apart from granting stronger levels of protection to the right to life and personal liberty.[53]

Phase IV can be characterized as the blossoming of the transformed view of the Constitution. In this phase, the CB judgments usher in an era of progressive interpretation, fostering a new understanding of the constitutional provision in question. Indeed, the decision in *Maneka Gandhi* has been considered so momentous, that RF Nariman J, speaking for a CB of five judges in *Mohd Arif v. Supreme Court of India*[54] expressly held that, after *Maneka Gandhi*,

48 KK Venugopal with Suhrith Parthasarathy and Suhasini Sen, *M.K. Nambyar: A Constitutional Visionary* (Ebury Press, Penguin Random House 2024) 58–63.

49 (1955) 1 SCR 777.

50 (1970) 1 SCC 248.

51 ibid [55].

52 ibid [50]–[54].

53 *Maneka Gandhi* (n 46) [6].

54 (2014) 9 SCC 737.

'[t]he wheel has turned full circle. Substantive due process is now to be applied to the fundamental right to life and liberty.'[55]

Such a progressive declaration, that due process protection applies to the right to life and personal liberty, would have been impossible to make in the *Gopalan* era. More importantly, the recognition of the right to privacy by a CB of nine judges in the case of *KS Puttaswamy*[56] ('right to privacy' case) was, as RF Nariman J declared in his judgment, largely possible because of the transformed understanding of fundamental rights and of Article 21.[57]

Apart from this, a range of socio-economic rights are today recognized by the SCI and implemented such as the right to health, right to shelter and right to education. They are direct beneficiaries of this transformation in the understanding of fundamental rights and Article 21.[58]

Another branch of constitutional law where this trend of the incremental development of important principles is noticeable is the collection of cases on the basic structure doctrine.[59] In 1951, the provisional Parliament passed the First Amendment to the Constitution. One of the measures was to immunize land reform laws from any sort of constitutional challenge. To that end, a new Article 31-A and an Article 31-B along with the Ninth Schedule were introduced to serve this purpose.[60]

After the provisional Parliament passed the First Amendment to the Constitution, the SCI was seized of a constitutional challenge to this Amendment in the case of *Sankari Prasad Singh Deo v. Union of India.*[61] The First Amendment, the Court found, did not violate any provision of Article 368 of the Constitution, and it was thus held to be a valid constitutional amendment.

---

55 ibid [28].

56 *KS Puttaswamy (Privacy-9J) v. Union of India* (2017) 10 SCC 1.

57 ibid [502], [525].

58 See, S Muralidhar, 'The Expectations and Challenges of Judicial Enforcement of Social Rights' in Malcolm Langford (ed), *Social Rights Jurisprudence: Emerging Trends in International and Comparative Law* (CUP 2008) 102–124; Rehan Abeyratne, 'Socioeconomic Rights in the Indian Constitution: Toward a Broader Conception of Legitimacy' (2014) 39 Brook J Intl L 34–42.

59 For an overview of the issues concerning the basic structure doctrine see, Madhav Khosla, 'Constitutional Amendment' in Sujit Choudhry, Madhav Khosla and Pratap Bhanu Mehta (eds), *The Oxford Handbook of the Indian Constitution* (Oxford University Press 2016) 232–50.

60 See Rohan J Alva, *A Constitution to Keep: Sedition and Free Speech in Modern India* (HarperCollins 2023) 132–34.

61 1951 SCC 966.

In another case from that time, *State of Bihar v. Kameshwar Singh*,[62] Dr BR Ambedkar who appeared for a group of zamindars whose landholding was directly affected by these amendments, valiantly but unsuccessfully, endeavoured to persuade the Court that regardless of the nature of the First Amendment, it ought to examine whether substantively speaking, the amendment was consistent with constitutional ethos. Incidentally Dr Ambedkar had shepherded the First Amendment in the provisional Parliament as the country's first Law Minister in 1951. A year later, in the SCI, he was arguing for the law that it sought to protect, to be struck down.[63] These cases can be categorized as being part of 'Phase I' as mentioned earlier.

By the 1960s, the winds of change were clearly blowing. In *Sajjan Singh v. State of Rajasthan*,[64] Mudholkar J as part of a CB was moved to observe that, in the life of the nation, it is paramount to know whether the 'basic features' of the Constitution ought to 'endure for all time—or at least for the foreseeable future or whether they are no more enduring than the implemental and subordinate provisions of the Constitution.'[65] The development and articulation of a doctrine for examining the validity of a constitutional amendment on substantive grounds was applied in the *Golaknath* case.[66] In essence, by a majority of 6:5, CJI K Subba Rao, speaking for the majority, held that a constitutional amendment could be declared unconstitutional, if it violated or abridged fundamental rights.

Thus far, the only method of judging the validity of a constitutional amendment was to see whether the procedure laid down in Article 368 had been complied with. The effect of the amendment was not a consideration for its validity. This changed with the *Golaknath* case. Fundamentally now, the court had to examine both the propriety of the procedure by which the amendment was passed and its actual effects on the stability and continued vitality of the Constitution. These cases fall in 'Phase II'.

---

[62] (1952) 1 SCC 528.

[63] See, Rohan J Alva, 'When the Basic Structure Doctrine was First Argued before the Supreme Court of India in 1951', (*BarandBench* 22 December 2023) <https://www.barandbench.com/columns/when-the-basic-structure-doctrine-was-first-argued-in-1951-in-the-supreme-court-of-india> accessed 25 February 2025.

[64] (1965) 1 SCR 933.

[65] ibid 969; See also, Arvind Datar, 'Seeds of Basic Structure First Sown by Justice JR Mudholkar' (*BarandBench*, 11 February 2023) <https://www.barandbench.com/columns/legal-notes-arvind-datar-seeds-basic-structure-first-sown-justice-jr-mudholkar> accessed 25 February 2025.

[66] *IC Golaknath v. State of Punjab* (1967) 2 SCR 762.

'Phase III' was when the SCI decided to temper the applicability of the newly minted doctrine in constitutional law. On 24 April 1973, a thirteen-judge Bench in *Kesavananda Bharati v. State of Kerala*,[67] by a majority of 7:6 held that a constitutional amendment could not violate or impact the basic structure of the Constitution. This enunciation of the basic structure doctrine adopted a middle path approach, by stating that constitutional amendments could be passed to alter features of the Constitution, but the basic structure of the Constitution itself could not be altered.

'Phase IV' applies to those categories of cases that applied the basic structure doctrine to review constitutional amendments on substantive grounds. Thus, decisions ranging from *Minerva Mills v. Union of India*[68] where, amongst others, a portion of Article 31C was struck down for violating the basic structure doctrine, to the *Supreme Court Advocates-on-Record Association v. Union of India*[69] popularly called the 'NJAC Case' in 2015. In the latter case, a CB struck down the 99th Amendment to the Constitution, which sought to dismantle the Collegium system and introduce an NJAC for appointing judges to the SCI and HCs. It was held that the NJAC, as proposed, removed judicial primacy in the appointments process, thus violating the basic structure.[70]

Ebb and Flow in Constitution Bench Judgments: Patterns, Challenges and Implications

This normative categorization of how a doctrine is enunciated by a CB is useful because it helps in articulating the basic premise which lies at the heart of a CB judgment. At its core, CB judgments seek to attach a certain truth to the meaning of the Constitution or iron out the creases that have crept into certain branches of the law. This can occur in one of two ways. In the first, a mode of juristic thought as set out initially is consolidated over time, as noticed in the previous section. In the second case, CB judgments go through periods of ebb and flow with regard to constitutional doctrine. The ebb and

---

67 (1973) 4 SCC 225.

68 (1980) 3 SCC 625.

69 (2016) 5 SCC 1.

70 For a critical analysis see, Rehan Abeyratne, 'Upholding Judicial Supremacy in India: The NJAC Judgment in Comparative Perspective' (2017) 49 *George Washington International Law Review* 569. See also the essays in this book by AP Shah and Madan Lokur.

flow in juristic doctrine is revealing in those cases where CB judgments are subsequently overruled. Consider a recent example.

In 2023, a CB of five judges in *NN Global Mercantile (P) Ltd v. Indo Unique Flame Ltd*,[71] held that an arbitration agreement in relation to a contract which was not stamped as per the Indian Stamp Act, could not be acted upon by the parties, since such a contract was unenforceable. Thus, no party could rely on such an arbitration agreement till the time the deficiency in the stamping of the document was remedied. In less than a year, this judgment was overruled by a CB of seven judges by the decision titled *In Re: Interplay Between Arbitration Agreements Under the Arbitration and Conciliation Act 1996 and the Indian Stamp Act 1899*.[72] Clearly this larger Bench found fault with the judgment of five judges and acted with alacrity to remedy the situation.

However, in other instances, the SCI has taken quite some time to overrule past decisions of CBs. For instance, in the 'right to privacy' case, the nine-judge Bench overruled the judgment of a CB from 1976 – *ADM Jabalpur v. Shivkant Shukla*. Here, it had been held that fundamental rights, more particularly under Article 21, can be suspended when an emergency is declared.[73] It is a different matter that the core of the judgment in *ADM Jabalpur* had been eviscerated by the 44th Amendment to the Constitution, which, amongst others, amended Article 359 and stipulated that Articles 20 and 21 of the Constitution can never be suspended during the time an Emergency has been declared.[74] Moreover, as a CB of nine judges in *IR Coelho*'s case had noted, later judgments, particularly the decision in *Maneka Gandhi*'s case had chipped away at the foundations of *ADM Jabalpur*.[75]

Yet, *ADM Jabalpur* existed purely because it had not been overruled. This decision of 1975 was only overruled in 2017, despite the deep scars it had inflicted on the stability of fundamental rights.[76]

---

[71] (2023) 7 SCC 1.

[72] 2023 INSC 1066.

[73] *ADM Jabalpur v. Shivkant Shukla* (1976) 2 SCC 521.

[74] HM Seervai, *Constitutional Law of India*, vol 2 (4th edn, 1996) 3083-3084.

[75] *IR Coelho v. State of Tamil Nadu* (2007) 2 SCC 1 [29]-[30].

[76] HM Seervai (n 74) vol 2, 2228. 'It is not possible for laymen and lawyers alike to speak of the judgments in the *Habeas Corpus Case* without strong emotion. The majority judgments gave a free charter to every petty Govt. servant to do his will against helpless people stripped by the Sup. Ct. of the protection of law.'

In some other instances, the ebb and flow occurs because of the absence of clarity on what the central holding of a CBs' judgment actually is. Here, judgments of CBs have created controversy rather than acting as a stabilizing force. Thus, the essential holding by a CB has to be correctly deciphered by later Benches.

In *TMA Pai Foundation v. State of Karnataka*,[77] a CB of eleven judges essentially held that the right to establish and administer educational institutions was guaranteed by Article 19 (1) (g) of the Constitution. This is the provision that makes it a fundamental right for all citizens, 'to practise any profession, or to carry on any occupation, trade or business.' However, quick on the heels of this decision, another CB of seven judges in *PA Inamdar v. State of Maharashtra*[78] had to be formed to explain the import of the decision in *TMA Pai*. Here are CJI Lahoti's prefatory observations from *PA Inamdar*:

> A Coram of 11 Judges, not a common feature in the Supreme Court of India, sat to hear and decide TMA Pai Foundation v. State of Karnataka. It was expected that the authoritative pronouncement by a Bench of such strength on the issues arising before it would draw a final curtain on those controversies. The subsequent events tell a different story . . . It was further pointed out that 'the decision raises more questions than it has answered . . .
>
> The prophecy has come true and while the ink on the opinions in *Pai Foundation* was yet to dry, the High Courts were flooded with writ petitions, calling for settlements of several issues which were not yet resolved or which cropped up post *Pai Foundation*. The 11 learned Judges constituting the Bench in *Pai Foundation* delivered five opinions. The majority opinion on behalf of six Judges was delivered by B.N. Kirpal, C.J. Khare, J. (as His Lordship then was) delivered a separate but concurring opinion, supporting the majority. Quadri, J., Ruma Pal, J. and Variava, J. (for himself and Bhan, J.) delivered three separate opinions partly dissenting from the majority. *Islamic Academy* [(2003) 6 SCC 697] too handed down two opinions. The majority opinion for four learned Judges was delivered by V.N. Khare, C.J. S.B. Sinha, J., delivered a separate opinion.[79]

---

77 (2002) 8 SCC 481.

78 (2005) 6 SCC 537.

79 ibid [2]–[3].

Indeed, this is one area of concern in CB judgments. The fact that multiple opinions are part of a judgment can make it difficult to distil the core holding of the judgment and the points of law on which the members of the Bench agree upon. This problem has been identified in other cases too, such as the decision of the SCI in *SR Bommai v. Union of India*,[80] where a CB of nine judges laid out the guidelines of how judicial review of declaration of emergency under Article 356 ought to be done. As has been pointed out by Soli Sorabjee, given the sheer number of opinions in this judgment, it is difficult to clearly define the central holding in this case.[81]

Legislative Pushback

It has also been the case that CB judgments have set off firestorms. The example that immediately comes to anyone's mind is the continuous battle between the Parliament and the SCI in relation to the basic structure doctrine.

In 1973, in *Kesavananda Bharati*, the Court had declared that the Parliament could not utilize its powers under Article 368 (the provision relating to amendment of the Constitution), to alter the basic structure of the Constitution. To overcome this judgment, the 42nd Amendment to the Constitution, amongst others, altered Article 368 (the provision that regulates the Parliament's power to amend the Constitution) by adding Article 368 (4) and 368 (5). Effectively, these articles once again conferred on the Parliament absolute powers to amend the Constitution.[82] A CB in *Minerva Mills v. Union of India*[83] responded and struck down these changes[84] and restored the primacy of the basic structure doctrine.[85] Through decisions such as these, the basic structure doctrine is firmly and securely embedded in Indian constitutional law.

This kind of legislative pushback to CB judgments has occurred recently as well, but with a different outcome.

80 (1994) 3 SCC 1.

81 See, Soli J Sorabjee, 'Decision of the Supreme Court in *S.R. Bommai v. Union of India: A Critique*' (1994) 3 SCC (Jour) 1.

82 See Seervai (n 74) 3169–71.

83 (1980) 3 SCC 625.

84 Fali S Nariman, *You Must Know Your Constitution* (Hay House 2023) 262–63.

85 See, Chintan Chandrachud, *The Cases That India Forgot* (Juggernaut Books 2019) 25–47.

In 2023, a CB of five judges in *Anoop Baranwal v. Union of India,*[86] held that when it comes to the appointment of Election Commissioners, a multi-member collegium comprising the Prime Minister, Leader of the Opposition and the CJI ought to be constituted, which will make such recommendations for appointment. Soon after this decision, the Parliament passed a law in which the panel constituted to recommend the appointment of Election Commissioners replaced the CJI with a Union Cabinet Minister nominated by the Prime Minister.[87] When this new law was challenged in the SCI, a two-judge Bench observed that since the judgment in *Anoop Baranwal* was to hold the field till such time a law governing the appointments of Election Commissioners was passed, the continuance of the law in question could not be suspended on the grounds that it runs contrary to this judgment.[88] As things currently stand, the CB judgment effectively lasted for less than a year.

Yet, there have also been instances when CB judgments have spurred the government into action. A good example of this is the CB judgment in *Satwant Singh Sawhney v. D Ramarathnam, Assistant Passport Officer, New Delhi.*[89] Here, the SCI, speaking through CJI K Subba Rao, held that the right to travel was a part of the right to life and personal liberty guaranteed by Article 21. Thus, the State could not arbitrarily take away a person's passport. The impact of this judgment was such that close on its heels, the Parliament swiftly enacted the Passports Act in 1967.[90]

Constitution Bench Judgments: From Dissent to Law of the Land

An interesting feature of CB judgments is that not infrequently, the dissenting view over a period of time is affirmed by a subsequent CB as having correctly declared the legal position.

Article 145 (5) clearly empowers the judges to deliver a dissenting judgment, when they choose to disagree with the judgment of the majority. The mix of CB judgments containing dissenting judgments is revealing.

---

86 (2023) 6 SCC 161.

87 Chief Election Commissioner and Other Election Commissioners (Appointment, Conditions of Service and Term of Office) Act 2023.

88 *Dr Jaya Thakur v. Union of India* 2024 SCC Online SC 406 [9].

89 AIR 1967 SC 1836.

90 Goel (n 30) vol no.1, Preface.

As we have already seen, approximately 326 CB judgments from 1950 to 2015 contained dissenting judgments. Historically, the CJI has been in dissent on thirteen occasions.[91] A contrary example, often cited by scholars, lawyers and judges alike, is that of K Subba Rao J.[92] When he became CJI, K Subba Rao ceased to write any dissenting opinion.[93]

In *Discordant Notes: The Voice of Dissent in the Court of Last Resort*,[94] a two-volume study of all the dissenting judgments delivered in the SCI, RF Nariman J, identifies key dissents in CB judgments, which later became the law of the land.[95] Some of them are discussed below to illustrate the path that a dissenting judgment travels from being the voice of a minority to that of a majority in the Court.

The most famous dissent is perhaps from the *Gopalan* case. Fazl Ali J was the sole dissenting judge. He took the view there was a degree of interconnectedness between fundamental rights and that Article 21 of the Constitution did in fact include certain features that strongly protected natural justice rights. As we saw, this was a viewpoint expressly rejected by the majority in *Gopalan*.[96] This dissent, a 'cry in the wilderness'[97] as it were of Fazl Ali J, later became the law of the land when it was accepted by a CB of eleven judges in the *RC Cooper* case.[98]

The other notable dissent of Fazl Ali J is in the case of *Romesh Thappar v. State of Madras*[99] and *Brij Bhushan v. State of Delhi*.[100] In these cases, Fazl Ali J dissented on the point that the preservation of 'public order' was integral to the structure of Article 19 (2) of the Constitution. However, in 1950, the ground

91 Giti Pratap, 'The Significant Minority: Thirteen Times Chief Justice of India Dissented in CB Cases' (*BarandBench*, 2 November 2023) <https://www.barandbench.com/columns/the-significant-minority-thirteen-times-chief-justice-india-dissented-constitution-bench-cases> accessed 25 February 2025.

92 Aparna Chandra, Sital Kalantry and William HJ Hubbard, *Court on Trial: A Data-Driven Account of the Supreme Court of India* (Penguin Random House India 2023) 75.

93 George H Gadbois Jr, 'Indian Judicial Behaviour' (1970) 3(5) *The Economic & Political Weekly* 166; Robinson et al, 'Interpreting the Constitution' (n 39) 31.

94 Rohinton F Nariman, *Discordant Notes: The Voice of Dissent in the Last Court of Last Resort* (Penguin Random House 2021).

95 Rohinton F Nariman, *Discordant Notes* (n 94) ch IV, 231–313.

96 *AK Gopalan* (n 46) 231–241

97 KS Puttaswamy (Privacy-9J) (n 57) [450].

98 Rohinton F Nariman, *Discordant Notes* (n 94) 240–41.

99 (1950) SCR 594.

100 (1950) SCR 605.

of 'public order' was not enumerated in Article 19 (2) as a specific ground to curb free speech. But his dissent was found so compelling that soon after this judgment, the Constitution was amended. By the First Amendment, Article 19 (2) was altered, to include 'public order' as a specific ground to limit the freedom of speech and expression.[101]

There are several other notable dissents in CB judgments that were later accepted by larger CBs. The dissenting judgment of Vivian Bose J in *State of Bombay v. The United Motors (India) Ltd*,[102] a case concerning the interpretation of Article 286 as it stood prior to the 6th Amendment (1956) to the Constitution, was later approved of by a seven-judge CB in *Bengal Immunity v. State of Bihar*.[103]

CJI BP Sinha's dissent in *Atiabari Tea Co Ltd v. State of Assam*,[104] on the interplay of taxes and inter-state trade and commerce, was approved by a nine-judge Bench in *Jindal Stainless Ltd v. State of Haryana*.[105] In the realm of the right to privacy, the dissent of K Subba Rao J (which was joined by JC Shah J) in *Kharak Singh v. State of Uttar Pradesh*[106] which made a strident argument in favour of privacy rights, was approved by a seven judge Bench in *Maneka Gandhi*.[107]

In the realm of reservation law, the dissent of K Subba Rao J in *T Devadasan v. The Union of India*,[108] on having unfulfilled vacancies for the weaker sections of society being carried forward to another year was approved by a seven-judge Bench in *State of Kerala v. NM Thomas*[109] and then by a nine-judge Bench in *Indra Sawhney v. Union of India*.[110]

---

[101] Rohinton F Nariman, *Discordant Notes* (n 94) 243. See also Alva (n 60) 127–28; Tripurdaman Singh, *Sixteen Stormy Days: The Story of the First Amendment to the Constitution of India* (Penguin Random House India 2020).

[102] 1953 SCR 1069.

[103] (1955) 2 SCR 603. See Rohinton F Nariman, *Discordant Notes* (n 94) 243–244.

[104] (1961) 1 SCR 809.

[105] (2017) 12 SCC 1. See Rohinton F Nariman, *Discordant Notes* (n 94) 249–258.

[106] (1964) 1 SCR 332.

[107] See Rohinton F Nariman, *Discordant Notes* (n 94) 262–267.

[108] (1964) 4 SCR 680.

[109] (1976) 2 SCC 310.

[110] 1992 Supp (3) SCC 217. See Rohinton F Nariman, *Discordant Notes* (n 94) 267–69.

The most recent example of a dissent in a CB judgment being approved of is the dissent of SC Agrawal J in *PV Narasimha Rao v. State.*[111] The point of dissent was that under Article 105 (2) of the Constitution, elected representatives who accept bribes for discharging their duties in the legislature do not enjoy immunity from prosecution.[112] In *Sita Soren v. Union of India,*[113] a CB of seven judges speaking through CJI DY Chandrachud faulted the majority opinion in *PV Narasimha Rao* and effectively upheld the principles enunciated in the dissent of Agrawal J. *Soren*'s case thus held that legislators do not enjoy immunity if they take bribes for performing their official functions in the legislature.

Some dissents often have a didactic dimension, which intends to convey to the majority of how its position may be misconceived and the peril it may bring to the future of constitutional stability. In this category, three dissents 'for the ages' come to mind. First, Venkatachalaiah J's (as he then was) dissent in the *Antulay* case;[114] where he emphasized the difference between an error of jurisdiction and an error of law within jurisdiction. Second, the dissent of DY Chandrachud J (as he then was) in the *Aadhaar* case;[115] in the context of the need to strictly abide by the procedure to be followed in case of Money Bills. Third, is the dissent by RF Nariman J in the Review Petition in the *Sabarimala Temple Entry*[116] case. Initially, by a 4:1 majority, the SCI had held that the exclusion of women between the ages of ten and fifty from the *Sabarimala* Temple was unconstitutional.[117] Subsequently, more than fifty review petitions were filed. On 14 November 2019, by a 3:2 majority, the CB hearing the review petitions, decided to keep them pending while referring broader constitutional questions on the true scope of Article 25 and Article 26 (provisions which relate to religious freedom) to a larger Bench. The majority argued that consolidating related petitions before a larger Bench would bolster public confidence and align with Article 145 (3). The dissent of Nariman J (for

[111] (1998) 4 SCC 626.

[112] See Rohinton F Nariman, *Discordant Notes* (n 94) 390–400.

[113] 2024 INSC 161.

[114] *AR Antulay v. RS Nayak* (1988) 2 SCC 602. See also Rohinton F Nariman (n 94) 380–90.

[115] *KS Puttaswamy (Aadhaar-5J) v. Union of India*, (2019) 1 SCC 1. See also, Rohinton F Nariman, *Discordant Notes* (n 94) vol 2, 516.

[116] *Kantaru Rajeevaru (Sabarimala Temple Review-5J) v. Indian Young Lawyers Assn.* (2020) 2 SCC 1. See also, Rohinton F Nariman, Discordant Notes (n 94) 517.

[117] *Indian Young Lawyers Association v. State of Kerala*, (2019) 11 SCC 1.

himself and Chandrachud J) strongly critiqued the majority's approach as an unwarranted departure from the narrow mandate of a review Bench. Nariman J cautioned against speculating about what future Benches might decide on related constitutional issues or pre-emptively referring these to a larger Bench. At the heart of these three dissents lay the urgent need to inform the majority of the mistake they may be committing.

Usually, judges, when they dissent, are not given to using caustic language. But as these dissents reveal, when pushed to a point, the judges have no other option but to be extremely critical with the hope that the majority realizes the error of its ways, and more particularly, a future Bench if it ever were to revisit the case realizes the principles that the dissenting judges were fighting hard to protect.

Epilogue

One of the major concerns, as we have seen, is that the multiplicity of opinions makes it difficult for a reader to adduce the central holding of a case. Since a CB ought to have a minimum of five judges, to have five different opinions makes it a herculean task to determine what are the principles the judges agree upon; what are the points of convergence and divergence; and, how can the differences in outlook of each judgment be reconciled. It may be too much to demand that CBs should have one judgment alone. For instance, in the 'right to privacy' case, the CB of nine judges at the end of the judgment, provided a precise summary of the conclusions that the Court had arrived at. Something similar had also been attempted in the *Kesavanada Bharati* case. But there, only nine out of the thirteen judges signed the official conclusion of the judgment, which reflected the key determinations of the majority. As a matter of practice, each CB judgment ought to contain a summary of the conclusions and determinations that have been arrived at by the Bench.

This will be helpful in at least three ways. As an institutional matter, lawyers and judges will be able to quickly grasp the essence of the case and the points of law that have been determined. Further, the public at large, who are impacted by these decisions, may better comprehend the full import of CB judgments. Finally, such a practice will, at least to some extent, help future Benches to determine the common points on which a particular CB agreed upon. Here, the task of future Benches will be made easier, for they will not need to conduct a fresh exercise to determine what the central holding of the judgment is.

Another suggestion is to decrease the length of CB judgments. A glance at the law reports from the early years shows that CB judgments were short and to the point. And they decided momentous questions of constitutional law. *Romesh Thappar*,[118] which laid the foundations of how the fundamental right to the freedom of speech is to be understood, is twelve pages long. *State of Madras v. Champakam Doraiarajan*,[119] the first judgment on the law on reservations, is nine pages long. The judgment of a CB of seven judges in *Nagpur Improvement Trust v. Vithal Rao,*[120] which examined the law on equality qua a person being subjected to different laws for the same action, is ten pages long.

Yet, recent CB judgments have been unusually long. The judgment of the nine-judge Bench in *Mineral Area Development v. M/s Steel Authority of India*[121] is 393 pages long. The judgment of the CB on marriage equality is 366 pages long.[122] Other CB judgments such as on the right to privacy and the judgment on the validity of the *Aadhar* scheme run into over a thousand pages.[123]

If, as William Shakespeare wrote in Hamlet, 'brevity is the soul of wit and tediousness the limbs and outward flourishes'[124] then shorter judgments may be helpful in powerfully conveying the law point that the CB seeks to settle.

In the life of the Indian republic, CB judgments have played an outsized role in shaping the direction of constitutional progress. Their impact is felt much beyond the immediate controversies that led to these decisions. CB judgments furthered the progressive evolution of the law and have made the Constitution more inclusive and protective of fundamental rights.

---

118 *Romesh Thappar* (n 99).

119 1951 SCR 525.

120 (1973) 1 SCC 500.

121 2024 INSC 554.

122 *Supriyo @ Supriya Chakraborty v. Union of India* 2023 INSC 920.

123 See Lokendra Malik and Yogesh Pratap Singh, 'Lengthy Judgments, Unlimited Arguments' (*BarandBench*, 29 July 2021) <https://www.barandbench.com/columns/lengthy-judgments-unlimited-arguments> accessed 25 February 2025.

124 William Shakespeare, *Hamlet* act 2, sc 2.

CB judgments have played a critical role in ensuring the successful working of the Constitution and the orderly development of the law. The structure and framework of the Constitution has to be infused with life and reason. The institution that has to perform this constitutionally sanctified role is the SCI. In a substantial measure, the working of the Constitution has been made successful by the working of the CBs in the SCI.

The Administration of the District Judiciary in India: Challenges and Opportunities

S RAVINDRA BHAT*

The Constitution of India arguably provides for a federal structure of government that treats the Union and the states as distinct. While the legislative and executive branches are separate for the Union and the states, the judiciary is a single pyramidical structure. The district judiciary[1] constitutes the foundational rung, exercising jurisdiction at the district level or in a more localized manner; the High Courts (HCs) constitute the middle rung, exercising original and appellate jurisdiction at the level of the State/Union Territory; and the Supreme Court of India (SCI) is at the apex level. Funding for court administration is provided by the states, and certain administrative aspects of the functioning of district courts are regulated by the states. In all other matters, the district courts are under the supervision of the HCs. The unitary character and set-up of the judiciary was a deliberate act on the part of the Constitution makers, for whom a single integrated judiciary was essential for uniform standards of judicial governance and judicial independence.[2]

Independence of the judiciary is a fundamental tenet of every democracy. The values of independence, impartiality and equality underpin public confidence in the judicial system. In this context, this essay examines the structure and independence of the district courts in India, their relationship with the HCs

* The author wishes to thank Raji Gururaj and Veda Singh for their substantive research support, suggestions and their invaluable editorial support.

[1] The term 'district judiciary' is used throughout this essay, instead of 'lower judiciary' or 'subordinate judiciary'. The SCI, in *High Court Bar Association, Allahabad v. State of Uttar Pradesh* 2024 INSC 150 observed that 'no Court of law is inferior to the other'.

[2] See Granville Austin, *The Indian Constitution: Cornerstone of a Nation* (Clarendon Press 1966) 184–185.

and the methods used to improve fairness and efficiency of the judicial process and guarantee access to justice, while ensuring that the conditions of service of judges and other employees are fair and reasonable. The essay will also address issues plaguing these courts, such as case pendency, inadequate judge strength, infrastructural inadequacies, difficult service conditions, problems with budgetary allocation and utilization and plausible efforts at mitigating them in a meaningful manner, so as to ensure access to justice and preservation of the independence of the judiciary.

Historical Context

In an early report predating the drafting of the Constitution,[3] the need to safeguard the independence of the district judiciary was highlighted. The Draft Constitutions of 1947 and 1948, however, did not include any express provisions on the theme. The omission became the focal issue in the Conference of Judges of the Federal Court and the Chief Justices (CJs) of the HCs held in March 1948. Their memorandum recommended a provision to place 'exclusively in the hands of the High Courts the power of appointment and dismissal, posting, promotion and grant of leave' of district judges.[4] The Drafting Committee accepted these recommendations and decided that for securing this end, a chapter relating to district judges and the district judiciary should be included in the Constitution.[5]

The provisions of the Constitution, as promulgated, do not explicitly guarantee the independence of the judiciary. However, the value emerges from a collective reading of several provisions.[6] The importance of this value as part of the basic

---

[3] See 'Report of the Joint Committee on Indian Constitutional Reforms' (vol 1, part 1, 1933-34) [337]; See also, Law Commission of India, 'One Hundred Eighteenth Report on Method of Appointments to Subordinate Courts/Subordinate Judiciary' (1986) 10 <https://cdnbbsr.s3waas.gov.in/s3ca0daec69b5adc880fb464895726dbdf/uploads/2022/08/2022080834.pdf> accessed 16 February 2025.

[4] See, Subhash C Kashyap, *The Framing of the Indian Constitution: A Study* (vol 5, 2nd edn, Universal Law Publishing 2006) 505.

[5] ibid 714–715; Dr Ambedkar, in his reply to the debate on the draft provisions, stated that the amended provisions were framed with the 'object to place the whole of the civil judiciary under the control of the High Court.'; See, Constituent Assembly Debates, 16 September 1949, vol 9, para 9.142.228 <https://www.constitutionofindia.net/debates/16-sep-1949/> accessed 16 February 2025.

[6] See Constitution of India 1950, arts 50 (Separation of the Judiciary from the Executive), 124 (Establishment and Constitution of the Supreme Court), 125 (Salaries of Judges), 146 (Appointments of Officers and Servants, and Expenditure of the Supreme Court), 211 (Restriction on Discussion of Judges' Conduct in the Legislature), 217 (Appointment and Conditions of Office of a Judge of a High

structure of the Constitution, was enunciated by thirteen judges of the SCI in *Kesavananda Bharati v. State of Kerala*.[7] The principle has since been reiterated in other decisions of the SCI since then, with the focus primarily being on the independence of the HCs.[8] Recently, in *All India Judges Association v. Union of India,* the SCI recognized that the independence of the district judiciary is 'equally a part of the basic structure of the Constitution'.[9] The SCI has further observed that the district judiciary is the edifice of the judicial system and it should be as strong as possible.[10]

Today, the district judiciary is acknowledged to be the 'backbone of the judicial system'.[11] It has a sanctioned strength of about 25,523 judicial officers (as of 30 June 2023)[12] who are the face of the judiciary for the common man, and the first and last avenues of relief for most. It is in the interest of judicial independence, impartiality and fairness that it is ensured that judicial officers and district judges are independent of executive control.[13]

Constitutional Scheme: Control over the District Judiciary is Vested in the High Courts

Articles 233 to 237 of the Constitution pertain to the district judiciary and are cited in a dedicated part of the Constitution.[14] Seervai writes that these provisions ensure that the initial appointment, posting, promotion, transfer, etc. of members of the district judiciary are placed under the protection of the HCs to 'insulate them from the pulls and pressures of political life'.[15]

Court), 220 (Restriction on Practice after being a Permanent Judge), 221 (Salaries, etc. of Judges), 227 (Power of Superintendence over all courts by the High Court), 229 (Appointments of Officers and Servants and the Expenses of High Courts), 233 (Appointment of District Judges), 235 (Control over Subordinate Courts vested in the High Court).

7 *Kesavananda Bharati v. State of Kerala* 1973 Supp SCR 1.

8 *SP Gupta v. Union of India* AIR 1982 SC 149 [26], [333], [343], *Union of India v. Sankalchand* AIR 1977 SC 2328 [12].

9 In *All India Judges Association* (2024) 1 SCC 546, the Court held: 'The independence of the District Judiciary must also be equally a part of the basic structure of the Constitution. Without impartial and independent judges in the District Judiciary, Justice, a preambular goal would remain illusory. The District Judiciary is, in most cases, also the Court which is most accessible to the litigant.'

10 *All India Judges Association v. Union of India* (2002) 4 SCC 247.

11 *All India Judges Association v. Union of India* 2024 (n 9)

12 Calculated as per figures from Supreme Court of India, 'Annual Report 2022–23' (vol 2, 2023).

13 See *State of West Bengal v. Nripendra*, 1966 (1) SCR 771.

14 Constitution of India 1950, part VI, ch VI.

15 HM Seervai, *Constitutional Law of India* (vol III, 4th ed, Law and Justice Publishing Co 2008) 3065.

Article 233 provides for the appointment, posting and promotion of district judges in the state by the governor of the state in consultation with the HC.[16] For positions (other than district judges) in the judicial service of the states, recruitments are to be made by the Governors of states in accordance with rules framed after consultation with the State Public Service Commission and with the HC exercising jurisdiction in relation to such state.[17] Such consultation is not an idle formality; the executive government, through the Governor, is bound to act upon the advice or recommendation of the HC.[18] In a case where the Governor appointed district judges on the advice of a cabinet sub-committee, without any discussion or counter-proposal by the HC, the appointment was held to be invalid for want of consultation with the HC.[19]

Under Article 235, control over district courts 'including the posting and promotion of, and the grant of leave to, persons belonging to the judicial service of a State and holding any post inferior to the post of district judge' is vested in the HCs.[20] The posting (transfer) of a district judge is also in the hands of the HC alone.[21] The three expressions, 'posting', 'promotion' and 'grant of leave' used in Article 235 are 'only illustrative in character and do not limit the extent of control exercised by the High Court over the officers of the subordinate judiciary.'[22]

The SCI has ruled that the HCs are duty-bound to insulate judicial functioning within their territory from being demoralized by brow-beating, stone-walling or bullying, whether by litigants or by their counsel.[23] It is the duty of the judges of superior courts to ensure that the independence of the judiciary is not compromised, and every judicial officer feels that he can freely and

---

16 The Constitution of India 1950, arts 233 (1), (2).

17 The Constitution of India 1950, art 234.

18 *State of Bihar v. Bal Mukund Sah* (2000) 4 SCC 640.

19 *State of Kerala v. A Lakshmikutty* (1986) 4 SCC 632.

20 The Constitution of India 1950, art 235; See also *State of Assam v. Kuseswar* AIR 1970 SC 1616, 1619.

21 *State of Assam v. Ranga Md*, 1967 (1) SCR 454; See also, *State of Assam v. Kuseswar Saikia* 1969 (3) SCC 505.

22 *Madan Mohan Choudhary v. State of Bihar* 1999 (1) SCR 596. See *Chandra Mohan v. State of Uttar Pradesh* 1967 (1) SCR 77, *Hari Dutt Kainthia v. State of Himachal Pradesh* (1980) 3 SCC 189, and Prem *Nath v. State of Rajasthan* 1967 (3) SCR 186.

23 *Mahabir Prasad Singh v. Jacks Aviation Pvt Ltd* 1999 (1) SCC 37; *Yoginath D Bagde v. State of Maharashtra* (1999) 7 SCC 739.

fearlessly give expression to his own opinion.[24] HCs have a duty to protect the judges of the district and sessions courts from any action which may undermine the administration of justice.[25]

High Courts Exercise Supervision, Not Control over Decisions in Individual Cases

HCs, which number twenty-five in the country, are at the apex of the judicial structure within the territories of each state or union territory.[26] Pursuant to Article 227 of the Constitution, the HCs exercise supervisory jurisdiction over the district judiciary. This power is not confined to the administrative sphere; it also includes judicial supervision.[27] It is only when a district court's order violates the fundamental basic principles of justice and fair play or a patent or flagrant procedural error has crept in or where the order results in manifest injustice, that the supervisory jurisdiction of the HC is justified.[28] Another judgment[29] describes this jurisdiction as extending 'to seeing that an inferior Court or Tribunal functions within the limits of its authority', in the exercise of which, the HC does not act as an appellate court. This jurisdiction allows for calling for returns from district courts, issuance of general rules and prescription of forms to regulate their practice and proceedings, and determination of the manner and form in which book entries and accounts shall be kept.[30] Significantly, this power cannot be limited or curtailed by enacted law.[31]

---

24 *VK Jain v. High Court of Delhi* (2008) 17 SCC 538.

25 This has been done through the invocation of Article 215 of the Constitution and Section 15 of the Contempt of Courts Act 1971, for example, in *Delhi Bar Association v. State of Gujarat* (1991) (3) SCR 936.

26 To name a few, provisions of the Civil Procedure Code, 1908; The Bharatiya Nagarik Suraksha Sanhita 2023 (BNSS, which replaced the Criminal Procedure Code 1973), the Family Courts Act 1984; the Motor Vehicles Act 1988, etc.).

27 In *Waryam Singh v. Amar Nath* 1954 SCR 565, the SCI held that the 'power of judicial superintendence to the High Courts apart from and independently of the provisions of other law conferring revisional jurisdiction on the High Courts.'

28 *Timbak Gangadhar Telang v. Ram Chandra Ganesh Bhide* (1977) 2 SCC 437.

29 *Mohd Yunus v. Mohd Mustaqim* (1983) 4 SCC 566.

30 Constitution of India 1950, art 227 (2).

31 *State of Gujarat v. Vakhatsinghji Vajesinghji Vaghela* AIR 1968 SC 1481, where the SCI declared that 'Article 227 of the Constitution gives the High Court the power of superintendence over all courts and tribunals – throughout the territories in relation to which it exercises jurisdiction. This jurisdiction cannot be limited or fettered by any Act of the State Legislature. The supervisory jurisdiction extends to keeping the subordinate tribunals within the limits of their authority and to seeing that they obey the law.'

The HCs' duties to supervise district and sessions courts include the duty to monitor the progress and trial of cases and to prescribe timelines within which cases must be disposed.[32] The power of superintendence has inherent limitations, even in the administrative field. HCs cannot 'pass a judicial order in a particular manner as that would certainly amount to interfering with the independence of the subordinate judiciary'[33] and 'cannot interfere with the day-to-day functioning of the other Courts by directing that only certain cases should be decided out of turn within a time frame.'[34]

Administrative Duties of the High Courts

The HCs, in conjunction with the judges of the district courts, holistically administer the district judiciary. The HCs have duties, *inter alia*, to evaluate the performance of district judges and judicial officers; make rules for premature retirement; monitor and manage case load and pendency; determine the appropriate judge strength and fill in vacancies; evaluate budgetary proposals, and oversee and develop court infrastructure, amongst others. Additionally, HCs are tasked with allied functions such as the robust provision of legal aid services in each district, juvenile justice administration and alternative dispute resolution (ADR) mechanisms, amongst others.

This presents a complex, interwoven administrative landscape on the ground, where judges both of the HCs and the district courts are not just engaged in the task of judging, but also in sustaining the institution of the judiciary itself and safeguarding its independence and efficacy by actually carrying out the groundwork for the same. The various administrative roles and challenges of the district judiciary are addressed in greater detail below.

Recruitments for the District Judiciary

The First Law Commission expressed concern at the judicial system's inability to recruit competent and capable personnel and also highlighted the delay

---

32 The right to a speedy trial has been declared as a fundamental right by the SCI in *AR Antulay v. RS Nayak* [1991] Supp (3) SCR 325. See also *Hussain v. Union of India* [2017] 2 SCR 626.

33 *Jasbir Singh v. State of Punjab* 2006 (8) SCC 294.

34 *High Court Bar Association, Allahabad v. State of Uttar Pradesh* 2024 INSC 150.

in recruitment of judges of the district courts.[35] Acknowledging this, the SCI directed that certain allowances should be mandatorily provided to judges at all levels.[36] The SCI further restructured the judicial cadre through recruitments by (a) promotion from amongst civil judges on the basis of merit-cum-seniority through a suitability test; (b) promotion through a competitive examination; and (c) direct recruitments from eligible legal practitioners on the basis of a written test and *viva voce* conducted by the HCs.[37] As on date, the cadre of district judges is recruited by promotion to the extent of sixty-five per cent quota (based on seniority); ten per cent based on merit in performance in a departmental test and twenty-five per cent from amongst legal practitioners.

The cadre of civil judges is drawn entirely from an open recruitment process consisting of a written test and interview process, managed by the HCs. The SCI has tasked the HCs with ensuring that vacancies in the judicial cadre are filled in a timely manner, because any delay therein impacts the administration of justice and limits access to justice.[38]

Performance Evaluation

The HC is empowered to frame applicable rules for promoting officers, determine seniority, prescribe norms of judicial conduct, determine infractions and impose penalties. In the course of these functions, the HC can also recommend the premature retirement of any judicial officer found to be inefficient, after a certain number of years.

The HCs use the system of 'annual confidential reports' (ACRs) to evaluate the officer's work and potential as the basis for deciding future career

---

35 Law Commission of India, 'Fourteenth Report on the Reform of Judicial Administration' (1958) <https://patnahighcourt.gov.in/bja/PDF/UPLOADED/BJA/MISC/263.PDF> accessed 21 February 2025.

36 *All India Judges Association v. Union of India* [1991] Supp (2) SCR 206. These allowances and perks included access to library and allowance to purchase law journals; a residence; a residential office; transportation to and from the court; allowance to the district judge who was tasked to inspect courts within their jurisdiction on a monthly basis, etc. The SCI also recommended the setting up of a judicial pay commission.

37 *All India Judges Association v. Union of India* (2002) (n 10).

38 *Malik Mazhar Sultan (1) v. Uttar Pradesh Public Service Commission* [2006] 3 SCR 689.

advancement.[39] The ACR-recording process for members of the district judiciary allows for wide discretion to be exercised. This discretion is limited only in some cases, with certain HCs choosing to adopt a marking-based system.

The ACR-recording processes impact the working of judges. Wrong assessments, for example, may impact promotions and result in the denial of advancement to deserving officers, and instead reward undeserving persons; delayed ACRs also negatively impact the morale of judges. This, in turn, results in disillusionment amongst the talented. Inspection Judges Committees, besides interacting with officers in short interviews, should additionally visit the courts to see their actual functioning. A fair, timely, and objective assessment of the officer is needed. Every judicial officer has a right to be informed of every entry in the ACR within a reasonable period, whether it is a 'poor, fair, average, good or very good' entry.[40] It has been recognized that inspecting judges (of the HCs) must adopt an element of objectivity while assessing the work and conduct of the judicial officers (who have to work under difficult and trying circumstances) and exercise caution before acting on ill-conceived or motivated complaints, as it seriously jeopardizes the efficient working of the district courts.[41]

Another issue that adversely impacts the functioning and efficiency of the district judiciary is the assignment of non-judicial work to judges and judicial officers, over and above the administrative duties assigned to them. Judicial officers are often sent on deputation to tribunals, quasi-judicial bodies, commissions and other government offices. This poses a difficulty in their holistic evaluation and adversely impacts career progression, as the ACRs only take into account the judicial work that was last carried out. Many judges are also assigned concurrent charge of other courts, over and above their regular duties. There is a need for a mechanism to account for non-judicial work/additional charge carried out. Weightage may be assigned for administrative/non-judicial work, as well as concurrent charge as a component of the ACR. These aspects have rightly been highlighted in a recent report of the National

---

[39] In *High Court of Punjab and Haryana v. Ishwar Chand Jain* (1999) 4 SCC 579, the SCI described the importance of this function.

[40] *Sujata Kohli v. Registrar General, High Court of Delhi* (2020) 14 SCC 58.

[41] *High Court of Judicature at Allahabad Through Registrar v. Sarnam Singh* (2000) 2 SCC 339 and *Registrar, High Court of Madras v. R Rajiah* (1988) 3 SCC 211.

Court Management Systems (NCMS) Committee[42] and will require close monitoring and implementation.[43]

Discipline, Misconduct and Penalties

An important dimension of 'control and supervision' of judicial officers and district judges extends to ensuring that they adhere to prescribed codes of conduct and are beyond reproach.[44] Consequently, any complaints received are inquired into, initially by a vigilance department (of each HC). These reports are then considered by a committee of HC judges. A HC judge, by way of a Full Court meeting, is nominated to conduct the inquiry against the judicial officers after charges are formally drawn and the reply to such charges is received. Upon considering the comments and defence of the officer and application of the mind to the findings recorded in the inquiry,[45] the appropriate penalty is imposed through a Full Court resolution, which is then given effect to by the Governor. The task of inquiring into complaints and charges of misconduct, including corrupt practices is to be seriously undertaken, as it has a direct bearing on the faith of the litigants in the judiciary;[46] at the same time, it has been emphasized that the judgments/orders of judges, *per se*, cannot be the premise of charges, based on complaints by disgruntled litigants or mischievous elements.[47]

---

42 The need for a national-level court management systems planning body, set up pursuant to directions of the SCI, was recorded in *Imtiyaz Ahmad v. State of Uttar Pradesh* 2012 (1) SCR 779. The NCMS was set up under the overall control of the CJI, by an office order, dated 2 May 2012 to 'enhance timely justice'.

43 See Sub-Committee of the NCMS, Supreme Court of India, 'Baseline Report on Human Resource Development Strategy in the District Judiciary' (2024) 9 <https://cdnbbsr.s3waas.gov.in/s3ec0490f1f4972d133619a60c30f3559e/uploads/2024/11/2024111432.pdf> accessed 21 February 2025.

44 The SCI, in *Baradakanta Misra v. High Court of Orissa* (1976) 3 SCC 327, underlined long ago that 'control is vested in the High Court to effectuate the purpose of securing independence of the subordinate judiciary and unless it included disciplinary control as well, the very object would be frustrated. The word "control" is accompanied by the word "vest" which shows that the High Court is made the sole custodian of the control over the judiciary.'

45 The SCI characterized the nature of application of mind succinctly in *The Registrar General, High Court of Karnataka v. M Narasimha Prasad* 2023 INSC 342: '(i) whether the charges stood proved; (ii) whether the findings of the inquiry officer are reasonable and probable and not perverse; (iii) whether the Rules of procedure and the principles of natural justice have been followed'. The HC is enjoined to ensure that penalty is not 'disproportionate, especially in the light of the gravity of the misconduct, his past record of service and any other extenuating circumstances.'

46 *High Court of Judicature through its Registrar v. Udai Singh* (1997) 5 SCC 129.

47 See *Ramesh Chander Singh v. High Court of Allahabad* 2007 (4) SCC 247 [12]: 'This Court on several occasions has disapproved the practice of initiation of disciplinary proceedings against officers of the subordinate judiciary merely because the judgments/orders passed by them are wrong.'; See also, *Abhay Jain v. The High Court of Judicature for Rajasthan* (2022) 13 SCC 1.

Premature Retirement

The HC is tasked with the responsibility of objectively determining whether, having regard to the overall work and performance, a judicial officer is fit to be continued in service. The criteria which the HC applies in such cases is a review of the entire record, of service and performance of the individual, complaints received, the conduct of the officer, etc. The Court is to determine whether, in public interest, the officer's service deserves to be discontinued.[48] This task is assigned typically to a committee of three senior judges who scan the record and submit their report to the full court, which then deliberates and decides on the further course of action. The SCI has ruled that such orders of premature or compulsory retirement are not punitive[49] or stigmatic;[50] they are to be based on a fair appraisal of the materials on the record and must not be arbitrary.[51] Further, a premature retirement order is not a termination (based on any misconduct). Therefore, the officer is entitled to all terminal and consequential benefits, such as pension, gratuity, etc. Orders of compulsory or premature retirement are subject to judicial review.[52]

Addressing Pendency and Devising Case Management Strategies

Over the years, the number of cases instituted by litigants has steadily increased, with a consequent increase in pendency being carried forward each year. As on 30 June 2023, 44,047,503 cases were pending before the district judiciary, of which 75.59 per cent were criminal cases.[53] Of this total pendency, 4,178,581, that is, 9.48 per cent of the cases have been pending for over ten years, with several states recording a greater percentage of pending cases over ten years old.[54]

---

48 *State of Uttar Pradesh v. Batuk Deo Pati Tripathi* 1978 (3) SCR 131.

49 *Baikuntha Nath Das v. Chief Medical Officer* 1992 (1) SCR 836.

50 *RK Mahajan v. Chief Justice of HP* 1995 Supp (3) SCC 655; *Sujata Kohli* (n 40).

51 *Madan Mohan Chaudhary v. State of Bihar* 1999 3 SCC 396.

52 *Swami Saran Saksena v. State of Uttar Pradesh* 1980 (1) SCC 12.

53 10,750,921 civil cases, and 33,296,582 criminal cases. Data from the Supreme Court of India 'Annual Report 2022–23' (n 12). For a comparative perspective as to case disposal figures, see NCMS, 'Baseline Report on Human Resource Development Strategy' (2016) <https://cdnbbsr.s3waas.gov.in/s3ec0490f1f4972d133619a60c30f3559e/uploads/2024/01/2024011748.pdf> accessed 10 October 2024.

54 ibid.

The reasons for the staggering pendency are multifarious; yet the discussion of pendency and arrears, for decades, has centred around engagement on the 'capacity' crisis in India's judicial ecosystem or the 'supply-side' factors. The efficiency of the judiciary has traditionally been measured as a function of the number of cases instituted, disposed and carried over as pendency in a year.[55] The oft-cited conclusion in scholarship is that the low rate of case disposal is directly caused by the low judge-population ratio, judicial vacancies and resulting heavy caseload on a daily basis,[56] the corollary being that if the judge-population ratio improves, pendency will reduce.[57]

As far back as in 1958, the Law Commission noted that final adjudication of a dispute necessarily implies that some time must lapse from the date of institution of a suit. The Report rightly noted that the time so taken would depend on several factors, such as the nature of the suit, the number of parties and witnesses, the complexity of the case, etc. The Report further highlighted that merely calculating average figures for case disposal timelines and then determining what constitutes arrears on that basis, is a misleading standard. If comparatively lighter suits are disposed of and heavier suits are allowed to remain pending, the figures of average duration may be relatively low, which is not a realistic representation of the time that the judicial system fairly needs.[58] Subsequent recommendations and efforts to reduce case pendency have focused on the *ad hoc* imposition of an ideal time frame within which cases must be disposed of.[59] Such *ad hoc* impositions, while being idealistic,

---

55 Aashita Dawer, 'Analysing Judicial Efficiency of Indian Courts' (Centre for Social and Economic Progress, 2022) <https://csep.org/wp-content/uploads/2022/06/Analysing-Judicial-Efficiency-of-Indian-Courts-_F-1-1.pdf> accessed 21 February 2025; Notably, this study (unlike earlier literature) uses pendency data from Supreme Court of India, Annual Reports (2015–2019), much like the primary data used in this essay.

56 ibid. See also, Law Commission of India, 'One Hundred and Twentieth Report on Manpower Planning in Judiciary' (1987) <https://cdnbbsr.s3waas.gov.in/s3ca0daec69b5adc880fb464895726dbdf/uploads/2022/08/2022080852.pdf> accessed 21 February 2025; and Law Commission of India, 'One Hundred and Twenty-Seventh Report on Resource Allocation for Infra-structural Services in Judicial Administration' (1988) <https://cdnbbsr.s3waas.gov.in/s3ca0daec69b5adc880fb464895726dbdf/uploads/2022/08/ 2022080875-1.pdf> accessed 21 February 2025; See also NCMS, 'Baseline Report on Human Resource Development Strategy' (n 53)

57 Dawer (n 55). This economic study of judicial efficiency used factors such as judge-population ratio, socio-economic factors (state domestic product per capita) and substantive and procedural law (complexity of criminal and civil cases), as determinants of legal case pendency rates.

58 Law Commission of India, 'Fourteenth Report' (n 35) 130–136 [4], [8]-[9].

59 See Law Commission of India, 'Report No. 253, Commercial Division and Commercial Appellate Division of High Courts and Commercial Courts Bill, 2015' (2015), 21 [2.5.4] <https://cdnbbsr.s3waas.gov.in/s3ca0daec69b5adc880fb464895726dbdf/uploads/2022/08/2022081674.pdf> accessed 21 February 2025.

do not scientifically help reduce the build-up of arrears, and can often set unachievable targets.

Some inroads to address the issue of case pendency in a more empirically informed and scientific manner have only recently been made. The recent NCMS Committee Report on the issue of arrears takes into account localized statistics for each case type, in each HC, to devise a template for realistic timelines that may be targeted.[60] Such an empirical approach accounts for inherent limitations in the judicial system, such as infrastructural constraints, or cases not being ready for hearing on account of procedural defects. If meaningfully implemented at the district level with greater granularity of considerations, the issue of case pendency may be addressed in an incremental manner going forward.[61]

Determining Judge Strength and Filling Vacancies

Analysis of data on judge strength over the last three years reveals that the average vacancy rate in district courts (as reported by the HCs under whose superintendence they function) has consistently been a little over twenty per cent.[62] The persistent rate of judicial vacancies, particularly at the district courts, has often been cited as one of the primary reasons for case pendency and mounting arrears. This linkage has been questioned through some recent empirical studies.[63] A quantitative study[64] of a dataset of more than 1,700 Indian district courts between 2010 and 2018 found that the performance of these courts was linked not just to the working strength of the courts, but also more qualitatively to the practices of court administration adopted. The study revealed that focusing on the nature of cases filed, case categorization, the

[60] Sub-committee of the NCMS, SCI, 'Defining Arrears: 2024 Report of the NCMS Sub-Committee on Defining Arrears' (2024) <https://cdnbbsr.s3waas.gov.in/s3ec0490f1f4972d133619a60c30f3559e/uploads/2024/11/2024111276.pdf> accessed 14 November 2024.

[61] ibid.

[62] Calculated based on primary data from SCI, 'Annual Report 2020–21' (2021), SCI, 'Annual Report 2021–22' (2022), SCI, 'Annual Report 2022–23' (vol 2 2023).

[63] See, Varsha Aithala, Anushka Sachan, Srijoni Sen, Himanshu Payal and Chiranjib Bhattacharya, 'Decision Time: Illuminating Performance in India's District Courts' *Data & Policy* 6 (2024) e32 <https://doi.org/10.1017/dap.2024.24> accessed 5 October 2024.

[64] ibid. This study used a specific quantitative measure for calculating court performance – the median number of days it takes a district court to decide a case, with independent variables such as age categorization, age of case, case management and judicial strength (working strength, term and workload).

procedural stages and improving the quality of 'judicial hours' (i.e., increasing the time available to judicial officers for judicial work by necessarily reducing non-judicial and administrative responsibilities)[65] will better serve strategies mitigating case pendency and have a stronger impact on efficiency, rather than centering reforms on the number of judges alone.[66]

Court Infrastructure

Infrastructure is a key determinant of judicial efficiency. In *All India Judges Association v. Union of India*,[67] the SCI observed that it was 'imperative upon the State to provide the judicial wing the requisite infrastructure commensurate with the constitutional obligation of the judiciary.'[68]

District courts are the most accessible and most widely used recourse for litigants at the grassroot level in India. However, severe infrastructural limitations are pervasive, both in terms of quantity of courtrooms available, as well as quality of court facilities. In the Shetty Commission Report, 1999, it was observed that there have even been incidents of falling ceiling plasters, narrowly missing the head of the judge.[69]

A Report of October 2023 noted that there were several challenges, such as insufficient furniture in court complexes, affecting the functionality of court staff.[70] Of the judicial officers surveyed, 44.5 per cent reported that they used their own means of transport to fulfil official responsibilities; forty-one per cent of court staff lacked access to a computer facility with a functional printer; facilities such as an extra monitor, UPS backup, LAN ports/access to stable internet facilities were also not consistently and uniformly available across the district courts.[71] Other issues included the

---

65 See also NCMS, 'Baseline Report on Human Resource Development Strategy' (2016) (n 53).

66 Aithala, Sachan, Sen, Payal, Bhattacharya, 'Decision Time: Illuminating Performance in India's District Courts' (n 63) 15.

67 (2018) 17 SCC 555.

68 ibid [3].

69 Shetty Commission Report, 'Pay Structure of the Judicial Officers of the Subordinate Judiciary' (1999).

70 Jeet Singh Mann, *Empirical Study to Evaluate the Delivery of Justice Through Improved Infrastructure* (Scheme of Action Research and Studies on Judicial Reforms Department of Justice, Ministry of Law and Justice, October 2023) 169–174, <https://www.researchgate.net/publication/382563619_Empirical_study_to_evaluate_the_delivery_of_Justice_through_Improved_Infrastructure> accessed 21 February 2025.

71 ibid.

lack of electronic display facilities for cause lists and other court information, and lack of e-filing facilities. Of the judicial officers surveyed, eighty per cent lacked access to a computerized court library; and there was a lack of video conferencing facilities.[72]

A report by the NCMS sub-committee's *NCMS Baseline Report on Court Development Planning System (Infrastructure and Budgeting)*, identified standard requirements for a court complex, both at the HCs as well as the district courts. These included minimum size requirements, physical accessibility standards and upgradation of IT infrastructure.[73] The 2023 *State of the Judiciary* report[74] highlighted a cumulative shortage of 4,250 courtrooms at the level of the district judiciary across the country.[75] In terms of residential accommodation, there was a shortage of 6,021 units across the country for district judges.[76] These numbers, when compared with the total sanctioned strength of judges at the district judiciary (25,188 as of March 2023), present a sobering figure.

The 2023 *State of the Judiciary* Report further notes some concerning statistics as to infrastructural facilities. In terms of inclusive and accessible infrastructure, only 13.1 per cent of district court complexes have a childcare room or facility. Only as many as fifty per cent of district-court complexes have ramps for persons with disabilities (PwDs). Other infrastructural support such as tactile paving and wheelchairs are available in less than thirty per cent of the court complexes.[77]

In respect of IT facilities, the NCMS Sub-Committee's Report on court infrastructure and budgeting delineates specific requirements for digitization of decided cases, indexation for easy retrieval, authentication of digitized records, weeding out of paper records and processes for e-filing, e-service and

---

72 ibid 175–180.

73 Sub-Committee of NCMS, SCI 'Court Development Planning System: Infrastructure and Budgeting' (2012) <https://cdnbbsr.s3waas.gov.in/s3ec0490f1f4972d133619a60c30f3559e/uploads/2024/01/2024011747.pdf> accessed 18 February 2025.

74 Centre for Research & Planning, SCI, 'State of the Judiciary: A Report on Infrastructure, Budgeting, Human Resources and ICT (November 2023) <https://cdnbbsr.s3waas.gov.in/s3ec0490f1f4972d133619a60c30f3559e/documents/misc/state_of_the_judiciary.pdf> accessed 21 February 2025.

75 ibid 192–193.

76 ibid 194–195.

77 ibid.

e-hearing.[78] The transition from paper files to digital files, and the move from traditional courts to e-courts is a necessity in the long term.[79] Digitization of records and establishment of e-courts will enhance productivity and efficiency, particularly in the context of severe space constraints and the enormity of case pendency at the district courts. A concerted effort is needed in respect of improving infrastructure facilities, closely tied in with reforms in budgeting and financial allocation for the district judiciary.

Budgeting and Financial Allocation

Budgets for the judiciary in India have been based on past and recurring expenses and have not involved a scientific planning process with short-term and long-term goals for improvements in manpower and infrastructure. The National Commission to Review the Working of the Constitution, in 2001, noted that '[i]n the past 50 years, there has been no proper allocation of funds commensurate with the increase in population, legal awareness, increase in legislation.'[80] This observation may now also be supplemented with the enormous increase in litigation across the states. The report further noted, 'The result is that there is, in terms of international Covenants and resolutions...a clear violation of the basic structure of the Constitution... '.[81]

Budgets for the judiciary have been confined primarily to establishment costs, covering salaries, allowances and minimum operational costs of the judiciary, and do not provide for long-term capacity-building. In 1977, Entry 11-A was introduced in the Concurrent List of 7th Schedule of the Constitution of India by the 42nd Amendment Act of 1976. By this amendment, the subject 'Administration of Justice: Constitution and organisation of all courts, except Supreme Court and High Courts' was brought under the concurrent purview of the union and the states, that is, both the union and the states are

[78] See Sub-Committee of NCMS, 'Court Development Planning System' (2012) (n 73).

[79] Paperless courts have been set up and are successfully operational in several states including Delhi, Uttarakhand, Punjab and Haryana, and Rajasthan. The state of Odisha recently became the first state to have paperless courts in the districts; See '100 Paperless Courts in Districts in 3 Months: Chief Justice of Orissa High Court' (*The New Indian Express*, 9 May 2023); See e-Committee, SCI 'Paperless Courts' <https://ecommitteesci.gov.in/project/paperless-courts/> accessed 21 February 2025.

[80] National Commission to Review the Working of the Constitution, 'A Consultation Paper on Financial Autonomy of the Indian Judiciary' (2001) <http://lawmin.nic.in/ncrwc/finalreport/v2b2 1.htm> accessed 10 October 2024.

[81] ibid.

empowered to legislate and govern this field. However, it was reported that states were still lacking in their contribution to court budgets.[82]

In the Union Budget 2023–2024, the allocation for the Ministry of Law and Justice was Rs 4,752 crore – approximately only 0.1 per cent of the total budget estimate.[83] Out of this estimate, Rs 1,061 crore was allotted for infrastructure facilities for the judiciary.[84] In *All India Judges Association v. Union of India*,[85] the SCI observed that strengthening of court infrastructure requires immediate attention in the form of planning, enhanced budgeting and structured implementation or execution of plans. The Court further took note of the fact that states had been allocating a mere one per cent of their total budget to the judiciary.[86]

The Centrally Sponsored Scheme (CSS) for Development of Infrastructure Facilities for the Judiciary mandates financial assistance by the Centre to the states and the union territories for the construction of court buildings, residential accommodations for judicial officers, toilet complexes and digital computer rooms in district courts.[87] As per the CSS Guidelines, allocation of funds to states/UTs by the Centre is restricted to the budgetary provision available under the Scheme during the financial year.[88] This budgetary provision is contingent on the actual working strength.[89] Such a mechanism fails to account for long-term planning and augmentation of judicial facilities, and results in practical difficulties, as states may only seek disbursal of additional funds *after* increasing the working strength, without the infrastructure or facilities for additional judges first being set up.[90] Budget allotment should

---

[82] See NCMS, SCI, 'Policy & Action Plan' (September 2012) <https://cdnbbsr.s3waas.gov.in/s3ec0490f1f4972d133619a60c30f3559e/uploads/2024/01/2024011772-1.pdf> accessed 21 February 2025.

[83] Budget Division, Ministry of Finance, 'Expenditure Budget 2023–2024' (2023) <https://www.indiabudget.gov.in/budget2023-24/doc/eb/allsbe.pdf> accessed 18 February 2025.

[84] ibid.

[85] *All India Judges Association* 2018 (n 67).

[86] ibid.

[87] Ministry of Law and Justice, Government of India, 'Revised Guidelines for Implementation of the Centrally Sponsored Scheme' (19 August 2021) <https://bhuvan-nyayavikas.nrsc.gov.in/documents%2FimpDocs%2F10_Revised--CSS-Guidelines-dated-19-08-2021.PDF> accessed 22 April 2025; See also, 'Report of the Arrears Committee 1899-1990' (1990) <https://dakshindia.org/wp-content/uploads/2016/08/Malimath-89-90.pdf> accessed 11 October 2024.

[88] Ministry of Law and Justice, 'Revised Guidelines for Implementation of the CSS' (n 87) [5].

[89] Centre for Research & Planning, 'State of the Judiciary: A Report on Infrastructure, Budgeting, Human Resources and ICT' (n 74) 49.

[90] ibid.

correspond to the sanctioned strength of judges, so that States may submit their demands for funds prior to the recruitment of new judicial officers.[91]

The success of budgets depends on linking financial outlays to time-bound outputs and outcomes through performance indicators, rather than estimate financial requirements based on past trends alone. Courts should prepare an annual budget proposal with holistic information, including the number of expected incoming cases for a year by case type, projected increase in litigation on account of the enactment of new laws or the introduction of amendments to existing laws, the available material resources, number of pending cases, etc. It is important to acknowledge that this is an intensive process that demands significant time on the part of judges and judicial officers, both at the HCs and the district courts and resources for onboarding of external members with financial expertise.

Judicial Training and Sensitization

The Law Commission of India's 117th Report highlighted the need for comprehensive judicial education, including both pre-service and in-service training for judges.[92] The First National Judicial Pay Commission (1996) identified several goals for judicial education, which include building self-confidence and a strong judicial work culture; instilling ethics and constitutional values; enhancing judicial performance and administration; updating legal knowledge and adapting to evolving demands; developing soft skills, analytical abilities, and management skills; and promoting gender sensitivity, etc.

The SCI emphasized the importance of in-service training, leading to the establishment of the National Judicial Academy (NJA) in Bhopal, Madhya Pradesh and state judicial academies (SJAs) in each state.[93] The NJA brings together judges from across the country to provide them a forum to jointly identify the major obstacles facing the administration of justice and develop appropriate solutions. The SJAs are established by each state. They are headed

[91] ibid 49.

[92] Law Commission of India, 'One Hundred and Seventeenth Report on Training of Judicial Officers' (1986) <https://cdnbbsr.s3waas.gov.in/s3ca0daec69b5adc880fb464895726dbdf/uploads/2022/08/2022080883-2.pdf> accessed 11 October 2024.

[93] The impetus for this initiative, in practical terms came from a resolution of the CJs' Conference, held on 18–19 September 1992.

by the CJ of the concerned HC, alongside monitoring by a committee of three to five HC judges. The faculty is drawn from sitting and retired HC and district court judges, academics and legal practitioners. State judicial academies typically conduct training courses, which include the foundation training for newly recruited civil judges, which has the longest duration (twelve months); likewise, judges who are promoted to the cadre of district judges also undergo mandatory training.

Despite the immense value of judicial training and education, apart from the state-specific judicial service rules that require judicial officers to undergo training, there are no rules/guidelines governing the administration and functioning of judicial academies. SJAs presently do not have permanent faculty, and the primary burden of conducting and coordinating training sessions and workshops falls upon judges and judicial officers. This means that training is conducted in an *ad hoc* manner, and there are fewer opportunities for faculty to collaborate and devise well thought-out training materials.[94] Writing workshops, which would be immensely beneficial for district judges and judicial officers, are few and far between.

With the rise of digital courts, the use of innovative educational tools and an online learning platform can also help make training sessions more comprehensive and frequent and address specific training needs. Specialized training for judicial officers appointed in special courts is also required.[95] These needs all require the involvement of IT personnel, academically trained faculty and technical members with specialized knowledge. Judges alone would be unable to meet all training and educational needs, with limited time on their hands and limited expertise in pedagogical methods.

Additional Duties of Judges

In addition to the core administrative functions elaborated above, HC judges, district-court judges and judicial officers are also saddled with additional responsibilities by way of statutory creation and other *ad hoc* mechanisms. These roles, although important for the judicial system, put a further burden on judges and impact the time available to them for judicial work.

---

[94] NCMS, 'Baseline Report on Human Resource Development Strategy in the District Judiciary' (2024) (n 43) 37.

[95] ibid 43.

Establishing of Special Courts

Special courts are predominantly a statutory creation, which require diversion of judicial capacity for specialized case categories and/or adherence to specified timelines. They are governed by the Special Courts Act of 1979, in conjunction with the legislation by which the special jurisdiction is created. These courts have limited jurisdiction, often relating to a specific enactment; for instance, family matters,[96] atrocities against SCs and STs,[97] narcotics,[98] corruption,[99] commercial suits,[100] etc. The SCI, by way of its directions has also played a role in the establishment or discontinuation[101] of special courts on numerous occasions; for instance, a series of directions were issued for the setting up of special courts in various states to expedite trials dealing with criminal cases in which members of Parliament (MPs) or legislative assemblies (MLAs) are involved.[102]

The Fourteenth Finance Commission recommended setting up of 1,800 Fast Track Courts (FTCs) between 2015 and 2020, to deal with several case categories including heinous crimes, civil cases relating to women, children and senior citizens, persons with HIV/AIDs, etc.[103] The management of these courts falls under the domain of the state governments, in consultation with the respective HCs. As on October 2024, 846 FTCs are functioning across the states.[104] Another category of courts, namely Fast Track Special Courts

---

[96] Family Courts Act 1984, s 3.

[97] Scheduled Castes and the Scheduled Tribes (Prevention of Atrocities) Act 1989, s 14.

[98] Narcotic Drugs and Psychotropic Substances Act, 1985, s 36.

[99] The Prevention of Corruption Act 1988, ch II.

[100] The Commercial Courts Act, 2015.

[101] In *Brij Mohan Lal v. Union of India* (2012) 6 SCC 502, the SCI had *inter alia* directed the states that they shall not take a decision to continue FTCs on an *ad hoc* and temporary basis; rather they would need to decide either to bring the FTC Scheme to an end or to continue the same as a permanent feature in the state. Reportedly, a number of states thereafter, opted to discontinue the scheme; See, Government of India, Ministry of Law and Justice (*Lok Sabha Unstarred Question No. 1476*, 27 November 2019) <https://sansad.in/getFile/loksabhaquestions/annex/172/AU1476.pdf?source=pqals> accessed 11 October 2024.

[102] *Ashwini Kumar Upadhyay v. Union of India* (2024) 1 SCC 185; in another instance, the SCI in *In Re: Expeditious Trial of Cases under Section 138 of N.I. Act 1881* 2022 SCC OnLine SC 649, directed pilot special courts to be set up in five states with the highest pendency of cheque-bounce cases under Section 138 of the Negotiable Instrument Act 1881.

[103] Fourteenth Finance Commission, 'Report of the Fourteenth Finance Commission' (2014) <https://fincomindia.nic.in/asset/doc/commission-reports/14th-FC/14thFCReport.pdf> accessed 11 October 2024.

[104] 'Fast Track Courts Dashboard' (*Department of Justice*, October 2024) <https://dashboard.doj.gov.in/

(FTSCs), have also been established, for instance for the speedy disposition of cases under the Protection of Children from Sexual Offences (POCSO) Act, 2012 (pursuant to a direction by the SCI to implement the Criminal Law Amendment Act, 2018). As of May 2024, 755 FTSCs including 410 exclusive POCSO (ePOCSO) Courts were reported to be functional across India, and more than 2,53,000 pending cases have been disposed of.[105] Notably, each of these FTSCs require one judicial officer and seven staff members, diverted from the existing judicial strength and working capacity of the courts.[106]

These specialized courts have largely failed in their objective of quicker disposal of cases, as illustrated by the statistics of case disposal by POCSO courts and commercial courts, respectively. According to recent studies, over 2.43 lakh POCSO cases were pending trial in FTSCs as of 31 January 2023.[107] Between 2019 and 2023, the pendency of POCSO cases increased exponentially by eighty-three per cent.[108] As per the Administrative Guidelines for Implementation of the FTSC Scheme, 2019, each FTSC for POCSO cases was expected to dispose of at least 165 cases in a year; the data, however, showed that only fifty-seven cases were being disposed by each FTSC in a year.[109] Studies in Andhra Pradesh, Assam, Delhi, Maharashtra and Karnataka further indicate that none of the Special Courts currently established exclusively try POCSO cases. The courts therefore have several structural defects, not being set up in a child-friendly manner to prevent the exposure of children to accused persons, contrary to Section 32 of the POCSO Act.[110]

---

fast-track-court/ftc_functional> accessed 11 October 2024.

[105] 'FTSCs at a Glance' (*Department of Justice*, 1 July 2024) <https://doj.gov.in/fast-track-special-court-ftscs/> accessed 11 October 2024. See also, 'Fast Track Courts Dashboard' (n 104).

[106] Ministry of Law and Justice, 'Administrative Guidelines for Implementation of the Scheme on Fast Track Special Courts (FTSCs) for Expeditious Disposal of Cases of Rape and Protection of Children from Sexual Offences (POCSO)' (2023) <https://cdnbbsr.s3waas.gov.in/s35d6646aad9bcc0be55b2c82f69750387/uploads/2024/01/20240121490725560.pdf> accessed 11 October 2024.

[107] India Child Protection Fund, 'Justice Awaits: An Analysis of the Efficacy of Justice Delivery Mechanisms in Cases of Child Sexual Abuse in India' (2023) <https://counterviewfiles.wordpress.com/wp-content/uploads/2023/12/justice-awaits.pdf> accessed 7 November 2024.

[108] ibid 18.

[109] ibid 20.

[110] Sonia Pereira and Swagata Raha, 'Structural Compliance of Special Courts with the POCSO Act', Centre for Child and the Law, NLSIU (eds), 'Implementation of the POCSO Act, 2012 by Special Courts: Challenges and Issues (February 2018) <https://ccl.nls.ac.in/wp-content/uploads/2021/10/8.-Implementation-of-the-POCSO-Act-2012-by-speical-courts-challenges-and-issues.pdf> accessed 7 November 2024.

Commercial courts were set up under the Commercial Courts Act, 2015, to enhance India's ease of doing business and facilitate quicker, more efficient resolution of commercial disputes. The Commercial Courts Act identifies twenty-two distinct categories of 'commercial disputes.' It further provides strict timelines for filing of pleadings, framing of issues and document production requests. Owing to the introduction of the Act, there has been a substantial increase in the number of cases that the designated judges have to adjudicate upon, often without any corresponding changes to judicial infrastructure and capacity. Adopting an extremely wide definition of 'commercial disputes' has essentially brought all civil disputes of a certain pecuniary value under the ambit of the commercial Benches/commercial courts, exacerbating the case load. The periodic reduction of the pecuniary threshold[111] has also contributed to the tremendous increase in the workload of commercial courts, to subsume more than three quarters of all civil disputes being litigated in the country.[112] Disposal rates across all states in commercial courts have been found to be less than ten per cent.[113]

The reasons for the failure of such specialized courts in addressing case pendency are manifold. The case load for the diverted case types are heavy, and there have been no changes to the legal process to enable FTCs to dispose of the cases quicker than a regular court. The supportive infrastructure to enable quicker disposal of cases is also lacking. In several instances, there is an acute disconnect between statutory timelines for case disposal and the realistic time taken for the legal process to be completed in a meaningful manner. For example, Section 309 of the Code of Criminal Procedure (CrPC)[114] was amended to impose a time limit of two months for the disposal of rape cases, from the date of filing of the chargesheet. In respect of POCSO cases, a one-year timeline is stipulated under the POCSO Act. A recent study, however,

---

[111] Commercial Courts Act 2015, s 2 (1) (i) (amended in 2018) defines 'Specified Value' as 'in relation to a commercial dispute, shall mean the value of the subject-matter in respect of a suit as determined in accordance with Section 12 which shall not be less than three lakh rupees or such higher value, as may be notified by the Central Government.'

[112] See generally, Sudhir Krishnaswamy and Varsha Mahadeva Aithala, 'Commercial Courts in India: Three Puzzles for Legal System Reform' (2020) 11(1) *Journal of the Indian Law Society* 20–47. See also, Vijay Kumar Singh, and Aratrika Deb, 'Resolution of Commercial Disputes in India: A Review of the Commercial Courts Act, 2015' (2022) 8(1) *National Law School Business Law Review* 49–80.

[113] Ameen Jauhar and Vaidehi Mishra, 'Commercial Courts Act, 2015: An Empirical Impact Evaluation' (Vidhi Centre for Legal Policy, 2019) <https://vidhilegalpolicy.in/wp-content/uploads/2019/07/CoC_Digital_10June_noon.pdf> accessed 7 November 2024.

[114] Bharatiya Nagarik Suraksha Sanhita, 2023, s 346.

found that the average time actually taken for disposal was 509.78 days.[115] The study further found that, out of the average time period, the evidence stage alone consumes about 183 days.[116]

Any criminal trial realistically needs time for framing of charges, recording of evidence and pronouncement of the final judgment. Delays of various kinds are often unavoidable. Holistic capacity building, increase in budgets for courts, devising efficient case management mechanisms, reduction in diversion of judges from core judicial functions, timely filling of vacancies, adequate training for judges handling specialized case types and infrastructural developments must all be addressed to ensure quicker case disposal. Such reforms are necessary across the legal system, rather than merely setting up special courts for special case types.

Legal Aid

The Legal Services Authorities Act, 1987 (LSAA) forms the fundamental framework for facilitating legal assistance and establishing various bodies dedicated to this cause. The hierarchy of authorities under this Act include the National Legal Services Authority (NALSA) which is headed by the CJI, with an Executive Chairman (who is invariably the senior-most SCI judge after the CJI), and is responsible for allocation of funds to the other authorities under the Act. Then, there are the State Legal Services Authorities, which are responsible for implementing NALSA's directives at the state level and are managed by the CJ of the HC as Patron-in-Chief, and an Executive Chairman (senior-most HC judge after the CJ). Every district also has a District Legal Services Authority and Taluk Legal Services Committee, which functions at the district and taluk levels respectively, with active involvement of district judges.

At all three levels, the focus is on promoting legal aid camps, providing education about legal rights and facilitating dispute resolution through Lok Adalats (which bind parties as if decided by a decree of the court).[117] The state

---

[115] Apoorva, Aditya Ranjan, Sandeep Bhupatiraju, Shareen Joshi, Daniel L Chen, 'A Decade of POCSO: Developments, Challenges and Insights from Judicial Data' (*Vidhi Centre for Legal Policy*, 17 November 2022) <https://vidhilegalpolicy.in/research/a-decade-of-pocso-developments-challenges-and-insights-from-judicial-data/> accessed 7 November 2024.

[116] ibid.

[117] These have been introduced as effective ADR mechanisms and are constituted to resolve pending

and district committees ensure access to justice by empanelling lawyers, who in turn can provide legal representation to individuals lacking financial means to file or defend cases. The state committees and district committees are manned by district judicial officers who act as administrators and policy implementers.

Alternative Dispute Resolution (ADR) Mechanisms

Section 89 of the Civil Procedure Code was introduced in 2002 to promote alternative methods of dispute resolution.[118] Pursuant to this, a number of mediation centres were set up during the period of 2005–2011 by various HCs, and several HCs also set up district-level mediation centres. These centres are administered by judicial officers, a sizeable number of whom are trained as mediators. As on December 2024, 1221 mediation centres existed across the country, deploying a total of 3271 judicial officers as mediators (along with 6685 lawyers and 575 others also deployed as mediators), disposing of 72,461 cases by way of mediation.[119]

Undeniably, 'court-annexed' mediation initiatives have had an impact on the nature of litigation in India, discernibly in urban cities such as Delhi, Chennai, Bangalore and Mumbai (which have several court-annexed centres).[120] However, there exists no uniform method of audit for ADR centres, no consistent methods and effectiveness of the mediators accredited, and data collection and presentation. The Mediation Act, 2023 (not yet notified) has attempted to fill this gap; yet the institutional framework needed to perform that task has not yet become functional. The impact of the diversion of judicial resources to supervise and administer ADR mechanisms also requires greater study.

---

cases and disputes by encouraging and facilitating amicable settlements. As per section 21 of the Legal Services Authorities Act, 1987, they have the effect of binding the parties as if they were decided through a decree of court.

[118] Inserted by Civil Procedure (Amendment) Act 1999, s 7 (w.e.f. 1 July 2002).

[119] As per data available on the official NALSA website: 'Settlement through Mediation, April 2024 - December 2024', (National Legal Services Authority) <https://nalsa.gov.in/statistics/settlement-through-mediation-report/settlement-through-mediation-report-april-2024-to-december-2024> accessed 22 April 2025.

[120] See, Alok Prasanna Kumar, Ameen Jauhar, Kritika Vohra, Ishana Tripathi, 'Strengthening Mediation in India A Report on Court-Connected Mediations' (*Vidhi Centre for Legal Policy*, December 2016), <https://vidhilegalpolicy.in/wp-content/uploads/2019/05/26122016_StrengtheningMediationinIndia_FinalReport.pdf> accessed 10 October 2024.

Juvenile Justice Committees

The 2013 Conference of Chief Justices[121] mooted the constitution of Juvenile Justice Committees (JJCs) by all HCs. These committees consist of three to five HC judges who convene in periodic intervals of four to six weeks. JJCs have made significant contributions in the area of administration of juvenile justice laws and rights of children. The areas covered include monitoring administrative mechanisms, infrastructure, rehabilitation and reintegration of children in conflict with the law, as well as children in need of care and protection.

The JJCs are envisaged to help navigate the legal process and the criminal justice system. They are expected to regularly assess the status of compliance with judicial and legislative mandates. Specialized training programmes and events are organized to bring about awareness and sensitize important stakeholders; state level consultations are organized, in which all district units send representatives to report on the need for support or share outcomes of past resolutions. These culminate in an annual meeting organized by the national JJC, headed by a judge of the SCI.

Towards a Framework for More Effective Judicial Administration and Management

The preceding two sections indicate in broad terms, the various administrative duties and responsibilities of the HC, in relation to its constitutional role of supervision of the district judiciary. Core administrative functions that are necessary to sustain the judicial system include recruitment of judicial officers and district judges, filling in of vacancies in a timely manner, maintenance of discipline in the judicial cadre, evaluating performance by judges and judicial officers, management of caseload and pendency, infrastructure development, financial planning and budgetary allocation and imparting judicial education and training. Additionally, district judges and judicial officers also devote significant time and energy in the implementation of special social welfare legislations, such as the Juvenile Justice Act (through JJCs), and the LSAA (through state- and district-level legal services authorities). They also set

[121] 'Minutes of the Chief Justices' Conference held on 5–6 April 2013' <https://cdnbbsr.s3waas.gov.in/s3ec0490f1f4972d133619a60c30f3559e/uploads/2024/04/2024042439.pdf> accessed 11 October 2024.

up and administer robust ADR mechanisms. All these responsibilities are intrinsic to judicial administration and are fundamental to preserving the ideals of judicial independence, separation of powers and equality and fairness in justice delivery – all elements of the basic structure of our constitutional scheme.

Judges and judicial officers have the fundamental duty, at an individual level, to do justice in the cases before them, to the parties before them. The work of judging, alongside managing overloaded judicial dockets and providing well-reasoned decisions within reasonable timelines, is a demanding role. Judicial administration, over and above, demands enormous time and resources that judges sometimes are hard pressed for, and lack expertise in. This section elaborates on these challenges and proposes certain recommendations.

Need for Distinct Administrative Cadres

Issues such as case pendency, arrears management, determination of judge strength and filling of vacancies, as well as budgeting and infrastructural development, all require customized solutions. A top-down, one-size fits all approach has, time and again, proved unworkable. Imposing uniform timelines for disposal of cases, or common categorization of cases across the board, does a disservice to the rich district-specific data that can be analysed and harnessed.

The primary challenge to such empirically informed approaches is the lack of uniform, comparable judicial data with sufficient granularity. The National Judicial Digital Grid (NJDG) was launched in 2015 as a facet of the larger e-Committee Project (launched in 2007) by the Ministry of Law and Justice in collaboration with the SCI e-Committee to create a digital repository for judicial data at all levels. The NJDG provides real-time consolidated figures on institution, disposal and pendency across all courts in India.[122] In a bid to promote transparency, this data is accessible to the public, albeit on limited

---

[122] The SCI also launched the 'Integrated Judicial Upgradation and Reforms on Infrastructure and Services', in short 'iJuris', integrated into the NJDG database, which aims to cover online updation and monitoring of statistics of the district judiciary. It is reported that data based on a dynamic questionnaire has been called for from all the HCs and district courts to examine the current state of the infrastructure and human resources of the judiciary on 26 April 2023 and continues to be updated. How this mechanism will integrate with the NJDG database and be accessible to the public, remains yet to be seen; See, Centre for Research & Planning (n 74) 182.

parameters. While NJDG data is extensive, the limited temporal aspect of the data, that is, that it can only be viewed as on the present day and cannot be extracted for a past date or across a uniform time period (by non-institutional stakeholders), limits the usage of this data in analytical models. The NJDG platform also provides data on delay determinants but is wholly dependent on the accuracy with which the designated staff performs this data-entry role. A large proportion of judicial orders are uploaded belatedly due to limited infrastructure, inadequate capacity and challenges faced during digitization of handwritten files.[123] As per the NJDG data on 3 November 2024, a total of 70,013,441 orders had not been uploaded.[124]

The proximate remedy for accurate data collection and analysis would be to institute in each district a cadre of judicial court staff who are trained statisticians and data analysts, to replace the reliance on court staff who are temporarily diverted for this purpose, or even judicial officers who are overburdened. This cadre of specialized staff could work solely on streamlining data collection and categorization, carry out statistical analysis to identify trends and causes for judicial delays, and contribute towards policy recommendations to combat pendency, both at the level of the individual court (in the context of its unique capacities and constraints), and at the macro level, for state-wide or nation-wide implementation. Similarly, distinct cadres may also be set up for IT services which would manage the digital infrastructure in courts, and for other duties that are purely administrative in nature. Such a cadre could be comprised of individuals with judicial understanding or experience, alongside technical training and required skills.[125]

The delegation of such roles to separate cadres would perform three functions: first, ensuring consistent and accurate data collection and analysis, which in turn would lead to empirically sound policy recommendations; second, freeing up judicial time to be spent on core judicial functions; and third, augmenting the capacity of court staff and officials who can take charge of a technical area of administration and work collaboratively with judges and members of

---

[123] Orders may also not be uploaded owing to the nature of the case; for instance, in cases relating to crimes against women, involving a minor or a child in conflict with the law etc., where the identity of the complainant is protected by law.

[124] 'Alerts' (*National Judicial Data Grid*, 3 November 2024) <https://njdg.ecourts.gov.in/njdg_v3/> accessed 3 November 2024.

[125] Similar recommendations for a distinct cadre for 'technology and data analysis' were made in NCMS, 'Baseline Report on Human Resource Development Strategy in the District Judiciary' 2024 (n 43) 82.

the executive and legislative branches (as in the case of budgeting needs, for example), to improve judicial efficiency.

In the Indian context, any court management cadre related suggestion would require careful delineation of responsibilities to the limited extent of judicial management, while still retaining the control and responsibility of the district courts and supervision of the HCs as prescribed in the Constitution.[126]

Instituting stringent mechanisms for case flow management, that is, a system for empirically analysing which cases are to be prioritized for early disposal, will play a large part in addressing pendency. The methodology of case flow management itself also requires greater analysis and consideration. With the rapid digitization of district courts and availability of more granular data, opportunities are ripe to optimize these strategies.

Judicial Impact Assessment

The issues plaguing judicial administration are compounded by the lack of a comprehensive process in place for analysing the impact of new legislations on the judiciary. As far back as in 2005, a report was submitted to the SCI, on the need for judicial impact assessment of new legislations. It was recommended, *inter alia*, that 'the financial memorandum attached to each bill must estimate the budgetary requirement for meeting the expenses of the additional litigation that may arise out of the new bill when it is passed by the legislature. The said budget must mention the number of civil and criminal cases likely to be generated by the new Act, how many courts are necessary, how many judges and staff are necessary and what is the infrastructure necessary . . .'[127] Following this recommendation, the SCI issued directions to the Central

---

[126] The institution of a professional specialized agency was suggested in *L Chandra Kumar v. Union of India* (1997) 3 SCC 261, in the context of administering tribunals and has found mention in various government reports subsequently. For a discussion on this aspect, see, Pratik Datta and Suyash Rai, 'How to Start Resolving the Indian Judiciary's Long Running Backlog' (*Carnegie Endowment for International Peace*, 9 September 2021) <https://carnegieendowment.org/research/2021/09/how-to-start-resolving-the-indian-judiciarys-long-running-case-backlog?lang=en> accessed 10 October 2024; A specialized corporation (the National Judicial Infrastructure Corporation) was proposed in 2021 by the then CJI to modernize the Indian judiciary's infrastructure, but such reform remains to be enacted. See, Dhananjay Mahapatra, 'CJI Plans National Corporation to Modernise Judicial Infrastructure' (*The Times of India*, 5 June 2021).

[127] 'Report of the Task Force on Judicial Impact Assessment' (15 June 2008) <https://wbja.nic.in/wbja_adm/files/Report%20of%20the%20Task%20Fprce%20on%20Judicial%20Impact%20Assessment.pdf> accessed 10 October 2024, 1-2.

Government,[128] and a detailed report was prepared on the question of judicial impact assessment.[129]

The 2005 Report noted that every legislation enacted by the Parliament adds to the burden of state courts, since the subject of '[a]dministration of justice, constitution and organization of all the subordinate courts' is enumerated under the Concurrent List in the Constitution of India. The major brunt of the burden of administering and enforcing new legislations is borne, in most cases, by the district and sessions courts in each state. Pursuant to Article 117 (3), bills are required to be accompanied with a financial memorandum only if they involve expenditure from the Consolidated Fund of India. Similarly, under Article 207 (3), a financial memorandum must accompany bills placed before state legislatures, where funds are to be drawn from the Consolidated Fund of the state. Where any authority or agency is created under the proposed legislation, the expenses for establishment and maintenance are provided from the budget of the sponsoring ministry.

In practice, however, funds for the implementation of laws, irrespective of whether they are central laws, state laws or laws enacted under the Concurrent List, are primarily drawn from the state exchequer. The Task Force on Judicial Impact Assessment, for example, examined a number of financial memoranda attached to central bills presented in the Parliament, which invariably stated that the expenditure on the courts were to be borne by the state governments. The Task Force noted that Section 138 of the Negotiable Instruments Act, 1881 that had been introduced in 1989 resulted in 25 lakh cases being added to the case load of the district courts, which had to saddle the entire burden.[130]

Recently, the SCI considered the issue of burgeoning litigation caused by the enactment of the Maharashtra Slum Areas (Improvement, Clearance, and Redevelopment) Act, 1971. The NJDG data revealed that a total of 1,612 cases under the legislation were pending before the Bombay HC, of which 135 cases were over ten years old. While the Act was a beneficial legislation intended to provide basic housing, the Court noted that the 'propensity and the proclivity of the statute to generate litigation are worrisome.'[131] The Court went on to direct the HC to initiate *suo motu* proceedings for a performance audit of the

[128] *Salem Advocates Bar Association (II) v. Union of India* (2005) 6 SCC 344.

[129] 'Report of the Task Force on Judicial Impact Assessment' (2008) (n 127).

[130] ibid 61.

[131] *Yash Developers v. Harihar Krupa Co-operative Housing Society Limited* (2024) 9 SCC 606 [51].

legislation, with a focus also on the judicial impact vis-à-vis achieving the social justice goals of the beneficial legislation.[132]

Performance audits would also be useful for commercial courts and ADR mechanisms where they are mandated to assess whether they have had the impact of delivering speedy justice, as envisioned. Such exercises are valuable in enhancing access to justice and managing the docket in a sustainable manner. However, they cannot be conducted in an *ad hoc* manner, pursuant to directions issued by the courts in individual cases or for particular legislations.

Streamlined processes involving the requisite officers with knowledge of judicial administration and the needs of the district judiciary, as well as scientific experts, statisticians and members of the executive branch, have not thus far been set up for the purpose of conducting judicial impact assessments as a procedural requisite.

The fundamental challenge, again, is the non-availability of the required data on judicial management and performance at different levels. A second difficulty is the lack of an independent body/dedicated cadre capable of collating and analysing information, identifying variables and drawing up realistic estimates through economic models and statistical interpretation. The need of the hour is to set up a joint mechanism of the judicial and executive branches at the national and state levels, staffed by well-trained, empirical social science research personnel, court administrators and financial experts.

Conclusion

The field of judicial administration is vast and complex. At the same time, it is the most fundamental determinant of judicial independence, fairness and equality in justice delivery, and consequently, ensures adherence to the rule of law. The processes, procedures and methodologies of judicial administration, in that sense, represent the actual working of the Constitution on the ground.

While the functioning of the HCs and the SCI have garnered wide attention, the details of administration of the district courts are under-studied. Uneven workload, vacancies and inadequate case management systems have been found to be causes for inefficiency in the system.[133] Improving data collection methods

132 ibid [65].

133 NCMS, 'Baseline Report on Human Resource Development Strategy' (2016) (n 53).

and accessibility of the said data will play a decisive role in reforming judicial administration at the district level. Policy solutions for case management, capacity building, infrastructure planning, etc. need to be data-driven and localized to impact justice outcomes for the common individual.

A look at recent case disposal figures at the level of the district judiciary is indicative of the sheer extent of the workload that judges are faced with. Between 1 July 2022 and 30 June 2023, a total of 25,514,157 cases were disposed of by the district judiciary across 710 districts.[134] Efforts need to be made to fill judicial vacancies and bolster judge strength, but this alone will not mitigate pendency and arrears. The judiciary's capacity also needs to be strengthened through the creation of distinct cadres for core administrative tasks such as statistical analysis, development and management of IT facilities, developing inclusive and accessible infrastructure and scientifically determining budgets. Such augmentation of judicial capacity will enable long-term planning and allow meaningful policies to be framed for revolutionizing judicial administration.

The burden on the district judicial officer (who is tasked with administrative and executive functions in addition to judicial duties) has to be empirically and holistically understood, so as to develop strategies that optimize 'judicial hours' and minimize leakages of time towards other responsibilities – whether quasi-judicial or administrative. Speaking relatively, the HCs too need to be free of duties keeping judges away from the core task of judging. Now more than ever, in the seventy-fifth year of the Republic and the promulgation of the Constitution, new ideas and proposals grounded in empirical study have to be implemented swiftly across all areas of judicial administration to enhance the independence and efficiency of the judicial system.

[134] There has been an upward trend in disposal rates since the global pandemic; 22,448,718 cases were disposed of in 2021–2022 and 10,696,042 in 2020–2021. Calculated based on primary data from Supreme Court of India, 'Annual Report 2020–21' (2021), Supreme Court of India, 'Annual Report 2021–22' (2022), Supreme Court of India, 'Annual Report 2022–23' (vol 2 2023).

Social Action Litigation

AN INTERVIEW WITH UPENDRA BAXI

This interview was conducted by the Editor over a few sittings. It covers a broad range of issues concerning the Supreme Court of India's (SCI) public interest litigation (PIL) jurisdiction. Professor Baxi has been a close observer of the SCI for over five decades and was also a participant in the early years of its evolution. He is a leading academic whose views have influenced the thinking of several generations of legal scholars, lawyers and judges.

The Editor's remarks and questions are in italics. The footnotes presented in first-person narrative have been provided by Professor Baxi.

Editor: *The notion of class action and representative petitions in the area of law and poverty could perhaps be traced to the Kerala (Legal Aid to the Poor) Rules, 1957.*[1] *The concept of PIL finds mention in the 1971 Report of the Gujarat Legal Aid Committee chaired by Justice PN Bhagwati as a sitting judge of the Gujarat High Court.*[2] *In his capacity as that Committee's chair, he had visited the USA, the UK and certain European countries to observe the legal aid systems then prevalent in those countries.*

We then have the 1973 Report Processual Justice to the People *of the Expert Committee on Legal Aid, chaired by Justice VR Krishna Iyer, which refers to PIL.*[3] *You had the occasion to comment on this Report in a critique published in the pages of* Economic and Political Weekly. *Finally, we have the 1977 Report of the two-member Juridicare Committee comprising Justices Krishna Iyer and Bhagwati*

1 Kerala Legal Aid (to the Scheduled Castes and Scheduled Tribes and to the Poor) Rules 1957.

2 PN Bhagwati, *Report of the Legal Aid Committee: Appointed by the Government of Gujarat Under Government Resolution, Legal Department, No LAC-1070-D Dated 22nd June 1970* (Government Central Press, Government of Gujarat 1971).

3 VR Krishna Iyer (Chairperson), *Report of the Expert Committee on Legal Aid: Processual Justice to the People* (Ministry of Law, Government of India Press, May 1973) <https://nvli.in/report-expert-committee-legal-aid-processual-justice-people> accessed 24 February 2025.

titled Report on National Juridicare: Equal Justice – Social Justice,[4] *which specifically talked of PIL as a tool for legal aid to the poor. It enclosed a draft Legal Services Authorities Bill (which too mentioned PIL as one of the functions of the central authority).*

On the judicial side, the expanded notion of standing began sometime in 1975 (MV Dabholkar[5] authored by Iyer J) *and in 1978* (Sunil Batra[6] and Charles Sobraj cases[7] – again authored by Iyer J). *However, it was not until February 1979 (when the coalition Janta government at the Centre was already shaky) in* Hussainara Khatoon[8] *that Justice Bhagwati appears to have formally launched the PIL jurisdiction. Justice Iyer too dealt with PILs but left the Supreme Court soon thereafter in November 1980.*

There is a point of view that the Supreme Court was 'atoning' for its endorsement of the Emergency in ADM Jabalpur[9] *and* Union of India v. Bhanudas Krishna Gawde[10] *particularly considering that Justice Bhagwati was a part of the majority*[11] *in the* ADM Jabalpur *case. The other point of view is that with a weak coalition at the Centre, the political environment was such that some of these judges found the necessity to exercise judicial power to shore up the image of the judiciary as a 'people's court'.*[12] *What are your thoughts on this?*

---

4 PN Bhagwati and VR Krishna Iyer, *Report on National Juridicare Equal Justice – Social Justice* (Justice Affairs, Department of Legal Affairs, Ministry of Law 1978).

5 *Bar Council of Maharashtra v. MV Dabholkar* (1976) 2 SCC 291 [24]. The Bench comprised of VR Krishna Iyer, Ranjit Singh Sarkaria, AC Gupta and Syed Murtaza Fazal Ali JJ observed: 'We wish to put beyond cavil the new call to the lawyer in the economic order. In the days ahead, legal aid to the poor and the weak, public interest litigation and other rule-of-law responsibilities will demand a whole new range of responses from the Bar or organised social groups with lawyer members. Indeed, the hope of democracy is the dynamism of the new frontiersmen of the law in this developing area and what we have observed against solicitation and alleged profit-making vices are distant from such free service to the community in the jural sector as part of the profession's tryst with the people of India.'

6 *Sunil Batra v. Delhi Administration* (1978) 4 SCC 494 ('Sunil Batra'). The majority opinion was delivered by Chandrachud, Fazal Ali, PN Shinghal and DA Desai JJ (authored by DA Desai J). A separate concurring opinion was delivered by VR Krishna Iyer J which is the longer opinion.

7 *Charles Sobraj v. Supdt. Central Jail Tihar*, New Delhi (1978) 4 SCC 104 (VR Krishna Iyer, DA Desai and Chinnappa Reddy JJ).

8 *Hussainara Khatoon (I) v. Home Secy., State of Bihar* (1980) 1 SCC 81. The majority opinion was authored by PN Bhagwati J (for himself and Koshal J).

9 *ADM Jabalpur v. Shivkant Shukla* (1976) 2 SCC 521.

10 *Union of India v. Bhanudas Krishna Gawde* (1977) 1 SC 834. The majority opinion was delivered by Jaswant Singh and AN Ray JJ with M Hameedullah Beg J delivering a separate concurring opinion.

11 The majority comprised of AN Ray CJ, MH Beg, YV Chandrachud and PN Bhagwati JJ. HR Khanna J gave the dissenting opinion.

12 Anuj Bhuwania, *Courting the People: Public Interest Litigation in Post-Emergency India* (CUP 2017). See Upendra Baxi, 'Farewell to Adjudicatory Leadership?: Some Thoughts on Dr. Anuj Bhuwania's

Prof. Baxi: The Reports that you refer to, do reflect the angst of the Indian legal system and are well worth reading even now. I was however critical of the 1973 Report in a piece that I wrote in the *Economic and Political Weekly.*[13] In my book, *The Indian Supreme Court and Politics* (1980),[14] I have suggested that the constitutionalizing of judicial populism and the rise of new judicial activism (as a collective phenomenon beginning from the late 1970s) emerged as a response to the Court taking a long and hard look at having delivered *ADM Jabalpur v. Shiv Kant Shukla,*[15] a decision which meekly accepted suspension of Articles 14, 19 and 21 fundamental rights but was construed to mean so total as even forbidding habeas corpus on the ground of mistaken identity. In commenting on the *Batra* case in my 1980 book, I had highlighted the intervention of a human rights group, in what was the earliest stages of social action litigation (SAL):

> *Batra* also marks a maturity of judicial concern for conditions of detention. For the first time in its history, the Chief Justice of India (Beg, C. J.) visited with his brethren (Justices Krishna Iyer and Kailasam) the Tihar Jail (on January 23, 1978) to ascertain the actual conditions; and the memorandum prepared by the Chief Justice was used as a basis for reasoning by the Court. If not for the first time, *Batra* also furnished the relatively new 'processual feature' in that the Court permitted the 'Citizens for Democracy', a voluntary group concerned with human rights, to formally intervene in the case.[16]

"Courting The People: Public Interest Litigation in Post-Emergency India": In Memoriam: Justice Prafulchandra Natwarlal Bhagwati' (2017) *NLUD SLJ*, 1-19.

13 The criticism related to the Committee's approach to its task, confusion of thoughts, metaphors and sloganeering, ignorance of limitation of resources while providing recommendations, ignorance of social inequality, failure to define the actual problem, impracticable recommendations and the failure to provide a 'workable scheme'. Upendra Baxi, 'Legal Assistance to the Poor – A Critique of the Expert Committee Report' (5 July 1975) 10 (27) *The Economic and Political Weekly* 1081; the Committee did not issue any public questionnaire or invite evidence from the public, which explained the lack of empirical data upon which affected the suggestions, it ignored practical realities about the legal profession, that there were unworkable recommendations, and that there was no scheme for implementation were some of the issues with the report, S Muralidhar, *Law, Poverty and Legal Aid: Access to Criminal Justice* (LexisNexis Butterworths 2004) 57–59.

14 Upendra Baxi, *The Indian Supreme Court and Politics: The Indian Supreme Court in Its Socio-Political Context* (Eastern Book Co 1980).

15 When *ADM Jabalpur v. Shiv Kant Shukla* was being argued, the entire Bar was scared. When YV Chandrachud J asked the lawyers if they were challenging the Second Emergency and its constitutionality, none of them said yes. No one knew if or when the Emergency was going to be lifted. While his moral heroism is exceptional, from the perspective of legal reasoning, I think Khanna J's opinion in *ADM Jabalpur* is overrated.

16 Baxi, *The Indian Supreme Court and Politics* (n 14) 238.

While it might seem that the entire Court was acting collectively, in fact there was a lot of disagreement and division among the judges. We had the Justice Chandrachud and Justice Bhagwati factions, which had their differences. Soon after the Emergency was revoked, there were also clear tensions between the so-called Janata and Congress-appointed judges.

In any event, the judges were transformed by the experience of the Emergency and were aware of what they failed to do in that period. So essentially, Justice Bhagwati and Justice Chandrachud were atoning. One should not forget that in the summer of 1975, Justice Krishna Iyer was the vacation judge in the Supreme Court, and he ordered a conditional stay of the judgment of the Allahabad High Court invalidating the election of the sitting Prime Minister Indira Gandhi. This meant that she could continue to function as a Prime Minister but not vote in the Parliament.[17] He gratuitously suggested that 'a quick acting legislature' could always amend a draconian law.[18] He was not an advisor to Mrs Gandhi; he was a judge of the Supreme Court. Anyway, in launching PIL, Justice Krishna Iyer was also atoning to some extent. Justice Bhagwati was certainly in a 'never again' mode. And there, the fact of an anti-Emergency coalition government helped. I believe that it is not only litigants who want justice. Judges also want to find and create opportunities to do justice.

Editor: *How much of the evolution of PIL can be attributed to the personal/political philosophies of Justice Iyer and Justice Bhagwati?*

Prof. Baxi: Undoubtedly, individual philosophical worldviews of the judges matter because these often influence judicial action. At the same time, they are under a duty to observe some canons of judicial discipline, which ought to temper judicial creativity and craftsmanship. How this is to be done is not an easy question and therefore judicial opinions have to be read very closely to grasp how this happens. Justice Iyer transformed the judicial imagination and made it into a vehicle to serve the have-nots and the labouring classes.

---

[17] See also, *Indira Gandhi v. Raj Narain* (1975) 2 SCC 159. This case unanimously held that the 39th Amendment was invalid, owing to violation of the basic structure limitations. This exceptional moment is not usually noticed. Which summit court has ever held an amendment constitutionally void at the height of the declared Emergency? See Baxi, *The Indian Supreme Court and Politics* (n 14) 238 for a fuller discussion.

[18] *Indira Gandhi v. Raj Narain* (n 17).

His abiding concern was to make the Constitution and the judicial review process responsive to suffering. He, whenever the occasion arose, adapted the Constitution to people's conditions and aspirations. He often quoted Bapuji's promise to wipe every tear from every eye, till I had to tell him in private that the judicial handkerchief is tattered and, when excessively used, can only spread glaucoma!

I must confess that Justice Krishna Iyer revelled in being an injudicious judge – if I may say so. He was not an ordinary person who carried this sense of common law discipline. He did not care about bourgeois law. Indeed, in his extrajudicial writings, he contrasted justices who were merely the 'shopkeepers of justice' from the 'missionaries', the activist justices with animated visions of social justice. He had not much affection for the non-enterprising brethren, and he showed it. I would think that Justice Iyer was a deeper thinker and a more reflective, reflexive, progressive judge than Praful Bhai (Justice Bhagwati), who in my view was very pragmatic.[19] While he shared, to a large extent, the judicial philosophy of Justice Iyer, he believed in hurrying slowly. As a master craftsperson, Praful Bhai too sculpted the doing of justice in his own way. He would watch how much activism the Bar and the other judges could bear.

Both were wordsmiths. Justice Bhagwati wrote good and even great prose when he wanted to, but Justice Iyer had virtually no boundaries on the use of language. His verbosity, though, often made others confused and people would run for the dictionary!

If you were to ask me, to pithily state the difference between these two giants, Justice Iyer was a veritable constitutional tsunami, whereas Praful Bhai pursued powerful diplomacy of human rights and justice through various constitutional gales and undercurrents. [20] However, if you ask me, his writing

---

[19] Bhagwati J seemed to follow the legal philosophy of the new pragmatists. Early philosophical pragmatists such as William James emphasized the concrete aspects of concepts as a basis for ascertaining whether they are 'good in the way of belief'. The new pragmatists such as Richard Posner who extended this philosophy to jurisprudence were legal philosophers. The new pragmatists rejected the idea that cases are solved by abstracted, overarching principles in favour of a theory of adjudication as creative problem-solving. The new pragmatists do not think that compromise is a bad word. They believe that if a compromise is based on certain principles, it's not a bad thing. There are some good compromises and some rotten compromises. They believe in compromise in the principled way. Principled pragmatists say all of life is a compromise and we should not make the best the enemy of the good. See, Charles L Barzun, 'Three Forms of Legal Pragmatism' (2018) 95(5) *Wash U L Rev* 1003.

[20] It might be interesting to note that Soli Sorabjee led a movement of the Bombay Bar, saying neither

a personal letter to Mrs Gandhi on her re-election in 1980 was not something that I appreciated even then.

Editor: *It is evident that in the initial phase, PIL was largely driven by the judges themselves. For example, the* Sunil Batra, Charles Sobraj, Prem Shankar Shukla,[21] Veena Sethi[22] *cases where the letters/telegrams/postcards would be addressed to individual judges such as Justice Iyer and Justice Bhagwati and would then be converted into PILs before them. Was there a strategic attempt by PIL petitioners to target a few Benches, which then led to resentment among other judges?*

Prof. Baxi: If you are talking of social action litigation or 'SAL' petitions, Murali, yes, SAL began with letters being written to specific judges. But this practice was soon changed, and all letter petitions were addressed or marked to the CJI, who then assigned it largely to Court No. 2, but some to other courts as well. The 'resentment' was not only due to the headlines, media coverage and the SAL linkages to investigative journalism, but some of the judges said as much and explicitly in their concurring opinions, which are in fact (what I describe as) 'disguised dissents'; my favourite example is that of Justice RS Pathak in *Bandhua Mukti Morcha*.[23]

Krishna Iyer J nor Bhagwati J should be among judges of the SCI. At least a hundred lawyers of the Bombay Bar opposed their elevation. It is important to note that during his tenure at the SCI, Bhagwati J continued to be a member of a Committee of Experts of the International Labour Organization, and after his retirement, went on to serve in several international bodies including the United Nations Human Rights Committee.

21 *Prem Shankar Shukla v. Delhi Administration* (1980) 3 SCC 526 ('Prem Shankar Shukla'). Bench comprised of VR Krishna Iyer, RS Pathak and O Chinnappa Reddy JJ.

22 *Mrs. Veena Sethi v. State of Bihar* (1982) 2 SCC 583. Bench comprised of DA Desai and PN Bhagwati JJ.

23 RS Pathak J in his concurring opinion said: 'I think the time has come to state clearly that all communications and petitions invoking the jurisdiction of the Court must be addressed to the entire Court, that is to say, the Chief Justice and his companion Judges. No such communication of petition can properly be addressed to a particular Judge. When the jurisdiction of the Court is invoked, it is the jurisdiction of the entire court. Which Judge or Judges will hear the case is exclusively a matter concerning the internal regulation of the business of the Court, interference with which by a litigant or member of the public constitutes the grossest impropriety. It is well established that when a division of the Court hears and decides cases it is in law regarded as a hearing and a decision by the Court itself. The judgment pronounced and the decree or order made are acts of the Court, and accordingly they are respected, obeyed and enforced throughout the land. It is only right and proper that this should be known clearly to the lay public. Communications and petitions addressed to a particular Judge are improper and violate the institutional personality of the Court. They also embarrass the judge to whom they are personally addressed. The fundamental conception of the Court must be respected, that it is a single indivisible institution, of united purpose and existing solely for the high constitutional functions for which it has been created. The conception of the Court as a loose aggregate of individual Judges,

Now looking back, it is evident that epistolary jurisdiction became an important addition to the existing work of the Court.

A characteristic feature of PIL was the expanded notion of 'standing'. The democratization of standing was normatively elaborated by a seven-judge Bench of the Supreme Court (5:2) in the *First Judges'* case (*SP Gupta v. Union of India*).[24] Interestingly, the entire Bar was the petitioner in this case. In his separate concurring opinion in that case, Justice Bhagwati gave a detailed exposition of the expanded notion of standing. I think this was the first ever statement on what I would call the 'democratization of standing'. By expanding standing in a case where the Bar itself was the petitioner, the Court ensured that the Bar would accept it.

Editor: *Would you like to elaborate why you preferred using the terminology SAL as opposed to PIL?*

Prof. Baxi: I have always distinguished and preferred SAL to the more voguish term 'PIL'.[25] The label PIL has slipped into Indian juridical diction

to one or more of whom judicial access may be particularly had, undermines its very existence and endangers its proper and effective functioning.'; *Bandhua Mukti Morcha v. Union of India* (1984) 3 SCC 161 [54]; see Upendra Baxi, 'Uprooting Injustice, Organizing Negation: The Enduring Legacy of Justice P.N. Bhagwati' in Mool Chand Sharma (ed), *Law, Justice and Judicial Power: Justice P.N. Bhagwati's Approach* (Oak Bridge 2019).

24 In the *First Judges'* case (*SP Gupta v. Union of India* AIR 1982 SC 149, 191–92) Bhagwati J, extended the doctrine of locus standi and observed as follows: 'In cases of this kind it would not be possible to say that any specific legal injury is caused to an individual or to a determinate class or group of individuals, what results in such cases is public injury that the act or acts complained of cannot necessarily be shown to affect the rights of determinate or identifiable class or group of persons; Public injury is an injury to an indeterminate class of persons. In these cases, the duty which is breached giving rise to the injury is owed by the State or a public authority not to any specific or determinate class or group of persons, but to the general public. In other words, the duty is one which is not correlative to any individual rights. Now if breach of such public duty were allowed to go unredressed because there is no one who has received a specific legal injury or who was entitled to participate in the proceedings pertaining to the decision relating to such public duty, the failure to perform such public duty would go unchecked and it would promote disrespect for the rule of law. It would also open the door for corruption and inefficiency because there would be no check on exercise of public power except what may be provided by the political machinery, which at best, would be able to exercise only a limited control and at worst, might become a participant in misuse or abuse of power. It would also make the new social collective rights and interests created for the benefit of the deprived sections of the Community meaningless and ineffectual.' The Bench in *SP Gupta v. Union of India* consisted of seven judges. The judges who were in the majority were PN Bhagwati, AC Gupta, SM Fazal Ali, VD Tulzapurkar and DA Desai JJ. The dissenting judges were Murtaza Fazal Ali (partially, as he agreed on some issues but dissented on others) and RS Pathak JJ.

25 Upendra Baxi, 'Taking Suffering Seriously: Social Action Litigation in the Supreme Court of India'

as effortlessly as all Anglo-American conceptual borrowings readily do. But while labels can be borrowed, histories cannot. PIL represents for America a distinctive phase of socio-legal development for which there is no counterpart in India; and the salient characteristics of its birth, growth and decay are also distinctive to American history. PIL efflorescence in the US owed much to substantial resource investment from the government and private foundations; PIL work was espoused by specialized public interest law firms. The issues within the sway of PIL in the US concerned not so much state repression or governmental lawlessness but rather civic participation in governmental decision-making. Nor did PIL groups there focus pre-eminently on the 'rural poor'. And, typically, PIL sought to represent 'interests without groups', such as, consumerism or environment through well-established mechanisms like 'lobbying'. In brief, the PIL movement in the US (given the nature of state and federal politics) largely marched with public advocacy outside courts. Thus, the concept of class action arose in the regulatory field.

I concluded my essay 'Taking Suffering Seriously',[26] which has undergone many editions under the same title, with the following words that still matter: 'For these who take people's sufferings seriously, there is no rejoicing; even revolutions provide transient occasions of celebration.' Thus, SAL is at best, as Rajeev Dhavan has observed (in words more applicable to PIL), an 'establishment revolution'; still, it nourishes hope in an otherwise darkening landscape of Indian law and jurisprudence.'[27]

I believe that keeping SAL distinct from PIL would enable us to better articulate a socially responsible criticism of SAL.[28] PIL can be appropriated by special interests (such as the resident welfare associations in which courts act as slum demolition apparatuses, or rather 'governance machines' – to here deploy Grigio

(1985) 4 *Third World Legal Studies* art 6 107-132, 107, 108–09 <http://scholar.valpo.edu/twls/vol4/iss1/6> accessed 24 February 2025.

[26] Baxi, 'Taking Suffering Seriously' (n 25) 107, 108–09.

[27] Professor Surendra Agarwal, however, was the first to cite the very same American law review sources that I had cited to advance a contrary thesis to name the Indian phenomenon as PIL! In a personal conversation, he aggravated the analytic and historical tasks by revealing that change of names did not affect the phenomenon. The conflation between SAL and PIL has caused much scholarly and judicial confusion and mischief; it is my firm belief that not every PIL is an SAL. In fact, it was the SAL opening that made PIL on a large scale possible. See Baxi, 'Taking Suffering Seriously' (n 25).

[28] See, Upendra Baxi, 'The Avatars of Judicial Activism: Explorations in the Geography of (In)Justice' in Surinder K Verma and Kusum (eds), *Fifty Years of the Supreme Court of India: Its Grasp and Reach* (OUP and Indian Law Institute 2000) 156–209; Upendra Baxi, 'Demosprudence and Socially Responsible/Response-able Criticism: The NJAC Decision and Beyond' (2016) 9 WB NUJS L Rev 153-172, 3–4.

Agamben's term). Judges can also appropriate SAL to increase their judicial power. But SAL was never intended by its founding judges to help property-owners (or 'propertiat', to deploy Justice Krishna Iyer's vivid imagery); it was specifically intended to transform the conditions of life for the constitutional have-nots – the disadvantaged, depressed, disenfranchised and disabled India peoples.[29] The questions before the Court in any SAL case are *the rights of the rightless*, or as Hannah Arendt put it, the human 'right to have rights'.[30]

Anuj Bhuwania's argument is that PIL has sometimes led to judicial populism and overreach. However, I think that these developments are a necessary evil, when traditional legal avenues have often systematically failed to protect fundamental rights of the have-nots, left behind even by agrarian reform measures so vociferously pursued in the first quarter century of Indian independence. For me, the moral authority of the judiciary to intervene on behalf of the people – especially the marginalized – is central, while Bhuwania's critique emphasizes procedural irregularities and the erosion of legal norms. While Bhuwania flays the procedural laxity and potential authoritarianism of the judiciary in PIL cases, I continue to emphasize SAL's broader emancipatory role, fully recognizing its occasional repressive role. Bhuwania argues for restraint. I urge judicial activism in SAL as a necessary force for social justice. In devising SAL as a distinct category, I have in mind underlying philosophical orientations: SAL foregrounds the transformative and emancipatory potential of litigation as a means of addressing systemic social injustice, while PIL, particularly in later years, pleads efficiency and equity for the general pursuit of public interest of the community.[31]

---

29 My terms like the above articulation and the expression 'epistolary jurisdiction' have often been used during the foundational days of the SAL, though not openly credited to me – at that time, the Court followed the rule that only eminent jurists, by definition non-Indian jurists, would be cited.

30 Hannah Arendt, *The Origins of Totalitarianism* (Harcourt Brace 1973) ix. See also, Jeffry C Isaac, 'A New Guarantee on Earth: Hannah Arendt on Human Dignity and the Politics of Human Rights' (1996) 90(1) *Am Polit Sci Rev* 61–73. On a related but distinctive perspective see, Jacques Rancière, 'Who Is the Subject of Human Rights' (2004) 103(2–3) *South Atlantic Quarterly* 307 (a text that requires reiterated reading); and Slavoj Žižek, 'Against Human Rights' (2005) 34 *New Left Rev* 115, 115–31; Andrew Schaap has recently argued that: 'Ranciere provides a more adequate basis for understanding the politics of human rights (such as that of the sans papiers) than is afforded by Arendt's conception of the political'. See his 'Enacting the Right to Have Rights: Jacques Rancière's Critique of Hannah Arendt' (2011) 10(1) *Eur J Polit Theory* 22–45 <https://www.researchgate.net/publication/254089371 Enacting_thein_right_to_have_rights_Jacques_Ranciere's_critique_of_Hannah_Arendt> accessed 24 February 2025.

31 Some early cases well illustrate the scope of SAL, an analysis of this (even if not exhaustive) must include the following: from the *People's Union for Democratic Rights v. Union of India* (1982) 3 SCC 235 (Asiad Workers' Case) to the 'settlement' of the Bhopal gas tragedy law suits (including the very recent, and cursory, dismissal of Union of India's review petition).

SAL is deeply rooted in the idea of structural injustice and empowerment of the violently marginalized people and communities, and its focus is on social transformation through judicial intervention. On the other hand, PIL engages a broader category of cases where the 'public interest' concerns – environmental degradation, public health, education, governance and administrative efficiency. Generally, in this broader sense, PIL addresses important middle-class concerns which may have incidental spill-over effects on constitutional underclasses. On the other hand, SAL is more steadfast, with a focus on its beneficiaries.[32] That is what SAL is, in fact, all about – a process of continuous co-learning about the social realities of law and justice in a constant flux. Indeed one way of describing this relationship of co-learning by the 'oathed' and 'unoathed' citizens. In SAL, the learning was about redressing the impact of the specific pathologies of power – what I have recently named democidal acts of power.

In both, the judicial function is broadened from mere *interpretation* of the laws to the task of judicial *protection*. It is the device of directions under Article 32 and Article 142 that brings the courts closer to, what I call, judicial co-governance of the nation. The judiciary, in this case, is particularly seen as stepping into the role of a protector of fundamental rights where other branches of government fail. I term this as continuing 'socialization of the Indian Constitution'. Indeed, with SAL and PIL, we go back to the concepts of law as justice – the latter reminiscent of Jahangir's bell.[33]

Editor: *You are quoted as saying: 'If in the seventies lawyers and judges achieved a proper conception of judicial power as people's power, in the eighties the SAL movement innovated a more direct unmediated form of people-judiciary partnership'[34] If you were to revisit the above comment, would you still maintain that the reference was to the judiciary as a whole and not just a few judges with a certain political ideology? And when we say 'people', do we mean people of all classes and castes?*

---

32 Later on, I used the word 'rightslessness'. Although normatively, the Constitution gives you rights under Part III, in reality, the four Ds are without rights – Depressed, Disadvantaged, Disenfranchised and Disabled.

33 Sonia Cardenas, *Chains of Justice: The Global Rise of State Institutions for Human Rights* (University of Pennsylvania Press 2014).

34 Upendra Baxi, *On Judicial Activism, Legal Education and Research in a Globalising India* (Capitol Foundation Society 1996) <http://opac.cusat.ac.in/cgi-bin/koha/opac-search.pl?q=Provider:Capital%20Foundation%20Society> accessed 24 February 2025.

Prof. Baxi: On the first part of the question, there were ideological differences amongst individual judges. However, a few of them were adroit at exploring the potential of epistolary jurisdiction and evolving creative ideas such as continuing mandamus and socio-legal commissions of enquiry.[35] Many new avenues also rapidly opened up, such as environmental jurisprudence, feminist concerns – especially violence against women – adding to the traditional portfolio of judicial activist concerns, such as agrarian reforms, limits of Parliamentary supremacy and the rise of administrative law and jurisprudence. We also ought to note the role of investigative journalism,[36] the rise of a civil rights Bar[37] and of similar animations in social movements towards effective uses of law (especially through human rights associations such as People's Union for Civil Liberties and People's Union for Democratic Rights).

The second part of the query, whether we understand 'people' as including people of all castes and classes across the board, poses a profound jurisprudential issue. No doubt the general concept of people is very abstract. In reality there exist only 'peoples' rather than 'the people'. Concrete contexts emerge when differentiation and disagreement, and even violent conflicts, occur among 'peoples'. The conflicting conceptions came to be characterized differently – say, by reference to 'people' and 'peoples' or, as the famous political thinker Seyla Benhabib used to say, between the 'concrete' and the 'abstract' other.[38]

My colleague and friend Bhuvan B Pande constantly talked about *Saakaar* and *Niraakaar* jurisprudence.[39] I extend this insight to constitutional judicial review. The Court has used both the forms in SAL and PIL, although the proportions vary and are indeed at times problematic.

Editor: *Do you view SAL/PIL contributing to the alteration in the perception of judicial power vis-à-vis the other two branches? Can it be said that lawyers*

---

35 See Baxi, 'Taking Suffering Seriously' (n 25).

36 For example, in *Sheela Barse v. State of Maharashtra* 1983 AIR SC 378. (PN Bhagwati, RS Pathak and Amarendra Nath Sen JJ).

37 *People's Union for Democratic Rights v. Union of India* (1982) 3 SCC 235; *Union of India v. Association for Democratic Reforms* (2002) 5 SCC 294; *Saheli, A Women's Resource Centre v. Commissioner of Police, Delhi Police Headquarters* (1990) 1 SCC 422; *Consumer Action Group v. State of TN* (2000) 7 SCC 425.

38 See, Seyla Benhabib, 'The Generalized and the Concrete Other' in Dianna T Meyers (ed), *Women and Moral Theory* (Rowman & Littlefield 1987) 57–72.

39 It is a theory of forms lurking here! *Saakaar* is, of course, embodied, formed, and *Niraakaar*, the unformed and the abstract. In between or outside may lie *Bhayankar*, and the *Vikaar*. We have developed some imagery of the former in discourses of terror but not of horror. Do either SAL or PIL discourse help in this respect?

have played a significant role in the development of PIL, or does it continue to be dominated by individual judges?

Prof. Baxi: The trouble is that there are not enough studies of this – ideological, institutional and developmentalist. There are no jurimetrics or judicial studies. The Bar, of course, plays an important part in developing PIL.

There have been several phases of PIL. These also overlapped. Each phase saw a different role for judges and lawyers. The first phase of PIL is what I call bureaucratization. In this phase, you create a public cell, designate officials in the courts and so on. Then comes the second phase of professionalization. It is the Bar, which criticized SAL in its early stages, that became the chief beneficiary of PIL, which became highly professionalized.

In the third phase, the Court began to distinguish between public interest litigation on the one hand and private interest litigation, publicity interest litigation, profit interest litigation, political litigation and frivolous litigation on the other. This phase saw summary dismissals with heavy fines of political or publicity litigation (abuse of judicial process).

The fourth phase of PIL is important. I call it 'farming out'. You give the case out to institutions such as the National Human Rights Commission, Child Rights' Commission, the Green Tribunal. And now Dhananjay Chandrachud's Court has started a new pattern – you give it to the Executive – for example, the direction that the Cabinet Secretary shall head a commission to decide on aspects of marriage equality.

The fifth phase is that of appointing a near-permanent amicus.[40]

In certain cases, some counsel specialize in PIL to the extent of forming special centres or institutes for PIL and, on the other hand, there exist specialist single-issue solo lawyers.[41] In the middle of the spectrum are lawyers concerned with different issues, such as the autonomy and dignity of sexual

[40] For example, Mr Harish Salve in environmental cases, as in the case of *MC Mehta v. Union of India* Writ Petition (Civil) No 13029 of 1985.

[41] Here, I must make a special mention of VM Tarkunde J who founded the PUCL. The contributions of women lawyers, including Indira Jaising and Rani Jethmalani and of Marudhar Mridul in the Rajasthan HC, Prashant Bhushan, Sanjay Parikh, S Muralidhar and R Venkataramani (presently Attorney General for India), deserve mention. There are many other early stalwarts (like Ramesh Garg, Shyamlha Pappu, Kapila Hingorani and Lily Thomas) that one would wish to name but space constraints relentlessly intrude. All I can say here is that the contributions of the Bar, of which I have mentioned only a few, are truly legendary.

minorities, violence against women, SCs and STs, corruption in governance, environmental and ecological matters, prisons and custodial centres and delivery of health services and goods and services. Educational service and pension matters, specially form a valiant enclave of PIL.

Editor: *The relaxed rules of standing, dispensing with formal pleadings and affidavits by PIL petitioners, the appointment of commissioners for fact-finding, experts for scientific reports and the deployment of the device of 'continuing mandamus' form the very essence of PIL. We have Justice Hidayatullah's comment in 1984 that 'PIL would result in the annihilation of all procedure'.*[42] *And now we are at a stage where there are elaborate PIL rules of the Supreme Court*[43] *and High Courts*[44] *(thanks to the 2010 judgment in* State of Uttaranchal v. Balwant Singh Chaufal*)*[45] *that excessively rigidify the entire process and also threaten to saddle 'frivolous', 'non-serious' PILs with exemplary costs.*[46] *This too, has been driven by the judiciary. Would you agree that we have come a full circle on this? Does this not have a somewhat 'chilling effect' on PILs and PIL petitioners?*

Prof. Baxi: I doubt that the 2010 decision has had a nation-wide chilling effect. Of course, what is frivolous and vexatious should not be decided in frivolous and vexatious ways! What you seem to have in mind in terms of rigidness and infallibility is studied in European contexts – a theory of 'juridification'. What is meant by them is not crystal clear, but the juridification of social relations seems a primary concern. Were we to deploy the juridification concept, a threshold denial of a PIL petition may ring some alarm bells, particularly as there seems no possible 'review' of the decision, or if the court fails to give good decisions for dismissal. On the other hand, there seems no good reason to deny claims based on justice and rights in a SAL letter petition.

---

[42] Justice Hidayatullah, 'Highways and Bylanes of Justice' (1984) 2 (1) SCC (Jour) 1.

[43] Chief Justice of India, 'Compilation of Guidelines to Be Followed for Entertaining Letters/Petitions Received in This Court as Public Interest Litigation' (Supreme Court of India 2003) <https://cdnbbsr.s3waas.gov.in/s3ec0490f1f4972d133619a60c30f3559e/uploads/2024/01/2024011510.pdf> accessed 24 February 2025.

[44] These rules can be viewed on the websites of individual HCs.

[45] *State of Uttaranchal v. Balwant Singh Chaufal* (2010) 3 SCC 402. Bench comprised of Dalveer Bhandari and Mukundakam Sharma JJ.

[46] Unfortunately, even serious PILs by highly regarded grassroots persons have been saddled with unconscionable costs by the dismissing court. In *Himanshu Kumar v. State of Chhattisgarh* (2023) 12 SCC 592, cost of Rs 5 lakhs was imposed on Himanshu Kumar, an activist working on tribal rights. In *Campaign for Judicial Accountability and Reforms v. Union of India* WP (Crl) No 169 of 2017, order dated 1 December 2017, cost of Rs 25 lakhs was imposed on Prashant Bhushan.

Editor: *Looking at PILs over the last five decades, is the shift in the political and philosophical outlook of judges discernible and does that explain the shifting agendas and priorities of the PILs that get entertained and are persisted with and those that don't?*

Prof. Baxi: Again, one must study the comparative growth rates of SAL and PIL across various periods. My impression is that there are lots more PIL cases than SAL, but the exact ratio needs to be worked out. Pending such an empirical study, one would only have shifting opinions on the issues you raise. Also, the question of 'shifting agendas and priorities' may be viewed from different perspectives, namely, social, economic and political impact (area or region wise), and also unintended yet cumulative impacts need to be analysed from the standpoints of the activists/movements or individual actors and institutions.

Editor: *There have been 'Green Benches', 'Social Justice Benches' of the Supreme Court (a pattern that is sometimes followed even in the High Courts, which used to sit on a certain day in the week to deal with PILs exclusively). Then with a change in the CJI, these were discontinued. Certain PILs are persisted with by particular judges, after whose retirement they vanish from the Court's docket for years on end. Thus, the issues of continuity, consistency and finality continue to plague the PIL jurisdiction. What are your thoughts on this?*

Prof. Baxi: I do not have data on SAL or PIL petitions thus 'vanishing' but I know, as I have pointed out, some of these cases are 'farmed out'. Sometimes the 'farming out' orders are to deal with and dispose of these cases, and sometimes, the agencies concerned are asked periodically to report the matter to the Supreme Court (as notably, with the *Agra Protective Home* case[47]).

But if you are right and some cases vanish altogether from the sight, this is a serious matter which the Registrar (Judicial) should report to the CJI in the Supreme Court, and the Chief Justices of the High Court; and where the petitioner-in-person or an advocate is involved, the reason why the petitions did not get listed or why the individuals did not pursue the matter should be enquired into. It is the administration of justice that suffers from vanishing petitions or litigations. Eternal vigilance, to vary the saying, is the

---

[47] *Upendra Baxi v. Union of India* (1998) 9 SCC 388. Bench comprised of JS Verma, BN Kirpal and Khare JJ.

price of doing justice. There must be a constant effort at bringing back before the Court issues that require its close monitoring through the device of 'continuing mandamus'. The responsibility for this must lie with the present generation of the Bar. I do not know whether the doctrines prohibiting of 'indoor management'[48] that amounts to 'maladministration' have ever been extended to SAL/PIL co-governance of the nation. If one were to look at the formation and cessation of special Benches, one gets the impression that it is all the prerogative of the CJI. So entrenched is this prerogative, that even the so-called judges' revolt in 2018 did not contest it!

'Consistency and finality' continue to plague the PIL jurisdiction. But these are also missing elsewhere, in other domains of adjudicatory power! And one is not sure whether these may be always considered the best judicial virtues!

More important are issues of systemic transformation – legislation and adjudication ought to usher in a certain order amidst change. Adequate law reform planning is the need of the day. It must be carried out with a pre-legislative human rights, environment and target beneficiaries impact assessment.

Editor: *The role of the* Amicus Curiae *in some of the major PILs concerning the environment (*MC Mehta *cases),*[49] *the forest conservation cases (*TN Godavarman*)*[50] *has come for criticism particularly with the control of the proceedings being ceded by the Court to the Amicus Curiae. After the unfortunate ruling in 1988 in the* Sheela Barse *case, where the Supreme Court refused to let the frustrated Petitioner withdraw the case (since it was making no progress) and substituted her with the Supreme Court Legal Aid Committee,*[51] *we have had PIL petitioners in several cases being displaced by the Amicus Curiae, who then controls the entire proceedings. Did you anticipate this in the 1980s when you were an active participant in the SAL movement?*

[48] The doctrine of indoor management is that outsiders are bound to know the external position of the company but are not bound to know its indoor management. It is also known as the Turquand Rule, as this doctrine was founded in the case of *Royal British Bank v. Turquand* (1856) 6 E&B 327.

[49] There have been several landmark judgments concerning the environment in which MC Mehta (*MC Mehta v. Union of India*, Writ Petition (Civil) No.13029/1985) was initially the Petitioner, and thereafter, it became an omnibus case name for environmental cases.

[50] It started with a petition being filed in 1995 with regard to the protection of forests; this was later turned into an omnibus case in which issues regarding environmental protection could be filed.

[51] *Sheela Barse v. Union of India* (1988) 4 SCC 226 (MN Venkatachaliah and Ranganath Misra JJ)

Prof. Baxi: This goes beyond any reasonable anticipation! The normal judicial practice is, as you know, to appoint an *amicus* for a specific case. The decision to take over the management of all forests is an extreme example of both hermeneutical and administrative adjudicatory governance. This may necessitate an appointment of a whole-time amicus team of lawyers and specialists, but this is not what the Court accomplished. Besides, the *amicus* was a legal counsellor, not necessarily a specialist in wildlife and forests, let alone climate change and forest resource management.[52]

I recall the *Sheela Barse* case rather vividly. Perhaps, she expressed her angst rather vociferously; still there was no justification for what I call the 'nationalization' of her petition. She had to invest her own personal resources to travel several times from Bombay to Delhi to face absent proceedings (the hearings were frequently adjourned!). Substituting her with the Supreme Court Legal Aid Committee was unfortunate and sent a wrong signal, deterring the filing of even genuine PILs. They could have instead asked the defaulting states to defray her expenses or requested a local lawyer to argue the matter. The sad part is that even after such substitution, the case did not make any substantial progress.[53]

Editor: *There has been a tendency to over-centralize in the Supreme Court issues concerning the whole country. One example is the PIL concerning the forests (*TN Godavarman*),[54] which is gargantuan. When you have just one Bench dealing with all the incidental issues concerning the entire country, it becomes, from a practical point of view, unmanageable. Either because the Court does not have the time or because it is not inclined or even worse, because the amicus curiae thinks the issue is not very important, there is a tendency to leave out a large number of issues. The reluctance of the Supreme Court to permit the High Courts to deal with the issue means that several individual groups and petitioners are standing in an unending queue in this one court hoping to be heard. Grave miscarriages of justice are, in this scenario, inevitable. What are your thoughts on this?*

---

52 Armin Rosencranz and Sharachchandra Lélé, 'Supreme Court and India's Forest' (2008) 43(5) *Econ & Polit Wkly* 11–14; Mihika Poddar and Bhavya Naha, '"Continuing Mandamus"– A Judicial Innovation to Bridge the Right-Remedy Gap' (2017) 10 *NUJS L Rev* 555.

53 After the replacement of the Petitioner with the Supreme Court Legal Aid Committee, the Court passed some directions. In *Sheela Barse v. Union of India* (1995) 5 SCC 654, the cases were sent to the respective HCs for monitoring of the implementation of orders.

54 *TN Godavarman Thirumupad v. Union of India* (2006) 1 SCC 1.

Prof. Baxi: I agree with you. First, all of the environmental litigation was concentrated in the Supreme Court 'Green' Bench headed by Justice Kuldip Singh. Indeed, centralization is a trend. But then we must ask ourselves: Why does centralization arise? I remember Prof. Duncan Derrett, a legendary teacher at the School of Oriental and African Studies, London, who taught Hindu law and wrote about state, law and religion. He was also puzzled by why people go to the Supreme Court, even in family law cases. He wrote that people go to the 'summit' Court because they feel the ultimate wisdom resides there. He called this a Brahmanical conception of truth and knowledge. The truth resides with the wise men, and the higher you go, the greater is the chance of your receiving truth, wisdom or enlightenment. Sometimes, one feels that this view is entirely credible; and yet, a wholly cultural reductionism of the judicial process is also discomforting, to say the least.

Editor: *What are your thoughts on* suo motu *jurisdiction so often exercised, not just in the Supreme Court by individual judges but the High Courts as well? What does it tell us about individual judges and Chief Justices? How is this consistent with the first rule of natural justice?*

I believe that *suo motu* is a different category from public interest and very far from SAL. The principle behind SAL was: let the State be less lawless and let the people have more rights. A question that comes up is what is the distinction between *suo motu* jurisdiction and regular jurisdiction. Is *suo motu* available to any judge or just the Chief Justice? So, is *suo motu* akin to PIL? Is *suo motu* bound by any limits? Is *suo motu* a doctrine?

Suo motu is a common law jurisdiction and is to be used sparingly because of the vast constitutional and SAL/PIL jurisdiction, and because of the review and curative proceedings, not to speak of the vast discretionary power assumed additionally by Article 142 prowess to issue directions and orders to 'do complete justice'. I will be happy to be proven wrong when I say that there has been no efflorescence of comparative empirical studies concerning the direction and impact of this expansion of the jurisdiction of the constitutional 'summit' courts.

In my understanding, whether judicial intervention in SAL matters through the *suo motu* device is apt or not depends on the judicial determination on the issue and how far it advances constitutional justice and human rights of the constitutional have-nots. In SAL situations the question stands reversed; it is no longer a question of judicial discretion or power but one of judicial duty. It is the question of why is *suo motu* judicial action so infrequent!

Editor: *On 'judicial fatigue', we have had the phenomenon of the Supreme Court sending PILs that have been pending with it for several years to the different High Courts*[55] *consigned to judicial history, with no follow-up. What are your thoughts on this?*

Prof. Baxi: As you know, the Supreme Court of India has a wide and vast jurisdiction, which has continued to expand thanks to Article 142,[56] the epistolary jurisdiction of SAL, the PIL creeping jurisdiction, the curative jurisdiction. The jurisdiction to determine its own jurisdiction is a kind of inherent constitutional power – a power writ large across the basic structure doctrine[57] as well.

Yet, both SAL and PIL may involve the issue of judicial or constitutional fatigue of the Bench and the Bar. Such fatigue is often induced by the processual matters such as long drawn arguments, adjournments and structural issues. The slow-moving state of governance has caused a state of judicial delay and arrears. How far activist recourse to judicial action exacerbates this state of affairs or contributes to its rapid deterioration are matters on which sustained cross-sectoral multilogue is necessary, even as we race to the centenary of the Constitution. Constitutional fatigue is a negative factor in the Indian development as far as the French maxim '*plus* ça *change, plus c'est la même chose* ('the more things change, the more they stay the same)' continues to rule and reign.[58]

Editor: *Much of the record of PIL cases (which included valuable reports of experts), whether in the High Courts or the Supreme Court (other than judgments and orders), are unavailable to the public. Strangely, even lawyers, civil society*

---

[55] *Safai Karamchari Andolan v. Union of India* (2014) 11 SCC 224. The Bench delivering the judgment consisted of P Sathasivam, Ranjan Gogoi and NV Ramana JJ.

[56] Article 142 gives the SCI discretionary power to pass any order necessary to provide complete justice in a case.

[57] The basic structure doctrine holds that certain fundamental features of the Constitution such as the supremacy of the Constitution, the rule of law and the independence of the judiciary cannot be amended or abrogated by the Parliament through a constitutional amendment. This doctrine was carved out by the SCI in *Kesavananda Bharati Sripadagalvaru v. State of Kerala* (1973) 4 SCC 225.

[58] Jean-Baptiste Alphonse Karr, *Les Guêpes* (1849).

groups and PIL petitioners appear to be reluctant to share these records with one another or place them in the public domain. What might be your thoughts on this?

Prof. Baxi: We should also collect the best practices in PIL from each state. For instance, the PIL Portal in the Orissa High Court[59] is a welcome beginning and can be replicated in other High Courts. Even as regards archiving of judicial records, the Orissa example[60] could be emulated.

Editor: *There has been a debate on the Court getting into issues that it is either unable (jurisdictionally) or incompetent (through lack of expertise) to deal with (such as interlinking of rivers, replacing single-stroke engines with CNG). On the other hand, PIL has contributed significantly to the development of environmental jurisprudence (*MC Mehta *case), triggering legislation in the area of women's rights against sexual harassment at the workplace (*Vishaka *case*[61]*) bringing about positive changes in criminal law and procedure (vulnerable witness courtrooms in cases of sexual violence), transparency in elections (APDR-filing of affidavits by candidates disclosing criminal antecedents), recognition and enforcement of the rights of the differently abled (*Patan Jamal Vali *case*[62]*) and the rights of gender and sexual minorities (*NALSA[63] and Navtej Johar[64] *cases). It is difficult, therefore, to not retain optimism regarding the promise of PIL. What are your thoughts on this?*

Prof. Baxi: I think I have responded to this question earlier, albeit in the context of the distinction I draw between SAL and PIL. But your question concerns, more directly, the experience of difficulties that some brethren have articulated and often even say in public, either through thinly veiled or disguised dissents. As I said earlier, there was a lot of unease, on the very same grounds that are now expressed by some judges, on SAL, and later PIL – the grounds of time-management, orders of continuous mandamus, directions in a given case, lackadaisical or nil compliance by the administration or the

---

59 'High Court of Orissa, PIL Portal' (High Court of Orissa) <https://orissahighcourt.nic.in/pil-portal/> accessed 24 February 2025.

60 'Centre for Judicial Archives, Odisha' (High Court of Orissa) <http://112.133.226.244/judicial_arc/> accessed 24 February 2025.

61 *Vishaka v. State of Rajasthan* (1997) 6 SCC 241.

62 *Patan Jamal Vali v. State of AP* (2021) 16 SCC 225.

63 *National Legal Services Authority v. Union of India* (2014) 5 SCC 438.

64 *Navtej Singh Johar v. Union of India* (2018) 10 SCC 1.

political executive, overall impact on the ground of judicial decision and use of contempt powers for enforcement/implementation.

Justice ES Venkataramiah expressed these anxieties early on by enunciating 10 questions regarding public interest ligation and its overall wisdom, but these were never taken up for hearing or answered by an appropriate Bench in the matter.[65] In *Ramakrishnan*'s case, he famously posed the wider question – basic for some constitutional ears but not all.[66] He said, if executive fails, we go to legislature, when legislature fail, we go to courts; where does one go when the Court fails us? However, as far as I know, even as CJI, he did not revisit his ten questions on PIL!

All this shows a valid sense of anxiety. But it is also a fact that sometimes the self-same judge who raises this kind of anxiety one day, happily takes up a case of PIL the next day! It seems that while there is some anxiety even today, judges and courts have accepted, overall, the PIL as a legitimate function of the judiciary. The volume of such litigation, the time it takes, its management and overall impact on the ground have to be studied empirically, not according to one's descriptive tastes (or like/dislike impression, both as to reasoning and impact). Still, this may suggest that only the most important matters may be thought fit for this jurisdiction. The question is: how does the master of roster decide that the matter is important? I wonder ...

All said and done, SAL/PIL are here to stay as forms of judicial action to invigilate implementation of constitutional rights, provisions and directions, and it is decidedly the best thing that has happened to the Constitution in the wake of lifting the internal Emergency of 1975–76.

---

[65] *Sudipt Mazumdar v. State of Madhya Pradesh* (1983) 2 SCC 258.

[66] *National Textile Workers' Union v. PR Ramakrishnan* (1983) 3 SCC 105.

Part II

The Court and Criminal Law: Practice and Procedure

SEEN FOUR CHIEF JUSTICES; YET TO SEE JUSTICE
1500 DAYS AND COUNTING
©MANJUL

The Supreme Court, Criminal Laws and Procedure

REBECCA MAMMEN JOHN

Introduction

Criminal procedure constitutes a domain where two modes of governance operate simultaneously – that of the 'law' and that of the 'police'. In his historical-legal analysis of preventive policing powers, Markus D Dubber offers 'law' and 'police' as distinct modes of governance.[1]

> 'Police is the mode of governing a macro household - manifested in police ordinances and other commands, to govern the prince's subjects, and tracts (and manuals) of police science, to advise the prince in the exercise of his power. Law is the mode of governing a democracy - manifested in constitutions and published norms, binding on governor and governed alike. The state under police is the police State . . . the state under law is the law state. '[2]

Dubber argues that both the 'law' and 'police' operate simultaneously in the modern State and are not necessarily in conflict with the other. However, the difference is foundational: the 'law' State historically emerged as a consequence of the Enlightenment critique of the 'police' State, and marked a shift '. . . from prudence to justice, from discretion to duty, from arbitrariness to principledness, from guideline to norm, from competence to legitimacy'.[3]

---

1 Markus D Dubber, *Preventive Justice: The Quest for Principle*, (Andrew Ashworth, Lucia Zedner, and Patrick Tomlin eds.), Prevention and the Limits of the Criminal Law, 2013.

2 Dubber (n 1) 48.

3 Dubber (n 1) 63.

Importantly, the reality of the 'police' State – occurring within and owing to the margin of discretion of policing – always exceeds that of the 'law' State, requiring the court to remedy the injury arising from this excess. In the ensuing negotiation that occurs in the courtroom, there are two kinds of processes at play. In the first instance, the court wields the law to either legitimize, or, to curtail the 'excess' of policing. While doing so, the litigant – most crucially in criminal law, the accused – is either transformed into a rights-bearing subject or a subject-without-rights (i.e, a subject to be disciplined, condemned and incarcerated).

One may alternatively view the role of the court through the balancing-interests framework borrowed from constitutional theory. At every stage of criminal procedure, the court considers competing interests – on the one hand, individual rights such as liberty, privacy and right against self-incrimination, and on the other hand, public order and prerogative of the state. Through this balancing exercise, the court settles on different configurations of the scope of rights and the scope of state power.

The criminal process, as laid down in the Code of Criminal Procedure, 1973 (CrPC) is a codification of legal and procedural practices, primarily of two institutions: the police and the courts. The CrPC provides 'a machinery for the punishment of offenders against substantive criminal law'.[4] It is a code of procedure and defines the powers of the police as well as its limits. It also defines the functions and powers of the court in supervising and regulating the exercise of police powers, besides regulating the contours of criminal trials and appeals.

This essay is divided into four sections. In the first section, the essay looks at the procedural landscape commencing with the registration of a first information report (FIR), arrest of an accused, remand, bail, filing of chargesheet, framing of charge and some post-charge provisions including recording statement of the accused under Section 313 and invocation of provisions like Sections 311 and 319 of the CrPC. The next section argues that the various interventions of the Supreme Court of India (SCI), particularly in matters of personal liberty, are marred by inconsistency and often betray a pro-State bias. The third section examines the Court's jurisprudence on the right against self-incrimination, as an illustrative example of its approach to constitutional rights vested in criminal procedure. Finally, in the last section, the essay examines the

[4] *In Re: Ganesh Narayan* (1889) 13 Bom. 590.

dissonance between judicial pronouncements and judicial realities owing to the systemic distance of the SCI from the ground. It further argues that the many institutional gaps of the Court in understanding issues on the ground have often aggravated problems instead of resolving them. The references in this essay are to the criminal laws preceding the new laws introduced with effect from 1 July 2024.

Mapping a Trial

This part of the essay maps out the various stages of a criminal trial by examining the balancing exercise and the resultant configurations of rights and state power arrived at by the SCI for every stage. The following analysis reveals that the Court's decisions on the law governing the pre-trial stages often prejudices the rights of the accused by operating on the prosecution's turf, whereas its decisions as regards the post-charge stage appear more balanced. This is illustrated through a critical reading of landmark judgments where the Court has defined the contours of the procedural landscape.

Registration of an FIR

The registration of an FIR under Section 154 of the CrPC by the police on receipt of a complaint is the first step wherein the criminal process is initiated. While the use of the word 'shall' in Section 154 (1) made registration mandatory, the qualifying phrase of 'information disclosing a cognizable offence' gave the police, in effect, discretion to determine whether a particular complaint was to be registered as an FIR. In practice, the registration and investigation of a case became dependent on extraneous factors including the class position of the complainant and the nature of power welded by the proposed accused. This malaise was recognized by the SCI in its landmark judgment in *Lalita Kumari*.[5] It held that the registration of FIR was mandatory and granting discretion to police officers in this regard would be antithetical to public order and to the rights of victims.[6] It further clarified that reasonableness or credibility of information was not a condition precedent to registration of a case.[7] However, the Court appears to have diluted its own

[5] *Lalita Kumari v. State of Uttar Pradesh* (2014) 2 SCC 1.

[6] ibid [53].

[7] ibid [79].

ruling by making the preliminary enquiry prior to registration, discretionary.[8] The judgment in *Lalita Kumari* is demonstrative of the Court diluting the enforceability of its own ruling.

Quashing

One may also consider here the Court's position on the permissibility of judicial termination of an ongoing investigation. Notably, the magistrate has no power to stop an investigation.[9] The accused person has the option of invoking the inherent jurisdiction of the High Courts (HCs) under Section 482 of the CrPC, 1973 to seek 'quashing' of the FIR and proceedings thereunder. One may seek a similar relief through the writ jurisdiction of the HC under Article 226 of the Constitution, or of the SCI under Article 32. In its judgment in *Bhajan Lal*,[10] the SCI followed previous judgments to call for judicial restraint in granting extraordinary relief under Section 482 of the CrPC or Article 226 of the Constitution. It laid down an illustrative list of seven categories of cases that were fit for quashing. These were broadly based on the ground of the offence not being made out from the averments in the FIR and/or evidence collected; allegations in the FIR being inherently absurd and improbable; express statutory Bar on the institution and continuance of the impugned proceedings; or proceedings being maliciously instituted.[11] The *Bhajan Lal* Court, in laying out the seven categories, improved upon a previous line of precedents that failed to clarify the precise width of discretion in quashing matters.

However, the ruling in *Bhajan Lal* has not been consistently followed by either the SCI itself or even the HCs.[12] This dissonance is reflected in its recent

---

[8] ibid [83]. In *Lalita Kumari*, the Court after stating in [120.1] that registration of FIR is mandatory if the information discloses commission of a cognizable offence, went on to state in [120.2], [120.6] that 'in which cases preliminary enquiry is to be conducted will depend on the facts and circumstances of each case'. It also set out illustratively the categories of such cases.

[9] *State of Haryana v. Bhajan Lal*, (1992) Supp (1) SCC 335 [36], [49].

[10] ibid.

[11] ibid [102].

[12] On the one hand, the SCI's own pronouncements, even preceding *Bhajan Lal*, have observed that cases should be quashed when the FIR does not disclose a cognizable offence (see for instance State of *West Bengal v. Swapan Kumar Guha* (1982) 1 SCC 561; *Madhavrao Scindia v. Sambhajirao Chandrojirao Angre* (1988) 1 SCC 692). On the other hand, it has consistently refrained from quashing cases at a preliminary stage even if there is no material to substantiate the allegations.

decisions in *Arnab Manoranjan Goswami v. State of Maharashtra*[13] and in *Neeharika Infrastructure v. State of Maharashtra*.[14] In *Goswami*, the Court was hearing an appeal against the HC's order rejecting an interim application for bail in a petition for quashing under Article 226 read with Section 482. The HC's rejection was based on the availability of alternate remedy under Section 439 limiting its jurisdiction under Article 226, in line with a precedent of the Apex Court.[15] The *Goswami* Court held that where the offence was not *prima facie* made out from the averments in the FIR, the court in its writ jurisdiction should consider granting bail based on settled bail jurisprudence.[16] The Court once again framed its balancing exercise between the public interest in fair investigation and the constitutional duty of the courts to protect individual liberty, and settled on the wide discretion of higher courts in granting bail in quashing petitions; it implored the HCs to be more vigilant in protecting personal liberty and preventing abuse of process.[17]

In complete contrast to this, the judgment in *Neeharika Infrastructure,* passed in the same year as *Goswami*, hailed the importance of the 'right' of police officers to investigate and emphasized on a strict standard of judicial restraint in interference with investigations in its jurisdiction under Article 226 of the Constitution and Section 482 of the CrPC.[18] The *Neeharika Infrastructure* Court further deplored the practice of HCs granting interim protection from arrest or interim stay on investigation in quashing petitions and observed that such interim orders needed to provide reasons. It went to the extent of observing that such 'blanket orders' affected the rule of law by 'scuttling' investigations.[19] Thus, in *Neeharika Infrastructures*'s balancing exercise, the position is placed firmly in favour of unfettered police discretion in investigation and a strong disapproval of judicial interference at this stage.

The problem of inconsistency aside, this predominantly pro-executive pattern of behaviour reveals a compelling fetish to put people through the trial system.

---

[13] *Arnab Manoranjan Goswami v. State of Maharashtra* (2021) 2 SCC 427; DY Chandrachud J wrote for the Bench which included Indira Banerjee J.

[14] *Neeharika Infrastructure v. State of Maharashtra* (2021) 19 SCC 401; MR Shah J wrote for the Bench which included DY Chandrachud and Sanjiv Khanna JJ.

[15] *State of Telangana v. Habib Abdul Jeelani* (2017) 2 SCC 779.

[16] *Arnab Manoranjan Goswami* (n 13) [63]-[66].

[17] ibid [67].

[18] *Neeharika Infrastructure* (n 14) [13].

[19] ibid [20]-[21].

Trial and the punitive consequences of criminal procedure become the rule, and relief at earlier stages the exception. This deference to executive discretion is unfortunately a recurring feature of the Court's record on criminal procedure.

Arrest

An early instance of the SCI placing safeguards for effecting arrests was *Joginder Kumar.*[20] Here, the Court framed the competing interests as human rights versus rising crime rates and individual rights versus social interest.[21] It then proceeded to carry out the balancing act by identifying principles of justified exercise of the police's power to arrest – such as flight risk, evasion of process by the accused, prevention of further commission and gravity of offence. The Court emphasized on arrest only in cases of necessity to enable the police to either prevent commission of offence or to investigate crime.[22] Thus it was not sufficient for the arrest to be a lawful exercise of power. It had to be an exercise *justified* by necessity.[23] The *Joginder Kumar* Court referred to Articles 21 and 22 of the Constitution to identify three requirements at the time of arrest: first, to inform a friend or a family member of the arrested person; second, to inform the arrested person of his right to inform a friend/ family member; and third, an entry to be made in the diary about who has been informed of the arrest.[24]

---

[20] *Joginder Kumar v. State of Uttar Pradesh* (1994) 4 SCC 260; At the time of the judgment, s 41 of the CrPC – which provides the police with the power to arrest without warrant – provided wide discretion to an officer to arrest a person 'who has been concerned in any cognizable offence, or against whom a reasonable complaint has been made, or credible information has been received, or a reasonable suspicion exists, of his having been so concerned'. The text of the provision did not place any effective fetters on police discretion, leaving this task to the courts on a case-by-case basis.

[21] *Joginder Kumar* (n 20) [8]-[9].

[22] Reference was made in this context to the guidelines recommended in the Royal Commission Report on Criminal Procedure from the United Kingdom and in the third Report of the National Police Commission.

[23] *Joginder Kumar* (n 20) [20].

[24] ibid [21]-[23]; Following the judgment of the Court in *Joginder Kumar*, the Law Commission recommended amendments to s 41 and introduction of provisions of pre-arrest notice in various reports. See, Law Commission of India, 152nd Report, (Ministry of Law and Justice, 1994), 51; Law Commission of India, 144th Report (Ministry of Law and Justice, 1996), 15; Law Commission of India, 177th Report (Ministry of Law and Justice, 2001) 100; In 2008, the Parliament accepted the recommendation of the Law Commission in 177th Report, and amended the CrPC to bifurcate the power of arrest based on the prescribed punishment. For offences punishable with a term of up to seven years, the power of arrest was to be exercised only when the officer has 'reasons to believe' that the person has committed the offence and has considered arrest necessary for prevention of further commission, proper investigation,

The Court expanded on this framework in the case of *DK Basu,*[25] where it was hearing a public interest litigation on custodial torture and death.[26] Faced with the stark reality of police discretion and its violent effects on the ground,[27] there was a need to enable the police to 'deal with the criminals in an efficient and effective manner',[28] but this could not make custodial violence and torture permissible. Thus, the end goal of deploying violence (effective investigation and crime prevention) might be valid, but the means were found to be illegitimate.[29] If the problem, then, is one of illegitimate means, the remedy lies simply in modifying training and behavioural patterns of police personnel.[30] However, in attempting a 'balancing exercise' the *DK Basu* Court faltered in observing: 'The right to interrogate the detenus, culprits or arrestees in the interest of the nation, must take precedence over an individual's right to personal liberty.'[31] In other words, curtailment of liberty of

---

prevention of tampering of evidence, prevention of intimidating witnesses or ensuring presence in court. for offences punishable with a term beyond seven years, the power of arrest was to be exercised if the officer had 'reasons to believe' on the basis of information that the person had committed the offence. Further, the amendment introduced Section 41-A, which requires, in cases where arrest is not required under Section 41(1), a police officer to issue notice directing the person against whom a reasonable complaint has been made or credible information has been received or a reasonable suspicion exists that he has committed a cognizable offence, to appear before him or at such other place as may be specified in the notice. The person is bound to comply with the notice and the officer shall not arrest him in case of compliance, except when he considers arrest necessary for reasons to be recorded in writing. See Criminal Procedure Code (Amendment) Act, 2008, Act no. 5 of 2009). Thus, the *Joginder Kumar* Court, in its writ jurisdiction, drew upon Part III rights in the Constitution to circumscribe the limits of discretionary power of arrest given in the CrPC. Exercise of police discretion was now required to meet the standards of both legality and legitimacy.

25 *DK Basu v. State of West Bengal* (1997) 1 SCC 416.

26 The letter was sent by DK Basu, a Kolkata-based human rights lawyer who founded the Legal Aid Society of West Bengal, a private body which till date offers a wide range of free legal services. Basu went on to become a judge of the Calcutta HC.

27 *DK Basu* (n 25) [31].

28 The Court needed to diagnose the problem before it offered a remedy. It did this curiously by framing the context, not in the excesses of police discretion, but one placed firmly on the turf of policing. The occurrence of crime is a crucial threat to the social order, and the Court recognized the challenging nature of policing due to proliferation of criminal activity – 'deteriorating law and order situation, communal riots, political turmoil, student unrest, terrorist activities and among others the increasing number of underworld and armed gangs and criminals.'

29 *DK Basu* (n 25) [28].

30 ibid [29]. Importantly, the Court in [30] referred to other governmental agencies like the Directorate of Revenue Intelligence, Directorate of Enforcement, Coastal Guard, Central Reserve Police Force, etc. and mandated in [37] that the preventive measures laid down would apply with equal force to such other governmental agencies as well.

31 ibid [33].

the arrestee is legitimate owing to an implied presumption of guilt. The only concern for the court remains the legitimacy of means, that is, the procedure for arrest. Accordingly, the guidelines framed by the Court are procedural in nature.[32] This is not a critique of the guidelines, but a critique of the Court's analysis that reduces the legitimacy requirement to a question of legitimate means alone.

The Court analyzed the new provisions regarding arrest – introduced by way of amendment[33] following the judgment in *Joginder* – in *Arnesh Kumar v. State of Bihar.*[34] The *Arnesh* Court reiterated the need for justification of arrest beyond its mere legality, but contextualized it in police practices on the ground that continued to view citizens as colonial subjects and deployed arrest as a tool of harassment and oppression. To remedy this, the validity of arrest was now to be subjected to the test of proportionality.[35] Given that the Court recognized the harms of excessive discretion on the ground, it laid down concrete guardrails on the margin of discretion involved in arrest, by providing directions for strict compliance with the amended Section 41 (1) and the notice requirement under Section 41-A.[36] These directions were aimed at embedding the necessity test in bureaucratic practices of the police.[37] Thus, the *Arnesh* Court, in recognizing the reality of police discretion in arrest, concretized what was an abstract principle in *Joginder Kumar* and provided remedies for violation of its directions (contempt of court in case of police officers, departmental action for magistrates).[38]

---

32 ibid [35].

33 Criminal Procedure Code (Amendment) Act, 2008 (Act No. 5 of 2009).

34 *Arnesh Kumar v. State of Bihar* (2014) 8 SCC 273.

35 ibid [6].

36 ibid [11]. See, *DK Basu* (n 25).

37 The *Arnesh* Court further held the Magistrates responsible for not holding the police accountable for practices of arbitrary arrests [6]. It issued directions to Magistrates to scrutinize reasons of arrest submitted in writing by the police officer when authorizing detention, and to record its own satisfaction about the necessity of arrest [11].

38 Non-compliance with the directions in *Arnesh Kumar* led to the decision in *Satender Kumar Antil v. Central Bureau of Investigation* (2022) 10 SCC 51 [21], [23], [26], [73(b)], [73(c)]. In *Antil*, the Court reiterated that the requirements of Section 41(1) and 41-A as well as the Arnesh Kumar directions were binding on courts, and non-compliance with any of them would inure to the benefit of the accused person in bail hearings. It further directed all state governments and union territories to issue standing orders to comply with the mandate of Section 41-A.

Remand

In *Madhu Limaye*,[39] one of the Court's earliest interventions, the Court deprecated the practice of Magistrates passing remand orders in a routine and mechanical manner without considering the legality of arrest or applying judicial mind to the grounds for extending custody.[40] In framing the balancing exercise – between individual liberty and prerogatives of investigation – it emphasized on the importance of the Magistrate independently applying its mind and not adopting the narrative of the police mechanically.[41]

The Court elaborated on this framework in the case of *Anupam J Kulkarni*.[42] Here, the Court was asked to decide the question whether a Magistrate could remand an accused to police custody after the expiry of the initial period of fifteen days. The court ruled that police custody and prolonged detention are 'generally disfavoured by law', since the accused needs to be protected from improper methods of interrogation.[43] Therefore, the period of detention beyond the first fifteen days has to be in judicial custody and not police custody. Further, the Magistrate is required to 'judicially scrutinize' the material placed before it by the police, to determine the necessity of police custody in the first fifteen days and record its reasons for authorizing such detention.[44]

Thus, the balancing exercise carried out in *Anupam Kulkarni* is rooted in the realities of excessive discretion – from practices of 'doubtful legality', like filing incomplete chargesheets, to the widespread prevalence of custodial violence. The balancing, once again, hinges on the Magistrate's ability to apply their judicial mind to the necessity of police custody.

The Court's recent pronouncements in the cases of *Pankaj Bansal*[45] and *Prabir Purkayastha*[46] have placed emphasis on the constitutional right of the accused

---

39 *In the matter of Madhu Limaye* (1969) 1 SCC 292.

40 ibid [12].

41 In other judgments, the Court has observed that purely mechanical remand orders would render the detention illegal, and a writ of habeas corpus may be maintainable against such detention (See, *Manubhai Ratilal Patel v. State of Gujarat* (2013) 1 SCC 314.

42 *Central Bureau of Investigation v. Anupam J Kulkarni* (1992) 3 SCC 141.

43 ibid [10].

44 ibid [4], [8], [10].

45 *Pankaj Bansal v. Union of India* (2024) 7 SCC 576.

46 *Prabir Purkayastha v. State (NCT of Delhi)* (2024) 8 SCC 254; A unique feature of the judgment is the reproduction in the main body a 'pictorial form' of the handwritten remand order of the Additional Sessions Judge with interpolations as to time that formed a crucial basis for holding the arrest itself to be unlawful [5].

to be informed of the grounds of arrest in writing under Article 22 (1). Further, the Court in *Prabir Purkayastha* held that 'grounds of arrest' are different from 'reasons for arrest' and while the latter are purely formal in nature, the former must contain case details that necessitated arrest. The Court also held that the purpose of informing the arrested person the grounds of arrest is salutary and would be effective only if the arrested person could consult his advocate, oppose police remand and seek bail.

Remand cannot and must never be a mechanical exercise, and the *Prabir* Court took exception to the fact that the accused was produced at 6 a.m., in the absence of his lawyer of choice, for the sole purpose of circumventing these constitutional protections. These issues had been raised before the HC but they were summarily dismissed, causing the SCI to remind the HC of its duties as a constitutional court. In both cases, the arrest and consequent remand were set aside and quashed.

The issue of need and necessity of arrest, introduced by the *Joginder Kumar* Court in 1994, was raised again before the SCI in *Arvind Kejriwal v. Directorate of Enforcement*[47] and later in *Arvind Kejriwal v. Central Bureau of Investigation*.[48] While in the former, the Bench comprised Sanjiv Khanna and Dipankar Datta JJ, in its holistic interpretation of Section 19 of the Prevention of Money Laundering Act (PMLA), 2002,[49] referred the matter to a larger Bench; in the latter, Ujjwal Bhuyan J, in his separate but concurring judgment, ruled that in the facts of the case there was no need or necessity to have arrested the accused and the arrest betrayed a 'caged parrot' behaviour on the part of the investigating agency – a euphemism to describe the political nature of the case and how the agency was acting on the instructions of its political masters.[50]

Bail

As stated earlier, the law on remand, arrest and bail is a singular domain where the commitment of courts to the Constitution's fundamental principles of liberty and due process is tested. While the next section of the essay undertakes

---

[47] *Arvind Kejriwal v. Directorate of Enforcement* (2025) 2 SCC 248.

[48] *Arvind Kejriwal v. Central Bureau of Investigation* 2024 SCC Online SC 2550.

[49] Prevention of Money Laundering Act, 2002 (Act No. 15 of 2003).

[50] The other judge on the Bench was Surya Kant J.

a closer analysis of the SCI's record in bail matters, this part only looks at the broader doctrinal position as stated by the Court itself. It consistently refers to Article 21 of the Constitution for affirming, what in some sense is the first principle of liberalism – that is, protection against arbitrary deprivation of personal liberty. In *State of Rajasthan v. Balchand*,[51] the Court offered the simplest articulation of the principle: 'The basic rule may perhaps be tersely put as bail, not jail, except when there are circumstances suggestive of fleeing from justice or thwarting the course of justice or creating other troubles in the shape of repeating offences, or intimidating witnesses and the like . . .'.[52]

The object of pre-trial detention, the Court has held categorically, is not punitive.[53] However, the question of granting or denying bail is left entirely to the discretion of the trial judge.[54] This sheer breadth of judicial discretion in the balancing exercise has resulted in bail jurisprudence being marked by arbitrariness, contradiction and ambiguity.[55]

The SCI had, in *Hussainara Khatoon*,[56] underscored the need for reforms in the bail system, a theme it revisited in *Antil*,[57] while deprecating this 'culture' of incarceration as a colonial inheritance and condemning indiscriminate arrests as draconian.[58] It issued extensive directions for trial courts to deal with bail applications.[59] The Court created categories of offences and leaned towards

---

51 *State of Rajasthan v. Balchand* (1977) 4 SCC 308.

52 ibid [2].

53 See *Gurbaksh Singh Sibbia v. State of Punjab* (1980) 2 SCC 565; *Sanjay Chandra v. CBI* (2012) 1 SCC 40.

54 *Dataram Singh v. State of Uttar Pradesh* (2018) 3 SCC 22.

55 On the one hand, practices of bail are not bound by any bright-line standards and emerge from the political economy of a heterogenous trial court system. On the other hand, trial courts are guided in two ways – the first is through guidelines and directions laid down in pronouncements, whereas the second is the signalling effect of the higher courts' own behaviour in matters of bail.

56 *Hussainara Khatoon (1) v. Home Secretary, State of Bihar* (1980) 1 SCC 81.

57 *Satender Kumar Antil* (n 38).

58 ibid [5].

59 The Court categorized offences into four groups: (A) offences punishable with less than or up to seven years' imprisonment; (B) offences punishable with death, life imprisonment or imprisonment of more than seven years; (C) offences punishable under special statutes that impose restrictive bail conditions (For instance, Section 37, Narcotic Drugs and Psychotropic Substances Act, 1985; Section 43-D(5), Unlawful Activities (Prevention) Act, 1967; Section 45, Prevention of Money Laundering Act 2002; Section 212(6), Companies Act, 2013.); (D) economic offences not covered by special statutes. For category A, the accused was to be ordinarily granted bail on appearance before the court after issuance of process. For categories B and D, the bail applications were to be decided on merits. For category C, the bail applications were to be similarly decided on merits in compliance with the restrictive conditions. Further, bail applications were to be decided within two weeks of being filed.

immediate release for those involved in offences punishable with up to seven years' imprisonment.[60]

Chargesheet and Completion of Investigation

The chargesheet or final report[61] is 'an opinion or intimation of the investigating officer to the concerned court that on the material collected during the course of investigation, an offence appears to have been committed by the particular person or persons, or that no offence appears to have been committed.[62] The question whether the chargesheet filed by the police is 'complete' is significant in considering whether a detained accused person is entitled to default bail under Section 167 of the CrPC. In a recent judgment, *Sharif Ahmed*,[63] the SCI held that a chargesheet is considered complete if the alleged offence is *prima facie* made out based on the annexed evidence and the sufficiency of the prosecution case does not depend on further evidence.[64] Section 173 (8) of the CrPC empowers the police to conduct further investigation. However, when an investigating agency informs the court that it would be filing supplementary chargesheets based on further investigation, the court should decide the issue of completeness of the original chargesheet before taking cognizance. This judicial scrutiny is critical since it directly affects fair trial rights of the accused. This is precisely what the SCI has often failed to see.

Consider, for instance, the restricted view taken by the SCI in *CBI v. Kapil Wadhawan*,[65] where it cancelled the default bail granted to the accused. The Court refused to consider that the claim of the original chargesheet being complete had to be tested against the nature and volume of pending investigation. In such instances, a court has two options. It may either

---

[60] The *Antil* Court diagnosed the problem as follows: two-thirds of the prison population in India are undertrial prisoners, and a majority of them do not require arrest since they are charged for offences punishable with less than seven years' imprisonment. Further, a majority of prisoners belong to socio-economically marginalized backgrounds.

[61] In the framework of the CrPC, 1973, there are two kinds of cases – complaint cases and state (also referred to colloquially as police cases) cases. In complaint cases, the magistrate is empowered to take cognizance of the offence based on the complaint under Section 190. So far as state cases are concerned, on completion of investigation, the investigating officer is required to forward to the magistrate a final report, or chargesheet, under Section 173 (2).

[62] *Dablu Kujur v. State of Jharkhand* (2024) 6 SCC 758 [14].

[63] *Sharif Ahmed v. State of Uttar Pradesh* 2024 SCC Online SC 726.

[64] ibid [13].

[65] *CBI v. Kapil Wadhawan* (2024) 3 SCC 734.

choose to be hyper-technical in its assessment of whether a chargesheet is complete, or it could assess whether the chargesheet reflects a thorough and complete investigation of the role of each accused and about each fact and circumstance in the knowledge of the investigating agency at the time of filing the chargesheet. The Courts' reluctance to evaluate chargesheets against a more robust idea of 'completeness' reflects an ostensible disregard for personal liberty.

That the trial courts have received scant guidance from the SCI in this regard, is perhaps exemplified by the Court's judgment in *Ritu Chhabaria*.[66] The Court deprecated the practice of filing piecemeal chargesheets without completion of investigation for the sole object of defeating the right of default bail.[67] It further observed, crucially, that Section 167 was not a mere procedural formality but flowed from Article 21 itself, since it is a safeguard in the face of the stark power imbalance between the accused individual and the investigating agency.[68] Curiously, a few days after the judgment, a recall application was filed and mentioned before the Chief Justice of India's (CJI) Bench. Before the matter went to the regular Bench as per established procedure, the CJI's Bench indefinitely stayed the operation of the judgment.[69] The signaling effect of this turn of events is evidently the persistence of police practices of 'doubtful legality' that the *Anupam Kulkarni* Court as well as the *Ritu Chabbaria* Court precisely diagnosed and deprecated.

Summoning to Framing of Charge

After the Magistrate takes cognizance and summons the accused person,[70] the accused enters appearance for the first time before the trial court and becomes entitled to receive a copy of the chargesheet, statements of witnesses and other documents forwarded to the court. Generally, the investigating officer only forwards inculpatory material to the court and excludes material that favours

[66] *Ritu Chhabaria v. Union of India* 2023 SCC Online SC 502.

[67] ibid [28].

[68] ibid [35].

[69] *Directorate of Enforcement v. Manpreet Singh Talwar* 2023 SCC Online SC 751.

[70] In a series of important judgments, the SCI has stressed on the seriousness of summoning since it initiates the criminal legal machinery in motion, and held that a summoning order must reflect application of mind by the court regarding its satisfaction on whether sufficient grounds exist to issue process. See, *Chief Enforcement Officer v. Videocon International* (2008) 2 SCC 492; *Bhushan Kumar v. State (NCT of Delhi)* (2012) 5 SCC 424; *Pepsi Foods v. Special Judicial Magistrate* (1998) 5 SCC 749; *Sunil Bharti Mittal v. CBI* (2015) 4 SCC 609.

the accused, although the same has been collected during investigation. Since charge is framed by the court based on the chargesheet and the materials forwarded by the police, the accused ought to have access to all materials collected during investigation to enable the court to take a wholesome view of the case at the stage of charge.

This is particularly important, since the Court, in *Debendra Nath Padhi*, held that the accused had no right to produce any material in his defence at the stage of charge, with a narrow exception carved out for material of unimpeachable quality at the sole discretion of the court.[71] This foreclosure of the right of an accused to produce evidence at the stage of discharge should be remedied by a right of fair disclosure, where the investigating agency is obliged to supply exculpatory material in its possession. To require otherwise would lead to suppression of such material, giving rise to the charge of prosecutorial misconduct.

However, while the Court in *Siddharth Vashisht* has recognized that fair disclosure by the police is part of the fundamental right of the accused to a fair trial under Article 21,[72] it has not required disclosure of exculpatory material to the accused person at the stage of charge. There has been a limited attempt by the Court to place guardrails on police discretion in this regard and limit its potential of misuse. *In Re: To Issue Certain Guidelines Regarding Inadequacies and Deficiencies in Criminal Trials* was a decision where the Court held that at the stage of charge, the accused is entitled to seek a list of relied and un-relied upon documents seized by the investigating agency.[73] This is not a foolproof measure, since exculpatory material is often camouflaged in police records and not formally seized. Further, the Court does not specify any consequences for the prosecution for non-disclosure.

However, even this limited safeguard was further narrowed by the Court in *Ponnusamy*.[74] The Court held here that the accused may seek copies of un-relied documents and other exculpatory material through Section 91 of the CrPC only *after* the framing of charge. *Ponnusamy* effectively curtailed

71 *State of Orissa v. Debendra Nath Padhi* (2005) 1 SCC 568; *Rukmini Narvekar v. Vijaya Satardekar* (2008) 14 SCC 1.

72 *Siddharth Vashisht @ Manu Sharma v. State of NCT Delhi* (2010) 6 SCC 1 [27].

73 *In Re: To Issue Certain Guidelines Regarding Inadequacies and Deficiencies in Criminal Trials v. The State of Andhra Pradesh*, Suo Moto Writ (Crl) No. 1/2017, order dated 20 April 2021.

74 *P Ponnusamy v. State of Tamil Nadu* (2023) 12 SCC 666.

the right of the accused to seek and use these un-relied documents (usually favouring them) to effectively argue for bail or discharge.

Thus, unlike the *Brady* disclosure standard in the United States (US),[75] which requires disclosure of all material (inculpatory and exculpatory) to the accused even when not requested, and non-compliance being a violation of the due process clause of the US Constitution, the SCI recognizes a much narrower standard. This compels the defence to operate on the turf of the prosecution at the stage of framing charge, which squarely affects their fair trial rights. Once again, this jurisprudence reveals a strong intent to put people through the punitive rigours of the trial process and to make them suffer its liberty-limiting implications during the pendency of proceedings. It also betrays a tendency of judicial deference to the investigating agency before the commencement of trial.

The Court, in various judgments, has held that when framing charge, a magistrate should apply their mind and look at the 'broad probabilities' of the case.[76] A court can look at such broad probabilities only if the accused is entitled to all materials in the possession of the prosecuting agency, including exculpatory material, at the stage of charge. Trial, of course, commences with the framing of charge.[77]

Victim's Participation

Any analysis of the SCI's record in criminal procedure must consider its treatment of the victim, the third stakeholder in the criminal justice system besides the prosecution and the accused. There are three broad issues that emerge: the problem of poorly conducted investigation and prosecution in a system where victims are not afforded a concrete, identifiable locus of their own; the victims' navigation of a system that is often alienating and hostile; and, finally, the predicament of victims of minority identities. The third issue has been raised most prominently by the women's movement, inasmuch as the patriarchal worldview undergirding the practice of law – by the police and the courts – leads to a redoubling of the violation that the victim seeks remedy for in the first place.

---

[75] *Brady v. Maryland* 373 US 83, 87 (1963).

[76] *Union of India v. Prafulla Kumar Samal* (1979) 3 SCC 4; *Dilawar Balu Kurane v. State of Maharashtra* (2002) 2 SCC 135.

[77] *Common Cause v. Union of India* (1996) 6 SCC 775; *Hardeep Singh v. State of Punjab* (2014) 3 SCC 92.

Both the legislature[78] and the judiciary have responded to these issues by focusing on two categories of rights – participatory rights and compensation. In its landmark judgment in *Bhagwant Singh*,[79] the SCI recognized that the victim/informant does not 'fade away' once an FIR is registered, and that the right to be informed of the conclusion and outcome of investigation was implicit in the act of lodging an FIR. The *Bhagwant Singh* Court directed the Magistrate to issue notice to the victim/informant when the police files a closure report. This was done to give an opportunity to the victim/informant to be heard and to 'protest' against such closure. As *Abhinandan Jha* had already recognized the right of the victim/informant to file a protest petition against a closure report,[80] the *Bhagwant Singh* direction allowed for the right to be meaningfully accessed.

In *Delhi Domestic Working Women's Forum*,[81] the Court recognized that harassment by the police as well as the hostility of the trial infrastructure were some of the systemic issues faced by victims of sexual violence. The guidelines framed by the three-judge Bench focused on access to legal representation, compensation and anonymity during trial. In subsequent judgments, the SCI has recognized that victims have an 'unbridled' right to participate in every stage of the trial.[82] It has, however, clarified that the participation of the victim does not dilute the primacy given to the prosecutor, and the victim's role is restricted to assisting the latter.[83]

Trial

The SCI's jurisprudence on provisions governing trial reflect a different nature of balancing. Given the adversarial model, the trial court acts as an independent arbiter, not so much balancing police discretion and individual liberty, but ensuring fair and equal opportunity to the prosecution and the defence to present their case. This section looks at three provisions – Sections 313, 319 and 311 of the CrPC – to illustrate the point. While in pronouncements on

---

78 See, CrPC, 1973, ss 372, 439(1A), 357A, 357B and 357C. See also, Scheduled Castes and Scheduled Tribes (Prevention of Atrocities) Act, 1989, s 15A.

79 *Bhagwant Singh v. Commissioner of Police* AIR 1985 SC 1285.

80 *Abhinandan Jha v. Dinesh Mishra* (1967) 3 SCR 668.

81 *Delhi Domestic Working Women's Forum v. Union of India* (1995) 1 SCC 14 [15].

82 *Jagjeet Singh v. Ashish Mishra* (2022) 9 SCC 321.

83 *Rekha Murarka v. State of West Bengal* (2020) 2 SCC 474.

Sections 313 and 319, the Court has largely upheld principles of fair trial and prevented abuse, its record on Section 311 has been less consistent.

Section 313 of the CrPC imposes a duty on the court, after prosecution evidence is led and concluded, to bring home to the accused all the incriminating circumstances against him, thereby giving him an opportunity to explain the same. It affords an opportunity to the accused to test the veracity of the prosecution case and offer cogent explanations to what is viewed as incriminating evidence. In *Sharad Birdhichand Sarda*,[84] the SCI reiterated the law laid down in *Hate Singh Bhagat Singh*,[85] that the circumstances of the offence which were not put to an accused under Section 313 cannot be used against him. In doing so, the Court reiterated the fundamental objective of the section, which was to provide the accused a fair opportunity to be heard. The judgment also noted that responses made by the accused will not be used to convict him, as the statement is not on oath.

Section 319 of the CrPC provides the power to the court to summon individuals who were not originally charged but whose involvement surfaces as the trial progresses. This power needs to be used with great care and circumspection, and courts have consistently held that the power to summon additional persons during trial must be sparingly used, since its overuse could lead to serious miscarriage of justice. In *Hardeep Singh*, a Constitution Bench of the Court held that the test for summoning under Section 319 was a higher threshold than that applied at the initial stage.[86] In *Shankar*,[87] the SCI held that to summon additional accused persons during trial, the evidence should be such that if it goes unrebutted it should result in the conviction of the person who is sought to be summoned.

Section 311 of the CrPC empowers a court to summon any material witness and examine him or recall and further examine a witness who has already been examined, when it is found essential for the dispensation of justice. In *Mohanlal Shamli Soni*,[88] the Court stated that the language of the section gave

[84] *Sharad Birdhichand Sarda v. State of Maharashtra* AIR 1984 SC 1622.

[85] *Hate Singh v. State of Madhya Bharat* 1951 SCC 1060.

[86] *Hardeep Singh* (n 77) [106]. Citing *Hardeep Singh*, recently a two-judge Bench in *Satbir Singh v. Rajesh Kumar* 2025 INSC 416, while reiterating that the standard for invoking Section 319 CrPC requires more than a prima facie case, held that additional accused can be summoned based on witness's statement without cross-examination.

[87] *Shankar v. State of Uttar Pradesh*, AIR 1962 SC 1154.

[88] *Mohanlal Shamli Soni v. Union of India* AIR 1991 SC 1346.

vast discretion to the judge and could not be restricted in its usage. However, this provision has often been used to favour the prosecution, as in the case of *Rajendra Prasad*.[89] Here, the Court upheld the order of the trial court, which had allowed the prayer of the prosecution to recall three witnesses for recording further evidence at the stage of final arguments. It held that the exercise of such power cannot be dubbed as filling a lacuna in the prosecution case. The Court declined to accept the contention of the accused that the prosecution cannot be permitted to fill up gaps in the case once the defence had highlighted them at the stage of the final arguments.

In sharp contrast to this, in the case of *Ram Mehar*,[90] relating to the trial of 148 workers of the Manesar factory of Maruti Suzuki Limited, where a similar application under Section 311 was moved by the accused, the Court invoked the principles of speedy trial and held that a criminal trial did not singularly centre around the accused, but also the victim who represents the 'collective'. It observed, '[T]he cry of the collective may not be uttered in decibels which is physically audible in the court premises, but the court has to remain sensitive to such silent cries and agonies, for society seeks justice.'[91] It spoke of the need to balance the interest of the victim with the rights of an accused, ignoring the fact that the accused were overburdened by long periods of incarceration, poverty and other disadvantages.

Whose Liberty Does the Court Protect?

The positions taken by the SCI in matters of criminal procedure and trials, as briefly outlined above, bring to mind the enduring observation made by HR Khanna J in *ADM Jabalpur*: '[T]he history of personal liberty...is largely the history of insistence upon procedure.'[92] The insistence on procedure and fair trial protocols is important for protecting the rights of both the accused person as well as the victim. In today's political landscape of restrictive regimes and compromised institutions, the question invariably emerges: who does the Court protect? Or rather, in what circumstances does the SCI deem a citizen worth protecting?

---

89 *Rajendra Prasad v. Narcotic Cell, Delhi* AIR 1999 SC 2292.

90 *State of Haryana v. Ram Mehar* (2016) 8 SCC 762.

91 ibid [42].

92 *Additional District Magistrate, Jabalpur v. Shivakant Shukla* (1976) 2 SCC 521 [583].

This section makes the argument that the record of the SCI in its interventions at various stages of the criminal process is marred by inconsistency. The Court usually adopts a pro-liberty approach when matters are at the later stages of trial – after the accused has suffered the tribulations of the criminal process, while it tends to be far more pro-executive in the earlier stages of the process. Another pattern of inconsistency is between cases of similar nature: a product of a judge-centric system that vests excessive discretion under the pretext of procedural flexibility.

As argued in the previous section, the Court has a tendency to compel citizens to suffer the punitive rigours of the criminal process before granting relief. This lends itself to drawing a comparison of sharp contrast with the conduct of the SCI in the case of *Goswami*, both in how the proceedings took place and the judgment that the proceedings resulted in. The then President of the Supreme Court Bar Association was even compelled to write a letter addressed to the CJI, remarking on the 'extraordinary urgent listing' of Goswami's case before a vacation Bench of the SCI. The letter, written in November 2020, observed that the immediate listing and hearing of Goswami's plea was an example of 'selective listing' by the Registry, particularly in light of the pandemic and the obstructed functioning of the courts.[93]

In the judgment that followed, the SCI made several lofty pronouncements regarding 'human liberty'[94] and the role of the courts in protecting such liberty, going so far as to say that 'deprivation of liberty for a single day is one day too many'.[95] In the same breath, the Court cautions itself, observing that it must be 'mindful of the deeper systemic impact of [its] decisions'.[96] This word of caution slipped into the judgment also requires reference: it is intended to serve as a reminder for the SCI of its place in the hierarchy of courts and the effect of its decisions on the courts below. In *Goswami's* case, the SCI observed that the HC had abdicated its responsibility as a Constitutional court, and it was for that reason that the SCI was required to interfere. However, this is the same court which often displays reluctance in upholding robust HC orders.

93 '"Selective Listing" of Matters: SCBA President Writes to Supreme Court Against Urgent Listing of Arnab Goswami's Case' (*LiveLaw*, 10 November 2020) <https://www.livelaw.in/top-stories/selective-listing-of-matters-scba-president-writes-to-supreme-court-against-urgent-listing-of-arnab-goswamis-case-165751> accessed 28 August 2024. See also, the essay by P Sainath in this book.

94 *Arnab Manoranjan Goswami* (n 13).

95 ibid [68].

96 ibid.

While both the letter and spirit of the judgment form the keystone of criminal jurisprudence, it is curious as to whom such principles are applied to and the circumstances in which the SCI chooses to apply them. After all, this is a Court which, in the context of the restrictive bail regime under the Unlawful Activities (Prevention) Act, 1967 (UAPA), has said that the fundamental principle of 'bail is the rule, jail is the exception' would not be applicable and speaks of the 'intention of the Legislature to make bail, the exception and jail, the rule'.[97] It may be noted that regardless of the fetters on the grant of bail under the UAPA, the SCI is the highest constitutional court, and in any event, the burden to prove a case still rests on the prosecution and can never shift.

We may have reference to a case where the Madras HC granted regular bail[98] to several members of the banned organization Popular Front of India by way of a thorough and well-reasoned judgment. The Union of India approached the SCI in a challenge to the order, and the order was set aside; the accused persons were directed to surrender despite the chargesheet having already been filed, usually considered a ground for grant of bail.[99] Grounds for cancellation of bail are based on well-established principles culled out by the SCI itself in various judgments: 'Bail once granted should not be cancelled in a mechanical manner without considering whether any supervening circumstances have rendered it no longer conducive to a fair trial to allow the accused to retain his freedom by enjoying the concession of bail during the trial.'[100] In this case, no supervening circumstances were shown to the Court that could have justified cancellation.

It is also worth noting that the same Bench, just two days after making the above pronouncement and setting aside a comprehensively reasoned, fiercely pro-liberty judgment of a HC, orally remarked in court that 'in bail matters SCI should not interfere. That is my opinion. It should rest and end with the HCs'.[101]

---

97 *Gurwinder Singh v. State of Punjab* 2024 INSC 92 [18].

98 *Barakathullah v. Union of India* (2023) 2 LW (Cri) 665.

99 *Union of India v. Barakatullah* 2024 SCC Online SC 1019.

100 *Dolat Ram v. State of Haryana* (1995) 1 SCC 349 [4].

101 'Bail Matters Should End in High Court; We Should Not Interfere: Justice Bela Trivedi of Supreme Court' (*BarandBench*, 24 May 2024) <https://www.barandbench.com/news/bail-matters-should-end-in-high-court-we-should-not-interfere-justice-bela-trivedi-of-supreme-court> accessed 28 August 2024.

The reluctance to uphold legally sustainable HC judgments is also seen in the orders passed in the State's appeals against the bail granted to three accused persons in the Delhi Riots conspiracy case by the Delhi HC. The judgment delivered by the Delhi HC is lucid, detailed and deals extensively with the interpretation of the UAPA. The SCI – first, by way of an interim order – has held that the ruling of the Delhi HC may not be used as precedent and may not be relied on by 'any of the parties in any of the proceedings'.[102] The final order, passed nearly two years after the interim order and the release of the three accused persons, confirms that the HC judgments may not be treated as precedent, as 'the idea was to protect the *State* against use of the judgment on enunciation of law qua interpretation of the provisions of the UAPA Act in a bail matter' (emphasis supplied). This is an absurd and illogical dictum that betrays a fearful court – a court whose independence may be called into question.

There is a troubling trend of interference with orders granting bail at an interim stage, which extends to an outright stay on the release of the accused person. Considering the sheer volume of cases pending before the Court, the relief granted or withheld at the interim stage often has a far more permanent effect than intended. Again, it may be relevant to return to the SCI's own estimation of its position in the hierarchy of courts – the pattern of its decision-making invariably seeps into the courts below, and it must be alert to the same. For instance, a vacation Bench of the Delhi HC stayed the release of a prominent political opposition leader without so much as having read the order of the Sessions Court granting bail.[103] It is now not uncommon for the State and its various investigating agencies to request a court to stay its own order of release, or to seek delayed implementation of an order granting bail in order to enable the State to approach a higher court. It must be seen where these easy curbs on liberty stem from, and whose liberty gets curbed.

---

[102] *State of NCT of Delhi v. Devangana Kalita*, SLP(Crl.) No. 4289/2021, order dated 18 June 2021.

[103] Nupur Thapliyal, 'Delhi High Court Stays Arvind Kejriwal's Bail, Says Trial Court Didn't Properly Appreciate ED Case & Materials' (*LiveLaw*, 25 June 2024) <https://www.livelaw.in/high-court/delhi-high-court/delhi-high-court-stays-arvind-kejriwals-bail-says-trial-court-didnt-properly-appreciate-ed-case-material-261391> accessed 29 September 2024; While granting bail to Gautam Navlakha, the Bombay HC stayed its own order of December 2022 for three weeks to allow the NIA to file an appeal. This stay was extended by the SCI twice until it was vacated in May 2024 in *Gautam Navlakha v. National Investigation Agency*, SLP(Crl.) No. 9216/2022, order dated 14 May 2024.

The SCI later adopted a course of self-correction and reiterated that bail orders ordinarily should not be stayed without hearing the accused.[104] Soon thereafter, in a series of judgments,[105] the Court found its constitutional voice by reiterating that both bail and the right to a speedy trial were constitutional rights granted to an accused under Article 21, and prosecuting agencies could not excessively rely on embargos in special statutes to plead that bail be denied. These orders had the desired rippling effect, freeing HCs and trial courts of the burden of acting as mouthpieces of the prosecution and enabling them to grant bail.

It will thus be seen that a vicious cycle is at play here: the SCI falters in the first instance by overturning well-reasoned judgments of the HC and by placing unnecessary fetters on courts below. This incentivizes the HCs and trial courts to pass unsustainable orders that excessively concede space to the prosecution. Over a period of time, this builds up to a crisis in jurisprudence where individual rights are so withered that the SCI is compelled to intervene and course correct. Thus, while there have been public comments about the need for trial courts to 'not play it safe' in matters of personal liberty,[106] it is evidently the conduct of the Apex Court that whittles down the margin of discretion for the courts below. Relief and a robust defence of constitutional rights becomes a moment of exception, which can only be accessed in the SCI in extraordinary circumstances, as opposed to it being a routine feature of jurisprudence.

Right Against Self-Incrimination in Criminal Procedure

Part III of the Constitution – specifically in Articles 20, 21 and 22 – expressly recognizes a set of fundamental rights at stake in criminal law. The importance of these rights cannot be overstated, since penal consequences are the most stringent restriction on rights (in a proportionality analysis). While it is not possible to offer a complete account of this jurisprudence, this section focuses on the Court's jurisprudence around the right against self-incrimination

[104] *Parvinder Singh Khurana v. Directorate of Enforcement* 2024 SCC Online SC 1765.

[105] *Manish Sisodia v. Directorate of Enforcement* 2024 SCC Online SC 1920; *K Kavitha v. Directorate of Enforcement,* 2024 SCC Online SC 2269); *Vijay Nair v. Directorate of Enforcement* 2024 SCC Online SC 3597.

[106] 'Trial Judges Play Safe by Not Granting Bail, Says CJI Chandrachud' (*The Times of India*, 29 July 2024) <https://timesofindia.indiatimes.com/india/trial-judges-play-safe-by-not-granting-bail-says-cji-chandrachud/articleshow/112091451.cms> accessed 26 August 2024.

as illustrative of its approach to constitutional questions/challenges in the context of criminal procedure.

The SCI's jurisprudence on the right against self-incrimination in Article 20 (3) has largely been a restrictive one. This jurisprudence deserves a close reading because of the proximity of several foundational principles of criminal law to the right against self-incrimination. While Article 20 (3) involves several important issues, this section focuses on how the Court has dealt with rights of the accused during an investigation, focusing on the interpretation of the phrase 'be a witness against himself'.

The first landmark judgment of the Court in this regard was in *MP Sharma v. Satish Chandra.*[107] The eight-judge Bench was asked to determine the constitutionality of search warrants on the grounds of Article 19 (1) (f)[108] and 20 (3). The petitioners relied on the US Supreme Court's judgment in *Boyd v. United States*[109] to argue that forcible search and seizure of incriminating documents amounts to compelled production, which is prohibited by the principle against self-incrimination.

In *MP Sharma,* the Court held that compelled production of documents is prohibited by Article 20 (3), but recovery of incriminating documents in a police raid is not. It then proceeded to cite *Boyd* and *Entick v. Carrington*[110] for the proposition that only illegal searches violate the right against self-incrimination.[111] It held that our constitutional framework does not distinguish between legal and illegal searches, and incriminating documents recovered in search and seizure proceedings were not protected by Article 20 (3). The reason for this is threefold: first, search and seizure is 'an overriding power of the State for the protection of social security and that power is necessarily regulated by law'; second, there is no right to privacy in the Indian Constitution unlike the 4th Amendment; and third, these powers are regulated by law and subject to magisterial supervision.[112] Thus, there is a legal

[107] *MP Sharma v. Satish Chandra* AIR 1954 SC 300.

[108] The fundamental freedom to acquire, hold or dispose of property was subsequently omitted by the Constitution (44th Amendment) Act 1978.

[109] *Boyd v. United States* 116 U.S. 616 (1886).

[110] *Entick v. Carrington* (1765) 19 St Tr 1029.

[111] *MP Sharma* (n 107) [14]-[15].

[112] ibid [17].

presumption of the constitutional validity of police powers exercised under magisterial supervision.

The right against self-incrimination was further restricted by subsequent Constitution Bench judgments in *Kathi Kalu Oghad*[113] and *Shyamlal Mohanlal Choksi.*[114]

In *Kathi Kalu Oghad*, the majority judgment, authored by CJI BP Sinha, offered two reasons for excluding compelled production of fingerprints or handwriting samples of accused from the ambit of Article 20 (3): first, this data is not incriminating by itself, and hence an accused be compelled to provide it;[115] and second, the expression 'to be a witness' refers to personal knowledge of the accused. This excludes compelled production of a document which does not contain 'statement conveying his personal knowledge relating to the charge against him';[116] self-incrimination would include information based on the accused's personal knowledge. Fingerprints or signatures are not personal knowledge/testimony in this sense, since it does not depend on the accused's 'volition'; CJI Sinha understood volition as mutability.

The partially dissenting opinion authored by Das Gupta J disagreed with this second reason. The reasoning here was that the right against self-incrimination is justified on the ground that testimonial compulsion disincentives the police officer from diligent search for evidence for ascertaining the truth *and* might make the accused give false evidence that misleads the investigation.[117] Since compelled production of fingerprint or handwriting sample does not result in either and is not incriminating by itself, it is not prohibited by Article 20 (3).[118]

Both opinions offer different formulations of the same proposition – the unreliability of an accused's disclosure-in-custody is significantly enhanced by use of coercion/violence by the police. Subsequent confirmation in Section 27 and fingerprints/signatures production as per the majority opinion are able to offset this unreliability by a putatively independent/objective (immutable)/

---

[113] *State of Bombay v. Kathi Kalu Oghad* AIR 1961 SC 1808. It was decided by an eleven-judge Bench, with BP Sinha, JR Mudholkar, K Subba Rao, KN Wanchoo, NR Ayyangar, Raghubar Dayal, PB Gajendragadkar, Syed Jaffer Imam JJ in the majority and AK Sarkar, KC Dasgupta, SK Das forming the minority.

[114] *State of Gujarat v. Shyamlal Mohanlal Choksi* AIR 1965 SC 1251.

[115] *Kathu Kalu Oghad* (n 113) [112].

[116] ibid [11].

[117] ibid [28].

[118] ibid [31]-[32].

external evidence. Thus, as long as the 'truth' of coerced testimony is confirmed, the element of violence/involuntariness is not anathema.

In *Shyamlal Mohanlal Choksi,* the Court held that the right against self-incrimination was not applicable to orders made by a police officer under Section 94 of the CrPC 1898 (Section 91 of the CrPC 1973) during investigation.[119]

This line of judgments must be considered alongside the Court's ruling in *Pooran Mal v. Director of Inspection (Investigation)*,[120] that evidence obtained in an illegal search and seizure procedure is admissible. These early pronouncements of the SCI on the scope of Article 20 (3) consistently affirm this doctrinal position – that the principle against self-incrimination is only in service of efficient investigation, as opposed to being rooted in bodily autonomy, dignity and privacy. Jurisprudentially then, there is a dissonance between the constitutional intolerance of torture[121] and the taint of coerced testimony. This also forecloses the scope for an effective constitutional challenge to laws like the Criminal Procedure (Identification) Act, 2022 that has been widely critiqued for being violative of rights of personal liberty, bodily integrity, free expression, self-incrimination and privacy.

This is somewhat remedied in the SCI's interpretation of Article 20 (3) in *Selvi v. State of Karnataka.*[122] Given the legal question of constitutionality of narco-analysis methods before it, the *Selvi* Court was compelled to directly address the relation between voluntariness and nature of evidence that was subtextual in the previous cases. The *Selvi* Court reiterated the justification of Article 20 (3) on grounds of false testimony that misleads the investigation;[123] it then observed that Article 20 (3) is a guarantee against third-degree methods of eliciting information, based on guarantees of individual dignity and bodily integrity in Article 21.[124] It then faced the impasse of the distinction between testimonial/communicative evidence and physical/real evidence that *Oghad*

[119] *Choksi* (n 114) [19]. However in *Nandini Satpathy v. PL Dani* 1978 (2) SCC 424 [19], the SCI held that insisting on a woman appearing in a police station to answer interrogatories 'in flagrant contravention of the wholesome proviso to Section 160 (1) of the CrPC'. The *Nandini Satpathy* Court also recognized that the fundamental right against self-incrimination under Art 20 (3) was inviolable and that the person being questioned can refuse to answer a question if they reasonably apprehend self-incrimination.

[120] *Pooran Mal v. Director of Inspection (Investigation)* AIR 1974 SC 348.

[121] See *DK Basu v. State of West Bengal* AIR 1997 SC 610.

[122] *Selvi v. State of Karnataka* (2010) 7 SCC 263.

[123] ibid [102].

[124] ibid [103].

had drawn, whereby the polygraph or a Brain Electrical Activation Profile (BEAP) test results would be physical evidence. The court used *Oghad*'s 'personal knowledge' test to hold that these test results ultimately reveal knowledge of a testimonial character (that can be directly or circumstantially incriminating). Though physiological responses are involved, the test result directly relates to the sphere of mental privacy of the accused, which is protected by Articles 21 and 20 (3). Finally, since the accused has no 'conscious control' over the result of a polygraph/BEAP test that they consent to, such test result by itself is inadmissible except on subsequent confirmation under Section 27 of the Indian Evidence Act.[125]

Thus, in following *Oghad*, the *Selvi* Court articulated the testimonial/physical evidence typology and reformulated the test of distinction from personal knowledge (rooted in mutability–voluntariness–reliability) to mental privacy (rooted in bodily integrity).

Despite this clear shift in *Selvi*, the Court's jurisprudence has remained tethered to the withered form of the right against self-incrimination that is subservient to the prerogatives of investigation. This was most blatantly seen in the Court's judgment in *Ritesh Sinha*.[126] The *Ritesh* Court was asked to decide two issues. The first one – on whether it was constitutionally permissible to compel the accused to give his voice sample during investigation – was answered in the affirmative by squarely relying on the mutability/personal knowledge test of *Kathi Kalu Oghad*.[127] The second issue was whether a Magistrate could direct collection of voice samples of an accused in the absence of a statutory provision granting such power. Remarkably, the Court observed that since there was no legislation that granted such powers to the Magistrate, it would invoke its powers under Article 142 of the Constitution to temporarily fill the 'void'.[128]

Thus, the Court relied on the ratio of *Kathi Kalu Oghad*, invoked a purported necessity and declared that the rigours of criminal procedure cannot be allowed to 'inconvenience' the prerogatives of investigation. There is an odd conflation of investigation with 'justice' in the Court's disregard for procedural safeguards.

---

[125] ibid [264].

[126] *Ritesh Sinha v. State of Uttar Pradesh* (2019) 8 SCC 1.

[127] ibid [9].

[128] ibid [16], [27].

The Court's judgment in *Ritesh Sinha* came in the aftermath of its landmark judgment in *Justice KS Puttaswamy (Privacy-9J) v. Union of India,*[129] recognizing a fundamental right to privacy. The *Ritesh* Court's complete disregard for privacy rights is not a contradictory development, given that the judgment in *Puttaswamy* finds no space in its several hundred pages to articulate the privacy rights in criminal procedure.

Going forward, this jurisprudence – of a severely diminished form of right against self-incrimination, and nearly unfettered police discretion – grants an alarmingly wide leeway for investigating agencies to seize and retain digital devices (mobile phones, computers and other electronic devices) from any individual, including persons who may not even be finally charge-sheeted. This practice, already widely prevalent, has been challenged before the SCI in a writ petition in October 2022, wherein the Court has asked the Central Government to frame guidelines on the issue.[130]

Conclusion

In conclusion, this essay calls for a principled court that is uniformly committed to its independence, the people's rights and procedure established by law, while not being subject to the vagaries of personal ideology or external political pressure.

The systemic distance of the SCI from the actual operation of the criminal process results in outcomes that do not necessarily remedy the issues that are placed before it. This distance is, in part, a consequence of the hierarchy of the courts and also the narrowing scope of interference as a case makes its way to the SCI. The Court deals largely in its appellate jurisdiction and is rarely, if ever, in direct contact with the actual operation of the procedure that it adjudicates.

This distance is exemplified by the SCI's emphasis on monitoring certain kinds of cases. Special courts dealing with cases under the Prevention of Corruption Act, 1988 have disproportionately fewer cases than other Sessions Courts, which deal with all manner of serious criminal cases including murder, rape, dacoity and so on. The daily cause list of these special courts when

[129] (2017) 10 SCC 1.

[130] *Foundation for Media Professionals v. Union of India,* WP(Crl.) 395/2022.

compared to that of other Sessions Courts is alarmingly uneven. Further, a subset of courts has been created to deal with cases involving Members of Parliament (MPs) and Members of Legislative Assemblies (MLAs), at both the magisterial and sessions levels. These are needless stratifications of the lower judiciary that exist as a direct consequence of the SCI's obsessive focus on corruption – focus that is excessive and disconnected from the structural issues of the criminal justice system.

Consider also, for instance, the Court's attempt to administrate the criminal process and the constitution of special Magistrate courts for conducting trials of cases under Section 138 of the Negotiable Instruments Act.[131] The constitution of special Magistrate courts for conducting trials was done as a 'pilot study' of one year. The establishment of these courts involved the transfer of cases to the special courts; and a year later, after the pilot study was disbanded, the cases were required to be transferred back to the regular Magistrate courts already designated for hearing only those cases that were under Section 138 of the Negotiable Instruments Act. This transfer and re-transfer – albeit done with the best intentions of streamlining the judicial docket – led to great disarray and also placed additional responsibility on an already overburdened judicial administration.

Finally, one may point to certain institutional gaps in the functioning of the SCI that exacerbate this dissonance from ground realities. The first of these is a tendency of the SCI to act without transparency or accountability. This essay has looked at some of these instances – the manner in which the judgment of the Court in *Ritu Chhabaria* was stayed; the inconsistency in quashing criminal cases with similar facts; or the use of certain categories like 'gravity of offence' to concede and defer to executive power. Given that the apex court is supposed to offer leadership and enable the lower judiciary to affirm constitutional principles that undergird the criminal process, this pattern of conduct has aggravated existing problems on the ground, leading to lazy and misdirected prosecutions and reduced accountability of lower courts.

Another institutional gap is polyvocality: the SCI itself speaks in different voices, and one Bench does not necessarily follow or consider the judgment laid down by a previous Bench. This tendency of treating judgments as

---

[131] *In Re: Expeditious Trial of Cases under Section 138 of N.I. Act, 1881* 2022 SCC Online SC 649.

expressions of personal ideology or cults of personality leads to an undisciplined jurisprudence. This becomes particularly important when personal liberty is at stake.

The call for a principled court is not a call for homogeneity. The call is, instead, for consistency in commitments while preserving its polyvocal nature – reasoned, competing interpretations, which, in turn, allow for rigour in adjudication.

Cartoon © Satish Acharya. Reproduced with permission.

Normalizing the Exception: Deviant Legislation and the Supreme Court

NITYA RAMAKRISHNAN*

Common law rules such as the presumption of innocence, the right against self-incrimination, and the right to a fair defence have always been regarded as integral to criminal justice in civilized societies. Statutes that deviate from these safeguards may be aptly termed 'deviant'. India has had a perennial stream of deviant laws – those that authorize preventive detention, those that reverse the burden of proof, those that permit self-incrimination in police custody, those that disentitle bail and allow for extended pre-charge detention. Standard criminal procedure is now seen as an obstacle to public order, and the State's police power has grown without let or hindrance since Independence.

Critiques of the State as inherently unjust have stemmed from the inevitable abuse of its power. On the other hand, legal theory has attempted to redeem the collective and the social compact by ascribing to the law a civilizing control upon those that wield state power. To fulfil this role though, the law must be more than the mutable text. It must be a brooding spirit, akin to what Vivian Bose J speaks of in *Anwar Ali Sarkar*,[1] while testing a special law abridging normal criminal process against the spirit of the Constitution:

> [W]hat is the history of these provisions? They arose out of the fight for freedom in this land and are but the endeavour to compress into a few pregnant phrases some of the main attributes of a sovereign democratic republic as seen through Indian eyes. There was present to the collective

* Invaluable assistance in research and editing was provided by Stuti Rai and Ishit Patel.

1 *State of West Bengal v. Anwar Ali Sarkar* AIR 1952 SC 75 (*Anwar Ali Sarkar*). The majority opinion was delivered in separate opinions by BK Mukherjea, N Chandrasekhara Aiyar and Vivian Bose JJ. Separate short concurring opinions were delivered by Fazal Ali and Mahajan JJ. Separate dissenting opinions were delivered by Patanjali Sastri and SR Das JJ (partly dissenting).

> mind of the Constituent Assembly, reflecting the mood of the peoples of India, the memory of grim trials by hastily constituted tribunals with novel forms of procedure set forth in ordinances promulgated in haste because of what was then felt to be the urgent necessities of the moment. … The whole proceedings were repugnant to the peoples of this land and, to my mind, Article 14 is but a reflex of this mood.
>
> What I am concerned to see is not whether there is absolute equality in any academical sense of the term but whether the collective conscience of a sovereign democratic republic can regard the impugned law, contrasted with the ordinary law of the land, as the sort of substantially equal treatment which men of resolute minds and unbiased views can regard as right and proper in a democracy of the kind we have proclaimed ourselves to be. …[2]

Expressed while striking down a law that allowed the State to treat those accused of similar crimes differently, these words nevertheless proclaim fidelity to a greater principle in a democracy, not to be abandoned in the exigencies of state policy. The State's police function affects the citizen most vitally. This would, arguably, call for some non-negotiables – a kind of 'basic structure' of criminal due process. Alas, it appears that such an inviolate scheme has, by and large, not been endorsed by the Supreme Court.

The **Grundnorm** – *Text or Transcendent Principle?*

The words 'procedure established by law' in Article 21 of the Indian Constitution[3] are the words that civilize state power over individual life and liberty. In the very year of its inception, the Supreme Court was called upon to decide whether these words signify a spirit beyond the text, or merely authorize the State's lawmakers to prescribe any procedure to enable deprivation of life or personal liberty. This was in *AK Gopalan v. State of Madras*,[4] a challenge to the Preventive Detention Act, 1950 passed by the Parliament.

---

2 ibid [86] (Vivian Bose J).

3 Constitution of India 1950, art 21 states: 'Protection of life and personal liberty – No person shall be deprived of his life or personal liberty except according to procedure established by law.'

4 AIR 1950 SC 27; The majority opinion was delivered by Hiralal Kania CJ, M Patanjali Sastri, Mehr Chand Mahajan, Bijan Kumar Mukherjea and Sudhi Ranjan Das JJ. Fazl Ali J dissented.

Preventive detention, as a measure, was challenged as deviating from the spirit of fairness and liberty pervading the Constitution. The specific terms of the statute were also challenged as violating Articles 13, 19, 21, and 22 of Part III of the Constitution (Part III).

Deprivation of liberty during peacetime without a trial, without the actual commission of any offence and by a mere executive order, has been abhorred in democracies. But executive detention abounded in colonial India and continues in free India.

Six judges heard the challenge raised directly in the Supreme Court under Article 32 by AK Gopalan, one of the country's tallest communist leaders,[5] detained under the Preventive Detention Act. A majority of 5:1 rejected the challenge and upheld the law. They repelled the notion that there was any immutable spirit beyond the literal text of Article 21, and ruled that 'procedure established by law' meant procedure prescribed by a law enacted by a competent body. The text of such law, if in conformity with the text of the constitutional prescription, would be a procedure established by law under Article 21.

Gopalan was the trendsetter that determined whether, within the Indian polity, anything could, on first principles, be considered anathema to 'procedure established by law', and whether there was 'due process' in any immutable sense. The judgment laid down many propositions some of which were later overturned, but its ratio – that personal liberty in India is in thrall to State-made law – remains effectively unchanged.

Article 22 of the Constitution provides for preventive detention and prescribes a procedure for effecting the same which, if followed by the law made by the legislature, was the end of the matter. 'Due process', understood as 'just process' in the USA, was inapplicable to the Indian Constitution, from which the phrase was deliberately omitted, noted Gopalan.

---

[5] See Granville Austin G, *Working a Democratic Constitution: A History of the Indian Experience* (Oxford University Press 2003) 58. Austin writes 'A Kerala native, member of the Congress Socialist Party in the thirties, and by 1951 president of the Communist Party's All-India Kisan Sabha, A. K. Gopalan had been in and out of jail since 1947, allegedly for threatening the police in a speech and otherwise speaking his mind. Each time the conviction had been set aside. After having been detained again, Gopalan was detained further under the Preventive Detention Act of 1950.'; See also, KG Kannabiran, *Wages of Impunity* (Orient Blackswan 2004) 30. In his book *Wages of Impunity*, KG Kannabiran recounts that, on 15 August 1947, all prisoners were released by the Madras government, except AK Gopalan, who was kept in solitary confinement. Despite being in jail, he innovated a way of celebrating the dawn of independence in jail.

Indeed, it was after much debate in the Constituent Assembly that the phrase in Article 21 'procedure established by law' was chosen over 'due process of law' which is found in the American Constitution. Dr BR Ambedkar argued against the term due process saying that it 'might lead to an excessive encroachment of judicial power over legislative intent, thereby disrupting the balance that must exist in a democratic system.'[6]

Thus, in *Gopalan*, even Patanjali Sastri J, who did not equate procedure *established* by law with procedure *prescribed* by law, found in the Constitution no immutable principle of fairness against invasion of personal liberty.

The minority judgment of Fazl Ali J read natural justice and fairness into the term 'law', and the Fundamental Right to freedom of movement under Article 19 (1) (d) into 'personal liberty' under Article 21.

In the event, the Supreme Court upheld not only executive detention in principle but also provisions allowing for an indefinite period of detention, repeat detention orders on grounds even disapproved by the Advisory Board, denial of a hearing before the Advisory Board and denial of access to its report. Section 14 of the Act, which barred disclosure of grounds of detention to a court, was unanimously struck down, because it went against the express words of Article 22 (5) that the detenu be informed of the grounds of detention and it also prevented any meaningful challenge.

As we shall see presently, though many of the premises of the majority decision in *Gopalan* were overturned, the new jurisprudence has countenanced even more drastic departures from the norms of criminal justice. A glimmer of an alternate view is sometimes seen, like lights along a distant shore.

Special Criminal Procedure, Anwar Ali Sarkar and Kathi Raning Rawat

Cooper[7] (eleven judges) and *Maneka Gandhi*[8] (seven judges) overturned *Gopalan* on the test of state action. Both read an interconnected scheme into

---

6 For a detailed discussion on these debates see Rohan Alva, *Liberty After Freedom: A History of Article 21: Due Process and the Constitution of India* (HarperCollins 2022); See also, Tripurdaman Singh, *Sixteen Stormy Days: The Story of the First Amendment to the Constitution of India* (Vintage Books 2020).

7 *Rustom Cavasjee Cooper v. Union of India* (1970) 1 SCC 248. C Shah, SM Sikri, M Shelat, V Bhargava, GK Mitter, CA Vaidialingam, KS Hegde, AN Grover, P Jaganmohan Reddy and D Dua JJ comprised the majority. The opinion was authored by Shah J. AN Ray J dissented.

8 *Maneka Gandhi v. Union of India* (1978) 1 SCC 248. The majority opinion was delivered by MH Beg CJ, YV Chandrachud, PN Bhagwati, NL Untwalia, S Murtaza Fazal Ali, VR Krishna Iyer and PS Kailasam JJ, with PN Bhagwati J writing for himself, NL Untwalia, S Murtaza Fazal Ali JJ, and with separate opinions authored by YV Chandrachud, VR Krishna Iyer, PS Kailasam JJ and MH Beg CJ.

the Fundamental Rights of Part III. Neither of these iconic cases were to do with criminal law, but both relied upon an exposition of Article 14 in *Anwar Ali Sarkar*.

The West Bengal Special Courts Act, 1950 contained a special procedure, lacking many safeguards of the Code of Criminal Procedure (CrPC). A pre-independence Ordinance, now enacted by the state, the Calcutta HC had struck it down as arbitrary, and the state appealed.

Anwar Ali Sarkar was one of the earliest cases where a deviation from normal criminal law called for the Supreme Court's attention. While ruling that arbitrariness was antithetical to the equality clause of Article 14, it recognized that 'law' in Article 21 means:

> ...[A] State-made law, but it must be a valid and binding law having regard not merely to the competency of the legislature and the subject it relates to, but it must not also infringe *any of the fundamental rights guaranteed under Part III of the Constitution* ...[9] (emphasis supplied)

The court noted serious deviations from normal criminal procedure. For instance, an accused could be convicted of an offence for which no charge was framed or notice given. However, it was not for these deviations that the Act was struck down. In fact, the court ruled that trial by jury was only a statutory provision, and could be dispensed with by a law. Whether any rights under the CrPC could be so integral to Article 21 that a departure from these would be wrong in principle, was a question that did not engage the court.

The majority in *Anwar Ali Sarkar* reiterated the *Gopalan* view that the Indian Constitution had 'not chosen to adopt' the due process concept,[10] and that 'a competent legislature [is] entitled to alter the procedure in criminal trials in such way as it considers proper'.[11] However, it struck down the Special Courts Act for failing the test of valid classification. Whimsicality, as to who the special procedure would apply to, was held to offend Article 14.

---

9 *Anwar Ali Sarkar* (n 1) [45] (BK Mukherjea J)

10 ibid [81] (Fazl J).

11 ibid [45] (Mukherjea J).

Understanding the test of Article 14 as valid classification, a similar Ordinance in Saurashtra[12] was upheld the same year in *Kathi Raning Rawat.*[13] This time, a majority of 4:3 held that the preamble to this Ordinance provided clarity on the offences or classes of cases that were to be tried by the special procedure. It was incidentally noticed that some of the more egregious provisions found in the West Bengal law were absent from the Saurashtra Ordinance.

Kathi Raning Rawat also emphasized that a valid law under Article 21 must be a reasonable law under Article 14.[14] The minority held that the preamble could not be factored in as 'guidance'.

Anwar Ali Sarkar and *Kathi Raning Rawat* both expressly observed that certain classes of offences or their aggravated forms may call for a departure from ordinary law.

Vivian Bose J, who struck down the West Bengal law with the majority in *Anwar Ali Sarkar,* also struck down the Saurashtra Ordinance with the minority in *Kathi Raning Rawat.* Both times he discarded the classification test altogether.[15] His is a unique note, bringing to bear upon constitutional appraisal the imperatives of democracy. Bose J rejected the positivist interpretation of Article 21.

> … In my opinion, "law" as used in Article 14 does not mean the "legal precepts which are actually recognised and applied in the tribunals of a given time and place" but *"the more general body of doctrine and tradition from which those precepts are chiefly drawn, and by which we criticise them"*[16]
>
> … We find men accused of heinous crimes called upon to answer for their lives and liberties. We find them picked out from their fellows, and however much the new procedure may give them a few crumbs of advantage, in the bulk they are deprived of substantial and valuable privileges of defence which others, similarly charged, are able to claim. It matters not to me, nor indeed to them and their families and their friends, whether this be

---

12 *Saurashtra State Public Safety Measures (Third Amendment) Ordinance, 1949* (Saurashtra Ordinance).

13 *Kathi Raning Rawat v. State of Saurashtra* AIR 1952 SC 123 (Kathi Raning Rawat); the majority opinion was delivered in separate opinions by M Patanjali Sastri, Fazl Ali, Mukherjea, SR Das JJ. Dissenting opinions were delivered by Chandrasekhara Aiyar, Mahanjan, and Bose JJ.

14 ibid [7] (Patanjali Sastri CJ).

15 Vivan Bose J concurred with the majority on a different point.

16 *Anwar Ali Sarkar* (n 1) [87] (Vivian Bose, J).

done in good faith, whether it be done for the convenience of Government, whether the process can be scientifically classified and labelled, or whether it is an experiment in speedier trials made for the good of society at large. It matters not how lofty and laudable the motives are. *The question with which I charge myself is, can fair-minded, reasonable unbiased and resolute men, who are not swayed by emotion or prejudice, regard this with equanimity and call it reasonable, just and fair, regard it as that equal treatment and protection in the defence of liberties which is expected of a sovereign democratic republic in the conditions which obtain in India today?* I have but one answer to that. On that short and simple ground I would decide this case and hold the Act bad.[17] (emphasis supplied)

*Preventive Detention Pre-*Cooper

Gopalan ruled that the Parliament could provide for preventive detention for longer than three months without reference to an Advisory Board, and indeed without any upper limit for detention. It was after a 1951 amendment to the Act that the government was obliged to release the detenu if the Advisory Board disapproved the detention. If approved, however, the detention could continue forever. This power of indefinite detention once approved was challenged in *S Krishnan.*[18] Though a majority of 4:1 held it permissible, Vivian Bose J penned a sharp dissent. Soon thereafter, the Parliament itself was driven to fix an upper limit of one year for the operation of a preventive detention order, and of five days for supplying the detenu with the grounds of detention.

The Paradigm Shift

In *Cooper,*[19] the Banking Companies (Acquisition and Transfer of Undertakings) Act, 1969 (Bank Nationalisation Act) was challenged successfully. *Gopalan*'s view that state action could only be judged by its stated object was totally negated.

[17] ibid [93] (Vivian Bose J).

[18] *S Krishnan v. State of Madras* AIR 1951 SC 301; the Bench consisted of Kania CJ, Patanjali Sastri, Mahajan, Bose and Das JJ.

[19] *Cooper* (n 7).

Gopalan had held that though preventive detention may affect free movement under Article 19 (1) (d), it could only be tested as a restriction of personal liberty under Articles 21 and 22. In fact, in the absence of personal liberty, all other incidents of liberty ceased to exist. So, even if the right to movement under Article 19 (1) (d) is impaired by preventive detention, the test will not be whether the restriction is reasonable as required by Article 19 (5), but only whether it is by a law passed by a competent legislature under Articles 21 and 22, which need not be tested for reasonableness.

Cooper now held that this view was wrong:

> ...Part III of the Constitution weaves a pattern of guarantees on the texture of basic human rights. The guarantees delimit the protection of those rights in their allotted fields: they do not attempt to enunciate distinct rights.[20]

The Bank Nationalisation Act was struck down as violating both Articles 19 (1) (f) and 31 (2), no longer seen as mutually exclusive tests. An evolution of this view, virtually exalting Part III to due and just process, was to come a decade later in *Maneka Gandhi* – but eventful years intervened.

The Tumultuous Period (1969–77)

In the years that followed *Cooper*, preventive detention came into its own as a political weapon. It happened like this. The Maintenance of Internal Security Act (MISA), originally an Ordinance, was passed by the Parliament in July 1971. Later, in the wake of the external Emergency of the Indo-Pak War, the Defence of India Act, 1971 (DIA) and Rules thereunder (DIR) were enacted. The DIA and DIR 1971 were substantially the same as the colonial era Defence of India Act and Rules, 1939 – which were an early example of the twin restrictions on grant of bail that are now seen so commonly.[21] Barring one section, these new preventive detention laws were upheld by the Supreme Court.[22]

---

20 ibid [61-62] (Shah J).

21 I am grateful to Ms Kirti Awasthi for her excellent research paper on this topic, which she generously shared with me.

22 See section titled 'MISA and More'.

The internal Emergency of June 1975 was declared even without revoking the external Emergency, though the war had long ended. MISA and the DIR were used to jail the political opposition and abridge civil liberties. The Proclamation of Emergency by the Presidential Order of 25 June 1975, which suspended fundamental rights and barred legal remedies, was upheld by the Supreme Court in the *Habeas Corpus Case*[23] (with a sole shining dissent). Prior to this, several High Court (HCs) had enforced the writ of *habeas corpus* even in the face of the Proclamation. *Maneka Gandhi* came in 1978, after the people of India had consummately rejected all that the Emergency signified in the Lok Sabha elections of March 1977.

MISA and More

By the time MISA and the DIA were taken to the Supreme Court, *Cooper* had been decided. The challenge could now be based on Article 14 (after *Anwar Ali Sarkar*) as well as Article 19 (after *Cooper*), besides Articles 21 and 22. Section 17A, added to MISA by DIA, permitted an Indian citizen to be detained for up to two years without reference to the Advisory Board. If approved by the Board, detention could extend to three years, or until the lapse of the DIA, whichever was later. Seven judges in *Shambhunath Sarkar*[24] unanimously struck down Section 17A. They ruled that for preventive detention longer than three months, review by an Advisory Board, under Article 22 (4) (a), was a salutary safeguard. Parliament's power under Article 22 (7) (a), to do away with the safeguard, should not be exercised, as had been done here, by simply reproducing the words in the Union and Concurrent lists as grounds for application of Section 17A.[25] Other grounds of challenge were not dealt with as detention was quashed on the invalidation of Section 17A.

It is possible, perhaps likely, that the idea of a valid law as 'reasonable' found in *Anwar Ali Sarkar*, *Kathi Raning Rawat* and *Cooper* had entered the verdict in

---

[23] *ADM Jabalpur v. Shivakant Shukla* (1976) 2 SCC 521; The majority consisted of AN Ray CJ, Beg, Chandrachud and Bhagwati JJ. The sole dissenting opinion was by HR Khanna J.

[24] (1973) 1 SCC 856; The Bench consisted of Shelat Acting CJ, Hegde, Ray, Reddy, Khanna, Mukherjea, and YV Chandrachud JJ.

[25] See Constitution of India 1950, sch VII, list I, entry 9: 'Preventive detention for reasons connected with Defence, Foreign Affairs, or the security of India; persons subjected to such detention'; See also, Constitution of India 1950, sch VII, list III, entry 3: 'Preventive detention for reasons connected with the security of a State, the maintenance of public order, or the maintenance of supplies and services essential to the community; persons subjected to such detention.'

Shambhunath Sarkar. If so, however, the effect did not last long. Just over a year later, the rest of MISA was fully upheld by the Supreme Court in *Haradhan Saha*[26] in one voice, spoken through CJI AN Ray.[27]

Neither fairness as spoken of by *Anwar Ali Sarkar* and *Kathi Raning Rawat*, nor the test of reasonableness imposed by Article 19 (5) were of any avail against the text of State-made law. The stage was set for the Emergency of 1975-1977.

ADM Jabalpur and the Suspension of Fundamental Rights

Dissenters and political opponents were jailed under MISA, DIA and other executive powers. In one fell swoop, the Proclamation of Emergency by the Presidential Order of 25 June 1975 suspended all fundamental freedoms. The Supreme Court, in *ADM Jabalpur*,[28] held by a majority of 4:1 that there was no remedy available in the face of such an order by the executive: 'The supremacy of the law means that the faith of civil liberty depends on the man who has to administer civil liberty much more than on any legal formula.'[29]

From *Gopalan* to *ADM Jabalpur*, for all the varied formulations, the freedom of the individual remained but an incident of executive caprice couched as executive or legislative wisdom, into which courts would not enter.

The lone dissenting judge did try and find a crevice in the wall thrown up by the executive and his brother judges thus:

> Even in the absence of Article 21 in the Constitution, the State has got no power to deprive a person of his life or liberty without the authority of law … life and liberty are priceless possessions which cannot be made the plaything of individual whim and caprice …[30]

---

[26] (1975) 3 SCC 198. The Bench consisted of Ray CJ, Reddy, Mathew, Beg, and Alagiriswami JJ.

[27] ibid [30].

[28] *ADM Jabalpur* (n 23).

[29] ibid [93] (Ray CJ).

[30] ibid [530] (HR Khanna J).

The More Things Change, the More They Remain the Same (1977–1980)

Forty-Fourth Amendment of the Constitution

The Emergency ended with the March 1977 elections. The Forty-Fourth Amendment was brought in to reverse some of its depredations. 'Internal disturbance' was no longer a ground on which an internal Emergency could be called, the cause had to be of the order of an 'armed rebellion'. Articles 20 and 21 could not be suspended during any declared Emergency, even rights under Article 19 could only be suspended during an external aggression and not during an internal Emergency.[31] No Emergency could be continued without the Parliament's periodic approval. Article 22 was amended, removing the Parliament's power to pass any law allowing indefinite detention, and stipulated against detention beyond two months without the approval of the Advisory Board;[32] but this last amendment was never brought into force.

None of these changes prevented the State from amending the Constitution a decade later to suspend all rights, including the right to life, in the insurgency-affected Punjab.[33] The people of Punjab formally remained without the constitutional right to life for as long as five years. Text is easily changed!

Maneka Gandhi and 'Due Process'

In 1978, Maneka Gandhi, whose passport was impounded by the Central Government,[34] challenged the action as an arbitrary invasion of her fundamental rights to life, liberty and free movement. Seven judges of the Supreme Court, in five opinions, now spoke eloquently of the integral scheme of protection against hostile state action under Part III.[35] In practical terms, the passport remained with the Registrar of the Supreme Court, pending the personal hearing that the government promised. However, the case is

---

31 The Constitution (Forty-Fourth Amendment) Act 1978.

32 Current provision reads as originally drafted.

33 See: the Constitution (Fifty-Ninth Amendment) Act 1988. To the best of the author's knowledge, this amendment has not been challenged before any court.

34 In a bid to prevent her leaving the country, during a probe by the Shah Commission of Inquiry before which she had been summoned

35 *Maneka Gandhi* (n 8).

generally taken as having brought into Indian public law the requirement of 'due process'.[36]

Nandini Satpathy: CrPC as Due Process

In the same year that *Maneka Gandhi* effectively read due process into Part III, a three-judge Bench in *Nandini Satpathy*[37] saw a convergence between the CrPC and the Constitution. As said before, *Anwar Ali Sarkar* did not examine how particular aspects of the CrPC checked with Article 21, except to say that trial by jury was a mere statutory right which could be taken away. *Nandini Satpathy* recognized that some CrPC provisions were, in substance, constitutional protections. They signified 'procedure established by law' because their very content was due process, and not because they were passed by a competent legislature.

Though the judgment notes that the CrPC was liable to change, it does suggest that there are abiding constitutional values in criminal law, which should not be eroded by slight and subtle alterations in the statute.[38]

Preventive Detention Post Maneka Gandhi and Nandini Satpathy

MISA was repealed in 1978, and the DIA lapsed in 1977.

The National Security Act (NSA), yet another preventive detention law, was brought in as an Ordinance, and then enacted by the Parliament in 1980. The legendary trade unionist, AK Roy, challenged this law. The Supreme Court turned down the plea that an Ordinance was not 'law' which could restrict liberty.[39] It also repelled his case that the purported grounds for detention under the Act were a mindless repetition of the entries in Lists I and III,[40] that it excessively delegated the power to detain persons, and contained other drastic clauses. Changes made by the Forty-Fourth Amendment to Article 22,

---

36 *Maneka Gandhi* (n 8) [7] (PN Bhagwati J).

37 *Nandini Satpathy v. PL Dani* (1978) 2 SCC 424; the Bench consisted of VR Krishna Iyer, Jaswant Singh and VD Tulzapurkar JJ.

38 ibid [21, 34].

39 *AK Roy v. Union of India* (1982) 1 SCC 271 [19] (YV Chandrachud CJ); the Bench consisted of YV Chandrachud CJ, PN Bhagwati, AC Gupta, VD Tulzapurkar and DA Desai JJ.

40 A ground on which Section 17A MISA was struck down in *Shambhunath Sarkar* (n 24).

neither notified nor complied with, were unsuccessfully pleaded by Roy.[41] Significantly, he argued that the detenu was bereft of due process rights before the Advisory Board, such as cross-examination and right to counsel. In other words, the procedure for executive detention was impugned in light of the 'due process' that had recently entered our jurisprudence and deviance from which was arguably unsustainable.

The unanimous view of the Supreme Court remained what it had been three decades back in *Gopalan* – the text of Article 22 exempted preventive detention from the imperatives of criminal due process.[42]

The Supreme Court did allow the detenu to give evidence in rebuttal, as Article 22 and NSA did not *expressly* bar the same. Otherwise, the court relied on *Haradhan Saha,* which upheld MISA (a *pari materia* law), although in the six years since that judgment India had been badly seared by executive highhandedness. And despite a sea change in fundamental rights jurisprudence, there was little difference in how executive detention was viewed by the court. The text of Article 21 conferred a right which was conditional upon the text of State-made law. So, *Gopalan* lives.

After *Gopalan* found that preventive detention did not offend any constitutional principle, there really has been no looking back for the Indian State. One publication lists about 50 central and state laws of executive detention in the country.[43]

While the odd provision may have been struck down, most challenges to the *vires* of preventive detention laws have been unsuccessful. Powers of externment have, on occasion, been invalidated.[44] The Supreme Court has also held that detention should first be challenged before the HCs unless there are 'satisfactory' reasons to straightaway move the Supreme Court.[45]

---

[41] The minority of two judges issued a mandamus directing the central government to notify them within a period of two months, without setting aside the detention.

[42] *AK Roy* (n 39) [86] (YV Chandrachud CJ).

[43] Surendra Malik and Sudeep Malik, *Supreme Court on Preventive Detention Laws* (2nd edn, Eastern Book Company 2019).

[44] See *State of Madhya Pradesh v. Thakur Bharat Singh*, AIR 1967 SC 1170, where Section 3(1) of the Madhya Pradesh Public Safety Act 1959 limiting the movement of citizens was struck down as violating Article 19 (1) (d); See also, *State of Madhya Pradesh v. Baldeo Prasad* AIR 1961 SC 293, striking down the CP and Berar Goondas Act, 1946. The Bench consisted of BP Sinha CJ, JL Kapur, PB Gajendragadkar, K Subba Rao and KN Wanchoo JJ.

[45] *Union of India v. Paul Manickam* (2003) 8 SCC 342 [22]; the Bench consisted of Doraiswamy Raju and

Detention itself has often been set aside, and a body of law on its technical compliance has been developed by the Supreme Court. In a case where a detenu was kept in continuous preventive detention for years on end, simply by serving a fresh detention order close on the heels of the HC invalidating the earlier one, the SCI directed that any fresh order served on the detenu be held in abeyance for a week, to let him avail of any anticipatory remedy.[46]

The rub really is that the relief, if any, comes only after a good part of the detention is over. A recent study of challenges to detention under various preventive detention laws in the Supreme Court between the years 2000 and 2019, has this to say:

> On an average, the Supreme Court gave its decision after the detenu spent a period of 344 days in detention, of which 111 were attributable to the Supreme Court.[47]

The Age of Terror

Since the mid 1980s, terrorism has been viewed as the single greatest threat to the nation state. International discourse on terror has led to the emergence of the 'security state'.

The Narcotic Drugs and Psychotropic Substances Act (NDPS) of 1985 permitted evidence of a statement recorded during investigation by an officer of the Narcotics Control Bureau.[48] This broke a 100-year-old tradition of an 'institutionalised presumption'[49] against confessions of guilt to investigators. It was only in 2020 that the Supreme Court held any such statement under the NDPS Act to be inadmissible in terms of Section 162 CrPC, and Sections

---

Arijit Pasayat JJ.

46 *Farooq Ahmad Bhat v. State of Jammu and Kashmir* W.P. (Crl) 2 of 2013, order dated 22 March 2013.

47 Shrutanjaya Bharadwaj, 'Preventive Detention, Habeas Corpus, and Delay at the Apex Court: An Empirical Study' (2020) 13(2) *NUJS Law Review* 12; The study also finds that 'On an average, the Supreme Court gave its decision after the detenu spent a period of 528 days agitating the habeas corpus petition at the Supreme Court level alone,' and further that these decisions were given on average 'after a period of 953 days calculated from the date of detention order or actual detention (whichever is earlier)'.

48 Narcotic Drugs and Psychotropic Substances Act 1985, s 67.

49 *Aloke Nath Dutta v. State of West Bengal* (2007) 12 SCC 230 [102], which refers to Sections 24 to 26 as constituting an 'institutionalised presumption against confession extracted by police or in police custody'. The Bench consisted of SB Sinha and Dalveer Bhandari.

25 and 26 Indian Evidence Act.[50] The NDPS model of letting into evidence self-incrimination by suspects has been adopted in a more detailed form by successive anti-terror laws.

After various special laws for notified areas in the early 1980s, the Terrorist and Disruptive Activities (Prevention) Act, 1987 (TADA) was brought for the whole of India. Anti-terror laws have always had provisions restricting release on bail. In sum, release on bail is barred unless a court, on perusing the prosecution's material, finds reason to believe that an undertrial is not guilty. These conditions were also introduced to the NDPS in 1989.[51]

The *vires* of TADA came up before a Constitution Bench in *Kartar Singh*.[52] The chief focus was deviance from the norms of criminal procedure. The Supreme Court held that the Parliament was competent to pass the law, whether it fell within 'criminal law' in the Concurrent List, or 'defence of India' in the Union List. The Executive's assessment of a dire threat to national security, as spoken to on the floor of the Parliament, was taken note of.

Kartar Singh, like *Nandini Satpathy* earlier, acknowledged that the protections in the CrPC and the Evidence Act against self-incrimination in police custody flowed from Articles 20 (3) and 21. The Court also noted the rising lawlessness of the law enforcement agencies.

The divergence, between the majority of three and the minority of two, arose on TADA's departure from a hitherto cardinal rule of Indian law, to allow into evidence confessions recorded by the police, against both the maker and others tried as co-accused or co-conspirators. The majority ruled that the departure was justified, as 'terrorists' were a distinct class of offenders. Lamenting the practice of torture, however, the majority, through S Ratnavel Pandian J, framed guidelines to be followed when the Superintendent of Police recorded confessions.[53] The minority of two was unswayed by the State's rhetoric. It held that the rule against self-incrimination was a non-negotiable element of due process, which is not in thrall to 'policy or rationale or object of the Act'.

---

50 *Tofan Singh v. State of Tamil Nadu* (2021) 4 SCC 1; the majority consisted of Rohinton F Nariman and Navin Sinha JJ.

51 Narcotic Drugs and Psychotropic Substances Act 1985, s 37.

52 *Kartar Singh v. State of Punjab* (1994) 3 SCC 569; The majority comprised S Ratnavel Pandian, MM Punchhi, and SC Agrawal JJ. The minority opinions were by K Ramaswamy and RM Sahai JJ.

53 ibid [253, 257] (Pandian J).

> The class of offences dealt by TADA may be different than other offences but the offender under TADA is as much entitled to protection of Articles 20 and 21 as any other. The difference in nature of offence or the legislative competence to enact a law did not affect the fundamental rights guaranteed by Chapter III. [...] Section 15 cannot be held to be valid merely because it is as a result of law made by a body which has been found entitled to make the law. The law must still be fair and just as held by this Court. A law which entitles a police officer to record confession and makes it admissible is thus violative of both Articles 20(3) and 21 of the Constitution.[54]

Safeguards Slacken

Even the token safeguards in special laws invariably slacken over time. In *Devender Pal Singh*,[55] the Court found that the confession was materially contradicted by clear facts. Yet, a majority of 2:1 held that a confession was true if it was voluntary. Thus, the well settled distinction between two separate conditions for relying upon a confession – truth and voluntariness – collapsed into one as implying the other, and the test became far less rigorous. In *Gurdeep Singh*,[56] a confession was accepted as voluntary even though it had been recorded when the accused was handcuffed and surrounded by a posse of armed guards.

TADA lapsed in 1995 amidst widespread protests against its misuse. With the enactment of Prevention of Terrorism Act 2002 (POTA), the controversy surrounding confessions to the police resumed. POTA had changed a bit from TADA's scheme. Under Section 32 of POTA, a confession recorded by the police could only be used against the maker, and not against others tried as co-accused or conspirators. Also, the guidelines given by the Supreme Court in *Kartar Singh* were statutorily drafted into POTA. The SCI upheld the constitutionality of Section 32 in *People's Union for Civil Liberties*.[57] However, in *Navjot Sandhu*,[58] often referred to as the Parliament Attack case, which was

---

[54] ibid [456] (RM Sahai J).

[55] *Devender Pal Singh v. State of NCT of Delhi* (2002) 5 SCC 234; The Bench consisted of MB Shah, BN Agrawal and Arijit Pasayat JJ.

[56] *Gurdeep Singh v. State* (2000) 1 SCC 498; The Bench consisted of KT Thomas and AP Misra JJ.

[57] *People's Union for Civil Liberties v. Union of India* (2004) 9 SCC 580; The Bench consisted of S Rajendra Babu and GP Mathur JJ.

[58] *Navjot Sandhu v. State (NCT of Delhi)* (2005) 11 SCC 600; The Bench consisted of P Venkatarama Reddi and PP Naolekar J.

tried under POTA, the reliability of a confession was linked to the scrupulous observance of custodial rights, access to a lawyer and remand to judicial custody. The SCI ruled out the confessions recorded by the police in that case as non-compliant with basic safeguards, and also found their tone unnatural and involuntary. The two-Judge Bench, though bound by *Kartar Singh*, doubted the wisdom of permitting police-recorded confessions, a course fraught with danger, as India lacked the systemic checks in place in the West where confessions made to the police are sometimes allowed into evidence.

The government is meant to scrutinize the record and see whether a case should really be tried under the harsh procedure of a terror law. A court cannot try such a case without a prior 'sanction' for prosecution from the government. This is theoretically held to be a great safeguard. Yet, sanction is generally accorded for the asking with next to no scrutiny. On a rare occasion, a HC held the sanction invalid and the trial vitiated. It discharged the accused. The Supreme Court stayed their release, expressing doubt about the appropriateness of a discharge in an appeal against conviction.[59] This, though the powers of an appellate court expressly include the power to discharge.[60]

The State Exempted

The 13 December 2001 attack on the Parliament was a classic terror strike. Indeed, it was the *raison d'etre* of the Prevention of Terrorism Ordinance (POTO) of 24 October 2001 being enacted as POTA by a joint session of the Parliament on 24 March 2002. POTO contained a code on interception of communications with the peremptory mandate that interceptions contrary to it must be destroyed and ruled out of evidence. The prosecution in the Parliament Attack case relied heavily on wiretaps without complying with the POTO regime on interception. Still, the Supreme Court allowed the wiretaps in evidence, upon the reasoning that on the date of the interceptions the police had not added the POTO sections to the FIR.[61] Inconvenient safeguards were thus avoided by simply omitting POTO from the FIR. In time for the police to record confessions, however, POTO was added.

If the accused are acquitted of the terror charges, could a confession recorded

---

59 *State of Maharashtra v. Mahesh Kariman Tirki* (2022) 10 SCC 207.

60 Code of Criminal Procedure 1973, s 386 (b) (i).

61 *Navjot Sandhu* (n 58) [155].

by the police under the special law still be used to convict them under the IPC? This question arose after the Rajiv Gandhi assassination case.[62] A five-judge Bench answered the reference by ruling that because the trial had been held under the special procedure, the confessions could still be read to prove the other IPC offences.[63]

The law does speak of a 'trial under' that Act but, given that the drastic provision allowing into evidence a confession to the police was upheld solely on the strength of terrorists being a distinct class, should those adjudged innocent of terror be subjected to the added disadvantages of the special procedure merely because they were tried for those offences?

An asymmetry loaded against the individual and in favour of the State is found not only in the statute, but also in the interpretation given to it by the courts.

After POTA

POTA was repealed in 2004. Simultaneously, the Unlawful Activities (Prevention) Act, 1967 (UAPA) was amended to incorporate some POTA offences. Though it classified terrorism as a distinct offence, the procedure was still the CrPC. This change was not to last. After the Mumbai attacks of 26 November 2008, the Parliament brought into UAPA most of POTA, other than confessions to the police.[64] The National Investigation Agency Act, 2008 (NIA Act) set up a central agency with the power to take over the investigation of any of the offences mentioned in the schedule to the Act, including the UAPA, from the local police. Following a judgment of the Supreme Court, all the scheduled offences, whether or not investigated by the NIA, will now be subject to the special procedure and tried by the special courts under the NIA Act,[65] which bars many remedies.[66] Grant or rejection of bail by the trial court is subject to an appeal to a two-judge Bench of the HC. HCs are divided on

---

62 *State v. Nalini* (1999) 5 SCC 253; The Bench consisted of KT Thomas and DP Wadhwa and SSM Quadri JJ.

63 *Prakash Kumar v. State of Gujarat* (2005) 2 SCC 409; The Bench consisted of RC Lahoti CJ, BN Agrawal, HK Sema, GP Mathur, PK Balasubramanyan JJ. See also *State v. Nalini* (n 62).

64 However, many other laws continue to have that provision. For instance, see Maharashtra Control of Organised Crimes Act, 1999, s 18.

65 *Bikramjit Singh v. State of Punjab* (2020) 10 SCC 616; The Bench consisted of RF Nariman, Navin Sinha and KM Joseph JJ.

66 National Investigation Agency Act 2008 Act, s 21 bars a revision to the HC as well as the HC's original power to grant bail.

whether an accused against whom charge has been framed can file an appeal, or have any remedy at all in a higher forum.[67] Denial of any remedy against framing of charge will lead to a near impossibility of release on bail, as it would imply a *prima facie* case, upon which bail is barred by UAPA.

Liberty Shortchanged

A host of laws now have additional restrictions on release on bail, including UAPA, Maharashtra Control of Organised Crime Act (MCOCA), Gujarat Control of Terrorism and Organised Crimes Act, 2015 (GujCTOCA) and Prevention of Money Laundering Act 2002 (PMLA). The text of the restrictions has led to varied expositions by the Supreme Court in the last years. In *Watali*,[68] a two-judge Bench ruled that the bail provision of UAPA eases the burden on the prosecution, as its case must be taken to be true unless rebutted. Considering that there is no rebuttal at the pretrial stage, does this mean there is to be no release on bail at all? *Watali* also ruled that once charge is framed a *prima facie* case is to be assumed, making a case for bail more onerous.

Watali read Section 43D '(5), UAPA – 'shall not be released on bail ... if the Court ... is of the opinion that there are reasonable grounds for believing that the accusation against such person is prima facie true' – as being similar to Section 21(4), MCOCA – '... no person ... shall, if in custody, be released ... unless ... the Court is satisfied that there are reasonable grounds for believing that he is not guilty of such offence and that he is not likely to commit any offence while on bail'.

In *KA Najeeb*,[69] a three-judge Bench of the Supreme Court took the view that the UAPA wording is a lower threshold for the accused than the MCOCA/

[67] Bombay, Chhattisgarh and Allahabad HCs hold there is an appeal under the NIA Act; See *Lt Col Prasad Purohit v. NIA* Criminal Appeal No 112 of 2018, order dated 5 March 2019 (Bombay HC), *Nishant Jain v. State of Chhattisgarh* CRA No 961 of 2021, order dated 22 September 2021 (Chhattisgarh HC), and *Hussna v. NIA*, 2016 SCC OnLine All 970; Some HCs hold that a HC has supervisory jurisdiction, see *Dimchuingam Ruangmei v. National Investigation Agency* 2022 SCC OnLine Megh 522, *Ayaz Ahmed v. Union Territory* Crl A 13 of 2022, order dated 16 February 2023 (HC of Jammu and Kashmir), *Ghulam Mohammed Bhat v. NIA* Criminal Appeal No 416 of 2012, order dated 18 April 2012 (Delhi HC); Still others do not recognize any remedy at all, see *Londhoni Devi v. State* (2013) SCC OnLine Gau 407.

[68] *NIA v. Zahoor Ahmad Shah Watali* (2019) 5 SCC 1; the Bench consisted of AM Khanwilkar and Ajay Rastogi JJ.

[69] *Union of India v. Najeeb* (2021) 3 SCC 713; The Bench consisted of NV Ramana, Surya Kant and Aniruddha Bose JJ.

NDPS version. It also held that a *constitutional court* is not bound by this restriction, and can release a person on bail if the promise of speedy trial, implicit in such statutes, is not met by the criminal justice system.

Yet, another two-judge Bench in *Gurwinder*[70] read down *Najeeb* as turning on the facts of the case, that is, purely upon an assessment that the erstwhile absconding Najeeb, in custody for five years, was unlikely to be sentenced to more than eight years, as was awarded to the co-accused who had already stood trial. *Gurwinder* declared that jail is the rule and bail the exception under UAPA.

Other judgments have held that a terrorist act must be shown to be in contemplation, on the basis of evidence with probative value, before a prima facie case can be inferred to deny bail.[71] This ratio was ignored in *Gurwinder.* In *Mazhar Khan,* the probative value of the only material, a pure custodial statement inadmissible under Section 162 CrPC, and Sections 25 and 26 Evidence Act, was not assessed. Upon the *Watali* reasoning that the prosecution's story must be taken as true, bail was denied.[72] Still, other judgments hold *Guwinder* as restricted to its own facts.[73]

Extended Pre-charge Detention

Unlike the normal law, where it is possible for an undertrial to get what is known as 'default bail' in 60 or 90 days if no charge-sheet is filed by the prosecution,[74] deviant laws give trial courts the discretion to extend the time to file a charge-sheet. Courts may grant this, if the public prosecutor justifies the 'continued detention' of the accused by showing the investigation done until then and the need for more time to complete it. The SCI has held that bare information to the accused of the application seeking extension, without any written notice would suffice.[75] Also, there is the view that details of the

---

[70] *Gurwinder Singh v. State of Punjab* (2024) 5 SCC 403 [45]. The Bench consisted of MM Sundresh and Aravind Kumar JJ.

[71] *Vernon v. State of Maharashtra* (2023) 15 SCC 56 [35]–[37]; The Bench consisted of Aniruddha Bose and Sudhanshu Dhulia JJ.

[72] *Mazhar Khan v. National Investigation Agency* (2024) 6 SCC 627.

[73] *Sheikh Javed Iqbal v. State of Uttar Pradesh* (2024) 8 SCC 293; See also *Jalaluddin Khan v. Union of India* (2024) 10 SCC 574.

[74] Code of Criminal Procedure 1973, s 167(2).

[75] *Sanjay Dutt v. State* (1994) 5 SCC 410; the Bench consisted of AM Ahmadi, JS Verma, PB Sawant, BP Jeevan Reddy and NP Singh JJ.

investigation and grounds for extension may be kept a secret from the accused like the case diary.

An account of investigation till date is not like a case diary but instead akin to an application for a remand. Without this information, an accused will be unable to oppose continued incarceration. On occasion, when there has been a blatant violation of the opportunity to oppose extension of time to file the charge-sheet, the Supreme Court has given relief to the accused.[76]

Proliferation of Deviant Laws

Today, aside from preventive detention, there are so many deviant laws in India that the normal runs the danger of becoming the exception. PMLA is the latest in this series and also carries onerous bail conditions. A two-judge Bench of the Supreme Court in 2018 had actually struck down these conditions as reversing the presumption of innocence without 'any compelling state interest' (*Kartar Singh* had justified a similar provision in TADA as necessitated by compelling state interest).[77]

Within months, the Parliament reintroduced these very conditions with cosmetic changes.[78] A three-judge Bench has now upheld it.[79] PMLA reverses the burden of proof with no riders,[80] and the SCI has validated the same with a laconic reduction of the greatest bulwark of liberty to a *mere* rule of evidence.

> Indeed, in a criminal trial, the principle of innocence of the accused/offender is regarded as a human right ... However, that presumption can be

[76] *Jigar v. State of Gujarat* (2023) 6 SCC 484; The Bench consisted of Ajay Rastogi and AS Oka JJ.

[77] *Nikesh Tarachand Shah v. Union of India* (2018) 11 SCC 1 [46]–[47]; The provision was struck down also on the ground that it required the Court to determine if the accused was innocent, not of the offence of money laundering but connected offences (under Part A of the Schedule, PMLA) which had resulted in proceeds of crime. This resulted in the arbitrary distinction where an accused who is tried for both money laundering and predicate offences simultaneously, or who is charged only with the predicate offences but tried along with others accused of money laundering, would have to satisfy s 45 to be released on bail, whereas a person being tried only for money laundering, or only the connected offence in an ordinary trial, would not. The Bench consisted of Rohinton F Nariman and SK Kaul JJ.

[78] The changes were brought about vide the Finance Act 2018, s 205. The change in the provision was that the bail conditions would be restricted to PMLA offences alone, and excluding connected offences unlike earlier.

[79] *Vijay Madanlal Choudhary v. Union of India* (2023) 12 SCC 1; The Bench consisted of AM Khanwilkar, Dinesh Maheshwari and CT Ravikumar JJ.

[80] Prevention of Money Laundering Act 2002, s 24.

> interdicted by a law made by the Parliament/Legislature. It is well-settled that statutory provisions regarding presumptions are nothing but rule of evidence (sic).[81]

PMLA goes further than even anti-terror laws, allowing the Directorate of Enforcement (ED) to compel statements on oath from anyone, including those to be prosecuted by the selfsame ED.[82] Would it not be a classic case of compelled self-incrimination when used by ED against an accused? The SCI returned an incomprehensible answer: if the statement is made after arrest, 'whether the protection given to the accused who is being prosecuted for the offence of money laundering, of Section 25 of the Evidence Act is available or not, may have to be considered on case-to-case basis being rule of evidence' (sic).[83] Having declared that ED officials are not police officers, even though they may arrest, detain, interrogate and prosecute,[84] *Vijay Madanlal* said that Section 25, which applies only to statements recorded by police officers, may apply as chance dictates. *Tofan Singh's*[85] recognition of what would constitute a police official for attracting the protection of sections 25 and 26 of the Evidence Act, though squarely applicable to the ED, was noticed but differentiated in *Vijay Madanlal.*

Some Accused Less Equal than Others?

An account of the SCI would be incomplete without noting the contrariety that marks its discourse on liberty and criminal law.

Some provisions of the Scheduled Castes and Scheduled Tribes (Prevention of Atrocities) Act, 1989 ('Atrocities Act') were struck down and others

---

[81] *Vijay Madanlal Choudhary* (n 79) [339].

[82] Prevention of Money Laundering Act 2002, s 50.

[83] *Vijay Madanlal Choudhary* (n 79) [449]; See also, Nitya Ramakrishnan, 'Undue Process: Here's What's Wrong with the Supreme Court's PMLA Judgment' (*The Wire*, 3 August 2022) <https://thewire.in/law/undue-process-heres-whats-wrong-with-the-supreme-courts-pmla-judgment> accessed 4 March 2025.

[84] Customs officials who may prosecute duty evaders are given powers to arrest prosecute and record statements under Section 108 of the Customs Act, 1962. In a series of judgments of the 1950s and 1960s, they were held not to be police officers while doing so; See *State of Punjab v. Barkat Ram* AIR 1962 SC 276; However, most of those prosecutions were punishable with fine alone and they seldom carried long imprisonment.

[85] *Tofan Singh* (n 50).

reinterpreted by a two-judge Bench in *Subhash Kashinath*.[86] Section 18 of this Act expressly prohibits grant of anticipatory bail. *Subhash Kashinath* held that this bar would not apply if there was no prima facie case against the accused. In other words, by this judgment, the statutory bar, far from stopping a petition for anticipatory bail at the threshold, enabled a court to consider whether there was indeed a case to justify an arrest.

Subhash Kashinath was premised upon the inevitable arbitrariness in arrests and police highhandedness, lamented by commission after commission and the irredeemable hardship and humiliation that an arrest inflicts upon the detenu. Indeed, the Supreme Court went to the extent of making a sociological assessment that wrongful prosecutions under the Atrocities Act will only serve to worsen caste distinctions in society.

Subhash Kashinath concluded that a blanket denial of anticipatory bail was an unconscionable deprivation of liberty. Although the court noted similar provisions in other laws such as the UAPA and NDPS, it distinguished those laws because they imposed additional conditions on even post-arrest bail, which were absent in the Atrocities Act. The reasoning is incomprehensible.

If the operative logic is police high handedness, indiscriminate arrests or absence of a prima facie case, this may equally apply to those arrested under the UAPA or similar statutes. In fact, the deficiencies of our investigative agencies would cast doubt on the wisdom of even the additional restrictions on regular bail in these laws. Why then should an accused under the UAPA be bereft of a protection from arrest if there is no prima facie case?

In the event, there was a public furore calling it a dilution of the safeguards intended for Dalits, and the judgment of the two-judge Bench in *Subhash Kashinath* was later reviewed. Many of its directions were recalled by a three-judge Bench, but the interpretation of Section 18 was maintained.[87] Even today anticipatory bail is granted to those accused under the Atrocities Act on the count that a prima facie case is absent, though the statute bars the remedy altogether.[88]

---

86 *Dr Subhash Kashinath Mahajan v. The State of Maharashtra* (2018) 6 SCC 454; the Bench consisted of AK Goel and UU Lalit JJ.

87 *Union of India v. State of Maharashtra* (2020) 4 SCC 761 [54]; The Bench consisted of Arun Mishra, MR Shah and BR Gavai JJ.

88 *Dhanraj Aswani v. Amar S Mulchandani* (2024) 10 SCC 336.

Hundreds remain in jail for years on end only to be found utterly innocent of any terror crime, but they are denied the remedy of pre-arrest bail as given to persons accused under the Atrocities Act. Reference has earlier been made in this essay that anti-terror terror laws are considered an exception. It is time to revisit this logic, for although the seriousness of a crime is relevant, innocent victims of police arbitrariness are found more in terror cases as the statistics of the low conviction rates will show.[89] Would wrongful prosecutions under terror laws not serve to increase alienation and hinder the fight against extremism?

Disturbed Areas and AFSPA

Indians in Jammu and Kashmir and in the North-East certainly seem to be less equal. The AFSPA has continuously operated in parts of the North-East since 1958, and in Jammu and Kashmir since the 1990s. The declaration of these areas as 'disturbed' under AFSPA by the Central or State Government,[90] and the power of military personnel to shoot at sight and even kill someone only suspected to be acting in contravention of orders,[91] has been upheld by the Supreme Court. This was done on the count of the Parliament's legislative competence as to the subject matter and upon the fond hope that the executive will be strictly guided by necessity as spelt out in the law.[92] Impunity by way of a pre-condition of executive sanction to prosecute armed personnel has been also upheld.[93] The likely alienation of the people of regions branded 'disturbed' and the danger of unaccounted military power was noted by the Supreme Court in passing.[94] Yet, no corrective or binding legal principle resulted – only a list of pious guidelines that the State can barely be held down to.

Whimsicality of Principle

If the textual reference in Article 22 to 'preventive detention' has impressed the Supreme Court time and again to hold it valid, surely there is no textual

89 'UAPA Case Data Suggests That Process Is Indeed the Punishment' (*The Wire*, 20 July 2022) <https://thewire.in/government/uapa-case-data-process-punishment-home-ministry-rajya-sabha> accessed 4 March 2025. See also: NCRB Crime in India Reports for 2018–2021. See also, National Crime Records Bureau, 'Crime in India Report 2018' to National Crime Records Bureau, 'Crime in India Report 2021'.

90 Armed Forces (Special Powers) Act 1958, s 3.

91 ibid, s 4 (a).

92 *Naga People's Movement of Human Rights v. Union of India* (1998) 2 SCC 109 [35], [46], [53]–[58].

93 ibid [52].

94 ibid [39].

basis to suggest that the presumption of innocence can be unconditionally done away with,[95] or that compelled self-incrimination is permissible or to justify the departure from normal safeguards.

The UAPA distinguishes between 'terrorist' and 'unlawful' activities, the former being subject to harsher procedure, stiffer bail conditions and more severe penalties. Some activities are to be dealt with by imposing a ban on an organization, without criminal prosecution. Other acts are liable to prosecution. All these distinctions have been blurred in practice. Provocative utterances are routinely equated with terrorist conspiracies by the police and the NIA. Even where HCs may have noticed these distinctions, the SCI has reversed the decision.[96]

The Pushback

An account of the SCI would also be incomplete without noting its introspection and the palliatives that it tries to fashion. The dissent in *Kartar Singh*, the observations against confessions recorded by the police in the *Parliament Attack* case, and periodic directives for release of undertrials held under draconian laws are indeed lights along a distant shore.

A marked attempt by the SCI to civilize PMLA is also discernible of late in three distinct ways. *First* by delineating the powers of arrest.[97] Written reasons for arrest under PMLA[98] (and UAPA)[99] have been held necessary, which may be judicially reviewed.[100] *Second,* bail remains the rule even in PMLA, and there is a right to bail if the trial is delayed for no fault of the accused.[101] Only after the preliminary burden is discharged by the prosecution does the onus shift to the accused to show that she is not guilty and entitled to bail.[102] *Three,*

---

95 Strict liability offences are known to law. They normally carry short terms and are reliant upon proof of other facts unlike the bare reversal of proof by the Prevention of Money Laundering Act 2002, s 24.

96 See *Union of India v. Barakathullah* 2024 INSC 452, reversing the grant of bail by the Madras HC in *Barakathullah v. Union of India* 2023 SCC OnLine Mad 6337.

97 Prevention of Money Laundering Act 2002, s 19.

98 *Pankaj Bansal v. Union of India* (2024) 7 SCC 576.

99 *Prabir Purkayastha v. State* 2024 SCC OnLine SC 934 [17].

100 *Tarsem Lal v. Directorate of Enforcement* (2024) 7 SCC 61.

101 *Manish Sisodia v. Directorate of Enforcement* 2023 SCC OnLine 1393; See also *Javed Gulam Nabi Shaikh v. State of Maharashtra* 2024 SCC OnLine SC 1683, See also *Prem Prakash v. Union of India* 2024 SCC OnLine SC 2270 [14]–[15].

102 *Prem Prakash* (n 101).

a statement recorded under Section 50 PMLA when an accused is already in custody cannot be used as evidence.[103]

Yet, alongside this comes a narrow interpretation, denying to women summoned to record a statement under Section 50 PMLA, the protection given to women under the CrPC that investigators may only question them at their place of residence.[104]

The Bottom Line

The Minister of State for Home has said in the Rajya Sabha that between the years 2016 and 2020, there were 24,134 undertrials in Indian jails in UAPA cases alone.[105] As per data published by the National Crime Records Bureau, 4,324 people were held in preventive detention at the end of 2022.[106] Statistics for other deviant laws are not readily available. Reports suggest that many arrested under these laws are social activists.[107] Journalists are being routinely picked up under the UAPA.[108]

Just as the people of Punjab were denuded of all fundamental rights on the pretext of fighting insurgency in the 1980s-90s, other parts of the country like the North-East, Jammu and Kashmir, and tribal areas in Chhattisgarh have been in a 'state of exception'[109] for decades, without a declared emergency. The right to judicial remedy, especially *habeas corpus,* is illusory in these regions.

---

[103] *Prem Prakash* (n 101) [29], [32].

[104] *Abhishek Banerjee v. Directorate of Enforcement* (2024) 9 SCC 22.

[105] 'UAPA Case Data Suggests That Process Is Indeed the Punishment' (n 89).

[106] Nation Crime Records Bureau, 'Prison Statistics India 2022' (2023) 33 <https://ncrb.gov.in/uploads/nationalcrimerecordsbureau/custom/psiyearwise2022/1701613297PSI2022ason01122023.pdf> accessed 4 March 2025; Statistics for other deviant laws are not readily available.

[107] See generally, Coordination of Democratic Rights Organizations 'The Terror of Law: UAPA and the Myth of National Security' (*People's Union for Democratic Rights*, 28 May 2012) <https://www.pudr.org/publications/the-terror-of-law-uapa-and-the-myth-of-national-security/> accessed 4 March 2025; See also 'Lawless Roads: A Report on TADA, 1985–1993' (*People's Union for Democratic Rights*, September 1993) <https://www.pudr.org/publicatiosn-files/1993-Sep-Lawless%20Roads.pdf> accessed 4 March 2025; See also, Preeti Verma (ed), 'The Terror of POTA and Other Security Legislation: A Report on the People's Tribunal' (Human Rights Law Network, March 2004) <https://www.slic.org.in/uploads/2019/03/The-Terror-of-POTA-and-Other-Security-Legislation.pdf> accessed 4 March 2025.

[108] Geeta Seshu, 'Behind Bars: Arrests and Detention of Journalists in India 2010-2020' (*Free Speech Collective*, 24 December 2020) <https://freespeechcollective.in/behind-bars-arrests-and-detentions-of-journalists-in-india-2010-2020> accessed 4 March 2025.

[109] Carl Schmitt's construct, which simply put, is the arrogation of power by the ruling dispensation on the pretext of 'praxis'.

State-sponsored vigilantism against left-wing extremism in Chhattisgarh was condemned by the SCI,[110] but the practice carries on. The AFSPA, with shoot at sight powers to the armed forces has been used against our citizens in the North-east and in Jammu and Kashmir for decades. There is nothing to suggest that any of these measures have strengthened the Indian polity. The sheer profusion of such laws speaks against their efficacy.

Unlike countries where emergency laws remain a near permanent feature, India has, on occasion, reversed deviations from the norm in the text of the law – usually by a political decision. But the reprieve has seldom lasted. Judicial disapproval, if at all, has been through a minority.

The State's arrogation of power through AFSPA, TADA, POTA, UAPA, PMLA and more has been unvaryingly endorsed by the SCI. With the result that the executive is able to weaponize the laws against democratic opponents. A culture of impunity and majoritarianism has grown under the shroud of national security.

Enhancing the content of fundamental rights in theory has not prevented an uncritical assumption that personal liberty threatens national security. Allowing this discourse to pass unchecked through the spread of deviant laws has entrenched this view in our institutions, with no value added to Indian life. The exception is fast turning into the norm.

The textual safeguards are as inadequate as they are inconsequential. The bare reality of deviant laws is the inevitability of abuse, empirically well established by now. It is high time the SCI interrogated the State's rhetoric.

---

[110] *Nandini Sundar v. State of Chhattisgarh* (2011) 7 SCC 547 [57]–[58].

Cartoon © Satish Acharya. Reproduced with permission

Crime and Punishment: The Uncertain Trajectory of Sentencing

VRINDA GROVER

The notion of '*just deserts*' or a sentence proportional to the offender's culpability is a principle which, with passage of time, has become applicable to criminal jurisprudence.[1] A review of the Supreme Court of India's (SCI) judgments overwhelmingly suggests that there is considerable variance in the judicial approach to sentencing.[2] One significant challenge, under the criminal law regime in India, stems from the absence of statutory guidelines on sentencing.[3] This essay traces the evolution of principles on sentencing through an analysis of SCI's judgments over the last seventy-five years, mainly in cases involving the death penalty. A comparative law analysis is attempted to examine how that might contribute to the evolving jurisprudence in the area.

Death Penalty: Theatre of Sentencing Debates

Given the irreversible nature of the punishment, the need for guidelines for the award of capital punishment assumes significance. With the moral weight of the convict's biological life resting heavy on the judicial mind, judges have sought some guidance to ensure fairness in the sentencing process.[4]

In *Jagmohan Singh v. State of Uttar Pradesh*,[5] a five-judge Bench of the SCI,

1 *State of Karnataka v. Puttaraja* (2004) 1 SCC 475.

2 *Santosh Kumar Satishbhushan Bariyar v. State of Maharashtra* (2009) 6 SCC 498.

3 The SCI in *State of Punjab v. Prem Sagar* (2008) 7 SCC 550 [2] succinctly observed: 'In our judicial system, we have not been able to develop legal principles as regards sentencing. The superior courts except making observations with regard to the purport and object for which punishment is imposed upon an offender, had not issued any guidelines. Other developed countries have done so. At some quarters, serious concerns have been expressed in this behalf.'

4 *Santosh Kumar Satishbhushan Bariyar* (n 2).

5 *Jagmohan Singh v. State of Uttar Pradesh* (1973) 1 SCC 20.

in 1973, explained that the Indian Penal Code, 1860 (IPC) strictly defines offences and provides the maximum punishment for each offence, while giving the courts considerable discretion in the matter of awarding sentences. The Court held that with the solitary exception of Section 303 IPC,[6] this discretion was available to the courts in regard to all offences punishable with death (as an alternate sentence) in the IPC. Significantly, in *Jagmohan,* a unanimous Court speaking through RS Palekar J negatived the challenge to the constitutionality of the death penalty as a 'cruel and unusual form' of punishment.

In February 1979, a three-judge Bench of the SCI, speaking through Krishna Iyer J in *Rajendra Prasad v. State of Uttar Pradesh* by a 2:1 majority,[7] held that the special reasons necessary for imposing the death penalty must relate to the criminal and not to the crime. The *Rajendra Prasad* court viewed the observations in *Jagmohan* as 'incidental observations without concentration on the sentencing criteria'. Later in the same year – 1979 – it was argued before a two-judge Bench hearing the appeal by one *Bachan Singh*[8] that the trial court could not have awarded him the death sentence since the 'special reasons' were not in conformity with the ratio of *Rajendra Prasad.*

One of the judges on the Bench hearing the *Bachan Singh* appeal (Kailasam J) held that the ratio of *Rajendra Prasad* was contrary to the judgment of the Constitution Bench in *Jagmohan.* The Bench then directed the matter to be placed before a larger Bench for resolving the 'doubts, difficulties and inconsistencies' pointed out by Kailasam J. *Bachan Singh* then became the lead matter in the batch of cases before a Constitution Bench, which was once again asked to pronounce on the constitutional validity of the death penalty.[9]

In 1980, a five-judge Bench of the SCI in *Bachan Singh v. State of Punjab,*[10] (the majority speaking through RS Sarkaria J, with PN Bhagwati J being

---

[6] Section 303 IPC made it mandatory for death sentence to be awarded to a life convict committing murder. In *Mithu v. State of Punjab* (1983) 2 SCC 277, the SC struck down this provision as unconstitutional as it rendered the stage of sentencing contemplated in Sec 235(2) CrPC and the 'special reasons' mandate of Sec 354(3) CrPC meaningless and otiose.

[7] *Rajendra Prasad v. State of Uttar Pradesh* (1979) 3 SCC 646. The majority comprised VR Krishna Iyer and DA Desai JJ and the dissenting judge was AP Sen J.

[8] *Bachan Singh v. State of Punjab* Criminal Appeal 273 of 1979.

[9] *Bachan Singh v. State of Punjab* (1980) 2 SCC 684 [4]-[7].

[10] *Bachan Singh* (n 10).

the lone dissenter[11]), while not willing to strike down the death penalty as unconstitutional, attempted to limit its imposition to the 'rarest of rare' cases. The *Bachan Singh* Court went on to categorize a non-exhaustive list of aggravating and mitigating circumstances that might have to be considered by a court when dealing with cases involving the death penalty. This was consistent with the statutory mandate of Section 354 (3) of the Code of Criminal Procedure (CrPC).[12] The statute required the imposition of the 'ultimate punishment' to be justified through 'special reasons'. The balancing exercise required the courts, in the sentencing phase, to shift the focus from the gravity of the crime to the person convicted for committing the crime.

The *Bachan Singh* majority was acknowledging the changed legislative policy since *Jagmohan*, which appeared to bolster the view that life imprisonment was the norm and death sentence the exception.[13] Also, it was clearly influenced by the decision in *Maneka Gandhi v. Union of India*,[14] where a seven-judge Bench had held that Articles 14, 19 and 21 were not to be interpreted in watertight compartments. The principle of reasonableness was set to pervade all the three Articles 'with the result that the procedure contemplated by Article 21 must be "right and just and fair" and not "arbitrary, fanciful or oppressive"; otherwise it should be no procedure at all and the requirement of Article 21 would not be satisfied.'

Bachan Singh clearly distinguished judicial discretion guided by crystallized principles from untrammelled or unguided discretion of judges based on individual biases or proclivities.[15] It is only the former strand of discretion that *Bachan Singh* found constitutionally valid. In doing so, it impliedly upheld the principle that similarly situated persons should receive similar sentences in criminal law for the same offence. Else, judicial discretion not rooted

---

[11] ibid [213]-[214]. When the judgment was pronounced on 9 May 1980, he issued a separate two-paragraph dissenting order holding that Section 302 IPC was unconstitutional and void and stated that he would give his reasons 'on the day on which the Court reopens after the summer vacations'. Ultimately, his detailed dissenting opinion came to be delivered more than two years later, on 16 August 1982, in *Bachan Singh v. State of Punjab* (1982) 3 SCC 24.

[12] Code of Criminal Procedure 1973, s 354 (3) – 'When the conviction is for an offence punishable with death or, in the alternative, with imprisonment for life or imprisonment for a term of years, the judgment shall state the reasons for the sentence awarded, and, in the case of sentence of death, the special reasons for such sentence.'

[13] Significantly, it took note of the provisions of the International Covenant on Civil and Political Rights (ICCPR) ratified by India since *Jagmohan*.

[14] *Maneka Gandhi v. Union of India* (1978) 1 SCC 248.

[15] *Bachan Singh* (n 9) [165]-[166].

in crystallized principles could culminate in different outcomes – death or life.[16] The *Bachan Singh* majority perhaps did not account for the individual proclivities of judges that challenge the uniform and fair exercise of judicial discretion – an issue discussed in some detail later in the essay.

Jagmohan and *Bachan Singh* echoed the view that the impossibility of laying standards is at the very core of criminal law as administered in India. *Jagmohan* and *Bachan Singh* contrasted the Indian legal framework with that of the United States (US) by highlighting the absence of constitutional mandates, such as in the Eighth Amendment in the US Constitution,[17] and consequently refused to liberally apply the test of reasonableness for testing the vires of the death sentence, in a manner similar to the 'due process' test in the US.

A little over three years after *Bachan Singh*, the debate on sentencing resurfaced before a three-judge Bench in *Machhi Singh v. State of Punjab*.[18] The Court emphasized that a balance sheet of aggravating and mitigating circumstances will have to be drawn up in the process of deciding whether to award capital punishment.[19] It further expanded on the doctrine of 'rarest of rare' by adding two crime-centric elements to aid in its determination – the uncommon nature of the offence, and whether the circumstances of the crime were such that it leaves no alternative other than the death penalty in order to do justice.[20]

In 1989, a two-judge Bench of the SCI in *Allauddin Mian v. State of Bihar*,[21] mandated a separate 'sentencing hearing' to effectuate the discernment of 'special reasons' under Section 235 (2) of the CrPC. The focus in the separate hearing, which was to take place after the conviction was pronounced, would be the person convicted of the crime and not just the crime. This was reiterated in 2009 by a two-judge Bench in *Santosh Bariyar*, which viewed the expression 'rarest of rare' as an 'exceptionally narrow opening provided in the domain of this negative precept' and that this opening is also qualified by another condition, 'when the alternative option is unquestionably foreclosed'.[22]

---

16 The view taken by the US Supreme Court in *McGoutha v. California* 402 US 183 (1971), that there are an infinite variety of cases and facets to each case that make general standards of punishment 'meaningless boilerplate', or an unnecessary statement of the obvious, resonated with the SC in *Jagmohan's* case.

17 'Excessive bail shall not be required, nor excessive fines imposed, nor cruel and unusual punishments inflicted.'

18 *Machhi Singh v. State of Punjab* (1983) 3 SCC 470.

19 ibid [38].

20 ibid [39].

21 *Allauddin Mian v. State of Bihar* (1989) 3 SCC 5.

22 *Bariyar* (n 2) [58].

The *Santosh Bariyar* Court noted that the extremely uneven application of *Bachan Singh* had created a lot of uncertainty in death penalty sentencing in India. It was found that the balance-sheet approach did not eliminate arbitrariness. The *Santosh Bariyar* court also held, as *per incuriam*, seven previous decisions of the SCI, including *Ravji v. State of Rajasthan*,[23] which had observed that it was the 'gravity of the crime but not the criminal' that was germane for determining the appropriate punishment.[24]

Again in 2012, in *Sangeet v. State of Haryana*,[25] a two-judge Bench of Madan B Lokur and KPS Radhakrishnan JJ, noted the unevenness in the sentencing jurisprudence. The same two-judge Bench in 2013, in *Shankar Kisanrao Khade v. State of Maharashtra*,[26] noted that the SCI had failed to apply the *Bachan Singh* test even-handedly in all cases. The Bench regretted that, in those cases, the relevant mitigating factors were not evaluated before the death sentence was awarded. One of the judges on the Bench, Radhakrishnan J, was categorical that the balancing test of *Bachan Singh* was 'not the correct test in deciding whether capital punishment be awarded or not'.[27] He proposed a three-pronged test – crime test, criminal test and 'rarest of rare' (R-R) test, which was to be applied by the sentencing court in the separate hearing following the conviction. According to Radhakrishnan J, even if the crime test and the criminal test are fully satisfied, the Court will still have to apply the R-R test, which depended on a society-centric perception (whether society will approve the awarding of death sentence to certain types of crimes or not) as opposed to a judge-centric perception.[28] The separate concurring opinion

---

[23] *Ravji v. State of Rajasthan* (1996) 2 SCC 175; The convict in *Ravji* was executed without following the law laid down by the Constitution Bench in *Bachan Singh*, an irreversible and fatal decision that is a stark reminder of arbitrariness and infallibility that infiltrates sentencing in death penalty cases.

[24] ibid [24].

[25] *Sangeet v. State of Haryana* (2013) 2 SCC 452.

[26] *Shankar Kisanrao Khade v. State of Maharashtra* (2013) 5 SCC 546.

[27] ibid [51].

[28] ibid [52]. The Court observed: 'While applying that test, the court has to look into variety of factors like society's abhorrence, extreme indignation and antipathy to certain types of crimes like sexual assault and murder of intellectually challenged minor girls, suffering from physical disability, old and infirm women with those disabilities, etc. Examples are only illustrative and not exhaustive. The courts award death sentence since situation demands so, due to constitutional compulsion, reflected by the will of the people and not the will of the Judges.' The *Khade* judgment also called upon the Law Commission of India to examine whether 'death penalty is a deterrent punishment or is retributive justice or serves an incapacitative goal.'[148]. More recently, in a review petition in *Rajendra Pralhadrao Wasnik v. State of Maharashtra* (2019) 12 SCC 460 [43], the SCI clarified that the test in *Bachan Singh* was not of improbability of reformation, but that of 'probability of reform and rehabilitation and not its possibility or its impossibility.' as a facet of Section 354 (4), CrPC, and thus called upon the State to place evidence

of Madan Lokur J in *Khade*, while not expressing any disagreement with the view of Radhakrishnan J, observed that 'death penalty and its execution should not become a matter of uncertainty nor should converting a death sentence into imprisonment for life become a matter of chance.'[29]

Public opinion in a given case may run against the cardinal principles of rule of law and constitutionalism, by which the courts are nonetheless bound. In *Chhannu Lal Verma v. State of Chhattisgarh*,[30] the 262nd Law Commission Report which called for the elimination of the death penalty from the statute books for all offences other than terrorism and waging war[31] was cited with approval, to caution against media trials bleeding into the justice dispensation machinery by putting undue pressure on the judiciary. It is arguable that inherent in the caution expressed by the Court against media trials pressurizing the Court in matters of sentencing, is an implicit disapproval of the test of society-centric 'rarest of rare' determination as expounded in *Khade*. However, the move away from the balancing test as propounded by *Khade* has also not been followed in subsequent cases, and the Court has reverted back to drawing up the balance sheet for imposing death penalty, as in the case of *Mukesh v. State of NCT of Delhi*.[32] Interestingly, in *Chhannu Lal Verma*, Kurian Joseph J, speaking for the majority, noted that 'capital punishment has failed to achieve any constitutionally valid penological goals' and that the need for the death penalty as a punishment should be reviewed. [33] In his dissent only on this point, Deepak Gupta J

on record in this regard in all cases. It was noted on analysis of various precedents that the State's initiative in collecting such critical evidence has been sparse.

29 *Shankar Kishanrao Khade* (n 26) [148].

30 *Chhannu Lal Verma v. State of Chhattisgarh* (2019) 12 SCC 438 [23]-[25]; In *Dhananjoy Chatterjee v. State of West Bengal* (1994) 2 SCC 220 [15], which was a much publicized case of a rape and murder of an 18-year-old in Calcutta allegedly by the security guard of the apartment complex, the Court observed: 'Imposition of appropriate punishment is the manner in which the courts respond to the society's cry for justice against the criminals. Justice demands that courts should impose punishment befitting the crime so that the courts reflect public abhorrence of the crime. The courts must not only keep in view the rights of the criminal but also the rights of the victim of crime and the society at large while considering imposition of appropriate punishment.' The convict was hanged to death; The above observations were followed in *Jaikumar v. State of Madhya Pradesh* (1999) 5 SCC 1 [21],while affirming the death sentence awarded to a 22-year-old male convicted of murdering his sister-in-law and niece in a brutal manner. According to the Court, they did not find any balancing factor since the aggravating factors 'are aplenty and galore without any mitigating circumstances'. The Court refused to consider the young age of the accused and the probability of his reformation as mitigating factors.

31 Report 262 of the Law Commission of India on Death Penalty, 2015.

32 *Mukesh v. State of NCT of Delhi* (2017) 6 SCC 1.

33 *Chhannu Lal Verma* (n 30) [24].

opined that 'since the Constitution Bench in *Bachan Singh* v. *State of Punjab* has upheld capital punishment, there is no need to re-examine the same at this stage.'[34]

High-profile, politically sensitive cases invariably generate surcharged and polarized media trials, which influence public opinion.[35] The intense pressure of populist opinion is also reflected in the tension between different organs of the State in the context of execution of death sentences. There are at least three instances where the State Legislatures denounced or attempted to pass a resolution to denounce the imposition of death sentence in politically sensitive cases – Punjab (Balwant Singh Rajoana sentenced to death for murder of Beant Singh, former Chief Minister of Punjab);[36] Jammu and Kashmir (Afzal Guru sentenced for conspiracy in the Parliament attack);[37] and Tamil Nadu (the Rajiv Gandhi assassination case).[38] Among these instances, it is Afzal Guru alone who has been executed thus far.[39] It is becoming increasingly commonplace for shrill calls for hanging of accused in rape cases to be unleashed even at the stage of arrest and investigation.[40] Where such rhetoric, alarm and social anxiety shapes public consciousness, can this then be tapped

34 *Chhannu Lal Verma* (n 30) [28]-[29].

35 One early instance of this is in the *Nanavati* case, which stands well-documented in *Mumbai Fables* by Gyan Prakash. The campaign supporting the main accused Naval Commander KM Nanavati resulted in the jury declaring him not guilty. Despite this, the Court handed down a conviction which was upheld till the SCI. He was nevertheless pardoned by the Governor of Bombay. One fallout was the movement towards the end of jury trials in criminal cases in India; See Gyan Prakash, *Mumbai Fables* (Princeton University Press 2011).

36 'Amit Shah in Lok Sabha says no pardon for Rajoana' (*The Times of India*, 4 December 2019).

37 'Afzal Guru resolution: Vote put off after uproar in J&K Assembly' *(NDTV*, 28 September 2011). <https://www.ndtv.com/india-news/afzal-guru-resolution-vote-put-off-after-uproar-in-j-k-assembly-468893> accessed 8 March 2025.

38 'TN Assembly calls for clemency' *(The New Indian Express*, 16 May 2012*)*; See also, J Balaji, 'Assemblies cannot seek clemency for death-row convicts: Achary' (*The Hindu*, 17 November 2021).

39 Once executed on 9 February 2013, Afzal Guru's body instead of being handed over to his family was buried in the premises of the Tihar jail. Sandeep Joshi and Ashok Kumar, 'Afzal Guru hanged in secrecy, buried in Tihar Jail' (*The Hindu*, 9 February 2013). It would be relevant to add that the Supreme Court has, in the context of dignity to an executed convict, in *Parmanand Katara (Pt) v. Union of India* (1995) 3 SCC 248 [3], held that the right to dignity under Article 21 of the Constitution extends not only 'to a living man but also to his body after his death'.

40 'Kolkata Welcomes Death Verdict for Dhananjoy,' (*The Hindustan Times*, 4 August 2004); "We Demand Death Penalty': Father of Woman Murdered by Live-in Partner in Delhi,' (*The Hindustan Times*, 15 November 2022); 'Students' Bodies Demand Death Penalty' (*The Times of India*, 19 August 2024). In response to the rape and death of a trainee doctor in RG Kar Medical Centre, the West Bengal Government introduced a bill with stringent provisions for cases of sexual assault, including death penalty for rape. See Shiv Sahay Singh, 'West Bengal passes Aparajita Women and Child Bill for stringent punishment in cases of sexual assault' (*The Hindu*, 4 September 2024).

into by judges as a measure of societal will, to configure sentencing for heinous crimes? Can a solemn judicial task of sentencing a convict be left at the mercy of the vagaries of political expediency for public appeasement?

Individualized Judge-Centric Sentencing Is an Anathema to Due Process

The lack of 'principled sentencing' by the SCI was illustrated in *Khade*, where the Court undertook an extensive review of its judgments in cases of rape and subsequent murder of a minor. It noted that the same mitigating factors that were relied upon to commute death sentence to life imprisonment in some of the cases were discounted in others where the sentence was confirmed. For example, the young age of the accused was not considered in *Dhananjoy Chatterjee v. State of West Bengal*[41] (twenty-seven years), *Jai Kumar*[42] (twenty-two years) and *Shivu*[43] (two accused, aged twenty and twenty-two years). The possibility of reformation was also ruled out without any expert evidence in *BA Umesh*[44] and *Mohd Mannan.*[45] Conversely, the benefit of possible reform was considered without any expert evidence in, *Nirmal Singh,*[46] *Mohd Chaman,*[47] *Raju,*[48] *Bantu,*[49] etc. The acquittal or life sentence awarded by the High Court (HC) was not considered an adequate mitigatory circumstance in *Satish*[50] and *BA Umesh*, but the opposite finding was arrived at in *State of Tamil Nadu v. Suresh.*[51] It is also pertinent to note that the Bench in *Khade* categorically states that the courts have failed in their duty to consider mitigating factors (criminal test) in several cases relating to the death sentence, examples include

41 *Dhananjoy Chatterjee* (n 30).

42 *Jai Kumar v. State of Madhya Pradesh* (1999) 5 SCC 1.

43 *Shivu v. Registrar General, High Court of Karnataka* (2007) 4 SCC 713.

44 *BA Umesh v. State of Karnataka* (2011) 3 SCC 85; His sentence was later commuted based on grounds of delay in adjudication of mercy petition and solitary confinement in *BA Umesh v. Union of India* (2022) SCC Online SC 1528.

45 *Mohd Mannan v. State of Bihar* (2011) 5 SCC 317; his sentence was later commuted based on lack of effective hearing on sentencing and post-conviction mental illness in *Mohd. Mannan v. State of Bihar* (2019) 16 SCC 584.

46 *Nirmal Singh v. State of Haryana* (1999) 3 SCC 670.

47 *Mohd Chaman v. State (NCT of Delhi)* (2001) 2 SCC 28.

48 *Raju v. State of Haryana* (2001) 9 SCC 50.

49 *Bantu v. State of Uttar Pradesh* (2008) 11 SCC 113.

50 *State of Uttar Pradesh v. Satish* (2005) 3 SCC 114

51 (1998) 2 SCC 372.

Nathu Garam,[52] *Jumman Khan*,[53] *Dhananjoy Chatterjee* and *Kamta Tiwari*.[54]

The reality of unguided sentencing becomes stark when the discernible trends in the judgments of individual judges of the SCI (either heading the Bench or steering the majority) are examined. A report published in 2015[55] by the Asian Centre for Human Rights picked up 33 decisions delivered by Arijit Pasayat J involving the death penalty. He had confirmed the death sentence in fifteen cases[56] (including four cases[57] in which lesser sentences/acquittals were enhanced to death sentence) and upheld acquittal in eight cases. He commuted the death sentence in seven cases and remitted three cases to the HCs to again decide on the sentence as the death penalty had not been imposed. It is crucial to note that the decisions in five cases out of the sixteen in which death penalty was confirmed by Pasayat J, have since been declared as *per incuriam*.[58] In stark contrast, MB Shah J who was in the SCI at the same time did not confirm the death penalty in any of fifteen cases adjudicated by him. He commuted the death sentence in twelve cases, did not enhance life imprisonment to death penalty in any case, did not alter acquittal by the HCs into death penalty in any case and did not remit back any case to the HCs on the quantum of sentence.

---

52 *Nathu Garam v. State of Uttar Pradesh* (1979) 3 SCC 366.

53 *Jumman Khan v. State of Uttar Pradesh* (1991) 1 SCC 752.

54 *Kamta Tiwari v. State of Madhya Pradesh* (1996) 6 SCC 250.

55 Asian Centre for Human Rights, *India: Death in the Name of Conscience* (May 2015), <http://www.uncat.org/wp-content/uploads/2019/05/deathinthenameofconscience.pdf.> accessed 28 August 2024.

56 *Ankush Maruti Shinde v. State of Maharashtra* AIR 2009 SC 2609; *Bantu* (n 49); *Devender Pal Singh v. State of NCT of Delhi* (2002) 5 SCC 234; *Krishna Mochi v. State of Bihar* (2002) 6 SCC 81; *Mohan Anna Chavan v. State of Maharashtra* (2008) 7 SCC 561; *Rameshbhai Chandubhai Rathod v. State of Gujarat* (2009) 5 SCC 740; *Shivaji @ Dadya Shankar Alhat v. State of Maharashtra* (2008) 15 SCC 269; *Shivu v. High Court of Karnataka* (n 13); *State of Rajasthan v. Kheraj Ram* (2003) 8 SCC 224; *State of Uttar Pradesh v. Sattan @ Satyendra* (2009) 4 SCC 736; *State of Uttar Pradesh v. Satish* (n 50); *Sushil Murmu v. State of Jharkhand* (2004) 2 SCC 338; *Bablu @ Mubarik Hussain v. State of Rajasthan* (2006) 13 SCC 116; *Bani Kanta Das v. State of Assam* (2009) 15 SCC 206; *MA Antony @ Antappan v. State of Kerala* (2009) 6 SCC 220.

57 *Ankush Maruti Shinde v. State of Maharashtra* (n 56); *State of Rajasthan v. Kheraj Ram* (n 56); *State of Uttar Pradesh v. Sattan* (n 56); *State of Uttar Pradesh v. Satish* (n 50).

58 *Ankush Maruti Shinde* (n 56); *Bantu* (n 49); *Mohan Anna Chavan v. State of Maharashtra* 2008 (2) ALT (Cri) 329; *Shivaji @ Dadya Shankar Alhat v. State of Maharashtra* AIR 2009 SC 56; *State of Uttar Pradesh v. Sattan* (n 56); During this period, SB Sinha J did not uphold the death sentence in any of the 17 cases he decided. In three, he acquitted the accused. 'Full Court Reference in the memory of Late Hon'ble Justice SB Sinha' 5 <https://cdnbbsr.s3waas.gov.in/s3ec0490f1f4972d133619a60c30f3559e/uploads/2024/01/2024011953.pdf> accessed 22 April 2025.

The decision in *Krishna Mochi v. State of Bihar*[59] warrants a more detailed discussion since the three-judge Bench of the SCI that delivered it included Pasayat J and MB Shah J (the third judge was BN Agrawal J). The majority comprising Pasayat J and Agrawal J confirmed the death sentence. Shah J, on the other hand, acquitted one of the accused and commuted the sentence of the other to life imprisonment.[60] Shah J noted several infirmities in the investigation conducted by just one officer, who was neither examined at the trial nor his diary brought on record; the informant was not examined; and only one witness identified one of the accused and even this was not corroborated. For the majority, however, these infirmities were insufficient to negate the case of the prosecution and could not even constitute mitigating factors for sentencing. In *Ravi v. State of Maharashtra*,[61] the dissenting judge Subhash Reddy J commuted the death sentence, whereas the majority comprising Surya Kant J and RF Nariman J were so overwhelmed by the brutality of the offence that it appears to have cited *Bachan Singh* only to carve out a 'brutality' exception.[62]

Personal beliefs and matters of faith of the judges are likely to impinge on their decision-making and may indirectly contribute to arbitrariness, which is already pervasive in judge-centric sentencing. Numerous studies and research papers have highlighted globally that religious beliefs often lead to strong positions on the issue of death penalty.[63] However, apart from one study,[64] not much research has been conducted in India to explore this aspect.

The problem with individualized judge-centric sentencing should not be viewed as questioning the need for a polyvocal Court. As a safeguard, it is suggested that in cases where the punishment being considered is the death penalty, it should require a unanimous decision, in a Bench of more than two judges. Not only would this be a strong safeguard against arbitrary sentencing,

---

59 *Krishna Mochi v. State of Bihar* (n 56).

60 The case concerned the death of thirty-five persons of a particular community in Gaya, Bihar, by members of the proscribed organization Maoist Community Centre (MCC).

61 *Ravi v. State of Maharashtra* (2019) 9 SCC 622.

62 ibid [62].

63 Monica K Miller and R David Hayward, 'Religious Characteristics and the Death Penalty' (2007) 32 Law and Human Behavior 113.

64 Centre on the Death Penalty, *Matters of Judgment* (National Law University Delhi Press 2017) <https://www.deathpenaltyproject.org/wp-content/uploads/2018/06/Matter-of-Judgment.pdf.> accessed 28 November 2024.

but also respect the polyvocality of the court as a treasured principle not to be buried under the weight of numerical majorities.

Sentencing Encroaching on Statutory Remission – Principled Approach or Stop-Gap Adjustment?

Section 302 IPC, provides two alternate forms of punishment for the offence of murder– death or imprisonment for life. The decision in *Gopal Vinayak Godse v. State of Maharashtra*[65] held that '[a] sentence of transportation for life or imprisonment for life must prima facie be treated as transportation or imprisonment for the whole of the remaining period of the convicted person's natural life.' Thus, unless the convict receives the benefit of remission or commutation, a sentence for life imprisonment means that a convict shall serve the sentence till the end of his natural life, as reiterated in *Maru Ram v. Union of India*[66] and *Sangeet.*

The power to grant remission and commutation under Sections 432 and 433, Code of Criminal Procedure (CrPC)[67] was qualified in 1978 by the insertion of Section 433A CrPC,[68] which barred the application of the aforesaid provisions to a convict whose death sentence is commuted or who has been sentenced to life imprisonment for an offence for which death sentence was a possible punishment, till the time the convict has served at least fourteen years imprisonment. This was further clarified in *State of Rajasthan v. Mukesh Sharma*,[69] which held that the period of fourteen years in Section 433A CrPC was a minimum criterion, and states were competent to make Rules for exercise of power under Sections 432 and 433 CrPC, which require a convict to serve more than fourteen years of sentence for consideration for remission and commutation.

The apprehension expressed in *Rajendra Prasad v. State of Uttar Pradesh*[70] and *Dalbir Singh v. State of Punjab*[71] – that a commuted sentence might result in

---

65 *Gopal Vinayak Godse v. State of Maharashtra* AIR 1961 SC 600.

66 *Maru Ram v. Union of India* (1981) 1 SCC 107.

67 s 473, 474 in the newly enacted Bharatiya Nagarik Suraksha Sanhita (BNSS).

68 BNSS s 475.

69 *State of Rajasthan v. Mukesh Sharma* (2019) 14 SCC 273.

70 *Rajendra Prasad v. State of Uttar Pradesh* (1979) 3 SCC 646.

71 *Dalbir Singh v. State of Punjab* (1979) 3 SCC 745.

further remissions after completion of fourteen years and that the possibility of such 'leniency' in case of grave crimes might result in increased award of the death sentence – led a three-judge Bench of the SCI in *Swamy Shraddhananda*[72] to substitute death penalty with life imprisonment without remission for a specified number of years beyond fourteen years. It was clarified, however, that in doing so the Court was not infringing on the powers of the President and the Governors to grant pardons and remissions under Articles 72 and 161 of the Constitution.[73] Thus, the decision in *Swamy Shraddhananda* set the stage for the imposition of irrevocable sentences of life imprisonment for twenty or thirty years or the remainder of one's natural life.

The correctness of the view taken in *Swamy Shraddhananda* was deliberated upon by the Constitution Bench in *Union of India v. V Sriharan.*[74] The majority opinion by FM Ibrahim Kalifulla J was for himself, CJI HL Dattu, and PC Ghose JJ. It upheld the view taken in *Swamy Shraddhananda*. UU Lalit J (for himself and AM Sapre J) dissented, questioning the creation of a sentence between life imprisonment and death sentence – an exercise that belonged 'specifically to the legislature.'[75] Further, the dissent pointed out that putting punishment beyond remission in reality 'will not be conducive to the reformation of the person and will in fact push him into a dark hole without there being semblance of the light at the end of the tunnel.'[76]

The fact that remission orders of the Executive have been subject to judicial review does not justify the Court crafting a new punishment to bridge the gap between life imprisonment and death sentence. The majority view in *Swamy Shraddhananda*, by forging such a sentence, has not only forayed into the legislative domain of stipulating punishment but also infringed the clemency power statutorily vested in the Executive – a power that is exercised at the post-sentencing stage, upon considerations of factors beyond those raised at the stage of sentencing before the court.[77] This discussion would

---

72 *Swamy Shraddhananda (2) v. State of Karnataka* (2008) 13 SCC 767; The Bench comprised of BN Agrawal, GS Singhvi and Aftab Alam JJ.

73 The sentence awarded by the Court in such cases was held to be a bar against exercise of power under Sections 432 and 433 CrPC only, i.e., statutory remission.

74 *Union of India v. Sriharan* (2016) 7 SCC 1.

75 ibid [273].

76 ibid [284].

77 In *Manoj v. State of Madhya Pradesh* (2023) 2 SCC 353, the SCI, speaking through a three-judge Bench, opinion authored by SR Bhat J, has stated that serious concerns persist against the decision in *Shraddhananda*, which was upheld by a slim majority in *Sriharan* (n 74), and the issue is to be reconsidered at the appropriate time.

remain incomplete without mentioning that over the last decade, different states have notified remission policies curbing the right of convicts to be considered eligible for remission, primarily on the basis of the heinous nature of offences.[78]

'Adequacy' of Sentence – Proportionality Principle in Sentencing

The SCI, while acknowledging that sentencing must consider varied penological goals of rehabilitation, reformation and deterrence, has on multiple occasions emphasized that the principle of proportionality must always guide the court while adjudicating on the quantum of punishment.[79] It has held that an 'appropriate sentence' is one which provides 'adequate punishment',[80] which is measured in terms of the punishment being proportionate to the offence. Sentencing is thus at its core a punitive exercise, even though the punishment imposed may take a form that encourages reformation and rehabilitation of the convict.

In *Jameel v. State of Uttar Pradesh*, the Court summarized sentencing as a process which must use 'deft modification' to be stern where necessary yet temper the law with mercy where warranted.[81] However, in the absence of empirical data in India with regard to the impact of sentencing on society, 'courts go by their own perception about the philosophy behind the prescription of certain specified penal consequences for particular nature of crime.'[82] However, the deftness of the modification in sentencing has been largely lost and substituted by judge-centric sentencing.

---

[78] Certain offences categorized as being heinous are excluded under the remission policies of many states (See, Remission Policy for the State of Gujarat, 2014 <https://www.scobserver.in/wp-content/uploads/2023/09/2014-Gujarat-Remission-Policy.pdf> accessed 20 April 2025. In an instance from Kerala, where a Government Order excluded certain classes of prisoners from remission, the SCI held that such blanket exclusions are arbitrary, see *Joseph v. State of Kerala* 2023 INSC 843. Recently, the Tamil Nadu Prison Rules have also been amended to the effect that no persons convicted for sexual offences under the Protection of Child from Sexual Offences Act, 2012 shall be eligible for remission, notified vide GO (MS) No. 61 dated 4 February 2025, Home (Prison-V) Department, Government of Tamil Nadu.

[79] *Soman v. State of Kerala* (2013) 11 SCC 382; *State of Madhya Pradesh v. Babulal* (2008) 1 SCC 234; *Puttaraja* (n 1).

[80] *State of Madhya Pradesh v. Najab Khan* (2013) 9 SCC 509.

[81] *Jameel v. State of Uttar Pradesh* (2010) 12 SCC 532 [15].

[82] *Narinder Singh v. State of Punjab* (2014) 6 SCC 466 [15].

The absence of rationale for imposing varied sentences for similar crimes came to the fore yet again in the peculiar case of *Uggarsain v. State of Haryana.*[83] The HC of Punjab and Haryana had sentenced seven persons convicted under different offences to the period already undergone in custody. The SCI was critical of the HC not finding 'any distinguishing feature in the form of separate roles played by each of them' and held that 'the imposition of the "sentence undergone" criteria, on persons having served varying periods of time amounted to an aberration, and the sentencing is for that reason, flawed.'[84]

Judicial Innovation in Sentencing

In *Dilbag Singh v. State of Punjab*,[85] Krishna Iyer J had advocated for the need to steer away from the rigid prescription of punishments in the IPC towards meaningful and productive sentences which seek to achieve the goal of sentencing justice and not mechanically seek to achieve the notion of prison justice. For this purpose, the Court called upon the Chief Probation Officer, Punjab, to file a report at the appellate stage to enable the Court to consider the issue of sentencing.

Dilbag Singh was later followed in *Ved Prakash v. State of Haryana*,[86] where it was held that it was the duty of the sentencing court to be 'activist enough' at the trial stage to do full justice by discovering all relevant material for the purpose of sentencing. It was held that the social background and personal factors of the crime-doer are imperative for sentencing, and courts had not paid requisite attention to the same. These early efforts by the Court to provide for just sentencing have now evolved as the guiding principles for the nature of material and information to be considered and assessed at the pre-sentencing hearing.[87]

---

83 *Uggarsain v. State of Haryana* (2023) 8 SCC 109.

84 ibid [16].

85 *Dilbag Singh v. State of Punjab* (1979) 2 SCC 103.

86 *Ved Prakash v. State of Haryana* 1981 (1) SCC 447.

87 In *Karan v. State of Madhya Pradesh* (2022) 18 SCC 368, the Court directed for orders of the probation officers to be placed before it to arrive at the appropriate sentence, as well as psychological evaluation and a social worker's report; The Delhi HC in *State v. Bharat Singh* (2015) 217 DLT 640 (DB) and *Vikas Yadav v. State of Uttar Pradesh* (2015) 218 DLT CN (1) set out an elaborate procedure which required the probation officer to gather the relevant facts of the person convicted and submit a report to the sentencing court.

In *Manoj v. State of Madhya Pradesh*,[88] the SCI in 2023, issued detailed guidelines to ensure that information about the social milieu of the accused is placed before the trial court at the time of sentencing, after citing the duty of the State to elicit necessary material about mitigating and aggravating circumstances. It also noted that the State's obligation is heightened in the social context of India where many convicts receive inadequate or ineffective legal defence. The Court further lamented that in many cases it made efforts at the appellate stage to gather material relevant to the circumstances of the convict at the time of the commission of the offence, which due to the passage of time is often 'too little too late'.[89] In such circumstances, the gravity of the offence tends to naturally dominate the judicial consideration in the absence of proper material regarding mitigating circumstances. The Court made it incumbent upon jail authorities to provide a fresh psychiatric and psychological report regarding the progress of reformation in jail and the onset of any mental illnesses post-conviction. It recorded that while some courts call for the probationer's report and reports from jail authorities at the stage of sentencing, it was not a uniform practice and contributed to the 'patchwork jurisprudence' on the death penalty in India.[90]

Pursuant to the judgment in *Manoj*, the SCI has permitted Project 39A housed then in the National Law University, Delhi, to access and interview a death-row convict, to conduct a psychological evaluation and bring on record relevant material through an expert regarding the mitigating circumstances in the case.[91] The directions in *Mohd Arif*[92] mandating open court hearing of Review Petitions against the death penalty by a minimum of three judges,[93] are yet another illustration of judicial innovation to infuse the sentencing process with a more humane approach, giving every opportunity to the death-row convict to place on record material to seek commutation of the death penalty.[94]

---

[88] *Manoj v. State of Madhya Pradesh* (n 77).

[89] ibid [246].

[90] ibid [244].

[91] *Muhammed Ameer-ul-Islam v. State of Kerala* SLP (Crl.) Diary No. 30957/2024, order dated 16 July 2024.

[92] *Mohd Arif v. Registrar, SC of India* (2014) 9 SCC 737.

[93] The Supreme Court Rules also mandate that a case involving the death sentence shall be heard by a Bench of not less than three judges. See Supreme Court Rules, 2013, ord 6, r 3, 4.

[94] To understand the significance of this additional step, it is important to note that there have been numerous instances where convicts – whose death sentences were upheld through the dismissal of

Justice Miscarried

There have been cases of death-penalty prisoners later found to be juveniles at the time of their alleged crimes or acquitted after decades of imprisonment, which highlight profound flaws in the criminal justice system. These instances reveal deep-seated issues, including unreliable evidence, procedural lapses and inadequate legal representation, which result in years of wrongful incarceration under the constant threat of execution.

In 2019, in *Ankush Maruti Shinde*,[95] six prisoners who had been on death row for sixteen years were acquitted. Deprecating the conduct of the investigating team and the prosecution, the SCI arrived at a finding that the prisoners had been falsely implicated in the case. The Court also ordered a departmental investigation against the investigating team. Further, the Court ordered the State to award a compensation of Rs 5 lakh each to the prisoners as well as a re-investigation into the case. There have also been other acquittals where the prisoners had spent in the range of seven to thirteen years on death row.[96]

The Juvenile Justice Act, 2000 was retrospectively amended to incorporate Section 7A of the Juvenile Justice Act, 2000 (JJ Act, 2000) and Rule 12 (3) of the Juvenile Justice (Care and Protection of Children) Rules, 2007 (JJ Rules, 2007), providing that a claim of juvenility may be raised before any court at any stage, including after the final disposal of the case. Pursuant to this, it was held in *Upendra Pradhan v. State of Orissa*, that a claim of juvenility as per the procedure established under the JJ Act 'can be taken before any Court at any point of time'.[97] This has led to two prisoners on death row being declared

---

Special Leave Petitions and Review Petitions, and whose mercy pleas were rejected by both the President and the Governor—were later granted commutation or even acquitted after their cases were reopened pursuant to the *Arif* mandate. See *MA Antony v. State of Kerala* (2020) 17 SCC 751 (commutation); *Sanjay v. State of Uttar Pradesh* 2025 INSC 317 (acquittal); *Ankush Maruti Shinde v. State of Maharashtra* (2019) 15 SCC 470 (acquittal).

[95] *Ankush Maruti Shinde* (n 94).

[96] *Prakash Nishad @ Kewat Zinak Nishad v. State of Maharashtra* 2023 INSC 561 (thirteen years); *Irfan @ Naka v. State of Uttar Pradesh* 2023 INSC 758 (nine years); *Rajesh v. State of Madhya Pradesh* 2023 INSC 839 (seven years); *Chotkau v. State of Uttar Pradesh* (2023) 6 SCC 742 (ten years); *Rahul v. State of NCT Delhi* (2023) 1 SCC 83 (nearly eleven years); *Ramanand alias Nandlal Bharti v. State of Uttar Pradesh* 2022 INSC 1075 (twelve years); *Jaikam Khan v. State of Uttar Pradesh* (2021) 13 SCC 716 (four prisoners, nearly eight years).

[97] *Upendra Pradhan v. State of Orissa* (2015) 11 SCC 124, reiterated in *Makkella Nagaiah v. State of Andhra Pradesh* (2023) 9 SCC 807.

juvenile and released.[98] One of them, Narayan Chetanram, who at the time of arrest was twelve years and six months, was finally released after having spent twenty-eight years in custody, twenty-five of which were on death row.[99] There have also been cases of convicts serving life imprisonment, later found to be juveniles at the time of commission of the crime, who were ordered to be released by the SCI after having spent a range of four to eight years in custody.[100]

Systemic Discrimination: A Grim Reality

It is undeniable that Indian society continues to be stratified by inequalities of caste, class, religion, gender, ethnicity, sexuality and other markers of marginalization, and this systemic discrimination also bleeds into the experience of sentencing, whether knowingly or otherwise. An analysis of execution of death-row convicts by Project 39A reveals a telling tale about the marginalized status of such death-row convicts[101] and the comparative non-imposition of the death sentence on convicts from better socio-economic origins. Empirical evidence thus points to a disturbing pattern that the infliction of the capital sentence intersects structural discrimination in our society. Thus, while seeking reports from jail authorities and probation officers, courts must be attentive that the same could also suffer from systemic biases and prejudice, and the counter-majoritarian court must be alert to such systemic shortcomings in the tools it employs. Perhaps, this is where the skill and perseverance of judicial deftness in the modification of sentences would be put to its most challenging test.

---

[98] *Narayan Chetanram Chaudhury v. State of Maharashtra* 2023 INSC 298; *Karan @ Fatiya v. State of Madhya Pradesh* 2023 5 SCC 504 (five years in custody); More recently, in *Om Prakash v. State of Uttarakhand* 2025 INSC 43 a prisoner whose death sentence was commuted to incarceration until he attained sixty years of age by the President of India was released by the SCI on being found to have been a juvenile on the date of the crime.

[99] Katherine Deborah Joy, 'Free at Last: The Story of a Child Who Spent 25 Years on Death Row & Emerged a Free Man' (*Article 14*, 17 April 2023) <https://article-14.com/post/free-at-last-the-story-of-a-child-who-spent-25-years-on-death-row-emerged-a-free-man--643c9fb92953e> accessed 29 November 2024.

[100] *State of Madhya Pradesh v. Ramji Lal Sharma*, 2024 INSC 747 (four years); *Pawan Kumar v. State of Uttar Pradesh* 2023 INSC 1012 (four years and six months).

[101] Project 39A, 'Socio Economic Profile' *Death Penalty India Report Summary*, (National Law University, 2016) 19 <https://static1.squarespace.com/static/5a843a9a9f07f5ccd61685f3/t/5b4ced7b1ae6cfe4db494040/1531768280079/Death+Penalty+India+Report_Summary.pdf> accessed 28 August 2024.

The idea of punishment and notion of sentencing also needs to be revisited and evaluated from a broader perspective in the context of prolonged and widespread incarceration of undertrial prisoners in India.[102] It is argued that undertrial incarceration is a form of *de facto* sentencing of accused persons on account of refusal and inability of courts to grant bail, when the allegations are prima facie heinous, or under special laws, where the process itself becomes the punishment[103] and sentencing is rendered meaningless. In this regard, the SCI has repeatedly[104] held that prolonged undertrial incarceration amounts to imposition of punishment even prior to conviction, as recently highlighted in the judgment of *Kalvakuntla Kavitha v. Directorate of Enforcement*, where it was held that '[r]elying on the various pronouncements of this Court, we had observed in the case of *Manish Sisodia* (supra)[105] that the prolonged incarceration before being pronounced guilty of an offence should not be permitted to become punishment without trial.'[106]

As statutory stipulations in special laws for terrorism, money-laundering and organized crime place stringent and at times insurmountable conditions for securing bail, undertrial detention overcrowds jails across India. There is an urgent need for the SCI, as the guarantor of personal liberty and constitutional safeguards, to resuscitate the maxim 'bail is the norm and jail an exception'. Further, as a facet of Article 21, the Court needs to develop jurisprudence to award compensation for prolonged undertrial incarceration, as victims of State excesses and false implication do not have the wherewithal to litigate suits for malicious prosecution and damages.

---

[102] Siddhartha Lamba, *Study on Functioning of Undertrial Review Committees From April to June 2020* (Common Wealth Human Rights Initiative 2022) 32-34 <https://www.humanrightsinitiative.org/download/1646661499CHRI%20Working%20of%20UTRC%202022%20Report.pdf> accessed 21 August 2024; *In Re: Inhuman Conditions in 1382 Prisons* (2016) 3 SCC 700.

[103] *Naresh Kumar v. State of Haryana*, Criminal Appeal No(s). 1722/2010, order dated 22 February 2024.

[104] *Abdul Rehman Antulay v. RS Nayak* (1992) 1 SCC 225; *Mohd Muslim v. State (NCT of Delhi)* 2023 SCC OnLine SC 352: para. 4; *Union of India v. KA Najeeb* (2021) 3 SCC 713.

[105] 2024 INSC 595.

[106] *Kalvakuntla Kavitha v. Enforcement Directorate* 2024 SCC OnLine SC 2269.

The Way Ahead for Individualized, Principled Sentencing

While *Dilbag Singh* emphasized the need for judicial innovation to usher in non-institutional reformation of convicts, the seeds it had sown in calling for community participation in reformation now find statutory basis in the form of community service as a prescribed punishment under the Bharatiya Nyaya Sanhita, 2023.[107] Although, there is a fair amount of ambiguity regarding the nature and scope of 'community service' and how it will be enforced. However, the retention of the death penalty as a form of punishment, further aggravated by the prescription of death penalty for a greater number of offences[108] and codification of the mandatory minimum period of twenty years as a sentence for life[109] in the new penal code, without any debate or consideration on the 'disquiet and unease' repeatedly expressed by the SCI,[110] is worrisome. For it is not just a missed opportunity to provide for more principled sentencing, which conforms to the due process requirement, but also a signal from the State that the response to crime will be harsher punishment. The political clamour for mandatory death sentences,[111] and the death penalty being introduced for sexual offences[112] while assuring no deterrence, offers a spectacle to the public that distracts from seeking accountability and allows the State to abdicate its responsibility to end impunity.[113]

The experience, in the United Kingdom (UK), of establishing a Sentencing Council' pursuant to the mandate of Coroners and Justice Act, 2009 and the Sentencing Act, 2020; and, in the United States (US), the issuance of US Sentencing Commission Guidelines in 2004[114] (made recommendatory

---

107 Bharatiya Nyaya Sanhita 2023 (BNS), ss 202, 209, 226, 303, 355, 356.

108 BNS ss 70, 103, 111, 113.

109 BNS s 6.

110 *Santosh Kumar Satishbhushan Bariyar* (n 2).

111 Saikat Kumar Bose, 'Explained: Mamata Banerjee"s New Law for Death Penalty in Rape Cases' (*NDTV*, 3 September 2024) <https://www.ndtv.com/india-news/aparajita-bill-rg-kar-medical-college-rape-murder-explained-mamata-banerjees-new-law-for-death-penalty-in-rape-cases-6481371>; PTI, 'Mob Rule Being Created as Politicians Aassuring Death Penalty for Culprits: SC Judge Abhay Oka' (*The Indian Express*, 1 September 2024).

112 BNS, s 70(2).

113 There is little to no engagement on this aspect with the findings of the 262nd Law Commission Report before legislating on the death penalty in the BNS.

114 United States Sentencing Commission, *Federal Sentencing Guidelines Manual* (2005) .

in nature by *US v. Booker*[115]) followed by the Federal Sentencing Guideline Manual of 2005[116] provide some formulaic solutions to judge-centric sentencing. However, these standardized templates may not lend themselves to easy replication in the Indian context, where structural location of the convict and systemic discrimination permeating the criminal legal system would require a deliberative humanistic approach through individualized, principled sentencing, to ensure equitable and just sentencing.

Judicial innovation by the Court in death-penalty sentencing has contributed salient principles in the sphere of Indian criminology and penology. These principles which were developed in the context of the death sentence, could be relied upon for application across the board for sentencing in all criminal cases, albeit with deft modification to suit the gravity of the offence and the range of punishment prescribed. The sensitivity and care required to ensure individualized, principled sentencing is a safeguard against unguided discretion and arbitrariness and a guarantee of due process to which all convicts are entitled, and the Court is bound under Articles 14 and 21 of the Constitution of India.

---

[115] *United States v. Booker* 543 US 220 (2005).

[116] United States Sentencing Commission, *Federal Sentencing Guidelines Manual* (n 114).

Part III

The Court and Equality

Cartoon © Manjul.

Article 30 and the Supreme Court: A Liberal and Wider Interpretation with a Few Exceptions

FAIZAN MUSTAFA

The protection of minorities is indeed the hallmark of a civilization. Lord Acton added a dimension: 'The most certain test by which we judge whether a country is really free is the amount of security enjoyed by minorities.'[1] If there is one word that can appropriately describe India, it is 'diversity'.[2] India is all about heterogeneity (and not homogeneity). There are 1,600 speech communities in India and 350 tribal groupings and over 3,000 castes. As the Supreme Court of India (SCI) turns seventy-five, it is important from both the purely scholarly point of view as well as the point of view of ordinary citizens to critically examine the jurisprudence developed by the highest court of India in upholding and preserving our rich diversity, because the rights of minorities are an important facet of Indian Constitution's diversity management. Articles 25 to 30 encapsulate the important constitutional value that respects minority rights in the contexts of religion, language, script and culture as well as the rights of minorities to establish and administer institutions of their choice.

What has been the response of the SCI to the protection of minority rights in terms of their educational and cultural rights? How has the Court defined minorities and minority institutions? How have various terms used in Article 30 been interpreted? What kinds of regulations can the State bring in to restrict the rights of minorities or how much of governmental control would

---

[1] Lord Acton , 'The History of Freedom in Antiquity, (*Acton Institute*, 26 February 1877) <https://www.acton.org/research/history-freedom-antiquity> accessed 27 August 2024.

[2] CJI Kirpal started his majority judgment in *TMA Pai Foundation v. State of Karnataka* (2002) 8 SCC 481, 529 with the statement, 'India is land of diversity...'.

be constitutionally permissible? Why cannot minorities be given the right to maladminister their institutions? What is the relationship between Articles 29(2)[3] and Article 30(1)[4]? What is the indicia to determine the minority character of an institution? These are some of the issues on which the SCI's response is to be critically evaluated.

Rationale of Minority Rights

Venkatarama Aiyar J, in *In Re Kerala Education Bill,*[5] the first leading case on minority rights, observed:

> It is well known that during the Middle Ages, the accepted notion was that Sovereigns were entitled to impose their own religion on their subjects, and those who did not conform to it could be dealt with as traitors. It was this notion that was responsible during the 16th and 17th centuries for numerous wars between nations and for civil wars in the continent of Europe, and it was only latterly that it came to be recognized that freedom of religion is not incompatible with good citizenship and loyalty to the State, and that all progressive societies should respect the religious beliefs of their minorities. It is this concept that is embodied in Articles 25, 26, 29 and 30 of the Constitution.[6]

Sixteen years later, in *Xavier's*[7] case, the Court explained the rationale of Articles 25 to 30 thus:

> These provisions enshrined a befitting pledge to the minorities in the Constitution of the country whose greatest son had laid down his life for the protection of the minorities. As long as the Constitution stands as it is today, no tampering with those rights can be countenanced. Any

---

[3] *Constitution of India*, 1950, art 29(2): 'No citizen shall be denied admission into any educational institution maintained by the State or receiving aid out of State funds on grounds only of religion, race, caste, language or any of them.'

[4] *Constitution of India*, 1950, art 30(1): 'All minorities, whether based on religion or language, shall have the right to establish and administer educational institutions of their choice.'

[5] *In Re Kerala Education Bill* AIR 1968 SC 956.

[6] *In Re Kerala Education Bill* 990.

[7] *Ahmedabad St Xavier's College Society v. State of Gujarat* (1974) 1 SCC 717.

> attempt to do so would be not only an act of breach of faith, it would be constitutionally impermissible . . .[8]

Recently by a 4:3 majority, the path for the declaration of minority character of the Aligarh Muslim University (AMU) was possibly opened by the SC,[9] by overturning more than a five-decade old judgment in *S Azeez Basha v. Union of India*.[10] Writing for the majority, CJI DY Chandrachud observed, Article 30 (1) is a 'special right' and basically a 'facet of the principle of non-discrimination against minorities'.[11] He went on to observe that distinct and diverse languages and religions have inherent value, and minorities should not be at any disadvantage due to their numbers.[12] SC Sharma J, in his opinion that partly concurs with the majority and on few points with the dissenting judges, also accepted that Article 30 'is a guarantee that embeds cultural diversity, secularism and fairness on the canvas of the Constitution'.[13] SC Sharma J also opined that 'this diversity is not a coincidence in India and is a product of the inherent genetic build of Indian society'.[14] Surya Kant J, like CJI Chandrachud, too emphasized the autonomy of minority institutions. In his dissenting opinion, he said that the unique nature of Article 30 lies in its broader protection against State intervention.

Not Just Conservation of Religion and Culture

In the *Kerala Education Bill* case, where the first non-Congress government of the Indian Republic tried to control and rather than assimilate minority institutions and President of the country asked for the SCI's advisory opinion, the Court in explicit words clarified that the right under Article 30 was not confined to religious minorities only: 'Article 30(1) gives certain rights not only to religious minorities but also to linguistic minorities. In the next place, the right conferred on such minorities is to establish educational institutions of their choice. It does not say that minorities based on religion should

8 ibid 771.

9 *Aligarh Muslim University v. Naresh Agrawal* 2024 SCC Online SC 3213

10 *S Azeez Basha v. Union of India* AIR 1968 SC 662.

11 *Aligarh Muslim University* (n 9) [50].

12 ibid [54].

13 ibid [5].

14 ibid [6].

establish educational institutions for teaching religion only, or that linguistic minorities should have the right to establish educational institutions for teaching their language only.'[15] It was clarified that the right was not limited to just conserving religion, language and culture but also extended to modern, liberal and secular education as well.[16] These rights are not available just to religious minorities but also to linguistic minorities[17] and go much beyond the preservation of religion and language.

In *Xavier's,*[18] the SCI held that religious minorities had the right to establish educational institutions to conserve language, script or culture under Article 29 (1), whereas Article 30 (1) allowed them to establish educational institutions 'of their choice' and for any purpose unconnected with language, script or culture.[19] The expression 'of their choice' is too wide and cannot be restricted.[20] Article 30 has nothing to do with theological institutions like Madrasas or Vedic institutions, which are governed by Article 26.[21]

Definition of Minority

The most fundamental question on Article 30 related to the definition of the term 'minority' has been authoritatively decided by the SCI; but doubts are raised time and again. The expression 'minorities' has been employed only

---

15 *In Re Kerala Education Bill* (n 5) [23].

16 ibid. It was noted that: '...the article leaves it to their choice to establish such educational institutions as will serve both purposes, namely, the purpose of conserving their religion, language or culture, and also the purpose of giving a thorough, good general education to their children'.

17 Since linguistic minorities too have identical rights under Article 30, these rights cannot be termed as appeasement of religious minorities. A Hindi speaking Brahmin of Uttar Pradesh can establish and administer Hindi-medium minority educational institutions in Tamil Nadu.

18 *Ahmedabad St Xavier's College Society* (n 7). The Court referred to the decision in *Rev Father W Proost v. State of Bihar* AIR 1969 SC 465.

19 *Ahmedabad St Xavier's College Society* (n 7) 742. The Court in *Xavier's* further said that the whole objective of conferring the right on minorities under Article 30 was to ensure that there would be equality between the majority and the minority. If the minorities did not have such special protection, they would be denied equality; The recent judgment of the SCI in the *Aligarh Muslim University* case was also unanimous on this issue – that minorities' rights were not confined to the protection of language and culture, *Aligarh Muslim University* (n 9) [54].

20 In fact, religious institutions can be established by both the majority as well as minorities under Article 26 of the Constitution.

21 Ruma Pal J, *TMA Pai Foundation v. State of Karnataka* (2002) 8 SCC 481 [375]: 'Right to set up an educational institution to impart religious instruction is under Article 26 (a) which says that every religious denomination or any section thereof shall have the right to establish and maintain institutions for religious and charitable purposes, and not under Article 30(1)'.

at four places in the Indian Constitution. Although the heading of Article 29 uses the word 'minorities', it is missing in the text of the provision. It is therefore possible to understand Article 29 as not being confined to just minorities. Then again, although the expression 'minorities or minority' has been employed in the heading of Article 30 and clauses (1) and (2), the term itself has not been defined in the Constitution.

Under international norms, the most obvious definition of minorities and majorities is in terms of numbers, or what is said to be the 'numerical inferiority test'. A minority is a group that is numerically smaller than the majority in the society, or any group that is less than fifty per cent of the given population. But under the 'powerlessness test', the non-dominant status of the group is also looked at to recognize it as a minority group if that group is powerless in the power structure of the State. United Nations' Special Rapporteur Francesco Capotorti argues that minorities are groups that possess distinct and stable ethnic, religious and linguistic characteristics. The crucial point is that, firstly, these characteristics differ from the rest of the population, and secondly, that these groups wish to preserve their distinctive identity even if this identity does not conform to the norms and the values of the majority.

The SCI has consistently maintained that, since Article 30 has used the terms 'religious' and 'linguistic' minorities together and since states were originally carved out on the linguistic basis, minorities are to be defined at the level of the state. In *Kerala Education Bill* itself, the Court did not accept the argument that minorities were to be decided at the local area or district level where the institution was located. It has preferred the numerical inferiority test over the powerlessness test.

In *TMA Pai*, the majority again reiterated State as the unit[22] for the determination of a group's minority status. Quadri J, in a partly concurring judgment did use the term 'non-dominant' but concurred with the numerical inferiority test and state as unit.[23] Ruma Pal J, in her powerful dissenting judgment, observed that defining minorities for the purposes of Article 30 would depend on the law in question – if it were central law, minorities be nationally defined, if state law, then at the level of state.[24] A better proposition

[22] *TMA Pai Foundation* (n 24) 553.

[23] ibid 620; Having referred to the expression 'non-dominant', Quadri J concurred with the majority on the state as unit.

[24] ibid 649.

would be to define religious minorities nationally; whereas, for the linguistic minorities, states should be the unit.

In *Bal Patil*,[25] the Court refused to recognize Jains as a minority and favoured assimilation of minorities. The Allahabad High Court had similarly refused to consider Muslims as a minority.[26] *Bal Patil*'s regressive judgment not only furthers the assimilationist argument but also wrongly concludes that no new religious minority would now be entitled to be recognized as a religious minority and receive the protection of Article 30.[27]

Establishment: Narrow and Wider Meaning

There is considerable confusion on how to determine whether an institution is or is not a minority institution. In *Azeez Basha*, the SCI accepted that the expression 'educational institution' would include even a university[28] that has now been reiterated in *Aligarh Muslim University*. *TMA Pai* had also accepted that the protection of Article 30 is available to education at all levels.[29] Way back in *Kerala Education Bill*, the SCI had categorically said that it was within the power of the minorities to expand their choice as much as they wanted. The SCI observed, 'It is said that the dominant word is "choice" and the content of that Article is as wide as the choice of the particular minority community may make it.'[30]

In *Azeez Basha*, the SCI opined that the expression in Article 30, 'establish' means 'bring into existence'[31]. This was despite CJI Wanchoo's acknowledgment

---

[25] *Bal Patil v. Union of India* (2005) 6 SCC 690 [33]: 'It was not in contemplation of the framers of the Constitution to add to the list of religious minorities. The Constitution through all its organs is committed to protect religious, cultural and educational rights of all. Articles 25 to 30 guarantee cultural and religious freedoms to both majority and minority groups. Ideal of a democratic society, which has adopted right of equality as its fundamental creed, should be elimination of majority and minority and so called forward and backward classes. Constitution has accepted one common citizenship for every India.'

[26] *Committee of Management, Anjuman Madarsa Noorul Islam Dehra Kalan, Ghazipurv. State of Uttar Pradesh* (2007) 4 All LJ 370.

[27] The Indian Constitution does not prohibit the birth of new religions. After *Bal Patil,* the government itself recognized Jains as a minority. Even Hindus are a religious minority in some states and union territories, and certainly can be a linguistic minority in any state. See Faizan Mustafa, 'Hindus as Minority: Government's Affidavit is Consistent with Constitution' (*The Indian Express*, 30 March 2022).

[28] *S Azeez Basha* (n 10) [21].

[29] *TMA Pai Foundation* (n 21) 591, 711.

[30] *In Re Kerala Education Bill* (n 5) 979.

[31] *S Azeez Basha* (n 10) [25].

that the word 'establish' has several other connotations as well, such as 'to ratify', 'to found', 'to confirm' or 'to settle', as defined in several dictionaries or used in foreign jurisdictions.[32] The Court after having noted the prior history of AMU, which was amongst the earliest of the renowned minority educational institutions, reached the strange conclusion that the university was brought into existence by an Act of the central legislature. In other words, AMU was not established by Muslims and could not be recognized as a minority institution. The Court also held that, in view of the recognition accorded to the degrees awarded by AMU, the Muslim community had waived its minority character.[33]

Within two years, a six-judge Bench in *Very Rev Mother Provincial*, *sub-silentio* overruled *Azeez Basha* when it accepted 'to found' as another meaning of the word 'establish' in Article 30.[34] The Court effectively rejected the narrow view of *Azeez Basha* on at least two counts. It held that the establishment of an educational institution can be ascertained from the 'intention' of the minority community 'to found an institution' of their choice and 'for the benefit of a minority community by a member of that community'.[35] The Court observed, 'Article 30(1) has been construed before by this Court. Without referring to those cases, it is sufficient to say that the clause contemplates two rights that are separated in point of time. The first right is the initial right to establish institutions of the minority's choice. Establishment here means the bringing into being of an institution and it must be by a minority community. It matters not if a single philanthropic individual with his own means, founds the institution or the community at large contributes the funds.'[36] Thereafter, the eleven-judge Bench in *TMA Pai* cited *Very Rev Mother Provincial* with approval.[37]

Recently, the *Aligarh Muslim University* judgment explicitly overruled the narrow construction of the word 'establishment' in *Azeez Basha*. CJI Chandrachud clarified the meaning of the term 'establish' thus:

---

32 ibid.

33 *S Azeez Basha* (n 10) [21], [22], [26].

34 *State of Kerala v. Very Rev Mother Provincial*, (1970) 2 SCC 417 [8].

35 ibid.

36 ibid.

37 *TMA Pai Foundation* (n 21) [196].

> the word 'establish' as used in Article 30(1) cannot and should not be understood in a narrow and legalistic sense. The words used in clause (1) of Article 30 have to be interpreted in view of the object and purpose of the article, and the guarantee and protection it confers. The guarantee and protection are not dependent on the basis or the manner in which the legal requirements were/are complied with, rather it concerns the persons who have founded and created the establishment. The incorporation by a statute or the procedure and requirements in law are not determinative factors.[38]

CJI Chandrachud went on to explain the distinction between 'establishment' and 'incorporation' when he said:

> The words 'incorporation' and 'establishment' cannot be used interchangeably. They connote different meanings. 'Incorporation' signifies the legal existence of the institution. In contrast, 'establishment' signifies the founding or bringing into existence of the institution. The possibility of distinguishing the establishment and incorporation of universities arose with the advent of teaching Universities. Two kinds of institutions were incorporated as teaching universities. They consisted of institutions which were established and incorporated at the same time, and institutions in which the establishment of the institution predated its incorporation. Universities in the latter category, however, were teaching colleges converted into teaching universities.[39]

Another question involved is the indicia of minority institutions. While this was left unanswered in *TMA Pai*, the SCI has laid down the indicia of a minority institution in *Aligarh Muslim University*. The majority led by CJI (on his behalf and on behalf of Sanjiv Khanna, JB Pardiwala and Manoj Misra JJ) suggested the following factors to be taken into account in determining the minority character:

> a. Ideation: to look at the genesis or ideation or brain behind the idea. The person taking initiative must belong to the minority community.[40]

---

[38] *Aligarh Muslim University* (n 9) [95].

[39] *Aligarh Muslim University* (n 9) [94].

[40] *Aligarh Muslim University* (n 9) [135].

b. Purpose: The intent must be to found an institution 'predominantly for the minority community'.[41]

c. Implementation:[42] Other factors to be taken into account would be collection of funds, getting land, construction of buildings and governmental approvals. Presence of religious symbols or religious instructions is not necessary, as fully aided minority institutions may not have religious instruction due to the prohibition in Article 28.[43]

d. Administration: It is not necessary that administration must be vested in the minority itself. The right to administer is the consequence of establishment.[44]

Surya Kant J too agreed with the majority that presence of others does not adversely affect minority character if a 'sprinkling of outsiders' is there in the administration.[45] The dissenting judges, Dipankar Datta and SC Sharma JJ emphasized the 'pervasive control' on administration as a major yardstick to decide the minority character. They preferred a substantial presence of minorities in such bodies and in exclusive decision-making in administrative matters.[46] If a genuine minority institution does not have its own so-called 'pervasive control' over administration and includes in its administration members of other communities, it cannot be penalized for such inclusion or acceptance of greater governmental oversight. Unlike religious institutions under Article 26, institutions of secular education under Article 30 may require administrative bodies of professionals and experts.

---

41 *Aligarh Muslim University* (n 9) [136]; Dissenting judge SC Sharma J agreed with the majority on purpose [169].

42 *Aligarh Muslim University* (n 9) [137], [133].

43 Surya Kant J in essence largely highlighted almost similar factors.

44 *Aligarh Muslim University* (n 9) [138]; It also held: 'To do otherwise, would amount to converting a consequence to a pre-condition.'

45 *Aligarh Muslim University* (n 9) [177], [182], dissenting opinion of Surya Kant J. As a matter of fact, 'sprinkling of outsiders' was used in *Kerala Education Bill* in the context of students, not governing bodies.

46 By over-emphasizing the communal character of the institution as a condition precedent to claim minority character, the dissenting judges went against the nine judge Bench judgment in *Ahmedabad St Xavier's College Society* where the Court had observed that 'the right to administer is to be tempered with regulatory measures to facilitate smooth administration'.

Pre-Constitution Institutions

Another related issue to the establishment debate has been the issue of protection to the pre-constitution institutions. In *Kerala Education Bill*, CJI SR Das had no doubt that pre-constitution institutions too were entitled to the protection of Article 30.[47] Subsequent SCI Benches also followed this liberal interpretation. In *SK Patro*,[48] the Court held that, though the concept of citizenship of India was not there prior to the commencement of the Constitution, yet if the persons setting up educational institutions in pre-Constitution era were residing in India and if they formed a well-defined religious or linguistic minority, the institutions established by them would be entitled to rights under Article 30.[49] With difficulty, the Jesuits of Ranchi[50] and Christians of Bhagalpur[51] were able to prove that these minority institutions were established not by foreigners but by Indian residents in the pre-Independence era. Similarly, in *St Stephen's*,[52] a prestigious pre-Constitution college in Delhi was held as a minority institution only after the Protestants of Delhi were able to demonstrate that the college was established by Indian residents and not foreigners.

Interestingly, while Arya Samaj is not a religious minority as it is a part of the Hindu religion, the DAV College in Jalandhar is considered as a minority institution in Punjab because of its medium of instruction being Hindi but without the kind of strict scrutiny to which Christian institutions are subjected.[53] Sindhi institutions too have been held as minority institutions.[54] The Court emphasized the significance of Article 30 when it held that every linguistic minority may have its own social, economic and cultural limitations, and it has a constitutional right to conserve such culture and language.[55]

---

[47] *In Re Kerala Education Bill* (n 5) 978.

[48] *Right Rev Bishop SK Patro v. State of Bihar,* (1969) 1 SCC 863.

[49] ibid 869.

[50] *Rev Father W Proost* (n 18).

[51] *Right Rev Bishop SK Patro* (n 48).

[52] *St Stephen's College v. University of Delhi* (1992) 1 SCC 558.

[53] *DAV College v. State of Punjab* (1971) 2 SCC 269.

[54] *Sindhi Education Society v. Chief Secretary, Government of NCT of Delhi* (2010) 8 SCC 49 [8]. Writing for the Court, Swatanter Kumar J held that there was no dispute that the Society was a minority institution and it enjoys the status of linguistic minority.

[55] *Sindhi Education Society* (n 54) [112].

St Stephen's also involved the issue of minority character of not only a pre-Constitution institution but of one that was governed by a regulatory statutory framework. Yet, it was held as an institution established by a minority and was thus entitled to Article 30 rights. It was authoritatively held that regulation by statute (in this case of Delhi University Act, 1922) does not in any way lead to loss of rights under Article 30. Unlike *Azeez Basha*, *St Stephen's* considered the significance of historical antecedents of the institution to ascertain its minority character. The Court inferred the Christian character of the college from the history of St Stephen's College rooted in the Christian community. Characteristics such as its 'name, emblem, motto, the establishment of a chapel and its religious instruction in the Christian Gospel for religious assembly'[56] and '. . . the presence of a larger number of Christian members of the Church of North India on it'[57] were noted by the Court.

Non-Minority Students

Admission of non-minority students in no way dilutes the minority character of an institution. In the *Bombay Educational Society* judgment,[58] the Court invalidated the policy to restrict admission in the English-medium minority schools to those children whose mother tongue was English, as the same would be contrary to Article 29 (2) and discriminate on the basis of language.[59] *TMA Pai* too approved *Kerala Education Bill* on the proposition that admission of non-minority students would not affect the minority character of an educational institution.[60]

---

[56] *St Stephen's College* (n 52) [34].

[57] ibid [35]. In *Aligarh Muslim University* (n 9) [133], it was held that there is no necessity to prove either the presence of religious symbols within the minority institutions or the imparting of religious instruction as in fully-aided government institutions, and that such an instruction may not be given due to the prohibition of Article 28.

[58] *Bombay Education Society v. State of Bombay*, 1955 SCR 568.

[59] CJI SR Das *In Re Kerala Education Bill* (n 5) [22] observed: 'By admitting a non-member into it the minority institution does not shed its character and cease to be a minority institution. Indeed the object of conservation of the distinct language, script and culture of a minority may be better served by propagating the same amongst non-members of the particular minority community. In our opinion, it is not possible to read this condition into Article 30(1) of the Constitution.'

[60] *TMA Pai Foundation* (n 21) 560.

Governmental Regulations, Governmental Aid and Minority Character

Article 30 jurisprudence of the SCI is largely about the kind of regulations the government can legitimately impose in respect of minority institutions. *Kerala Education Bill* itself was an attempt to control minority institutions. In *SK Patro*, an order of the Deputy Director of education that imposed an obligation on the school to constitute a managing committee to control, administer and manage affairs was under challenge. There have been some decisions restricting the scope of governmental regulations, but then there have been decisions that allowed substantial governmental control in the name of regulations.

An important aspect is what regulations may be placed by the government on providing aid to a minority institution. The Court in *Kerala Education Bill* was conscious of the fact that, without aid, no educational institution could really survive. It said, 'No educational institutions can in actual practice be carried on without aid from the State and if they will not get it unless they surrender their rights they will, by compulsion of financial necessities, be compelled to give up their rights under Art. 30 (1) . . .'[61]

The Court also observed that the '[l]earned Attorney-General concedes that reasonable regulations may certainly be imposed by the State as a condition for aid or even for recognition.' There is no right in any minority, other than Anglo-Indians, to get aid, but, he contends, that if the State chooses to grant aid then it must not say – 'I have money and I shall distribute aid but I shall not give you any aid unless you surrender to me your right of administration'. The State must not grant aid in such a manner as will take away the 'fundamental right of the minority community under Article 30 (1).'[62] Grant of aid, thus, cannot be tied to the surrender of the minority character of a minority institution. The liberal approach of the Court in *Kerala Education Bill* is clearly reflected in the observation of CJI SR Das that the State cannot impose such 'onerous' conditions for granting aid for minority educational institutions for receiving aid, such that the minority community is forced 'to surrender their constitutional right of administering educational institutions of their choice.'[63]

---

[61] *In Re Kerala Education Bill* (n 5) [31].

[62] ibid.

[63] *In Re Kerala Education Bill* (n 5) [26].

This view was subsequently affirmed in *TMA Pai* and *PA Inamdar*,[64] holding that aided institutions do not lose minority rights by accepting state aid. *TMA Pai* did make a distinction between aided and unaided institutions and the kind of autonomy they are entitled to. It was held that while the unaided institutions have maximum autonomy, aided institutions do not lose their minority character on receiving aid, although conditions may be imposed that are 'related to the proper utilization of the grant and fulfilment of the objectives of the grant.'[65] Ruma Pal J reiterated the Court's consistent approach on the issue of aid when she observed that the State cannot compel a minority institution to give up its right under Article 30 (1) as part of the restrictions for 'grant-in-aid'.[66]

In the case of aided non-minority institutions, greater regulation is permissible for promoting good, efficient and sound administration, and to prevent maladministration, for proper maintenance of high standards for education, including conditions for admissions and reservations and for the protection of the interests of staff. Further, general laws of the land are applicable to minority institutions, such as taxation, sanitation, social welfare, economic regulation, public order and morality.[67] But the Court was categorical in clarifying that although regulations and checks are necessary to ensure good administration, it has to be ensured that an aided institution 'does not become a government-owned and controlled institution'.[68]

The SCI in *TMA Pai* held that, where there is aid by the government, autonomy may be diluted, as Article 29 (2)[69] would apply,[70] and conditions could be laid down for recognition, such as for maintaining the standard of education. The Court observed that the conditions, however, should not directly or indirectly defeat the protection conferred by Article 30, such as by: (a) denying recognition solely due to it belonging to a minority; or

[64] (2005) 6 SCC 537.

[65] *TMA Pai Foundation* (n 21) [143].

[66] ibid 662.

[67] *TMA Pai Foundation* (n 21) [137].

[68] ibid [72].

[69] *Constitution of India*, 1950, art 29 (2): 'No citizen shall be denied admission into any educational institution maintained by the State or receiving aid out of State funds on grounds only of religion, race, caste, language or any of them.'

[70] *TMA Pai Foundation* (n 21) [91].

(b) imposing regulations aimed at or having the effect of depriving the institution of its minority status.[71]

In *Sidhrajbhai*,[72] the SCI held that the condition that church mission teachers training schools should surrender eighty per cent of seats to government nominees was violative of Article 30. It further held that the rights guaranteed under Article 30(1) are declared in 'absolute' terms, unlike the reasonable restrictions on freedoms guaranteed under Article 19(1).[73] But this view was not accepted in subsequent decisions.[74] Finally, in *TMA Pai Foundation*, CJI Kirpal himself widened the scope of the regulations.[75]

The problem with post-*Sidhrajbhai* judgments has been on the determination of reasonableness. Shah J had observed in *Sidhrajbhai* that the right under Article 30 cannot be 'whittled down by so-called regulative measures conceived in the interest not of the minority educational institution, but of the public or the nation as a whole.'[76] In *Lily Kurian*,[77] the Court held that regulations cannot be justified in the name of general public interest and they must be only in the interests of the concerned minority. However, 'the moment one goes beyond that and imposes, what is in truth, not a mere regulation but an impairment of the right to administer, the Article comes into play and the interference cannot be justified by pleading the interest of the general

---

[71] Ibid [103].

[72] *Rev Sidhrajbhai Sabhai v. State of Gujarat* AIR 1963 SC 540.

[73] Ibid [10]; MB Shah J further held that:

> [R]egulations which may lawfully be imposed either by legislative or executive action as a condition of receiving grant or of recognition must be directed to making the institution while retaining its character as a minority institution effective as an educational institution. Such regulation must satisfy a dual test-the test of reasonableness, and the test that it is regulative of the educational character of the institution and is conducive to making the institution an effective vehicle of education for the minority community or other persons who resort to it [15].

[74] *Ahmedabad St Xavier's College Society* (n 7); *All Saints High School v. Government of Andhra Pradesh* AIR 1980 SC 1042; *DAV College* (n 53).

[75] *TMA Pai Foundation* (n 21) [107].

[76] *Rev Sidhrajbhai Sabhai v. State of Gujarat* (n 72) [15]; Shah J also propounded the dual test mentioned above to examine the constitutionality of a governmental regulation. This test has been consistently reiterated by the SC including in *TMA Pai*. It has also been approved by the eleven-judge Bench in *Aligarh Muslim University* that any regulation, to be valid today, has to satisfy that test.

[77] *Lily Kurian v. Lewina* (1979) 2 SCC 124; In this case, the State's power to regulate was again clarified and it was held that the State could certainly make regulations for the proper administration of Article 30 institutions and such institutions in the name of autonomy could not indulge in maladministration. The Court observed that 'Article 30(1), though couched in absolute and spacious terms in marked contrast with other fundamental rights in Part III, has to be read subject to the regulatory power of the State.' Further, 'Article 30(1) is not a charter for maladministration; regulation, so that the right to administer may be better exercised for the benefit of the institution, is permissible.' [27] [36].

public; the interests justifying interference can only be in the interests of the minority concerned.'[78] And that 'the State may "regulate" the exercise of the right of administration, but it has no power to impose any "restriction" which is destructive of the right itself.' This important point on the purpose of regulation was subsequently diluted in spite of the dual test in *Sidhrajbhai* being reiterated in a number of subsequent decisions.

Xavier's noted that the Court has consistently held that 'it is not only permissible but also desirable to regulate everything in educational and academic matters for achieving excellence and uniformity in standards of education.'[79] Accordingly, in *Xavier's*, the Court allowed regulations for ensuring proper utilization of funds, preventing anti-national activity, laying down qualifications or conditions of service, imposition of conditions of compliance with the principles of natural justice before terminating the service of teachers, ensuring that the appointment of teachers is from a panel prepared by the State or University, in addition to the qualifications for entry of students, students' hygiene and physical training and the age of superannuation of teachers.

But these observations have eventually led to the substantial dilution of minority rights and undermined the administrative autonomy of the institutions under Article 30, as subsequent Benches of the Court upheld several intrusive or restrictive governmental regulations. Thus, the inclusion of the principal and staff on the board of management of a minority college were considered valid in *Gandhi Faiz-e-Azam College*;[80] approval of outside or external authorities for the disciplinary action against the employees of minority education institutions was considered valid in *All Saints High School*.[81] The right of management of minority institution was diluted in *Frank Anthony School*[82] in the name of 'fairness' to the employees. In *Christian Medical College*,[83] labour laws were held to be applicable to minority institutions as well; *St John Teachers Training Institute*[84] extended the applicability of rest of the general laws of the country even in respect of unaided institutions; minority institutions' freedom

[78] *Lily Kurian* (n 77) [36].

[79] *Ahmedabad St Xavier's College Society* (n 7) [46].

[80] *Gandhi Faiz-e-Azam College Shahjahanpur v. University of Agra* (1975) 1 SCC 283.

[81] *All Saints High School* (n 74).

[82] *Frank Anthony Public School Employees Association v. Union of India* (1986) 4 SCC 707.

[83] *Christian Medical College Hospital Employees Union v. CMC Vellore Association* (1987) 4 SCC 691.

[84] *St John's Teachers Training Institute (for Women) v. State of Tamil Nadu* (1993) 3 SCC 595.

to devise their curricula was severely curtailed in *English Medium Students Association*;[85] in *Bihar Madarsa Board*,[86] governmental takeover of minority institutions on the ground of maladministration was again reiterated and regulation aimed to ensure 'efficiency and discipline of the institution' was also upheld.[87]

Recognition and No Right to Affiliation

Just like governmental aid, there is no right to get recognition or affiliation. But such onerous obligations cannot be justified for granting or withholding recognition or affiliation. On the issue of affiliation, neither there is a fundamental right to affiliation nor a minority institution can be deprived of its minority character to get an affiliation. Such institutions cannot be compelled to give up the right of management to get affiliation. The Court observed in *St Stephens* that 'in the first place, it may be stated that the State or any instrumentality of the State cannot deprive the character of the institution, founded by a minority community by compulsory affiliation since Article 30 (1) is a special right to minorities to establish educational institutions of their choice.'[88] *TMA Pai* also endorsed this view that affiliation and recognition must be available to every institution that fulfils the prescribed conditions for such affiliation. Such terms cannot be imposed as a condition of grant of affiliation or recognition such that institutional autonomy and the objective of establishing the institution are completely destroyed.[89]

No Right to Maladminister

The SCI has reiterated that minorities under Article 30 have no right to maladminister their institutions. It has therefore recognized the powers of the State to insist on proper safeguards to: (a) to prevent maladministration; (b) to maintain fair standards of teaching; or (c) to ensure excellence of the institutions. CJI SR Das emphasized the importance of efficient administration of minority institutions in *Kerala Education Bill* and considered it an integral part of excellence. It was observed that:

---

85 *English Medium Students Association v. State of Karnataka* (1994) 1 SCC 550.

86 *Bihar State Madrasa Education Board v. Madrasa Hanifa Arabic College* (1990) 1 SCC 428.

87 *Virendra Nath Gupta v. Delhi Administration* (1990) 2 SCC 307.

88 *St Stephen's College* (n 52) [41].

89 *TMA Pai Foundation* (n 21) [36].

> The right to administer cannot obviously include the right to maladminister. The minority cannot surely ask for aid or recognition for an educational institution run by them in unhealthy surroundings, without any competent teachers, possessing any semblance of qualification, and which does not maintain even a fair standard of teaching or which teaches matters subversive of the welfare of the scholars. It stands to reason, then, that the constitutional right to administer an educational institution of their choice does not necessarily militate against the claim of the State to insist that in order to grant aid the State may prescribe reasonable regulations to ensure the excellence of the institutions to be aided.[90]

If universities prescribe the curriculum for examinations, they must be followed, subject however to special subjects that the minority institutions may seek to teach; and to a certain extent, the State may also regulate the conditions of employment of teachers and the health and hygiene of students. Such regulations do not bear directly upon the administration as such, although they may indirectly affect it. The Court has consistently held that the minority institutions cannot be allowed to fall below the standards of excellence expected of educational institutions, or under the guise of exclusive right of management, to decline to follow the general pattern. It also held that while the management must be left to them, they may be compelled to 'keep in step with others.'[91]

Minority Reservation in Minority Institutions

There has been some confusion on the relationship between Article 29 (2) and Article 30 (1) of the Constitution, particularly in respect of aided minority institutions. Though *Kerala Education Bill* talked of just 'sprinkling of outsiders' in minority institutions, yet the issue remained unresolved till 1992 when *St Stephen's* restricted the right of minorities to reserve seats for the minorities to the maximum limit of fifty per cent. *TMA Pai* lifted this fifty per cent upper limit[92] and held that institutions, particularly private unaided

[90] *In Re Kerala Education Bill* (n 5) [31].

[91] *TMA Pai Foundation* (n 21) [109], citing *Very Rev Mother Provincial* (n 38); In *St Stephen's* also, the Court explained the ambit and extent of the right to administer when it observed that the right to administer does not include the right to maladminister [59].

[92] *TMA Pai Foundation* (n 21) 584.

ones, have a right to admit students based on a rational and fair system of their own, subject to minimum qualifications and systems of computing equivalence between different kinds of qualifications that may be prescribed.[93] The Court further approved the decision in *St Stephen's,* upholding the right of the institutions to select students as a part of the right to administer, but not to the extent that the institution could serve the exclusive advantage of the minority community.[94]

Islamic Academy[95] left it to the state to determine the quantum of reservation depending upon the course and needs of the minority. After *TMA Pai* lifted the fifty per cent upper limit of reservation imposed by *St Stephen's*, the Parliament through the 93rd Constitutional Amendment inserted Article 15 (5) and excluded minority institutions from the ambit of constitutional reservations.[96] In 2019, Article 15 (6) was inserted with an identical language of exclusion of Article 30 institutions. This exclusion was necessary to maintain the fifty per cent upper limit of reservations. The SCI, in *Sindhi Educational Society*, has also held that the state's insistence on the implementation of reservation for SC/ST prior to grant of aid is not applicable to minority institutions.

Common Admission Tests and NEET

The right to admit students of their choice has been consistently held as part of the right to administer minority educational institutions. The SCI has held that reasonable restrictions on the right to admit students can certainly be imposed, but the welfare of the minorities ought to be kept in view. In *St Stephens*, the Court was categorical that the right to select students is very much a part of administration of the institution: 'The right to select students for admission is a part of administration. It is indeed an important facet of administration. This power also could be regulated but the regulation must be reasonable just like any other regulation. It should be conducive to the welfare of the minority institution or for the betterment of those who resort to it.'[97]

---

93 ibid 540.

94 ibid 575.

95 *Islamic Academy of Education v. State of Karnataka* (2003) 6 SCC 697.

96 The amendment was upheld by the five-judge Constitution Bench in *Ashok Kumar Thakur v. Union of India* (2008) 6 SCC 1.

97 *St Stephen's College* (n 52) [60].

The SCI, in *St Stephen's,* quoted Mathew J's observations in *Xavier's* that minorities have the right to admit their own candidates to maintain the minority character of their institutions. This was said to be 'the necessary concomitant right which flows from the right to establish and administer educational institutions in Article 30.'[98] Mathew J held it to be the right of parents when he observed, 'The parents are entitled to have their children educated in institutions having an atmosphere congenial to their own religion.'[99]

When the National Eligibility cum Entrance Test (NEET) was introduced by the Medical Council of India (MCI), a three-judge Bench led by CJI Altamas Kabir in *Christian Medical College,*[100] by a majority of 2:1, opined that the MCI does not have right to conduct NEET and rights under Article 30 cannot be taken away by notifications of the MCI and Dental Council of India (DCI). The right to admit students was yet again held as an essential facet of the right under Article 30 and it was also reiterated that so long as the process of admission to such institutions is transparent and merit is adequately taken care of, such right cannot be interfered with, except in cases of maladministration or lack of transparency.[101]

In 2016, not only a review of CJI Kabir's judgment was allowed but the dissenting judge of the 2013 judgment, Anil Dave J, made NEET compulsory even prior to a full hearing of the case.[102] In 2020, a three-judge Bench led by Arun Mishra J upheld NEET.[103]

The NEET judgment, in fact, has also in a way gone against the *TMA Pai* decision that had categorically held that unaided private minority institutions would have maximum autonomy. A minority professional college can admit, in their management quota, a student of their own community/language in

---

[98] ibid [95]

[99] ibid.

[100] *Christian Medical College Vellore v. Union of India* (2014) 2 SCC 305.

[101] ibid [157].

[102] NEET not only seems to be an assault on the autonomy of universities and higher-education institutions, particularly private unaided ones but it also seems to not be contributing to promotion of merit. It is ironic that, while in all other areas, including industrial relations, the government is going for deregulation, in the case of education, over-centralization is becoming a harsh and painful reality. In the name of NEET, the rights of unaided private institutions and minority institutions cannot be violated, as no regulation can annihilate the minority character; See, Faizan Mustafa, 'NEET Neither Student Friendly, Nor Merit Promoting' (*The Hindu*, 16 May 2020).

[103] *Christian Medical College Vellore Association. v. Union of India* (2020) 8 SCC 705.

preference to a student of another community even when the other student is more meritorious. No such right exists for non-minorities.[104] However, *inter se* merit of minority students cannot be ignored. In *Islamic Academy*, it was held that the institutions that have a special feature and that have been admitting only students of their own community but have a fair and transparent admission procedure for at least twenty-five years can seek an exemption from the common admission test.[105] The Mishra J led Bench did not agree to any such exemption.

Conclusion

Since the SCI itself had emphasized the special significance of Article 30 and termed it as 'an article of faith' in *Lily Kurian*[106], a 'sacred obligation' in *Kerala Education Bill*,[107] 'the conscience of nation' in *Xavier's College*[108]; 'an absolute right' in *Sidhrajbhai*,[109] the Court would hopefully continue to liberally interpret this all-important fundamental right. The determination of minority character of Aligarh Muslim University by the three-judge Bench, as per the law laid down by the seven-judge Bench, would be the litmus test of the direction that SCI would take in future on the issue of minority rights under Article 30.

---

104 *Islamic Academy of Education* (n 95) 727.

105 ibid 729.

106 *Lily Kurian (n 77).*

107 *In Re Kerala Education Bill* (n 5) 986.

108 *Ahmedabad St Xavier's College Society* (n 7) 744.

109 *Rev Sidhrajbhai Sabhai v. State of Gujarat* (n 72) 547.

Supreme but Pro-Caste: How the Jurisprudence of the Supreme Court of India Preserves and Protects India's Caste System

G MOHAN GOPAL

Some say that they should be satisfied with the abolition of untouchability only, leaving the caste system alone. The aim of abolition of untouchability alone without trying to abolish the inequalities inherent in the caste system is a rather low aim.

Dr BR Ambedkar

As a judge of the Kerala High Court (HC), VR Krishna Iyer J, in *Kunhu Mohammed v. JK Ummayithi*,[1] remarked that '[i]n the inevitable chemistry of social change Courts certainly are not anti-catalysts'.[2] In the quarter century since the year 2000, the Supreme Court of India (SCI) has, belying this expectation, doubled down on its 'anti-catalyst' role in the 'inevitable chemistry of social change' with respect to India's epochal struggle to annihilate caste.

Notwithstanding its rhetoric about a casteless society, in the seventy-five years of its existence, the SCI has protected and preserved the caste system. It has been an anti-catalyst in two ways: first, by suitably redefining three foundational legal concepts (caste, religion and Hindu); and second, by eviscerating reservation, which, as conceived by Dr Ambedkar, is the intended constitutional weapon of caste destruction.

1 1969 KLR 629.

2 ibid [1]; See Fali S Nariman and Rajeev Dhavan, 'The Supreme Court and Group Life' in BN Kirpal (ed), *Supreme But Not Infallible: Essays in Honour of the Supreme Court of India* (Oxford University Press 2004) 274. In the publication to commemorate the first fifty years of the SCI, titled *Supreme But Not Infallible*, Fali S Nariman and Rajiv Dhavan point out that '[I]n the controversial area of traditional group rights, affirmative action, personal laws, and gender justice, the [Supreme] Court has been high sounding whilst adroitly avoiding a too courageous pursuit of the ends of egalitarian justice . . .' They added that the Court needed to heed the aforementioned words of Krishna Iyer J.

Conscious that there is no generally accepted definition of caste, this essay offers a new definition from a legal point of view. The definition distinguishes between social groups (communities), organically formed by individuals coming together on one hand, and the *varna-jaati* category that is imposed top-down on social groups on the other.

Caste (the *varna–jaati* system) is defined here as a political system of governance that vests and divests civil, political, social and economic rights of individuals through a three-part process: (i) individual rights are de-recognized and extinguished and rights are limited to group rights derived exclusively from the social group to which the parents of a person belong and change of social group is prohibited; (ii) social groups in turn are categorized into five hierarchical categories; and (iii) categories one to four are vested with varying degrees of civil, political and economic rights and privileges, whereas category five communities are divested of all rights and privileges and are instead placed under numerous civil, political and economic liabilities and disabilities. They are stripped of their humanity and citizenship. The final authority to decide the categorization of individual social groups, the roles, rights, liabilities and disabilities of members of each category as well as the relationships between categories is controlled by category one. Inter-marriage between categories or change of the category into which one is born is prohibited. The total stripping of individual and group civil, political and economic rights of the population placed in category five enables their unhindered social, economic and political exploitation. The caste system is thus an oligarchy, rule by the few (categories one to four) of the vast majority of people (category five). As in the case of other systems of despotism, the caste system is justified by the claim that it is divine in origin.

As the caste system is a system for vesting, divesting and regulating rights of individuals and social groups, it is a political system of government rather than a religious system or a social system. In effect the *varna–jaati* system is a system of unequal citizenship. A system of government may be defined as a structure for establishment and operation of institutions to distribute power and govern people by defining and regulating rights, claims, privileges, disabilities and liabilities. These are the practical functions of the *varna–jaati* system. The *varna–jaati* system should therefore also be recognized for what it is in its essence: a form of government.

As an autocratic and oligarchic form of government, the *varna–jaati* system is in direct conflict with the democratic form of government established by the Constitution based on equal citizenship. The SCI presents itself as a 'neutral arbiter' in this titanic struggle between oligarchy and democracy, 'finding a *stable equilibrium* between justice to the backwards, equity for the forwards and efficiency for the entire system' (emphasis supplied).[3] Regrettably, however, behind this rhetoric, the SCI's 'stable equilibrium role' has not been neutral. The SCI has instead produced a social 'stasis' – a stable equilibrium of social stagnation in which no annihilation of caste can possibly occur and the oligarchic caste social order can continue to reign by default, with minor cosmetic changes to better fit it within the fashions of the day.

Constitutions constitute the bridge on which standards of axios[4] are brought over from society into the legal system – sometimes harmoniously, at other times in a contentious manner. This essay discusses not only precedents but also judicial doctrines as well as the axiology and the social context from which they are derived. It is written in the hope that in the coming quarter century, as our Republic stands at the cusp of a century of Independence, a diverse and inclusive SCI would have reversed course and deployed the Constitution to finally annihilate caste.

Constitutional 'Weapons of Caste Discrimination'

A small band of members from caste-oppressed communities as well as minority communities, led by the indomitable Dr BR Ambedkar, were faced with the task of creating a Constitution which would provide a springboard for democratizing India. They had the formidable challenge of working in a Constituent Assembly dominated by powerful, conservative members from

3 *M Nagaraj v. Union of India* (2006) 8 SCC 212 [44]; The relevant portion reads: 'Backward Classes seek Justice. General class in public employment seeks equity. The difficulty comes in when the third variable comes in, namely, efficiency in service. In the issue of reservation, we are being asked to find a stable equilibrium between justice to the backwards, equity for the forwards and efficiency for the entire system. Equity and justice in the above context are hard concepts. However, if you add efficiency to equity and justice, the problem arises in the context of the reservation.'

4 Axiology means means a branch of knowledge dealing with how society attributes value and worth to something. It stems from two Greek words – 'axios', derived from the Latin word 'axioma' and the Greek word 'axioma', meaning, literally 'that which is thought worthy or fit', and from 'axioun' meaning 'to think worthy'; and from '-ology', a 'word-forming element indicating "branch of knowledge, science,"' (https://www.etymonline.com/search?q=axios). *General Theory of Value* by Ralph Barton Perry (1926) says that a value is 'any object of any interest'. Perry identified eight 'realms' of value: morality, religion, art, science, economics, politics, law and custom. Ralph Barton Perry, *General Theory of Value* (Longmans, Green and Company 1926) 124.

caste-privileged backgrounds. They did not succeed in full measure. The result was a compromise that fell short of the expectations of the caste-oppressed including Dr Ambedkar who demanded the total 'annihilation' of caste (i.e., the *varna–jaati* system of vesting and divesting rights through categorization of communities into five categories of citizenship). Quite miraculously, however, they managed to include in the Constitution powerful provisions to help in the goal of annihilation of caste, which I would like to term as 'weapons of caste destruction', that are a vital sheet anchor for the democratization of the Indian social order and the advancement of social justice.

For instance, Article 17 abolishes, forbids and criminalizes the practice of untouchability, and Article 25 vests freedom of religion in the 'individual' and not in groups. This is a radical rejection of the *varna* system, which does not recognize the individual except as a member of a group and vests all claims, privileges, liabilities and disabilities exclusively in groups. Further, Article 25 makes the right to religion subject to other fundamental rights.

Chief among the provisions that prohibit caste discrimination is Article 15, which prohibits discrimination on grounds only *inter alia* of religion, *caste*, place of birth or residence with respect to access to and use of nine enumerated public areas and facilities (access to shops, public restaurants, hotels and places of public entertainment; use of wells, tanks, bathing ghats, roads and places of public resort maintained wholly or partly out of State funds or dedicated to the use of the general public). Article 16 prohibits discrimination, inter alia, on the basis of religion, *caste*, descent or place of birth or residence in respect of any employment or office under the State. Article 29 (2) prohibits discrimination with respect to 'admission into any educational institution maintained by the State or receiving aid out of State funds' on grounds only inter alia of religion or *caste*.

Article 335 mandates that 'the claims of the members of the Scheduled Castes (SCs) and the Scheduled Tribes (STs) *shall be taken into consideration*, consistently with the maintenance of efficiency of administration, in the making of appointments to services and posts in connection with the affairs of the Union or of a State' (emphasis supplied).[5] There are provisions under which seats in the Lok Sabha, state assemblies, panchayats and municipalities

---

[5] Later in this essay, I make the point that this has wrongly been read by courts to mean that such claims shall not be considered unless they maintain efficiency of administration.

are reserved for SCs and STs.[6] Article 46 provides that the State shall promote with special care the educational and economic interests of the weaker sections of the people, and, in particular, of the SCs and the STs and shall protect them from social injustice and all forms of exploitation.

The Varna–Jaati *Distinction*

Before Independence, and in the early days after Independence, courts did not make a rigorous distinction between '*varna*' and '*jaati*'. The terms 'caste', '*varna*', '*jaati*' and 'class' were used interchangeably. These words were treated as just different names for the same phenomenon.[7] For instance, in *Gopi Krishna Kasaudhan v. Musammat Jaggo*, the Privy Council observed:

> The Shastras dealing with the Hindu Law of marriage do not contain any injunction forbidding marriages between persons belonging to different divisions of the same *varna*; and neither any decided case nor any general principle can be invoked which would warrant such a prohibition ... There exists no doubt a disinclination to marry outside the sub-caste, inspired probably by a social prejudice; but it cannot be seriously maintained that there is any custom which has acquired the force of law.[8]

In 1965, the SCI, in *Amireddi Rajagopala Rao v. Amireddi Sitharamamma*,[9] while noting that '[t]he claim of a concubine who was a respectable woman of the Brahmin caste and her illegitimate sons for maintenance was allowed in *Hargovind Kuari v. Dharam Singh*'[10] in the same context, went on to also describe '*Swairini* as a woman who abandons her own husband and goes to another man of her own *varna* out of love for him.'

---

[6] The Constitution of India 1950, arts 243-D (panchayats), 243-T (municipalities), 330 (Lok Sabha), 332 (state assemblies).

[7] *Jaati* is used to refer in the vernacular to the social identity of pagans and *varna* to refer to the social identities of the caste-privileged.

[8] *Gopi Krishna Kasaudhan v. Musammat Jaggo* 1936 SCC OnLine PC 25, 303; In *Kashi Nath v. Bhagwan Das* 1947 SCC OnLine PC 31, the Privy Council was examining whether a duly solemnized marriage between Bawan Das and Lachmi Kuer was valid. It was conceded before the court that the marriage was valid 'if the Golwaras, the caste to which the third wife belonged, was a sub-caste of the Vaishya caste, of which the Agarwalas were a sub-caste.'

[9] *Amireddi Rajagopala Rao v. Amireddi Sitharamamma* 1965 SCC OnLine SC 265.

[10] *Hargovind Kuari v. Dharam Singh* (1884) ILR 6 All 329.

The Supreme Court's Approach to Caste

Continuing the view set out by SCI in a long line of judgments, a five-judge Constitution Bench in *State of Punjab v. Davinder Singh*[11] discussed the caste system in great detail. The Court said:

> 62. Everyone is born as Shudra i.e. to work and slowly each one of them elevates himself to a higher status of Vaishya, Kshatriya and Brahmin on the strength of his talent, quality, character and nature.
>
> 63. It means the duties of Brahmins, Kshatriyas, Vaishyas and Shudras were distributed according to their qualities (guns) and nature (and not by birth). All people have different nature and characteristics. Their personality is shaped according to their qualities (gunas). Thus, different professionals duties are suited to persons of different nature and character. Since the center of society is God (Parmatma), everyone (atma) works according to their intrinsic qualities to sustain themselves and the society.
>
> 64. According to the varna system no one is to be considered as lower or higher, rather it is preached that everyone is equal fragment and a part and parcel of Him, the Almighty. Gita nowhere preaches that the aforesaid varnas are on the basis of birth and are not interchangeable. However, with the passage of time, the varna system deteriorated and the people started labelling these varnas on the basis of birth, ignoring the nature and characteristics of a person which is exactly the opposite to what is preached in Gita. The varnas were given the nomenclature of castes in a very loose manner.
>
> 65. Later, children of Brahmins started calling themselves as Brahmins, irrespective of whether they possessed the corresponding qualities or not. Similarly, the children of other varnas also adopted the varna of their father ignoring their own nature, talent and qualities. When this system grew rigid and birth based, it became dysfunctional.
>
> 66. In short, what is intended to be conveyed is that according to Gita there is no caste system and the varna system (categorization) referred to therein is quite distinct, based upon persons nature and qualities. Thus, there was no caste system in ancient India i.e., Bharat. The misconstruction of the

---

[11] 2024 INSC 562.

varna system as a caste system was a social defect that crept in with time and was not considered to be good as it divided the society and brought about discrimination and inequality.

A four-point judicial doctrine emerges from these judgments, which is in sync with the axiological views of the caste-privileged in India:

(i) The *varna* system is a 'laudable'[12] system of categorization of people according to their profession, talent, qualities, nature, abilities and consciousness, intended to provide a balanced structure to society and bring out the best in every person. *Varna* is not caste. *Varna* is a sound and social order of ancient India. It is not caste.

(ii) *Jaati* is different from *Varna. Jaati* is caste. It is a common name for the infinite variety of ethnic, indigenous social identities of pagan communities which are divisive and anti-social identities. The use of *jaati* as a synonym for pagan social groups carries the implication that these communities are separate species from *homo sapiens*.

(iii) The caste (*jaati*) system emerged later in India as a result of the deterioration and petrification of the *varna* system. The caste (*jaati*) system created social problems such as untouchability, and other bad practices prevailing in the Indian society, divided it and brought about discrimination and inequality. To create social unity and cohesion amongst the people, the separate existence of these pagan social groups should be destroyed and they should be merged into the *varna* framework of four identities. Needless to say, such an intention is nothing short of cultural and ethnic cleansing and genocide.

(iv) In the constitutional regime, there is no caste system. It seeks to move the country into a casteless society. However, in the name of social welfare to uplift the depressed and the backward classes, we again fell into the trap of caste system.

The SCI's approach to caste closely mirrors the Vedic–Brahmanical axiology that preserves *varna* as a 'laudable' social order.

The SCI's approach to the theory of caste does not pay attention to the

[12] *KC Vasanth Kumar v. State of Karnataka* 1985 Supp SCC 714, 785.

axiology of the anti-caste movement, an exemplar of which was Narayana Guru of Kerala, according to whom *jaati* meant '*janma reeti*', that is, mode of birth, making it synonymous with 'species'. As *Homo sapiens* have only one method of birth, all humans belong to the same *jaati*. On this basis, Narayana Guru calls for the total rejection of all claims of *jaati* difference as they amount to an attempt of sub-speciation of human beings.[13] Article 38 (2) of the Constitution calls for equality between groups. Social groups should be free to form and transform as their members wish and function in accordance with the core values of liberty, equality, fraternity and dignity set out in the Preamble to the Constitution. This view is both complementary to Dr Ambedkar's call for representative democracy on the basis of due and adequate representation of all communities and in sync with the constitutional vision.

The Supreme Court on Religion

In *Commissioner, Hindu Religious Endowments, Madras v. Sri Lakshmindra Thirtha Swamiar of Sri Shirur Mutt (Shirur Mutt* case*)*, the SCI defined religion as 'a matter of faith with individuals or communities', which is not necessarily theistic.[14] Religion was defined as consisting not only faith and belief but what could also lay down a code of ethical rules for its followers to accept; it could prescribe rituals and observances, ceremonies and modes of worship regarded as integral parts of religion, and these forms and observances might extend even to matters of food and dress. The Court held that the expression 'practice of religion' in Article 25 'not only protects the freedom of religious opinion' but also guarantees 'acts done in pursuance of a religion and this is made clear by the use of the [aforementioned] expression'.[15] What constituted an 'essential part of a religion' for the purposes of Article 26 (b)

---

[13] Narayana Guru further explains that since *varna* is a statement of the status, rights and responsibilities of the four different *jaatis* created in the Rig Veda, and as there are no *jaati* differences, *varna* becomes null and void. What remains in this framework is '*samudaya*' (communities, social groups), which are organically self-formed groups that are constantly in a state of flux being created, altered, merged and dissolved in response to individual human agency, exercising their right to association under Article 19 (1) (c). They would include religious, cultural and civil-society groups. As *varna* and *jaati* are the sole sources of hierarchy and social division, once *varna* and *jaati* are gone, there is no framework for hierarchy or categorized division or sub-speciation between samudayas or people. See Dr T Bhaskaran (ed), *Sree Narayana Guru Vaikhiri* (Kummathunadu SNDP Union, 2000).

[14] *Shirur Mutt* case 1954 SCR 1005 [18] (Mukherjea J); The judgment of the court was delivered by BK Mukherjea J, a renowned expert on religious law who became the Chief Justice of India on 23 December 1954, some eight months after delivering this judgment.

[15] ibid [19].

had primarily to be ascertained with reference to the 'doctrines of that religion itself'.[16] Without providing adequate reasons, the SCI rejected an individual-centred definition of religion, saying that it could not be considered 'precise or adequate' and expressed 'great doubt' whether such definition could have been in the minds of the Constitution makers.[17] The individual-centred approach would have given pagan religions the right to recognition as religion and would not have allowed the emergence of a Hindu religion consolidated under a priesthood. Staying within the fundamental caste/*varna* principle that rights should be vested in groups, but never in individuals, the SCI's definition of religion limited protected religion to organized groups. Thus, the SCI's definition of religion in the *Shirur Mutt* case makes the Vedic–Brahmanical idea of religion India's national idea of religion.

As a result, individuals and groups that reject the idea of organized religion are unable to get legal recognition and constitutional protection as religion, and, worse, are unilaterally and wrongly declared and treated as part of Hinduism. For example, the Kerala HC has in at least three cases rejected the faith, beliefs and practices of followers of Narayana Guru as Hindus,[18] whereas, on 8 October 1925, Narayana Guru had said that 'there is no such religion as Hinduism'.[19]

The Supreme Court on Defining Hinduism

Article 25 (2) (b) of the Constitution of India defines the word 'Hindu' as including 'persons professing the Sikh, Jaina or Buddhist religion.' The word

[16] ibid [20]; The Court further held that 'no outside authority has any jurisdiction to interfere with their decision in such matters . . . A law which takes away the right of administration from the hands of a religious denomination altogether and vests it in any other authority would amount to a violation of the right guaranteed under clause (d) of Article 26.'

[17] ibid [18].

[18] In *Bhargavan v. Thankappan* 1989 (1) KLT 719, the Kerala HC rejected the claim that in the faith and belief of claimants, Narayana Guru is God. In *MK Santo v. State of Kerala* 2002 (2) KLT 481, the Kerala HC held that disciples of Narayana Guru did not constitute a religious denomination. The Kerala HC, in effect acting as an ecclesiastical court, held in *KK Purushothaman v. N Santhamma* 2016 (3) KLT 679 that Narayana Guru was a social reformer and 'is not an avatar of God', and that Narayana Guru's statute cannot be treated as a temple. In *Acharya Jagdishwaranand Avadhuta v. Commissioner of Police* (1983) 4 SCC 522, the SCI held that although 'Ananda Marga' is not a separate religion by itself, it subscribed to the ideas of Hinduism and is a religious denomination under the Hindu religion. In *Bramchari Sidheswar Shai v. State of WB* (1995) 4 SCC 646, Ramakrishna Mission was found not to be a separate religious denomination but part of the Hindu religion; in *SP Mittal v. Union of India* (1983) 1 SCC 51, it was held that the followers of Sri Aurobindo's teaching do not constitute a separate religious denomination.

[19] Dr T Bhaskaran (ed), *Sree Narayana Guru Vaikhiri* (Kummathunadu SNDP Union, 2000) 18.

is defined likewise in various statutes,[20] which creates a presumption that the enumerated persons would be Hindus unless proved to the contrary.[21]

A Constitution Bench of the SCI in *Sastri Yagnapurushdasji v. Muldas Bhudardas*[22] adopted a legal definition of 'Hinduism', which declares in effect that Hinduism is a Vedic religion. The issue before the Court was whether the Swaminarayan sect is a religion distinct and separate from the Hindu religion. In deciding this, the Court had to answer the question: who are the Hindus and what are the broad features of the Hindu religion? In answering the question, the SCI held, without any legal, theological or historical basis, that while 'a certain amount of divergence' is noticeable in the teaching of Hindu saints and religious reformers, 'underneath that divergence lie certain broad concepts which can be treated as basic' and 'the first among these basic concepts is the acceptance of the Vedas as the highest authority in religious and philosophic matters.'[23] This SCI definition of Hindu imposes faith in the Vedas on those whose spirituality has nothing to do with the Vedas but were involuntarily classified as Hindus starting in the first (1951) Census of newly independent India. By imposing faith in the Vedas on them, SCI has kept the caste (*varna–jaati*) system alive as the *varna–jaati* system is created by the *Purushasuktam* of the Rig Veda by postulating four distinct methods of birth (*jaatis*) for humans.

The SCI's 1996 judgment in *Dr Ramesh Yeshwant Prabhoo v. PK Kunte* (*Hindutva* case) took it to the next level saying that the word 'Hinduism' or 'Hindutva' are to be understood as 'depicting a way of life of the

---

[20] The Hindu Marriage Act 1955, the Hindu Adoption and Maintenance Act 1956, the Hindu Minority and Guardianship Act 1956, and the Hindu Succession Act 1956. The broad definition is 'any person who is a Hindu by religion in any of its forms or developments, including a Virashaiva, a Lingayat, or a follower of the Brahmo, Prarthana or Arya Samaj; any person who is a Buddhist, Jain or Sikh by religion, and any other person . . . who is not a Muslim, Christian, Parsi or Jew by religion.'

[21] In *Ganpat v. Returning Officer* AIR 1975 SC 420, the SCI observed: 'Hinduism is so tolerant and Hindu religious practices so varied and eclectic that one would find it difficult to say whether one is practising or professing Hindu religion or not.'

[22] 1966 SCC OnLine SC 198.

[23] In *Vidya Varuthi Thirtha v. Balusami Ayyar* AIR 1922 PC 123, the Privy Council, speaking through Ameer Ali J noted that in southern India, where 'the diffusion of Aryan Brahmanism was essential for bringing the Dravidian peoples under the religious rule of the Hindu system, colleges and monasteries under the names of the Mutt were founded under spiritual teachers of recognized sanctity.'

Indian people.'[24] In other words, it was synonymous with 'Indianisation',[25] obliterating the differences between all the cultures coexisting in the country. Between these various judgments, we see a merging of the idea of Vedism–Brahmanism with the idea of Hinduism, and the idea of Hinduism merging with the idea of India.

Eviscerating Reservation to Protect the Varna *Order*

As it is demographically difficult to attack reservation in the political space, the main battle against reservation has been successfully waged in courts. Reservations in pre-Independence era were part of the political machinations of monarchs and the British to secure the support of social groups and stay in power. However, the purpose of constitutional reservation was to secure representative democracy (*swaraj*) and equality of social groups so that the *Varna* oligarchy that rules India could be dismantled. It was this that led the Drafting Committee of the Constituent Assembly, led by Dr Ambedkar, to insert the word 'backward' into Article 16 (4) between the words 'in favour of any' and 'class of citizens'. This was meant to limit reservation to only those communities who had been marginalized and pushed into backwardness due to social discrimination under the caste system.[26]

Through its pronouncements over these seventy-five years, the SCI has effectively stalled reservation from achieving its original purpose – to secure equality between social groups through representative democracy and the dismantling of the oligarchy. In *MR Balaji v. State of Mysore*[27] the SCI considered it necessary to emphasize that 'Article 15 (4) like Article 16 (4)

[24] *Dr Ramesh Yeshwant Prabhoo v. PK Kunte* (1996) 1 SCC 130, 161. The *Hindutva* case raises serious questions about whether Hinduism is a religion at all for the purposes, for example, of Articles 25 and 26 of the Constitution when the SCI itself says: 'No precise meaning can be ascribed to the terms 'Hindu', 'Hindutva' and 'Hinduism'. The words 'Hinduism' or 'Hindutva' are not necessarily to be understood and construed narrowly, confined only to the strict Hindu religious practices unrelated to the culture and ethos of the people of India, depicting the way of life of the Indian people . . . Unless the context of a speech indicates a contrary meaning or use, in the abstract the terms 'Hinduism' or 'Hindutva' cannot be confined merely to describe persons practising the Hindu religion as a faith . . .'

[25] ibid 159.

[26] Perhaps the most important part of this intervention by Dr Ambedkar in the Constituent Assembly was his statement that the 'control of the administration' by one or a few communities should disappear. There can be no room for doubt that Dr Ambedkar was explicit that the purpose of reservation is to end oligarchy.

[27] 1963 Supp (1) SCR 439.

is an enabling provision; it does not impose an obligation, but merely leaves it to the discretion of the appropriate Government to take suitable action, if necessary.' It was reiterated in *CA Rajendran v. Union of India*[28] that Article 16 (4) confers 'a discretionary power on the State to make a reservation of appointments in favour of backward class of citizens which, in its opinion, is not adequately represented in the Services of the State'[29] This contradicts Dr Ambedkar's express reference in the Constituent Assembly to Article 16 (4) as a fundamental right while discussing the definition of the word 'backward' in this provision.[30]

On the eve of his retirement, VR Krishna Iyer J, in *Akhil Bharatiya Soshit Karamchari Sangh v. Union of India* questioned the rationale of reservations by observing:

> The success of State action under Art. 16 (4) consists in the speed with which result-oriented reservation withers away as, no longer a need, not in the ever widening and everlasting operation of an exception [Art. 16(4)] as if it were a super-fundamental right to continue backward all the time. To lend immortality to the reservation policy is to defeat its raison d'être; to politicise this provision for communal support and Party ends is to subvert the solemn undertaking of Art. 16 (1), to casteify 'reservation' even beyond the dismal groups of backward-most people, euphemistically described as SC & ST, is to run a grave constitutional risk. Caste, ipso facto, is not class in a secular State.[31]

In *Indra Sawhney v. Union of India*,[32] a nine-judge Constitution Bench of the SCI was examining the validity of a central government notification that

---

[28] AIR 1968 SC 507.

[29] ibid [6]; It was reiterated by the SCI in *Mukesh Kumar v. State of Uttarakhand* AIR 2020 SC 992 that, 'it is abundantly clear from the judgments of this Court in *Indra Sawhney v. Union of India,* 1992 Supp (3) SCC 217, *Ajit Singh (2) v. State of Punjab* (1999) 7 SCC 209; *M Nagaraj v. Union of India* (2006) 8 SCC 212; and *Jarnail Singh v. Lachhmi Narain Gupta* AIR 2018 SC 4729 that Articles 16 (4) and 16 (4-A) are enabling provisions.

[30] Dr Ambedkar said: 'That I think if I may say so, is the justification why the Drafting Committee undertook on its own shoulders the responsibility of introducing the word "backward" which, I admit, did not originally find a place in the fundamental right in the way in which it was passed by this Assembly.' Nor has the SCI adverted to the detailed argument that Articles 15 (4) and 16 (4) are indeed fundamental rights made by the eminent constitutional jurist Prof. Mahendra P Singh nearly three decades ago; See MP Singh, 'Are Articles 15 (4) and 16 (4) Fundamental Rights?' (1994) 3 SCC Jour 33.

[31] *Akhil Bharatiya Soshit Karamchari Sangh v. Union of India* (1981) 1 SCC 246 [22].

[32] *Indra Sawhney v. Union of India* 1992 Supp (3) SCC 217.

provided inter alia twenty-seven per cent reservation for 'Other Backward Classes' (OBCs) in employment. The majority,[33] in interpreting the word 'backward' in Article 16 (4), concluded as follows:

(a) A caste can be and quite often is a social class in India. If it is backward socially, it would be a backward class for the purposes of Article 16 (4). Among non-Hindus, there are several occupational groups, sects and denominations, which for historical reasons are socially backward. They too represent backward social collectives for the purposes of Article 16 (4).

(b) Neither the Constitution nor the law prescribe the procedure or method of identification of backward classes. Nor is it possible or advisable for the court to lay down any such procedure or method. One can start the process with the castes, wherever they are found, apply the criteria (evolved for determining backwardness) and find out whether it satisfies the criteria. If it does – what emerges is a 'backward class of citizens' within the meaning of and for the purposes of Article 16 (4).[34]

(c) It is not necessary for a class, in order to be designated as a backward class, to be similar to the SCs and STs.

(d) 'Creamy layer' can be, and must be, excluded.

(e) It is not correct to say that the backward class contemplated by Article 16 (4) is limited to the socially and educationally backward classes referred to in Article 15 (4) and Article 340. It is much wider. The accent in Article 16 (4) appears to be on social backwardness. Of course, social, educational and economic backwardness are closely inter-twined in the Indian context.[35]

---

[33] BP Jeevan Reddy J speaking for himself and, MH Kania CJ, Venkatachaliah, Ahmadi JJ with S Ratnavel Pandian and PB Sawant JJ, writing separate opinions concurring with the majority. The dissenting judges, Dr TK Thommen, Kuldip Singh and RM Sahai JJ wrote separate opinions.

[34] The SCI makes it clear here that while a caste is a class and may be a backward class if it fulfils required backwardness criteria, non-caste classes can also be backward classes if they meet the eligibility criteria. In *R Chitralekha v. State of Mysore* AIR 1964 SC 1823, the SCI followed *MR Balaji v. State of Mysore* AIR 1963 SC 649 to hold that '(i) the caste of a group of citizens may be a relevant circumstance in ascertaining their social backwardness; and (ii) though it is a relevant factor to determine the social backwardness of class of citizens, it cannot be the sole or dominant test in that behalf – caste is only a relevant circumstance in ascertaining the backwardness of a class.'

[35] *Indra Sawhney* (n 29) [796]–[797].

In other words, SCI disconnected reservation from caste reservation, opening it up to those who were not victims or survivors of the *varna–jaati* system. According to the Court, there is no mandatory relationship between caste and backward class. The Court took the view that 'distress' that Article 16 (4) reservation seeks to alleviate is *not* a distress that is unique to castes, that is, caste oppression and caste discrimination. The distress is 'backwardness', whatever may be its cause.

In *Ram Singh v. Union of India*,[36] while negativing the demand for reservation for Jats, a dominant caste in many states in northern India, the SCI expressed the view that an affirmative action policy could not be only on the basis of historical injustice and that it must also identify 'new emerging groups' so that they may recover 'lost ground' in claiming preference and benefits on the basis of historical prejudice. This regressive definition of Backward Class seeks a complete break with the constitutional history of reservation as a tool for representation to annihilate the monopoly of the caste oligarchy on state power.

The Bane of Creamy Layer

Over the last seventy-five years, the SCI has changed the character of reservation by viewing it as a tool for 'an entirely different purpose: upliftment' of classes (not necessarily castes) who are socially and educationally backward due to poverty. It began with the judgment in *State of Kerala v. NM Thomas*,[37] where the majority, speaking through Krishna Iyer J commented that the benefits of reservations were by and large 'snatched away by the top creamy layer of the "backward" caste or class, thus keeping the weakest among the weak always weak and leaving the fortunate layers to consume the whole cake.'[38]

---

[36] (2015) 4 SCC 697.

[37] (1976) 2 SCC 310.

[38] ibid [124]; Krishna Iyer J referred to a research conducted by the AN Sinha Institute of Social Studies, Patna, that revealed 'a dual society among harijans, a tiny elite gobbling up the benefits and the darker layers sleeping distances away from the special concessions' with the bonanza going to the 'higher' harijans. The second problem with reservations, according to the majority, was that the claim was overplayed extravagantly in democracy by large and vocal groups whose burden of backwardness had been substantially lightened with time, and measures of better education and more opportunities of employment, 'but wish to wear the "weaker section" label as a means to score over their near-equals formally categorised as the upper brackets'. Lastly, there had to be a constant process of objective re-evaluation of progress registered by the 'underdog' categories lest a once deserving 'reservation' should be degraded into 'reverse discrimination'.

This was, in a sense, echoing what the Court had said in 1962 in *MR Balaji*.[39] In *KC Vasanth Kumar v. State of Karnataka*,[40] the Court held that for identifying socially and educationally backward classes 'the only criterion which can be realistically devised is the one of economic backwardness . . .'[41]. It added that 'Class poverty, not individual poverty, is therefore the primary test.'[42] This was then built on in *Indira Sawhney* where Jeevan Reddy J queried: 'If some of the members are far too advanced socially (which in the context, necessarily means economically and, may also mean educationally) the connecting thread between them and the remaining class snaps. They would be misfits in the class. After excluding them alone, would the class be a compact class. In fact, such exclusion benefits the truly backward.'[43] This trend of analysis had the predictable impact of blocking the strongest sections and individuals of non-oligarchic communities from gaining access to key positions in the State from which they are excluded by social discrimination at the hands of the oligarchy.

What was begun by Krishna Iyer J has unfortunately now been applied wrongly to the SCI by a seven-judge Bench in *Davinder Singh*.[44] While CJI DY Chandrachud (speaking for himself and Manoj Misra J) talks of states having to determine backwardness of a group on the yardstick of 'inadequacy of effective representation', four other concurring judges[45] opined that, in order to achieve real equality, the state should exclude the creamy layer among the SCs and STs from the benefit of affirmative action.[46] The exclusion of the creamy layer from OBC and SC reservation serves only one purpose – it reduces their chances of securing positions and overcoming caste prejudice. It weakens the caste-marginalized community by reducing its representation.

More recently, in upholding the constitutionality of ten per cent reservation for economically weaker sections (EWS), in *Janhit Abhiyan v. Union of*

---

39 *MR Balaji* (n 27); The Court observed that the measure of financial assistance proposed by the state government may 'afford relief to and assist the advancement of the Backward Classes in the State, because backwardness, social and educational, is ultimately and primarily due to poverty.'

40 *KC Vasanth Kumar* (n 12) 734.

41 ibid [26].

42 ibid [80].

43 *Indra Sawhney* (n 29) 724.

44 *Davinder Singh* (n 11).

45 BR Gavai, Vikram Nath, Pankaj Mithal and Satish Chandra Sharma JJ.

46 The lone dissenting judge was Bela Trivedi J.

India,[47] the SCI has gone a further step and not only totally delinked reservation as a policy tool from the issue of representation but made it a tool to be used for reserving jobs and education seats for the caste-privileged. The majority, speaking through Dinesh Maheshwari J, observed:

> Reservation is an instrument . . . not only for inclusion of socially and educationally backward classes to the mainstream of society but, also for inclusion of any class or section so disadvantaged as to be answering the description of a weaker section. In this background, reservation structured singularly on economic criteria does not violate any essential feature of the Constitution of India.[48]

Reservation on the Basis of Population Share

Dr Ambedkar in constitutional fora, starting with the Round Table Conferences in London in 1930, demanded reservation that was proportionate to the population and adequate (i.e., adequate to be effective for small communities whose population share may be very small) representation. It is part of history now that the Indian National Congress led by Mahatma Gandhi strongly opposed this demand.

In the very first year of our Constitution, the Madras HC faced a challenge by Champakam Dorairajan to the 'Communal Government Order' of the Madras government, which proposed reservation in medical college seats for communities based, *inter alia*, on their numerical strength. While striking down the GO, the HC observed that this move was 'shipwrecked on the language of Article 15 (1) of the Constitution'.[49] This view was upheld by the SCI.[50] The truth is that social justice was shipwrecked on the rock of oligarchy in this case as by striking down the system of reservations SCI restored a Brahmin monopoly over admission to medical and engineering colleges in the then Madras Presidency. Ignoring this complex legacy, the SCI in *Indra*

---

[47] (2023) 5 SCC 1.

[48] ibid 177; Bela M Trivedi and JB Pardiwala JJ wrote separate concurring opinions, while Ravindra Bhat J, writing for himself and CJI UU Lalit , dissented; This judgment is contrary to the widely accepted 'difference principle' that 'differences or inequalities in the distribution of the primary goods of income and wealth and powers and positions of office and responsibility are to be arranged so that they are to the greatest benefit of the least advantaged.'; See Samuel Freeman, 'The Argument for the Difference Principle and the Four Stage Sequence' (*Stanford Encyclopedia of Philosophy*, 24 October 2023) <https://plato.stanford.edu/entries/original-position/difference-principle.html> accessed 12 March 2025.

[49] *Champakam Dorairajan v. State of Madras* (1950) 63 LW 895, 916.

[50] *State of Madras v. Champakam Dorairajan* AIR 1951 SC 226.

Sawhney held that the expression 'adequate representation' in Article 16 (4) of the Constitution cannot be read as 'proportionate representation'. The SCI's refusal to accept population share as a basis for providing reservation has effectively negated representative democracy and constitutes a crucial part of the defence of the *varna* oligarchy and the *varna* social order.

Reservation for the Caste-Oppressed Cannot Exceed Fifty Per Cent

In *MR Balaji*, the SCI introduced the idea of limiting reservation to fifty per cent. In dealing with the constitutional validity of sixty-eight per cent reservation in admission to engineering and medical colleges (fifty per cent for OBCs, fifteen per cent for SCs and three per cent for STs), the Court observed:

> If under the guise of making a special provision, a State reserves practically all the seats available in all the colleges, that clearly would be subverting the object of Article 15 . . . Speaking generally and in a broad way, a special provision should be less than 50%; how much less than 50% would depend upon the present prevailing circumstances in each case.[51]

The introduction was more in the form of a doctrine than in the form of a rule. It is again based on *ipse dixit* rather than any sound legal principle. However, as in the case of the Krishna Iyer J doctrine on creamy layer, the Gajendragadkar J doctrine on fifty per cent limit has had a powerful influence in confining the demand for due and adequate representation for all communities in proportion to their population coming from some eighty-five per cent of the population to fifty per cent of opportunity, leaving the remaining fifty per cent to just fifteen per cent of the population as a 'general category', which in practical terms is treated in many parts of the country as a category exclusively for the caste-privileged. This is the 'stable equilibrium' that *Nagaraj* was referring to. But it is not representative democracy.

Some twenty-nine years later, *Indra Sawhney* entrenched the fifty per cent limit for reservation (subject to limited exceptions) as law stating that 'reservation of a majority of seats was never envisaged by the founding fathers.'[52]

---

51 *MR Balaji* (n 27) [34].

52 *Indra Sawhney* (n 29) [808]; It was clarified that 'reservation under Article 16 (4) do not operate like a communal reservation. It may well happen that some members belonging to, say Scheduled Castes get selected in the open competition field on the basis of their own merit; they will not be counted against the quota reserved for Scheduled Castes; they will be treated as open competition candidates.'

The Bogey of Reservations Being a Threat to Efficiency

Article 335 of the Constitution requires the claims of SCs and STs for appointments to posts under the government to be taken into consideration 'consistently with the maintenance of efficiency of administration'. This has, and for reasons explained below, wrongly been construed by the SCI, in a catena of cases, beginning with *T Devadasan v. Union of India*[53] as a constraint on Articles 16 (4) and 15 (4) so that 'there is no reverse discrimination'.[54]

However, the history of Article 335 tells a different story. The debates in the Constituent Assembly over the Draft Article 296 (later Article 335) show that it was never intended as a constraint on Article 16 (4). It is a positive exhortation to maintain representation of minorities in public employment including by taking such steps as are needed to overcome any possible negative impact on efficiency (such as by providing training) so that impact on efficiency does not become a constraint for representation. It was never intended to establish a limitation on reservation.[55] This becomes clear when reservation is seen as a necessary remedy against oligarchy. Any reduction in reservation will only preserve the oligarchy which would be a constitutionally abhorrent impact.

The judgment of Jeevan Reddy J in *Indra Sawhney*, while agreeing that Article 335 cannot be read as a mandate for efficiency in administration,[56] stated as a demurer that in certain posts, given the nature of the duties, merit 'alone

---

53 (1964) 4 SCR 680 [25]; The Court opined that '[w]hile Article 335 is mandatory in character, Article 16 (4) is directory and permissive.' Further the state may not 'make such reservation for such Castes and Tribes, if it thinks that the implementation of Article 335 meets a given situation'.

54 In *Ajit Singh v. State of Punjab* AIR 1999 SC 3471 [18] it was held that Article 335 had been incorporated 'so that the efficiency of administration is not jeopardized.'

55 Article 16 (4) is about all communities securing a due share of public employment in proportion to their population share as a fundamental right, regardless of the overall size and strength of administration. It includes persons who are not minorities. On the other hand, Article 335 only refers to SCs/STs. Therefore, these two provisions deal with two distinct populations. Further Article 335 does not refer to the merit of the staff appointed to ensure representation. Article 16 (4) does not refer to efficiency.

56 *Indra Sawhney* (n 29) 751; To quote the relevant portion: 'Maybe, efficiency, competence and merit are not synonymous concepts; maybe, it is wrong to treat merit as synonymous with efficiency in administration and that merit is but a component of the efficiency of an administrator. Even so, the relevance and significance of merit at the stage of initial recruitment cannot be ignored. It cannot also be ignored that the very idea of reservation implies selection of a less meritorious person. At the same time, we recognise that this much cost has to be paid, if the constitutional promise of social justice is to be redeemed.'

counts', and in such event, 'it may not be advisable to provide for reservations.'[57] Again, this is an unjustified narrowing of the goal of representation of all communities so as to dismantle the oligarchy.

These judgments make it appear that the SCI is deploying Article 335 to constrain the recruitment of SCs/STs and backward classes in public employment without properly understanding the concepts of merit and efficiency as well as the overarching goal of dismantling the oligarchy. The consequence is the erosion of the transformative nature of reservation as 'a weapon of caste destruction', preserving the *varna* social order, thereby keeping India in social stasis.

Making Data Mandatory for Reservations but a Social Census to Collect Data Is Not Mandatory

Decennial censuses between 1881 and 1931 collected detailed information on the communities of British India and Indian princely states. The 1941 census, which was held in the middle of the Second World War, was limited in nature, and community-level census data was not published. The 1931 census was therefore the last census with community-wise data. Although there is no provision in the Constitution mandating it, the SCI in *Nagaraj* stipulated that a pre-condition for providing reservation was for the government to have data on backwardness, inadequate representation of communities and the impact of proposed reservation on administrative efficiency.[58] The result is that backward classes have been put in a quandary.

The government cannot be compelled to provide reservation because the SCI has held that there is no right to reservation; the concerned government

---

[57] ibid [838]; To quote: 'For example, technical posts in research and development organisations/ departments/ institutions, in specialties and super-specialties in medicine, engineering and other such courses in physical sciences and mathematics, in defence services and in the establishments connected therewith. Similarly, in the case of posts at the higher echelons, e.g., professors (in Education), pilots in Indian Airlines and Air India, scientists and technicians in nuclear and space application, provision for reservation would not be advisable.'

[58] *M Nagaraj* (n 3) 44; The Court said: 'The State is not bound to make reservation for SCs/STs in matters of promotions. However, if they wish to exercise their discretion and make such provision, the State has to collect quantifiable data showing backwardness of the class and inadequacy of representation of that class in public employment in addition to compliance with Article 335. It is made clear that even if the State has compelling reasons, as stated above, the State will have to see that its reservation provision does not lead to excessiveness so as to breach the ceiling limit of fifty per cent or obliterate the creamy layer or extend the reservation indefinitely.'

has the power to decide whether to provide reservation. On its part, the government has a ready excuse for not providing reservation. They need not do so till they have the required data that has been mandatory by the SCI. The net result is that reservation as a means for the transformation of the country to a representative democracy has been put on hold by the SCI.

SC and OBC Groups Can Be Further Sub-Categorized

Categorization of communities as castes is the instrument through which the caste system controls society. As the *varna* system fears the vesting of power in the SCs and OBCs on par with the privileged *varnas*, there is a vested interest in breaking solidarity and creating disunity within these groups so they can be weakened and their threats reduced. The *EV Chinnaiah*[59] judgment that rejected SC sub-categorization was right in taking the view that, within the existing constitutional framework, it is not possible to sub-categorize SCs. Unfortunately, this has been undone in *Davinder Singh*.[60]

Conclusions and the Way Forward

This essay has argued that, in terms of substantive law, the SCI has protected and preserved the caste system (framed as '*varna*') in two ways: first, by laying down a caste-friendly interpretation of the law in three crucial areas (definitions of caste, religion and the term Hindu); and second, by repressing reservations, a powerful weapon of caste destruction through judicially crafted restrictions that are blocking representation. The Court's claim is that this is being done to establish a 'stable equilibrium' by balancing between competing demands for 'justice to the backwards, equity for the forwards and efficiency for the entire system'.[61] In my view, the stable equilibrium has become a graveyard for social justice.

---

[59] Accepting the findings of the Ramachandra Raju Commission that there was *inter se* backwardness among the SCs in matters of reservation in education and appointment, the state government promulgated the Andhra Pradesh Scheduled Castes (Rationalisation of Reservations) Ordinance, 1999, which later was replaced by an Act. A five-judge Constitution Bench in *EV Chinnaiah v. State of AP* (2005) 1 SCC 394 struck down the law holding that a further classification of SCs/STs would result in tinkering with the Presidential List. It would also amount to reverse discrimination and violate of Article 14. Only the Parliament could amend the Presidential List under Article 341 of the Constitution to exclude or add SCs.

[60] *Davinder Singh* (n 11).

[61] *M Nagaraj* (n 3) [44] (Kapadia J).

If our apex court remains an unrepresentative body which functions as the *varna* oligarchy's sentinel on the *qui vive*, the constitutional design for representative democracy will not be realized.

The next generation '*swaraj*' is to have marginalized communities, long excluded from power, secure their share of power in the Indian state through representative democracy. Reducing the excess share of power of a small oligarchy to ensure that *all* communities have due and adequate representation is not reverse discrimination – it is *reversing* discrimination to secure equality and democracy.

Cartoon © Adhwaryu.

The Top Court and the Troubled Countryside

P SAINATH*

'All the judges of the Supreme Court do not have the power of our local havildar.'

'A single constable here can make or break us,' Chunni Lal Jatav, a survivor of the 1992 Kumher massacre in Rajasthan's Bharatpur district, told me.

'The judges of the Supreme court listen to learned lawyers of both sides and interpret the law. Our havildar makes his own laws. He can do almost anything,' he said, speaking to me in Kumher in 1999.

Chunni Lal was also very sceptical about the Kumher massacre case ever going as high as the Supreme Court of India (SCI). And he was not wrong. It took over a decade for the police to even file a chargesheet. He himself did not live to see a special SC/ST court in Bharatpur pass sentence on the accused – *31 years later*. In September 2023, the special court sentenced nine people to life imprisonment and acquitted forty-one others. In Kumher, they would tell you that those forty-one included some of the main culprits and brains behind the massacre.

As many as thirty-two of the eighty-three accused had died during this three-decade period. And on 20 March 2024, the Rajasthan HC at Jaipur suspended the sentence on those nine awarded life imprisonment.[1]

Chunni Lal's prophecy of the case not making it to the SCI has come true. Though, I guess it still can. As of now, the government of Rajasthan has not even appealed against the special court verdict. How likely is that to happen?

* The author would like to thank Anindita Mukherjee and Sriya Sridhar for their energetic assistance and invaluable inputs.

1 Ashish Mehta, 'HC Suspends Sentence of All 9 Convicts of Kumher Massacre' (*The Times of India*, 21 March 2024).

Well, the state of Rajasthan has filed appeals in less than one per cent of the cases of acquittal by the special courts between 2017 and 2021.[2]

Chunni Lal's point about the power of his local havildar has a ring of both sadness and truth to it. He was clear that when it came to poor rural people from marginalized communities, interest at the higher courts would always be limited. Chunni Lal was a villager, but had spent some time in Jaipur. He was aware of one more thing that most of us are not. That the High Court (HC) in Jaipur is the only one in the country that has a huge statue of 'Lord Manu' on its campus.[3] Sure, you can also see a statue of Ambedkar, but not on the premises. Babasaheb stands outside the Court's boundary walls, at a road corner where he seems to be directing traffic, not justice.

Even though the case of the Kumher '*kaand*' may never reach the SCI in the lifetime of its survivors, others have. Like that of the 1985 Karamchedu massacre in Andhra Pradesh's Bapatla district. Upper caste landlords murdered six Madigas, raped three women, and grievously injured many others. The atrocity displaced hundreds of that Dalit community of mainly agricultural workers from the village. The attackers also looted and burned their homes. A district court sentenced 159 perpetrators to life imprisonment. This was struck down by the AP HC on grounds of 'benefit of doubt.' And twenty-three years after the massacre, the SCI sentenced just one person to life imprisonment and thirty others to three years each.[4]

The Tsundur massacre of August 1991 also reached the SCI. At least eight persons from the Mala community (who are Dalits) were slaughtered by upper caste gangs in the fields of Tsundur village which is today in Bapatla district. Their bodies were hacked to pieces, stuffed into gunny bags and thrown into the Tungabhadra drain. As many as 212 people were charged in a total of twelve separate cases. All of them were acquitted by the Andhra Pradesh HC in 2014.[5] That is, twenty-three years after the massacre.

---

2 'Dalits Demand Filing of Appeal Against Kumher Massacre Acquittal Judgment' (*The Hindu*, 29 April 2024).

3 In 2023, the SCI dismissed a petition to have the statue removed, asking petitioners to approach the Rajasthan HC. The petition in relation to the statue is said to be the longest pending writ petition in the HC. The statue stands; Awstika Das, 'Supreme Court Dismisses PIL Petition Seeking Removal of Statue of Manu in Rajasthan High Court' (*LiveLaw*, 24 February 2023) <https://www.livelaw.in/top-stories/supreme-court-sc-dismisses-public-interest-litigation-pil-petition-removal-statue-manu-manusmriti-rajasthan-high-court-222441> accessed 24 February 2025.

4 *State of Andhra Pradesh v. Rayaneedi Sitharamaiah* (2008) 16 SCC 179.

5 *Chidipudi Srinivasa Reddy v. State of Andhra Pradesh* Criminal Appeal No 1021 of 2011, order dated 22 April 2014

The top Court stayed the acquittals in July 2014.[6] Meanwhile, thirty-three of the accused have died. The case is still pending in the apex Court. This, despite appeals by rights groups in 2022 for a speedy trial and conclusion to the case.[7]

Like in Kumher, and Karamchedu, the victims in Tsundur were Dalits. Poor rural people from marginalized communities. When you are from one of these groups, or from a religious minority like the Muslims, it is extremely difficult to access the highest echelons of justice. And sometimes when you do, it could be worse than 'justice delayed is justice denied.' It might be justice devastated. For the victims, the process is the punishment. Or further punishment. But the same process can also serve as a silent pardon for the perpetrators.

And there have been other massacres where, like in Kumher, the case never made it to the top Court. The 1987 massacre of seventy-two poor Muslims in Maliana in Uttar Pradesh, for instance. In March 2023, the district court in Meerut set free all thirty-eight accused on the grounds that there was no evidence against them. The appeal against the decision is pending before the Allahabad High Court.[8] But given that it is thirty-six years since the massacre, it is hard to predict its success.

The Nellie massacre of 1983 in Assam saw some 2,000 Bengali Muslims slaughtered by caste Assamese Hindus and other communities. Four decades later not a single culprit has faced justice.[9] It made no splash in the apex Court. As a piece in *Scroll.in* put it 'in the years that followed, 688 first information reports were filed for the Nellie massacre, resulting in just 299 chargesheets and no prosecution – the state administration had not thought it necessary to press for justice.'[10] Kilvenmani, Neerukonda, Laxmanpur Bathe – the list is long and dishonourable. In many such cases, the courts have lamented lapses in investigation. But it is hard to find any instance where someone has been held accountable for them.

---

6 *State of Andhra Pradesh v. Modugula Mallikarjuna Reddy* SLP (Crl) Nos 5353–5361 of 2014, order dated 30 July 2014).

7 Sumit Bhattacharjee, 'Rights Group Seeks Speedy Trial of Tsundur Massacre Case' (*The Hindu*, 5 August 2022).

8 'Maliana Massacre of '87: UP Challenges Court's Decision' (*The Times of India*, 22 August 2023).

9 Arshad Ahmed, '"They Slaughtered Us": 41 Years On, Nellie Massacre Survivors Now Say Justice Is Not for Them' (*Maktoob Media*, 18 February 2024) <https://maktoobmedia.com/features/they-slaughtered-us-41-years-on-nellie-massacre-survivors-now-say-justice-is-not-for-them/> accessed 24 February 2025.

10 Ipsita Chakravarty, 'Why Was Assam's Nellie Massacre of 1983 Not Prevented, Despite Intimations of Violence?' (*Scroll.in*, 18 February 2017) <https://scroll.in/article/829682/why-was-assams-nellie-massacre-of-1983-not-prevented-despite-intimations-of-violence> accessed 24 February 2025.

It is a struggle just to get to the SCI. That it is too often a losing battle, surely has much to do with the victims being poor rural people. And even more to do with their social backgrounds – their caste or religious minority status.

Look at India's giant army of undertrials. What are their backgrounds? In the media, barring a brilliant series in *The Wire*, there have mostly only been a few one-off stories. And those often lack the depth and punch required to place the issue on the national agenda.

Here's what we learned in 2022 from a minister's reply in the Parliament. Out of 5,54,034 prisoners in our jails, 4,27,165 of them, or seventy-seven per cent, were undertrial prisoners.[11] And that the Prison Statistics Report India, 2022, recorded that Dalits, Adivasis and other marginalized castes from Other Backward Class groups accounted for sixty-six per cent of all the undertrials.[12] In Uttar Pradesh, that figure is over seventy-five per cent. The undertrials tend to be mainly rural people with little access to legal aid.[13]

But their problems do not end there. *The Wire* – whose correspondent Sukanya Shantha has made a major impact on the issue with her investigative work on state-sanctioned caste-based discrimination and segregation in Indian prisons – shows how much deeper the mess goes. 'In several states, prison manuals still dictate that labour within the prison should be assigned on the basis of caste.'[14]

These regressive practices have been around in Indian prisons for over a century. It was only in July 2024, though, that the top Court acted. A division Bench of the SCI headed by CJI DY Chandrachud indicated it would direct the Ministry of Home Affairs (MHA) to appoint a nodal officer to do away with caste-based discriminatory practices in India's prisons.[15]

---

11 Rohini Roy, 'Undertrial Prisoners in India: Why Are 66% from Marginalised Castes?' (*The Quint*, 24 December 2022) <https://www.thequint.com/news/law/indias-undertrial-prisoners-why-are-are-66-percent-from-marginalised-castes> accessed 24 February 2025.

12 Shreehari Paliath, 'Despite Campaign, India Saw Number of Prisoners Increase in 2022' (*Scroll.in*, 15 December 2023) <https://scroll.in/article/1060246/despite-campaign-india-saw-number-of-prisoners-increase-in-2022> accessed 24 February 2025.

13 'Over 75% of Undertrials in UP from SC, ST, OBC Groups, Centre Tells Parliament' (*The Wire*, 15 March 2023) <https://thewire.in/rights/uttar-pradesh-75-percent-undertrials-sc-st-obc> accessed 24 February 2025.

14 Sukanya Shantha, 'From Segregation to Labour, Manu's Caste Law Governs the Indian Prison System' (*The Wire*, 10 December 2020) <https://thewire.in/caste/india-prisons-caste-labour-segregation> accessed 24 February 2025.

15 '"Most Disturbing", Supreme Court Says of Caste-Discrimination Sanctioned by Prison Manuals' (*The Wire*, 10 July 2024) <https://thewire.in/caste/most-disturbing-supreme-court-caste-discrimination-prison-manuals-pil> accessed 24 February 2025; On 3 October 2024, the SCI delivered the judgment

If you are rural and poor, from an oppressed social group and seeking justice – and that could only happen if and when those at the very top can be accessed. And if and when they act to make justice possible.

I could not then and cannot now help being provoked by Chunni Lal's wisdom. I really wonder:

Does the SCI have a vision, or even just a simple, clear perspective of rural India? Do hundreds of millions of poor rural Indians have the same access to it that urban people do? If they do not, should the court be bothered about that? Or is that someone else's problem?

Does the SCI have a sense of the realities of rural life? The occasional judgment – like some on the importance of the Directive Principles of State Policy (DPSPs) – seems to suggest they do try to engage with those realities. Yet, several judgments suggest otherwise. Like, for instance, those judgments on Aadhaar, panchayat election eligibility, farmers protests and more.

If the SCI did take a good look at rural India, it would understand that perhaps the single most important feature of power in the countryside was and is: impunity. Impunity in the functioning of every branch of government and administration. Impunity which drives the actions of the dominant castes and classes of a region. Experience has taught them that they can get away with any outrage. Well, almost always.

A brutal example of that came on 3 October 2021, when the jeep of Ashish Mishra ran over farmers in a protest march in Banbirpur village of Uttar Pradesh's Lakhmipur Kheri district. Four farmers and a journalist died, ten were injured and three people from the jeep convoy were beaten to death by enraged protestors. Ashish Mishra claimed he was not in his car at the time. He is the son of Ajay Mishra 'Teni' – then Union Minister of State for Home Affairs.

---

in *Sukanya Shantha v. Union of India* 2024 INSC 753 where the SCI held that all the provisions in jail manuals that allow caste-based discrimination in prison are unconstitutional. The Court also directed all the states and UTs to revise their jail manuals/rules in accordance with this judgment within three months. The Court has kept the case pending for monitoring.

A Special Investigation Team (SIT) probing the atrocity called the killing of the four farmers and the journalist 'a planned conspiracy'. The district court at Lakhimpur Kheri denied him bail. At that point it looked like justice was on its way.

Everyone, though, was acting under the pressure of a massive farmers' movement. One that had taken shape as the largest peaceful protest in the world. That too, one they organized at the height of the COVID-19 pandemic. Tens of thousands of farmers were still camped at Delhi's borders. Their stir would last fifty-three weeks and conclude on 26 November 2021. That is, after the Union Government repealed the three farm laws they were fighting against.

By February 2022, Mishra was out on bail. Thanks to an order that, strangely, the State of Uttar Pradesh did not appeal against.[16] After some to-ing and fro-ing between the Allahabad High Court and the SCI, he is now out on bail at the behest of the SCI, with his bail conditions having been steadily relaxed.[17] Meanwhile, the trial drags on.

In the villages of Lakhimpur Kheri, many now fear Ashish Mishra is invincible. They believe his father can get him out of the worst of situations.

In the case of Karan Bhushan Singh, it was his father Brij Bhushan who faced serious charges. Brij Bhushan was accused of sexual harassment by some of the country's leading sportswomen. To get around the growing storm, the ruling party gave a poll ticket to his son rather than to Brij Bhushan himself. Karan Bhushan, the merest novice, sailed through in UP's Kaiserganj constituency in June 2024. (His father had won the same Kaiserganj seat six times). Karan Bhushan won by a margin of over 1.5 lakh votes in an election where other ruling party stalwarts were laid low in the same state.

So perhaps the people of Kaiserganj might be forgiven for believing what Chunni Lal Jatav did in Kumher. That the local havildar or strongman, has powers greater than those of any court.

While matters drag on in the courts, the voters of Lakhimpur Kheri did

---

[16] Krishnadas Rajagopal, 'Supreme Court Asks Why UP Didn't Appeal against Ashish Mishra's Bail' (*The Hindu*, 30 March 2022).

[17] *Ashish Mishra alias Monu v. State of UP* SLP (Crl) No 7857 of 2022. Vide order dated 25 January 2023, bail was granted with certain conditions being imposed that were thereafter relaxed in orders dated 26 September 2023 and 22 July 2024.

manage to hand out some degree of punishment to those they believed guilty. Ajay Mishra 'Teni' was defeated in the Lok Sabha elections of 2024. He had sailed through in the same constituency in 2014 with a victory margin of 1.1 lakh votes. And nearly doubled that margin in 2019 to 2.18 lakh votes. A cousin of the journalist who died in that attack told the media that the 'public has done justice to the departed souls.' But, he points out, it still remains 'half justice.'[18] By which he implied that the people have done their half. Only the Courts are yet to move on the remaining half.

The SCI's approach to the three farm laws – first surfacing as Ordinances in June 2020 at the height of the COVID-19 pandemic – was strange. It failed to gain the confidence of the tens of thousands of protestors at Delhi's gates. Firstly, the three laws appeared to have been drafted in corporate boardrooms. Secondly, they were rammed through the Parliament in a bizarre manner. They did not go to the Standing Committee on Agriculture, nor to any select committee as demanded by scores of Member of Parliament (MPs). They were just bulldozed through.

There was no need, no urgency for such an action. There was also plain fraud. It was clear to the government that they did not have the votes in the upper house. So, eight members of the Rajya Sabha were suspended for a week by Deputy Chairman Harivansh Singh and ejected for their 'disruptive' behaviour. However, video footage showed one or two of them very much in their seats, raising points well within the rules of the house.

KK Ragesh, one of those MPs accused of being 'in the well of the house…and not in his seat in the gallery at that point of time,' was simply not there. And this is clearly visible on Rajya Sabha TV footage. He was in his seat raising the demand for a division of vote on the numerous amendments brought to the Bill by opposition members. He was nonetheless ejected.

Ragesh summed up the unfairness of the bills to rural people, especially to farmers, this way:

> [They are the] Farmers' Produce Trade and Commerce (Promotion and Facilitation) Bill, 2020, Farmers (Empowerment & Protection) Agreement

---

[18] Shikha Salaria, 'Ajay Mishra Teni Defeated by SP Candidate, Lakhimpur Kheri Victims' Kin Say 'Public Delivered Justice' (*The Print*, 5 June 2024) <https://theprint.in/politics/ajay-mishra-teni-defeated-by-sp-candidate-lakhimpur-kheri-victims-kin-say-public-delivered-justice/2118200/> accessed 24 February 2025.

> of Price Assurance and Farm Services Bill, 2020 and the Essential Commodities (Amendment) Bill — in Parliament. All three Bills were inter-connected.
>
> The first two give corporates opportunity to trade in agricultural commodities while entering into agreements with farmers without any government intervention. The third provides corporates the opportunity to stock as much as they wish agricultural commodities that come to them through procurement and contracts. The government has created opportunities for corporates to procure commodities at cheap prices, hoard the stock and create artificial shortages, and possibly sell them later at exorbitant prices. The three laws will facilitate looting of farmers and consumers; the Centre has legitimized hoarding and black market with them.[19]

Immediately after the ejection of the eight members, it was announced that the laws had been passed by 'voice vote.' Now, Rule 252 of the Rajya Sabha is clear that if a voice vote is challenged, even by a single member, then the Speaker would have to move to a division of vote. Besides, the very first words of Rule 252 are: 'On the conclusion of a debate, the Chairman shall put the question…'

In this case the 'debate' was simply muffled. And eight of those calling for a division of vote were ejected from the proceedings.

The SCI, rightly concerned by the mass of humanity surging at the Capital's doorsteps and their welfare, decided to set up its own committee of experts to study the laws. This team would also negotiate with government and farmers and make recommendations. The Court therefore stayed the implementation of the three laws till January 2021. And directed the Committee to submit their recommendations within two months of its first sitting.

This path angered the farmers. They denounced the four committee members as stooges of the government and of the corporations that stood to benefit from the laws.

---

19 KK Ragesh, 'Rules, Precedent Were Ignored to Push Through Anti-farmer Bills in Rajya Sabha' (*The Indian Express*, 2 October 2020).

So strong was the farmer reaction that Bhupinder Singh Mann one of the members (from Punjab) quit the team a day after it was set up in January 2021.[20] With that, the Committee was truncated by twenty-five per cent before its first meeting was held. Farmer unions pointed out that all the four members were people who had publicly expressed very strong support to the laws. And had done so in interviews, in newspaper articles they wrote, and on television programmes.

The spate of petitions, PILs, before the court challenging the three laws, had not sought the setting up of any committees. They wanted the highest court of the land to rule on the constitutionality of the laws – something it never did. There were very serious issues of law involved.

For one, both laws barred the jurisdiction of civil courts and created purely executive mechanisms for dispute resolution. They empowered, in the first instance, the Sub-Divisional Magistrate and granted appellate powers to the District Collector, instead of creating independent authorities with judicial members, fixed terms and procedures.

Surely, this suspends the farmers' right to judicial remedy?

Who but the SCI is competent to rule on that? Instead, the apex Court chose to set up its 'expert' committee. As one who covered the farm protests and was delighted when the Court stayed the laws, I was baffled. Why was the Court so comfortable in dealing with a bunch of pro-corporate armchair experts, while being so reluctant to connect with the thousands of farmers, poor, ordinary Indians from villages in deep rural India. Why could it not see their questions on the laws as legitimate and demanding a ruling on constitutionality?

If the Court really wanted the opinion of experts, why did it not look at the Report of the National Commission of Farmers (NCF), popularly known as the 'Swaminathan Commission?' That Commission was chaired by the nation's most distinguished agricultural scientist ever. Indeed, the farmers were demanding the implementation of the main recommendations of what was in fact a government-appointed commission.

The NCF's recommendations were seen as pro-farmer and as not favourable to private corporations, particularly those headed by India's two richest men. They were the result of years of work – with the widest possible consultation

[20] 'BKU Leader Mann Recuses Himself from SC Committee on Farm Laws' (*The Hindu*, 14 January 2021).

of all affected sections. Including the unions representing millions of farmers in this nation. If there are two English words that almost every single Indian farmer knows, those would be 'Swaminathan Commission Report.' The Court could at least enquire why the Government of India would not have a single day's dedicated discussion on the Swaminathan report in the Parliament.

Yet here was the SCI asking a quartet of quacks to produce in two months a report that was going to surpass in substance what the eight-member Commission had toiled for years to produce: five reports (in six volumes between December 2004 to October 2006). A Commission that had produced the only document in independent India approaching anything like a blueprint for Indian agriculture.

There is something Kafkaesque about it. The Government confronting the farmers came to power first in 2014 promising to implement the NCF report's main recommendations. Especially those on the Minimum Support Price. In power, it dismissed the report as unfeasible and warned it would distort market prices. It battled the peasants for fifty-three weeks – in which time 726 of the farmers died in the protestor camps. And then in February 2024, some four months after his death – conferred the Bharat Ratna on Prof MS Swaminathan. In short, it valorized the man, having villainized his work.

Meanwhile, the farmers struggle had forced the Government to repeal the laws in November 2021. A victory as embarrassing to the Court as to the Government. The apex Court shelved its own 'expert' report and stayed silent. One of the aggrieved 'experts,' though, released it in March 2022. Every word in it confirmed farmer union predictions about its being a tool of governments and corporates. It was, as one farmer at Singhu told me – 'a sarkar-corporate *chalisa*.'

The peasantry still lives in great insecurity – seeing the corporate interests driving those laws now being introduced through the backdoor. On February 12, 2024, we set a dubious record. India became perhaps the first nation to use drone warfare against its own farmers (or any civilians for that matter). The drones were not just about surveillance. They were also equipped with tear gas canisters which they dropped on protesting farmers.[21] Again, it was the peasantry across the country who responded, not the courts. There is every

---

21 Vijaita Singh, 'Haryana Police Is First Force to Use Drones for Tear Gas' (*The Hindu,* 13 February 2024).

reason to believe that farmers played a decisive role in some seventy seats lost by the ruling party in the 2024 Lok Sabha elections.

Arnab Goswami is a celebrity television anchor, founder and managing director, and editor-in chief of Republic TV. And probably the highest paid mediaperson in India. Based out of NOIDA, he is a powerful figure in New Delhi. Goswami was arrested in November 2020 in a 2018 case of abetment to suicide of Anvay Naik, an interior designer. Naik's suicide note had alleged non-payment of dues by three persons, including the TV personality.

Journalist Siddique Kappan is from Kannamangalam, a village of fewer than 8,000 people in Kerala's Malappuram district. Kappan was arrested in October 2020 while on his way to Hathras (Uttar Pradesh) to report on the gangrape and death from her injuries of a nineteen-year-old Dalit girl.[22] An atrocity that swiftly gained national notoriety. At the time of his arrest, he was working with a Malayalam news portal, *azhimukham.com*, and was the Secretary of the Kerala Union of Working Journalists, Delhi unit.

Arrested on 5 October 2020, it was forty-five days before he got to talk to his lawyer for five minutes. And that, as one report pointed out, 'with a petition in the Supreme Court, an application before the magistrate in Mathura, and another application in the apex court – before he finally got to even speak to the lawyer, let alone officially sign him as his legal representative.'[23]

Arnab Goswami was arrested on 4 November 2020. His case shot up to SCI within hours of being denied bail by the Bombay HC on 9 November of the same year. On 11 November the SCI granted him bail.[24]

Kappan was arrested, along with three others, under Section 151 of the CrPC, which allows an arrest to prevent commission of a cognizable offence.[25] The

---

[22] Nellore Sravani, 'My Life Continues to Be an Open Jail: Kerala Journalist Siddique Kappan' (*The Hindu*, 29 January 2024).

[23] Apoorva Mandhani, 'After 43 Days in UP Jail, Kerala Journalist Finally Gets to Talk to Lawyer for 5 Mins on Phone' (*The Print*, 18 November 2020) <https://theprint.in/india/after-49-days-in-up-jail-kerala-journalist-finally-gets-to-talk-to-lawyer-for-5-mins-on-phone/546781/> accessed 21 February 2025.

[24] *Arnab Manoranjan Goswami v. The State of Maharashtra* (2021) 1 SCC 802.

[25] Mandhani, 'After 43 Days in UP Jail, Kerala Journalist Finally Gets to Talk to Lawyer for 5 Mins on Phone' (n 23).

Kerala Union of Working Journalists filed a petition of habeas corpus in the SCI on 6 October 2020.

The authorities in Uttar Pradesh struck back almost immediately. The very next day, on 7 October, an FIR was registered in Mathura, charging Kappan with Section 124A of the Indian Penal Code (sedition). Also, with 153A (promoting enmity between different groups on grounds of religion, etc). And with 295A (deliberate and malicious acts, intended to outrage religious feelings of any class by insulting its religion or religious beliefs) of the Indian Penal Code (IPC). All these, along with provisions of the Unlawful Activities (Prevention) Act (UAPA) and the Information Technology Act.[26]

Six months later, he was also charged under the Prevention of Money Laundering Act, 2002 (PMLA) as well, by the Enforcement Directorate. And all he was doing was his job as a journalist.

Kappan faced three years of hell following his arrest. He contracted the coronavirus while in prison in 2021. Though his condition was terrible and though people were dying in thousands in Uttar Pradesh during that phase of the COVID-19 pandemic, the authorities resisted taking him to the hospital. Finally, following a major outcry, Siddique Kappan was taken to the KM Medical College hospital in Mathura. There, he told me, though in no condition to run off anywhere, he was chained to a hospital bed. And provided with a bottle and told he should urinate into that rather than make repeated trips to the bathroom. A SCI order had to be obtained to have him transferred to AIIMS, Delhi. He barely survived the ordeal.

In February 2021, Kappan was given five-days interim bail to visit his ailing mother.[27] The process and travel meant he could only spend two and a half days with her. It was the last time he saw her. She died when he was back in prison and could not attend her funeral.

On 9 September 2022, Kappan was granted bail in the UAPA case by the SCI.[28] Which also ordered him not to leave Delhi without the trial court's permission. And to record attendance at a police station every Monday.

---

26 ibid.

27 Debayan Roy, 'Supreme Court Allows Journalist Siddique Kappan to Visit His Ailing Mother in Kerala for Five Days' (*BarandBench*, 15 February 2021) <https://www.barandbench.com/news/litigation/supreme-court-allows-siddique-kappan-to-visit-ailing-mother-for-five-days> accessed 21 February 2025.

28 *Sidhique Kappan v. State of Uttar Pradesh*, SLP (Crl.) No. 7844 of 2022, order dated 9 September 2022.

On 23 December the same year, the Allahabad HC granted him bail in the money laundering case.[29] But he was finally released on bail only on in February 2023.[30] That is, fully four months after the apex Court order and forty days after that of the Allahabad HC. It took him six weeks before he could return to his home in Kerala. There too, he had to report to a local police station every Monday. Kappan is back in Delhi, but still makes trips to Lucknow every now and then to attend court hearings.

No conditions were attached to the bail swiftly granted to Arnab Goswami. He has never been detained or jailed since. He was not required, unlike Kappan, to surrender his passport.

It's not as if the top Court's attention was never drawn to its differing approach in the two cases. As *LiveLaw* reported, as early as December 2020, Senior Advocate Kapil Sibal told the SCI that he would draw on its order in the Arnab Goswami case to seek Kapan Siddique's release. 'In Arnab Goswami's case, your lordships have interfered when the bail application was pending. I will rely on that,' he told the apex Court.[31]

CJI DY Chandrachud had said while granting bail to Goswami: 'If we don't interfere in this case today, we will walk on a path of destruction.'[32]

But it would still be another two years before Siddique Kappan walked out of incarceration on bail.

As Kappan told *The Hindu* in January 2024, his absence left his five-member family in a precarious financial situation. He was their sole breadwinner. With his wife busy making visits to the courts, the education of his three children took a hit.[33] Paying their tuition fee posed serious problems. Meanwhile, he was unable to retain or return to his job after his release on bail. Which means he is now having to earn a living as a freelancer.

---

29 *Sidhique Kappan v. Directorate of Enforcement*, Criminal Misc. Bail Application No. 13642 of 2022, order 23 December 2022.

30 Ratna Singh, 'Siddique Kappan Released on Bail after More than Two Years in Jail' (*BarandBench*, 2 February 2023 <https://www.barandbench.com/news/siddique-kappan-released-bail-after-two-years-jail> accessed 22 February 2025.

31 '"In Arnab Goswami's Case, Your Lordships Interfered When Bail Was Pending: I'll Rely On That": Sibal During Siddique Kappan Case' (*LiveLaw*, 2 December 2020) <https://www.livelaw.in/top-stories/siddique-kappan-arnab-goswami-kapil-sibal-supreme-court-166697> accessed 22 February 2025.

32 Debayan Roy, '"If We Don't Interfere in This Case Today, We Will Walk on a Path of Destruction"', Supreme Court Grants Bail to Arnab Goswami' (*BarandBench*, 11 November 2020) <https://www.barandbench.com/news/supreme-court-grants-bail-to-arnab-goswami> accessed 22 February 2025.

33 Nellore Sravani, 'My Life Continues to Be an Open Jail: Kerala Journalist Siddique Kappan' (n 22).

Post filing of the FIR on 6 May 2019 – representatives of Goswami visit the police station on his behalf. Till date, Goswami has not been compelled to visit himself.[34] Investigation was stalled for one year from the date of the FIR being filed. The Naik family does not appear to have succeeded in getting Goswami to pay them. Though, apparently, correspondence from Goswami's company suggests they were willing to pay the Naiks Rs 39.01 lakhs.[35]

Kappan was for a while quite bewildered by what was happening to him. But then, he told a conference in Hyderabad in January 2024, 'I understood. I happen to be a Muslim, a Keralite and a journalist. A perfect combination required for a person to be labelled a terrorist in this country.'[36]

That poignant and tragic statement ought to disturb the rest of us. Those of us who believe that all are equal in the eyes of the law. Kappan certainly was not. Certainly not anywhere near being equal with Arnab Goswami. The top Court seemed content to walk that 'path of destruction' in his case.

The then President of the Supreme Court Bar Association, Dushyant Dave, wrote a letter to the top court saying he wished to lodge 'a strong protest' against what appeared to be preferential treatment. Dave also said, 'the likes of Goswami get special treatment while ordinary Indians are made to suffer, including imprisonment, which are many times illegal and unauthorized.'[37]

Rural and non-metro journalists bear the brunt of their industry's rapaciousness. On 24 March 2020, as Prime Minister Modi gave 1.4 billion people four hours' notice to a national lockdown, there was one silver lining to the chaotic gloom. The media were declared an essential service.

Declaring them as such allowed journalists to do their jobs. It also meant that the jobs they held were in some measure protected. They could not be arbitrarily taken away from them.

But as we know, thousands of journalists – many of them rural and small town – were brutally retrenched by managements of multiple corporate-controlled

---

[34] 'Arnab Goswami Exempted from Personal Appearance in Anvay Naik Suicide Case In Alibaug Court' (*LiveLaw*, 10 April 2021) <https://www.livelaw.in/news-updates/arnab-goswami-anvay-naik-suicide-bombay-high-court-personal-appearance-172415> accessed 21 February 2025.

[35] *Arnab Manoranjan Goswami v. The State of Maharashtra* (2021) 2 SCC 427 [11].

[36] Nellore Sravani, 'My Life Continues to Be an Open Jail: Kerala Journalist Siddique Kappan' (n 22).

[37] 'Arnab Goswami Case: Dushyant Dave Writes To SC on "Selective Listing of Matters"' (*The Wire*, 10 November 2020) <https://thewire.in/law/arnab-goswami-supreme-court-petition-selective-listing> accessed 20 February 2025.

media houses. The Delhi Union of Journalists and the National Alliance of Journalists believe – and drew the attention of the courts to this – over 3,000 journalists and three to five times that number of non-journalist media workers were sacked between the start of the lockdown and May 2022.[38] They were on the streets at a time when there was nothing to save them. Over 720 journalists (again, mostly rural and non-metro) also died of the coronavirus, most of whom received no medical support at all from their employers. And their families ended up in debts of lakhs of rupees borrowed to cover their hospitalization and other medical expenses.

The SCI has sometimes intervened very positively in the rural or non-metro sphere. In actions bringing benefit and hope to thousands of people. But problems arise from the follow up or lack of it.

Look at, for example, *G Sundarrajan v. Union of India*[39] – the case of the Kudankulam Nuclear Plant, the largest nuclear power station in India. Work on setting up the plant began in March 2002, but faced strong opposition from local fishing communities. People had in fact been resisting the idea since it was first proposed in 1979.

In 2011, a severe crackdown on the protestors saw the government of Tamil Nadu file some 350 cases against peaceful demonstrators. Nearly 9,000 people were charged with sedition. And, astonishingly, almost 13,000 with waging war against the state.[40] SP Udayakumar, leader of the agitation, was named as the Number 1 accused in over 300 FIRs.[41]

The section criminalizing the creation of 'disaffection towards the Government established by law' (124A) entered the Indian Penal Code (1860) through an

---

[38] 'Journalists Write to Parliamentarians Demanding Formation of National Media Commission' (*NewsClick*, 9 December 2021) <https://www.newsclick.in/Journalists-Write-Parliamentarians-Demanding-Formation-National-Media-Commission> accessed 20 February 2025.

[39] *G Sundarrajan v. Union of India* (2013) 6 SCC 620.

[40] R Ramasubramanian, '"Please Help Me Get My Passport Back Too," Anti-Nuclear Protestor Pleads with Sushma Swaraj' (*Scroll.in*, 17 June 2015) <http://scroll.in/article/734792/please-help-me-get-my-passport-back-too-anti-nuclear-protestor-pleads-with-sushma-swaraj> accessed 24 February 2025.

[41] Arun Janardhan, '8,856 'Enemies of State': An Entire Village in Tamil Nadu Lives Under Shadow of Sedition' (*The Indian Express*, 11 September 2016) <https://indianexpress.com/article/india/india-news-india/kudankulam-nuclear-plant-protest-sedition-supreme-court-of-india-section-124a-3024655/> accessed 24 February 2025.

amendment in 1870. The very first case of sedition would be heard only two decades later, in 1891, in the HC of Calcutta. In 1897, Bal Gangadhar Tilak became perhaps the first Indian to be convicted on that count by the Bombay HC.[42]

The first case of sedition in Tamil Nadu handing out severe sentences came in 1908. Freedom fighters Subramaniam Siva and VO Chidambaram Pillai were convicted on this ground. Though VO Chidambaram was the second accused, he was sentenced to transportation for life. Siva, to transportation for ten years.[43]

As Sundarrajan puts it, the Jayalalithaa government in two years piled on more cases of sedition than had the British Raj in the Madras Presidency in seventy-seven years (1870 to 1947). Besides, the Madras Presidency was a much larger geographical entity than the present-day Tamil Nadu state. While the nearly 9,000 people charged with sedition between 2011 and 2013 lived within just a twenty to thirty kilometre radius of Kudankulam in Tirunelveli district.

As the issue gained momentum, it landed up in the SCI.

The Court was appalled by both the scale and the intensity of this crackdown on peaceful protestors. On 6 May 2013, the SCI ordered that:

> Endeavour should be made to withdraw all the criminal cases filed against the agitators so that peace and normalcy be restored at Kudankulam and nearby places, and steps should be taken to educate the people of the necessity of the plant which is in the largest interest of the nation particularly the State of Tamil Nadu.[44]

The Court's order on withdrawal of the cases was a welcome relief. The judgment, though, clearly assumed the plant was in the 'largest national interest.' And that people opposed to it lacked understanding. They needed to be 'educated' on its benefits.

The State Government did not comply at once as it was required to. This compelled the protestors to move the Madras HC, asking it to punish the government for contempt.

---

[42] *Queen-Empress v. Bal Gangadhar Tilak & Keshav Mahadev Bal* (1897) ILR 22 Bom 112.

[43] The Madras HC commuted both sentences to transportation for six years. *In Re:O Chidambaram Pillai v. Unknown* 1 IND CAS 36; *In Re: Subramania Siva v. Unknown* 1 IND CAS 22.

[44] *G Sundarrajan* (n 39) [244.14].

Following this, the government dropped 213 of the roughly 350 cases. The protestors petitioned the SCI in 2014. They pointed out that all the cases had not been withdrawn despite the apex Court's explicit order. However, the SCI left it to the authorities to take the process further.[45]

A new government of Tamil Nadu withdrew twenty-six cases in September 2021.

Next, another thirty-four cases were withdrawn, and further action was dropped in eight more, subsequently. It was only under two cases that a few people were convicted. Some of whom were involved in a local conflict with rival villagers that had nothing to do with the agitation. The Madras HC quashed another five cases and the Radhapuram court disposed of three more. With 291 cases disposed of – there are still about 59 pending. That is thirteen years after they were filed, and eleven years after the SCI ordered all the cases be dropped. Thousands in the villages there have suffered intimidation, harassment, loss of jobs or income.

So while the SCI's intervention was at one level admirable, the follow up on its orders was not.

Kudankulam dragged into sunlight a process plaguing the countryside for a long time. What an Ambedkar might have called the lawlessness of law. Suddenly, with the agitation against the nuclear plant gaining worldwide media attention, the *explosive scale* of that ugly process – hundreds of cases and countless FIRs – was now out in the open.

The FIRs seemed a work of comic art and the nature of their content was fascinating. They would begin 'Udayakumar and 3,500 others'. Or, 'Udayakumar and 3,000 others'. Or, 'Udayakumar and 2,000 others…' (This particular number of 2,000 figures repeatedly in FIRs filed within days of each other). Also: 'Udayakumar and others' (which gave the police license to pick up as many others as they wished). 'Jeyakumar and 2,000 others'. 'Bose and 2,000 others.' 'Michael Rayappan and 2,000 others', 'Mathan and 2,000 others', 'Karikolraj Nadar and 2,000 others'…

Since 'others' numbered many unnamed thousands, the police could pick up anyone they wished, on any day, at any time they wished. It is impossible to fully estimate how many thousands were harassed, tormented, even tortured

45 *G Sundarrajan v. Union of India* (2014) 6 SCC 776.

over several years in this extraordinary example of process-as-punishment.

In just weeks towards the end of 2011, you can find mind-boggling numbers of FIRs lodged. Including a period when one was being filed every day against the same persons under the same sections.

An interesting commentary in *The Economic & Political Weekly* made the point that 'Prime Minister Manmohan Singh, Chief Minister J. Jayalalithaa, the Tirunelveli district collector and the Superintendent of Police and many other officials had regularly met the people charged with sedition and waging war against the government of India. Many of the ministers too have met the members of the struggle committee regularly.' The *EPW* quotes SP Udayakumar as posing the question: 'Doesn't that make them co-conspirators in our crime?'[46]

Around 2011, eerily similar situations unfolded in Odisha and Andhra Pradesh. The manner of leveraging law to intimidate and torment was not very different. Some top police officers of those states even kindly explained it to mediapersons.

An IG-rank officer in Tamil Nadu would tell *The Indian Express* five years later in 2016 that usually such cases would be closed in six months with the noting *Further Action Dropped*. But that this kind of repression was needed in the [non-violent, peaceful] Kudankulam agitation. Because 'we needed to keep a check on the villagers. Retaining these charges will help douse their anger; over 8,000 people booked under charges will scare them to not initiate similar protests again.'

Asked about further action, he said there was nothing to be probed or charge sheeted. 'These were all cases to scare them. When I look back after five years, I see that those 121 and 124A charges on 8,000 random people did serve the purpose.'[47]

I was served similar wisdom in Odisha when talking to a top police officer about the severe crackdowns in Kalinganagar, Jagatsinghpur and Koraput. I had asked how it was that there were ridiculous charges like 'theft of a buffalo' against an Assistant Professor of Chemistry involved in a peaceful protest.

---

[46] S Senthalir, 'Silent Emergency in Koodankulam' (2012) 47 (31) *The Economic and Political Weekly* 23–26.

[47] Arun Janardhanan, '8,856 "Enemies of State": An Entire Village in Tamil Nadu Lives under Shadow of Sedition' (*The Indian Express*, 12 September 2016).

'You need to understand, sir,' he explained. Perhaps as he was a very short while away from retirement, he spoke more freely. 'These are bad fellows; they are involved in all sorts of things. But you see, when we take them to court, the serious charges are often dismissed by the judges as unsustainable. Therefore, we need a judicious mix of charges that will keep them out of mischief as they will be reporting to court or police station. These things are needed.'

And indeed, it did prove effective to a degree in keeping people on a leash – by wrecking their lives. Many in Kalinganagar could neither retain their jobs, nor find new employment. Week after week, they would be visiting their lawyers, the local station or a court proceeding. An educated Adivasi couple who had little or no interaction with police prior to the agitation against the Tata Steel Plant in Kalinganagar, would have forty or more cases against them – dragging on for years. This was also the stir which, in 2006, saw fourteen Adivasis killed in police firing.[48]

In 2011, in neighbouring Andhra Pradesh, protestors against two thermal power plants in Srikakulam district were met with a similar ferocity in firing and in filing of FIRs. Police brought cases against over 2,000 people in Kakarapalli and against 1,729 in Sompet. As many as six people, three each in Sompet and Kakarapalli villages, died in police firing.[49]

Among the 2,000 against whom cases were brought, were two agricultural labourers – Chandramma aged eighty and Manickiamma, seventy-eight. Both frail and ailing woman who were barely able to walk even with their handsticks. Yet, they were hauled off to the lock up where they spent thirteen days. The issue became a cause célèbre when *Eenadu* reported that despite their obvious inability and weakness, they were charged with, among other things, attempt to murder. That too, of a police party and thermal plant officials.

Where do we stand today in 2024 on this appalling criminalization of dissent? My guess: the retired Odisha police officer must be wishing he were still in service. Today, few judges would throw out the 'serious charges' he was so aggrieved by.

---

[48] Prafulla Das, 'Resistance and Tragedy' (*The Frontline*, 26 January 2006).

[49] ML Narasimha Reddy, 'North Coastal Andhra Is Boiling' (*Eenadu*, 27 November 2011); ML Narasimha Reddy, 'They Destroy Lives, Harass Us When Questioned' (*Eenadu*, 28 November 2011); ML Narasimha Reddy, 'Questioning Begets Harassment' (*Eenadu*, 28 November 2011).

In the absence of a solid jurisprudence of accountability, no one gets hauled up or punished. No one has ever been pulled up for shamelessly flouting the SCI's orders in the Kudankulam case. Or in other cases, too. The police and local authorities get away with anything, even with repeating their abuse of power with impunity in exactly the same ways. This means the only recourse India's rural poor have is not to the Courts, but to public protest. And the untrammelled and now unquestionable power of agencies entrusted with maintaining law and order, helps the criminalization of dissent achieve pandemic status in the countryside. Which suggests dissent and the protests it generates, are going to be criminalized on a scale we cannot at this point begin to imagine.

Since July 1991, we have every day been in violation of the Constitution. Through economic policy, laws and political action. Especially, in contravention of the DPSP. The brunt of the consequences of those violations have been and continue to be borne by hundreds of millions of rural Indians. And of course by the urban poor, a large number of who are rural migrants now in wretched city slums.

The tragedy is greater when we learn that the SCI has from time to time proclaimed the importance of the DPSPs. Sadly, it has also produced judgments which diminish their worth.

The Court has more than once in the past few decades exhorted the State and all of us, to grasp the significance of the DPSPs. One judgment in 2010 lamented that: 'Of late, there has been a visible shift in the courts approach in dealing with cases involving the interpretation of social welfare legislations. The attractive mantras of globalization and liberalization are fast becoming the *raison d'etre* of the judicial process and an impression has been created that the constitutional courts are no longer sympathetic towards the plight of industrial and unorganized workers.'[50]

People can be forgiven that impression. After all, it arises in major part from the judgments rendered by the SCI itself.

---

50 *Harjinder Singh v. Punjab State Warehousing Corporation* (2010) 3 SCC 192 [30] (Singhvi J).

In the DPSP, we as a nation committed to 'eliminate inequalities in status, facilities and opportunities, not only amongst individuals but also amongst groups of people.' From 1991, we have in a full-blooded manner, cynically constructed, legitimized, normalized – even valorized, gross inequalities – social, economic, political and more. The mildest of welfarist measures for the poor are scoffed at as 'freebies' and 'sops' by the media and the elite.

Top researchers at the World Inequality Lab are telling us that this spectacular rise of inequality makes 'the "Billionaire Raj" headed by India's modern bourgeoise more unequal than the British Raj headed by the colonialist forces.'[51] It also squarely places India among the most unequal countries in the world.

They bring us that revelation around the same time that *Forbes* magazine, oracle of the global super-rich, confirms it from another angle. *Forbes* tells us that as on 16 July 2024, we had 211 dollar billionaires whose cumulative net worth was USD 1,056.7 billion. That is a figure more than a fourth of India's GDP. Close, in fact, to a third. India did not have a single dollar billionaire till the mid 1990s.

There is great concentration of wealth even *within* our billionaires. The top ten account for USD 414 billion of the total USD 1,056.7 billion. That is, almost forty per cent of their total, combined billionaire net worth. Indeed, the top five in this grand list of 211 alone account for USD 308.5 billion of that total. Or almost a third of that combined billionaire net worth.

At that point, it is no longer about concentration of wealth in the top one per cent. India's 211 ultra rich make up 0.000015 per cent of the population. The World Inequality Lab also tells us: 'nearly 90% of the billionaire wealth in 2022-23 is held by UCs [upper castes].'[52]

Surely not what the authors of the Constitution had in mind while calling on the State in Part IV to ensure that '*the operation of the economic system does*

[51] Nitin Kumar Bharti et al, 'Income and Wealth Inequality in India, 1922–2023: The Rise of the Billionaire Raj' (2024) World Inequality Lab Working Paper 2024/09 <https://wid.world/www-site/uploads/2024/03/WorldInequalityLab_WP2024_09_Income-and-Wealth-Inequality-in-India-1922-2023_Final.pdf> accessed 20 February 2025.

[52] Nitin Kumar Bharti et al, 'Towards Tax Justice and Wealth Redistribution in India: Proposals Based on Latest Inequality Estimates' (2024) World Inequality Lab Issue Brief 2024/01 <https://wid.world/document/towards-tax-justice-and-wealth-redistribution-in-india-proposals-based-on-latest-inequality-estimates-world-inequality-lab-issue-brief-2024-01/> accessed 20 February 2025.

not result in the concentration of wealth and means of production to the common detriment;' This country abolished wealth tax in the Union Budget 2016-2017. Our present levels of inequality are a shocking comment on what we have been up to as a nation since 1991. (Or perhaps, on a smaller scale, from the 1980s). A terrifying departure from the DPSPs which tell us that it is the duty of the State to:

> 38. 1[(1)] ... promote the welfare of the people by securing and protecting as effectively as it may a social order in which justice, social, economic and political, shall inform all the institutions of the national life.

And that the State will also:

> 38 2[(2) ... in particular, strive to minimise the inequalities in income, and endeavour to eliminate inequalities in status, facilities and opportunities, not only amongst individuals but also amongst groups of people residing in different areas or engaged in different vocations.] 39. The State shall, in particular, direct its policy towards securing— (a) that the citizens, men and women equally, have the right to an adequate means of livelihood; (b) that the ownership and control of the material resources of the community are so distributed as best to subserve the common good.

Alas, the wealth, means of production and the material resources of all communities are today held in fewer hands than ever before in our history. 'The common good' simply doesn't come into it. The judgments of the apex Court seem more aligned with the worldview of that very ruling elite in whose hands so much of wealth and resources are concentrated. More so, when it comes to issues like 'development.' It takes the ruling elite's definition of that as its own. It seems to embrace the worldview of the narrowest elite as being in 'the largest interest of the nation.' The top Court seems unable to take note of more advanced and less selfish measures such as human development.

India, after thirty years of huge 'wealth creation,' stands at 134 in the United Nations Human Development Index 2022. That is out of 193 countries. We rank an appalling 111 out of 125 nations in the Global Hunger Index 2023.[53] In the Global Gender Gap Report 2024 we are at 129 out of 146

---

[53] Klaus von Grebmer et al, '2023 Global Hunger Index: The Power of Youth in Shaping Food Systems'

countries surveyed.[54] That is, eighteenth from the bottom. In the Environmental Performance Index 2024, India stands at 176 out of 180 nations surveyed.[55] Fifth from the bottom. We do rank third, though, in the Forbes Billionaires list.

Surely, these indexes must find a place in a twenty-first century notion of 'development.' The values related to these clearly exist in the DPSPs, in our Constitution. They do not seem to inform the Court's view of Development.

The SCI, it must be said, has had some of its finest moments in issues largely rural related. Like in the case of the midday meals scheme in schools. Which might have remained largely confined to Tamil Nadu but for the Court's powerful intervention. In November 2001, the apex Court told all state governments to launch this programme in their schools within six months.[56] The rest is history. The benefits that brought to millions of children and their poor families cannot be overstated. For me that is *the* glorious moment in the saga of the SCI and rural India.

However, it was also the period as Singhvi J put it, when 'The attractive mantras of globalization and liberalization [were] fast becoming the *raison d'etre* of the judicial process.'[57]

Embracing the worldview of the elite – hardly what the Constitution asks us to do – brings its own baggage. It embeds attitudes towards the poor, the marginalized – and the common good – which spring from that worldview. At its best, it nurtures a paternalism that sees the rural masses as simple folk, less than literate, who need to be 'educated.' Who require guided enlightenment. As in the Kudankulam case. Or in some of the SEZ battles.

In its less-than-benevolent avatar, it seems more severely paternalistic. As

---

(2023) Welthungerhilfe <https://www.globalhungerindex.org/pdf/en/2023.pdf> accessed 21 February 2025.

[54] Kusum Kali Pal, Kim Piaget and Saadia Zahidi, 'Global Gender Gap Report 2024' (2024) World Economic Forum <https://www.weforum.org/publications/global-gender-gap-report-2024/> accessed 21 February 2025.

[55] Sebastián Block et al, '2024 Environmental Performance Index' (2024) Yale Center for Environmental Law & Policy <https://epi.yale.edu> accessed 21 February 2025.

[56] *People's Union for Civil Liberties v. Union of India* (2007) 1 SCC 728; After this, in 2014, the Social Justice Bench (SJB) of the SCI, presided over by Madan Lokur J, passed various orders related to food security, drought management and compensation, malnutrition, midday meals, etc. In the food–security-related case, a continuing mandamus was also issued by the Bench in *Swaraj Abhiyan v. Union of India* (2016) 7 SCC 498; *Swaraj Abhiyan v. Union of India* (2018) 12 SCC 170.

[57] *Harjinder Singh* (n 50).

when it comes to welfare-related issues like the Aadhaar ID. Or when it comes to eligibility restrictions in the panchayats. Like, for instance, the two-child norm in states such as Haryana that excludes millions of women from running for office. Or the requirement that candidates be debt-free, educated and in possession of a functional toilet—that potentially excludes every marginalized group imaginable, and was upheld in *Rajbala v. State of Haryana*.[58]

Unsurprisingly, the Court's paternalism leads to deeply patriarchal outcomes. The Court had this to say of the Haryana amendments in *Javed v. State of Haryana*:

> It was also submitted that the impugned disqualification would hit the women worst, inasmuch as in the Indian society they have no independence and they almost helplessly bear a third child if their husbands want them to do so. This contention need not detain us any longer. A male who compels his wife to bear a third child would disqualify not only his wife but himself as well. We do not think that with the awareness which is arising in Indian women folk, they are so helpless as to be compelled to bear a third child even though they do not wish to do so.[59]

In such cases it is the fault of that villager if she is not educated. It is her fault if she is poor. And there is no excuse for a lack of restraint in overproducing children. It is also, in other ways and cases, the fault of the poor if they're hungry. The selective sympathy of this two-track approach jells strongly with the ruling elite's neoliberalism of these past thirty years. Oddly, that neoliberal ideology still hugely dominates a country with a welfare constitution.

The DPSPs are neither flawless nor a panacea for all ills. By their own admission they are not 'enforceable by any court.' They do assert, though, that these principles are 'nevertheless fundamental in the governance of the country and it shall be the duty of the State to apply these principles in making laws.'

While meant to be guiding principles for generations of legislators, they can be ignored or mischievously interpreted by governments using a few of them as a tool. The latter because the principles evolved in a hotly contested political

---

[58] *Rajbala v. State of Haryana* (2016) 2 SCC 445.

[59] *Javed v. State of Haryana* (2003) 8 SCC 369 [63].

environment – and some had to reflect the political compromises of the day. Like for instance, the prohibiting of 'the slaughter, of cows and calves and other milch and draught cattle.'

That's a 'principle' today being wildly misused, where whole municipalities are imposing bans on the sale/consumption of any kind of meat. That, in a country where the National Family Health Survey 4 (2005–06) pointed out – seventy-five per cent of Indians are non-vegetarian. The next round of the NFHS (2019-21) revealed that the number of people who had never consumed non-vegetarian food actually declined between the two surveys. NFHS 5 showed that an 'overwhelming 83.4 per cent of men and 70.6 per cent of women in the 15-49 age group eat non-vegetarian food daily, weekly or occasionally.' Higher than the 78.4 per cent for men and 70 per cent for women in NHFS-4.[60]

The Indian population figure in the Census, viewed religion-wise, suggests that at least forty-three per cent have no ideological or religious taboos on the consumption of beef. Which figure too, does not include the millions of Hindus who regularly consume it. Also, the laws brought in by some states have ensured that the menace of, and damage caused by, stray cattle rank high among the problems of farming communities in those states.

In our times, the Principles also become a problem when the right to work and livelihood lands us no further than a limited rural employment guarantee scheme. Or when that to Education ends up in the flawed and truncated Right to Education (RTE).

So the DPSPs are far from being a magic bullet, or even just benign, pious principles. Yet, they might be the best we have at this point. Their very nature of generality means they could be interpreted otherwise. That is, more progressively – as their authors intended – than just in terms of an NREGs or an RTE. The DPSPs do tell us of a society that can be, maybe even should be. They also offer a platform of principles around which movements for Justice can be built. And not just reactionary movements like those resulting in the slew of anti-cow slaughter laws in some states.

Movements for justice built around them could also be a unifying platform. The 2024 elections remind us that ordinary people, especially those from the

---

[60] Harikishan Sharma, 'More Men Eating Non-Veg than before: Health Survey Data' (*The Indian Express*, 17 May 2022).

marginalized communities, are conscious of and concerned about threats to the Constitution. To its more basic vision. It is easier to build social awareness and unity around the DPSPs of the Constitution than around the manifesto of any one political party.

If the Fundamental Rights are, as some say, the heart of the Constitution, the Preamble and DPSPs are its soul. At least to this legally untrained citizen desperate to have his country live up to the explicit or implied promise of at least a handful of them. Right to work, Right to Food, Right to Education, Right to Livelihood, Health and Shelter…

Which brings us back to the question at the start of this essay.

Does the SCI have a vision, or even just a simple, clear perspective of rural India? Do hundreds of millions of poor rural Indians have the same access to it that urban people do? If they do not, should the court be bothered about that? Or do they think that is someone else's problem? Does the SCI have a sense of the realities of rural life?

I see little to rejoice at in the answers these questions throw up. Can the SCI treat the DPSPs more seriously beyond re-emphasizing their importance from time to time? I believe it can. But that would call for embracing those Principles as earnestly as the Court sometimes asks us to.

Even when the top Court comes up with great judgments, it is ill-equipped to oversee their implementation. Which mostly leaves the affected and afflicted with only one option: public protest. The least the SCI can do – and enjoin every other court in the nation to also do – is to protect that right to protest. Instead, we have gone headlong in the reverse direction – in criminalizing dissent.

I confess I have no legal background at all, let alone any claim to being an expert on the Constitution of India. And am so, perhaps, exposing my naivete in these matters.

But in forty-four years as a journalist, I have covered the very masses the Constitution exhorts us to worry about. In thirty-one of those, I have been a full-time rural reporter. And every single time I am in the field and see the victims of a forced displacement; each time I am on the road with distressed migrants; every farmer, weaver, carpenter and other household I have visited that have seen suicide deaths driven by deep agrarian distress; every encounter with ecological refugees; all those rural employment guarantee sites I have been to where girls aged eleven to thirteen wear full sarees pretending to be fourteen or above in their desperation to obtain physically bruising work in forty-five degrees Celsius or higher; every caste atrocity, each blatant injustice and inequality it has been my misfortune to cover, I recall and long for the Constitution of India's vision and promise of 'justice, social, economic and political…'.[61]

[61] Constitution of India 1950, Preamble.

Cartoon © SanitaryPanels.

Reflections on Gender Discrimination and Women Lawyers

AN INTERVIEW WITH INDIRA JAISING

The Editor met Ms Jaising for a long conversation about her career and the ways in which she has seen the Supreme Court of India (SCI) change over five decades, her experiences as a pioneering woman lawyer, and the cases that she has been involved in that have contributed to the development of the law.

The footnotes presented in first-person narrative have been provided by Ms Jaising.

Editor: *You started to appear in the Supreme Court in the early 70s. As one among the very few women who were in the Court then, how did you find it receiving women lawyers?*

Ms Jaising: I find the easiest way in which I can describe myself is by the generation to which I belong. The fact of the matter is that I was born in 1940, before the Constitution was framed. So, I cannot claim to be one of the founding mothers of the Constitution of India, but I do claim to be one of its founding daughters. It is the era into which I was born that has influenced my entire life as a professional, as a human being, as a person in every sense of the word. I am definitely a product of my times. I came into the profession with no expectations. I looked upon it as a service-oriented profession. The task, which I set out for myself, was to acquire the necessary skills. Although I did a master's degree in law, and was a fellow at the School of Advanced Legal Studies, London, I never saw my future as an academic. My ambition was to be a litigator. I grew up believing that the democracy in which I lived would never go away but my task was to work for the implementation of social and political rights. I wanted to work with the directive principles of state policy, which I saw as a product of the freedom movement.

My first case in the Supreme Court was *Workmen v. Firestone Tyre & Rubber*[1], a case relating to labour law. Fascinating case, a fascinating judgment. It dealt with the issue of reinstatement of a dismissed worker that plagued the labour movement in India. Common law does not have the concept of reinstatement at all. If anybody's services are terminated, the only relief you can get is compensation. These are the kinds of issues that absorbed my mind because they gave me these incredible opportunities to depart from the framework of common law or to depart from the framework of contract law and move towards a different concept of law for the people.

The Industrial Disputes Act, 1947 had been amended with the introduction of Section 17B into the Act,[2] which completely entrenched the right to reinstatement and talked about wages to be paid not only for the period when the workmen were wrongfully denied employment but during the pendency of legal proceedings.

The *Firestone* case was argued in Court No.5 of the Supreme Court before two male judges – Justice CA Vaidyalingam and Justice ID Dua. Mr MC Setalvad, far senior to me, the former Attorney General for India, was representing the industry, and I was representing the workers. I do not think that the judges perceived me as 'just a woman', but they saw me as a woman representing the cause of labour and social justice. So, immediately, I had a double identity. Partly for that reason, I think that I had a very good reception in the Court. I also got excellent feedback from Mr MC Setalvad himself, who was highly appreciative of the arguments that I had made in Court.

In answer to your question on the attitude of courts that were predominantly male, I would say that male judges love to patronize young women lawyers; they are a source of amusement to male judges. If the women succumb to this, then they face no discrimination. In my own case, I found that the older I got, and the more successful I was at asserting myself, the more discrimination I faced. There is a culture of sycophancy that exists in our courts till today. Should you depart from it, you become an outsider. The discrimination comes in very subtle forms. Women cannot be prevented from arguing in court, but

---

1 *Workmen of Firestone Tyre & Rubber Co of India (P) Ltd v. Management* (1973) 1 SCC 813.

2 Industrial Disputes Act 1947, s 17B (as amended by Act 46 of 1982, s 11, effective 21 August 1984) involving the payment of full wages to workman pending proceedings in higher courts.

their work can be invisible. They are not the 'eminent jurists' or the 'great lawyers' of the country, the leaders of the Bar.

Editor: *There appears to be a typecasting of women lawyers as there is a general tendency to go to them with matrimonial cases. You appear to have broken that stereotype by commencing your practice with representing trade unions and workmen.*

Ms Jaising: I joined a very mainstream law firm, Mulla & Mulla, in Bombay, and that is the place where I had picked up my skills. When I was going to court, I could see lawyers like Mr Fali Nariman and Mr Ashok Desai arguing every day, and I knew the difference between good advocacy and bad advocacy and I could see how to navigate the court. After a few years in the High Court, I decided to shift to the Supreme Court and gravitated towards the chamber of Mr RK Garg. The kind of work he was doing attracted me. It was a mix of labour law and constitutional law. This is the kind of practice you do not see in the Supreme Court today. They were a group of solid seniors, Mr DP Singh, Mr Suresh Agarwal, Mr Garg and Mr MK Ramamurti. It is rare now to find seniors collaborating in this way. And for me, that was critical. Nowadays, I find that the seniors are highly competitive. If three or four of them are appearing in the same matter, they do not seem willing to have a common conference or to share their mandate with each other.

Mr Garg's office was involved in a lot of trade union work. Mr MK Ramamurti was known for his association with trade unions, and Mr Garg for his work on civil liberties. It was the collective work and the bonding between lawyers that I found very attractive. But I soon found that while there was space for me as a woman, there was no space for me as a woman lawyer in that framework. So, after one year, I took a call that the Supreme Court was not the place for me, and I returned to Bombay. I started working with a prominent trade union lawyer, Mr KT Sule, and also handled my own work. He was a member of the Communist Party of India (Marxist). His main interest was to defend the trade unions. I learnt a lot of my labour law from him. Mr GB Pai used to always be on the other side, for the management. In those days, there was a clear demarcation between those who represented labour and those who represented management. It was our ideology that drove our work. Today, however, you will find lawyers appearing both for management and labour. The early years of the Court were exciting times. New law was being created by the interpretation of the provisions of the Constitution. There is no doubt about the fact that when you represent deprived sections of the community, you are forced to be creative in your arguments, as the letter of the law has not much to offer them. These days I find arguments have become like mantras, repeated in every case in exactly the same way.

Editor: *When the labour law judgments of the 60s are referred to, the name of Justice PB Gajendragadkar invariably comes up. He is viewed as having contributed to the progressive jurisprudence in labour law in the Supreme Court*[3] *which perhaps paved the way for later development. Which of the judges did you see at that point in time in the Supreme Court responding favourably to such cases? Do you think these judgments had a role in shaping the labour law movement of those times?*

Ms Jaising: I would argue that the foundation of labour law in India was laid in the *Western Indian Match Company* case.[4] The real challenge was to get away from the 'hire and fire' policy of the common law, and this case achieved that result. The case went on to lay the foundation of reinstatement in work, building on the foundation of security of tenure. There is no doubt that judgments of the Court channelled the development of the labour movement in the country towards an acceptable form of dispute resolution. When employers were exploitative, the workers had nowhere to turn to but the courts. This is the essence of democratic lawyering in court. In *Firestone*, none of the judges were really known to be pro-labour, and yet, the judgment was a milestone in the journey for security of tenure for workers. Justice Krishna Iyer's judgment in *Gujarat Steel*[5] again helped the working class. Much later, when there were retaliatory closures of industrial establishments, the provisions of the Industrial Disputes Act were successfully defended by lawyers like the late Mr MK Ramamurthy and myself in *Meenakshi Mills*.[6] We also had the judgment in *National Textile Workers Union*[7] where workers were given the right to participate in management, which in any case is one of the

---

3 For a detailed discussion, see essay by K Chandru in this book.

4 *Western India Match Co. Ltd. v. Workmen*, AIR 1964 SC 472.

5 *Gujarat Steel Tubes Ltd v. Gujarat Steel Tubes Mazdoor Sabha* (1980) 2 SCC 593.

6 *Workmen of Meenakshi Mills Ltd v. Meenakshi Mills Ltd* (1992) 3 SCC 336; where the constitutionality of s 25N of the Industrial Disputes Act 1947, pertaining to restriction on employer's right to retrench workmen was upheld. The essay by K Chandru in this book also discusses some of these cases.

7 *National Textile Workers Union v. PR Ramakrishnan* (1983) 1 SCC 228.

directive principles of state policy. Hence there is no doubt that the Supreme Court has shaped not only labour law but the labour movement of the country.

One thing that has worsened is the adjournment culture in the Supreme Court. In a labour matter before the Bench of Justice Krishna Iyer and Justice Bhagwati, about the closure of a mill, I protested when Mr Murlidhar Bhandare[8] sought an adjournment. I explained that I had come all the way from Bombay with the workers having collected money for my airfare. I insisted that Mr Bhandare's client should be made to compensate for this as a condition for the adjournment. The judges agreed.

Unfortunately, the adjournment culture continues to this day. Delays in the Supreme Court are largely on this account. The legal system is discredited, and it is the litigants who suffer.

Editor: *I distinctly remember your teaming up with Senior Advocates KG Kannabiran and K Chandru in 1990 and exposing through a cover-story in* The Lawyers *of the misdemeanours of V Ramaswami J when he was the CJ of the Punjab and Haryana HC.*[9] *The rest, as they say, is history.*[10] *Many years later, you also led a pioneering effort to bring transparency and fairness to the process of designation of senior advocates. You have asked for rules that ensure merit-based selection, greater transparency and accountability.*[11] *I think you have also said that you would rather do away with the system of senior advocates altogether. What motivated you to take up this cause? And are you satisfied with the response of the Supreme Court?*

Ms Jaising: Apart from being sycophantic, the legal profession is monopolistic, dynastic and resistant to change. I am a first-generation lawyer. In representing

8 Mr Bhandare, who was a senior lawyer, also taught part-time at the Government Law College, Bombay.

9 A cover story on the allegations of corruption against V Ramaswami J along with the full text of the internal audit report of the Punjab & Haryana HC indicating corruption was published. Indira Jaising, KG Kannabiran, K Chandru, 'Judicial Misconduct?' (1990) The Lawyers, 5th vol. no.4, 4.

10 For a detailed discussion, see the essay by Raju Ramachandran in this book.

11 In *Indira Jaising v. Supreme Court of India* (2017) 9 SCC 766 and *Indira Jaising v. Supreme Court of India* (2023) 8 SCC 1, guidelines were formulated for the designation of Senior Advocates by a Bench comprising of three judges. Certain doubts were expressed regarding the correctness of the guidelines in these two decisions by a two-judge Bench in *Jitender @ Kalla v. State (Govt. of NCT of Delhi)* 2025 INSC 249 which was directed to be placed before the CJI to constitute a Bench of appropriate strength. A three-judge Bench constituted for this purpose in *Jitendra Kalla v. State (Govt. of NCT of Delhi)* 2025 INSC 667 has done away with the points-based system for evaluating Senior designation.

the working class and the disadvantaged in courts, I had no role models. This worked to my advantage, and I could gather my own community of like-minded lawyers. This is what led to the formation of the *Lawyers Collective*. Its members, who were invariably first-generation lawyers, went on to work for larger causes. Nepotism and 'legacy' appear to facilitate upward mobility at the Bar, which continues to be largely male-dominated.[12] Until recently, there were hardly any female seniors at the Bar. I was already designated in 1987 by the High Court of Bombay. I was determined to break this rule of dynasty to open up the profession to develop a younger generation of lawyers who will be the future of the legal profession. This is one of the cases of which I am most proud. There might be aberrations, which will require course correction, but the system should not be shut down.

Editor: *Are there other issues concerning the administration of the court that you have been concerned about?*

Ms Jaising: I have filed very few petitions in my own name, but all of them relate to the administration of justice. That is the canvas. Transparency and accountability were the motivations for filing the petition related to live streaming.[13] The court space should be gender friendly. Women lawyers upon becoming mothers are constrained to either discontinue altogether or limit their practice; and this adversely affects their chances of being recognized for being designated as Senior Advocates on par with their male counterparts. This is what led to the filing of the petition for a creche in the court premises.[14]

At the hearing, the Registry offered a 150 sq. ft space. I protested that this was too small. This led to the judges inspecting the premises and agreeing with us. Ultimately, a 3,500 sq. ft space was identified. It is good to see that the creche is used now both by women lawyers and staff who bring their children to the creche, as well as by male lawyers. I believe Justice Rohinton Nariman once said that the happiest place in the Supreme Court of India is the creche.

---

12 Academic articles have already been published by Marc Galanter, where he talked about the monopolistic lawyer, and it focused around the whole issue of super seniors; See, Marc Galanter and Nick Robinson, 'India's Grand Advocates: A Legal Elite Flourishing in the Era of Globalization' (2013) 20(3) Intl J Legal Prof <https://ssrn.com/abstract=2348699> accessed 29 November 2024.

13 *Indira Jaising v. Secretary General* Writ Petition (Civil) No 66 of 2018; It culminated in the judgment *Swapnil Tripathi v. Supreme Court of India* (2018) 10 SCC 639.

14 It was filed by my junior colleague, Anindita Pujari, in her own name. She would bring her infant daughter to the Court. The child and her caretaker would sit under a tree in the lawns of the SCI.

Editor: *It took thirty-nine years for the Supreme Court to have its first woman judge in Justice Fathima Beevi in October 1989. And that too, six months after she had completed her tenure as a High Court judge.*[15] *Do you think it is a myth that having women on the Bench means women's issues get better visibility, and the way they are understood is better? Would you agree that women judges also get co-opted into notions of patriarchy and feudalism which their representation is supposed to act against? Could you also comment on the complexity of the cross-cutting identity of a woman judge?*

Ms Jaising: I think it is a myth that women judges are better able to address women's issues. It is also a form of gender stereotyping. Many women internalize misogyny and are themselves victims of patriarchy. But there is a more fundamental reason to having women on the Bench, and that is the issue of equal representation in all institutions of decision-making. Representation is critical because it goes to the heart of democracy.

What we need is a critical mass of women in decision-making positions to ensure their visibility literally and ideologically. Look at Rwanda, which made fifty per cent reservation for women in Parliament. Then suddenly, you saw that not just fifty but sixty per cent women were elected to the Parliament. To understand the meaning of sensitization you need to understand the need for representation – it is linked to the question of sensitization. How can there be sensitization without representation? It is not possible.

One of my angsts has been that women want validation from male colleagues, whether at the Bar or on the Bench. I do not approve of it. I believe that there is a way of being yourself, being a woman, being a feminist, being a good lawyer and being a good judge. Recent dissents by women judges – for instance, Justice Bela Trivedi's dissent in the sub-categorization case[16] and Justice Nagarathna's dissent in the demonetization case[17] – are, according to me, instances of good judgment writing, which appear to underscore the importance of due process.

[15] She retired from the Kerala High Court on 29 April 1989 and was elevated to the SCI on 6 October 1989.

[16] *State of Punjab v. Davinder Singh* 2024 INSC 562

[17] *Vivek Narayan Sharma v. Union of India* (2023) 3 SCC 1, 126–183.

Editor: *How did the composition of the Benches affect the outcomes in some of the landmark cases on gender discrimination that you were involved in? For instance, the case of* Rupan Deol Bajaj.[18]

Ms Jaising: Rupan's case came up before a Bench of two male judges. She pointed out to me that, while the Supreme Court said that there should be a complaints committee and a woman should head the complaints committee,[19] why was it that when it came to this case, there was no woman on the Bench? Rupan Deol Bajaj's case went twice to the Supreme Court. First, on the issue of non-registration of an FIR.[20] The Bench consisted of two male judges, Justices AS Anand and MK Mukherjee. They directed that an FIR should be registered. The second time, when KPS Gill challenged the punishment awarded to him, it was a Bench presided over by Justice BN Srikrishna. The Court upheld the punishment.[21] So, then after it was all dusted and dry, I turned to Rupan and asked her, 'Do you still want a woman judge?'

Among the lesser-known facts is that Siddhartha Shankar Ray, the then Governor of Punjab, stepped into the witness box in the trial court to testify to the good character of KPS Gill. My cross-examination of him went like this:

'Rupan Deol Bajaj complained to you?'

'*Yes, she complained to me.*'

'You did conduct an inquiry?'

'*Yes, I conducted an inquiry.*'

'At the end of the inquiry, you issued a warning to him to say that you should not drink in public places?'

'*Yes, I did.*'

'Thank you very much.'

End of cross-examination. Now, as a cross-examiner, you should know when to end your cross-examination.

---

[18] Case involving the outraging of modesty, filed by a woman IAS officer against KPS Gill, then DGP Punjab, in which he was held guilty, and the conviction was upheld by the SCI.

[19] *Vishakha v. State of Rajasthan* (1997) 6 SCC 241 [17].

[20] *Rupan Deol Bajaj v. Kanwar Pal Singh Gill* (1995) 6 SCC 194.

[21] *KPS Gill v. State (UT Chandigarh, Administration) Through Secretary* (2005) 6 SCC 161.

When it comes to sexual harassment, male bonding is evident; male colleagues step forward and give evidence in favour of the accused. They find nothing wrong with misogynistic comments; for them, it is 'water cooler' talk.

I have to say that the young magistrate presiding over the trial court convicted him. Which was a big thing at that time. He went on to become a High Court judge.[22]

Editor: *Generally, in your experience, how have judges reacted to lawyers appearing for survivors in such cases?*

Ms Jaising: More than judges, it is usually the male defence lawyers who pillory women who go to the court. Many of them are misogynists and will do everything within their power to 'win a case'. You will hear every type of argument that is sexist, misogynist and male chauvinistic. As a woman lawyer, I feel that this is not only unfair to the client but also to me. And unfortunately, the judges do not stop them. When judges do not stop them, it falls on your shoulders to stop them. My journey has been a difficult one. It has led to my being also stereotyped as someone who is 'aggressive'. As a woman, to assert yourself is to be aggressive. A man in similar circumstances is not considered aggressive but 'successful'. In the obituary I wrote for Mr Fali Nariman, I said that he was one of the most aggressive lawyers I had met, and also the most successful.[23] So, why is it that when a man is aggressive, you are never told he's aggressive? But if a woman is aggressive, she is a shrew *and* she is aggressive.[24]

Editor: *You have also been a member of the CEDAW [Committee on the Elimination of Discrimination Against Women].*[25] *Do you think enough is being done on gender sensitization of judges? Do you think that this should be one of the parameters for the selection of judges?*

---

[22] Darshan Singh J, Judge, Punjab and Haryana HC.

[23] Indira Jaising, 'Indira Jaising Writes: Indian Law, After Fali S Nariman' (*The Indian Express*, 22 February 2024).

[24] See, Tushar Kohli, 'Indira Jaising Writes to the CJI on Subtleties of Gender Stereotyping, Suggests Combat Measures' (*The Leaflet*, 18 December 2024) <https://theleaflet.in/indira-jaising-writes-to-the-cji-on-subtleties-of-gender-stereotyping-suggests-combat-measures/> accessed 24 November 2024.

[25] Indira Jaising was a member of the United Nations' Committee on the Elimination of Discrimination Against Women (CEDAW) from 2009–2012.

Ms Jaising: CEDAW taught me that countries have not only to end discrimination against women but a duty to 'respect, protect and fulfil' our right to equality and non-discrimination based on sex. I believe there is only a symbolic change in our courts. Judges now pay lip sympathy to women's issues. But if symbols are not translated into action, they have no meaning. There is an articulated acceptance of gender in judgments of the court, which would include acceptance of same-sex relationships. It would include self-identification of trans people. It would include greater representation of women seniors. When, thanks to live streaming, one hears in real time the comments made by judges during hearings, the misogyny is palpable. For instance, the brazenness with which a High Court judge remarked to a woman lawyer who seemed to know much about the opposing party that soon enough she would know the colour of their underpants![26] The Supreme Court had to take *suo motu* notice of the case to undo the damage done by such comments to the image of the judiciary.[27] Where are such remarks coming from? This judge is unaware of judgments of the Supreme Court disapproving of such judicial behaviour.[28]

Even on issues like sensitivity to gender needs, my complaint to the Supreme Court to shift the washroom for males, which is presently next to the canteen, to the end of the corridor has met with a standard response that it has been forwarded to the PWD for necessary action. Do you know that there is no toilet for women on the second floor of the Supreme Court where law officers sit?

Editor: *It is remarkable that in his judgment in the case of the sexual harassment of a woman judicial officer in Madhya Pradesh, Justice Jagdish Khehar acknowledged how you had educated the Court on the appropriateness of the language used to describe your arguments.*[29] *Can you tell us more about this?*

---

[26] 'Why a Karnataka HC Judge Has Landed in Soup over His "Pakistan", "Undergarments" Remarks' (*The Firstpost*, 20 September 2024) <https://www.firstpost.com/explainers/karnataka-hc-judge-bengaluru-pakistan-undergarments-remarks-supreme-court-13817441.html> accessed 25 November 2024.

[27] *In Re: Remarks by High Court Judge During Court Proceedings* SMW (C) No 9 of 2024.

[28] *Aparna Bhat v. State of Madhya Pradesh* Criminal Appeal No 329 of 2021, order dated 18 March 2021; *In Re: Right to Privacy of Adolescents* Suo Motu WP (C) No 3 of 2023, order dated 20 August 2024.

[29] In paragraph 26 of the decision in *Additional District and Sessions Judge 'X' v. High Court of Madhya Pradesh*, (2015) 4 SCC 91, Justice Khehar noted: 'Every day is a matter of learning. Hearing of submissions in this case, we may say, was a matter of further understanding the sensitivities involved in a controversy of the present nature. We may venture to demonstrate this, by noticing a verbal exchange, during the course of hearing, between the counsel for the petitioner and that for the High Court. While

It is significant that the High Court judge who was charged with sexually harassing the woman judge was her administrative judge.[30] The asymmetry of power in that situation is obvious. However, she was no pushover and resisted his advances. Soon enough, she was victimized and transferred to a remote place. Her daughter was studying in Class 10, in a school that did not have a hostel. Although there was a rule that, in such a situation, the parent should not be transferred till Class 10 is complete, the woman judicial officer was still transferred. She was forced to resign but made an official complaint of sexual harassment to the CJI and the President of India. The High Court set up an enquiry committee of its own comprising judges from the same court. It is this decision that was challenged in the Supreme Court on the ground that the committee had to have judges from outside the court. The stakes for the High Court were high, as an adverse judgment would reflect poorly on the ability of the court to follow the law.

It was during this hearing that my opponent referred to one of my interventions as 'delightful'. I know no disrespect was meant to me, it could have been a genuine respect for me as a person but the fact is that I was appearing in court as a professional and the remark was gendered. I resented it and made my resentment known. For me, it is important to protest in real-time when

---

the learned counsel representing the High Court was on "his" legs, the learned counsel for the petitioner interjected to express "her" point of view. All through, during the process of hearing, submissions were advanced in a lively and respectful manner, and pointedly on the subject under consideration. Feeling that the thought being projected by the learned counsel was being disturbed by the intervention, the Bench accordingly exhorted the learned counsel, to go on unmindful of the interruption. The learned counsel for the High Court, well-meaning and deferential as he always is, responded by observing, "The interjections by the learned Senior Counsel for the petitioner, are always delightful". The learned Senior Counsel for the petitioner, had serious objection to the term, "delightful" used, with reference to "her". She questioned, the use of the term, "delightful" by posing to the learned Senior Counsel, whether similar interjections by men, were also considered by him as delightful. Why then, she questioned, should "her" interjection be found "delightful". In expressing her view, she went on to describe the response of the learned Senior Counsel as "sexually coloured". Having given our thoughtful consideration to the response of the learned counsel for the petitioner, we may only say, that she may well be right. There is a lot to be learnt, from what she innocuously conveyed. Her sensitivity to the issue, one may confess, brought out to us, a wholly different understanding on the subject. It is, therefore, that we have remarked above, that the evaluation of a charge of sexual harassment, would depend on the manner in which it is perceived. Each case will have to be decided on its own merits. Whether the perception of the harassed individual was conveyed to the person accused, would be very material in a case falling in the realm of oversensitivity. In that, it would not be open to him thereafter, to defend himself by projecting that he had not sexually harassed the person concerned, because in his understanding the alleged action was unoffending.'

[30] The judge was later exonerated both a three-member Committee set up by the SCI and by the Committee set up by the Rajya Sabha under the Judges (Inquiry) Act. A more detailed discussion can be found in the essay by Raju Ramachandran in this book.

you are offended by a sexist remark rather than look for *ex post facto* solutions, hence I protested. I am happy to say that the judges understood that it was my perception that mattered in the matter of sexism in court, not just that of the person who meant it well as a compliment maybe.

Editor: *It is not a coincidence, is it, that you have taken up many cases concerning sexual harassment of women by judges?*

Ms Jaising: No. I have gone on record to say that I myself have been sexually harassed in the corridors of the Supreme Court, which are incidentally so narrow and crowded that they provide ample opportunity to sexually harass a woman and get away with it as being an innocent accident. Sometimes sitting in a court waiting for a case, you suddenly realize that you are being stared at by a male colleague who should be focusing on court proceedings instead.

One of the biggest issues in the judiciary is the sexual harassment of women judges. A very big issue. The dirty secret of the judiciary. Then what is this talk of sensitivity all about? I have personally handled four cases of women judges who have been sexually harassed.

I have already referred to the case of the woman district judge from Madhya Pradesh. Very few people know about the impeachment proceedings.[31] The inquiry committee set up gave the judge a clean chit, applying the standard of 'beyond reasonable doubt'[32] which is a criminal law standard. That was incorrect. It has to be on a balance of probabilities. That was the case in which I cross-examined four sitting judges of the High Court.[33] One of them blatantly admitted that he had not even read the papers before signing the document that he had signed.

There is an interesting postscript to this case. Accepting her plea, in a separate

---

[31] An impeachment motion, signed by fifty-eight members, was submitted to the Rajya Sabha Chairman. In April 2015, the Rajya Sabha Chairman, after admitting the motion, set up an investigation panel. On 15 December 2017, the report of the Committee constituted under the Judges Inquiry Act 1968 was tabled in the Rajya Sabha, and the judge was given a clean chit.

[32] 'Report of the Inquiry Committee in the Matter of: Motion for Removal of Justice Gengele, Judge, Madhya Pradesh High Court under Sub-Section (2) of Section 3 of the Judges Inquiry Act 1968' (Rajya Sabha, 2018) 69 <https://cms.rajyasabha.nic.in/documents/1631892021869.03_jic_gangele_report.pdf> accessed 29 February 2024.

[33] 'Indira Jaising's Address on Transformative Constitutionalism' (*Socio-Legal Review*, 28 July 2019) ISSN 0973-5216 <https://www.sociolegalreview.com/post/indira-jaising-s-address-on-transformative-constitutionalism> accessed 24 February 2025.

writ petition, that the choice presented to her of being a good mother or fulfilling her right to work was unfair and unconstitutional, the Supreme Court ordered her reinstatement.[34]

But the more important issue is why is there sexual harassment of women judges in the judiciary. One reason is that under Article 235 of the Constitution of India[35], a High Court has administrative control over the 'subordinate' judiciary. High Court judges can make or break any judge, including a woman, who is in the district judiciary.

But apart from that, it takes you back to the phenomenon of sycophancy expected by judges of the higher judiciary. The Annual Confidential Reports of judges of the district judiciary are written by the High Court judges. Their promotion prospects are dependent on them. While the Madhya Pradesh case involved sexual harassment, there are other things which may seem trivial but are disturbing. Like at a public function, they will require women judges to wear sarees of the same colour, stand at the entrance and throw flowers at the incoming judges. You are going to treat your women like that and then you are hypocritical enough to welcome the increase in the number of women in the judiciary.[36]

The Supreme Court had to take *suo motu* notice[37] of six women judges who were not confirmed by the Madhya Pradesh High Court. Four of them have been put back, and two are still struggling. There was also a recent news report of a complaint by a woman judge who threatened to commit suicide because no one was addressing her complaint of sexual harassment.[38] We know that

---

34 *Ms X v. Registrar General, High Court of Madhya Pradesh* (2022) 14 SCC 187; This case involved a woman judge (Additional District Judge) having to resign from her judgeship after a case of sexual harassment by a sitting HC judge, and this order accepting her resignation was challenged in the SCI. The Court, while directing reinstatement, held that her resignation could not be construed to be voluntary.

35 Constitution of India 1950, art 235: 'Control over Subordinate Courts: The control over district courts and courts subordinate thereto including the posting and promotion of, and the grant of leave to, persons belonging to the judicial service of a State and holding any post inferior to the post of district judge shall be vested in the High Court, but nothing in this article shall be construed as taking away from any such person any right of appeal which he may have under the law regulating the conditions of his service or as authorising the High Court to deal with him otherwise than in accordance with the conditions of his service prescribed under such law.'

36 Progressively, the number of women in the district judiciary, countrywide, has seen a marked increase in the recent years.

37 *Re Termination of Civil Judge, Class-II (Jr Division), Madhya Pradesh State Judicial Service* SMW (C) No 2 of 2023.

38 Omar Rashid, '"Harassment", Pleas and a Petition Dismissed in 8 Seconds: Behind Woman Civil Judge's Letter to CJI' (*The Wire*, 16 December 2023)

the then CJI took notice of the news report but we don't know the outcome of the case.[39]

Editor: *In the context of sexual harassment of women at the workplace, would you want to say anything about the case involving CJI Ranjan Gogoi?*

Ms Jaising: Unfortunately, the true facts will never be known since the enquiry report was kept under wraps. My speaking up on the subject had devastating consequences for me, but how much more would the woman herself have been devastated. The truth is, as I mentioned earlier, we have no satisfactory system of investigating allegations of sexual harassment against judges.

Editor: *You have handled the cases of Githa Hariharan[40] (parental rights) and Mary Roy[41] (property rights), which appear to be recognizing the agency of women. Would you say that these decisions, by coincidence, were rendered by judges who happened to be gender sensitive? What might have been your contribution to alter their perception?*

Ms Jaising: In my opinion, lawyers have a major contribution to make to the outcome of a case. Their conceptualization of the case on the drawing board and in their minds matters a lot. Ask the right questions and you will get the right answers. But I must tell you that, often, judges fight shy of answering a question directly. They do often come up with the right solution but the process of reasoning is not always robust. In that sense, these cases have left many things unsaid. All of them raised the question of the agency of women.

<https://thewire.in/women/civil-judges-letter-cji-sexual-harassment> accessed 24 February 2025; Her writ petition filed in the Supreme Court was dismissed on the ground that an Internal Complaints Committee was seized of the matter by a Bench consisting of Hrishikesh Roy and Sandeep Mehta.

[39] 'CJI Takes Note of Letter by Woman Judge Seeking "Permission to End Life" in Absence of Relief Against Sexual Harassment by District Judge' (*The Leaflet*, 15 December 2023) <https://theleaflet.in/judicial-accountability/cji-takes-note-of-letter-by-woman-judge-seeking-permission-to-end-life-in-absence-of-relief-against-sexual-harassment-by-district-judge> accessed 24 February 2025.

[40] *Githa Hariharan v. Reserve Bank of India* (1999) 2 SCC 228; A case where the SCI declared Section 6(a) of the Hindu Minority and Guardianship Act 1956, unconstitutional to the extent that it gave preferential guardianship rights to fathers over mothers, which violates Articles 14 and 15 of the Constitution of India.

[41] *Mary Roy v. State of Kerala* (1986) 2 SCC 209. In this case, the SCI held that Sections 16 and 19 of the Travancore Succession Act of 1092 are discriminatory against women by not providing them an equal share in the property of the intestate and hence violative of Articles 14 and 15 of the Constitution of India.

For me, *Githa Hariharan* was an open and shut case. The law says that the father is a natural guardian of a minor, and after him, the mother. What did the Court say? The judgment says that the words 'after him' will be interpreted to mean 'when the father is negligent'.[42]

Mary Roy again was for me an open and shut case. The law said in black and white that a daughter would inherit Rs 5,000 at maximum on the demise of her father, and the rest of the estate would go to the sons. As you know, Article 15 mandates that there shall be no discrimination based on sex alone and this was a case waiting to happen. We had a Bench of Justices RS Pathak and Bhagwati. I presumed that we would get an exposition of the law relating to equality for women. Instead, the judges said that the Travancore Christian Succession Act stood repealed since the Indian Succession Act automatically applied to the erstwhile territory of Travancore–Cochin.[43] I would think that the result of the case was just. Daughters and sons got equal rights to inheritance. However, an opportunity to state that any discrimination based on sex was unconstitutional was lost. The case sent shock waves in the State of Kerala. The Syrian Christian community is one of the wealthiest in Kerala. It is a land-owning, coffee-growing community. After that judgment, the daughters of the community started inheriting their share of the land. The case had a huge backlash. Lawyers started advising fathers to make wills disinheriting their daughters. Notwithstanding this, Mrs Mary Roy continued to support other women fighting for their share of land. Hence, although all these cases had a positive outcome, the issue of discrimination against women was not directly addressed.

Editor: *Would you like to reflect on the recent cases involving women and religion?*

Ms Jaising: It is necessary to talk about the more recent *Shayara Bano*[44] case, where too I appeared. None of the judges were willing to articulate a constitutional theory based on equality for women. Of the five judges, two dissented. One said what was bad in theology was bad in law.[45] It was Justice

42 *Githa Hariharan v. Reserve Bank of India* [39].

43 *Mary Roy v. State of Kerala* 1986(2) SCC 209 [6], [8].

44 *Shayara Bano v. Union of India* (2017) 9 SCC 1 (Triple Talaq case).

45 Opinion of Kurian Joseph J in *Shayara Bano v. Union of India* [1]–[27].

Nariman who came closest to saying the law was unconstitutional.[46] The difficulty for judges has always been the inability to separate law from religion in the domain of personal laws, all of which are based on religious texts. Equality for women in the domain of personal laws remains the unfinished agenda of the Supreme Court to seventy-five years after the Constitution of India came into force.

The *Sabarimala*[47] case raised a direct conflict between the right of women to equality on the one hand and the rights of religious establishments to manage their own affairs on the other hand. Women in the age group of 10 to 50 were not permitted to enter the temple. In a historic 4:1 judgment,[48] the Court held that they had a right to enter the temple and the rights under Article were guaranteed to 'all persons', and this expression obviously included women. This is the closest the Court has come to dealing with the conflict of rights of women to equality and religion. The discrimination was based on the fact that during those years women menstruate, and they are considered 'impure'.[49]

I was disappointed when the five-judge Bench decision in *Sabarimala* was referred to a Bench of nine judges for review.[50] Now you will understand why I said that de-linking religion from personal laws is the unfinished agenda of the Supreme Court – and unfinished agenda for social change, which was the demand on 'the other side of Independence'.

---

[46] The test of manifest arbitrariness was applied by Rohinton Nariman J to strike down triple talaq; *Shayara Bano v. Union of India* [102], [104].

[47] *Indian Young Lawyers Association v. State of Kerala* (2019) 11 SCC 1.

[48] There was a strong dissent by Indu Malhotra J who held that Article 14 could not be the only touchstone to test religious practices, that the practice of not allowing women of certain ages was an essential religious practice and that the argument equating not allowing entry of women to right against untouchability under Article 17 was misconceived; *Indian Young Lawyers Association v. State of Kerala* (2019) 11 SCC 1 [425]–[541].

[49] No civilized jurisprudence can accept that proposition, and the Court did not. Chandrachud J articulated best the historic fight for social justice, which began long before the Constitution had been drafted in *Indian Young Lawyers Association v. State of Kerala* [334]. 'Reading Dr Ambedkar compels us to look at the other side of the independence movement. Besides the struggle for independence from the British rule, there was another struggle going on since centuries and which still continues. That struggle has been for social emancipation. It has been the struggle for the replacement of an unequal social order. It has been a fight for undoing historical injustices and for righting fundamental wrongs with fundamental rights. The Constitution of India is the end product of both these struggles. It is the foundational document, which in text and spirit, aims at social transformation namely, the creation and preservation of an equal social order. The Constitution represents the aspirations of those, who were denied the basic ingredients of a dignified existence.'; This passage is memorable for it recognizes that social change is a continuous process, and courts must interpret the Constitution in the context of the aspiration for equality for women.

[50] See Rohan Alva's essay in this book.

Editor: *On the issue of medical termination of pregnancy, there was this Bench of Justices Hima Kohli and Nagarathna that initially allowed the prayer. However, when the Union of India came back to Court to say that one of the doctors in the medical board had observed that the foetus had a heartbeat, Justice Hima Kohli had a rethink.*[51] *When the matter went before a larger Bench, which refused permission to terminate the pregnancy, neither of the two women judges were part of it. What are your thoughts on this episode?*

Ms Jaising: I find this a breach of protocol. There is an unwritten convention that the differing judges who first heard the case must be part of the larger Bench. Moreover, it would be expected that in a matter of this kind, women judges would be on the case to bring a diversity of opinions to the Bench. Indian law thus far has not gone the American way of projecting the issue as pro-choice versus pro-life. It is unfortunate that despite the pregnant woman saying that she could not carry the burden of another child, she was refused permission to go ahead with the abortion. It was almost heartless to reject her case.

Editor: *On the Mahmood Farooqui case,*[52] *one would have expected a detailed judgment from the Supreme Court as the question, in the context of rape, was whether 'no means no' and that 'no does not mean yes'. What are your thoughts?*

Ms Jaising: I have written[53] on why the High Court judge as well as the Supreme Court, failed to distinguish between what are the elements of the

---

[51] In *XYZ v. Union of India* WPC No 1137 of 2023 vide order dated 9 October 2023, the Bench comprising Hima Kohli and BV Nagarathna JJ passed an order allowing a married woman to terminate her twenty-six-week pregnancy. In the same matter, a day later, on 10 October 2023, an application for recall was filed by the Union of India based on the report of one doctor of the Medical Board of the All India Institute of Medical Sciences, which said the foetus is 'viable'. The same Bench now pronounced a split verdict – Nagarathna J refused to interfere with the earlier order, Kohli J recorded her inclination to not allow the termination of pregnancy. Thereafter, the matter was placed before the CJI to constitute a Bench of three judges to decide the case. By an order dated 16 October 2023, a three-Judge Bench composed of CJI DY Chandrachud, JB Pardiwala and Manoj Misra JJ rejected the plea of termination on the basis that the child is viable and has a heartbeat. Interestingly, the CJI constituted the Bench leaving out both Kohli and Nagarathna JJ and also not including the other woman judge in the Court, Bela Trivedi J.

[52] In *Mahmood Faqooqui v. State (Govt. of NCT of Delhi)* (2017) 243 DLT 310, an order of conviction under Section 376(1) was overturned by the Delhi HC. Thereafter, In *X v. Mahmood Farooqui* 2018 SCC Online SC 3353, the appeal against the HC order was dismissed.

[53] Indira Jaising, 'Mahmood Farooqui's Acquittal Will Have Devastating Consequences for Rape Victims' (*The Hindustan Times*, 29 September 2017).

offence and what is the defence. When a woman asserted that she said 'no', the burden of proof shifts to the accused to prove that she indeed consented. Consent is then a defence that the accused can take; where is the question of the woman proving that hers was not a 'feeble' no! Apart from being a misogynist judgment, it was also legally incorrect. The court missed an opportunity to clarify this point.

There is another very important case which links with this – the pending case in the Supreme Court on marital rape.[54] Now we all know what happened in the Delhi High Court. One judgment held that the exception to Section 375 IPC was unconstitutional, the other that it was not.[55] But there was a third way. I am dealing with the case where under the existing law, a judge of the Karnataka High Court has allowed framing of charges against the husband, at the instance of a wife.[56] And I am defending that judgment. I think this presents an opportunity to creatively and constructively interpret the existing law. I am arguing that the outcome will depend on our conception of what marriage is. It is a partnership of equals which it must be, there is no question of an 'exemption' to the rape law in marriage, sexual intercourse is a matter of mutual desire to strengthen bonds of love and affection.

Editor: *There are times when Article 142 is used like in Vishaka,*[57] *which then triggers the law-making process. You took another approach with the Protection of Women from Domestic Violence Act, 2006. What is your general thinking on engaging the judiciary to fill the legal vacuum, or would you rather first have a law enacted and get the judiciary to take it further?*

Ms Jaising: Definitely the latter of the two. I believe that *Vishaka* is a judgment that has not achieved its stated aim. It was filed in the name of Bhanwari Devi, and she is still waiting for justice in the Rajasthan High Court.[58] Secondly, the issue of sexual harassment at the workplace falls primarily within the domain

---

[54] *Hrishikesh Sahoo v. State of Karnataka* SLP (Crl) Nos 4063–4064 of 2022.

[55] *RIT Foundation v. Union of India* (2023) 3 HCC (Del) 572; The Bench of Rajiv Shakdher and Hari Shankar JJ delivered a split verdict; Shakdher J being prepared to accept marital rape as an offence and Hari Shankar J disinclined to do so.

[56] *Hrishikesh Sahoo v. State of Karnataka* (2022) 2 KCCR 145.

[57] *Vishakha v. State of Rajasthan* (1997) 6 SCC 241.

[58] Sachin Saini, 'Bhanwari Devi: Justice eluded her, but she stands resolute for others' (*The Hindustan Times*, 17 September 2021).

of labour law. The inability to classify laws in their true domain can lead to the effort being frittered away.

While *Vishaka* brought into the public domain, the issue of sexual harassment in the workplace, it left a lot unsaid of the other situations in which it takes place. These may not be employment related but still are hierarchical and unequal. Statutes on the other hand are meant to deal with all kinds of hypothetical situations anticipated in advance, based on the felt needs of society on empirical data systematically collected. Laws are drafted through a proper consultative process that can account for the myriad of circumstances and situations in which such a law might apply. First you had *Vishaka*, then you got the Sexual Harassment of Women at Workplace (Prevention, Prohibition and Redressal) Act, 2013. The Act suffers from the same problems that the judgment does. There is no clarity under the Act whether the recommendations of the Fact-Finding Committee are binding, and whether, for example, the inquiry report will be accepted as a report under Article 311 of the Constitution of India.

A good example of a well drafted law is The Human Immunodeficiency Virus and Acquired Immune Deficiency Syndrome (Prevention and Control) Act, 2017, which is the only anti-discrimination law in this country today. It was *Lawyers Collective* that held a nationwide consultation on the law with the affected community.[59] Similarly the Protection of Women from Domestic Violence Act, 2005, was drafted in consultation with the community. I believe there is a need to constantly review the working of the statutes. Recently, the Supreme Court highlighted the need for reviewing the enacted laws for their effectiveness.[60]

Editor: *On the provision of legal aid and legal services through private initiatives, Lawyers Collective was among the pioneering efforts where lawyers offered their professional inputs on a pro bono basis. Where do you think our formal legal services system is failing? What are your views on improving access to justice in courts?*

Ms Jaising: So first, I will tell you the inspiration behind the setting up of Lawyers Collective. This comes from a trip which I had made to London

[59] Laws in consultation with the affected community are at least, in theory, dealing with the felt needs of the community. Lawyers Collective drafted the law, and the law says that no doctor can discriminate against any person who is HIV positive or deny medical service.

[60] *Yash Developers v. Harihar Krupa Co-operative Housing Society Limited* 2024 (9) SCC 606 [57]-[64].

at a point in time where the 'Law Centres' movement started in the mid 70s. Law Centres were set up within communities. This led to the Law Centres producing legal literature in simple English to make law accessible to the people. These were being funded by local counties and boroughs. This movement created a cadre of lawyers committed to the idea of legal aid. Criminal law in the United Kingdom has always been funded by legal aid, as no accused persons should go unrepresented for want of resources.

I agree that there is no actual shortage of funds for legal services in India.[61] It is the lack of spending on actual legal aid, that is, representation for people in need of lawyers, that is the issue. A lot of money is being spent on salaries for the staff and in organizing meetings of the authorities, apart from Lok Adalats.[62]

Although the Legal Services Authorities Act does not mandate it, by convention, the second senior-most judge of the Supreme Court is invariably nominated by the CJI as the Executive Chairperson of the NALSA (National Legal Services Authority).[63] There needs to be a separation of the judiciary from the administration of the legal services authorities (LSAs).

The formal legal aid system has been unable to attract the best available legal talent. Bright young lawyers, under supervision of the seasoned ones, can contribute to strengthening the work of the legal services authorities.

The criminal justice system should also be well-funded. We need to evaluate the effectiveness of the system of the Legal Aid Defense Counsel Scheme introduced by NALSA in 2022.[64]

---

[61] Raja Bagga, *Hope Behind Bars? Status Report on Legal Aid for Persons in Custody* (Commonwealth Human Rights Initiative 2018) 23, 77–78 <https://www.humanrightsinitiative.org/download/CHRI%20Legal%20Aid%20Report%20Hope%20Behind%20Bars%20Volume%201.pdf> accessed 22 November 2024; Soibam Rocky Singh, '15% of Funds Allocated to State Legal Services Stay Unused' (*The Hindu*, 10 September 2018) <https://www.thehindu.com/news/cities/Delhi/15-of-funds-allocated-to-state-legal-services-stay-unused/article24911399.ece> accessed 22 November 2024.

[62] Gursimran Kaur Bakshi, 'NALSA Says It Doesn't Have Funds but Accommodates Judges in 5-Star Hotels for Conferences: Justice Dipankar Dutta' (*LiveLaw*, 2 October 2024) <https://www.livelaw.in/top-stories/nalsa-says-it-doesnt-have-funds-but-accommodates-judges-in-5-star-hotels-for-conferences-justice-dipankar-dutta-271347> accessed 24 February 2025.

[63] Correspondingly, the second senior-most judge of the HC is invariably nominated by the CJ as the Executive Chairperson of the State Legal Services Authority.

[64] 'Legal Aid Defense Counsel System (Modified)' (The National Legal Services Authority, 2022) <https://nalsa.gov.in/acts-rules/guidelines/legal-aid-defense-counsel-system-2> accessed 24 February 2025.

It is a pity that even today, several undertrials in jail are going unrepresented. The one solution that is yet to be tried might be for NALSA to accredit law firms based on protocols to provide legal aid to accused persons.

That is not to say that the LSAs at present are not doing good work. I would like to mention one particular case where the Delhi High Court Legal Services Committee provided witness protection to a woman who was being intimidated to give up her complaint, by anonymizing her identity, relocating her and providing her with a new phone number to access legal services without being detected. These measures helped her through the case.

There are other tried and tested solutions. For instance, in the United States, there are students who attend Ivy League colleges by taking loans, but they get waivers of loans if they agree to do two or three years of public interest work. The exposure of one's early years in the profession stays with you. I have interns from all over the world who have worked with *Lawyers Collective*, and no matter where they are today, the experience has impacted their work as lawyers and they remain committed to providing *pro bono* legal services. Similarly, lawyers who have worked with *Lawyers Collective* have gone on to establish their own law practices, but they continue to integrate *pro bono* work in their legal practice

Another suggestion is that the Bar Council of India should amend its rules to permit paralegals to offer legal services to litigants and even appear before some of the tribunals.

Editor: *There is a view that in the recent past, there has been a communal element to appointments to the higher judiciary. Do you agree?*

Ms Jaising: It is no longer possible to argue that consultation with the judiciary for the appointment of judges means with the concurrence of the judiciary. It is relevant to discuss the case of Justice Victoria Gowri's appointment to the Madras High Court. Her appointment was challenged by a group of lawyers practising in the Madras High Court.[65] The question they raised was not only should a person be eligible for appointment but must also be suitable for appointment. The petitioners pointed out that, in her utterances as the General Secretary of the Mahila Morcha (women's wing) of the ruling party

[65] *Anna Mathew v. Supreme Court of India* Writ Petition (Civil) No 148 of 2023, order dated 7 February 2023.

at the Centre, she had spoken about white terror (Christian terror) and green terror (Islamic terror).[66] But the Court said, 'Oh, but the criteria laid down by the Constitution has been followed, she's got more than 10 years practice.' The real issue was: did she have a commitment to the values of the Preamble to the Constitution of India which was not addressed. That should answer your question on the communalizing of the judiciary.

I would also like to put on record that the kind of polarization that I have seen at the Bar is a new phenomenon of the last seventy-five years. Most agendas are political in nature and law reform is the casualty. It's the Bar itself which is getting increasingly communalized. We must remember that judges are drawn largely from the Bar.

Editor: *I would like us to discuss generally the issue of pendency and arrears in courts. It appears that with increased filing and not enough judges, the problem of delay in disposal of cases is only going to get worse. Compounding this, we have instances of cases taken out of turn and then occupying the courts' time to a disproportionate extent. What are your thoughts on where we are headed?*

Ms Jaising: I frankly think it is not enough for us to say that we do not have enough judges (although this is a fact). The legal profession, or the legal system as a whole, has reached its lowest ebb in the last seventy-five years by living in an adjournment culture. I have always held the view that the arrears are not a function of just the number of judges not being equal to the workload. Not all judges work at the same pace they are meant to. I have often walked into a courtroom during court working hours and found it empty either due to bad court management or due to an unanticipated adjournment. Tribunalization has not solved the problem, nor has arbitration. The adjournment culture has spread into these forums as well.

The legal profession is also a big contributor to this. More than eighty per cent of the work, in any court in the hierarchy is with just twenty per cent of the lawyers in that Bar. Recently, a junior lawyer was telling me that your ability to be heard in the Supreme Court depends on your ability to mention matters. This is the reason why Senior Advocates are engaged.

---

[66] Saurav Das, '"Problem of Christian, Love Jihad": A Future Judge's Bias Reveals Supreme Court Collegium's Enduring Opacity' (Article 14, 30 January 2023) <https://www.article-14.com/post/-problem-of-christian-love-jihad-a-future-judge-s-bias-reveals-supreme-court-collegium-s-enduring-opacity-63d73360b1296> accessed 24 February 2025.

I find that although some cases are taken up *suo motu* by the Supreme Court – and I do not resent the time they get in Court – they are either not taken to the logical end or they do not produce anything useful in terms of addressing the real issue. One such recent instance, the *RG Kar* case.[67] Also take Manipur,[68] where there has been no logical conclusion.

Reflecting on seventy-five years of the Supreme Court, the earlier progressive jurisprudence and acceptable standards of behaviour by judges, have, in my view, taken a downwards trajectory. This might be seen as a pessimistic conclusion. However, it is encouraging to see young lawyers being alive to the dangers posed to the ideas of the Constitution and values enshrined in its Preamble. I can see that many of them are actively representing those in need of their services. It is my hope that they will one day go on to become the judges of the future.

---

[67] *In Re: Alleged Rape and Murder Incident of a Trainee Doctor in RG Kar Medical College and Hospital, Kolkata and Related Issues* Suo Motu Writ (Crl) No 2 of 2024.

[68] *Dinganglung Gangmei v. Mutum Churamani Meetei* Special Leave Petition (Civil) Diary No 19206 of 2023.

Part IV

The Court and Substantive Laws

Cartoon © SanitaryPanels.

Labour Laws and the Supreme Court

K CHANDRU

Long before the Supreme Court of India (SCI) was established, labour laws were in existence.[1] However, the labour jurisprudence that could have been expected of the courts was still a work in progress. Before an attempt is made to review the decisions rendered by the SCI for over a period of seven and a half decades, it is necessary to have a certain historical background on the labour laws themselves and the issues they were attempting to resolve.

In this essay, the main focus will be on the decisions of the SCI interpreting various provisions of the Industrial Disputes Act, 1947 (ID Act), as much of the litigation in the labour law field emanated from this statute. This essay also seeks to examine the development of the law through particular areas like contract labour, child labour and women in the workforce.

The History of Labour Legislation in India

Much of the statute law in India is a continuation, with modifications and additions, of the laws introduced by the British. However, the provisions for workers' safety found in the labour law statutes in the United Kingdom prior to 1947[2] were absent in the corresponding statutes in India. As the British Empire expanded, there was also forced expatriation of indentured labour worldwide to far-off islands in the British colonies,[3] without any corresponding provisions for their welfare and safety. The ascension of Empress Victoria and the establishment of the British–Indian Empire in 1857 did little to improve the conditions of labour.

---

1 For instance, the Factory Act 1881.

2 Factory Act 1833; Workmen's Compensation Act 1906.

3 These workers found themselves in the rubber plantations in Malaya and in the tea and coffee plantations and sugarcane fields in South Africa, the Caribbean and even the Fiji Islands.

At the end of World War I, the International Labour Organization (ILO) was formed in 1919, and British India became a member. Gradually, some of the conventions and resolutions of the ILO intended to protect labour from exploitation were given effect to in different forms in India as well. Persistent uneasiness regarding the gross exploitation of Indian labour caused for a Royal Commission of Labour (RCL) to be appointed by the House of Commons. The RCL, after its visit and inquiries in India, submitted a report to the British Parliament in 1931. It noted that the need for organization among Indian workers was great and that nothing but a strong trade union movement would provide adequate protection for them.[4] The Report further noted that there was glaring exploitation and very little concern for the safety, health and welfare of the workers.[5]

The Trade Unions Act, 1926; Workmen's Compensation Act, 1923 (now renamed as Employees Compensation Act); Mines Act, 1923; and a few factory regulations were some of the statutes concerning workers that were subsequently introduced. The Trade Disputes Bill of 1929, when introduced in the Central Legislative Assembly, met with stiff resistance from the All-India Trade Union Congress (AITUC).[6] In the period between the two World Wars, the only labour legislation that merits mention is the Payment of Wages Act, 1936, which regulated the timely payment of wages without huge fines and deductions. The period in and around the year of Indian Independence witnessed the enactment of significant labour legislations including the Bombay Industrial Relations Act, 1946; the Industrial Disputes Act, 1947; the Industrial Employment (Standing Orders) Act, 1946; Factories Act 1948; and the Employees State Insurance Act, 1948.[7]

Article 23 of the Constitution of India prohibited bonded labour and Article 24 prohibited the employment of children in factories, mines and hazardous

---

4 *Report of the Royal Commission on Labour in India* (Central Publication Branch 1931) ch XXI; The Commission's report finally said: 'Everything that we have seen in India has forced upon us the conviction that the need of organisation among Indian workmen is great . . . Nothing but a strong Trade Union movement will give the Indian workman adequate protection . . . It is in the power to combine that labour has the only effective safeguard against exploitation, and the only lasting security against inhumane conditions.'

5 ibid.

6 The Trade Disputes Act did not recognize the right of the workers to have collective bargaining. Further, even the decisions of the labour fora were not enforceable against the employers. The statutory right of the workers to collective bargaining was also not provided for.

7 Some of the state legislatures also enacted special legislations like the Shops and Establishments Act, for instance, the Madras Shops and Establishments Act 1947.

employment. Part IV of the Constitution, prescribing directive principles of state policy, was essentially a socialist charter and had several provisions for protecting the interests of labour. This provided a springboard for the new Parliament to enact several labour legislations.[8]

The Industrial Disputes Act, 1947 provided for the investigation and settlement of industrial disputes and established the machinery for conciliation and adjudication in these matters. The decisions of the labour courts and industrial tribunals were subject to appeal before the Labour Appellate Tribunal (LAT), whose orders could be appealed to the Federal Court.

With the establishment of the SCI in 1950, and the subsequent abolition of the LATs, the SCI became the final arbiter of all industrial disputes. Having been groomed in civil disputes governed by the Code of Civil Procedure (CPC), the judges of the SCI in the early years borrowed heavily from the labour jurisprudence of various Commonwealth countries as well as the United States of America.[9]

An Overview of the Supreme Court's Labour Jurisprudence

The span of seventy-five years of the SCI can be divided into four different periods, and certain landmark decisions could be referred to justify and illustrate the approach adopted in those periods. During the first two decades (1950–70), the Court largely took a cautious approach. It must be noted that the SCI was almost the fourth and final tier of appeal for labour matters. Finding a 'substantial question of law of general importance'[10] as required under Article 133 was the aim of the Court.

The second phase covered the period from 1970 to 1990. The SCI showed a liberal approach that used Part IV of the Constitution as an interpretative tool.[11] The third phase was between 1990 and 2005. This saw the advent of liberalization, privatization and globalization (LPG). This not only affected

---

[8] For instance, the Employees Provident Fund Act 1952, and the Maternity Benefit Act 1961.

[9] *Bharat Bank Ltd, Delhi v. Employees of the Bharat Bank Ltd, Delhi* AIR 1950 SC 188, *DN Banerji v. PR Mukherjee* AIR 1953 SC 58.

[10] Constitution of India 1950, art 133.

[11] This period saw an upsurge in labour litigation and some legal engineering was adopted by certain judges, which created a degree of hope and faith in the legal system among the working class. Once again, this observation has to be seen in the context set out earlier, i.e., that the composition of the Benches also determined the outcome of the litigation.

decision-making but found wholehearted support in some of the Court's decisions.[12] The fourth phase, which began in 2006 and continues till date, has hardly had any significant decision contributing to the development of labour jurisprudence. The larger Bench references made in an earlier phase were not dealt with by succeeding Chief Justices of India (CJIs). Thus, the disposal rates of labour cases have seen a significant slowdown.

Right from the inception of the SCI, there have been two significant trends in the sphere of labour rights. One, the liberal trend, which invariably leaned towards labour; the other, the conservative school that maintained an interpretation that outright favoured capital and went beyond the letter and spirit of the law. It appears that while in the initial years, the definitions in the ID Act did not pose too much difficulty for the SCI to interpret, the fact is that even after seventy-seven years of that statute, there is a continuing uncertainty in the interpretation of those definitions in litigation. One is reminded of the warning administered by Krishna Iyer J that '[s]emantic luxuries are misplaced in the interpretation of "bread and butter" statutes.'[13]

Industry

Section 2 (j) of the ID Act defines 'industry' to mean 'any business, trade, undertaking, manufacture or calling of employers and includes any calling, service, employment, handicraft or industrial occupation or avocation of workmen'. Since 1952, there have been several decisions of the SCI interpreting the expression 'industry'. While one trend of decisions continued to define the term with a broader social perspective, the other attempted to narrow down its application so as to exclude several categories from the purview of the statute. In 1952, when a matter came from a municipality, the issue before the court was whether there should be a profit motive involved for an institution to be covered under the ID Act. A Constitution Bench, speaking through N Chandrasekhara Aiyar J, clearly laid down the legal proposition that to form an industry, one need not be doing a trade or business.[14] This was affirmed in a later decision by SK Das J.[15]

---

12 The established concepts and interpretations were questioned by some Benches and references were made to larger Benches, thereby creating a greater amount of uncertainty among and disappointment for the working class.

13 *Surendra Kumar Verma v. The Central Government Industrial Tribunal Cum Labour Court* (1980) 4 SCC 443, 447.

14 *DN Banerji v. PR Mukherjee* (1952) 2 SCC 619 [17].

15 *Baroda Borough Municipality v. Its Workmen* AIR 1957 SC 110.

In a subsequent case, in the context of whether a 'hospital' would come under the definition of 'industry', a three-judge Bench headed by PB Gajendragadkar J reiterated that institutions could not be excluded by reason of having a non-profit motive.[16]

Two distinct changes took place soon after the 1960s. First, the composition of the Court underwent extensive changes when most of the old guards left the SCI. Second, there were two significant developments at the national level. The first was the Indo-China border dispute resulting in a declaration of Emergency in 1962, and the second, the Indo-Pakistan war of 1965. During the former, many of the leaders of the leading trade union federation of workmen, the AITUC were detained under various detention laws. There were restrictions on trade unions and social movements. This had a bearing on the minds of judges when they were adjudicating labour disputes. Subsequent decades saw certain smaller Benches consistently doubting prevailing conceptions of the term 'industry'. At least three cases took diametrically opposite views. Gajendragadkar J was responsible for initiating this line of inquiry, stating that the expansive definition of industry required stricter demarcations.[17]

Once the line of distinction was started, it was easy for others to carry this battle further. Hidayatullah J, in a three-judge Bench, exempted the Madras Gymkhana Club from the application of the ID Act, stating that the element of trade or business was completely missing in a members' club.[18] Later, sitting in a six-judge Bench, Hidayatullah J wrote for the unanimous Court that a hospital was not an industry[19] and distinguished the earlier *Bombay Hospital*[20] case. The Court held that the hospital was not engaged in an economic activity, was run as a department of the Government, and that the treatment of persons was part of the functions of the Government.

---

16 *State of Bombay v. Hospital Mazdoor Sabha* AIR 1960 SC 610 (*Bombay Hospital* case).

17 *The National. Union of Commercial Employees v. MR Meher, Industrial Tribunal Bombay* AIR 1962 SC 1080; *University of Delhi v. Ram Nath* AIR 1963 SC 1873.

18 *Secretary, Madras Gymkhana Club Employees' Union v. Management of the Gymkhana Club* AIR 1968 SC 554.

19 *The Management of Safdarjung Hospital v. Kuldip Singh Sethi* (1970) 1 SCC 735; In *Dhanrajgirji Hospital v. Workmen*, (1975) 4 SCC 621, a subsequent Bench comprising of NL Untwalia and A Alagiriswami JJ, known for their conservative views on labour matters, did not lag behind and by following *Safdarjung Hospital* held that the Dhanrajgirji Hospital is also not an industry covered by the ID Act.

20 *Bombay Hospital* case (n 16); This was made by a three-judge Bench of the Court comprising Gajendragadkar, Subba Rao and KC Das Gupta JJ.

To know the mindset of Alagiriswami J, known for his conservative viewpoint on labour issues, it is enough if one looks at his dissenting opinion in *Sukhdev Singh v. Bagatram Sardar Singh Raghuvanshi*[21] where the SCI gave a liberal interpretation of the term 'State' within the meaning of Article 12 of the Constitution. The majority, headed by AN Ray J, held that a public-sector entity, whether created by or under a statute, if substantially owned by the government, would be a State within the meaning of Article 12. This expansion led to another area of litigation, that is, by public-sector employees who were given constitutional status. It also gave them an opportunity to question their service conditions on the touchstone of Part III of the Constitution.

Alagiriswami J in his dissent opined that the labour force was not as 'weak or helpless' as it had been in the nineteenth century. Referring to powerful lobbying activities in England and the United States, he commented that trade unions were coming up to the SCI even against interim orders of the industrial tribunals, turning the regulatory framework into a litigant's paradise.[22]

This observation of Alagiriswami J was not based on facts. Only a year earlier, the report of an expert committee headed by VR Krishna Iyer J found that it was the employers who were repeatedly approaching the SCI in order to delay the implementation of awards.[23] In 1983, a three-judge Bench headed by Chinnappa Reddy J observed that it was a pity that even public-sector establishments, which are instrumentalities of the State, were attempting to absolve themselves of any wrongdoing, thus wasting public time and money.[24]

This equivocation, over three decades, on interpreting the definition of 'industry' under the ID Act led to the decision of a seven-judge Bench in *Bangalore Water Supply and Sewerage Board v. R Rajappa*.[25] The decision was

---

21 (1975) 1 SCC 421.

22 ibid.

23 'Report of the Expert Committee on Legal Aid: Processual Justice to the People' (Ministry of Law, Justice and Company Affairs, Government of India May 1973); The Report showed that in 1960 about 550 appeals were filed by employers and workers in the SCI during 1955–59. Of these, 421 (or seventy-seven per cent) were filed by employers and 128 (or twenty-three per cent) by workers or their unions. The report noted that the Court took a long time to decide many of these cases, and sixty-three per cent of the 286 employer's appeals decided by the SCI were unsuccessful. In sixty per cent of the cases in which employers were unsuccessful, and for which information is available, the implementation of awards was delayed by two to six years.

24 *SK Verma v. Mahesh Chandra* (1983) 4 SCC 214.

25 *Bangalore Water Supply & Sewerage Board v. R Rajappa* (1978) 2 SCC 213.

by a 5:2 majority.[26] Divided on ideological lines, the majority held that an 'industry is a continuity, is an organized activity, is a purposeful pursuit – not any isolated adventure, desultory excursion or casual, fleeting engagement motivelessly undertaken. Such is the common feature of a trade, business, calling, manufacture- mechanical or handicraft based-service, employment, industrial occupation or avocation'.[27] The Bench urged the Parliament to appropriately define the term 'industry'. Taking a cue from the judgment, the Parliament redefined the term 'industry' under Section 2 (j) of the ID Act in the year 1982. However, the said amendment is yet to be notified, even after forty-two years. One explanation could be that no alternative remedies were provided for those categories excluded from the ID Act. The judgment has been doubted in cases thereafter.[28] Although a direction was issued in 2017 that the CJI should constitute a nine-judge Bench to reconsider the issue,[29] it was only in 2024 that the cases in the batch were listed before such a Bench. It could, however, not be taken up for hearing. The question remains whether, for nearly seventy-seven years, the definition of the term 'industry' should be allowed to remain uncertain. In this scenario, one can well imagine what the predicament of labour is in the courts today.

Despite the references to a larger Bench, several two-judge Benches started making exceptions for government-run departments under the plea that they were discharging sovereign functions. Just before his retirement K Ramasamy J, otherwise a very progressive judge, was the author of three decisions that sought to exclude the postal, telegraph and telephone services establishments from the ID Act on the ground that they were discharging

---

26 The majority comprised, apart from MH Beg CJ, Krishna Iyer J (who wrote the judgment), PN Bhagwati, DA Desai and YV Chandrachud JJ. The two dissenters were Jaswant Singh and Tulzapurkar JJ.

27 *Bangalore Water Supply & Sewerage Board* (n 25); The Court further observed that 'it is legitimate to project the value set of the Constitution, especially Part IV, in reading the meaning of even a pre-Constitution statute. The paramount law is paramount and Part IV sets out Directive Principles of State Policy, which must guide the Judiciary, like other instrumentalities, in interpreting all legislation.'

28 *Coir Board, Ernakulam, Cochin v. Indira Devi PS* (1998) 3 SCC 259; *State of Uttar Pradesh v. Jai Bir Singh* (2005) 5 SCC 1, with the Bench comprising DM Dharmadhikari, N Santosh Hegde, KG Balakrishnan, Arun Kumar and BN Srikrishna JJ.

29 *State of Uttar Pradesh v. Jai Bir Singh* (2017) 3 SCC 311, O Chinnappa Reddy J, post-retirement, criticized the frequent referral of cases to Benches, remarking that questioning the worker-oriented judgment in *Bangalore Water Supply* was akin to narrowly interpreting pro-weaker-section provisions like Articles 15, 16 and the Directive Principles; See O Chinnappa Reddy, *The Court and the Constitution of India* (Oxford University Press 2008) 187.

sovereign functions.[30] This was despite their being defined as 'public utility services' under Section 2 (1) (n) of the ID Act. By then most of these services were by and large privatized.

However, these attempts to shield sovereign activity were superseded by *Bangalore Water Supply*. Subsequent Benches, bound by the seven-judge decision, were therefore unable to subscribe to the view by K Ramaswamy J.[31]

The Industrial Relations Code enacted in 2020 retains the definition of the term 'industry' as declared by the seven-judge Bench in the *Bangalore Water Supply* case while at the same time excluding (i) institutions owned or managed by organizations wholly or substantially engaged in any charitable, social or philanthropic service; and (ii) any activity of the appropriate Government related to sovereign functions, including all the activities carried on by the departments of the Central Government dealing with defence research, atomic energy and space. However, as of the writing of this essay, the said Code has not been notified. There is still hope that the eight-decade-old battle over the definition of 'industry' will be laid to rest.

Retrenchment

A subsequent problem was the highly litigated question as to what constitutes the term 'retrenchment' within the meaning of Section 2 (oo) of the ID Act. The term, with the exception of voluntary retirement, retirement and termination on grounds of ill-health read as follows: '"[R]etrenchment" means the termination by the employer of the service of a workman for any reason whatsoever, otherwise than as a punishment inflicted by way of disciplinary action.'

In *State Bank of India v. N Sundara Money* (*Sundara Money*), while interpreting the provision, Krishna Iyer J underscored that welfare legislation demands a 'teleological purpose and protective intendment', not mere 'cold print' or 'grammatical construction'.[32] Highlighting the 'comprehensive definition' of the term, the Court held that 'termination embraces not merely the act . . .

30 *Sub-Divisional Inspector of Post, Vaikan v. Theyyam Joseph* (1996) 8 SCC 489; *Physical Research Laboratory v. KG Sharma* (1997) 4 SCC 257; *Bombay Telephone Canteen Employees' Association v. Union of India* (1997) 6 SCC 723.

31 *General Manager, Telecom v. S Srinivasa Rao* (1997) 8 SCC 767.

32 *State Bank of India v. N Sundara Money* (1976) 1 SCC 822.

but the fact of termination howsoever produced', and that the words 'for any reason whatsoever' were 'very wide and almost admit of no exception'.[33] Despite the attempt in another case by the employers and Chambers of Commerce, to have the issue reconsidered,[34] the decision in the *Sundara Money* case was eventually upheld by a Constitution Bench.[35] The employers did not litigate any further, since the Parliament came to their rescue and added a sub-clause in the form of Section 2 (oo) (bb) to the definition of the term 'retrenchment', which made the earlier interpretation unworkable.

Strike and Lock-Out

The term 'strike' is defined under Section 2 (q) and the term 'lock-out' under Section 2 (l) of the ID Act. Both required notices to be given by the respective parties. However, resort to either step during the pendency of conciliation or adjudication or the life of an award was prohibited and invited penalties, including imprisonment. Once an industry was declared a 'public utility service', then the issuance of a strike notice was mandatory, which would start the process of conciliation, failing which the matter would move to adjudication. During this period, resorting to a strike was made illegal. Although rare, one employer had a strike declared illegal through arbitration, leading to heavy penalties on the workers. The arbitrator's award was challenged in Court, despite the employer being private and typically outside writ jurisdiction. A Bench headed by Krishna Iyer J ruled that since strikes are governed by the ID Act, remedies must be sought within its framework, stating that tort claims by employers against workers have 'not found a place in the pharmacopoeia of Indian Industrial Law'.[36]

The right to strike was not treated as part of the workmen's arsenal by the SCI from the very beginning. In the case of a railway union leader, he was removed by an order of the railways under the Railway Services (Safeguarding of National Security) Rules, 1949. A challenge made to the removal order was negatived by a Constitution Bench of the SCI. TL Venkatarama Ayyar J,

---

[33] ibid; The Court was critical of the bank coming in appeal and observed that the matter could have been settled with half-a-month's pay, and instead took years to resolve.

[34] *Mgt of Karnataka State Road Transport Corporation v. M Boraiah* (1984) 1 SCC 244.

[35] *Punjab Land Development and Reclamation Corporation Ltd v. Presiding Officer, Labour Court, Chandigarh* (1990) 3 SCC 682.

[36] *Rohtas Industries Ltd v. Rohtas Industries Staff Union* (1976) 2 SCC 82.

speaking for the Court, held that while the appellants have a fundamental right to form associations under Article 19 (1) (c), they do not have a right to continued employment with the State and cannot claim a constitutional infringement when their services are terminated.[37]

This position was somewhat relaxed when another Constitution Bench subsequently held that government servants while in service were also entitled to the protection of the Fundamental Rights provisions under Part III of the Constitution. They had the right to form an association and demonstrate in furtherance of their demands, but that did not include the right to strike.[38] This position of law was further reinforced by subsequent judgments.[39]

Even conducting demonstrations and holding meetings on an employer's premises was denied to workers, as the SCI stated that '[t]he Indian Railways, though a State Undertaking, have the right to enjoy their properties like any private individual'. The Court further emphasized that '[t]here is no fundamental right to hold meetings in government premises', warning that allowing such action would lead to chaos.[40]

The Court also denied the right of the trade union to have access to the details of the financial workings of the banks in relation to their dispute demanding a profit-sharing bonus. The Court held that the fundamental right to form an association under Article 19 (1) (c), did not carry a concomitant right to seek information from the employer.[41]

In a case of a mass dismissal of workers for going on strike, a Bench headed by Krishna Iyer J intervened and held that all concerned could not be held guilty; those who were innocent bystanders should be given the relief of reinstatement with limited wages.[42]

Of late, various High Courts (HCs) have started issuing injunctions against

---

[37] *P Balakotaiah v. Union of India* AIR 1958 SC 232.

[38] *Kameshwar Prasad v. State of Bihar* AIR 1962 SC 1166.

[39] See *TK Rangarajan v. Government of Tamil Nadu* (2003) 6 SCC 581.

[40] *Railway Board v. Niranjan Singh* AIR 1969 SC 966; This was very surprising because the Railways own vast properties, including townships and huge labour colonies.

[41] *All India Bank Employees' Association v. National Industrial Tribunal* AIR 1962 SC 171.

[42] *Gujarat Steel Tubes Ltd v. Gujarat Steel Tubes Mazdoor Sabha* (1980) 2 SCC 593; Per Krishna Iyer J, 'we are not able to uphold the conclusion of the arbitrator that the punishment of dismissal was appropriate for the entire mass of workmen whose only guilt, as proved was nothing more than passive participation in the illegal and unjustified strike by not reporting for duty. The verdict is inevitable that the discharge is wrongful.'

public-sector employees going on strike in support of their demands. The view taken is that since the organization is a public-utility service, any strike will be illegal and so the Court can injunct them. Far from safeguarding the precious right to strike as a weapon in the armoury of the workers, the Courts have consistently denied any such collective bargaining in their favour.

Analysis of Decisions on ID Act

In the last seventy-five years, to its credit, the SCI did not, except once, strike down any provision of the labour laws enacted by the Parliament. The only time was in 1976, when the ID Act was amended and a new Chapter V-B was introduced, which brought in restrictions on the employers from laying off or retrenching workers, or closing establishments without prior permission from the appropriate government. authority. When striking down Section 25-O of the ID Act, which required industries to seek prior permission, the SCI went into a philosophical discourse and said that there should not be any doctrinaire approach to the problem of socialism. NL Untwalia J, writing for the Constitution Bench, observed that while the inclusion of 'Socialist' in the Preamble may encourage the courts to favour nationalization and State ownership, the prevailing economic structure, dominated by private ownership, necessitated a balanced approach.[43] But subsequent Constitution Benches upheld the provisions relating to prior permissions for retrenchment,[44] lay-off[45] and closure.[46]

At the same time, the impact of liberalization, privatization and globalization on the courts was enormous. Speaking for a Constitution Bench, VN Khare J emphasized that globalization and economic liberalization, rooted in frameworks like the World Trade Organization (WTO) and the General Agreement on Tariffs and Trade (GATT), would foster human development and bring a 'decent life' to society, and urged an alignment with global standards to boost India's growth.[47]

---

[43] *Excel Wear Etc. v. Union of India* (1978) 4 SCC 224; The Court further questioned whether socialism and social justice could be interpreted so expansively as to disregard the interests of shareholders, creditors, depositors and others connected to privately owned industries.

[44] *Workmen of Meenakshi Mills Ltd v. Meenakshi Mills Ltd* (1992) 3 SCC 336.

[45] *Papanasam Labour Union v. Madura Coats Ltd* (1995) 1 SCC 501.

[46] *Orissa Textile & Steel Ltd v. State of Orissa* (2002) 2 SCC 578.

[47] *Islamic Academy of Education v. State of Karnataka* (2003) 6 SCC 697; The Court went on to laud globalization and its effects. It wrote in its order that society had accepted pub-culture, and that sooner or

However, the Court's approach towards relief for labour was a matter for concern. Workers have virtually lost all hope of any resolution of their disputes in the four-tier appeal system in the more than four decades since the Court began entertaining appeals in labour matters. It is a telling commentary that almost all big industries and their workers have stopped moving the labour court system for the resolution of their disputes. The lifecycle of an award of a labour court resolving an industrial dispute might be just one year, but it takes more than two decades to get it confirmed by the highest Court. This has rendered the adjudication process redundant and explains why there are very few cases of collective disputes coming before the SCI today. Only disputes concerning non-employment of individual workers have been taken up in the fourth phase of the Court's functioning.

In 1958, the SCI had rendered a verdict[48] that prevented the labour court from reinstating a wrongly removed workman unless the employer's action suffered from want of good faith, or there was victimization or unfair labour practice, or the management was guilty of a basic error or a violation of a principle of natural justice, or when, on the materials before the court, the decision of the employer was wholly baseless or perverse. This meant that the labour court could not interfere, even where the punishment was disproportionate. The ruling deterred the labour court from appreciating the evidence recorded in a domestic inquiry. After more than ten years, the Parliament stepped in and introduced Section 11A into the ID Act, under which the labour courts were empowered to review the evidence recorded by a domestic tribunal and, in a given case, interfere with the punishment if found excessive.[49] The SCI, in *Workmen of Firestone Tyre and Rubber Company of India (Private) Ltd v. The Management*,[50] interpreted Section 11A as enabling the tribunal to judicially

---

later alcoholic beverages would be available even in small grocery shops. Calling socialism a 'catchword' from Indian history, Lakshmanan J observed that with the advent of liberalization, the view that Indian society was essentially 'wedded' to socialism was dissipating; See also Lakshmanan J's opinion in *State of Punjab v. Devans Modern Breweries Ltd* (2004) 11 SCC 26.

[48] *Indian Iron & Steel Co Ltd v. Their Workmen*, AIR 1958 SC 130.

[49] Introduced through the Industrial Disputes (Amendment) Act, 1971. This was to give effect to the resolution of the ILO that mandated that any decision of the employer in dispensing with the services of a worker should have approval by a third-party neutral arbiter.

[50] (1973) 1 SCC 813; In the words of the Court: 'Even in cases where a domestic enquiry has been held and finding of misconduct recorded, the Labour Tribunals have now full power and jurisdiction to reappraise the evidence and to satisfy themselves whether the evidence justifies the finding of misconduct. Even if the enquiry proceedings are held to be proper and the finding of misconduct is also accepted, the

review the decision of an employer in a domestic inquiry and interfere even on the question of the quantum of punishment.

It is indeed surprising that there are as many as twenty-five reported decisions of the SCI dealing with cases of 'errant' bus conductors not issuing tickets after collecting the fare. In these, the SCI seemed to take a high moral ground, that the morality of the worker was the determinative factor and not the quantum of money taken, and characterized the orders of reinstatement as 'misplaced sympathy'.[51] The excess amounts allegedly found on checking could be as meagre as one rupee to three rupees.[52]

In 1982, the Parliament introduced Section 17B in the ID Act to counter the extreme disadvantage faced by workmen when management was able to question the awards in the HCs and get a blanket stay on their enforcement for years on end. Under this Section, employers had to pay the last drawn wages pending the writ petition; further, the amounts paid were not liable to be recovered after the decision of the Court. The expression 'full last drawn wages' occurring in this provision resulted in differing interpretations by the HCs. It was left to the SCI to resolve it in 1999 by explaining the intent behind the amendment thus:

> The object underlying the provision is to relieve a certain extent the hardship that is caused to the workman due to delay in the implementation to the workman is in the nature of subsistence allowance which would not be refundable or recoverable from the workman even if the award is set aside by the High Court or this Court. Since the payment is of such a character Parliament thought it proper to limit it to the extent of the wages

Tribunal has now power to consider whether the punishment of dismissal or discharge was necessary for the type of misconduct of which the workman is found guilty. In such circumstances, the Tribunal can also give any other relief to the workman, including the imposing of a lesser punishment.'-

51 *Karnataka State Road Transport Corporation v. BS Hullikatti* (2001) 2 SCC 574; The Court noted that '[i]t is misplaced sympathy by the Labour Courts in such cases when on checking it is found that the Bus Conductors have either not issued tickets to a large number of passengers, though they should have, or have issued tickets of a lower denomination knowing fully well the correct fare to be charged. It is the responsibility of the Bus Conductors to collect the correct fare from the passengers and deposit the same with the Company. They act in a fiduciary capacity and it would be a case of gross misconduct if knowingly they do not collect any fare or the correct amount of fare.'

52 See *Regional Manager, UPSRTC, Etawah v. Hoti Lal* (2003) 3 SCC 605.

which were drawn by the workman when he was in service and when his services were terminated.[53]

Inconsistency Adding to Uncertainty

A survey of the decided cases reveals that the approaches of different Benches of the SCI on the aspect of misconduct and punishment awarded to a workman are widely divergent. On the issue of a workman using abusive language against the employer, one Bench headed by DA Desai J took the view that an isolated instance without blameworthy conduct could not justify dismissal from service,[54] while another Bench, speaking through N Santosh Hegde J was of the view that this kind of indiscipline, in the presence of subordinates, did not justify a lesser punishment.[55]

These diametrically opposite points of view are apparent even with regard to other forms of misconduct. In a case where a worker found sleeping on duty was dismissed, the Court agreed with the labour court that the punishment was disproportionate to the misconduct and sustained his reinstatement.[56] In a decision rendered on similar facts six years later, the Court justified the extreme punishment of dismissal.[57]

---

[53] *Dena Bank v. Kiritikumar T Patel* (1999) 2 SCC 106.

[54] *Rama Kant Misra v. State of Uttar Pradesh* (1982) 3 SCC 346; The Court noted that '[w]hen it is said that language discloses a threatening posture it is the subjective conclusion of the person who hears the language because voice modulation of each person in the society differs and indiscreet improper, abusive language may show lack of culture but merely the use of such language on one occasion unconnected with any subsequent positive action and not preceded by any blameworthy conduct cannot permit an extreme penalty of dismissal from service.'

[55] *Mahindra and Mahindra Ltd v. NB Narawade*, (2005) 3 SCC 134; The Court observed, 'We too are of the opinion that the language used by the workman is such that it cannot be tolerated by any civilized society. Use of such abusive language against a superior officer, that too not once but twice, in the presence of his subordinates cannot be termed to be an indiscipline calling for lesser punishment in the absence of any extenuating factor referred to herein above.'

[56] *Colour-Chem Limited v. AL Alaspurkar* (1998) 3 SCC 192; SB Majmudar J wrote that 'it must be held that the appellant was guilty of unfair labour practice. Such an act was squarely covered by Clause (a) of Item 1 of Schedule IV of the Act being legal victimisation, if not factual victimisation.'

[57] *Bharat Forge Co Ltd v. Uttam Manohar Nakate* (2005) 2 SCC 489; The Bench, speaking through SB Sinha J, held that 'The Labour Court evidently had taken recourse to Clause (g) of Item 1 of Schedule IV of the Act which ex facie was inapplicable. The said provision clearly postulates two situations, namely, (i) the misconduct should be of minor or technical character; and (ii) the punishment is shockingly disproportionate without having any regard to the nature of the particular misconduct or the past record of service of the employee.'

Compensation in Lieu of Reinstatement

While the usual remedy was reinstatement with back wages in cases of wrongful dismissal, the SCI increasingly began awarding compensation in lieu of reinstatement. This drew criticism, and the Court, speaking through GS Singhvi J expressed displeasure with the earlier approach to social welfare legislation and observed:

> The attractive mantras of globalization and liberalisation are fast becoming the raison d'etre of the judicial process and an impression has been created that the constitutional courts are no longer sympathetic towards the plight of industrial and unorganized workers . . . It need no emphasis that if a man is deprived of his livelihood, he is deprived of all his fundamental and constitutional rights and for him the goal of social and economic justice, equality of status and of opportunity, the freedoms enshrined in the Constitution remain illusory . . . [T]he approach of the courts must be compatible with the constitutional philosophy of which the Directive Principles of State Policy constitute an integral part and justice due to the workman should not be denied by entertaining the specious and untenable grounds put forward by the employer—public or private.[58]

Again, between 2004 and 2009, the Benches of the SCI, speaking through SB Sinha J in consecutive judgments, held that the duty lay with the worker and not the employer to show that he was not gainfully employed during the period of his dismissal.[59] A later Bench headed by RV Raveendran J distinguished the earlier judgments and held that 'while an employee cannot be asked to prove the negative, he has to at least assert on oath that he was neither employed

[58] *Harjinder Singh v. Punjab State Warehousing Corporation* (2010) 3 SCC 192. In a concurring opinion, AK Ganguly J observed that 'any attempt to dilute the constitutional imperatives in order to promote the so-called trends of "Globalisation", may result in precarious consequences. Reports of suicidal deaths of farmers in thousands from all over the country along with escalation of terrorism throw dangerous signal . . . At this critical juncture the judges' duty, to my mind, is to uphold the constitutional focus on social justice without being in any way misled by the glitz and glare of globalization.'

[59] *Madhya Pradesh Electricity Board v. Hariram* (2004) 8 SCC 246. This judgment was authored by SB Sinha J, and within a span of five years he reiterated this position in quick succession in *Allahabad Jal Sansthan v. Daya Shankar Rai* (2005) 5 SCC 124; *Manager, RBI, Bangalore v. S Mani* (2005) 5 SCC 100; *Uttar Pradesh State Brassware Corporation Ltd v. Udai Narain Pandey* (2006) 1 SCC 479; *Talwara Coop Credit & Service Society Ltd v. Sushil Kumar* (2008) 9 SCC 486; *Novartis India Ltd v. State of West Bengal* (2009) 3 SCC 124; *MD Balasaheb Desai Sahakari SK Ltd v. Kashinath Ganapati Kambale* (2009) 2 SCC 288.

nor engaged in any gainful business or venture and that he did not have any income. Then the burden will shift to the employer.'[60] This view was endorsed by another Bench headed by V Gopala Gowda J, which observed that 'once the employee shows that he was not employed, the onus lies on the employer to specifically plead and prove that the employee was gainfully employed and was getting the same or substantially similar emoluments'.[61] Very recently, a Bench headed by Abhay S Oka J attempted to walk a middle path, synthesizing both points of view and clarifying that while the initial burden was on the employee to show that he was not gainfully employed after dismissal, how this burden was discharged varied. An employee's assertion on oath would suffice if the employer failed to present contrary evidence.[62]

Labour and Service Interface

The 42nd Amendment to the Constitution introduced Article 323A by which Administrative Tribunals were to be established to deal with cases involving the conditions of service of Central and State Government employees. Eight years after the Amendment, the Parliament enacted the Administrative Tribunals Act, 1985 (AT Act) which, *inter alia*, established the Tribunals and divested the HCs of the jurisdiction to deal with those cases under Article 226 of the Constitution. Even pending matters before the HCs stood transferred to the Tribunals. The AT Act provided a direct appeal to the SCI against the orders of the Tribunals. This dramatically increased the workload of the SCI, with appeals not only from the orders of Central Administrative Tribunals but also the State Administrative Tribunals.

A seven-judge Constitution Bench of the SCI, while negativing the challenge to the constitutional validity of the AT Act in *L Chandra Kumar v. Union of India*, held that the power of judicial review of the HCs under Article 226 of the Constitution was also part of the basic structure of the Constitution.[63] Adopting a pragmatic approach, the SCI, using its powers under Article 142

---

[60] *JK Synthetics Ltd v. KP Agrawal* (2007) 2 SCC 433.

[61] *Deepali Gundu Surwase v. Kranti Junior Adhyapak Mahavidyalaya (D.Ed)* (2013) 10 SCC 324; The Benches headed by Gopala Gowda J reiterated this view in *Raghubir Singh v. Gen Manager-Haryana Roadways, Hissar* (2014) 10 SCC 301; and *Bhuvnesh Kumar Dwivedi v. M/s Hindalco Industries Ltd* (2014) 11 SCC 85.

[62] *Ramesh Chand v. Mgt of Delhi Transport Corporation* 2023 SCC Online SC 776.

[63] *L Chandra Kumar v. Union of India* (1997) 3 SCC 261. The SCI further mandated that such writ petitions would have to be decided by a Bench of two judges of the HC.

of the Constitution of India, then went on to carve out an intermediate tier of judicial review not provided in the AT Act. It required a party dissatisfied with the order of an Administrative Tribunal to first challenge it in a writ petition before the jurisdictional HC. Thereafter, the SCI could be approached, but only through a special leave petition.[64]

This pragmatic move not only delayed the final resolution of the dispute but significantly added to the costs of litigation, whether for employees or for the government. In general, the experiment with Tribunals has resulted in a lot of misgiving, and this has been acknowledged in several judicial pronouncements.[65]

Contract Labour

Before the introduction of the Contract Labour (Regulation and Abolition) Act 1970 (CLRA Act), the workers of the principal employer always had the right to question the deployment of contract labour and get the matter adjudicated by the Industrial Tribunal. A three-judge Bench headed by KN Wanchoo J wrote, 'If the contract had been malafide and a cloak for suppressing the fact that the workmen were really the workmen of the company, the tribunal would have been justified in ordering the company to take over the entire body of workmen and treat it as its own workmen.'[66]

The effect of the said decision was short-lived. The Parliament enacted the CLRA Act and thus removed the power of the industrial codes to order the abolition of contract labour while adjudicating industrial disputes by workmen.[67] The constitutional validity of the CLRA Act was upheld by a Constitution Bench of the SCI.[68]

---

64 Interestingly, the same approach has been adopted as with regard to the Armed Forces Tribunal, established under the Armed Forces Tribunal Act 2007. See, *Balkrishna Ram v. Union of India* (2020) 2 SCC 442.

65 *Madras Bar Association v. Union of India* (2014) 10 SCC 1; *Madras Bar Association v. Union of India* (2015) 8 SCC 583; *Rojer Mathew v. South Indian Bank Limited* (2020) 6 SCC 1; *Madras Bar Association v. Union of India* (2020) 7 SCC 416; *Madras Bar Association v. Union of India* (2021) 7 SCC 369.

66 *The Standard-Vacuum Refining Co of India Ltd v. Its Workmen* AIR 1960 SC 948.

67 *Vegoils Private Ltd v. The Workmen* (1972) 2 SCC 724.

68 *Gammon India Ltd v. Union of India* (1974) 1 SCC 596.

Taking advantage of the new enactment, many employers, including public sector and government departments, started outsourcing labour. Alarmed by this new trend, the SCI expressed dismay. Terming the practice as an 'archaic system' that is a 'relic of early capitalism', a Bench headed by Chinnappa Reddy J remarked that the steady revival of contract labour in the public sector was surprising, given that the sector was expected to function as a model employer.[69]

However, despite CLRA Act, there was still no clarity on the status of contract labour after abolition by a notification. In the context of the contract labour engaged in sweeping, cleaning, dusting etc. in Air India, a three-judge Bench headed by K Ramaswamy J ruled in 1997 that they were entitled to absorption in the establishment of the principal employer on a regular basis.[70] This relief, however, was short-lived. Within four years, a five-judge Constitution Bench in *Steel Authority of India Ltd v. National Union Water Front Workers*[71] reversed the *Air India* judgment and held that on abolition, the contract labourers could not seek regular employment with the principal employer.

The effect of this ambiguity today has encouraged unrestricted engagement of contract labour, both in the private and public sector. Today, the contract workforce in many industries far exceeds regular workers, and the outsourced labour stands excluded from the welfare net of labour legislation.

Migrant Workers

In at least three decisions,[72] the SCI had, over the years, referred to the importance of migrant workers and the need for the authorities to enforce the Inter-State Migrant Workers Act, 1979 (ISMW Act). However, the general observations in those judgments do not appear to have informed the orders that the SCI passed during the COVID-19 pandemic, when large-scale migration of workers from their cities of work to their villages caused much

---

69 *Catering Cleaners of Southern Railway v. Union of India* (1987) 1 SCC 700.

70 *Air India Statutory Corporation v. United Labour Union* (1997) 9 SCC 377.

71 (2001) 7 SCC 1.

72 *Labourers Working on Salal Hydro Project v. State of Jammu & Kashmir* (1983) 2 SCC 181; *Bandhua Mukti Morcha v. Union of India* (1984) 3 SCC 161; *People's Union for Democratic Rights v. Union of India* (1982) 3 SCC 235.

laws and were being exploited by the contractors. This was converted into a petition, and the labour commissioner was asked to visit the site and submit a report. A slew of directions were subsequently issued for minimum wages to be paid and for strict compliance with the provisions of the CLRA and the ISMW Acts.[75] The Court noted that the report of the Labour Commissioner recorded that children were also engaged in the project. While acknowledging that it was not possible, in the prevailing socio-economic conditions, to prohibit child labour altogether, the SCI, following its earlier judgment in the *Asian Games Village* case, reiterated that no child below the age of fourteen years should be employed in the project, and if so employed should be immediately disengaged. The Central Government thereupon issued instructions to that effect.[76]

Strangely, the SCI did not find the process of packing of matchsticks to be 'hazardous' and unsuited for the engagement of children. In a 1991 decision concerning the employment of child labour in the match works industry, the SCI appeared to endorse it by observing that 'the tender hands of the young workers are more suited to sorting out the manufactured product and process it for the purposes of packing.'[77] What made it worse was the gratuitous suggestion that 'in consideration of their special adaptability at least sixty per cent of the prescribed minimum wage for an adult employee in the factories doing the same job should be given to them'.[78]

The Court also appeared to be reluctant to substitute a child that was thus removed from a hazardous occupation with an adult from the child's family on the ground that it would 'strain the resources of the State'.[79] It stated that

---

[75] *Labourers Working on Salal Hydro Project v. State of J&K*, 1983 (2) SCC 181.

[76] The Child Labour (Prohibition and Regulation) Act (CLPR Act) was enacted in 1986, which in the Schedules listed out hazardous occupations and processes in which children are prohibited from working. The building and construction industry is listed under the prohibited processes by an amendment made as late as 2016. The CLPR Act still does not prohibit a child from being engaged to help his family in occupations or processes not included in the Schedule 'after his school hours and during vacation'. Also, since the definition of 'child' means a person who has not completed fourteen years of age, the law does not deter teenage children dropping out of school for employment in hazardous occupations and processes.

[77] *MC Mehta v. State of Tamil Nadu* (1991) 1 SCC 283. This was even while the Court noted that the 'employment of children within the match factories directly connected with the manufacturing process upto final production of matchsticks or fireworks should not at all be permitted'.

[78] ibid; This effectively legitimized engaging children in the process of packing matchsticks.

[79] *MC Mehta v. State of Tamil Nadu* (1996) 6 SCC 756.

it was sufficient for the appropriate government to deposit Rs 5,000 in a fund for each child employed in a factory, mine or other hazardous industries. The same approach was adopted in the case of bonded labour as well.[80]

Labour and Women

The SCI, as early as the late sixties frowned upon the action of an employer discharging women once they got married. The rationale was that 'work has got to be done as a team and presence of all those workmen is necessary, is in our opinion no disqualification so far as married women are concerned'.[81] However, even fifteen years later, the SCI was reluctant to invalidate the action of Air India in requiring its air hostesses not to marry within four years of service, and also prescribing different age criteria for retirement for men and women holding the same post of cabin crew.[82]

Twenty-two years later, the SCI was still reluctant to hold that the conditions of service that required air hostesses to retire from flight duties on international flights at the age of fifty, or opt for ground duties between the ages of fifty and fifty-eight, when their male counterparts could continue on flight duties until fifty-eight, was discriminatory.[83] Apart from the fact that a majority of air hostesses had accepted a settlement incorporating such conditions of service, what appears to have weighed with the SCI was that 'there is nothing objectionable for air hostesses to wish for a peaceful and tension-free life at home with their families in the middle age and avoid remaining away for long durations on international flights'.[84]

---

80 In *Bandhua Mukti Morcha v. Union of India,* (1997) 10 SCC 549, the directions issued in the Sivakasi match industries case were reiterated. However, the prayer for a complete ban on employment of children was rejected on the grounds that such a ban must 'begin from most hazardous and intolerable activities like slavery, bonded labour, trafficking, prostitution, pornography and dangerous forms of labour and the like'.

81 *Bombay Labour Union Representing the Workmen v. Messrs International Franchises Pvt Ltd* AIR 1966 SC 942. Speaking through PB Gajendragadkar J the Court observed that 'there is nothing to show that married women would necessarily be more likely to be absent than unmarried women or widows. If it is the presence of children which may be said to account for greater absenteeism among married women, that would be so more or less in the case of widows with children also.'

82 *Air India v. Nergesh Meerza* (1981) 4 SCC 335.

83 *Air India Cabin Crew Association v. Yeshaswinee Merchant* (2003) 6 SCC 277.

84 ibid; The fact that a relatively small group of fifty-three air hostesses in executive posts had raised this challenge just before they attained fifty years of age, whereas 684 of the total of 1,138 air hostesses in

To complete the trilogy, we have the judgment in 2011 of the SCI affirming the verdict of the Delhi HC,[85] which upheld the decision of Air India to both increase the flying age of air hostesses to fifty-eight on par with their male counterparts and bring parity in the cadres of inflight supervisors/pursers and air hostesses.[86] The Court now held that notwithstanding the decisions in *Nargesh Meerza* and *Yeshaswinee Merchant*, 'Air India was at liberty to adopt the revised promotion policy which was intended to benefit all the employees.'[87]

When a nurse belonging to the military nursing service of the Indian Army sought to be discharged due to her getting married during probation, the SCI invalidated it on the ground that she ought to have been given 'a chance to prove her ability in the two years following the marriage'.[88] However, when the rule providing for discharge on marriage itself was challenged by another woman employee belonging to the military nursing service under Article 32, the SCI dismissed the writ petition, giving her the liberty to challenge the order of release given by the authority.[89] Later, her challenge was rejected by the Delhi HC.[90] Thus, it is clearly seen that the Court was not willing to examine the larger question of the connection between marriage and the capability required to continue in service. The same yardstick was not adopted for men in uniform.

In the initial stages, the provisions of the Maternity Benefit Act, 1961 (MB Act) were interpreted progressively in line with the constitutional mandate. When the MB Act provided for twelve weeks leave with wages, the Court directed payment of eighty-four days wages, even in the case of daily wage women workers. It did not allow an attempt at deduction of wages for the

---

the worker category had not questioned it was another factor that weighed with the Court.

85 Order dated 8 October 2007 in WP (C) Nos 983-987 of 2006.

86 *Air Cabin Crew Association v. Union of India*, (2012) 1 SCC 619.

87 ibid.

88 *Lieutenant (Mrs) Indira Kumari Kartiayoni v. The Maha Nideshak, Raksha Mantralaya, Shastra Sena Chikitsa Seva, New Delhi* (1991) 3 SCC 11; TK Thommen and RM Sahai JJ noted that 'if she succeeded in proving that she was good enough to remain in service, notwithstanding the marriage, if marriage was a handicap she was entitled to be retained in service in terms of the President's Order. But that opportunity was not given to her ... the appellant is entitled to prove that she can continue her efficiency record in the period after the marriage. She has to be given that opportunity.'

89 *Lt Mrs C Reethama Joseph v. Union of India* (1997) 10 SCC 721.

90 *Lt Mrs C Reethama Joseph v. Union of India* 2012 SCC OnLine Del 96.

weekly off restricting wages to seventy-two days.[91] When the Life Insurance Corporation of India (LIC) terminated the services of a probationer on the ground that she had applied for maternity leave, the SCI did not hesitate to set aside her termination and held that any test or scrutiny regarding pregnancy of an employed woman was illegal.[92]

Equally, the SCI supported the cause of female bartenders in the liquor bars in Delhi. It not only struck down the applicable Delhi excise rule preventing female bartenders from being hired on the grounds of gender discrimination, but also reduced their age of recruitment from twenty-five to twenty-one.[93]

On the other hand, the SCI upheld a Haryana law that disqualified a candidate for the post of *sarpanch*, in those reserved exclusively for women, from contesting if she had three or more children.[94] Thus, the Court approved of the government-mandated two-child norm, which placed the woman in a rural household at a distinct disadvantage compared to her male counterpart. Inexplicably, the Court remarked, 'We do not think that with the awareness which is arising in Indian women folk, they are so helpless as to be compelled to bear a third child even though they do not wish to do so. At the end, suffice it to say that if the legislature chooses to carve out an exception in favour of females it is free to do so but merely because

---

[91] *B Shah v. The Presiding Officer, Labour Court* (1977) 4 SCC 384; Jaswant Singh J, sitting with Krishna Iyer J, wrote that 'in interpreting provisions of beneficial pieces of legislation like the one in hand which is intended to achieve the object of doing social justice to women workers employed in the plantations and which squarely fall within the purview of Article 42 of the Constitution, the beneficent rule of construction which would enable the woman worker not only to subsist but also to make up her dissipated energy, nurse her child, preserve her efficiency as a worker and maintain the level of her previous efficiency and output has to be adopted by the Court'; The same spirit was followed in *Municipal Corporation of Delhi v. Female Workers (Muster Roll)* (2000) 3 SCC 224.

[92] *Mrs Neera Mathur v. Life Insurance Corporation of India*, (1992) 1 SCC 286; The Court, speaking through KJ Shetty J, observed that 'when we are moving forward to achieve the constitutional guarantee of equal rights for women the Life Insurance Corporation of India seems to be not moving beyond the status quo. The case on hand illustrates this typical attitude of the Corporation.'

[93] *Anuj Garg v. Hotel Association of India* (2008) 3 SCC 1; Within a decade, in *Indian Hotel and Restaurant Association (AHAR) v. The State of Maharashtra* (2019) 3 SCC 429, they also struck down the rule preventing engagement of dance girls in the liquor bars in Maharashtra. In both decisions, the SCI did not hesitate to refer to several decisions of the US Courts in their support, while in the past it had always tried to avoid following their decisions.

[94] *Javed v. State of Haryana* (2003) 8 SCC 369, Speaking for the Bench, RC Lahoti J wrote: 'The challenge to the constitutional validity of Section 175(1)(q) and 177(1) fails on all the counts. Both the provisions are held intra vires the Constitution. The provisions are salutary and in public interest.'

women are not excepted from the operation of the disqualification it does not render it unconstitutional.'[95]

Conclusion

A review of the last seven and a half decades of labour law decisions of the SCI reveals a distinct reluctance to interpret labour legislation to favour the workers. A conscious attempt appears to have been made to progressively whittle down the scope of the relief that could be granted to them, unmindful of the inordinate delays in deciding such cases. The Court appears also to be not mindful of the unequal playing field where the procedures and tiers of challenge in the judicial hierarchy appear to favour the party with the greater litigating power. One can imagine the frustration of a wrongfully terminated worker, succeeding after two decades of litigation, being denied reinstatement and having to settle for compensation, and that too not of the full back wages. The Court's track record in recognizing the rights of casual and contractual workers has also not been consistent with the philosophy underlying the Directive Principles of State Policy.[96]

For this state of affairs, one cannot blame the judiciary alone. The State and its enterprises have progressively reduced the intake of employees on a regular basis. Much of the work of an establishment, not limited to maintenance and upkeep, is now being outsourced. Even sanitation work, like the cleaning of sewers, is now outsourced and the municipal corporations seek to avoid liability for deaths occurring on account of such hazardous employment.[97] The new Labour Code, which is yet to be notified, does little to rectify the imbalance arising out of employees being placed legislatively at a distinct disadvantage

---

[95] ibid; This trend has unfortunately continued in *Rajbala v. State of Haryana* (2016) 2 SCC 445, where another Bench upheld a rule that prevented persons who had not completed matriculation from contesting for the post of *sarpanch*.

[96] The judgment of the Constitution Bench in *State of Karnataka v. Uma Devi* (2006) 4 SCC 1 rendered illegal the employment of lakhs of employees in government establishments, appointed without following the Rules in question, despite having worked for more than two, and sometimes, even three decades.

[97] Until the judgment of the SCI in *Safai Karamchari Andolan v. Union of India* (2014) 11 SCC 224, there was total indifference displayed by the governments both at the Centre and the states in effectuating the Employment of Manual Scavengers and Construction of Dry Latrines (Prohibition) Act, 1993; See also *Delhi Jal Board v. National Campaign for Dignity and Rights of Sewerage and Allied Workers* (2011) 8 SCC 568, *Dr Balram Singh v. Union of India* 2023 SCC OnLine SC 1386.

vis-à-vis employers. We are yet to see an SCI that will not glibly defer to such changes in legislative policy that sit at odds with the constitutional promise in the Preamble and the Directive Principles of State Policy. It is sad commentary that there is very little in terms of legal precedent that a worker can cite in their favour before a labour court or tribunal even after seventy-five years of the SCI. This calls for institutional introspection.

EMBARRASSMENT.
THAT'S WHAT STOPPED INDIA FROM MAKING ME, THE GREAT INDIAN BUSTARD, ITS NATIONAL BIRD. THE FEAR OF EMBARRASSMENT FROM BEING MISSPELLED AS 'GREAT INDIAN B*STARD.'
I'LL TELL YOU WHAT'LL EMBARRASS INDIA A LOT MORE THAN A SPELLING MISTAKE.
THAT A ONCE-NATIONAL BIRD CONTENDER, AND THE STATE BIRD OF RAJASTHAN, IS ON THE VERY BRINK OF EXTINCTION!
THAT DESPITE KNOWING WHAT KILLS US— HABITAT LOSS, COLLISIONS WITH OVERHEAD TRANSMISSION LINES & WINDMILLS— NOTHING HAS BEEN DONE!
AND THAT THE GREAT INDIAN BUSTARD IS ALL SET TO BE THE FIRST BIRD TO GO EXTINCT IN INDEPENDENT INDIA!
SO, ARE YOU EMBARRASSED ENOUGH, OR SHOULD I PERFORM MY SIGNATURE COURTSHIP DANCE FOR A NON-EXISTENT MATE, AND EMBARRASS YOU FURTHER?
WELL, WHAT HAVE I TO LOSE? I'M THE GREAT INDIAN 'BUSTED'!
ROHAN

Consistently Inconsistent: Environmental Law and the Supreme Court

GAUTAM PATEL

Pity the Supreme Court. In a country as diverse in every aspect as India, it is no easy task to balance competing equities. From infrastructure and urbanization to forests, wildlife, demographics, languages, literature, regional concerns, climate, weather, topography, geography, water resources, politics, India perhaps more than any other country presents a bewildering array of choices.

In truth, India is not and never has been a unitary system, though it is a unified nation. It is, instead, an amalgam of widely disparate and even disjunctive systems of different hues. The unification of this enormous landmass, one-fifth the size of the United States, under a constitutional federal structure is a leap of faith – that, somehow, we will all manage to pull together towards a shared common objective. India differs from other wide-ranging environmental and ecological systems such as the US and other countries because added to the mix of complexity are a multitude of cultural, historical, sociological, linguistic and political contestations.

In this assessment, I do not propose to concern myself with the evolution of environmental policy in India. There are sufficient authoritative texts on that aspect.[1] Instead, I endeavour to evaluate the decision-making of the Supreme Court of India (SCI) against parameters defined by a jurisprudence it has itself developed. There is little to be gained, I believe, by asserting that SCI decisions do not completely meet constitutional mandates or do not sufficiently hew to the prescriptions of environmental science. My concern is with the development of jurisprudence; the constitutional imperative always

[1] Shyam Divan and Armin Rozencranz, *Environmental Law and Policy in India, Cases and Materials* (3 edn, , Oxford University Press 2022); Geetanjoy Sahu, *Environmental Jurisprudence and the Supreme Court* (Orient Blackswan 2014).

underlies the jurisprudence. The question that poses itself is whether this jurisprudence, developed over decades, lends itself to a discernible, identifiable pattern in decision-making.

It is perhaps unrealistic to expect a shared jurisprudential ideology whether at any given moment or even over a period of time. One reason is that the SCI does not sit *en banc* as one court of all judges. It cannot. Its work is split between various Benches and the assignment of judicial work – of every case – to a particular Bench is solely in the hands of the Master of the Roster', the CJI. Two Benches may, therefore, hear environmental cases at the same time and arrive at diametrically opposite conclusions. When this work is spread over time, measured in years and decades, the results are even more unpredictable. There is another influential factor at play – that of judicial activism, which I will consider briefly a little later in the discussion.

The quest, therefore, must be for a pattern of broad consistency based on jurisprudential principles sufficiently established to form binding precedent. Consistency is not the same as certainty; the former is but an approximation. True, a 'foolish consistency is the hobgoblin of little minds',[2] but departure from consistency outside of reason and logic is even more dangerous. One looks, therefore, for a *measure* of consistency, but neither certitude nor ideological fixity.

Indian courts cannot be expected to operate in jurisprudential silos isolated from the development of law across the globe. Foreign jurisdictions similar to ours often evolve principles on issues that arise here as well. In addition, there are the country's treaty obligations and international covenants. This is true not only of environmental law, but a raft of other areas of legal discourse: intellectual property law, human rights law, disability law, enforcement of foreign judgments, matrimonial law, internet and technology law, sports law, terrorism and security law, and even well-established fields like contract law, insolvency and company law. To be effective – and to be effectuated – foreign law can obviously not be applied directly to domestic jurisprudence. It must be incorporated one way or the other into *our* jurisprudence. We can accept that multilateral and bilateral treaties and agreements, international covenants and pacts, and 'customary' international law are all legitimate foundations for shaping substantive rights in India.

---

2 Ralph Waldo Emerson, 'A foolish consistency is the hobgoblin of little minds, adored by little statesmen and philosophers and divines' in *Self-Reliance, Essays: First Series* (1841).

In dealing with issues of human rights and the environment (among others), the SCI has often adopted a 'presumption of consistency', that is, striving to make domestic law consistent with international law. A discernible trend in environmental law cases is the incorporation and adoption of international principles into domestic environmental law by the SCI through judicial interpretation of international law, whether customary or treaty/convention-based.[3]

The issue therefore is not in the incorporation or the setting of a legal principle by adoption from international sources into the matrix of municipal environmental law. It is rather in the application of those principles, once established, repeatedly reaffirmed, to cases that come before the court. One does not expect consistency in the formulation of the law; but it is not unreasonable to demand some level of predictability – a halt to the incessant swinging of the pendulum – in the application of the law so enunciated.

To put it bluntly, the jurisprudence inverts the well-received four-tiered preferential hierarchy: first, environment; second, individual liberty; third, government; and fourth, big business. This categorization is no longer so neat; indeed, it is increasingly difficult to separate government from big business. But even if we maintain this segregation, scholars have found that environmental causes have always been suborned to the environmentally destructive demands of 'infrastructure', such as mega-dams, airports, highways and so on.[4]

A close study of three decades of SCI decisions between 1980 and 2010 showed that while the SCI supported issues raised by 'underdogs' such as environmental non-governmental organizations, prominent exceptions were cases challenging infrastructure projects.[5] As we shall see, it is in precisely

---

3 Some of the instances would be: *Vellore Citizens Welfare Forum v. Union of India* (1996) 5 SCC 647; *AP Pollution Control Board-I v. Prof MV Nayudu* (1999) 2 SCC 718; *AP Pollution Control Board-II v. MV Nayudu* (2001) 2 SCC 62 and (2001) 2 SCC 86; *MC Mehta v. Kamal Nath* (1997) 1 SCC 388; *Narmada Bachao Andolan v. Union of India* (2000) 10 SCC 664; *ND Jayal v. Union of India* (2004) 9 SCC 362; *Essar Oil Ltd v. Halar Utkarsh Samiti* (2004) 2 SCC 392; *Karnataka Industrial Areas Development Board v. C Kenchappa* (2006) 6 SCC 371; *Intellectuals Forum v. State of AP* (2006) 3 SCC 549.

4 Prashant Bhushan, 'Supreme Court and PIL: Changing Perspectives under Liberalisation,' *The Economic and Political Weekly* 38, no. 18 (1 May 2004); Prashant Bhushan, 'Misplaced Priorities and Class Bias of the Judiciary,' *Economic and Political Weekly* 44, no. 14 (4 May 2009).

5 Geetanjoy Sahu, 'Why the Underdogs Came Out Ahead: An Analysis of the Supreme Court's Environmental Judgments, 1980–2010,' *The Economic and Political Weekly* 49, no. 4 (25 January 2014). See also, the appendix to Sahu, *Environmental Jurisprudence and the Supreme Court*, which lists as many as 191 environmental judgments between 1980 and 2010.

this area that an intervention from the SCI is vital; and yet, it is here that we find a reluctance to come down on the side of the environmentalists. The jurisprudential inconsistency is apparent when one sets these decisions against the principles that the SCI itself repeatedly enunciates in the broadest possible terms. And it is that consistent inconsistency that exacerbates the threats to the environment rather than resolve it.

TN Godavarman Thirumulpad v. Union of India,[6] popularly known as *Godavarman* or the 'forest' case, is a long-running litigation in the SCI about India's forests. It has been continuously heard for three decades, and even as of August 2024, it features on the SCI cause lists in some form. Some commentators hold that this one litigation has almost single-handedly saved India's forests from widespread devastation. That is at least debatable. Rosencranz and Lele argue that it is a case of unmindful judicial activism and an encroachment on quotidian governance issues, but with hugely negative social, ecological and administrative consequences.[7]

Some of the many broad 'principles' that the SCI has adopted are critical to any evaluation: sustainable (often called 'balanced') development, often bundled up with inter-generational equity; the 'polluter pays' principle; the precautionary principle; and the doctrine of public trust. As we shall presently see, these are often cited as 'governing principles'. But in the context of massive infrastructure projects where environmental and ecological damage is the most severe and far-reaching in terms of geography, people's rights and displacement, and long-term impact, the SCI has, in direct contrast to other smaller and lower-footprint projects, been reluctant to intervene.[8] I consider some of the more recent decisions on three of these principles, setting them against earlier precedents.

Sustainable Development, Balanced Development and Inter-Generational Equity

In principle, 'sustainable development' is a concept that spans time. It weighs immediate needs against anticipated future demands. It is fundamentally

---

6 *TN Godavarman Thirumulpad v. Union of India*, Writ Petition (Civil) No 202 of 1995.

7 Armin Rosencranz and Sharadchandra Lele, 'Supreme Court and India's Forests,' *The Economic and Political Weekly* 43, no. 5 (2 February 2008).

8 Bhushan (n 4); Sahu (n 4).

a question of balance: setting present demands against an estimation of long-term or future impacts. The contexts vary from banking to fossil-fuel dependencies. The nature of the task gives it the alternative phraseology of 'balanced' development and 'inter-generational equity'. The latter tells us about competing equities. The public needs of today to be set up and weighed against the as-yet-unknown but reasonably anticipated demands of an uncertain future.

Above all, thinking about sustainable development must be guided by two principles – caution or circumspection is one, and erring on the side of the unknown must, logically, be the other. For fundamental to any proper application of this principle is an understanding of irreversibility. A natural resource diminished or gone may well be impossible to replace, restore or preserve, and might, too, suffer from the law of unintended consequences.

The phrase 'sustainable development' is used so frequently in judgments that tracing a line through its application is bewildering. For instance, in one order in the ongoing *Godavarman* forest case, the SCI said: 'Environmental justice could be achieved only if we drift away from the principle of anthropocentric to ecocentric.' In other words, 'human interest does not take automatic precedence and humans have obligations to non-humans independently of human interest.'[9] However, a different approach was discernible sixteen years earlier in *Vellore Citizens' Welfare Forum v. Union of India*,[10] where it was observed that: 'The traditional concept that development and ecology are opposed to each other is no longer acceptable. "Sustainable Development" is the answer.'[11] This view was reiterated later that year, in 1996, in *Indian Council for Enviro-Legal Action v. Union of India*.[12] Flash forward a decade to 2006, when the SCI went on to say in *Intellectuals Forum, Tirupathi v. State of Andhra Pradesh*[13] that 'In pursuit of development, focus has to be on sustainability of development and policies towards that end have to be earnestly formulated and sincerely observed.'[14]

---

9 See, *Centre for Environmental Law, WWF-India v. Union of India* (2013) 8 SCC 234 [44].

10 *Vellore Citizens' Welfare Forum v. Union of India* (1996) 5 SCC 647.

11 ibid [10]; The Court further observed: 'We have no hesitation in holding that "Sustainable Development" as a balancing concept between ecology and development has been accepted as a part of the customary international law though its salient features have yet to be finalised by the international law jurists.'

12 *Indian Council for Enviro-Legal Action v. Union of India* (1996) 5 SCC 281.

13 *Intellectuals Forum, Tirupathi v. State of Andhra Pradesh* (2006) 3 SCC 549.

14 ibid [84]. The Court appeared to have accepted that while all human beings have a fundamental right to a healthy environment, they have a 'corresponding duty of ensuring that resources are conserved and preserved in such a way that present as well as the future generations are aware of them equally'.

One cannot help wonder if sustainable development was 'the answer' in 1996, a jurisprudential declaration that could only have been binding, one that was followed for a decade until 2006, how did it cease to be the answer in the *Godavarman* order of 2012, one that explicitly rejected sustainable development as being 'too anthropocentric' an approach? Is sustainable development still normative environmental jurisprudence, or has it fallen by the wayside? And what precisely does preferring an 'ecocentric approach' mean? Given that every intervention by humankind in any form of development is bound to result in some degree of environmental and ecological damages, does the 'ecocentric approach' principle tell us that no such development should ever be considered?

We do not know.

Rationally, one would expect the SCI to reconcile these conflicting positions and provide guidance – one needed not only for eco-warriors but also project proponents.[15] The SCI does no such thing. Instead, it simply, and quite blithely, cites all these decisions in one fell swoop in a very recent judgment in the *Godavarman* series (2024).[16] While approving a tiger safari in the Corbett Tiger Reserve, the Court cited a number of authorities but appeared to hold that the approach while applying the principle of sustainable development has to be ecocentric and not anthropocentric. In a 2024 order in the same case, where the SCI was examining the irregularities (in India, a wondrous synonym for illegalities) in tree-felling and construction, especially in the Pakhrau area. The SCI promptly segued into a discussion of the public trust doctrine (including some decisions that are discussed a little later in this essay), chastized the forest minister and the Divisional Forest Officer, referred to the report of the Centrally Empowered Committee (CEC), invoked a principle of 'ecological restitution', reiterated its concern about the tiger and tiger habitats, and then proceeded to issue a raft of directions. These included *not* disturbing 'safaris which are already existing' including the one at Pakhrau; setting up of yet another Committee, and so forth. The Committee's concerns are to be whether the approach should be ecocentrism and not of anthropocentrism,[17] what activities should and should not be permitted in the buffer and fringe

---

[15] In another *Godavarman* case, this time of 2022 and relating to tree-felling in the context of the Delhi Metro, the SCI explicitly *reaffirmed* the sustainable development principle. See, *TN Godavarman Thirumulpad v. Union of India* (2022) 4 SCC 289 [48.9]

[16] *In Re: TN Godavarman Thirumulpad v. Union of India* 2024 SCC OnLine SC 243 [88–96].

[17] ibid [181D (iii) (a)].

zones, how many resorts should be permitted, and, having earlier noted that loud blaring music from resorts was undesirable, what restrictions on noise pollution ought to be placed.

This order in *Godavarman* cites, among many others, the decision in *Tata Housing Development Company Ltd v. Aalok Jagga.*[18] While the decision hinges on a statement of the public trust doctrine, it is worth noting for what it says regarding sustainable development (which, as I have said, is generally thrown into the mix as if salting a decision with every conceivable environmental law principle [the polluter pays principle was also included] on its own adds heft or improves the taste). The case came before the SCI from a 2017 order of the Delhi High Court (HC).[19] Tata Housing proposed a mixed-use development (with the somewhat over-the-top moniker of *Camelot*) in Punjab. It had sought and obtained environmental clearance from the state environmental impact assessment authority, an expert appraisal committee and the Ministry of Environment and Forests (MoEF),[20] which recommended the grant of an environmental clearance. It had called for a report from the regional office. This report had said that the project was within the catchment area of Sukhna Lake, following a Survey of India map. Tata Housing had claimed that the project did not affect the lake – the project site was 123 metres from the lake. Before the Delhi HC, a writ petition was filed inter alia claiming a violation of the Environment (Protection) Act, 1986. The HC directed Tata Housing to comply with certain statutory requirements. Tata Housing appealed to the SCI. The HC order was set aside and the case was transferred to the Delhi HC. In the second round, Tata Housing maintained that it had all the necessary clearances. This was disputed. The State Government (of Punjab) supported Tata Housing. The Union Territory of Chandigarh was in opposition *inter alia* on the basis that the project would adversely affect the lake. It was also argued that wildlife clearance was necessary. The Delhi HC allowed the writ petitions before it, and Tata Housing found itself in the SCI again.

While the decision has an elaborate discussion on the public trust doctrine (of which more a little later), the SCI held that sustainable development has come to be accepted as a 'viable concept' to eradicate poverty and improve the

[18] *Tata Housing Development Company Ltd v. Aalok Jagga* (2020) 15 SCC 784.

[19] *Sarin Memorial Legal Aid Foundation v. State of Punjab* 2017 SCC OnLine Del 7822.

[20] Now the MoEFCC, adding 'climate change' to its title.

quality of human life while 'living with the carrying capacity of supporting ecosystems'. *Vellore*, *Intellectuals Forum* and *Indian Council for Enviro-Legal Action* were all cited. The SCI held that such a development could not be permitted so close to a wildlife sanctuary; that would violate the public trust doctrine for it was within a no-go distance of ten kilometres from the Sukhna Wildlife Sanctuary.

As a straightforward case of being within a prohibited zone of a protected area (the wildlife sanctuary in question), a factual determinant, the case should have posed no great question of public law. The references to the sustainable development principle are entirely without relevant context and are stated in generalities – but with no recognition of the *Godavarman* 2012 ecocentrism over anthropocentrism preference. Instead, it was observed:

> 27. Humans as well as the wildlife are completely dependent upon environment for their survival. Humans are completely dependent on the environment. Like humans, the wildlife is also dependent on the environment for its survival and also gets affected by the environment. The relationship between humans and animals can be understood by the food-chain and food-web. The wildlife is affected by several reasons such as population, deforestation, urbanisation, high number of industries, chemical effluents, unplanned land-use policies, and reckless use of natural resources, etc.[21]

This is somewhat puzzling. The so-called 'conflict' is an invention, an imaginary tension between non-existent (and utterly unviable) antipodal absolutes if it is expressed in these terms. It fails to acknowledge an immutable truth: that *Homo sapiens* is the only species on the planet that destroys its own environment. Sustainability and balance are necessary only because humankind's footprint on the planet is so massive. Absolute ecocentrism of the stripe plugged here is a myth; and it cannot form the basis for making decisions that affect the basic human condition one way or the other.

This discussion would be incomplete without a study of the SCI's remarkable 2013 decision in *Orissa Mining Corporation Ltd v. Ministry of Environment and Forests*.[22] The case was something of an outlier. It pitted on the one side a

---

21 *Tata Housing Development Company Ltd* (n 18) [27].

22 *Orissa Mining Corporation Ltd v. Ministry of Environment and Forests* (2013) 6 SCC 476.

powerful heavy industrial mega-corporation, supported enthusiastically by a state government, against indigenous peoples. It correctly – and sensibly – set down a comprehensible delineation of 'sustainable development' – without ever using the phrase, and as a logical corollary to this, advanced the scope of environmental law to include the right to self-determination of local people in deciding what they did or did not want done to their environment. The judgment is refreshingly astonishing because it quietly and without much fuss totally rejects the top-down approach – something like saying 'our proposed development is good for you, you just don't know it and can't understand it' – that has been the end result of so much environmental litigation.

At stake was the survival of the local people of the Niyamgiri hills in Orissa, clearly an extremely fragile ecosystem. Sterlite, a major industrial enterprise, proposed an alumina refinery in Lajigarh *tehsil* of district Kalahandi. It claimed that no forest land was involved. A sister concern, Vedanta, sought permission to use several hundred hectares of land in the same area also for an alumina refinery. The State Government submitted a proposal to the MoEF to divert forest land, for a road and conveyor belt. It later withdrew this proposal. The MoEF granted a conditional environmental clearance delinking the refinery from the inevitable bauxite mining. The State Government produced another proposal to divert over 600 hectares of forest land for mining bauxite ore in two districts. In August 2010, the then MoEF passed an order refusing Stage II forest clearance for diverting these 600-odd hectares in the Lanjigarh bauxite mines. The Orissa Mining Corporation, a State Government entity, came to the SCI challenging the MoEF order. It said that the MoEF order nullified two previous orders, both in the *Godavarman* case, one relating to Vedanta,[23] and the other to Sterlite.[24]

The *Godavarman (Vedanta)* order of 23 November 2007 observed that the adherence to the sustainable development principle was a constitutional requirement but 'how much damage to the environment and ecology has got to be decided on the facts of each case',[25] that is, the only standard is no standard at all. Then comes the normal recitation:

> 6. On the other side, we have a picture of abject poverty in which the local people are living in Lanjigarh Tehsil including the tribal people. There is

[23] *TN Godavarman Thirumulpad (104) v. Union of India* (2008) 2 SCC 222.

[24] *TN Godavarman Thirumulpad (106) v. Union of India* (2008) 9 SCC 711.

[25] *TN Godavarman Thirumulpad (104)* (n 23) [3].

> no proper housing. There are no hospitals. There are no schools and people are living in extremely poor conditions which is not in dispute.
>
> 7. Indian economy for the last couple of years has been growing at the rate of 8 to 9% of GDP. It is a remarkable achievement. However, accelerated growth rate of GDP does not provide inclusive growth. Keeping in mind the two extremes, this Court thought of balancing development vis-à-vis protection of wildlife ecology and environment in view of the principle of sustainable development.[26]

What standard was being applied here? The SCI refused permission to the Vedanta–State Government joint venture, set out its own rehabilitation package and allowed the holding company (Sterlite) to apply if the company was agreeable to providing this 'rehabilitation'. The local people were reduced *en masse* to 'poverty', and therefore, presumably, without rights they could assert under the Constitution, but apparently to be grateful for an imposition of a corporate entity's perception of their needs.

Two years later, the MoEF rejected the forest clearance.

Three years later, on 18 April 2013, Orissa Mining Corporation's writ petition came to be decided. KSP Radhakrishnan J wrote for the three-judge Bench. Diametrically contrary to the previous two orders, his opinion had two central themes: the rights of indigenous or local people and their right to decide for themselves how they wanted their environment to be dealt with; and, whether said in so many words or not, what environmental protection and sustainability truly mean. The Bench noted the previous SCI clearance and Stage I approval, and then found that an expert committee constituted by the MoEF had reported a violation of tribal rights and community rights, and of forest laws. Importantly, the judgment rejected the top-down approach and, instead, recognized the inability of tribals, STs and traditional forest dwellers in taking legal action against development projects undertaken in their abode or forest. This dimension of ownership in natural resources – clearly an important component of sustainability – proved determinative to the outcome. The Court held the State to account, answerable for the protection of these rights, including identity, culture, religious practices and beliefs.

[26] ibid [6]–[7].

There is the clearest possible enunciation of the rights of the local people in forests and the natural resources of the land they occupy; the state is only a custodian, thus correctly marrying the public trust doctrine to sustainability. The local government, the gram sabha, had, as the SCI said, not taken into account any of these rights, especially the religious rights to worship a local deity. Not only was the project proponent required to correct defects but, far from 'adopting' a court-mandated 'rehabilitation' package, in what must be seen as an utterly extraordinary and exceptional leap of faith, the Court ordered a referendum to be conducted by the gram sabha.[27]

It does not use the phrase, but the judgment is a fine example of the deployment of free, prior and informed consent (FPIC) in environmental decision-making.[28]

As it turns out, the twelve gram sabhas spread over Rayagada and Kalahandi districts voted against the project in July–August 2013. That result was impossible but for the intervention of the SCI. From any perspective, the *Orissa Mining Corporation* case is a significant breakthrough in environmental law in this country. It fully (and correctly) rejects the lumping of all local people into one poverty-stricken class and the implicit suggestion that because they are poor, they do not have the capacity or even the right to self-determination. As a facet of the right to life, and of the guarantee of equality, the importance of this cannot be understated. Self-determination and the defence of environmental rights go hand in hand; they are not two sides of a coin, but rather both sit on one side. Analysed carefully, *Orissa Mining Corporation* sets a standard for environmental law that travels beyond weary shibboleths; and self-determination is crucial to this.

Another aspect that emerges is equally important, and this is the Court's refusal to accept that private enterprise's profit motive can ever substitute for legitimate governance. Take the construct as it was placed before the SCI – the abject poverty of the local people. That immediately pointed not to the need to allow the introduction of private enterprise pillaging the environment, but to the colossal and wholly unexplained failure in, or, more accurately, abandonment of every notion of governance.

---

[27] *Orissa Mining Corporation Ltd* (n. 22) [66-68].

[28] Parshuram Tamang, 'An Overview of the Principle of Free, Prior and Informed Consent and Indigenous Peoples in International and Domestic Law and Practices,' *Australian Indigenous Law Reporter* 9, no. 2 (2005) [111–116] <http://www.jstor.org/stable/26479590> accessed 17 August 2024.

It is interesting to contrast the SCI's approach in *Orissa Mining Corporation* with its decision relating to a copper smelting plant in Tamil Nadu. Tuticorin is the Dutch name for Thoothukudi, a very old port city on the Coromandel Coast of the Bay of Bengal, south-east of Chennai. There, Sterlite Industries (part of the Vedanta group) got approval from the state pollution control board to set up a copper smelting plant. The MoEF then granted conditional environmental clearance. The State Government and the State Pollution Control Board (SPCB) both approved the project. The MoEF's environmental clearance and the approvals by the SPCB were challenged in the Madras HC by an environmental voluntary organization. Meanwhile, Sterlite set up the plant. It went into production. Two other writ petitions came to be filed. At least one alleged ongoing pollution and industrial accidents. On 28 September 2010, a Division Bench heard all three petitions. It directed closure of the plant and said its employees were entitled to compensation under labour law. This judgment came up to the SCI. The resultant decision borders on the bizarre. The SCI had before it what was evidently a frontal environmental issue. There was no other issue at play at all. There is no examination of these. One of the questions was whether the plant could at all have been permitted in violation of an express condition, viz., that it not be located within twenty-five kilometres of any of the islands in the ecologically sensitive Gulf of Munnar. As an uncontroverted fact, the plant was within twenty-five kilometres of four of the twenty-one islands. This is of course the perennial dilemma, which once again awakens the ecocentrism versus anthropocentrism debate. Was it all right to condone this as a minor infraction since 'only' four islands were affected? Should not 'all' the islands have been in the 'no-fly-no-go' or hands-off area? The SCI preferred instead to enter into a discussion on the boundaries of judicial review, citing international authority to say blandly that the standards for judicial review in environmental cases are the same as those in all other cases. That is true; they are; but that is simply like saying that an environmental public interest litigation (PIL) is nothing but a writ petition with an expansion of the applicable law on locus. It takes us nowhere. More importantly, citing a study and therefore presumably applying the precautionary principle, the SCI found that there were in fact some deviations from the prescribed norms. Even while it acknowledged that there had been a misrepresentation and suppression of material facts, it held that 'to decline relief to the appellants in this case would mean closure of the plant of the appellants.'[29] The SCI invoked the 'polluter pays' principle and imposed a fine of Rs 100 crores on Sterlite 'to be spent on suitable measures for improvement of the environment, including water and soil'.[30]

This approach is egregious beyond description and belief. It is an entirely incorrect application of the 'polluter pays' principle, which is not meant to fine an *ongoing* polluter, or one who has deliberately acted contrary to law and permissions. 'You may pollute so long as you can pay for it' cannot possibly be a legal standard in law. There was no doubt about the transgressions; the SCI noted these. There was no doubt that the company was guilty of suppression and misrepresentation. What principle of equity or justice, let alone environmental law could be deployed in aid of a party like this. Also, note, too, the discrepancy in the numbers. The fine was of Rs 100 crores – a one-time, one-off deposit. The profits before depreciation, interest and tax for the financial year 2010–2011 were Rs 1,043 crores, an annual intake ten times the size of the fine.[31]

So much for ecocentrism.

After some unfortunate developments,[32] the case came up to the SCI again. In April 2018, the Tamil Nadu SPCB declined to renew the plant's consent to operate certificate for failing to adhere to the prescribed conditions. The Madras HC in 2020 dismissed writ petitions filed by Vedanta Limited, against the closure.[33] This judgment of the Madras HC was upheld by the SCI in 2024 in *Vedanta Limited v. State of Tamil Nadu*.[34] Vedanta was refused permission to reopen the plant. The Court acknowledged that closing the industry was not the preferred course of action. However, in light of the nature and recurrence of the violations, as well as the gravity of the environmental violations, keeping in mind that 'economic activities should not come at the expense of

---

29 *Sterlite Industries (India) Limited v. Union of India* (2013) 4 SCC 575 [48].

30 ibid [47].

31 The Court examined the annual report of the company in [47] to arrive at the fine amount.

32 ETB Sivapriyan, 'Act Against 17 Policeman for Thoothukudi Police Firing: Commission,' (*Deccan Herald*, 18 October 2022) <https://www.deccanherald.com/india/act-against-17-policemen-for-thoothukudi-police-firing-commission-1154835.html> accessed 13 July 2024; Upasana Sajeev, 'CBI Did Not Probe Thoothukudi Firing Incident Independently: Madras High Court' (*LiveLaw, 30 Jul 2024)*) <https://www.livelaw.in/high-court/madras-high-court/madras-high-court-thoothukudi-police-firing-cbi-failed-miserably-265000?from-login=241735> accessed 13 July 2024.

33 *Vedanta Limited v. State of Tamil Nadu*, WP No. 5756 of 2019 order dated 18 August 2020.

34 2024 INSC 175.

environmental degradation or the health of the population', both the statutory authorities and the HC had no alternative and that failing to take such action would have been a dereliction of their clear duty. [35]

The Precautionary Principle

The laziest trawl in any law database will throw up at least a hundred cases that cite the precautionary principle. Apparently first enunciated in *Vellore* – and constantly reaffirmed thereafter as the 'law of the land'[36] – the principle is stated thus: in environmental law, it is for the project proponent to show that the proposal is environmentally benign.[37] This is a matter of evidence, and is a reversal of the normal burden of proof rule, viz., that he who alleges must prove. Under the precautionary principle, it is not for the project opponent, the one who comes to court, but the project proponent, who defends the project, to show that the project is *not* environmentally hazardous, that is, that it is environmentally benign. The clearest enunciation of its implications is to be found in *AP Pollution Control Board v. Prof MV Nayudu.*[38] In a closely reasoned decision, M Jagannadha Rao J for the two-judge Bench, identified the rationale for this principle: the inherent uncertainty and lack of cohesion in science and expert scientific opinion. As the Court pointed out, in environmental cases, the environmental harm is anticipated and the principle is founded on scientific uncertainty; and hence the so-called 'reversal of burden of proof'.[39] He who wishes to alter the *status quo* must prove that it is environmentally safe to do so; he who wants to preserve the environmental *status quo* has no such burden.[40]

Tied to the precautionary principle is the administrative requirement of an environment impact assessment. The connection is obvious: to show, as the *Nayudu* decision said, the 'absence' of a 'reasonable' environmental or ecological concern, that is, that the project is benign. It is precisely this that weighed with

---

35 ibid [24].

36 *MC Mehta (Badhkal &Surajkund Lakes Matter) v. Union of India* (1997) 3 SCC 715; *Bittu Sehgal v. Union of India* (2001) 9 SCC 181.

37 *Vellore Citizens' Welfare Forum* (n 10) [11].

38 *AP Pollution Control Board v. Prof MV Nayudu* (1999) 2 SCC 718.

39 ibid [37].

40 ibid [38], [39].

SP Bharucha J in his finely reasoned dissent in *Narmada Bachao Andolan v. Union of India*,[41] where he wrote:

> 274. An adverse impact on the environment can have disastrous consequences for this generation and generations to come . . . While surveys and studies on the environmental aspects of the project have been carried out subsequent to the environmental clearance, they are not, due to what are euphemistically called 'slippages', complete . . . Given that the construction of the dam and other work on the project has already commenced, this factor must play a part in their deciding whether or not environmental clearance should be accorded. Until environmental clearance to the project is accorded by them, further construction work on the dam shall cease.

But if this is a question of evidence and of 'burden of proof', how is that burden to be discharged? No judgment of the SCI spells this out clearly. Even the *Nayudu* formulation is insufficient, for it speaks only of the absence of a 'reasonable' ecological concern. What is or is not 'reasonable' is unacceptably subjective. That cannot be a probative standard. There appear to be only two ways to 'discharge' this burden. One, by showing that the project conforms to statutorily mandated norms (especially for effluent, noxious emissions and so on); or, two, to show that the mandated norms are themselves unreasonable or impractical. How much effluent discharge into the Yamuna or the Ganga is 'reasonable'? Should there be *no* discharge into these rivers? One would imagine so; but what of the *Patalganga*, a relatively lesser riverine system in a major industrial belt in Maharashtra? Should it be held to the same standard?

It is interesting to note what transpired later in *Nayudu*. On 5 May 2000, the SCI recalled an earlier order of 13 April 2000 and itself appointed an expert to see 'whether the conditions prescribed by the Technical Committee' of the AP Pollution Control Board in 1997 'and any other safeguards and conditions can be sufficient to permit the commissioning of the project in question'.[42] It allowed the expert to make a site visit, and to take the assistance of the National Geophysical Research Institute as well. The SCI allowed for

---

41 *Narmada Bachao Andolan v. Union of India* (2000) 10 SCC 664.

42 *AP Pollution Control Board v. Prof MV Nayudu* (2001) 2 SCC 86.

objections to the report. The expert submitted his report, which was against the project proponent, and which therefore, filed its objections.

On 1 December 2000, the SCI delivered its second judgment in the *Nayudu* case (*Nayudu II*).[43] By now, it had the expert's report – that of the National Geophysical Research Institute and one by the National Environmental Appellate Authority. The Court found all three reports to be against Surana Oils and held that the Pollution Control Board cannot be directed to grant the necessary clearance.[44] The Court also directed that any other polluting industries within a ten-kilometre radius of the two lakes should not be permitted.[45]

While *Nayudu II* may have done the right thing for the right reasons, the question that remains, however, is whether it established a forensic methodology of reversing the burden of proof. The amplitude of the SCI's power – and its literally entering into the arena by commissioning reports for itself – are not avenues equally applicable to the rest of the judiciary. For instance, had this been a case before a civil court, can there be any doubt that some degree of formality would have had to attach to the process of, or by which, the reversed burden of proof could be held to have been discharged? Surely some cross-examination and testing by the well-known evidentiary principles would need to provide the normative balance on the aspect of discharging the 'burden of proof'? *Nayudu II* worked as it should because of the sloppiness of the project proponent, not because a structured, definable, predictable forensic approach was prescribed and followed. Indeed, what *Nayudu II* needed to do was two things: first, to prescribe a procedurally sound and predictable method for discharging a burden of proof; and, second, carving out an exception for the situations where that method could safely be jettisoned. In the hands of a less buccaneering project proponent, one with greater acuity (and possibly greater resources), the absence of a structured procedural law could render the legitimacy of the end result vulnerable.

On the one hand, therefore, there is a statement of a broad principle frequently deployed. On the other, there is consistently the uncertainty-inducing failure to lend precision to a fundamental legal concept. For no burden of proof can

---

[43] *AP Pollution Control Board II v. Prof M V Nayudu* (2001) 2 SCC 62.

[44] ibid [62]; What is curious, though, is that neither of these is discussed except in [31], where the contents are noted; and there is no discussion of the objections Surana Oils took to the 3 expert reports.

[45] ibid [75].

ever remain a burden without a sound procedural mechanism of discharging that burden. That mechanism must be a replicable template, and it must be set down as the law.

The Public Trust Doctrine

The public trust doctrine was first enunciated in *MC Mehta v. Kamal Nath*,[46] the legendary 'Span Motel' case. Kamal Nath, a former Minister of – ironically – the MoEF, had built a club or a resort on the banks of the River Beas in Himachal Pradesh, encroaching on forest land. This was later 'regularized' (once again, the effacing of law's boundaries by executive action).[47] Acting on a newspaper report, the SCI intervened, and applying the public trust doctrine, quashed the government approval and cancelled the lease. The motel was directed to pay compensation and to show cause why it should not be fined. A boundary wall was to be built (apart from other directions).[48]

Kamal Nath was from the year 1997. The scene shifts to 2009, when the SCI decided the *Fomento Resorts & Hotels Ltd v. Minguel Martins* case.[49] The challenge was, again, to a resort – this time in Goa. The Goa seat of the Bombay HC directed the demolition of part of the Cidade de Goa construction. The hotel company went to the SCI. One of the petitioners before the HC was the Goa Foundation. Before the SCI, the Goa Foundation specifically invoked the doctrine of public trust regarding public access to what was meant to be a public beach. The Court accepted the submission, reiterating the position settled by *Kamal Nath* (which it cited) and noting the adoption of the doctrine in other decisions since.[50] The hotelier was directed to maintain public access to the beach.[51]

---

[46] *MC Mehta v. Kamal Nath* (1997) 1 SCC 388.

[47] See, *K Ramadas Shenoy v. Chief Officer, Town Municipal Council, Udipi* (1974) 2 SCC 506 [30]: 'Illegality is incurable.'

[48] *Kamal Nath* (n.46) [34] 'Our legal system — based on English common law — includes the public trust doctrine as part of its jurisprudence. The State is the trustee of all natural resources which are by nature meant for public use and enjoyment. Public at large is the beneficiary of the sea-shore, running waters, airs, forests and ecologically fragile lands. The State as a trustee is under a legal duty to protect the natural resources. These resources meant for public use cannot be converted into private ownership.'

[49] *Fomento Resorts & Hotels Ltd v. Minguel Martins* (2009) 3 SCC 571.

[50] *MI Builders v. Radhey Shyam Sahu* (1999) 6 SCC 464, regarding an underground shopping complex in Lucknow; *Intellectuals Forum, Tirupathi (n 13)*.

[51] The basis of this judgment was altered by a statutory amendment, the Land Acquisition (Goa Amendment) Act, 2009. In an Article 32 petition challenging the Amendment, the Supreme Court upheld the validity of the amending Act in *Goa Foundation v. State of Goa*, (2016) 6 SCC 602.

In both *Kamal Nath* and *Fomento*, the SCI was seen to take strict action in direct consequence of an application of the public trust doctrine. But *Godavarman* 2024, though it cites both and more, and though it says that politicians and bureaucrats have 'thrown the public trust doctrine in the dustbin', does not follow through, except in the most desultory fashion.

Which brings me to two airports and a bird.

First, the bird. The Great Indian Bustard (GIB). It is today found only in parts of Rajasthan and Gujarat. It is notoriously (and genetically) short-sighted. Specifically, it cannot see power transmission lines below it. Electrocution results. On 19 April 2021, the SCI decided an Article 32 public interest writ petition brought to protect the GIB: *MK Ranjitsinh v. Union of India*.[52] Invoking the principle of sustainable development and the public trust doctrine (and referencing the *Godavarman* 2012 ecocentrism 'drift'), the Court delivered a decision that is as remarkable for its concision (coming in at a mere 14 pages) and its tight focus on the issue at hand – balancing the power transmission needs against ecological concerns. Detailed directions followed, including installing divertors, but the principal direction was to shift the powerlines underground.

For reasons that are difficult to discern, in 2024 in the very same case (it was kept pending),[53] the SCI reversed course. It did so in a judgment spanning 33 pages, couched in scintillating and often stirring prose. The public trust doctrine makes no appearance. The word 'sustainable' is used twenty-five times (sometimes in relation to energy and power). Since the issue was about solar power or energy, the decision strayed – there is really no other word for it – into climate change, and held, among other things, that the right to life, because it includes the right to a wholesome environment, also extends to the 'right to be free from the adverse effects of climate change'.[54]

Sample the Court's conclusions, which are baffling and utterly irreconcilable, with principles and doctrines said to be 'the law of the land'. The Court noted that there was no basis for a 'general prohibition' on the laying of transmission

---

[52] *MK Ranjitsinh v. Union of India* (2021) 15 SCC 1.

[53] *MK Ranjitsinh v. Union of India* 2024 SCC OnLine SC 570.

[54] ibid [35]. 'By recognizing the right to a healthy environment and the right to be free from the adverse effects of climate change, states are compelled to prioritize environmental protection and sustainable development, thereby addressing the root causes of climate change and safeguarding the well-being of present and future generations.'

lines for distributing solar power and that it was not feasible to have all of them 'underground'. It appears to have found an 'intricate interface' between protecting the GIB and 'protecting against climate change' while at the same time adding a caveat that this was 'not a binary choice between conservation and development' but a 'dynamic interplay' between the two compulsions![55] This newfound 'dilemma' called for a consultation with 'domain experts' and for the Court to be 'circumspect in issuing sweeping directions'.[56] Thus, the earlier directions were recalled and an expert committee appointed. The justification for this backtracking was: '. . . By leveraging scientific expertise and engaging stakeholders in meaningful consultations, this approach ensures that conservation efforts are grounded in evidence and inclusive of diverse perspectives.'[57]

It is difficult to know where to begin with a decision like this. The entire dialectic is faux, of positioning the survival of an admittedly endangered species, the GIB, against climate change solely because the power supply and transmission in question here was solar. Would it have mattered to the logic if it was thermal? Or nuclear? Latching on to solar power and then extrapolating to climate change, and then pushing further to pit the GIB against the possible damage to some other (unknown and unspecified) species is jurisprudential prestidigitation. It is a wholesale abandonment of the principles the SCI established and repeatedly reaffirmed. This judgment almost entirely ensures the extinction of the GIB.[58]

---

55 ibid [52]–[53].

56 ibid [61].

57 ibid. Further, in a parting shot of self-affirmation, the Court said: 'This approach allows for more nuanced decision-making tailored to the unique circumstances of each location, ensuring that conservation objectives are met in a sustainable manner.' [62].

58 ibid [52]. Every one of the thirteen reasons in [52] for not laying lines underground is linked to only one aspect, despite all the climate-change bedcovering: money. Some reasons are ludicrous ('it is difficult and time-consuming to detect faults with underground cables.') The entire lot seems to be copypasted from some submission. Grounds g, h, i and j are worth reproducing:

> g. Underground cables may give rise to environmental issues for many vulnerable species. They may also result in forest fires or other fires; h. The cost of laying underground cables is prohibitive. It is about 4 to 5 times higher than laying overhead transmission lines. The cost is estimated to run into thousands of crores. If the cables are undergrounded in their entirety, the cost of harnessing renewable energy would be prohibitive; i. Cables are not generally used for the evacuation of power from a generating station; j. The report prepared by the technical expert committee constituted by the Ministry of Power indicates that the undergrounding of transmission lines of 60kV and above is not technically feasible because any outage would result in large generation losses.

This is by no means an isolated instance. On 7 March 2024, the SCI stayed a Himachal Pradesh HC order of 9 January 2024 regarding the expansion of the Gaggal airport in Kangra.[59] The HC took into account the submission that the State Government was 're-examining' the issue and therefore said it would be inappropriate to let an airport expansion proceed in the meantime, including dispossessing project affected persons or demolishing their structures. Time and expense would be wasted, the HC said, if the decision was indeed re-assessed.[60] There was nothing 'blanket' or 'unjustified' in the HC order; if anything, the opposite. It was an order of circumspection and caution; and it did not decide rights. Nor did it completely steamroll the rights of those affected by the project.

The second airport in question is the one in north Goa, at Mopa in Pernem. The Mopa site and the Barazan plateau is of enormous ecological value, with a large variety of birds, mammals, and more. The adjoining forests of Tillari–Chandgad are said to be tiger habitats, and the entire region is part of the Radhangari–Sawantwadi–Dodarmarg–Bhimgad–Kali region spanning three states. It is here, on a tabletop amidst this forest, that the Mopa greenfield airport was proposed. The Federation of Rainbow Warriors and others challenged the grant of an environmental clearance to the project before the National Green Tribunal (NGT). The NGT affirmed the clearance but said further safeguards were necessary. Two appeals were filed to the SCI, one by Hanuman Laxman Aroskar and the other by the Federation of Rainbow Warriors.

The result was a decision that was remarkably clear-sighted and bold, one that hewed closely to every applicable principle of environmental law. The decision turned significantly on the environmental impact assessment (EIA) said to have been done for the project.[61] The SCI said that the failure to

[59] *The Principal Secretary v. Gaggal Airport Expansion Affected Social Welfare Committee*, SLP (C) No 1676 of 2024, order dated 7 March 2024.

[60] *Gaggal Airport Expansion Affected Social Welfare Committee v. The Principal Secretary*, CWP No 7846 of 2023, order dated 9 January 2024.

[61] *Hanuman Laxman Aroskar v. Union of India* and *Federation of Rainbow Warriors v. Union of India* (2019) 15 SCC 401; The decision closely analysed the entire schema and the principles underlying EIAs. It considered the Guidance Manual for airports. It then considered the failure to disclose the existence of surrounding forests, the existence of an eco-sensitive zone, the importance of public participation and so forth. On every aspect, it found the state government wanting. Section J of the judgment is captioned 'Environmental Rule of Law'. All the principles are incorporated here (including an invocation of international law).

disclose material information as required by the MoEF's EIA Notification of 2006, which was an independent code, had a 'cascading effect' on its purpose. The project proponent, that is, the State Government had failed to discharge its burden of establishing compliance and had not made the mandatory disclosures.[62] The Court explained that 'The basic postulate of the 2006 Notification is that the path which is prescribed for disclosures, studies, gathering data, consultation and appraisal is designed in a manner that would secure decision making which is transparent, responsive and inclusive.'[63] The SCI repelled the argument that the need for a new airport was 'paramount'. Noting that the Expert Appraisal Committee (EAC) had abdicated its functions, the Court reminded that 'while the need for a public project as significant as an international airport is duly factored into the decision making calculus, such development proceeds on a considered view of the importance of the prevailing state of the environment.'[64] The Court then proceeded to issue time-bound directions 'bearing in mind the need to bring about a wholesome balance between the development of infrastructure of an airport and the preservation of the environment.'[65]

A year later, on 16 January 2020, came round two; and if there is ever a case of being hoisted with one's own petard, this is probably it. *Aroskar II*[66] was a result of the MoEFCC moving the SCI to lift the stay on the Environmental Clearance. It seems that following *Aroskar I*, the State Government provided 'supplementary information' to the EAC, which 'revealed certain environmental features' – the existence of reserved forests (earlier denied); proposed reserve forests (also earlier denied); four rivers in Goa and one in Maharashtra; mangroves; the Western Ghat mountain range; and two wetlands. Forest areas in a radial distance of fifteen kilometres were *now* disclosed in three talukas in Goa and three in Maharashtra. And there were reserve forests in Mopa. *Aroskar II* extracted the MoEFCC's recommendations at length and then waxed eloquent on the concessionaire's zero-carbon programme. The petitioner's arguments covered a wide range of issues, including composition

---

62 The Court said: 'There can be no gambles with the environment: a "heads I win, tails you lose" approach is simply unacceptable; unacceptable if we are to preserve environmental governance under the rule of law.' *Aroskar* (n 61) [82].

63 *Aroskar* (n 61) [157].

64 ibid [161].

65 ibid; In [162], it directed the EAC to revisit the conditions subject to which it granted its EC on the basis of the concerns highlighted in the judgment. Till then, it suspended the EC.

66 *Hanuman Laxman Aroskar v. Union of India*, (2020) 12 SCC 1.

of the EAC (which had no members with expertise on ornithology or terrestrial ecosystem); the conflict of interest of the EIA consultant; need for factoring in the objections addressed during public consultation; and EAC's failure to fulfil its remit of 'revisiting the EC as mandated by the order of [the] Court.'[67]

The SCI rejected every one of these concerns. The answer regarding the composition of the EAC as a body is telling – there was not one environmentalist among the thirteen people. Merely saying 'scientific background' and 'domain knowledge' can hardly be sufficient. This is at odds with what follows, for the SCI strongly commended the inclusion in *future* EACs of persons with specialized knowledge of diverse disciplines in relation to environmental protection. On Eco-Sensitive Zones (ESZ), other than noting material, the judgment says nothing. On forestlands, it notes, among other things, that the earlier non-disclosure – which ought to have been fatal on an application of any principle in environmental law – has now been taken care of.[68] The judgment ended with the Court now finding it 'difficult' to hold that the project had failed 'to meet the standards which the court applies in the course of judicial review in environmental matters.'[69]

This is the sheerest casuistry. *Aroskar II* completely elided its specific and strongly-worded findings in *Aroskar I*. The question was *not* whether there were or were not forests; the forests were where they have always been, and for centuries. The question was whether it was legitimate to wholly omit mention of critical factors in the first EIA or whether this vitiated the entire process. Why else would *Aroskar I* have held that 'neither the decision-making process nor the decision itself' could pass legal muster? If neither the process nor its resultant decision passes the smell test, how then can there ever arise a question of after-the-event perfumery? Notably, *Aroskar II* does not even attempt – or dare – to invoke any principle in environmental law. It could not.[70]

---

[67] ibid [25].

[68] ibid [44.2].

[69] ibid [55].

[70] We can multiply these endlessly. *ND Jayal v. Union of India* (2004) 9 SCC 362, on the Tehri Dam is a case in point, a colossal disaster waiting to happen. Or the incredible mandamus compelling the interlinking of all of India's rivers within a decade, *Networking of Rivers, In Re*, (2012) 4 SCC 51.

The pattern of SCI decision-making in environmental litigations is, thus, consistently inconsistent. Even if one considers the pronouncements regarding climate change, these jurisprudential pendulum swings are in themselves not 'sustainable'. It is simply no longer possible to cling to the notion that large projects have no alternatives and to their altar must be sacrificed vital environmental and ecological concerns – questions of the survival of the planet. Our shared future depends on the careful preservation of our environment and ecology. This is not a narrow concern limited to our country. Governments will always promote big spending and large projects. It is up to us to demand viable alternatives. The SCI has, over time, developed rock-solid principles. In its hands lies the power to decide how firmly these are to be applied.

Cases that Have Shaped the Tax Landscape in India

ARVIND P DATAR*

This essay seeks to trace the development of tax jurisprudence in India through the lens of significant decisions of the Supreme Court of India (SCI) on taxation. The power to levy taxes, which is an attribute of sovereignty, as well as the limitations on such power, are governed by the Indian Constitution. In a federal polity as ours, the powers of taxation, both direct and indirect, stand divided between the Parliament and the state legislatures. This has posed its own interpretational challenges. The decisions of the Court on taxation offer a window into the manner in which the tax landscape in India, in the backdrop of our Constitutional framework, has evolved over a period of time. They also reflect the shifts in the Indian and global economy over the last seventy-five years.

Tax laws, *per se*, have two broad aspects. The first is the jurisprudential basis dealing with the levy and collection of taxes. The second is the socio-economic perspective. This essay seeks to examine the decisions of the Court from both perspectives.

The first part of the essay deals with the fundamentals of taxation and taxing powers under the Indian Constitution. The second part deals with the issues on taxation that the Court has dealt with over the last seventy-five years.

Distinction between 'Tax' and 'Fee' and the Components of Tax

The debate over whether a levy constitutes a 'tax' or a 'fee' has arisen primarily on account of the usage of these terms in the different entries in the Seventh Schedule to the Constitution of India. This Schedule sets out the topics on

---

*The author has been assisted by Karthik Sundaram and Harinarayanan K, Advocates, Madras High Court.

which the legislatures can make statutes in three lists: the Union List (List I), which sets out the topics on which the Parliament exclusively can make legislation; the State List (List II), which sets out the topics on which state legislatures exclusively can make legislation; and the Concurrent List (List III), which sets out the topics on which both the Parliament and the state legislatures can make legislation.[1] A specific reference has been made in Article 246 of the Constitution, which is titled 'Subject-Matter of Laws Made by Parliament and the Legislatures of State', to each of these three lists. The residual power of the Parliament to make laws on matters not enumerated in the State List is provided in Article 246 (4) of the Constitution and is set out in so many terms in Entry 97 of List I.[2]

The Union List as well as the State List have separate entries for different types of taxes and fees, separately enumerated. For instance, Entry 82 in the Union List provides for 'taxes on income other than agricultural income', Entries 83 and 84 on duties on customs, and duties on excise, respectively; whereas the State List has likewise separate entries for taxes on agricultural income (Entry 46), taxes on land and buildings (Entry 49), taxes on mineral rights (Entry 50), and so on. Both Lists have one entry each that pertains to 'fees in respect of any of the matters' enumerated in that list (Entry 96 in List I, Entry 66 in List II and Entry 47 in List III). When a challenge is laid to the constitutional validity of a statute (whether enacted by the Parliament or state legislature) that imposes a levy, one of the grounds invariably will be that the concerned legislative body lacked the 'legislative competence' to impose such a levy. It is in such context that it is usually sought to be argued that the nature of the levy is more likely a 'tax' or 'fee', and that accordingly the concerned legislature could not have enacted the statute imposing such a levy.

One of the early instances where the SCI was called upon to determine if the proposed levy under a statute was a 'tax' or a 'fee' was in *Commissioner, Hindu Religious Endowments v. Sri Lakshmindra Thirtha Swamiar of Sri Shirur Mutt*,[3] where the constitutionality of the Madras Hindu Religious and Charitable

---

1 While List I has 97 entries (numerically higher because of entries 2A, 92A, 92B), List II has 66 entries (numerically lower because of omissions of entries 11, 19, 20, 29, 36, 52 and 55) and List III has 47 entries (numerically may be higher on account of insertion of entries 17A, 17B, 20A, 33A). It is only List I that has a 'catch all' residual entry 97, which reads 'any other matter not enumerated in List II or List III including any tax not mentioned in either of those lists'.

2 Constitution of India 1950, schd VII, list 1, entry 97.

3 AIR 1954 SC 282.

Endowments Act, 1951, was under challenge. It was explained that a tax is an involuntary and compulsory extraction without the taxpayer's consent, under a coercive law, a fee is voluntarily paid for a specific purpose. That while taxes are imposed for a public purpose without reference to any special benefit to the taxpayer, fees are charges for specific services rendered by governmental agencies. Further, while taxes form part of the common burden of society, fees relate to the cost of a particular service benefiting individuals. On the facts of the case, it was held that the amount collected under Section 76 of the Act under challenge was a tax and not a fee. The conclusion therefore was that the Madras State Legislature lacked the competence to enact the provision.[4]

In 1999, the SCI was called upon to decide whether a fee for issuing a trade licence for running a lodging house, hotel, etc. by the Hyderabad Municipal Corporation was a tax and therefore invalid since it was not compliant with the procedural requirements of Sections 197 and 198 of the Hyderabad Municipal Corporation Act, 1955. Answering the question in the negative in *Secundarabad Hyderabad Hotel Owner's Association v. Hyderabad Municipal Corporation,*[5] the SCI held that the fees charged were not just for services rendered but have a large element of a 'regulatory fee levied for the purpose of monitoring the activity of the licensees to ensure they comply with the terms and conditions of the license'.[6] The levy was upheld by rejecting the contention that it was in fact a tax.

Moving on to the issue of the 'components of a tax', the Court in *Govind Saran Ganga Saran v. Commissioner of Sales Tax,*[7] held that the well-known components of a tax are: the character of the imposition known by its nature, which prescribes the taxable event attracting the levy; the taxable person; the rate of tax; and the measure of tax. The Court also held that if these components are not clearly and definitely ascertainable, it would be difficult to state that the levy is valid. This concept has been further elaborated in *Gujarat Ambuja Cements v. Union of India*[8] where the Court held that questions related

[4] The Court in *Jindal Stainless Ltd (3) v. State of Haryana,* (2017) 12 SCC 1 has held that the term 'tax' under Article 265 read with Article 366 (28) included imposts of every kind viz. tax, duty, cess or fees. The Court also held that a liability founded on the principles of contract could not be 'tax' in its technical sense, as a tax is necessarily an incident of sovereignty and in the nature of a compulsory extraction.

[5] (1999) 2 SCC 274.

[6] ibid 284. It was held that in case of a regulatory fee, no quid pro quo was necessary but the fee should not be excessive.

[7] 1985 Supp SCC 205.

[8] (2005) 4 SCC 214. In *State of Rajasthan v. Rajasthan State Chemists Association* (2006) 6 SCC 773, the Court has held that the four components of a tax referred above are inter-related having nexus with each other.

to legislative competence should be determined with reference to the object of the tax, which is essentially the character of the tax.

In 1973, an amendment was brought in Section 4 of the Central Excises and Salt Act, 1944, whereby the assessable value of excisable goods, which was ordinarily computed on the manufacturing price (i.e., manufacturing cost plus manufacturers profit), was expanded to include post-manufacturing expenses such as packing, storage, publicity, etc. Upholding the validity of the broader concept of 'assessable value', the SCI in *Union of India v. Bombay Tyre International Ltd*,[9] held that any standard of reference for the purpose of determining the measure of the levy, and any standard that maintains a nexus with the essential character of the levy, can be regarded as a valid basis for assessing the measure of the levy. The Court in *Mineral Area Development Authority v. SAIL*,[10] observed that the measure and levy of tax need not be 'direct and immediate'. The nexus has to be 'reasonable' and must have some relationship with the nature of levy. The Court has repeatedly said that in examining the validity of a fiscal levy, it will generally defer to the legislature that possesses a broad discretion in matters of fiscal levies.[11]

On the issue of 'rate of tax', the Court in *Pandit Banarasi Das Bhanot v. State of Madhya Pradesh*,[12] has held that it is not unconstitutional for the legislature to leave it to the Executive to determine details relating to the working of taxation laws, such as the selection of persons on whom the tax is to be levied, the rate that is to be charged, and the like.[13] The Court after identifying the essential components of a tax has also in certain cases, concluded that if there are no computation provisions, then the charge of tax itself will fail. The leading authority on this proposition is the decision in *Commissioner of Income Tax v. BC Srinivasa Setty*.[14]

---

9 (1984) 1 SCC 467. A further expansion of the concept of assessable value under the Central Excise law was upheld by the SCI in *Assistant Collector of Central Excise v. MRF Limited* AIR 1987 SC 701.

10 2024 SCC OnLine SC 1796.

11 See *Hoechst Pharmaceuticals Limited v. State of Bihar* (1983) 4 SCC 45.

12 (1959) 1 SCR 427.

13 Other important decisions of the Court concerning the rate of taxation, especially as regards the prescription of rates of tax in the Annual Finance Acts, are that in *Chatturam Horilram Ltd v. Commissioner of Income Tax* (1955) 2 SCR 290 and *Commissioner of Income Tax v. Elphinstone Spinning and Weaving Mills Co Ltd* (1960) 3 SCR 953.

14 (1981) 2 SCC 460. In this context, it is also important to refer to the decision of the Court in *Commissioner of Income Tax v. Ajax Products Ltd* (1965) 1 SCR 700, which holds that the subject is not to be taxed unless the charging provision clearly imposes the obligation.

Legislative Power and the Interpretation of Entries in the Three Lists

The Indian Constitution is the fountainhead from which flows both the legislative power to impose a tax and the limitations on such power. In many an instance, the question before the Court revolved around the interpretation and scope of the provisions conferring legislative powers to impose taxes.

In *Commissioner of Commercial Taxes v. RS Jhaver*,[15] the Court held that the entries in the various Lists of the Seventh Schedule must be given the widest possible interpretation. Hence, while making a law under any entry in the Schedule, the legislature would be competent to make all such incidental and ancillary provisions as may be necessary to effectuate the law. In the case of a taxing statute, it is open to the legislature to enact provisions that would check evasion of tax. Provisions for search and seizure are incidental to this power.

On the issue of interpretation of entries in the three lists to the Seventh Schedule, the question that arose was whether a single statute could be enacted by exercise of the powers conferred under two or more entries. In *Ujagar Prints (II) v. Union of India*,[16] the SCI held that if a legislation purporting to be under a particular legislative entry is assailed for lack of legislative competence, the State could seek to support it on the basis of any other entry within the legislative competence of the legislature. It is not necessary for the State to demonstrate that while enacting the law, the legislature was conscious of the source of its competence. Legislative competence could be demonstrated from a number of entries. An example of such a 'ragbag' legislation is the Finance Act, which is passed in the Parliament every year in its Budget session.

The question whether the expression 'industrial alcohol' appearing in Entry 8 of List II (State List) would include 'intoxicating liquor', thus permitting the states to enact legislation to collect excise duty on its manufacture, was answered in the negative by a seven-judge Bench of the SCI in *Synthetics and Chemicals Ltd v. State of Uttar Pradesh*.[17] Recently a nine-judge Bench of the SCI in *State of Uttar Pradesh v. Lalta Prasad Vaish*[18] reversed the

---

15 AIR 1968 SC 59.

16 (1989) 3 SCC 488.

17 AIR 1990 SC 1927; The Court held that the Indian Constitution did not recognize the theory of 'police power' as such and that the right to levy tax or imposts must be in accordance with the provisions of the Constitution.

18 2024 INSC 812; While CJI DY Chandrachud wrote the majority opinion for himself and Hrishikesh Roy, Abhay Oka, JB Pardiwala, Manoj Misra, Ujjal Bhuyan, Satish Chandra Sharma, Augustine George Masih JJ, BV Nagarathna J dissented.

earlier judgment by a majority of 8:1, holding that the said expression does accommodate all manner of 'intoxicating liquor' even if they may be harmful to human health.

The Union List and Its Interpretation

Some of the significant decisions of the SCI that interpret the scope of the entries in List I in the Seventh Schedule are *Elel Hotels & Investments Ltd v. Union of India*[19] on the scope of Entry 82 of List I dealing with the levy of Income tax; *Chhotabhai Jethabhai Patel v. Union of India*[20] and *Ujagar Prints (II)*[21] on the scope of Entry 84 of List I dealing with the levy of excise duty; *Central India Spinning and Weaving and Manufacturing Company v. Municipal Committee, Wardha*;[22] *MPV Sundararamier and Co v. State of Andhra Pradesh*[23] dealing with the scope of terminal taxes on goods and passengers under Entry 89 of List I; and *Vikas Sales Corporation v. Commissioner of Commercial Taxes*[24] on the scope of Entry 92A of List I dealing with taxes on the sale or purchase of goods in the course of inter-state trade or commerce.

The difference between the scope of the legislative entry and the manner in which the term might have been used in a fiscal statute has been the subject matter of consideration in *Elel Hotels*.[25] The constitutional validity of the Hotel Receipts Tax Act, 1980, which imposed a special tax on gross receipts of certain categories of hotels, was challenged on the basis of lack of legislative competence, as also violation of Article 14 and 19 (1) (g) of the Constitution. The Court held that the expression 'income' in Entry 82, List I cannot be subjected, by implication, to any restriction by the way in which that term might have been deployed in a fiscal statute. Negativing the challenge, it was held that what was sought to be brought to tax was in fact a 'tax on luxuries', which was within the legislative competence of the state legislatures.

---

19 (1989) 3 SCC 698.

20 AIR 1962 SC 1006.

21 In *Ujagar Prints (II)* (n 16), it was held that the jurisprudential basis for the 'pith and substance test' flows from Article 246 (1) of the Constitution where the expression 'with respect to' is juxtaposed with the power to make laws in respect of the legislative fields demarcated in the three Lists to the 7th Schedule to the Constitution.

22 AIR 1958 SC 341.

23 1958 AIR 468.

24 (1996) 4 SCC 433.

25 *Elel Hotels* (n 19).

Interpretation of Entries in the State List

The decisions in *State of Madras v. Gannon Dunkerley and Co. (Madras) Ltd*[26](*First Ganon Dunkerly* case); *Builders Association of India v. Union of India*[27] and *Gannon Dunkerley and Co v. State of Rajasthan*[28] are leading authorities on the scope of Entry 54 of List II dealing with the levy of taxes on sale or purchase of goods (as it stood prior to the Constitution [101st Amendment] Act, 2016). In the *First Gannon Dunkerly* case, the SCI considered Entry 48 in List II of the Seventh Schedule to the Government of India Act, 1935 (which corresponds to Entry 54 of List II) and held that the expression 'sale of goods' occurring therein is *nomen juris*, its essential ingredient being an agreement to sell movables for a price and property therein passing pursuant to that agreement. It was held that in a building contract that was indivisible, there was no separate sale of goods and that the provincial legislatures could not tax the supply of materials made as a part of such contract by treating it as a sale. This judgment necessitated the insertion of an amendment to Article 366[29] of the Constitution, in terms of which amendment, the transfer of property in goods involved in the execution of a works contract was deemed to be a sale. In *Builders Association of India*,[30] it was held that the object of inserting Clause 29A in Article 366 was to enlarge the scope of 'tax on sale or purchase of goods' to include the transfer, delivery or supply of goods.

On the scope of Entry 62 of List II dealing with taxes on 'luxuries', including taxes on entertainments, amusements, betting and gambling (as it stood prior to the Constitution [101st Amendment] Act, 2016), the SCI in *Godfrey Phillips India Ltd. v. State of Uttar Pradesh*,[31] held that the word meant the activity of enjoyment of or indulgence in that which is costly or which is generally recognized as being beyond the necessary requirements of an average member of society and not articles of luxury.[32]

---

26 (1959) 1 SCR 379.

27 AIR 1989 SC 1371.

28 (1993) 1 SCC 364.

29 Clause 29A defining 'tax on the sale or purchase of goods' was inserted by the Constitution (46th Amendment) Act 1982 which was inserted with effect from 2 February 1982.

30 *Builders Association of India* (n 27).

31 AIR 2005 SC 1103.

32 An earlier decision in *Express Hotels Pvt Ltd v. State of Gujarat* (1989) 3 SCC 677, held that the word 'luxuries' in Entry 62, List II cannot be limited merely to tax things tangible and corporeal but would encompass the element of extravagance or indulgence not confined to goods and articles but services and activities as well.

Tests and Interpretations under Article 246

Along the same lines, in *International Tourist Corporation v. State of Haryana,*[33] it was held that it was necessary to establish the legislative incompetence of the state legislature before the Parliament could claim exclusive legislative competence by resorting to the residuary power.

In the fourth decade of the Constitution, the SCI had to resolve the seeming conflict between the overlapping powers of the Union and the states. In *Federation of Hotels and Restaurants v. Union of India,*[34] the Court propounded the 'aspect theory', which has thereafter been the subject-matter of much discussion and debate. From a theoretical perspective, the 'aspect theory' can be seen as an exception to the 'doctrine of pith and substance', which is the primary rule. The Court concluded that the tax in question was essentially on expenditure and not on luxuries or sale of goods falling within the state's power.[35]

The Court deliberated on the scope of the residuary entry in Entry 97 of List I in *Union of India v. HS Dhillon (HS Dhillon).*[36] The issue was whether the amendments to the Wealth Tax Act, 1957 to include the capital value of agricultural land for the purposes of computing net wealth was beyond the legislative competence of the Parliament. The Court, by a majority of 4:3 held that there was a distinction between 'net wealth tax' and 'tax on property' and that the impugned levy was not a levy of tax on property, which fell under Entry 49 of List II of the Constitution. The Court held that the only question to be asked was whether the matter sought to be legislated on formed part of or was included in List II or in List III or was the tax sought to be levied mentioned in List II or in List III. If the answer was in the negative, it followed that the Parliament had the power to make laws with respect to that the matter or tax.[37]

---

33 (1981) 2 SCC 318.

34 AIR 1989 SC 1949.

35 The distinct aspect, namely, 'the expenditure' aspect of the transaction falling with the union power must be distinguished and the legislative competence to impose a tax thereon sustained. The 'aspect theory' has thereafter been applied by the Court in its decisions in *All-India Federation of Tax Practitioners v. Union of India,* (2007) 7 SCC 527 and *Union of India v. Mohit Mineral Pvt Ltd,* (2019) 2 SCC 599.

36 AIR 1972 SC 1061.

37 In *Commissioner of Wealth Tax v. Dr Karan Singh* 1993 Supp (1) SCC 500, the decision in *HS Dhillon* (n 36) was clarified. The context was the applicability of the Wealth Tax Act, 1957 to the State of Jammu and Kashmir. First it had to be examined whether the subject matter of the legislation formed a part of

Introduction of GST – the 101st Constitution Amendment Act

Article 246A, which has been introduced in the Constitution through the Constitution (101st Amendment) Act, 2016 fundamentally changes the constitutional structure related to taxing powers of the Union and state governments and empowers both the Parliament and state legislatures to make laws with respect to GST imposed by the union and the states. Prior to such amendment, there existed a complete separation of taxing powers of the union and the states under Article 246. There was no simultaneous conferment of taxing powers on the union and the states with respect to any specified field of taxation. This has changed with the 101st Constitution Amendment, which confers simultaneous powers on the Union and the states to make laws in respect of GST, as is the stated purpose of the 101st Constitution Amendment.

In *Union of India v. VKC Footsteps Pvt Ltd*,[38] it was held that since Article 246A itself defined the source of power as well as the field of legislation (with respect to goods and services tax), there was no need to travel to the Seventh Schedule to find out the appropriate entry with reference to which it could have been enacted. It was held that Article 246A 'embodies the constitutional principle of simultaneous levy as distinct from the principle of concurrence'.[39]

Limitations on Taxing Power

In *Kunnathat Thatehunni Moopil Nair v. State of Kerala*,[40] it was held that Article 265 imposed a limitation on the taxing power of the state. That tax cannot be levied by way of an executive fiat but can only be levied by way of a valid law, meaning that the levy of tax should be within the legislative competence of the legislature imposing the tax and is subject to the conditions

any entry under List II. If not, it was within the competence of the Parliament. It was not necessary to decide whether the impugned legislation fell within Entry 86 List I read with Entry 97 List I, or Entry 97 List I alone.

38 (2022) 2 SCC 603.

39 In *Union of India v. Mohit Minerals (P) Ltd.* (2022) 10 SCC 700, the Court, *inter alia*, held that the recommendations made by the GST Council were not required to be tabled in the legislature and therefore were not mandatory. Only the secondary legislation which is framed based on the recommendations of the Council under the provisions of the CGST Act (Section 166 of the CGST Act) and the IGST Act (Section 24 of the IGST Act) mandated tabling in the Parliament. In the same decision, the Court upheld the constitutional validity of the GST (Compensation to States) Act, 2017.

40 (1961) 3 SCR 77.

laid down in Article 13 of the Constitution of India.[41] The theme that the power to levy taxes is subject to constitutional limitations, especially in a federal polity such as ours, also finds resonance in the nine-judge-Bench decision in *Jindal Stainless Ltd (3) v. State of Haryana*.[42]

Some of the other constitutional limitations on the imposition of taxes are those which can be found in Articles 285 to 289 of the Constitution. In *In Re: Sea Customs Act*,[43] it was held that the intention of the Constitution-makers was that Article 285 would exempt all property of the Union from all taxes on property levied by a state or by any authority within the state. On the other hand, Article 289 contemplated that all property of the states would be exempt from all taxes on property that may be leviable by the Union. The SCI opined that both Articles 285 and 289 were concerned with taxes directly either on income or on property and not with taxes that may indirectly affect income or property. It further opined that the immunity granted to the states in respect of Union taxation did not extend to duties of customs, including export duties or duties of excise.[44]

'Nexus' and Territorial Extent of Tax Laws

In the context of our Constitution, when one speaks of the territorial limits of taxation or 'taxing nexus', the two primary articles of the Constitution that usually come into play are Article 245, which deals with the 'Extent of laws made by Parliament and by the Legislatures of States', and Article 286, which deals with 'Restrictions as to imposition of tax on the sale or purchase of goods'.

---

41 In *Hari Krishna Bhargav v. Union of India* (1966) 59 ITR 243, it was held that while a tax is not open to challenge on the ground that it is harsh or excessive, it is subject to the conditions laid down in Article 13 of the Constitution of India. In *Balaji v. Income Tax Officer* (1961) 43 ITR 393, the Court held that the combined and plain reading of Article 13 and Article 265 of the Constitution makes it abundantly clear that a law which is inconsistent with any of the provisions of Part III is void.

42 (2017) 12 SCC 1. In *Murthy Match Works v. The Assistant Collector of Central Excise* (1974) 4 SCC 428, it was held that unconstitutionality and not unwisdom of legislation, is the narrow area of judicial review. In the recent nine-judge decision in *Mineral Area Development Authority* (n 10), it was observed that Article 245 makes the exercise of legislative powers expressly subject to the provisions of the Constitution.

43 AIR 1963 SC 1760.

44 In *Andhra Pradesh State Road Transport Corporation (APSRTC) v. Income Tax Officer* AIR 1964 SC 1486, the Court held that even if the state owns the bulk of the capital of the APSRTC, the income of the corporation cannot be treated as 'income' of the state as a majority shareholder. Consequently, the immunity from taxation under Article 289 of the Constitution will not be available to the corporation.

In *State of Bombay v. RMD Chamarbaugwala*,[45] the SCI held that the Bombay Lotteries and Prize Competition Control and Tax Act (amended) being a law in relation to betting and gambling (Entry 34 of List II) and tax on betting and gambling (Entry 62 of List II) was within the competence of the state legislature. The Court also held that though the newspaper was published outside Bombay, it was widely circulated in Bombay and that there were collection agents in Bombay to collect entry forms and fees, and hence there was sufficient territorial nexus to entitle the state legislature to collect the tax.

In *Bengal Immunity Co Ltd v. State of Bihar*,[46] the Court observed that the expression 'extra-territorial operation', as appearing in Article 245 of the Constitution, can have two connotations: (a) a reference to law in respect of acts or events that take place inside the state but have operation outside; and (b) laws with reference to nationals of a nation state in respect of their actions outside the nation state. In the view of the Court, the expression 'extra-territorial operation' referred to the second situation referred above.

In *GVK Industries Ltd v. Income Tax Officer*,[47] the Court concluded that (a) the Parliament did not have the power to legislate for any territory other than the territory of India; (b) the Parliament was empowered to make laws with respect to aspects or causes that occur, arise or exist or may be expected to do so, within the territory of India, and also with respect to extra-territorial aspects or causes that have an impact on or nexus with India; and (c) that any laws enacted by the Parliament with respect to extra-territorial aspects or causes that have no impact on or nexus with India would be ultra-vires and would be laws made 'for a foreign territory'.[48]

---

[45] AIR 1957 SC 699.

[46] AIR 1955 SC 661.

[47] (2011) 4 SCC 36.

[48] The Court also noted that the Parliament is constitutionally restricted from enacting legislation with respect to extra-territorial aspects or causes that do not have, nor are expected to have any direct or indirect, tangible or intangible impact(s) on or effect(s) in or consequences for (a) the territory of India, or any part of India; or (b) the interests of, welfare of, well-being of or security of inhabitants of India, and Indians. On the issue of nexus or connection with India, the Court observed that while the same should not be subjected to prior tests such as 'sufficiency' or 'significance' or in any other manner requiring a predetermined degree of strength, the connection to India be real or expected to be real, and not illusory or fanciful, and that such determination is a mixed question of fact and law.

Retrospectivity of Tax Legislation

The broad principles relating to the retrospective operation of tax statutes as laid down in the decision of the Court in *RC Tobacco (P) Ltd v. Union of India*[49] are as follows:

(a) to violate constitutional norms, the retrospective operation of a fiscal statute should be unduly oppressive and confiscatory or discriminatory; and

(b) the period of retrospectivity and degree of unforeseen or unforeseeable financial burdens imposed for the past period are considerations though the length of time by itself is not decisive to affect retrospectivity.

When one speaks about retrospective legislation, one also needs to look at and examine the scope of validation acts passed by the legislature. On this issue, the SCI, in *Prithvi Cotton Mills Ltd v. Broach Borough Municipality*,[50] has held that the legislature can enact a validating law that re-enacts a statute that has been struck down by removing the defect therein pointed out by the Court. Further, such a validating statute can be made retrospective, thereby saving all actions taken under the 'struck down' statute. While the validating act is itself subject to judicial review, if the Court finds that the mischief or the defect pointed out by the Court, which led to the invalidation of the statute, has not been removed, the validating act would also become vulnerable to being struck down by the Court.

Cases Concerning Tax Legislation in the Initial Years of the Court

One issue that concerned the Court in the initial decade of the Constitution was the interpretation of Article 286 of the Constitution, which deals with 'restrictions as to imposition of tax on the sale or purchase of goods'. In *State of Bombay v. United Motors (India) Ltd (United Motors [India] Ltd)*,[51] the Court dealt with the validity of the Bombay Sales Tax Act, 1952 and the interpretation of the explanation to Article 286 (1) of the Constitution. It was

[49] (2005) 7 SCC 725.

[50] AIR 1970 SC 192.

[51] (1953) 1 SCC 514.

held that Article 286 (1) (a) read with the explanation prohibits taxation of sales or purchases involving inter-state elements by all states except the state in which the goods are delivered for the purpose of consumption therein. The latter state is left free to tax such sales or purchases; this power it derives not by virtue of the explanation but under Article 246 (3) read with Entry 54 of List II.

The decision in *United Motors (India) Ltd* was within a period of three years, overruled by a larger Bench of the SCI in *Bengal Immunity Co Ltd.*[52] It now held that the earlier decision did not affect only the parties before the Court, but the taxing rights of the state vis-à-vis the consuming public. It further held that Article 286 (2) placed a restriction on the taxing power of the states on sales or purchases in the course of inter-state trade or commerce and that unless and until such ban was lifted by the Parliament, no state in which the goods were delivered could levy a tax on sale or purchase in the course of inter-state trade or commerce.[53]

All the above cases dealt with the position prior to the Constitution (Sixth Amendment) Act, 1956, which omitted the explanation to Article 286 (1) and substituted the provisions of Article 286 (2) and 286 (3) of the Constitution. This Amendment also introduced Entry 92-A in List I to Seventh Schedule, which empowered the Parliament to make laws on the sale or purchase of goods other than newspapers in the course of inter-state trade or commerce.[54]

In *JV Gokal and Co v. Assistant Collector of Sales Tax*,[55] the Court held that the purchase of goods on the high seas against shipping documents for payment, before the goods cross the customs frontiers of India, is a 'sale in the course of import' for the purposes of Article 286 (1) (b) of the Constitution and could

---

52 *Bengal Immunity Co Ltd* (n 46).

53 In *MPV Sundararamier and Co* (n 23), the Court held that under Entry 54 of List II, the states were competent to enact laws levying tax on inter-state sales subject to the restriction under Article 286 (2) of the Constitution. In *State of Travancore–Cochin v. Shanmugha Vilas Cashewnut Factory, Quilon,* AIR 1953 SC 333, the Court dealt with the issue of interpretation of Article 286 (1) (b) of the Constitution and held that a sale in the course of export out of the country should be understood in the context of Clause (1) (b) as meaning a sale taking place not only during the activities directed to the end of exportation of the goods out of the country but also as part of or connected with such activities. The Court also held that the last purchase of goods made by the exporter for the purpose of exporting them to implement orders already received from a foreign buyer or expected to be received subsequently in the course of business, would not be covered within the scope of Article 286 (1) (b) of the Constitution.

54 The Central Sales Tax Act, 1956 was enacted with reference to Entry 92-A.

55 AIR 1960 SC 595.

not be subject to a levy of sales tax. The Court also held that the law in India was that the delivery of the 'bill of lading' when the goods were afloat was equivalent to the delivery of goods itself.

Decisions Reflective of the Prevailing Economic Policy

When the decisions of the Court on taxation over the last seventy-five years are examined, they appear to be responding to the prevalent social and economic policies. In the initial years, the primary issues of concern before the Court were those dealing with agricultural income, taxation of Hindu Undivided Family (HUF) income, etc. In *Andhra Sugars Ltd v. State of Andhra Pradesh*,[56] the SCI dealt with the issue of differential treatment of the factories producing sugar by means of vacuum pans, *khandsari* units producing sugar by open-pan process and cane growers using cane for the manufacture of jaggery, and whether they were reasonable and had a rational relation to the object of taxation. The Court held that while, ordinarily, purchase tax is levied with reference to the turnover, which is the aggregate of the purchase prices so paid, the occupier of a factory can be subjected to purchase tax by reference to the weight of goods purchased by them. It also held there are marked differences between the three classes of users of cane and their capacity to pay the tax, and that the legislature could reasonably treat the three sets of users of cane differently for purposes of levy.

In *Navnit Lal C Javeri v. KK Sen*,[57] while dealing with the constitutional validity of Section 12 (1B) read with Section 2 (6A) (e) of the Indian Income Tax Act, 1922, dealing with the taxation of 'deemed dividend', the Court held that while there must be some rational connection between the item taxed and the concept of 'income' when liberally construed, if the legislature realized that the private-controlled companies generally adopted the device of making advances or giving loans to their shareholders with the object of evading the payment of tax, it could step in to meet this mischief, and that, in that connection, it had created a fiction by which the amount ostensibly and nominally advanced to a shareholder as a loan was treated in reality for tax purposes as the payment of dividend to the said shareholder. The Court also held that given the mischief sought to be remedied, the taxation of 'deemed

[56] AIR 1968 SC 599.

[57] AIR 1965 SC 1375.

dividend' would fall within the legislative field assigned to the Parliament under Entry 82 of List I to the Constitution.

Lohia Machines Ltd v. Union of India[58] dealt with the interpretation of Section 80J (1) of the Income Tax Act, 1961 and the validity of Rule 9A of the Income Tax Rules, 1962. These provisions grant tax relief to new businesses in respect of 'capital employed' for tax exemption purposes. However, it excludes 'borrowed capital' in the computation of 'capital employed'. Such exclusion was challenged as being arbitrary, unreasonable, beyond the scope of the Act and as being in excess of the legal authority granted under the Income Tax Act. The Court held that the expression 'capital employed' has a variable meaning that may or may not include long-term borrowings and therefore, if the Central Board of Revenue makes rule or rules providing for the exclusion of long-term borrowings in computation of the 'capital employed', there can be no question of encroaching upon or remoulding the substance of the 'capital employed'. That would be clearly within the authority of the Central Board of Revenue to prescribe the manner or mode of computation of the 'capital employed'.

With the opening up of the Indian economy, globalization and increase in cross-border trade, the nature of issues that arise for consideration before the Court has undergone a drastic change. The Court, in the last two decades, has been dealing with a multitude of issues, such as tax treatment under Double Tax conventions, treatment of sale of shares in entities outside India that has an underlying business effect in India, treatment of payments made to overseas software suppliers and the operation of treaties containing a most favoured nation (MFN) clause.

In *Union of India v. Azadi Bachao Andolan*,[59] which is a seminal decision on the issue of the tax treatment under the India–Mauritius Double Tax Avoidance Convention, 1983 (DTAC), the Court held that Section 90 of the Income Tax Act, 1961, is specifically intended to enable and empower the Central Government to issue a notification for implementation of the terms of a Double Taxation Avoidance Agreement (DTAA). The very object of grafting the said two sections, that is, Section 4 and Section 5, with the expression 'subject to the provisions of the Act' is to enable the Central Government to

---

[58] AIR 1985 SC 421.

[59] (2004) 10 SCC 1.

issue a notification under Section 90 towards implementation of the terms of DTACs, which would automatically override the provisions of the Income Tax Act in the matter of ascertainment of chargeability to income tax and ascertainment of total income, to the extent of inconsistency with the terms of DTAC.[60]

Vodafone International Holdings (VIH) BV v. Union of India,[61] held that when it came to taxation of a holding structure, at the threshold, the burden was on the Revenue to allege and establish abuse in the sense of tax avoidance in the creation and/or use of such structure(s). In the application of a judicial anti-avoidance rule, the Revenue may invoke the 'substance over form' principle or 'piercing the corporate veil' test only after it is able to establish on the basis of the facts and circumstances surrounding the transaction that the impugned transaction is a sham or tax avoidance.[62]

Engineering Analysis Centre of Excellence (P) Ltd v. Commissioner of Income Tax[63] dealt with the contentious issue of whether payment(s) made to non-resident suppliers of software amounted to royalty payments, which were required to be subject to Tax Deduction at Source (TDS) in terms of Section 195 of the Income Tax Act, 1961. On the real nature of the transactions that fell for consideration by the Court, it opined that what was 'licensed' by the foreign, non-resident supplier to the distributor and resold to the resident

---

[60] The Court also upheld that validity of Circular No. 789 of 2000 on the basis that the clarifications were in line with the legal position and a Circular issued to set things on course by eliminating avoidable wastage of time of the assessing officers discharging the onerous public duty of collection of revenue cannot be faulted when the Circular does not in any confine the powers of the assessing officer with regard to any particular assessment. It merely formulates broad guidelines to be applied in the matter of assessment of the assessees covered by the provisions of the DTAC.

[61] 2012 (6) SCC 757.

[62] On facts, it was held that the case concerned a straightforward share sale. VIH (Dutch tax resident) acquired the entire share capital of CGP Investments (Holdings) Ltd (tax resident of Cayman Islands) (CGP), from Hutchison group (resident in Hong Kong). CGP indirectly owned sixty-seven per cent of Hutchison Essar Limited (HEL), the Indian telecommunication business. VIH acquired upstream shares with the intention that the congeries of rights, flowing from the CGP Investments (CGP) share, would give VIH an indirect control over the three genres of companies. The Court also held that Section 195 of the Income Tax Act casts an obligation on the payer to deduct tax at source from payments made to non-residents which payments are chargeable to tax. Such payment(s) must have an element of income embedded in it which is chargeable to tax in India. If the sum paid or credited by the payer is not chargeable to tax then no obligation to deduct the tax would arise. Shareholding in companies incorporated outside India (CGP) is property located outside India. Where such shares become subject-matter of offshore transfer between two non-residents, there is no liability for capital gains tax and consequently the question of deduction of Tax at Source would not arise.

[63] 2021 SCCOnline SC 159.

end-user, or directly supplied to the resident end-user, was in fact the sale of a physical object that contained an embedded computer program, and was therefore, a sale of goods.

In *Assessing Officer v. Nestle SA*,[64] the issue before the Court was whether there was any right to invoke the MFN clause when the third country with which India had entered into a DTAA was not a member of the Organization for Economic Co-operation and Development (OECD) yet (at the time of entering into such DTAA); and secondly, whether the MFN clause was to be given effect to automatically or if it was to only come into effect after a notification has been issued. The Court held that either the treaty concerned had to be legislatively embodied in Indian law through a separate statute, or get assimilated through a legislative device. Absent this step, treaties and protocols were *per se* unenforceable.[65]

Whether Royalty Is a 'Tax'

The vexed question whether royalty under the Mines and Minerals (Development and Regulation) Act, 1957 (MMDR Act) was a 'tax' was referred to a nine-judge Bench of the Court in 2011 in *Mineral Area Development Authority v. SAIL.*[66] There was a conflict between an earlier decision in *India Cement Ltd. v. State of Tamil Nadu*,[67] which held that royalty was in the nature of a 'tax' and that the state legislatures did not have the competence to levy tax on mineral rights, and, the decision in *State of West Bengal v. Kesoram Industries*,[68] where the Court clarified that there was an inadvertent error in the decision in *India Cement* and that royalty under the MMDR Act was not a 'tax'. The Court, by an 8:1 majority, in *Mineral Area Development Authority* concluded that royalty was not a tax; it was a contractual consideration paid

64 2023 SCCOnline SC 1372.

65 ibid [72]; The fact that a stipulation in a DTAA or a protocol with one nation, requires same treatment in respect to a matter covered by its terms, subsequent to its being entered into when another nation (which is member of a multilateral organization such as OECD), is given better treatment, does not automatically lead to integration of such term extending the same benefit in regard to a matter covered in the DTAA of the first nation, which entered into DTAA with India. In such an event, the terms of the earlier DTAA require to be amended through a separate notification under Section 90.

66 *Mineral Area Development Authority* (n 10) [5]; See also *Mineral Area Development Authority v. SAIL* (2011) 4 SCC 450.

67 (1990) 1 SCC 12.

68 (2004) 10 SCC 201.

by the mining lessee to the lessor for enjoyment of mineral rights. It was held that payments made to the Government could not be deemed to be a tax merely because the statute provided for their recovery as arrears.[69] The Court overruled the decision in *India Cement* and certain other cases to the extent of the observations made by thc Court in the reference.

Concluding Observations

From a jurisprudential perspective, the decisions of the Court in its early days constitute the building blocks upon which later case law jurisprudence in taxation has developed and evolved. While each individual decision referred to in this essay is important in its own right, the endeavour of this essay has not been to analyse or focus on any particular decision but rather see how these decisions have combined together to form the tapestry of tax jurisprudence in India.

While taxes are certain, what is more important is certainty in taxation as well as in the interpretation of tax laws. When one looks at the subject of tax certainty, the need of the hour is certainty in both tax policy as well as judicial interpretation of the fundamental concepts of taxation.

However, one issue that possibly requires introspection is the time period taken by the Court to revisit certain of its earlier decisions, which in the view of the Court do not reflect the correct legal position. The law is ever-evolving, and the Court needs to and is more than right in revisiting certain of its earlier decisions that, it believes, do not reflect the correct legal and jurisprudential position.

[69] *Mineral Area Development Authority* (n 10) [130]–[137], [365.1]; Entry 50 of List II does not constitute an exception to the position of law laid down in *MPV Sundararamier and Co* (n 23). The legislative power to tax mineral rights vests with the state legislatures. The Parliament does not have legislative competence to tax mineral rights under Entry 54 of List I, it being a general entry. Since the power to tax mineral rights is enumerated in Entry 50 of List II, the Parliament cannot use its residuary powers with respect to that subject-matter.

YOUR REPORT ON ME IS DEFAMATORY AND ILLEGAL! TAKE IT DOWN!

I LITERALLY JUST REPORTED THE FACTS
THE FACTS ARE DEFAMATORY AND ILLEGAL! TAKE THEM DOWN!
RACHITA
@sanitarypanels

Media Freedom

GAUTAM BHATIA

The Supreme Court of India (SCI) has often insisted that the media does not enjoy any special constitutional rights; rather, freedom of press is enfolded within the broader constitutional right to freedom of speech and expression guaranteed under Article 19 (1) (a) of the Constitution. A survey of media freedom as a part of looking back upon seventy-five years of the SCI's jurisprudence, thus, cannot be disentangled from the broader history and evolution of the jurisprudence around the right to free speech.

Indeed, right from the initial *Romesh Thappar*[1] and *Brij Bhushan*[2] cases, free speech jurisprudence has been shaped by cases brought by newspapers or by journalists. With that said, however, there are also domains that directly impact the media in a way that they do not impact other individuals or entities who may seek to exercise their rights to free speech. This essay, therefore, will survey both strands of jurisprudence: general free speech jurisprudence where the media has often been a protagonist, and those parts of free speech jurisprudence that specifically concern media freedom.

By way of historical context, it is important to note that the press in general – and newspapers in particular – played an important role in the Indian nationalist movement and the struggle for freedom in the first half of the twentieth century. While the origin of independent newspapers as the 'fourth estate', responsible for subjecting the record of the government and the administration to critique, goes back to the late eighteenth and early nineteenth centuries in India[3], a nationalist public sphere began to emerge in the early years of the twentieth century. The importance of the press to the nationalist cause can be gauged from the fact that the colonial British

1 *Romesh Thappar v. State of Madras* 1950 SCR 594.

2 *Brij Bhushan v. State of Delhi* 1950 SCR 605.

3 See Andrew Otis, *Hicky's Bengal Gazette: The Untold Story of India's First Newspaper* (Westland 2018).

government passed an increasingly draconian set of press acts throughout these years, subjecting the press both to prior restraints upon publication (through licensing and registration requirements, and also through pre-censorship), as well as to stringent post-publication laws, complete with criminal prosecution.

At the time of Independence and the framing of the Constitution, thus, India had a history both of a press that saw itself as independent of the ruling regime, as well as of press censorship that sought to curtail that independence. It is in this context that we must study the battles over media freedom in the post-colony under the framework of the Indian Constitution.

Freedom of Speech and the Media

It is perhaps significant that the first two cases on the freedom of speech decided by the SCI both concerned the press. *Romesh Thapar*[4] and *Brij Bhushan*[5] both involved the ban and/or seizure of certain magazines and periodicals, ostensibly on the grounds of maintaining public order (under the relevant provincial legislation).[6] In both those cases, the SCI struck down the impugned state action on the basis that public order was not – at the time – a ground on which the freedom of speech could be restricted. These cases were notable for the Court taking an approach to Article 19 (1) that sought to read the restrictions clause narrowly and invalidate state action that strayed beyond its contours; indeed, the Court noted so explicitly. This approach, however, was not to last: the Parliament (at that time, the provisional Parliament, which was the same as the Constituent Assembly) enacted the First Amendment with a specific view to overcome these judgments, and expand the scope of Article 19 (2).[7] The SCI also changed its approach in response, and over the years, became substantially more deferential to the State when it came to speech deemed to be 'subversive' or a threat to public order.[8] It was only many years later – in the 2015 *Shreya Singhal* case – that

---

4 *Romesh Thappar* (n 1).

5 *Brij Bhushan* (n 2).

6 *Brij Bhushan* was a more draconian case, as it involved pre-publication restrictions. The SCI ruled such restrictions to be per se unconstitutional. This position has never been formally overruled, but nor has it been subsequently endorsed by the Court.

7 The Constitution (First Amendment) Act 1951.

8 See *State of Bihar v. Shailabala Devi* 1952 SCR 654; *Ramji Lal Modi v. State of Uttar Pradesh* 1957 SCR 334; *Kedar Nath Singh v. State of Bihar* AIR 1962 SC 955.

the Court would go back to a narrow test for the restriction of subversive speech: that of incitement to imminent violence.[9]

Other than subversive speech, there are perhaps three domains where free speech jurisprudence directly impacts media freedom: hate speech, defamation (both civil and criminal) and privacy on the one hand and contempt of court on the other. Both the law of defamation (and in some cases, privacy claims) and the law of contempt have been deployed as means of 'lawfare' against the press in India[10] and abroad.[11] On both counts, regrettably, and with a few exceptions, the SCI's jurisprudence has been less than satisfactory.

The issue of hate speech has occupied significant attention of late, with the SCI handing down judgments attempting to define what hate speech is, as well as exercising continued supervision over ongoing cases involving hate speech. Indeed, the SCI's most elaborate consideration of the issue came in the context of a journalist, Amish Devgan, who was accused of calling a revered religious figure a 'robber' and a 'terrorist'.[12] The Court drew a link between hate speech and the denial of equal concern and respect to all sections of the society, and refused to quash the first information reports (FIRs) against Amish Devgan (while granting him interim protection). Soon after, a different Bench of the Court had an opportunity to apply these principles in a case involving a television programme called 'UPSC Jihad' on Sudarshan TV, which, it was argued, accused Muslims of writing the Union Public Service Commission (UPSC) exam for the purpose of subverting the administrative services from within, and attempted to make this point with graphics showing a bearded man in the backdrop of an exploding bomb. Although the Court did not deliver a final judgment on the issue, it did hear arguments at length (this essay's author was one of the counsels in the case), and it injuncted the programme from continuing further after four episodes had been aired.[13]

In the domain of defamation, in 2016, a two-judge Bench of the SCI upheld the constitutionality of criminal defamation law (at the time, sections 499 and 500 of the Indian Penal Code (IPC)).[14] The basis of the SCI's judgment was

[9] *Shreya Singhal v. Union of India* (2015) 5 SCC 1.

[10] The former Chief Minister (CM) of Tamil Nadu, J Jayalalithaa, was known to have filed more than 6,000 defamation cases in the course of her long tenure in power.

[11] The most famous example of this is of Lee Kuan Yeuw from Singapore.

[12] *Amish Devgan v. Union of India* (2020) 14 SCR 198.

[13] *Firoz Iqbal Khan v. Union of India* (2021) 2 SCC 591.

[14] *Subramanian Swamy v. Union of India* (2016) 7 SCC 221.

the need to 'balance' the right to free speech and the right to reputation. The judgment, however, left many questions unanswered: in particular, whether criminalizing defamation satisfied the test of proportionality (given that a civil remedy existed); whether the standard under section 499 of the IPC was consistent with the doctrine developed by the Court in *R Rajagopal v. State of Tamil Nadu*,[15] with respect to the need for 'actual malice' to be satisfied in a defamation claim involving public figures; and whether a more rigorous standard under criminal defamation (as opposed to civil defamation) satisfied the test of non-arbitrariness.[16] At the time of writing, however, criminal defamation continues to be on the statute books, now in the form of the new Bharatiya Nyaya Sanhita (BNS).

With respect to civil defamation, because of various structural reasons pertaining to the nature of civil litigation in India, the SCI has not had a significant occasion to develop legal doctrine. There is a general assumption that, in the absence of express codification, India continues to follow the common law of defamation (although its application, especially at the level of the trial courts, remains patchy). However, given that most defamation cases do not get to trial and a verdict on merits, the impact on speech and media freedom takes place at the stage of the *injunction*. In this respect, in the teeth of conflicting judgments at all levels of the judiciary (often unaccompanied by substantive reasoning), the SCI's recent reiteration of the hoary test in *Bonnard v. Perryman* is welcome.[17] It restrains courts from injuncting speech as long as the defendant can offer a plausible defence; the validity of the defence will be tested at trial, but in the meantime, the marketplace of ideas will not be closed off (the plaintiff's remedy, if successful, will be damages).[18] A uniform and consistent application of the test would constitute a substantial shot in the arm for media freedom in India, at least as far as resisting defamation suits (often in the form of strategic litigation against public participation

---

15 *R Rajagopal v. State of Tamil Nadu* (1994) 6 SCC 632; this case also considered the balance between privacy and free speech.

16 See Gautam Bhatia, 'The Supreme Court's Criminal Defamation Judgment: Glaringly Flawed' (*Constitutional Law and Philosophy*, 13 May 2016) <https://indconlawphil.wordpress.com/2016/05/13/the-supreme-courts-criminal-defamation-judgment-glaringly-flawed/> accessed 28 February 2025.

17 *Bloomberg Television Production Services India Pvt Ltd v. Zee Entertainment Enterprises Ltd* (2025) 1 SCC 741. See also, *Bonnard v. Perryman* (1891) 2 Ch 269.

18 *Bloomberg Television* (n 17) [8].

– SLAPP[19]) goes. However, it remains to be seen if the SCI's dictum will percolate down the judicial hierarchy.[20]

On the issue of contempt of court, the SCI has consistently adopted a vague and loose formulation that makes it difficult to predict what kind of speech will fall on the wrong side of the line. The Contempt of Courts Act, 1971 criminalizes the offence of 'scandalising the court'.[21] The Court's test, which broadly replicates the statutory provision – that is, whether speech has the 'tendency' to substantially interfere with the course of justice – leaves a lot to subjective play in the joints[22]; certain judges, for example, have even gone so far as to argue that calling a judgment a 'misdeed' amounts to contempt of court (albeit in dissent).[23] The impact of this is a chilling effect when it comes to writing about the Court in the media, which is difficult to measure in quantitative terms, but which is substantiated through anecdotal evidence and personal testimonies. The 'chilling effect' refers to a phenomenon where vague and indeterminate legal standards lead individuals to engage in self-censorship and refrain from engaging in even legitimate speech for fear of crossing a blurred and difficult-to-identify line.[24] The SCI's contempt of court jurisprudence has undoubtedly resulted in a chilling effect on speech *about* the Court.

This is reflected through a number of inconsistent judgments on the point that have created significant confusion about the scope of the offence. For example, in *In Re: Arundhati Roy*,[25] the SCI found the celebrated writer Arundhati Roy guilty of contempt and sentenced her to a symbolic 'one day' of imprisonment. Ironically, the speech for which Roy was arraigned was an accusation that the SCI was 'muzzling dissent' in respect of its ruling in the *Narmada* Dam

---

19 George W Pring and Penelope Canan, *SLAPPs: Getting Sued for Speaking Out* (Temple University Press 1996).

20 Ideally, the same set of considerations should apply to privacy claims.

21 See, Section 2 (c) (i), The Contempt of Courts Act, 1971.

22 See, *Re Arundhati Roy* AIR 2002 SC 1375; *D C Saxena v. Hon'ble Chief Justice of India* 1996 (5) SCC 216.

23 *In Re: Shri Sham Lal* (1978) 2 SCC 479, where CJI Beg initiated contempt proceedings against an editor for criticizing the now-notorious *Habeas Corpus* (*ADM Jabalpur*) judgment. CJI Beg was outvoted by two of his colleagues who decided to drop the proceedings but penned a lengthy dissent essentially defending his own judgment

24 The concept was articulated by the SC of the US in the landmark judgment of *New York Times v. Sullivan* 376 US 254 (1964) and later accepted by the SCI in *Shreya Singhal* (n 9).

25 *Arundhati Roy* (n 22).

case![26] A perusal of the Court's judgment reveals that what it considered more objectionable was not so much the potential that Roy's words had to *actually* obstruct the course of justice, but rather, the *substantive content* of her words that tended to lower the 'reputation' of the Court.

More recently, the comedian Kunal Kamra has found himself at the receiving end of contempt of court proceedings for a series of satirical tweets about the SCI's alacrity in granting bail to the TV presenter Arnab Goswami, compared to its seeming slowness in other cases.[27] The Attorney General, while sanctioning contempt proceedings, noted that Kamra's tweets had crossed the line from 'humour' to 'contempt'. A closer look at the tweets reveals that, in essence, Kamra suggested the existence of a two-tier justice system, where individuals with relative power and privilege received fast-track access to justice, while others did not. This is, of course, a long-standing critique of judiciaries in general and of the Indian judiciary in particular; but what appeared to have particularly angered Kamra's accusers was the irreverent manner in which he made this critique – for example, by comparing the judge hearing the case to an airline attendant serving champagne to first-class customers. This sense is buttressed by the fact that, at the same time, the Court also issued notice on contempt proceedings against the cartoonist Rachita Taneja, who, through her cartoons, had suggested that the ruling party exercised a larger-than-normal sway over the Court – again, a point about judiciaries and executives that scholars have frequently made, and continue to make.[28]

The *Kamra* and *Taneja* cases also suggest that the issue of contempt of court has to be understood in the context of modern-day social media, where critiques have the tendency to go 'viral'. While we do not yet have a judgment that expressly draws this link – and indeed, the Court has previously rejected the idea that different standards of restriction apply to online speech – it is equally clear that satirical critiques that might earlier have been restricted to small audiences, now have potentially vast audiences instead, depending

---

26 *Narmada Bachao Andolan v. Union of India*, Writ Petition No 319 of 1994.

27 *Abhyudaya Mishra v. Kunal Kamra* Contempt Petition (Crl) No. 2 of 2020 (*Kamra*). Kamra has again been prosecuted recently by being booked on criminal charges for his utterances during a stand-up comedy show about the Deputy Chief Minister of Maharashtra. He was granted interim protection from arrest by the Bombay High Court in *Kunal Kamra v. State of Maharashtra* in Criminal Writ Petition 2053/2025 by order dated 25 April 2025.

28 *Aditya Kashyap v. Rachita Taneja* Contempt Petition (Crl.) No. 4 of 2020 (*Taneja*).

on their virality. The spread of this form of critique, which is organically embedded within social media, is thus perhaps responsible for this spate of contempt cases.

As an addendum, it is important to flag a final set of cases: these are at the intersection of parliamentary privileges and free speech. In an early judgment (*MSM Sharma v. Shri Krishna Sinha*[29]), the SCI appeared to hold that parliamentary privileges overrode 'Part III' of the Constitution; thus, for example, if the Parliament adjudged that there had occurred a breach of privilege in reporting about itself and sought to punish the journalists involved, there was no scope to invoke Article 19 (1) (a) of the Constitution. This position, however, has been heavily critiqued and the judgment itself is arguably ambiguous on this point. In 2003, when the Tamil Nadu legislative assembly sought to arrest and imprison editors and journalists of *The Hindu* for reporting that they considered to be a breach of privilege, the SCI stayed the arrests and noted that, because of the gaps in reasoning in *MSM Sharma* and its potential conflict with a subsequent seven judge Bench decision, the entire matter had to be considered afresh.[30] The case was thus referred to a seven-judge Bench and was due to be heard in 2024 (it has not yet been heard). Until then, the constitutional position with respect to the intersection of parliamentary privileges and free speech remains in something of a limbo.

Issues of Media Freedom

Economic Regulation and Restriction

The early years of the Indian Republic – under a planned economy, with many goods being rationed – saw a series of cases that pertained specifically to the press. The most prominent amongst these was *Sakal Papers v. Union of India*, which saw a challenge to a price-per-page policy with respect to the press, as well as a cap upon the number of advertisements that a newspaper could carry.[31] As the SCI was faced with a case that squarely concerned itself with the issue of press freedom, it was able to focus on the role of newspapers – and more broadly, the media – in a newly-democratic society.

---

29 *MSM Sharma v. Shri Krishna Sinha* 1959 Supp (1) SCR 806.

30 *N Ravi v. Speaker, Legislative Assembly, Chennai* WP (Criminal) Nos. 206-210 of 2003.

31 *Sakal Papers v. Union of India* (1962) 3 SCR 842.

The Court noted that freedom of speech was vital to the functioning of a democracy, which was based on the communication and exchange of ideas.[32] As far as newspapers went, the ability of a newspaper to disseminate its ideas was closely linked to circulation, and circulation in turn was determined by price.[33] A price-per-page limit, as well as a restriction upon advertisements, in different ways, impacted the newspaper's price, and thereby, its circulation. Both policies, therefore, infringed the freedom of speech and were unconstitutional.[34]

Sakal Papers was significant because of the Court's acknowledgment that the media could be restrained in ways other than direct censorship, but also because of its reiteration of the approach to Article 19 (1) that read the restrictions clause as narrowly as possible: in *Sakal Papers*, the SCI rejected an argument that the policies were based on public interest (especially, that they were designed to allow smaller newspapers to grow and compete with larger newspapers), reasoning that 'public interest' was not a listed ground under Article 19 (2).[35] The argument that the policies were designed to promote the free speech of other newspapers was also rejected.[36] This is interesting, as *Sakal Papers* judgment was decided at the same time when the Court was growing more deferential to the State in the domain of 'subversive' speech (see earlier under 'Freedom of Speech and the Media'). In this context, the judgment in *Sakal Papers* might make more sense when we consider it to be a part of the Court's era of judicial pushback to redistributive economic policies that it felt were going too far; as with land reform laws[37], the government's primary argument in *Sakal Papers* was also based on economic redistribution – namely, that it was trying to break newspaper monopolies and create a more egalitarian space for news.[38]

The broad logic of *Sakal Papers* was subsequently upheld in a similar case involving restrictions on newsprint: *Bennett Coleman v. Union of India.*[39]

32 ibid.

33 ibid.

34 ibid.

35 ibid.

36 ibid.

37 This did not extent, however, to tax laws, where the SCI has always been significantly more deferential, including in cases involving taxes on newspapers. While the Court has held that confiscatory or punitive taxation will be hit by Article 19(1) (a), it has generally tended to uphold the specific tax under challenge; See, *The Indian Express Newspapers (Bombay) Pvt Ltd v. Union of India* 1985 (1) SCC 641.

38 For a political economy analysis of the early SCI's decisions in the domains of both civil liberties and land reform, see Sandipto Dasgupta, *Legalizing the Revolution: The Indian Constitution and the Creation of the Postcolony* (Cambridge University Press 2024).

39 *Bennett Coleman & Co. v. Union of India* (1972) 2 SCC 788.

Although, in a sign of the changing times, *Bennett Coleman* saw a detailed dissent by Mathew J, grounded specifically in egalitarian logic.[40]

Soon after, the liberalization of newsprint regulations – and subsequently, the liberalization of the economy as a whole – meant that the specific issues that arose in *Sakal Papers* and *Bennett Coleman* became redundant; and the cases themselves are now limited to their doctrinal value, abstracted from their facts. However, the fact that the media, as an institution, exists within the larger political economy, and not as an autarky, remains as relevant in the digital age as it did in the age of physical newspapers.[41] In that context, the judgments in *Sakal Papers* and *Bennett Coleman* perhaps represent a missed opportunity for the Court to take seriously the question that the *ability* to speak depends on who has control over the infrastructure of speech, which, in turn, is often a function of economic power. One cannot, therefore, consider questions of media freedom without considering questions of political economy and redistribution.[42] That fresh consideration, however, is still to come.

Subsequent cases did throw up related issues. One of the most interesting is the case of *LIC v. Manubhai D Shah*, where the SCI hinted at there being a right of reply within the pages of a newspaper.[43] This is something akin to the 'fairness doctrine' in the United States, which required television channels to give adequate air-time to both sides of a contentious issue.[44] *LIC v. Manubhai D Shah* was perhaps based on the understanding that newspapers – as parts of the infrastructure of speech – occupy a unique position of power when it comes to shaping the public sphere; consequently, they are bound by certain constitutional norms of fairness and equality when exercising that power. *LIC v. Manubhai D Shah*, however, was delivered in the context of very specific facts – an in-house government magazine – and probably for that reason, is a bit of an outlier; subsequent cases have failed to develop on, and take further, its logic.[45]

---

40 ibid (Mathew J).

41 Jack M Balkin, 'The First Amendment in a Second Gilded Age' (2018) 66(5) *Buffalo Law Review* 979.

42 For a discussion, see Gautam Bhatia, *Offend, Shock or Disturb: Freedom of Speech under the Indian Constitution* (Oxford University Press 2015).

43 *LIC v. Manubhai D Shah* (1992) 3 SCC 637.

44 See, e.g., the discussion in *Red Lion Broadcasting Co. v. FCC* 395 US 367 (1969).

45 LIC's refusal to carry, in its in-house magazine, an article by the Petitioner critical of its functioning formed the factual backdrop for the case. The Court struck down LIC's decision. But see, e.g., *The Secretary, Ministry of Information and Broadcasting v. Cricket Association of Bengal* (1995) 2 SCC 161, where something of this nature was upheld with respect to airwaves.

Reporting on Sub-Judice Cases

The extent to – and the manner in – which the media can report on sub-judice cases has always been a matter of some controversy (the most notorious example being the *Nanavati* case[46], which led to the abolition of the jury in India). An injunction reporting essentially amounts to '*prior restraint*' (that is, choking off the marketplace of ideas at the source), and because of its far-reaching character, is frowned upon in free speech jurisprudence.[47] The basic idea is that such an injunction ought to be granted only in the most extreme and unavoidable of circumstances, with the default remedy for illegal speech being *post-facto* damages or compensation.

In its *Sahara v. SEBI* judgment, popularly known as the 'Media Guidelines Case', the SCI sought to clarify the confused law on the issue by setting out the circumstances under which an injunction could be granted on reporting upon a sub-judice case.[48] The Court framed the issue as one that required a 'balance' between the right to free speech and the right to a fair trial under Article 21 of the Constitution.[49] It held that an injunction could be granted where there was a risk that the Article 21's right of fair trial would be violated by continued reporting on an issue.[50]

This ruling, however, created more problems than it resolved. To start with, there was a conceptual problem in the Court's approach. A ban on reporting on sub-judice cases on the basis of fair trial violations might make sense in a context where jury trials continue to exist. Juries are composed of lay persons who are trained neither in law nor in adjudication. However, in India, there are no more jury trials, in substantial part *because* of how media coverage influenced the outcome in a murder trial. The Court's reasoning, therefore, appears to suggest that even trained judges are susceptible to media influence in deciding cases. That might be partially true as a matter of sociological fact, but it is quite striking for the SCI to assume that judges are incapable of deciding cases free of media influence.

---

46 *KM Nanavati v. State of Maharashtra* AIR (1962) SC 605.

47 See the discussion by the Supreme Court of the US in *Nebraska Press Association v. Stuart* 427 US 539 (1976); See also, *Brij Bhushan* (n 2).

48 *Sahara India Real Estate Corporation v. Securities and Exchange Board of India* (2012) 10 SCC 603.

49 ibid; the Court opened with this observation in its first paragraph.

50 ibid.

Secondly, the SCI's doctrinal test is both wide and vague, resembling its test in contempt of court cases. It allows for wide discretion – especially at the trial level – when it comes to the grant of injunctions. This has been proven in the implementation: media gag orders are frequently granted at the trial court level, especially when there are cases against powerful political figures.[51] The *Sahara v. SEBI* judgment essentially lowers the threshold for an injunction on the one hand, and expands judicial discretion in granting it on the other, making it ripe for exploitation by powerful individuals who wish to suppress critical reporting.

The Media in the Digital Age

The rise of the internet has fundamentally altered the media landscape. Increasingly, across the world, the internet is becoming a significant source of news for an increasing number of individuals. News on the internet, however, is accessed in a structurally different way from how it is accessed in the physical world. The major difference is the existence of *intermediaries*, that is, platforms that host the content produced by both individuals and news organisations (e.g., X, Facebook, Instagram, etc). Intermediaries constitute a vital node of the online information network as they have the power to not only host content, but also, remove it, and thereby choke off access to the online marketplace of ideas. For this reason, governments have always been keen to control intermediaries; at the same time, attempts have also been made to ensure that laws are framed in a manner that intermediaries remain sufficiently independent from governments but continue to remain sufficiently accountable to the law.

This has been accomplished through what is called the 'safe harbour' principle. According to this principle, intermediaries are ordinarily not liable for content posted on their platform, except in certain specific instances. If this were not the case, intermediaries would be flooded with lawsuits for such content and would be unable to continue functioning: it is akin, for instance, to making the builder of a highway potentially liable in perpetuity for all accidents that take place on the said highway, and having them go to court to defend themselves

[51] Courts in Karnataka have been particularly regressive in this respect. See Umang Poddar, 'Why Does Karnataka See So Many Gag Orders Against the Media?' (*Scroll.in*, 13 April 2023) <https://scroll.in/article/1046157/why-does-karnataka-see-so-many-gag-orders-against-the-media> accessed 28 February 2025.

every time there is such an accident. If one replaces the physical highway with the online information highway, the similarities can be easily understood.

Different jurisdictions have disagreed over what the scope of the exceptions should be. In India, under the Information Technology Act, 2008 (IT Act) intermediaries retain safe harbour unless they have 'actual knowledge' that someone has posted illegal content on their platforms.[52] In *Shreya Singhal*, the SCI interpreted 'actual knowledge' to mean either a court order or a government notification.[53] The second condition is problematic, as it potentially means that intermediaries can lose safe harbour – thereby placing media freedom online at risk – solely on the basis of a government notification.

This has been reflected in a series of rules passed by the government that seek to tighten control over intermediaries, as well as online media companies, by imposing a series of regulations, failure to comply with which will result in the loss of safe harbour (or, in other cases, blocking of content under Section 69 of the IT Act). For example, in 2023, an amendment to the IT Rules established a fact check unit (FCU) (to be notified by the central government), whose task would be to flag 'fake, false or misleading' information concerning the central government. A potential consequence of non-compliance with the FCU's determination would result in the loss of safe harbour (although this was contested during court proceedings). The 2023 Amendment was challenged before the High Court of Bombay which, by a 2:1 majority, struck it down for being over-broad, vague, causing a chilling effect upon online speech, and insufficiently cognisant of the crucial role played by online intermediaries in facilitating free speech online.[54]

At the time of writing, the Union of India has challenged the judgment of the High Court, and the case is pending hearing before the Supreme Court. The nature of the case, however, demonstrates how the online sphere has thrown up a series of new challenges when it comes to media freedom, and how judges must grapple with concepts such as safe harbour and intermediary liability, which have no genuine analogue in the physical world. These challenges will only grow in the future, and the initial framework established by the *Shreya*

---

[52] See Information Technology Act 2008 s 79.

[53] *Shreya Singhal* (n 9).

[54] *Kunal Kamra v. Union of India*, 2024:BHC-OS:14371-DB. By way of disclosure, the present writer was involved in the case before the High Court of Bombay, representing one of the petitioners, the Association of Indian Magazines.

Singhal case may eventually have to be reconsidered in the interests of securing genuine media freedom in the digital sphere.

Conclusion

This essay has provided a broad overview – and a set of signposts – in order to understand media freedom over seventy-five years of the SCI. As with the SCI's record on free speech in general (many aspects of which implicate media freedom as well), the history is patchy and uneven. There are moments of conceptual clarity and doctrinal advance towards greater freedom, but these are interspersed by long periods of restrictive jurisprudence and deference towards the State. One of the particularly glaring gaps in the Court's jurisprudence has been its failure to grapple with the relationship between freedom of speech, an increasingly corporatized media sector, and the political economy. Early cases provided the Court an opportunity to think through these issues, but this opportunity was not sufficiently taken up. It is likely, however, that the near future will provide fresh opportunities to reconsider this issue in the context of the digital sphere. The digital sphere also throws up challenges of its own, the most significant of which is the ubiquity of intermediaries. In *Shreya Singhal*, the Court took a first stab at addressing this issue, but its analysis – as subsequent events have shown – left something to be desired. In the months and years to come, these issues will only grow in importance and significance, and increasingly, the Court will be called upon to adjudicate them. The second edition of this book, in another seventy-five years, should make for interesting reading!

Cartoon © Satish Acharya. Reproduced with permission.

The Tenth Schedule to the Indian Constitution: No Cure for Defections?

SUHRITH PARTHASARATHY

India's democracy, often hailed for its scale and endurance, has long been challenged by the peculiar and destabilizing phenomenon of political defections. Indeed, it is a feature that is as old as electoral democracy in the country. But it became a matter of national concern when multiple members of the Haryana Legislative Assembly swapped floors after the fourth general elections.[1] Notable among them was Gaya Lal, a member of the then Hassanpur Constituency, who shifted his allegiance between political parties three times within twenty-four hours, leading to the coining of the striking phrase, '*Aya Ram Gaya Ram*'. The Fifty-Second Amendment to the Constitution of India, with which the Tenth Schedule was introduced, was aimed at thwarting defections of this kind. But for all its avowed good intentions, the law has proven ineffective.[2] It has been so deeply marred by its intrinsic flaws that far from serving as a panacea to defections, it has placed in the hands of the Speaker of the House an irrepressible power. In the years since its introduction, the Tenth Schedule has morphed into a highly contentious instrument, often aided by the Supreme Court of India's (SCI's) interventions at varying stages of disputes – sometimes even at the very inception. Its effects have invariably undermined the basic thrust and essence of our democracy.

The failure of the anti-defection law in achieving its aims has been evident almost throughout its history, but its deleterious effects have been starker still in recent times. From the toppling of governments in Karnataka and Madhya Pradesh to the brazen deployment of horse-trading in states such as Manipur

---

1 Pradeep Sachdeva, 'Combating Political Corruption: A Critique of Anti-defection Legislation' (1989) 50(2) *Indian J Polit 'Sci, 157–168'*.

2 Chakshu Roy, 'The Anti-defection Law That Does Not Aid Stability' (*The India Forum*, 5 October 2022) <https://www.theindiaforum.in/law/anti-defection-law-does-not-aid-stability> accessed 25 February 2024.

and Goa, the Tenth Schedule has routinely been invoked not as much with a view to curbing defections as to orchestrate and manufacture legislative majorities where none exist. These cases invariably reach the SCI often as a tribunal of first instance; and the Court, for its part, either allows the situation at hand to fester, or takes over the entire administration of the law altogether, playing, in the process, the role an important political player and agent rather than that of an arbiter.

This essay seeks to demonstrate that in dealing with issues of 'anti-defection', the SCI plays an almost overt political role. It appears to straddle seemingly disinterested decision-making with that of a participant in the political process, aware of the attendant pragmatic considerations and expediencies, a task quite distinct from what the Constitution's makers envisaged.

The Terms of the Tenth Schedule and Its History

Until the Fifty-Second Amendment was introduced, the Constitution did not expressly use the phrase 'political party'. The basic purpose of the Amendment was to delineate the conditions under which a member of a House – either of the Parliament or of the State Legislative Assemblies – would be disqualified for defecting from one party to another. But its framing went beyond its stated goals, and the stipulations it made came to form a complex web. It provides that a member belonging to a political party would be disqualified from the membership of the House if he or she has voluntarily given up membership of such political party; or if he or she votes or abstains from voting in the House contrary to a direction issued by the political party to which he or she belongs without first seeking and obtaining prior permission of the party, and so long as such breach has not been condoned by the party within fifteen days of its occurrence. In all cases, a person is deemed to belong to the political party by which he or she was set up as a candidate for election.

In its original form, the Tenth Schedule provided for two broad exemptions to disqualification. First, in Paragraph 3, cases where one-third of the members of a 'legislature party' split to form a separate group (this provision was removed in 2003, through the Ninety-first Amendment to the Constitution). Second, cases where two-third of a party in the House decide to merge with another political party, with the condition that those members who do not accept the merger and continue to function as a separate group survive disqualification. This apart, the law also provides that the general rules of disqualification would not apply, among others, to the Speaker and Deputy Speaker of the Lok Sabha and State Legislative Assemblies who, on election to such post, resign from their party and do not join either their original party or another party while holding such post or if they have so resigned rejoin their original party after ceasing to hold their office.

Critically, the Tenth Schedule placed in the hands of the Speaker of the House a most significant power. Any question on whether a member ought to be disqualified under this law had to be decided by the Speaker of the House, and his or her decision was to be final. Separately, in Rule 7, the Tenth Schedule also provides that no court shall have jurisdiction over any matter connected with the disqualification of a member under the anti-defection laws.

It was immediately evident that while clear procedures were necessary to curb undemocratic horse-trading and party swaps, the dangers of regulation were such that it could equally hamper the right to free expression of legislative members and their ability to act based on their conscience and free will. When an effort was made in 1978 to curb crossvoting by legislators to thwart defections, Nani Palkhivala was scathing in his response:

> No greater insult can be imagined to the members of Parliament and the State legislatures than to tell them that once they became members of a political party, apart from any question of the party constitution and any disciplinary action the party may choose to take, the Constitution of India itself expects them to have no right to form judgment and no liberty to think for themselves, but they must become soulless and conscienceless entities who would be driven by their political party in whichever direction the party chooses to push them.[3]

But as Paras Diwan speculated in an article authored in 1979, if citizens were to ask themselves whether defections in legislatures that have occurred over the years were caused by a change of one's conviction or ideological proclivities, or by virtue of genuine disillusionment or disenchantment with the party a member belonged to; or whether the defections were products of

---

[3] NA Palkhivala, *Our Constitution Defaced and Defiled* (Macmillan 1964) 67.

something more sinister – perhaps of opportunism, even corruption – the answer would definitively have been in favour of the latter: 'The core of the matter is that these unprincipled and opportunistic defections have taken place for anything but conviction or change in ideology. They are based either on sheer opportunism or pecuniary or power gains. This is why the "Aya Ram and Gaya Ram" is the epithet applied by the people with contempt and disdain to the political defectors.'[4]

The Judgment in Kihoto Hollohan

Did the Tenth Schedule draw the line where it ought to have been drawn? The question came up for consideration when a challenge was mounted to it on various grounds, in *Kihoto Hollohan v. Zachillhu.*[5] it was argued, among other things, that (a) the amendment was destructive of the basic structure of the Constitution in that it violated the freedom of speech, right to dissent and freedom of conscience of elected members – rights that were critical to the sustenance of parliamentary democracy; (b) in barring judicial review, it had the effect of nullifying Articles 136, 226 and 227 of the Constitution and therefore ought to have been ratified by the legislature of the states under the proviso to Article 368 (2) of the Constitution before the bill could have been presented for presidential assent; (c) in view of this failure to secure ratification from the states, the entirety of the Fifty-Second Amendment was void; (d) even assuming this failure was not fatal, the other provisions of the Tenth Schedule were not severable from those that required state ratification, and hence, the amendment as a whole deserved to go; and (e) the investiture of the determinative and adjudicate jurisdiction in the office of the Speaker gave rise to a genuine apprehension of bias and partiality and therefore offended the essence of democracy.

Writing for the majority, for three of the five judges on the Bench, MN Venkatachaliah J rebuffed much of the petitioners' concerns.[6] He noticed that on the one hand there was the real and imminent threat to the very fabric of India's democracy posed by 'political behaviour conspicuous

[4] Paras Diwan, 'Aya Ram Gaya Ram: The Politics of Defection' (1979) 21 *J Indian L Inst* 291.

[5] *Kihoto Hollohan v. Zachillhu* (1992) Supp (2) SCC 651.

[6] The majority opinion was authored by MN Venkatachaliah J for himself, K Jayachandra Reddy and SC Agrawal JJ with JS Verma J authoring the dissenting opinion on behalf of himself and LM Sharma J.

by their utter and total disregard of well recognised political proprieties and morality',[7] but on the other that there were what he described as 'side effects', which might hurt 'honest dissenters and conscientious objectors'.[8] But in any experimental legislation there were always, he said, grey lines, which the court needed to darken and deepen through the act of interpretation. While it was true that the views of individual members, often differing within the same political party, can often bring about change, a political party by itself functioned on the basis of a set of shared beliefs. In words with far-reaching consequences, Venkatachaliah J said, freedom of members 'to vote as they please independently of the political party's declared policies will not only embarrass its public image and popularity but also undermine political confidence in it, which, in the ultimate analysis, is its source of sustenance – nay, indeed, its very survival.'[9]

Viewed in this way, a defection was nothing but a political and social evil. Much as Diwan had observed, Venkatachaliah J too was of the view that most floor-crossings did not belong to any sacred zone of conscience – which he saw as mere 'theoretical assumptions'[10] – but were products instead of more menacing objectives. For these reasons, he believed that the Court must defer to Parliament's wisdom. He then proceeded to answer the petitioner's argument that the difference between the conception of 'defection' and 'split' in the tenth Schedule was so artificial that it amounted to an 'outrageous defiance of logic'.[11] If floor-crossing by one member was bad, how could the same act by a collective group of one-third of elected members be seen as any better? Would it, quite to the contrary, not be an even more aggravated form of anti-democratic evil? But the Court dismissed this argument with ease. The premise in declaring an individual act of defection as forbidden is that the lure of office or money could have prevailed, it held. But a collective crossing of floors would amount to 'honest dissent'[12] and it was permissible

[7] ibid [33].

[8] ibid [34].

[9] ibid [44].

[10] ibid [49].

[11] ibid [50].

[12] Note the following excerpt from Diwan (n 4), 'Aya Ram Gaya Ram'. 'That a particular course of conduct commended itself to a number of elected representatives might, in itself, lend credence and reassurance to a presumption of bona fides,' wrote Venkatachaliah J. 'This presumption,' he added, 'might weaken based on the number of members sharing the action', but there was 'nothing capricious and arbitrary in this legislative perception of the distinction between "defection" and "split".'

for the legislature to raise a presumption of bona fides since a large group was engaged in the offending conduct.

However, the majority took a more favourable view on the argument that Paragraph 7 of the Tenth Schedule, in particular, breached the requirements of the proviso to Article 368 (2) of the Constitution. This proviso stipulated among other things that any change brought to Chapter IV of Part V or Chapter V of Part VI of the Constitution required ratification by the legislature of not less than one half of the States. In this case, the Fifty-Second Amendment had certainly not secured such ratification. The petitioners argued that properly construed the amendment nonetheless undermined the jurisdiction of the SCI and the High Courts (HCs) under Articles 136, 226 and 227 of the Constitution and therefore the additional requirement contained in the proviso to Article 368 (2) of the Constitution ought to have been met. It was clear from the discussion in the Parliament, the Court held, that Paragraph 7 was inserted into the Tenth Schedule to bar the jurisdiction of the courts. There was no need for an amendment to expressly alter the languages used in these articles; so long as their operation was affected, such change could only be brought about by confirming to the requirement contained in the proviso to Article 368 (2).

But the Court also found that the nullification of Paragraph 7 did not impinge on the other provisions contained in the Tenth Schedule. Those clauses, Venkatachaliah J wrote, were severable from Paragraph 7 in that they could survive by themselves. What is more, the finality attached to the Speaker's decision in Paragraph 6, the Court held, did not create a non-justiciable constitutional area. The Speaker's decision would be subject to the ordinary rigours of judicial review, and the SCI or a HC would be within their powers to test a decision so made on public law grounds, including violations of constitutional mandates, *mala fides*, infringement of principles of natural justice and perversity. But this finding came with a caveat: 'Judicial review,' wrote Venkatachaliah J, 'should not cover any stage prior to the making of a decision by the Speakers/Chairmen.'[13] In other words, no *quia timet* action – that is the grant of injunctions to prevent harm/injury – would be permissible, unless the consequences are grave and irreversible.

---

[13] *Kihoto Hollohan* (n 5) [111].

The Court's Responses in Practice and Its Role as a Political Player

In practice, however, the workings of the Tenth Schedule have undermined much of the hopes expressed by the majority in *Kihoto Hollohan*. Here, one can examine any number of examples, many of them from the recent past.

Among the earliest instances where the SCI was asked to intervene was in *Ravi S Naik*,[14] where chaos was created in the Goa State Assembly on account of the constitutionally suspect actions of a Deputy Speaker in dealing with petitions seeking disqualification of defecting members of legislative assembly (MLAs). One of the principles settled in this decision was that an MLA could be said to have 'voluntarily given up his membership' by his conduct even when he had not formally resigned.[15]

On 24 February 1998, the SCI passed an extraordinary order in *Jagdambika Pal*,[16] where it set the date and time for holding of a floor test in the state legislative assembly. The background was that elections to the Uttar Pradesh Legislative Assembly had been held in February 1998 and no clear majority had emerged. Twelve members of the Indian National Congress (INC) had allegedly defected to the Bharatiya Janata Party (BJP), which had secured 226 seats, as compared to 196 seats for the INC. When the Speaker appeared disinclined to decide on the disqualification of the defectors, the SCI was approached.

The SCI ordered that a special session would be summoned for a single point agenda of 'a composite floor test between the contending parties in order to see which part of the two contesting claimants of Chief Ministership[17] has a majority in the house.'[18] It mandated the result to be laid before the SCI on 27 February 1998 when the Court would assemble at 10.30 a.m. Extraordinarily, it directed that 'this order shall be treated to be a notice to all the MLAs, leaving apart the notices the Governor/Secretariat is [sic] supposed to

---

[14] *Ravi S Naik v. Union of India* 1994 Supp (2) SCC 641.

[15] ibid [11].

[16] *Jagdambika Pal v. Union of India* (1999) 9 SCC 95. The Bench comprised MM Punchhi, SC Agrawal and KT Thomas JJ

[17] The contest for Chief Ministership was between Kalyan Singh and Jagdambika Pal.

[18] *Jagdambika Pal* (n 15) [1]. Kalyan Singh secured 225 votes compared to the 196 received by Jagdambika Pal, thus concluding the six-day political drama that started when the twenty-two-member Loktantrik Congress withdrew its support from the Kalyan Singh Government.

issue'.[19] It was plain, even as early as 1998, that a Speaker could subvert the constitutional provisions that expected him to act in a responsible and non-partisan manner while dealing with petitions for disqualification under the Tenth Schedule.

One of the oft-exploited loopholes in the original Tenth Schedule was plugged in 2003, through the Ninety-First Amendment to the Constitution. Rule 3 had stipulated that where a split in a party resulted in one-third of the members of the House moving out of the party, such members would be exempt from disqualification. But the stated object and purpose underlying these changes, that is 'the desired goal of checking defections'[20] never fructified. Instead, the changes helped effectively validate bulk defections while declaring individual defections as illegal. The removal of Rule 3 was an answer to some of the 'severe criticism' that the clause had faced 'on account of its destabilizing effect on the Government'. But the merger exemption has continued to create a heap of issues.

A survey by Ritwika Sharma and Mayuri Gupta shows that between 1986 and 2004, out of a total of fifty-five decisions on petitions for disqualification that were studied by them, only six resulted in a successful claim.[21] Out of the forty-nine other cases, in thirty-eight instances, disqualification did not occur either as a result of a split, under the erstwhile Rule 3, or a merger that continues to remain exempted under Rule 4, or a combination of the two factors.

After the removal, in 2003, of Rule 3 from the Tenth Schedule, the topic of voluntarily giving up membership was revisited in *Rajendra Singh Rana v. Swami Prasad Maurya,*[22] where the SCI held that if an MLA gave a letter to the Governor to call on the Leader of the Opposition (LoP) to form the government, that too would be considered as having voluntarily given up the membership of the party. In another case, it was held that independent MLAs joining a coalition government would not lose their independent identity.[23]

---

[19] ibid [3].

[20] Statement of Objects and Reasons for the 91st Amendment Act, 2003.

[21] Ritwika Sharma and Mayuri Gupta, 'Anatomy of India's Anti Defection Law' (Vidhi Centre for Legal Policy, 24 November 2023) <https://vidhilegalpolicy.in/research/anatomy-of-indias-anti-defection-law/> accessed 24 February 2025.

[22] *Rajendra Singh Rana v. Swami Prasad Maurya* (2007) 4 SCC 270.

[23] *Ravi S Naik* (n 14). Seven INC legislators who had split away from the party, which had twenty seats in the forty-member Assembly to form the Goan People's Party (GPP), which then teamed up with the Maharashtrawadi Gomantak Party (MGP), which had eighteen seats under the banner of a Progressive Democratic Front (PDF), to form a coalition government. This coalition collapsed when MGP

En masse resignations of MLAs triggering the collapse of a government have received judicial imprimaturs in a series of recent decisions. Consider the SCI's order on 19 March 2020,[24] when the legislative assembly of the State of Madhya Pradesh found itself in a state of strife. Consider, in particular, the sequence of events, and how the Court wound up influencing political results not through a final, considered judgment, but through an interim measure.

A crisis had been triggered by the resignation of several members of the assembly from the INC, leading to the government seemingly losing its majority. The Speaker of the House on a preliminary evaluation of these resignations had scheduled a floor test for 26 March. This was a time when the country at large was striving to counter the ravaging effects of the COVID-19 health crisis. But even after the Speaker had announced his decision to convene the House on 26 March, petitions were filed in the SCI, including one by Shivraj Singh Chouhan, the leader of the BJP in the state. On 19 March, based on this plea, a two-judge Bench of the SCI advanced the floor test to March 20. At this hearing, the INC had contended that sixteen members who had allegedly resigned from the party were incommunicado and were held hostage at a resort arranged for by the BJP. The Chief Minister had already written to the Governor of the State pointing to a foiled attempt early in March 2020 to allure members owing allegiance to the INC, and efforts made by the BJP to arrange three chartered aircraft to whisk away members to Bengaluru.[25]

But the interim order passed by the Court did not deal with these contentions and the alleged efforts to subvert the Tenth Schedule.[26] Instead, it said that

withdrew its support on 4 December 1990, and the CM was compelled to seek a vote of confidence in the Assembly that was summoned on 10 December 1990. The leader of the INC staked a claim to form government under the banner of a Congress-Democratic Front (CDF), which included Sanjay Bandekar and Ratnakar Chopdekar who had defected from the MGP. On a petition by a leader of the PDF, the Speaker disqualified both of them. President's Rule was imposed thereafter. Meanwhile, the Bombay HC stayed the Speaker's disqualification order. On 25 January 1991, President's Rule was revoked, and Ravi S Naik was sworn in as CM. However, within a few weeks thereafter, on a petition filed by an MGP legislator, the Speaker disqualified Ravi S Naik on the ground of defection. More litigation ensued when the Speaker was removed from office and the Deputy Speaker, in his place, reviewed the orders disqualifying Bandekar and Chopdekar.

24 *Shivraj Singh Chouhan v. Speaker, Madhya Pradesh Legislative Assembly* 2020 SCC Online SC 486 (Bench comprising DY Chandrachud and Hemant Gupta JJ).

25 The phenomenon of chartering private aircraft to shepherd away MLAs to distant locations in exotic hotels has almost become routine.

26 *Shivraj Singh Chouhan v. Speaker, Madhya Pradesh Legislative Assembly* (2020) 17 SCC 1. It was also directed that the meeting of the House would be convened for the single agenda of testing the House's

'the submissions which have been urged before the Court would necessitate a judgement which would take some time to be delivered. The state of uncertainty in the State of Madhya Pradesh must be effectively resolved by issuing a direction for convening a floor test, bearing in mind the principles which have been enunciated in the decision of the nine-judge Bench of this Court in *SR Bommai v. Union of India*[27] and in the decision of the Constitution Bench in *Nabam Rebia v. Deputy Speaker, Arunachal Pradesh Legislative Assembly*.'[28] Accordingly, it directed, among other things, that the floor test would stand advanced to 20 March.[29] In this manner, even though the Speaker of the House was still evaluating the resignations and the validity thereof, the SCI had effectively rendered that process a *fait accompli* by directing the conduct of a floor test.[30]

Several questions emanate out of how the Court dealt with the crisis in Madhya Pradesh. Was the Court's intervention in what was essentially a political question justifiable? Could it enforce the Tenth Schedule to precipitate the fall of a democratically elected government? Was the Court correct in forcing the Speaker's hand even before he could decide whether the resignations made by rebel MLAs were made to circumvent the legislative process? Was the Court not undermining the Speaker's authority and independence by allowing for a coordinated resignation that had the effect of toppling and replacing the ruling government?

Questions of this kind arise virtually every time a group(s) of legislators shift across political lines, upsetting the arithmetic dividing the House. The complications emanating out of the Tenth Schedule were also evident in the

---

confidence in the government, that voting would take place by show of hands, and that the Director General of Police (DGP), Karnataka, as well as the DGP, Madhya Pradesh, would ensure that there shall be no restraint or hindrance whatsoever on any of the rebel MLAs taking recourse to their rights and liberties as citizens.

27 *SR Bommai v. Union of India* (1994) 3 SCC 1.

28 *Nabam Rebia v. Deputy Speaker, Arunachal Pradesh Legislative Assembly* (2016) 8 SCC 1.

29 *Shivraj Singh Chouhan v. Speaker, Madhya Pradesh Legislative Assembly* (2020) 17 SCC 1.

30 In the final judgment that followed, the Court accorded its reasons for these directions. It held here that it was unable to agree with submissions to the effect that the holding of a trust vote would short-circuit the jurisdiction of the Speaker on a matter of resignation and disqualification. On the claim that members had been whisked away to a resort in Karnataka with a view to defeating the rigours of the Tenth Schedule, the Court merely observed that while 'we increasingly see a breakdown in the composition and allegiances of the political party due to private allurements offered to Members as opposed to public policy considerations, the law may have to evolve to address these burgeoning evils.' It was to that end, the Court said, that it had mandated that these members be afforded sufficient security to participate freely in the trust vote.; *Shivraj Singh Chouhan* (n 25) [54].

SCI's judgment in January 2020, in *Keisham Megachandra Singh v. The Hon'ble Speaker, Manipur Legislative Assembly*,[31] where the SCI delved into a long-brewing crisis in the State of Manipur. In 2017, elections to the Manipur Legislative Assembly resulted in a hung house, with no single political party securing a majority. The BJP won twenty-one seats, and the INC were victorious in twenty-eight out of the total sixty available seats. The BJP nonetheless formed the government with the support offered by many smaller parties and independent members. On the new government taking over, a series of applications were filed before the Speaker of the House demanding that Thounaojam Shyamkumar Singh, who had been elected on an INC ticket but had joined the BJP soon after the results had been declared, be disqualified under the Tenth Schedule.

When the Speaker did not respond, the applicants approached the HC of Manipur. Initially, in September 2017, the HC expressed reluctance to fix a time table for the Speaker to dispose of the applications.[32] When it was approached again, in January 2018,[33] the HC held that by voluntarily giving up the membership of a political party, Shyamkumar Singh had indeed breached the Tenth Schedule. But despite these findings, the HC declined to disqualify the member holding that it could not issue a writ of *quo warranto* to the member, when the Speaker had still not acted on the applications for disqualification. In the further appeal, the SCI held[34] that if the Speaker did not decide a disqualification petition within a reasonable time, he would lose the shield of Paragraph 6 of the Tenth Schedule, and that the HC, in such an instance, could exercise the power of judicial review.[35]

---

[31] *Keisham Megachandra Singh v. The Hon'ble Speaker, Manipur Legislative Assembly* (2021) 6 SCC 503.

[32] The HC of Manipur declined immediate interference by holding that the issue of whether it could direct a Speaker to decide a disqualification petition within a fixed time frame was pending before a Bench of five judges of the SCI (likely to be the reference made in vide order dated 8 November 2016 in SLP(C) 33677/2015, titled *SA Sampath Kumar v. Kale Yadaiah*) and therefore, that these petitions ought to await further orders. In January 2018, new petitions were moved before the HC, seeking an express direction to disqualify Shyamkumar Singh.

[33] The petitions invoked Paragraph 2(1) (a) of the 10th Schedule and the 2007 judgment of the SCI in *Rajendra Singh Rana v. Swami Prasad Maurya* (2007) 4 SCC 270.

[34] *Keisham Megachandra Singh* (n 31).

[35] The Court also clarified its ruling in *Kihoto Hollohan* by holding that what was meant to be outside the pale of judicial review were only those *quia timet* actions that take the form of injunctions that are sought to prevent the Speaker from deciding on the ground of some perceived or apprehended danger. The limitations that *Kihoto Hollohan* speaks of do not apply, wrote RF Nariman J, to cases where judicial review is sought 'in aid of the Speaker arriving at a prompt decision as to disqualification under the provisions of the Tenth Schedule' *Keisham Megachandra Singh* (n 31) [30].

The Manipur case prompted the SCI to reflect on the general failure of the Tenth Schedule as a constitutional experiment. Writing for the Court, Nariman J found Verma J's dissent in Kihoto Hollohan to be 'prophetic'. Although he acknowledged that the Speaker's office was 'undoubtedly high', Verma J was clear that Articles 103 and 192 of the Constitution did not vest in him the authority to decide on election disputes – a genus of disputes no different from questions over a member's disqualification for defection. Verma J also viewed the Speaker's decision, in such context, to be suffering from the apparent vice of bias.[36]

The dangers of entrusting a quasi-judicial role with the Speaker – who belongs to a particular political party – were anticipated even earlier, in 1991. Political scientist NS Gehlot, in an illuminating article, pointed to at least five flaws that permeated through the anti-defection law.[37] One, there had been no public debate on any of its specific provisions and the Rajiv Gandhi-led government of the time had made no effort to seek consensus across political lines; two, the amendment was made largely to keep party-majority captive at the cost of individual dissent; three, it accorded an almost plenary power in the party's whip to ensure that members voted as instructed on all manners of issues, not merely those restricted to maintaining the party's majority; four, while the Tenth Schedule now recognized the political party as a unit, there were no independent measures taken to strengthen the inner workings and internal democracy of parties. Quite towards the contrary, defections in bulk had now been legitimatized through conditions such as mergers. Gehlot pointed to the example, among others, in Haryana where the Janata Party (JP) Chief Minister, Bhajan Lal, had defected to the Congress (I) with twenty-one

---

[36] Citing Lord Hewart's aphoristic phrase that justice must not only be done, but it must also be seen to be done, Verma J found that the Speaker, being an authority within the house, was susceptible to being biased. 'Rule of law has in it firmly entrenched, natural justice, of which, rule against bias is a necessary concomitant; and basic postulates of rule against bias are: nemo judex in causa sua – "A Judge is disqualified from determining any case in which he may be, or may fairly be suspected to be, biased"; and "it is of fundamental importance that justice should not only be done, but should manifestly and undoubtedly be seen to be done."' *Kihoto Hollohan* (n 5) [181]. It was for this reason, wrote Verma J, that in the Constitution, as originally adopted, the Speaker was not invested with powers to determine disputes concerning disqualification of members under Articles 103, 192 and 329. In now conferring in the Speaker these powers – with the added weightage of a finality to his decision – the 52nd Amendment had run afoul of the principles of democracy and free and fair elections, which are an integral part of the Constitution's basic structure.

[37] NS Gehlot, 'The Anti-defection Act, 1985 and the Role of the Speaker' (1991) 52 (3) *Indian Journal of Political Science* 327.

of his supporters from the JP. This meant that Lal retained power despite making a political switch.

The 'Merger' Exception

The basic objective of Rule 4 and its 'merger' provision is to allow for authentic amalgamations of different parties based on ideological alignments. But, in practice, it has often been invoked to condone wholesale defections by legislators, who, through colourable invocations of the merger rule, switch parties en masse with a view to toppling the government of the day. Consider recent examples of its use. In 2019, in Karnataka, seventeen MLAs from the INC and the Janata Dal (Secular) – which together had a coalition government in power – resigned from their membership. Their resignations were not accepted by the Speaker. But when the Government was tasked with establishing its majority through a no-confidence motion, the sixteen MLAs did not vote, and the Government fell. Eventually, the Speaker rejected the resignations and disqualified the members until the end of the Assembly's term in 2023. When the matter reached the SCI in *Shrimanth Balasaheb Patel v. Hon'ble Speaker, Karnataka Legislative Assembly*,[38] the Court upheld the disqualification but reversed the Karnataka HC's direction that such disqualification would continue throughout the term of the Assembly. As a result, those members joined the BJP, and contested the by-elections, leading to an eventual change in government. Here, too, the Court's role at the stage of adjudicating on interim relief played a salient role. In an order issued on 17 July 2019, a three-judge Bench presided over by CJI Ranjan Gogoi framed the question before the Court about whether, for those who sought to resign from office, the Speaker ought to first process the resignations which were filed well in time before the petitions and then move towards accepting the disqualification petitions; or if both of these decisions were to be adjudicated simultaneously.[39]

---

[38] *Shrimanth Balasaheb Patil v. Hon'ble Speaker, Karnataka Legislative Assembly* (2020) 2 SCC 595.

[39] The question framed was: 'The issue arising in the case is whether resignations submitted by Members of the Legislative Assembly at a point of time earlier than petitions for their disqualification under the Tenth Schedule of the Constitution should have priority in the decision making process or whether both sets of proceedings should be taken up simultaneously or the disqualification proceedings should have precedence over the request(s) for resignation.', *Pratap Gouda Patil v. State of Karnataka* (2019) 7 SCC 463 [3].

The Court noted that wide-ranging arguments had been advanced by counsel before it, touching on the text and purport of Articles 164, 190, 191, 212 and 361B and the Tenth Schedule of the Constitution. But these constitutional principles, it ruled, ought not to receive 'an exhaustive enumeration by the Court unless such an exercise is inevitable and unavoidable to resolve the issues that may have arisen in any judicial proceeding'.[40] By all means, this is an extraordinary thing for a constitutional court to say. It was effectively conceding that its job was to 'maintain the constitutional balance'[41] without in any way being constrained by what the text of the Constitution, in fact, mandated. Having said this, the Court proceeded to leave it to the discretion of the Speaker of the House to decide on the resignations within whatever timeframe the Speaker deemed fit, but this came with what might have, at first blush, appeared to be a bland rider: 'We also make it clear that until further orders the fifteen Members of the Assembly, ought not to be compelled to participate in the proceedings of the ongoing session of the House and an option should be given to them that they can take part in the said proceedings or to opt to remain out of the same.'[42]

A closer examination would reveal that the order scarcely balanced the parties' rights. For, if the resignations were held to be invalid, an individual member's defiance of the party whip would trigger disqualification under the Tenth Schedule.[43] Had the Court, rather than choosing to balance rights, examined what the Constitution said, it would have noted two things: one, that no member of a legislative assembly has an inherent right to resign from the house; two, a political party, acting through a party whip, has the authority to direct a member's presence in the house. By effectively allowing these fifteen members to abstain from participating in proceedings, the Court had nullified the basic thrust of the Tenth Schedule.

The interim modalities may have differed from how the Court approached the situation in Madhya Pradesh in 2020, but the upshot was the same: the

---

[40] ibid [4].

[41] ibid [5].

[42] ibid [7].

[43] Gautam Bhatia, 'Postscript: The Supreme Court's Problematic Order in the Karnataka Case' (Constitutional Law and Philosophy, 17 July 2019) <https://indconlawphil.wordpress.com/2019/07/17/postscript-the-supreme-courts-problematic-order-in-the-karnataka-case/> accessed 25 February 2025; Manu Sebastian, 'Why SC Order in Karnataka MLAs Case Goes Against the Spirit of Anti-Defection Laws?' (*LiveLaw*, 17 July 2019) <https://www.livelaw.in/columns/why-sc-order-karnataka-mlas-case-anti-defection-laws-146465> accessed 25 February 2025.

country's judiciary was effectively influencing how power might vest and be transferred in the states.

The Shiv Sena Case

The political turmoil in Maharashtra, where in 2022, forty out of a total of fifty-five MLAs from the Shiv Sena withdrew support to the coalition government formed by their party with the INC and the Nationalist Congress Party (NCP), bears close scrutiny. In a peculiar turn of events, both groups of legislature party members – the group who stayed in the coalition and those who exited it – claimed to represent the 'real' Shiv Sena. The facts leading up to this fallout are hugely revelatory on both the benefits and ills of the Tenth Schedule.

In November 2019, the Shiv Sena,[44] the NCP and the INC formed a post-poll alliance that they called the Maha Vikas Aghadi (MVA).[45] The MVA secured a majority and formed a government with Uddhav Thackeray as the Chief Minister. Soon thereafter, the Shiv Sena Legislature Party wrote to the Speaker of the Assembly that it had chosen Eknath Shinde as its group leader and had appointed Sunil Prabhu as the party's chief whip.

Up until June 2022, the MVA governed the State with little trouble. But news reports began to emerge that some of the MLAs from the Shiv Sena had been meeting BJP leaders with the aim of bringing down the government. With the office of the Speaker vacant at the time, its duties were being discharged by the Deputy Speaker Narhari Zirwal. What followed was a remarkable series of events. The Shiv Sena Legislature Party (SSLP) broke into two distinct factions, one with Udhav Thackeray at its helm and another with Eknath Shinde. Both factions claimed to represent the real and original Shiv Sena. With trouble brewing, the chief whip Sunil Prabhu, who remained a part of Thackeray's camp, directed all MLAs from the Shiv Sena to attend a meeting at Thackeray's residence on 21 June, which was blatantly disregarded by Shinde's camp. A resolution was passed at the 21 June meeting to remove Shinde from his position as group leader and replace him with Ajay Choudhari, and these changes were communicated to the Deputy Speaker.

---

[44] The Shiv Sena, which was formed in 1966, is recognized by the ECI as a 'state political party'. In January 2018, in an organizational election of the party, Uddhav Thackeray was elected as its party president.

[45] In the state elections that were held in the following year, out of a total of 280 seats, the BJP secured 116, the Shiv Sena 56, the NCP 53, the INC 44, and independent candidates 13.

Separately, some thirty-four MLAs who did not attend the meeting at Thackeray's residence, passed a counter-resolution confirming Shinde's position as the group leader, removing Prabhu as whip and appointing Bharat Gogawale in his place. These decisions were also communicated to the Deputy Speaker. Simultaneously, these thirty-four MLAs issued a notice to Deputy Speaker Zirwal stating that he no longer enjoyed their support and called on him to move a motion for his removal from office.[46]

On 23 June, Prabhu submitted petitions of disqualification under Rule (1) (a) of the Tenth Schedule to the Deputy Speaker, calling for disqualification of the Shinde camp MLAs who had violated the party whip. The Deputy Speaker, in turn, acting on these petitions, called on the thirty-four MLAs to submit their written submissions to him by 27 July. On that day, the Shinde faction approached the SCI under Article 32. Upon hearing the matter urgently, the Court passed the following interim order: 'Meanwhile as an interim measure, the time granted by the Deputy Speaker of the Assembly to the petitioners or other similarly placed Members of the Legislative Assembly to submit their written submissions up to today by 5.30P.M., is extended till 12.07.2022.'[47]

On the very next day, Devendra Fadnavis, the Leader of the Opposition, wrote to the Governor of the State, asking him to direct Thackeray to prove his majority.[48] Acting on this letter, the Governor convened the House and directed a floor test to be held on 30 June at 11.00 a.m.[49] On 29 June, a day before the proposed floor test, Prabhu approached the SCI seeking a stay of the same on the grounds that disqualification petitions against forty-two MLAs of the Shiv Sena were pending consideration before the Deputy Speaker, and needed to be decided first. However, the Court held that it did not 'find any ground to stay convening of the Special Session of the Maharashtra Vidhan Sabha on 30-6-2022, i.e, tomorrow at 11.00 a.m. with the only agenda of a

---

[46] These notices were issued under Article 179 (c) of the Constitution, read with Rule 11 of the Maharashtra Legislative Assembly Rules 2019. The Shinde-faction MLAs were taken away by air to Guwahati and lodged in a hotel until the floor test took place. See 'Mumbai-Surat-Guwahati-Goa-Mumbai: Shinde Sena's ten-day round trip to topple Maharashtra's Thackeray govt' (*The Times of India*, 2 July 2022).

[47] *Eknathrao Sambhaji Shinde v. Deputy Speaker, Maharashtra State Legislative Assembly* 2022 SCC Online SC 775

[48] Seven independent MLAs also wrote a similar letter to the Governor on the same day.

[49] Among other things, the business of the house, the Governor said, shall be conducted in such a way that the speeches, if any, are concluded in a short period of time and the trust vote is concluded on 30 June by 5.00 p.m. The Governor also wrote to the Secretary, Maharashtra Legislative Assembly, calling upon him to make necessary arrangements for the floor test.

trust vote', but added that 'the proceedings of the trust vote to be convened on 30-6-2022 shall be subject to the final outcome' of the litigation before it.[50]

Soon after the Court's order, Thackeray resigned from his position as Chief Minister. Shinde claimed to have the majority's support,[51] but before that could be tested on the floor of the House, elections to the post of Speaker were held, where Rahul Narwekar was elected to the post, based on the support of the Shinde-camp MLAs. On assuming office, Narwekar immediately recognized the appointment of Shinde as the leader of the SSLP and Gogawale as the party's Chief Whip. On 4 July 2022, in the vote of confidence that was moved in the House, Shinde proved his majority. Prabhu filed a fresh set of petitions against the thirty-nine MLAs led by Shinde under the Tenth Schedule. Contrasting petitions were filed by Gogawale against those from the Thackeray-faction for violating the whip that he had issued on the previous day. The new Speaker issued notices in the latter petitions alone.[52]

Eventually, various writ petitions over these disputes culminated in a hearing before a five-judge Bench of the SCI. The Court framed for itself a series of questions to answer. Notably, it was to decide to what extent a notice for removal of a speaker restricts them from continuing with disqualification proceedings under the Tenth Schedule of the Constitution, as held by the Court in *Nabam Rebia* the scope of the powers of judicial review under the Tenth Schedule; the amenability of intra-party decisions to review; and the ambit of the powers of the Election Commission of India (ECI) with respect to the determination of a split within a party.

The Court's answers are telling. In *Nabam Rebia*, a Constitution Bench, also of five judges, had ruled that it was impermissible for a Speaker to adjudicate

---

50 *Sunil Prabhu v. Principal Secretary, Governor of Maharashtra* 2022 SCC Online SC 776.

51 On 30 June, Fadnavis once again wrote to the Governor, this time staking claim over the majority of the House. Simultaneously, Shinde submitted a letter to the governor together with a resolution from thirty-nine MLAs from the SSLP authorizing him to initiate proceedings to form government in the state. He claimed, in this letter, that he had the support of 116 BJP MLAs and seventeen independents. The Governor invited Shinde to take oath as CM and called on him to prove his majority. In the elections to the post of the Speaker that followed, the BJP put forward the name of Rahul Narwekar, while Rajan Salvi from the Thackeray faction also threw his name into the hat. Prabhu, in seeking to continue to act as the Chief Whip of the Shiv Sena, directed its members to vote against Narwekar and to vote against the motion of confidence for the Council of Ministers headed by CM Shinde.

52 In the meantime, owing to the impasse over who the true Shiv Sena was, Shinde filed a petition before the ECI under the Election Symbols (Reservation and Allotment) Order 1968, seeking that the 'bow and arrow' symbol that belonged to the Shiv Sena be allotted to his faction. On 17 October 2022, the ECI passed an order granting the symbol to Shinde's group.

disqualification petitions under the Tenth Schedule after a notice of intention to move a resolution for their removal had been issued. The Thackeray-faction argued that this decision required reconsideration by a larger Bench of seven judges and the Court agreed. *Nabam Rebia*, it said, appeared to have been premised on a set of contradictions. For one, the judgment ran counter to the ruling of the larger Bench in *Kihoto Hollohan* because, there, the Court had held in categorical terms that there was no reason to doubt the independence and impartiality of the Speaker. Two, in *Nabam Rebia*, the Court referred to the debates of the Constituent Assembly in interpreting the term 'all the then members' used in Article 179 (c) of the Constitution but failed to observe that Dr BR Ambedkar had explained that this phrase meant 'all members who are members of Parliament and whose seats are not vacant, and it does not mean members sitting or present and voting'.[53] And finally, among other things, the judgment in *Nabam Rebia* had failed to examine whether the temporary disablement of the functions of the Speaker under the Tenth Schedule was prone to misuse by MLAs against whom disqualification petitions had been instituted; and whether a 'constitutional hiatus' in the operation of the Tenth Schedule came into place due to the speaker's temporary impairment.

But having referred *Nabam Rebia* for reconsideration by a seven-judge Bench, the Court still held that the ruling by itself did not affect the outcome in the Shiv Sena case. The Court held that far from injuncting the Deputy Speaker from acting on the petitions for disqualification, it had, through its interim orders, merely extended time to the members to file their written responses. In the meantime, though, the election to the post of the Speaker had taken place and Narwekar had assumed office. So, it fell to him to decide on the petitions, and the deputy speaker had effectively been divested of his powers to decide on whether the members ought to be disqualified under the Tenth Schedule.

On the separate question of whether the Governor was correct in calling for a floor test when Thackeray's majority was initially questioned, the Court ruled

---

[53] The provision stipulates that a member holding office as Speaker or Deputy Speaker of an Assembly may be removed from his office by a resolution of the Assembly passed by a majority of all the then members of the Assembly. During the framing, an amendment had been moved by Mohammad Tahir proposing that the phrase 'all the then members of the Assembly' be replaced with the phrase 'all the members of the Assembly present and voting'. This amendment was rejected. The Court in *Nabam Rebia* proceeded on this premise, but had not noticed, as CJI Chandrachud wrote, that the phrase 'all the then members of the Assembly' as used in other provisions of the Constitution had been subject to specific discussion, and that Dr Ambedkar had, in fact, clarified that the phrase had been used to indicate 'all members who are members of Parliament and whose seats are not vacant, and it does not mean members sitting or present and voting'.

in favour of the Thackeray camp that such action was impermissible since there must be some objective material in addition to a mere request to call for a floor test for the Governor to act on.

But what did this ruling, in fact, entail? Could *status quo ante* be restored? The Court held that it could not make such an order. Remember, in its interim order on 29 June 2022, the Court had declined a grant of temporary relief and refused a stay of the convening of the special session of the assembly that the Governor had called on the following day. It said that it had found no reasons to stall the session and that the trust vote would in any event be subject to the final outcome of the challenge. Ought this not to have meant a restoration of the old *status quo*? According to the Court, no, because Thackeray, on the refusal of the stay, had resigned from his Chief Ministership and had not, in fact, faced the floor test. The upshot therefore was this: the Court had found that the special session was illegally convened, but Thackeray was now disentitled from any relief because he had refused to participate in what was clearly an illegitimate session.[54]

In sum, what the Shiv Sena case shows us is that for all the good intentions of the Tenth Schedule, its workings depend on how the Court rules not only in its final judgment, but when its jurisdiction is first invoked. In this case, the Court's interim orders were so invasive to the natural process that by the time its final ruling came about, it wound up being a case where the existence of a right was established but no consequential relief could be granted.

Conclusion

Ultimately, the flaws inherent to the Tenth Schedule are so fundamental to its working that no court can really unravel them. In binding individual legislators to the party whip's directions, even on matters that are far from instrumental to the party's political position, the rights of these legislators – and as a result the rights of the constituents they represent – to free speech and expression stand infringed. And when this causes legislators to jump ship, they do so in

[54] The matter came back to the SCI when Narwekar did not adhere to the deadlines set out for decision on disqualification pleas with impunity. See 'Supreme Court extends deadline for Maharashtra Speaker Rahul Narwekar to decide disqualification pleas against NCP breakaway MLAs to February 15' (*The Hindu*, 29 January 2024). The displeasure of the SCI was to no avail since consequently, fresh elections were announced, which saw the return of the BJP-Shinde faction. This time, Fadnavis became the Chief Minister with Eknath Shinde and Ajit Pawar becoming Deputy-CMs.

groups, taking advantage of the merger exemption contained in Paragraph 4. The idea behind the exemption was to ensure that disqualification does not ensure when a party as a substantial whole – with the sanction of its leadership – wanted to be absorbed into another party. But what it has resulted in are cases where individual members come together to use it as a means to rebel against the party's governing leaders.

When matters reach the SCI, decisions are invariably made with the purported view to balancing the immediate political considerations. The Tenth Schedule might well be a democratic necessity. But if its effective implementation depends on intervention from the Court at every stage, it can scarcely achieve its aims. Some of the ways to potentially overhaul its workings is to, among other things, introduce a fairer decision-making process, involving an independent body or tribunal of judicially minded persons, with particular judicial oversight.[55] Timelines too will need to be written into the law. The merger exemption must either go, or the rules around it will have to be tightened to ensure that legislators do not use it as a means to oust a serving government and instead use it as a genuine measure aimed at party consolidation. The political party is today recognized as an integral unit by the Constitution. However, issues of internal party democracy cannot forever remain a chimera.

---

[55] The expectation that the Speaker will, in an adjudicating capacity under the Tenth Schedule, not act impartially is now a given. Even as of March 2025, the SCI was pulling up the Speaker of the Telengana Assembly for sitting on the complaints under the Tenth Schedule. See 'SC questions Telangana Speaker's 'delay' in deciding MLAs' disqualification pleas' (*The Indian Express*, 5 March 2025).

Judicial Review of Arbitral Awards

AMIT GEORGE*

Introduction

Fali Nariman, one of India's most distinguished jurists and an internationally recognized authority on international arbitration, once aptly reflected on the Indian Arbitration Act, 1940 (1940 Act), drawing from Russell's classic work on arbitration to highlight the enduring friction between two seemingly irreconcilable phenomena: the pursuit of justice, on the one hand, and the threat of endless litigation, on the other. His observation succinctly captures the challenges that plagued arbitration under the 1940 Act: 'In India we have had our Arbitration Act since 1940—it governs domestic and reaches out to foreign arbitrations as well; it is based on the 'high principle' and the party losing never lets the Court forget it!'[1]

Nariman further stated that arbitration under the 1940 Act rarely concluded with the issuance of the award. It often extended into prolonged litigation as parties routinely challenged awards in India's multi-tiered judicial system. He further remarked that there was a noticeable tendency among courts to approach arbitration with a distinct pro-court bias, adopting a mindset that was 'supervisory, almost schoolmasterly'.[2] This, he observed, reflected an 'indulgent and paternalistic' attitude towards arbitration.[3]

---

* I extend my sincere appreciation to Mr Rishabh Dheer, Advocate, for his varied insights and contributions which have been invaluable in the preparation of this essay, and without which it would not have come together as it has. I also extend my heartfelt gratitude to Ms Rupam Jha, Mr Dushyant Kishan Kaul, Ms Lakshmi Nair, Advocates, and my interns, Ms Aditi Bhojanagarwala, Mr Sparsh Jain, Mr Avirah V Amprayil and Mr Siddharth Narula, for their vital research assistance.

1 Fali S Nariman, 'Finality in India: The Impossible Dream' (1994) 10 (4) *Arbitration International* 373; Nariman further noted that: 'In India, arbitrations whether domestic or foreign, do not end at all: they go on and on, first before the Arbitrators; then, when everything appears to have ended with the award, they go on again in challenges to the award, which in a three-tier system like ours lasts for years.'

2 ibid 375; Nariman further stated that 'Indian lawyers have been accustomed to look for hidden deficiencies in awards and arbitration agreements, and our judges have not been too reluctant to find them.'

3 Fali S Nariman, 'India and International Arbitration' (2009) 41 *George Washington International Law Review* 367.

While India's journey in arbitration law may have been marred by inefficiencies, procedural delays and judicial overreach (discussed later in this essay), there has been a concerted push for positive reform, *albeit* with certain persisting inconsistencies, in the arbitration ecosystem, with the enactment of the Arbitration and Conciliation Act, 1996 (1996 Act) and subsequent amendments thereto.[4] Throughout this evolution of the arbitration landscape over the years, the Supreme Court of India (SCI) has played a pivotal role in shaping the course of the law in the country. While significant improvements have been driven by the SCI, its polyvocal character has led to legal uncertainties, that is, the diverse perspectives emanating from different benches have resulted in ambiguity as regards the scope of judicial intervention in arbitration.[5] This essay traces the journey of arbitration law in India and reflects on the SCI's role in shaping it over the past seventy-five years. It also briefly traces early setbacks encountered in the arbitration regime, the many ways in which India overcame these setbacks, and the turning points in arbitration law that culminated in the legal framework we have today. In the end, it proffers certain measures that would assist in further enhancing India's position as a global arbitration player.

Considering the period under review and the large amount of judicial precedent that must be engaged with, the scope of the present essay is confined to examining the SCI's approach to award-challenge proceedings over the years. The essay explores aspects intrinsically linked to the legal framework governing such proceedings such as the modification of awards, the requirement of reasons in either upholding or setting aside an award, the scope of the 'public policy' doctrine, and other grounds for judicial intervention with arbitral awards. As an arbitral award reflects the culmination of the arbitration process, an analysis of the jurisprudence generated in award-challenge proceedings provides a cogent barometer of the SCI's overall attitude towards alternative dispute resolution processes, in general, and arbitration, in particular.

---

[4] Arbitration and Conciliation (Amendment) Act 2015, No 3, Acts of Parliament, 2016 (India); Arbitration and Conciliation (Amendment) Act 2019, No 33, Acts of Parliament 2019 (India); Arbitration and Conciliation (Amendment) Act 2021, No 3, Acts of Parliament 2021 (India). See also, Arbitration and Conciliation (Amendment) Ordinance 2020 (India).

[5] See the section on 'Analysing Precedents: A Fluctuating Case of Uncertainty' for a detailed discussion on this aspect.

The Arbitration Act, 1940

Under the 1940 Act, judicial intervention was required at various stages in domestic arbitration. For instance, courts were required to initiate arbitral proceedings, confirm the existence of a valid arbitration agreement and an arbitrable dispute, extend the time for rendering an award, and provide judicial imprimatur to an arbitral tribunal's award before enforcing it.[6] This extent of judicial involvement led to 'widespread discontent over excessive judicial intervention in arbitral proceedings with attendant delays and uncertainty'.[7] It is perhaps for this reason that the law on modification and setting aside of an arbitral award, under the scheme of the 1940 Act, was termed as 'scattered' by the Law Commission of India LCI).[8] The court was vested with multiple options when dealing with an arbitral award:[9] It had the discretion to either fully accept or reject the award, or take an intermediate course by modifying or remitting it for reconsideration by the arbitrator.

In the context of the court's power to modify the award in terms of Section 15, it is interesting to note that the LCI, in its Report in 1978, termed the provision 'a salutary one' and recommended no changes to it.[10] If one compares this position with the Indian Arbitration Act, 1899 or even the English Arbitration Act, 1950, the court had no power to alter or amend an arbitral award.[11] It is noteworthy that the LCI, as early as 1978, was mindful of the potential ramifications of judicial interference in arbitration matters. This is particularly relevant today, given that court intervention and its impact on India's standing as an arbitration-friendly jurisdiction remains the subject of

---

6 Krishna Sarma et al, 'Development and Practice of Arbitration in India – Has it Evolved as an Effective Legal Institution' (Working Paper No 103, Stanford Center on Democracy, Development and the Rule of Law 2009).

7 Aloke Ray and Dipen Sabharwal, 'Indian Arbitration at a Crossroads' (*White & Case*, January 2007) <https://static1.squarespace.com/static/537e8bcbe4b09ac6c31f0ae6/t/53daf516e4b0e65009ffa151/1406858518409/LM_Arbitration+in+India.pdf> accessed 24 March 2025.

8 Law Commission of India, 'Seventy Sixth Report on Arbitration Act, 1940' (1978) 41 <https://cdnbbsr.s3waas.gov.in/s3ca0daec69b5adc880fb464895726dbdf/uploads/2022/08/2022080559-1.pdf> accessed 24 March 2025.

9 N Krishnamurthi, 'National Report for India (1977–1986) [Archived]' in Pieter Sanders (ed), *ICCA Yearbook Commercial Arbitration 1977* (vol II, Kluwer Law International 1977) 31–46.

10 The LCI discussed the 'need' for a provision that conferred upon courts the power to modify an arbitral award while discussing the history and position in England; See Law Commission of India 'Seventy Sixth Report' (n 8) 42.

11 *Russell on Arbitration* (1970) 314; See also *Hall v. Alderson* (1825) 2 Bing 426 and *Moore v. Buklin* (1837) L.J.Q.B. 20.

considerable debate. In its seventy-sixth Report, the LCI, *inter alia*, noted, *albeit* in the context of the court's power of remission,[12] that 'care has to be taken that scope is not created for unnecessary interference by the court'.[13]

No Requirement for a 'Reasoned' Award Under the 1940 Act

Under the 1940 Act, arbitrators were not obligated to provide reasons for their awards unless the parties expressly agreed otherwise. Distressed by significant financial losses suffered by the government on account of its inability to successfully challenge an unreasoned award, the Public Accounts Committee (1977–1978) recommended amending the 1940 Act to provide for reasoned awards.[14] The LCI, however, rejected this proposal outright,[15] *inter alia*, noting that it would increase the burden on arbitrators and the likelihood of more frequent challenges to awards.[16]

Subsequently, in 1989, a Constitution Bench of the SCI, in *Raipur Development Authority v. Chokhamal Contractors*,[17] was seized of the question of whether an award should be set aside or remitted solely on account of an arbitrator's failure to provide reasons in support of their decision.[18] Answering in the negative, the court held that an arbitral award rendered under the 1940 Act could not be set aside or remitted solely because it did not contain reasons. The court further noted that it was always open for the parties to include a provision in their arbitration agreement requiring the arbitrator to provide reasons in support of the award,[19] and the question of whether a non-speaking award should be

---

12 A plain reading of s 16 (power to remit award) would indicate that the courts' power to remit an award was confined only to the three specific grounds – related to the incompleteness of the award in terms of quantity, intelligibility, and legality – and not any other ground. Consequently, a remission ordered on grounds other than those explicitly mentioned would be beyond the scope of the court's authority and be invalid; See Law Commission of India 'Seventy Sixth Report' (n 8) 43.

13 Law Commission of India 'Seventy Sixth Report' (n 8) 46.

14 Public Accounts Committee, Sixth Lok Sabha, 'Ninth Report' (PAC No 548, September 1977) 201 [3.272].

15 See Law Commission of India 'Seventy Sixth Report' (n 8) [4.42–4.50].

16 Other reasons included the voluntary character of arbitration, the consideration of speed, and that in most arbitrations, arbitrators were laymen who could not be expected to insert reasons that may satisfy the legal requirements and the scrutiny of the court.

17 1989 (2) SCC 721.

18 As the 1940 Act did not explicitly mandate the provision of reasons in an arbitral award, the SCI, in an attempt to fill this gap, indicated that a non-speaking award was likely to cause suspicion in the mind of the judge before whom the award was challenged.

19 The court stated that 'it is open to the parties to the dispute to introduce a term either in the arbitration

set aside fell within the legislative realm and was best left to the Parliament.[20] Nonetheless, the Court expressed concern that the financial interests of the State were being prejudiced due to non-reviewable, non-speaking arbitral awards,[21] and urged government entities to include a provision for reasoned awards in their contracts, in the interest of public accountability.[22]

It is relevant to note at this juncture that, in contrast to the 1940 Act, the 1996 Act brought a significant change through Section 31 (3), which expressly requires arbitrators to provide reasons for their awards unless the parties agree otherwise.[23]

The 1940 Act: Some Progress and Many Pitfalls

Despite the evident limitations of the 1940 Act on the statutory plane, the SCI made effective interventions from the judicial perch. In *Renusagar Power Co. Ltd. v. General Electric Company* (*Renusagar*),[24] the SCI, *inter alia*, noted that a liberal construction of the provisions under the 1940 Act was required to facilitate the speedy resolution of disputes through arbitration. In this regard, the Court held as follows:

> The Statement of Objects and Reasons shows that the Act seeks to achieve speedy settlement of disputes arising from international trade through Arbitration. The Act is a successor to the Arbitration (Protocol & Convention) Act, 1937 ... The present Act was enacted, as its long title indicates, to give effect to the said New York International Convention on the Recognition and Enforcement of Foreign Awards to which India is a party.

---

agreement or in the deed of submission requiring the arbitrators to give reasons in support of the awards. When the parties to the dispute insist upon reasons being given, the arbitrator is, as already observed earlier, under an obligation to give reasons.'

20 *Delhi Airport Metro Express Pvt Ltd. v. DMRC Ltd.* (2022) 1 SCC 131, where SCI held that 'An arbitral award stating no reasons for its findings would make itself susceptible to challenge on this account'.

21 See PM Bakshi, 'Arbitrators and Reasoned Awards' (1990) 32 (3) *Journal of the Indian Law Institute* 400–402.

22 ibid.

23 Arbitration and Conciliation Act 1996, s 31 (3).

24 (1984) 4 SCC 679; See also, AK Bansal, 'Towards a New Law on International Arbitration in India' (1995) 12 (3) *Journal of International Arbitration* 67–72.

It is obvious that since the Act is calculated and designed to subserve the cause of facilitating international trade and promotion thereof by providing for speedy settlement of disputes arising in such trade through arbitration, any expression or phrase occurring therein should receive, consistent with its literal and grammatical sense, a liberal construction.'

While *Renusagar* highlighted the potential of arbitration in India, Fali Nariman, with his usual sobering yet witty candour, pointed out the real-world challenges that continued to bedevil Indian arbitration:

> I am often asked whether a foreigner can rely upon the arbitral process when dealing with India, and my answer is 'yes-if the foreigner has the tenacity and endurance to last out'. In the Indian legal system, there is ample-sometimes excessive-due process; and one has to be patient and persevering. If the foreigner can resist possible attempts by the Indian party to derail the arbitral process whilst it is in progress, and, after the arbitral process ends, successfully resist attempts to set aside (or not to enforce) the arbitral award, then a foreigner can justifiably rely upon the arbitral process when dealing with India: as was evidenced in the leading case of Renusagar Power Co. v. General Electric Co. (1993).[25]

In line with the aforesaid cautionary note, the challenges posed by the 1940 Act were compounded not only by its normative drawbacks but also by its implementation by all stakeholders, including the courts, which exacerbated the underlying problems.[26] An overzealous judiciary, eager to maintain its authority, led to a breakdown of the arbitration process which was otherwise envisioned to bring about a transformative change in dispute resolution in India.[27] Under the 1940 Act, courts had the power to stay legal proceedings where a valid arbitration agreement existed between the parties. This determination, however, hinged on two factors: first, whether the court was satisfied that there was no sufficient reason to refer the matter to arbitration, and second, whether the party requesting arbitration was 'ready and willing to do all things necessary for the proper conduct of the

[25] Fali S Nariman, 'India and International Arbitration' (n 3).

[26] Gourab Banerji, 'Judicial Intervention in Arbitral Awards: A Practitioner's Thoughts' (2009) 21(2) *National Law School of India Review* 39–53, 47.

[27] Vikram Raghavan, 'New Horizons for Alternative Dispute Resolution in India - The New Arbitration Law of 1996' (1996) 13 (4) *Journal of International Arbitration*, Kluwer Law International 5–42.

arbitration'.[28] Section 34 of the 1940 Act, therefore, opened the floodgates for not referring disputes to arbitration in many situations, effectively leading to increased judicial interference and frustrating the arbitration process.[29] For example, in *Ramji Dayawala v. Invest Import*,[30] the SCI exercised its discretion under Section 34 to refuse stay of the suit in that case, noting that the balance of convenience was in favour of settling the dispute in India.[31] While the decision faced criticism,[32] it reflected the Indian judiciary's reluctance to trust arbitrations conducted in a foreign jurisdiction.[33]

In addition, the statutory framework, too, was not equipped to tackle the impending deluge of issues.[34] In *Guru Nanak Foundation v. Rattan Singh & Sons*,[35] the SCI expressed its dissatisfaction with the inefficacy of the 1940 Act. Therefore, while the 1940 Act formalized arbitration as a dispute resolution process in India, its limitations largely undermined its effectiveness. Despite the SCI's occasional efforts to promote arbitration, as seen in *Renusagar*, frequent court intervention, the lack of consistency, and procedural ambiguities in the 1940 Act led to excessive technicality and delays.

Under the 1940 Act, arbitral awards increasingly began to be set aside if they were found to be inconsistent or not in accordance with the terms of the contract. Grounds for review, including the failure to consider material facts or evidence and the consideration of irrelevant facts or evidence

---

28 Indian Arbitration Act 1940, s 34.

29 Several reasons were advanced to deny a stay. For example, misconduct of party (*Uttar Pradesh Co-operative Federation v. Sunder Bros* 1966 SCC OnLine SC 228); suppression of facts (*Chartered Bank v. Commissioners for the Port of Cal* AIR 1978 Cal 239); difficult questions to decide, for which an arbitral tribunal was unsuited (*Bhuwalka Brothers Ltd v. Fatechand Murlidhar* 1950 SCC OnLine Cal 35); past conduct of the applicant (*Union of India v. Jaimspex Wires Traders* 1982 SCC OnLine Bom 259); applicant's lack of desire to pursue arbitration and an ostensibly narrow arbitration clause (*Ramani Mohan Barman v. Gouri Rani Barman* 1977 SCC OnLine Cal 10).

30 *Ramji Dayawala & Sons (P) Ltd v. Invest Import* (1981) 1 SCC 80.

31 Two SCI judgments, in *Michael Golodetz v. Serajuddin & Co* 1962 SCC OnLine SC 311 and *VO Tractoroexport v. Tarapore & Co* 1969 3 SCC 562, contained observations that a court could refuse to refer parties to an arbitration abroad if it was convinced it would be a drain on foreign exchange.

32 *See*, Fali S Nariman, 'International Commercial Arbitration: Arbitration Issues Relating to India' in NR Madhava Menon (ed), *Commercial Law and Arbitration: Reading Materials for a Refresher Course for Law Teachers* (National Law School of India University 1988).

33 *See*, *New Great Insurance v. Akitselskaleet* AIR 1964 Bom 71.

34 *See*, Darius J Khambata, 'Chapter 31: Arbitration in India: Quo Vadis?' in Cavinder Bull, Loretta Malintoppi and others (eds), *Arbitration's Age of Enlightenment?* (ICCA Congress Series No 21, Kluwer Law International 2023) 527–556. *See also* Tracy S Work, 'India Satisfies Its Jones for Arbitration: New Arbitration Law in India' (1997) 10(1) *Transnational Lawyer* 217–244.

35 (1981) 4 SCC 634.

(principles traditionally used in administrative law), started to surface.[36] These developments paved the way for a merits review and the incorporation of the *Wednesbury* principle into Indian arbitration law.[37] Deprecating this practice, jurists termed this an 'anathema to Indian jurisprudence'.[38] The stage was, thus, set for a comprehensive overhaul of the law, which paved the way for the Arbitration and Conciliation Act, 1996.

1996 Act: Transition to a New Regime

With the liberalization of the Indian economy and the advent of globalization, the provisions under the 1940 Act were no longer equipped to meet the evolving requirements of India's modern economic framework.[39] There was widespread demand across various sectors for an overhaul of the outdated arbitration laws[40] as they were widely considered archaic and insufficient to meet the demands of a modern economy.[41] The 1940 Act provided little contemporary value,[42] and the calls for reform were strongly supported by associations in business and commerce as well as the judiciary.

The need for a new legal framework in arbitration was also advocated by the CJI.[43] In furtherance of the same, in 1995, the Minister of Law, Justice and Company Affairs introduced a Bill in the Rajya Sabha to implement the UNCITRAL Model Law within Indian arbitration laws and also give statutory recognition to conciliation.[44] However, due to other legislative

---

36 *Associated Engineering Co v. Government of Andhra Pradesh* (1991) 4 SCC 93.

37 *KP Poulose v. State of Kerala* (1975) 2 SCC 236.

38 Fali S Nariman, 'Finality in India: The Impossible Dream' (n 1) 376; See also GK Kawatra and SL Khurana, 'Indian Arbitration Law Existing and Proposed' (1995) 12(3) *Journal of International Arbitration* 5–38, 26.

39 Although India's economic policy promoted free trade and investment, the existing system failed to keep pace as it did not provide appropriate efficient mechanisms for dispute resolution and was not seen as conducive to facilitating the growth of international commercial arbitration in India; See VS Deshpande, 'Foreign Award' in the 1958 New York Convention' (1992) 9 (4) *Journal of International Arbitration* (1992) 51.

40 Vikram Raghavan (n 27) 42. See Sunitha Phadnis and Dirk Otto, 'Law Relating to Recognition and Enforcement of Foreign Judgments and Arbitral Awards in India' (*AIR Journal*, 1995) Section 17.

41 Vikram Raghavan (n 27).

42 See PM Bakshi (n 21) 400.

43 AM Ahmadi, 'Inaugural Address to the Seminar on International Arbitration' (Indian Society of Arbitrators 11 November 1994)

44 GK Kawatra and SL Khurana, 'Indian Arbitration Law - Existing and Proposed' (1995) 12 (3) *Journal of International Arbitration* 5.

priorities, the Parliament did not take up the Bill. Consequently, when the Parliament was not in session, the President of India promulgated the new arbitration law through an Ordinance. There was, thus, a substitution of the 1940 Act by the 1996 Act[45] to, among other things, address the challenges posed by the contemporary international trade and commercial landscape.

The 1996 Act was designed to foster trade by 'a unified legal framework for the fair and efficient settlement of disputes arising in international commercial relations'.[46] It sought to address the needs of foreign investors and businesses and showcased Parliament's effort to harmonize India's legal system with its economic policy goals.[47] From the outset, the SCI emphasized the distinct and forward-looking nature of the 1996 Act. In *Sundaram Finance v. NEPC India*,[48] the Court categorically noted that the 1996 Act ought to be interpreted in light of the UNCITRAL Model Law– on which it was based – and should remain 'uninfluenced by the principles underlying the 1940 Act'.

Public Policy: A Beast to Mount, Fear or Ignore?

The term 'public policy', as incorporated under Section 34 of the 1996 Act, originates from the New York Convention, 1958 and other international treaties. Under the 1958 Convention, 'public policy' encompassed fundamental principles of law and justice, covering both substantive and procedural aspects. These included issues such as corruption, bribery, fraud and breaches of due process. Under the 1940 Act, courts would often use the catchall provision 'otherwise invalid' to conduct a merit-based review of an arbitral award. Under the 1996 Act, however, the legislature sought to limit judicial interference by providing for specific grounds for challenge. 'Public policy' was codified as a ground under Section 34 of the 1996 Act. Nonetheless, it has given rise to extensive litigation as its interpretation has fluctuated considerably over time (detailed below).

Indian courts have often engaged in intrusive judicial scrutiny of arbitral awards by invoking the ground of conflict with public policy, often referred

[45] See AK Ganguli, 'The Proposed Amendments to the Arbitration and Conciliation Act, 1996 – A Critical Analysis' (2003) 45 (3) *Journal of the Indian Law Institute* 5–6.

[46] Preamble to the Arbitration and Conciliation Act 1996.

[47] Vinay Reddy and V Nagaraj, 'Arbitrability: The Indian Perspective' (2002) 19 (2) *Journal of International Arbitration* 117–150.

[48] (1999) 2 SCC 479.

to as the 'unruly horse'.[49] The notion of public policy is inherently vague and incapable of a clear definition, making it an elusive and challenging concept to confine within strict legal boundaries.[50]

Given that 'public policy' was not a basis for setting aside arbitral awards under the 1940 Act,[51] it is particularly noteworthy that the SCI, as early as 1959, foresaw the risks, and accordingly cautioned against the expansive use of 'public policy' as a vague and nebulous ground for challenges to arbitral awards. In this context, the Court cautioned that public policy 'should only be invoked in clear and incontestable cases of harm to the public'.[52] While the Court simultaneously acknowledged that the concept could evolve under exceptional circumstances of a changing world, it advised restraint, in the interest of societal stability, to not make 'any attempt to discover new heads in these days'.[53] Similarly, in the context of an arbitral award issued under the 1940 Act, the SCI, in *Markfed Vanaspati & Allied Industries v. Union of India*,[54] while affirming a passage from *Russell on Arbitration* which, *inter alia*, stated that 'the paramount public policy is that freedom of contract is not lightly to be interfered with', noted that the Court should endeavour to 'honour and support the award as far as possible'.

Over time, the SCI adopted a broader interpretation of public policy, recognizing that what was once contrary to public policy in one era might not be so in subsequent generations.[55] In fact, the SCI, in *Murlidhar Aggarwal*

---

[49] *Richardson v. Mellish* (1824–34) All ER 258.

[50] Darius J Khambata, 'Chapter 10: Challenge and Enforcement of Awards: The Brooding Omnipresence of Public Policy' in Dushyant Dave, Martin Hunter and others (eds), *Arbitration in India* (Kluwer Law International 2021) 195–234; Percy H Winfield, 'Public Policy in the English Common Law' (1928–29) 42 *Harvard Law Review* 76.

[51] Darius J Khambata, 'Challenge and Enforcement of Awards' (n 50) 200. The author, however, notes that some 'stray decisions' under the 1940 Act refer to 'public policy'.

[52] *Gherulal Parakh v. Mahadeodas Maiya* (1959) SCC OnLine SC 4.

[53] ibid.

[54] (2007) 7 SCC 679.

[55] See Arthad Kurlekar and Gauri Pillai, 'To Be or Not to Be: The Oscillating Support of Indian Courts to Arbitration Awards Challenged Under the Public Policy Exception' (2016) 32 Arbitration International 179. To illustrate the oscillating interpretations of public policy by the SCI, contributing to the confusion around the nebulous concept of public policy, consider two rulings delivered on the same day (4 September 2014): *Anand Bros v. Union of India* (2014) 9 SCC 212 and *Oil & Natural Gas Corporation Ltd v. Western Geco International Ltd* (2014) 9 SCC 263. In *Anand Bros*, the Court observed that 'the scope of interference [by courts in arbitral matters] appears to be shrinking in its amplitude'. However, in *Western Geco*, the Court took a contrasting approach, broadening the definition of public policy to include 'all such fundamental principles as providing a basis for the administration of justice and enforcement of law', thereby expanding the grounds for judicial intervention.

v. State of Uttar Pradesh, stated that public policy 'would be almost useless if it were to remain in fixed moulds for all time'.[56] Subsequently, in *Central Inland Water Transport Corporation Ltd. v. Brojo Nath Ganguly*,[57] the Court held that public policy must be flexible and adaptable to societal changes, effectively allowing for a degree of 'judicial lawmaking'. The Court noted that a narrow interpretation of public policy would preclude the creation of new heads of public policy, whereas a broader view permitted judicial evolution. The Court favoured the latter broader approach. Pertinently, the Court, in *Murlidhar Aggarwal*, also held that judges bore the responsibility of determining public policy as it evolved and were not strictly bound by precedent. While acknowledging that judges may not always accurately interpret public policy, the Court held that, with the support of the Bar, it was suited for such a task, particularly considering the court's constitutional mandate to interpret and apply public policy.[58]

Analysing Precedents: A Fluctuating Case of Uncertainty

In *Renusagar*, the SCI, seized of an enforcement application for an arbitral award rendered in New York under the ICC rules, clarified the interpretation of Section 7 (1) (b) (ii) of the Foreign Awards (Recognition and Enforcement) Act, 1961 concerning the scope of the term 'public policy'. The Court was cognizant of the pro-enforcement bias and the need for attaining finality of arbitral awards. This led the Court to hold that 'public policy' could not be interpreted to include a review on the merits of the award, as would occur in an appellate proceeding. Accordingly, the Court held that neither the Foreign Awards Act nor the New York Convention provided for the inclusion of a mere violation of Indian law or contractual provisions within the meaning of 'public policy'. Instead, enforcement could only be refused if the award was contrary to: (i) the fundamental policy of Indian law, (ii) the interests of India, or (iii) justice or morality. While the Court did not define these terms explicitly, it was categorical that this interpretation of 'public policy' did not permit any review of the merits of an arbitral award.[59]

---

[56] (1974) 2 SCC 472.

[57] (1986) 3 SCC 156.

[58] *Murlidhar Aggarwal* (n 56).

[59] Notably, the Court distinguished between the award and its enforcement, noting that only the enforcement needed to comply with Indian public policy, not the award itself. This ensured that no merits review of the award could be conducted, because such a review would conflict with the principles of the New York Convention.

Pertinently, although the Foreign Awards Act was repealed with the enactment of the 1996 Act, the relevance of *Renusagar* has endured.[60] In fact, the dictum in *Renusagar* has justifiably been lauded internationally,[61] and the judgment is considered a seminal authority on the point that a court cannot review an award on its merits.[62] In the initial years following the enactment of the 1996 Act, Indian courts generally adhered to a 'narrow view' of judicial intervention in arbitral awards. In *Konkan Railway Co. Ltd. v. Mehul Construction Co.*,[63] the SCI, after referring to the adoption of the UNCITRAL Model Law and the Indian government's new liberalization policy, observed that the Parliament had enacted the 1996 Act with the objective of attracting 'the confidence of the International Mercantile community' and that 'under the new law the grounds on which an award of an arbitration could be challenged before the Court have been severely cut down'.[64] Thus, the narrower concept of 'international public policy', as established in *Renusagar*, was preferred even in cases involving domestic arbitral awards.

However, in a decision that was pregnant with consequence, in 2003, the SCI, in *Oil & Natural Gas Corp. Ltd. v. Saw Pipes* (*Saw Pipes*),[65] distinguished the standards for challenging domestic awards under Part I of the 1996 Act from those for enforcing foreign awards, and held that the narrower concept of public policy enunciated in *Renusagar* applied *only* to foreign awards.[66]

---

[60] Sidharth Sharma, 'Public Policy Under the Indian Arbitration Act: In Defence of the Indian Supreme Court's Judgment in ONGC v. Saw Pipes' (2009) 26 *Journal of International Arbitration* 133, 140.

[61] Lawrence F Ebb, 'Reflections on the Indian Enforcement of the GE/Renusagar Award' (1994) 10 (2) *Arbitration International* 141, 149.

[62] Alan Redfern and Martin Hunter, *Redfern and Hunter on International Arbitration* (6th edn, Oxford University Press 2015) ch 11; See Jahnavi Sindhu, 'Public Policy and Indian Arbitration: Can the Judiciary and the Legislature Rein in the "Unruly Horse"?' (2016) 58 (4) *Journal of the Indian Law Institute* 421, 427.

[63] (2000) 7 SCC 201.

[64] ibid.

[65] (2003) 5 SCC 705. The case concerned an arbitral award for liquidated damages due to delayed supply of pipes. Following a series of SCI judgments, the arbitral tribunal held that liquidated damages were payable only if the amount was a genuine pre-estimate of losses and not a penalty. The SCI, however, found the arbitral award erroneous and held that an award suffered from patent illegality when it was based on an incorrect proposition of law, erroneous application of law, or contravention of the terms of the contract. The Court, therefore, gave recognition to a broader interpretation of public policy *qua* challenges to domestic awards.

[66] In 2013, the SCI's judgment in *Shri Lal Mahal v. Progetto Grano Spa* (2014) 2 SCC 433 was the harbinger of the pivotal shift in Indian arbitration law. By doing away with 'patent illegality' as a ground for challenging foreign arbitral awards on the basis of public policy, the judgment was a catalyst in advancing India's reputation as an arbitration-friendly jurisdiction.

While it may be argued that *Saw Pipes* is not inconsistent with the Court's enunciation in *Renusagar* and merely reframes the notion of patent illegality in positive terms (i.e., illegality that goes to the root of the matter), it has nonetheless been criticized for expanding the scope of judicial intervention beyond the more restrained approach set out in *Renusagar*.[67] In fact, academics have noted that despite the SCI having held, in no uncertain terms, that the scope of challenge under the new Act was far lesser than the repealed 1940 Act,[68] *Saw Pipes* vastly enlarged the scope of award-challenge proceedings to more than what was available under the 1940 Act.[69] One of the most common criticisms of *Saw Pipes* is that it contradicts the clear language of Section 5 of the 1996 Act, which provides for minimal judicial intervention in arbitration matters. Critics argue that *Saw Pipes* undermined this legislative mandate by expanding the scope for judicial intervention.[70] In fact, Fali Nariman argued that the decision 'virtually set at naught the entire Arbitration and Conciliation Act of 1996 [...] and put the clock back to where we started under the old 1940 Act'.[71]

In *Saw Pipes*, the issue was whether a court could set aside an arbitral award that was patently illegal in contravention of the 1996 Act, or any substantive law governing the parties, or in violation of the terms of the contract. The Court answered in the affirmative. In its reasoning, the Court, in *Saw Pipes*, conflated procedural violations with jurisdictional errors and held that any breach of the 1996 Act would amount to a jurisdictional error by the arbitral tribunal. Moreover, the Court invoked Section 28 of the 1996 Act, which requires arbitral tribunals to decide disputes in accordance with the terms of the contract and the substantive law chosen by the parties. Accordingly, the Court held that a violation of the terms of the contract or the substantive law would constitute a breach of the 1996 Act, and characterized such breaches as 'patently illegal'.

At this juncture, it is apposite to note that while 'patent illegality' was not explicitly mentioned as a ground for setting aside an award under Section 34 of the 1996 Act at the time, the Court, in *Saw Pipes*, circumvented

67 See Darius J Khambata, 'Challenge and Enforcement of Awards' (n 50) 213.

68 See *Olympus Superstructures (P) Ltd v. Meena Vijay Khetan* (1999) 5 SCC 65.

69 PC Markanda, *Law Relating to Arbitration and Conciliation* (6th edn, Wadhwa and Co 2006).

70 Amelia C Rendeiro, 'Indian Arbitration and Public Policy' (2011) 89 *Texas Law Review* 699.

71 Sumeet Kachwaha, 'The Indian Arbitration Law: Towards a New Jurisprudence' (2007) 10 *International Arbitration Law Review* 13, 15.

this limitation by accepting the argument that 'patent illegality'[72] should be considered an additional ground under 'public policy'. This effectively obliterated the narrower interpretation set out in *Renusagar*.

Saw Pipes faced widespread criticism as it interpreted public policy in the broadest manner possible and effectively provided a 'by-pass' to unsuccessful parties in arbitration.[73] The SCI held that 'it would be clear that the phrase "public policy of India" is not required to be given a narrower meaning' and that an 'award which is, on the face of it, patently in violation of statutory provisions cannot be said to be in public interest'.[74] This interpretation is said to have made 'a significant dent in the jurisprudence of arbitration in India'.[75] Thus, a new ground of public policy evolved, unfettered by the requirement to demonstrate 'clear and incontestable harm to the public'[76] or to justify that evolving circumstances necessitated such a ground to prevent 'injury to public interest or welfare'.[77]

Thereafter, in *McDermott International Inc v. Burn Standard Co. Ltd.* (*McDermott*),[78] the SCI acknowledged that *Saw Pipes* had 'invited considerable adverse comments' and reiterated that courts played only a minimal supervisory role, confined to circumstances where the award was so unfair and unreasonable that it shocked the conscience of the court. However, the SCI did not reconsider *Saw Pipes*,[79] and instead introduced two additional grounds for setting aside an award, namely: (i) where the

---

72 Law Commission of India, 'Supplementary to Report No. 246 on Amendments to the Arbitration and Conciliation Act, 1996' (2015) <https://cdn.ibclaw.online/legalcontent/ACM/Reports/Supplementary-246th+Report+on+Amendment+to+the+Arbitration+and+Conciliation+Act-1996-Law+Commission+of+India-Feb%E2%80%992015.pdf> accessed 3 April 2025 [7.5]; *Saw Pipes* (n 65) opened the floodgates for judicial interference in domestic awards, on the ground of patent illegality.

73 Aloke Ray and Dipen Sabharwal (n 7) 2.

74 Saw Pipes (n 65); See also Jahnavi Sindhu (n 62) 423.

75 Sumeet Kachwaha, 'The Indian Arbitration Law: Towards a New Jurisprudence' (n 71) 15; See also Sumeet Kachwaha, 'Enforcement of Arbitration Awards in India' (2008) 4 *Asian International Arbitration Journal* 64, 70.

76 *Gherulal Parakh* (n 52); See also, Anirudh Hariani, 'Indian Arbitration and the Shifting Sands of Public Policy' 16(2) *Asian International Arbitration Journal* (Kluwer Law International 2020) 159–192.

77 *Murlidhar Aggarwal* (n 56); *Rattan Chand Hira Chand v. Askar Nawaz Jung (Dead) by LRs* (1991) SCC 3 67, [15].

78 (2006) 11 SCC 181.

79 In May 2006, two division benches of the SCI rendered judgments in *Centrotrade Minerals & Metals Inc v. Hindustan Copper Ltd* (2006) 11 SCC 245 and *McDermott* (n 78). While both judgments noted that *Saw Pipes* (n 65) had faced considerable criticism, the Court also noted that they were nonetheless bound by its precedent.

reasons provided were perverse in view of the evidence and (ii) where the award was vitiated by internal contradictions – both of which allowed for merit-based reviews.

Notwithstanding the clarification in *McDermott* that judicial interference should be minimal, certain contemporaneous decisions emanating from the High Courts (HCs) espoused a broad interpretation of 'patent illegality', effectively re-introducing the ground of 'patent error of law' into the Act.[80] In a further extension of the trend of expanding a merits review of arbitral awards, in the decision in *Numaligarh Refinery Ltd. v. Daelim Industrial Co. Ltd.*,[81] despite acknowledging that courts should generally refrain from interfering with findings of fact or substituting their own interpretation of the contract for that of the arbitrator, given the circumstances in that case,[82] the SCI extensively engaged with the merits of the findings in the arbitral award as though it were exercising appellate jurisdiction.

The highest crest in the rising judicial wave of expanding interference in arbitral awards in the regime under the 1996 Act was achieved in *Oil & Natural Gas Corporation Ltd. v. Western Geco International Ltd.* (*Western Geco*),[83] wherein the SCI noted that while *Saw Pipes* had enumerated various grounds of public policy, including 'fundamental policy of Indian law', it had not elaborated on its scope and meaning. Seizing the opportunity, the court held that adherence to a judicial approach, the principles of natural justice and reasonableness constituted integral aspects of the 'fundamental policy of India'. Furthermore, the court in *Western Geco* introduced the *Wednesbury* principle into Section 34 of the 1996 Act, which allowed courts to scrutinize arbitral awards more closely.[84] This empowered the judiciary to exercise discretion in assessing whether an arbitral award met the standard of reasonableness, thereby immeasurably expanding the scope of review under

---

80 *Jagmohan Singh Gujral v. Satish Ashok Sabnis* 2003 SCC OnLine Bom 335; *Bharat MN v. Satish Ashok Sabni* 2003 SCC OnLine Bom 348; *Damodar Valley Corporation v. Central Concrete & Allied Products Ltd* 2006 SCC OnLine Cal 660; *Vishal Exports Overseas Ltd v. IndAgro Synergy Ltd* 2007 SCC OnLine MP 204; There were, however, other decisions that resisted reviewing arbitral awards on the ground of error of law. See *MR Power Projects v. State of Arunachal Pradesh* 2008 SCC OnLine Gau 49; *National Highways Authority of India v. Afcons Infrastructure Ltd* 2008 SCC OnLine Del 738; *Centrotrade Minerals & Metals Inc* (n 79).

81 (2007) 8 SCC 466.

82 ibid.

83 *Western Geco* (n 55).

84 See, Darius J Khambata, 'Challenge and Enforcement of Awards' (n 50).

the public policy ground.[85] Such an expansive interpretation enabled courts to examine whether an arbitral tribunal had failed to draw a necessary inference or had reached an untenable conclusion, potentially justifying the setting aside of the award.[86] In view of the judgments enumerated hereinabove, it appears that courts have readily applied the 'shocking the conscience' test to set aside arbitral awards based on a merits review, rather than limiting its application to the exceptional cases that meet a high threshold warranting intervention.[87] Courts have also set aside awards where the decision of the arbitral tribunal was found to be in contravention of the terms of the contract.[88]

In this regard, the SCI's decision in *Associate Builders v. DDA*[89] deserves commendation as it made a laudable attempt[90] to neutralize the view taken in *Western Geco* and address the issue of excessive judicial interference by emphasizing that 'an award based on little evidence or on evidence which does not measure up in quality to a trained legal mind would not be held to be invalid on this score', and cautioned that courts could not act as appellate bodies to correct errors of fact in arbitral awards.[91] A close reading of the judgment provides ample guidance for courts to adopt a restrained approach in award-challenge proceedings and promote deference to arbitral findings. Therefore, notwithstanding some earlier decisions, including in *Saw Pipes*, certain principles regarding non-interference with arbitral awards have stood the test of time.[92]

It is also noteworthy that the Arbitration and Conciliation (Amendment Act), 2015[93] (the 2015 Amendment) added an Explanation to Sections 34, 48 and 57

[85] *Western Geco* (n 55) has been criticized for expanding the scope of judicial intervention, a move seen as a regression from India's pro-arbitration and pro-investment approach.

[86] See, Jahnavi Sindh (n 62) 423.

[87] See, *Centrotrade Minerals* (n 79).

[88] See, *Hindustan Zinc Ltd v. Friends Coal Carbonisation* (2006) 4 SCC 445; *Konkan Railway Corporation Ltd v. Oriental Construction Company Ltd* (2013) SCC OnLine Bom 238; *Maharashtra State Electricity Distribution Company Ltd v. Vijai Electricals* (2015) SCC OnLine Bom 297; *M/s Phoenix Yule Ltd v. Neyveli Lignite Corporation Ltd* (2014) SCC OnLine Mad 496; *TEMA India Ltd v. Engineers India Ltd* (2015) SCC OnLine Del 10221; *Uttar Pradesh Jal Nigam v. Anuj Construction Pvt Ltd* (2014) SCC OnLine All 12931; *Union of India v. JG Engineering Pvt Ltd* (2005) SCC OnLine Gau 52; *M/s Shivalik Foods v. Union of India* (2018) SCC OnLine J&K 42.

[89] (2015) 3 SCC 49.

[90] Arthad Kurlekar and Gauri Pillai (n 55).

[91] See, Jahnavi Sindhu (n 62) 423.

[92] See, *PR Shah Share & Stock Brokers (P) Ltd v. BHH Securities (P) Ltd* (2012) 1 SCC 594.

[93] Arbitration and Conciliation (Amendment) Act 2015, No 3, Acts of Parliament, 2016 (India).

of the 1996 Act clarifying that 'the test as to whether there is a contravention with the fundamental policy of Indian law shall not entail a review on the merits of the dispute'.[94] The Explanation was recommended by the LCI with the specific intent of counteracting the effect of *Western Geco*.[95] Following the 2015 Amendment, the SCI, in *Ssangyong Engineering v. National Highways Authority of India* (*Ssangyong*), unequivocally held that the contravention of a statute not linked either to public policy or public interest could not serve as a ground for setting aside an arbitral award, and that it was not permissible to invoke a statutory contravention under the guise of patent illegality to challenge an award.[96] Simultaneously, it is worth noting that although *Ssangyong* acknowledged that 'perversity' and 'irrationality' were no longer available as grounds for challenge under 'public policy of India', it held that these would 'certainly amount to a patent illegality appearing on the face of the award'.[97] This interpretation somewhat negates the Parliament's intention to remove *Wednesbury* unreasonableness as a ground under public policy and to restrict the scope of challenges to arbitral awards. It also contradicts the requirement under Section 34 (2A) of the 1996 Act that patent illegality must be evident 'on the face of the award'. This is because, as noted in *Ssangyong*, 'an award which ignores vital evidence' cannot ordinarily be tested on this yardstick since such omissions – of 'vital' evidence – are not typically apparent on the face of the award. Therefore, while the court, in *Ssangyong*, rejected the *Wednesbury* standard, it effectively allowed a limited test of perversity, in the context of domestic awards, to come in through the backdoor.[98]

Despite the 2015 Amendment, perversity and irrationality continue to be invoked to set aside awards, and courts often substitute their own interpretation of contracts for that of the arbitral tribunal. It is now well-settled that the terms of a contract are primarily for the arbitrator to decide, and courts, in award-challenge proceedings, do not sit in appeal over such findings unless the arbitrator's interpretation is so perverse that no fair-minded or reasonable person could have arrived at such a conclusion.[99] However, this cardinal rule

[94] Law Commission of India, 'Supplementary to Report No. 246 on Amendments to the Arbitration and Conciliation Act, 1996' (n 72).

[95] *Ssangyong Engineering v. National Highways Authority of India* (2019) 15 SCC 131.

[96] ibid.

[97] ibid.

[98] Anirudh Hariani (n 76).

[99] *National Highways Authority of India v. ITD Cementation India Ltd* (2015) 14 SCC 21.

continues to be sidestepped on occasion. For instance, the SCI, in *South East Asia Marine Engineering & Constructions v. Oil India Ltd.*, held that the tribunal's ostensible failure to read the contract as a whole was perverse.[100]

Foreign Awards and Public Policy

At this juncture, it would also be aposite to briefly survey the landscape with specific reference to foreign awards. It is relevant to note in this regard that when it comes to the enforcement of foreign awards, there are fundamental distinctions compared to domestic awards. First, while a domestic award is deemed final and enforceable unless challenged, a foreign award must go through an enforcement procedure where the court determines its enforceability before it can be executed in India.[101] Second, unlike in the case of domestic awards, courts are empowered only to refuse enforcement of a foreign award, but cannot set it aside.[102] In the context of foreign awards, Indian courts have historically tended to interpret 'public policy' as synonymous with 'law', largely influenced by Section 13 (f) of the Code of Civil Procedure, 1908. Section 13 (f) provides that a foreign judgment may not be recognized or enforced in India if it is based on a claim of 'a breach of any law in force in India'. The implications of such an attitude were apparent: nearly any foreign award could be denied enforcement by equating public policy with non-compliance with any Indian law.[103]

Fortunately, while interpreting the meaning of the phrase 'public policy' under the Foreign Awards (Recognition and Enforcement) Act, 1961,[104] the SCI, in *Renusagar*, addressed and dispelled these concerns. The Court clarified that the public policy test, as applied to foreign awards, should not be equated with all of Indian law; it would require 'something more than the violation

---

[100] *South East Asia Marine Engineering & Constructions Ltd v. Oil India Ltd* (2020) SCC OnLine SC 451.

[101] Although some may contend that requiring court enforcement of foreign awards results in potential delays, this review mechanism serves to expedite the enforcement process. This decreases the possibility of further litigation and ensures the finality of the award by deterring unnecessary appeals by parties.

[102] See, Sumeet Kachwaha, 'Enforcement of Arbitration Awards in India' (n 75) 70; See also, Harpreet Kaur, 'The 1996 Arbitration and Conciliation Act: Step Toward Improving Arbitration in India' (2010) 6 Hastings Business Law Journal 261.

[103] Vinay Reddy and V Nagaraj (n 47).

[104] Foreign Awards (Recognition and Enforcement) Act 1961, s 7 (1) (b) (ii): 'A foreign award may not be enforced under this Act [...] if the court dealing with the case is satisfied that [...] the enforcement of the award will be contrary to public policy.'

of the law of India' for a foreign award to be unenforceable. The Court set a high standard, stating that enforcement would only be refused if it conflicted with (i) the fundamental policy of Indian law, (ii) the interests of India, or (iii) justice or morality. This narrower interpretation was a progressive move and indicated that foreign arbitral awards should generally be upheld unless they seriously contravened core principles of Indian law. Furthermore, the Court distinguished between the award itself and its enforcement, noting that only the enforcement – not the award itself – should not conflict with the public policy of India. This ruled out any merits review of the award as that would have been contrary to the New York Convention. The Court also noted that other jurisdictions, too, applied a broader public policy standard for domestic awards and a narrower one for foreign awards. Finally, it held that 'public policy' in this context referred solely to the public policy of India, and did not include the public policy of any foreign country.

As far as the position under the 1996 Act is concerned, the SCI, in *Shri Lal Mahal*, reinforced a narrow interpretation of the public policy defence for foreign arbitral awards and unequivocally held that the law laid down in *Renusagar* would also be applicable to Section 48 (2) (b) of the 1996 Act. The Court clarified that for enforcement under Section 48, the expression 'public policy of India' should be construed narrowly, and that enforcement could only be refused where the award contravened the fundamental policy of Indian law, the interests of India, or justice or morality. Interestingly, the court went a step further and, despite the similarity in the underlying concept, distinguished the application of public policy under Section 48 (2) (b) from Section 34 (2) (b) (ii), noting that the application of the public policy doctrine under Section 48 (2) (b) should be more restrictive.[105]

The 246th Report of the LCI recommended a narrower formulation of public policy under Section 48 by excluding the 'interests of India'. This exclusion was intended to prevent interpretational misuse.[106] This recommendation

---

[105] *Shri Lal Mahal* (n 66); The SCI stated: 'Although the same expression "public policy of India" is used both in Section 34 (2) (b) (ii) and Section 48 (2) (b) and the concept of "public policy in India" is same in nature in both the Sections but, in our view, its application differs in degree insofar as these two Sections are concerned. The application of "public policy of India" doctrine for the purposes of Section 48 (2) (b) is more limited than the application of the same expression in respect of the domestic arbitral award.'

[106] Law Commission of India, 'Two Hundred and Forty-Sixth Report on Amendment to the Arbitration and Conciliation Act, 1996' (2014) <https://cdnbbsr.s3waas.gov.in/s3ca0daec69b5adc880fb464895726dbdf/uploads/2022/08/2022081615.pdf> accessed 24 March 2025 [37].

was promptly adopted, and the said expression was omitted in the 2015 Amendment.[107] Scholars have also noted that it is generally harder to prevent a foreign arbitral award from being enforced in India than it is to overturn a domestic arbitral award.[108]

Recently, the SCI, in *Avitel Post Studioz Ltd. v. HSBC PI Holdings (Mauritius) Ltd.*, reaffirmed the distinct standards applicable to a foreign award vis-à-vis a domestic award.[109] Nonetheless, despite best attempts to avoid interpretational vagaries in the enforcement of an arbitral award – including through the exclusion of 'interests of India' from Section 48 (2) (b) – the test of 'fundamental policy of India' has retained its inherent subjectivity. This subjectivity is further highlighted by two SCI judgments from 2020. In *Vijay Karia v. Prysmian Cavi E Sistemi SRL*,[110] a three-judge Bench reinforced the pro-enforcement bias of the New York Convention towards foreign arbitration awards and held that violation of a mandatory provision of a statute (the Foreign Exchange Management Act, 1999 in that case) would not breach the fundamental policy of Indian law.[111] In contrast, in *National Agricultural Co-operative Marketing Federation of India v. Alimenta SA*,[112] another three-judge Bench found that enforcing a foreign award (where damages had been awarded by the tribunal for breach of a contract) involving violations of the export control policy would constitute a breach of the fundamental policy of Indian law. Interestingly, despite both judgments concerning Indian laws on foreign dealings, they reached diametrically opposite conclusions. This demonstrates the overly subjective nature of the 'fundamental policy of Indian law' test.[113]

---

[107] Arbitration and Conciliation (Amendment) Act 2015, No 3, Acts of Parliament, 2016.

[108] VS Deshpande, 'International Commercial Arbitration and Domestic Courts in India' (1985) 2(1) Journal of International Arbitration 45.

[109] *Avitel Post Studioz Ltd v. HSBC PI Holdings (Mauritius) Ltd* (2024) 7 SCC 197.

[110] 2020 SCC Online SC 177.

[111] The Court confirmed that the object of Section 48 was to enforce a foreign award, subject only to specific well-defined exceptions. The Court clarified that the phrase 'was otherwise unable to present his case' in Section 48(1) (b) could not be interpreted expansively and noted that a failure to consider a material issue would not fall within its rubric; see, Darius J Khambata, 'Challenge and Enforcement of Awards' (n 50) 226.

[112] 2020 SCC OnLine SC 381.

[113] *Anirudh Hariani* (n 76).

What the Numbers Reveal

To carry out a data-based comparison of the extent of interference under the 1940 Act and the 1996 Act, an analysis of 176 decisions under the 1940 Act and ninety decisions under the 1996 Act, emanating from the SCI, was undertaken during the course of research for the present essay. Under the 1940 Act, 64.20 per cent of the arbitral awards surveyed (out of the sample size of 126) were found to have been upheld *in toto*. However, under the 1996 Act, only 52.22 per cent of the arbitral awards (out of a sample size of 90) were found to have been upheld *in toto*. A table fleshing out the aforesaid data, and revealing the extent and nature of interference under the 1940 Act and 1996 Act as reflected from the judgments of the SCI, is as under:

Nature of Interference	1940 Act	Percentage	1996 Act	Percentage
Award set aside as a whole	43	24.43%	24	26.67%
Award partly set aside	20	11.36%	19	21.11%
Award upheld in toto	113	64.20%	47	52.22%
Total decisions considered	**176**		**90**	

It is important to appropriately caveat the data reflected in the aforesaid table. Insofar as the 1996 Act is concerned, the table excludes decisions where only the interest awarded by the arbitral tribunal was assailed and subsequently set aside or modified. Insofar as the 1940 Act is concerned, in addition to the aforesaid exclusion, only instances of setting aside – and not the limited modification as contemplated under Section 15 of the 1940 Act – have been considered.

With the aforesaid caveats in mind, an analysis of the data reveals that the tendency to interfere with arbitral awards – at least in the context of a partial setting aside – has seen a significant upswing under the 1996 Act, quite contrary to the general understanding that the regime under the 1996 Act has seen a more hands-off approach to an arbitral award as compared to the regime under the 1940 Act.

Judicial Review of Arbitral Awards: The Good, the Bad, the Curative

In a recent decision, the SCI, in *Hindustan Construction Company Limited v. National Highways*,[114] held that '[b]y training, inclination and experience,

[114] (2024) 2 SCC 613.

Judges tend to adopt a corrective lens [... however,] that lens is unavailable when exercising jurisdiction under Section 34 of the Act'. Therefore, the Court was clear that the exercise of jurisdiction under Section 34 could not be equated with that of ordinary appellate jurisdiction.[115] This means that (i) an arbitrator is 'the ultimate master of the quantity and quality of evidence',[116] and that (ii) courts are proscribed from using contractual interpretation to circumvent the limited grounds under Section 34 and conduct a *de facto* review of the merits of an arbitral award.[117] The aforesaid reasoning adroitly captures the essence of the limited jurisdiction available with a court in award challenge proceedings after the enactment of the 2015 Amendment, and it is hoped that the rationale employed therein is employed consistently in future judicial precedent emanating from the SCI.

One area of contestation that has witnessed extensive debate in the recent past is regarding the permissibility of modification of arbitral awards. Over the years, the SCI has adopted inconsistent positions regarding the modification of arbitral awards. Illustratively, in cases such as *Tata Hydro-Electric Power Supply Co Ltd v. Union of India*,[118] *Oriental Structural Engineers Pvt Ltd v. State of Kerala*[119] and *Vedanta Limited v. Shenzhen Shandong Nuclear Power Construction Company Ltd*,[120] the Court permitted modification of the arbitral awards. Furthermore, in cases such as *JG Engineers Pvt Ltd v. Union of India*,[121] the Court, while exercising its power to partially set aside an arbitral award, held when 'an error is identified in some of the claims,

[115] *Dyna Technologies Pvt Ltd v. Crompton Greaves Ltd* (2019) 20 SCC 1.

[116] See, *Associate Builders* (n 89).

[117] See also, *National Highways Authority of India* (n 99).

[118] (2003) 4 SCC 172. While upholding the award, the Court modified the award in relation to the start date from which the rate of interest would apply, while keeping the rate of interest unchanged.

[119] (2021) 6 SCC 150. While the Court upheld the interest awarded by the arbitral tribunal due to delayed payments by the respondent in that case, it modified the rate of interest because it found the quantum awarded by the tribunal to be excessive.

[120] (2019) 11 SCC 465. The Court modified the rate of interest granted by the tribunal as it was deemed onerous. Accordingly, the Court reduced the interest rate of fifteen per cent that would apply after 120 days of delayed payment to a uniform rate of nine per cent for the entire INR component; for the EUR component, it set the rate at LIBOR plus three per cent points from the date of the arbitral award, noting that it would not be fair to charge the same interest rate for the INR and EUR components.

[121] (2011) 5 SCC 758. See also, *John Peter Fernandes v. Saraswati Ramchandra Ghanate* 2023 SCC OnLine Bom 676 and *National Highways Authority of India v. Additional Commissioner* 2022 SCC OnLine Bom 1688, which are judgments rendered after *Project Director NHAI v. M Hakeem* (2021) 9 SCC 1, where the arbitral award was partially set aside.

then the unaffected claims must be segregated and upheld'.[122] However, in another line of judgments, including *McDermott*,[123] *Project Director NHAI v. M Hakeem*,[124] *Larsen Air Conditioning and Refrigeration Company v. Union of India*[125] and *SV Samudram v. State of Karnataka*,[126] the Court espoused the principle of minimum judicial interference and cautioned that 'any attempt to carry out such a modification would amount to crossing the "*Laxman Rekha*"'.[127]

In view of the lack of a unified judicial approach that would, *inter alia*, ensure greater predictability in the enforcement of arbitral awards, a three-judge Bench of the SCI, in *Gayatri Balasamy v. M/S ISG Novasoft Technologies Ltd*,[128] has referred, to a larger Bench, the question of whether the powers under Section 34 and Section 37 of the 1996 Act include the power to modify an arbitral award, and whether such power can be implied from the power to set aside an award under Section 34.

While the legal framework surrounding the modification of arbitral awards is marred by confusion, the oft-cited principle of minimal interference with arbitral awards has also witnessed a recent – and well-publicized – setback. The SCI's judgment in *Delhi Metro Rail Corporation Ltd v. Delhi Airport Metro Express (P) Ltd.*[129] has attracted widespread criticism for setting aside an arbitral award in a curative petition. While non-interference with arbitral awards has long been a foundational principle, this judgment is a troubling departure from this position. The legal backdrop is equally unsettling. Initially, the single judge of the HC of Delhi upheld the arbitral award under Section 34, *inter alia*, observing that courts should refrain from interfering with awards as long as they are reasonable and plausible.[130] On appeal, the division Bench

[122] *JG Engineers Pvt Ltd* (n 121).

[123] In *McDermott* (n 78), the Court *inter alia* held that '[t]he court cannot correct errors of the arbitrators. It can only quash the award leaving the parties free to begin the arbitration again if it is desired.'

[124] *Project Director NHAI* (n 121).

[125] 2023 SCC OnLine SC 982.

[126] 2024 INSC 17.

[127] ibid.

[128] 2024 SCC OnLine SC 1681. The reference was answered in *Gayatri Balasamy v. M/S ISG Novasoft Technologies Ltd* 2025 INSC 605. It has been held by a 4:1 majority that courts under Sections 34 and 37 of the Act can modify arbitral awards in four limited circumstances: (i) where the award is severable (ii) to correct clerical/computational errors (iii) to vary post-award interest and (iv) under Article 142 for complete justice.

[129] (2024) 6 SCC 357.

[130] *Delhi Metro Rail Corporation v. Delhi Airport Metro Express (P) Ltd* 2018 SCC OnLine Del 7549.

partly set aside the award on the ground that it was perverse and patently illegal.[131] Reiterating the limited scope of judicial interference, the SCI restored the tribunal's award.[132] The subsequent review petition was dismissed outright.[133]

In an unprecedented move, however, the SCI allowed the curative petition on the ground that the arbitral award overlooked vital evidence and the specific terms of the termination clause, which resulted in a perverse and patently illegal outcome. While the Court's intervention may be viewed as justifiable from the fact-specific context that it operated in, invoking the usage of this remedy in the context of arbitration – where finality is a core tenet – and the Court's decision to engage with the matter at the curative stage, is concerning.

Despite such interference, the SCI noted that courts 'must be slow in interfering with a judgment delivered in exercise of powers under Section 37' of the 1996 Act. The usage of the word 'slow' emphasizes judicial restraint and implies that courts should exercise caution while interfering with judgments rendered under Section 37 of the 1996 Act. This term suggests a deferential approach towards arbitral awards. However, given the inconsistent positions on setting aside arbitral awards, the precise interpretation of the term 'slow' may be ambiguous and may lead to uncertainty in its application.

Curative petitions are an extraordinary remedy meant for exceptional cases where gross miscarriage of justice has occurred. Although the SCI appropriately clarified that the curative jurisdiction should not be used to open the floodgates and create another stage of court intervention, the decision nonetheless sends a negative signal to the international arbitration community.

Charting the Path Forward

Assessing Awards for Quality: A Challenge

Commentators note that minimal judicial intervention, one of the primary objectives of the Model Law, would only be effective when courts are confident that qualified arbitrators have been appointed and the arbitration proceedings

131 *Delhi Metro Rail Corporation v. Delhi Airport Metro Express (P) Ltd* 2019 SCC OnLine Del 6562.

132 *Delhi Airport Metro Express (P) Ltd v. Delhi Metro Rail Corporation* 2022 1 SCC 131.

133 *Delhi Metro Rail Corporation v. Delhi Airport Metro Express (P) Ltd* 2021 SCC OnLine SC 3613.

have been properly conducted.[134] It has also been stated that 'the secret to a relationship that is beneficial to both arbitral tribunals and people would be to encourage but not to interfere'.[135]

Arbitration in India lacks formal mechanisms for ranking arbitrators or evaluating the substantive quality of arbitral awards. Unlike in traditional litigation, arbitrators function within a relatively insulated framework. Arbitral awards are largely shielded by confidentiality principles which limit external evaluation of their quality. The absence of a ranking or quality benchmark poses challenges for parties in selecting arbitrators whose competence and impartiality are assured. As is evident from the discussion in the preceding part of the present essay, the extent of interference with arbitral awards by the SCI reflects a lingering distrust in the arbitration process being able to achieve a just result.

A structured, qualitative ranking system for arbitrators – grounded not merely in volume or length of service but also in factors such as expertise, efficiency, party satisfaction and impartiality – could improve transparency and accountability, as also instil greater trust in the arbitration process as a whole. Such a framework would provide objective criteria for determining arbitrators' suitability based on dispute-specific requirements. Without such benchmarks, the risk persists that parties may appoint arbitrators based more on reputation than actual expertise or field-specific competence, which may impact both the quality and finality of arbitral awards.

Whether Former Judges Make for Better Arbitrators?

The prevailing practice of courts largely favouring the appointment of retired judges as arbitrators has raised concern and has been viewed by some as an extension of patronage.[136] Under Section 11 of the 1996 Act, the law only requires that arbitrators meet qualifications in the arbitration agreement, and otherwise leaves their selection to the discretion of the appointing court.[137]

---

[134] Stephen York, 'India as an Arbitration Destination: The Road Ahead', (2009) 21(2) *National Law School of India Review* 77.

[135] Namrata Shah and Niyati Gandhi, 'Arbitration: One Size Does Not Fit All: Necessity of Developing Institutional Arbitration in Developing Countries' (2011) 6 *Journal of International Commercial Law and Technology* 239.

[136] Krishna Sarma et al (n 6).

[137] On the contrary, the typical practice followed by arbitration institutions is to ask arbitrators to indicate their areas of specialization in order to match them to relevant disputes.

Therefore, there is no systematic methodology followed by Indian courts while appointing arbitrators.[138] This can result in the appointment of retired judges as arbitrators who follow rigid court-like procedures or may lack field-specific experience or technical expertise, which can lead to delays in grasping complex issues.[139] Another recurring issue with appointing retired judges as arbitrators is the over-reliance on a select group of well-regarded former judges, which leads to limited availability of dates for hearings, especially with three-member tribunals.[140] This trend warrants reform to ensure that the legitimacy of the appointment process as enshrined under Section 11 of the Act remains intact.[141]

This approach also indicates a lack of trust in appointing lawyers or other professionals as arbitrators – a trend less prevalent in jurisdictions like the UK, where barristers and specialists from other disciplines often serve as arbitrators.[142] Similarly, in the American Arbitration Association's panels of arbitrators, a diverse group of professionals – including lawyers specializing in commercial arbitration, professors, and various industry experts such as accountants and managers – comprise the pool from which arbitrators are chosen. Such diversity is important for selecting arbitrators based on expertise suited to the specific field of dispute where retired judges may not always be the most appropriate choice.[143]

Practitioners also express concern over what they perceive as encroachment in the larger alternative dispute resolution field by former judges.[144] Concerns have been raised that this trend also compromises the perceived impartiality and independence of the alternative dispute resolution ecosystem within the country as a whole.[145]

The prevailing perception that only retired judges are competent to handle

---

138 Badrinath Srinivasan, 'Appointment of Arbitrators by the Designate under the Arbitration and Conciliation Act: A Critique' (2014) 49 (18) *The Economic and Political Weekly* 59.

139 ibid.

140 ibid.

141 See, Namrata Shah and Niyati Gandhi (n 135).

142 Anirudh Wadhwa and Anirudh Krishnan (eds), *Justice R.S. Bachawat: Law of Arbitration & Conciliation* (vol 2, 5th edn, LexisNexis Butterworths Wadhwa Nagpur 2010).

143 Krishna Sarma et al (n 6).

144 Sriram Panchu, 'Thanks to Our Judges, Darkness Now Clouds India's Mediation Playing Field' (*The Wire*, 13 June 2022).

145 ibid. See also, Sriram Panchu, 'By All Means, Let It Rain! Rain Is Welcome On The Entire Mediation Landscape, Not In Select Judicial Enclaves Questionably Acquired-A Response to Sr. Adv. K Kannan's Article' (*LiveLaw*, 26 June 2022).

arbitrations constrains the arbitration process. Expanding the pool to include experienced lawyers and specialists – an approach increasingly being adopted by various Indian arbitration institutions through their panel of arbitrators – could improve the overall efficiency in arbitration. In fact, L Nageswara Rao J, former judge of the SCI, also stated: 'Why is it only judges are appointed as arbitrators by the courts? For the past one and a half years after my retirement, I have been speaking at various podiums outside this country also that it is time that Indian courts should shed this habit of only appointing judges as arbitrators. There are legal professionals of various age groups who have experience in arbitration who should be appointed'.[146]

Alternative dispute resolution initiatives should prioritize development and resolution of disputes over other interests. This would mitigate the perception that alternative dispute resolution has become a channel of patronage for retired judges and help foster public trust in alternative dispute resolution. While retired judges undoubtedly bring to the table a wealth of legal knowledge and experience, an untrammelled preference for only one stream or source of appointment of arbitrators compromises the efficacy of the arbitration process.

The Role of the Bar

The role of the Bar in streamlining arbitration cannot be overstated, yet it is often overlooked. From selecting competent arbitrators to setting appropriate expectations with clients about the finality of awards and the limited scope of judicial review, lawyers play a pivotal role at every stage of arbitration proceedings. In India, litigants' tendency to pursue litigation and seek 'another bite at the cherry' all the way up to the SCI exacerbates the already overwhelming backlog of cases, and fosters a negative culture of litigation and appeals. This practice effectively reduces constitutional courts to mere appellate bodies and encourages litigants to 'gamble' on a different outcome at every possible level. As officers of the Court, lawyers bear a professional responsibility to avoid dilatory tactics that diminish the efficacy of arbitration as an alternative means of dispute resolution.

---

[146] L Nageswara Rao J during the Delhi Arbitration Weekend (7 March 2024), reported in Satyendra Wankhade, 'Courts Should Shed Habit of Appointing Only Retired Judges as Arbitrators: Justice L Nageswara Rao' (*BarandBench*, 9 March 2024).

Furthermore, Bar associations could consider developing training programs and certifications for lawyers engaged in arbitration – particularly for younger practitioners. Through such initiatives, Bar associations would not only foster specialized skills within the Bar but would also help cultivate an arbitration culture that avoids imitating court-like processes such as lengthy procedures as well as excessive formalities and that preserves arbitration as a quicker and more efficient alternative to traditional litigation.

Conclusion

The history of the SCI, in terms of how it has approached arbitration over the past seventy-five years, has been marked by an inconsistent approach, with different Benches taking divergent positions. This is reflective of the subject-matter dichotomy faced by the SCI as it frequently finds itself delving into intricacies of contractual interpretation and evidentiary issues in arbitration matters, notwithstanding its role as the constitutional court of last resort.

Although the SCI has, particularly after the enactment of the 1996 Act, generally espoused a policy of minimal judicial interference, significant inconsistencies persist. While there has been a noticeable shift in attitude, especially in reducing the distrust that previously clouded arbitral awards, the broader issue of judicial intervention remains unsettled and the numbers reveal a worrying picture. Certain instances of judicial interference by the SCI negatively affected India's standing as a viable seat for international commercial arbitrations, thereby necessitating the need for course correction by both the judiciary and the legislature.[147] This culminated in the 2015 Amendment, followed by several decisions of the SCI that further clarified the law on the limited scope of judicial intervention in arbitral awards to reinforce the pro-arbitration stance of Indian courts.[148]

Legislative reforms in the last decade have been important milestones in shaping arbitration in India. However, it must be recognized that legislative

---

[147] In a paper published by the Indian Council of Arbitration, PA Mohammed J (Retd.) wrote that '[t]he onward march in the field of foreign investment encouraging [the] private sector cannot be easily brushed aside. But the hurdles for such continuous development are always from within. The delay in bureaucratic actions, arbitration proceeding[s] and court procedure are some of the hurdles which forbid development.'; See, PA Mohammed, 'ADR and Law Ministry's Proposals for Amendment in the Arbitration and Conciliation Act, 1996' (Oct–Dec 2003) *ICA Arbitration Quarterly* 4, 5.

[148] See, for instance, *MMTC Ltd v. Vedanta Ltd* (2019) 4 SCC 163.

amendments alone are insufficient. Progress will only be achieved when the judiciary, legislature and other stakeholders undergo a corresponding attitudinal shift. In this endeavour, the SCI's pivotal role, and the role of courts in general, is evident from the fact that matters concerning patent illegality or public policy are predominantly governed by judicial discretion. Simultaneously, a more objective application of the public policy test is necessary. The golden rule – that an arbitral award, whether domestic or international, must be enforced unless exceptional circumstances exist – must be reinforced. This will minimize court interference and promote the finality of arbitral awards. Therefore, by resisting the temptation to reassess the merits of arbitral awards, courts can help position India as a preferred arbitration destination.

It is laudable that Indian courts have taken steps to address long-standing inefficiencies by setting up dedicated Arbitration Benches to tackle the backlog. While India has gained momentum in developing institutional arbitration across the country in recent years, much remains to be done. To ensure that India emerges as a preferred destination for arbitration, courts must resist the temptation to reassess the merits of awards.

In 2021, the then CJI remarked that, '[a]ll the Foreign Investors requested only one thing. They said that they were ready to invest but were afraid of litigation […] In case by any chance, they get themselves involved in litigation, they want it to be resolved easily, amicably and without any time lag so that their investment is saved'.[149] The statement reflects the foreign investors' concerns about the unpredictability of litigation in India. Only time will tell whether these concerns have been effectively addressed or if the narrative of improvement is merely theoretical, with little tangible progress on the ground. Whether India will succeed in becoming an internationally coveted seat for commercial arbitration – an ambition that has only been partially realized so far – remains to be seen. The coming years will reveal if India can consistently build, maintain, and strengthen its pro-arbitration stance – and the SCI will continue to play a critical role in this endeavour.

[149] Shruti Kakkar, '"Litigation Costly, Tedious, Time-Consuming": CJI Ramana Encourages Arbitration & Mediation' (*LiveLaw*, 20 August 2021).

Part V

The Court, the Bar and Legal Education

I'M LIVE FROM THE LOCAL COURT WHERE TWO LAWYERS ARE ENGAGED IN A PHYSICAL ALTERCATION. LADY JUSTICE, ANY COMMENTS?
NEWS
CONSTI TUTION
COULD I HAVE MY BLINDFOLD BACK PLEASE?
NEWS
CONSTI TUTION

The Supreme Court Bar

Background Note

S MURALIDHAR

There are at least three types of lawyers practicing before the Supreme Court of India (SCI). We have Senior Advocates who are recognized under Section 16 (2) of the Advocates Act,[1] Advocates-on-Record (AoRs) whose registration and functioning are governed by the Supreme Court Rules, 2013 (made by the SCI, with the approval of the President of India, under Article 145 of the Constitution[2]) and non-AoRs.

All three categories are governed in their functioning by the rules made by the Bar Council of India (BCI) under Section 15 of the Advocates Act. The admission and enrolment of advocates, including Senior Advocates, their disqualification and removal from the roles, and the disciplining power of the conduct of advocates, are all governed by the BCI Rules. Apart from their accountability to the courts in general under the Advocates Act and the BCI Rules, the AoRs registered on the rolls of the SCI are answerable to it and can be removed from the rolls of AoRs under the Supreme Court Rules.[3]

The designation of either an AoR or non-AoR as a Senior Advocate takes place in terms of the provisions of Order IV, Rule 2 of the Supreme Court

---

1 Advocates Act 1961, s 16(2).

2 In order to become an AoR, an advocate not being a Senior Advocate, and being enrolled with a State Bar Council, and not within four years on the date of commencement of training for one year with an AoR, passes an examination conducted every year by the SCI. It is only an AoR who is qualified to file pleadings, including petitions, affidavits and a vakalatnama for a party in the SCI. The AoRs can also address the Court.

3 Supreme Court Rules 2013, Ord 4, r 10.

Rules, 2013.[4] The SCI has further issued guidelines in 2023 for this purpose.[5] The Court has, on the judicial side, in *Indira Jaising v. Supreme Court of India*,[6] laid down the model guidelines that are required to be adopted and suitably modified by the High Court (HC) for designating advocates as Senior Advocates. No Senior Advocate can appear in the SCI unless instructed by an AoR.[7] A non-AoR again has to be instructed by an AoR in order to be able to address the Court.

At present, there are around 650 Senior Advocates and 3500 AoRs, apart from non-AoRs.[8] The Supreme Court Bar Association (SCBA), which comprises all three categories of advocates, has on its rolls over 7,000 'resident members (active)'. The membership process entails advocates having to undergo a screening.[9] Although the elections to the SCBA are held once a year, and the number of women lawyers registered with it has shown a steady increase, the SCBA is yet to have a woman lawyer as President.[10]

The Government of India is represented in the SCI by the Attorney General for India (AG), the Solicitor General of India (SG) and as many as Additional Solicitor Generals for India (ASG), instructed by a multitude of AoRs and non-AoRs who are on the 'panel' of the litigation wing of the Central Government.[11] Each of the States and Union Territories also have their 'standing counsel' regularly practicing before the SCI. Litigants who are unable to afford the costs and fees for pursuing cases can approach the

---

4 Usually, the Full Court, comprising of all the judges of the SCI, will meet to decide upon applications invited through a public notice from among advocates.

5 'Guidelines for Designation of Senior Advocates' (Supreme Court of India, effective 2023) <https://main.sci.gov.in/pdf/LU/17072023_042844.pdf> accessed 23 November 2024.

6 *Indira Jaising v. Supreme Court of India* (2017) 9 SCC 766; (2023) 8 SCC 1; Certain doubts were expressed regarding the correctness of the guidelines in these two decisions by a two-judge Bench in *Jitender @ Kalla v. State (Govt. of NCT of Delhi)* 2025 INSC 249 which was directed to be placed before the CJI to constitute a Bench of appropriate strength. A three-judge Bench constituted for this purpose in *Jitendra Kalla v. State (Govt. of NCT of Delhi)* 2025 INSC 667 has done away with the points-based system for evaluating Senior designation.

7 Supreme Court Rules, 2013, Ord 4, r 2(a) (ii).

8 Not all of these advocates are in active practice. Also, some of them might be 'outstation' lawyers who were regular practitioners in the HCs and other courts elsewhere in the country, but who may travel to the SCI to appear in the cases filed there.

9 SCBA Rules, r 5 (v) (a); There could be a situation where the lawyer appearing in the SC is not necessarily a member of the SCBA.

10 It has had women Vice-Presidents and candidates for the post of President.

11 This is referred to as the Central Agency and has an office within the premises of the SCI. Government of India is among the major litigants in the SCI.

Supreme Court Legal Services Committee functioning in the terms of The Legal Services Authorities Act, 1987 for assistance. The SCI also has a panel of lawyers, from which the Court might appoint one in select cases to assist the Court as *amicus curiae*.

The SCI on the judicial side has been closely monitoring the enrolment of the members to the SCBA and the conduct of its elections. In a series of orders, in the *BD Kaushik* case, it has mandated the 'one Bar, one vote' rule with a view to ensuring that the office bearers of the SCBA are from among the regular practitioners of the SCI.[12] It has also, by an order dated 2 May 2025, mandated that at least 1/3rd of the Executive Committee and Senior Executive Members of the SCBA should be reserved for women. [13] Recently, it constituted a committee headed by a former judge of the SCI which has submitted its report regarding further reforms in the electoral process.[14]

---

12 *Supreme Court Bar Association v. BD Kaushik* (2011) 13 SCC 774.

13 *Supreme Court Bar Association v. BD Kaushik*, Miscellaneous Application Diary No. 13992/2023, order dated 2 May 2025.

14 Debby Jain, 'Former Supreme Court Judge-Justice L Nageswara Rao To Head Committee Constituted For Proposing Electoral Reforms In SCBA' (*Livelaw*, 25 February 2025) <https://www.livelaw.in/top-stories/supreme-court-former-sc-judge-l-nageswara-rao-to-head-committee-for-recommendations-on-scba-electoral-reforms-284957> accessed 30 March 2025. The Committee has since submitted its report. See, *Supreme Court Bar Association v. BD Kaushik* (n 13).

Advocates of the Supreme Court

AN INTERVIEW WITH MEENAKSHI ARORA

In the following interview conducted by the Editor in the month of December 2024 in virtual mode, Ms Meenakshi Arora, Senior Advocate, reviews the working of the above system in general, apart from the issue of conduct and ethics of advocates practicing before the SCI. Ms Arora topped the AoR exam held in 1989 and was designated as a Senior Advocate by the SCI in 2013.

Editor: *Over the years, the number of AoRs qualifying in the written exam and being registered as such with the SCI has shown a marked increase. Since 2021, the number of AoRs registered every year has been 253, 260, 198 and 356, respectively. With there not being enough work for all of them, there is every possibility of many of them 'lending their names' for the filing of petitions, for a fixed fee, without actually being involved in the preparation and presentation of the case. Is this phenomenon rendering the institution of the AoR redundant?*

Ms Arora: With an increased filing of cases, and the current pendency as you know is nearly 83,000 cases, you definitely need a proportionate increase in the number of AoRs. With the standards of the AoR exam being quite stringent, there is a whole section of advocates who are not willing to sit for the exam but use the services of an AoR, for a small fee, for filing cases and also arguing them. According to me, that practice is required to be completely discouraged. The object of having lawyers of a required degree of competence and knowledge handling cases in the SCI and being answerable to it cannot be defeated by permitting lawyers who do not go through the same rigorous test, to practice in the SCI.

I remember in our time as AoRs, we invariably drafted the petitions and pleadings ourselves. It would never leave our desk without being thoroughly vetted by us. Now the formats set out in the Rules make the task easier. But you are right, a large number of AoRs only lend names now. And they do not essentially practice in the SCI. And sometimes, the judges find that they are not present, alongside the arguing counsel, as they should be, when the case is heard.

I also think that the AoR institution must itself command the respect from the court. The fact is that at least eighty per cent of the work in the SCI is handled by the AoRs themselves. I do believe they are at the receiving end when something goes wrong in the Court and are not given their due.

Editor: *You are then saying that the institution of AoR needs to continue but has to be better regulated.*

Ms Arora: I would say that the SCI will not survive without that institution. As I said, although the exam to qualify as an AoR is a difficult one, we find that Special Leave Petitions (SLP) are poorly drafted. But just imagine what they would be like if you took away the institution of AoR. You have some AoRs who are excellent and there are some that are average. That, I suppose, is inevitable in any system. I am impressed though by the increasing number of bright young AoR.

Editor: *Of late, the instances where the Court is pulling up an AoR or even a Senior Advocate for either misrepresentation or material particulars in a petition or affidavit before the Court are increasing.*[15] *These point to the fact that at least at the level of the SCI, it involves the participation of a number of players, including the litigants and lawyers, in the preparation of the case, and not just the AoRs. One suggestion that has been made to the SCI in a recent case, where it is contemplating framing guidelines, is for the petition/pleading to be accompanied by, even at the time of filing, a certificate issued by the person on whose instructions the AoR drafted the petition/pleading that it was on the basis of the instructions given by the person issuing the certificate.*[16] *Do you think this will help?*

---

[15] *Jitender @ Kalla v. State (Government of NCT of Delhi)*, 2025 INSC 249; Another Bench comprising of Bela Trivedi and Satish Chandra Sharma JJ also berated an AoR for not remaining present during the hearing and for filing a second SLP without disclosing the earlier dismissal of an SLP against the same order and delivered a split-verdict on the action to be taken against the AoR. See Sucheta, 'SC delivers split verdict on acceptance of unconditional apology by errant Advocates; Matter to be placed before CJI' (*SCCOnline Times*, 18 April 2025) <https://www.scconline.com/blog/post/2025/04/18/contempt-of-court-sc-spilt-verdict-acceptance-apology-advocates-sc-legal-news/> accessed 21 April 2025.

[16] However, in the judgment in *Jitender @ Kalla* (n 15), the said suggestion has not been accepted; In *Supreme Court Bar Association v. State of Uttar Pradesh* 2025 INSC 364, a Bench of Bela Trivedi and Satish Chandra Sharma JJ mandated how appearances of lawyers should be reflected in the Court's orders by limiting it just to the arguing counsel and one assisting counsel/AoR for every party. This has caused considerable consternation and misgivings by the Bar since there are always a number of lawyers involved in the preparation of the case for presentation in SCI and their being given due credit is justified.

Ms Arora: The petitions that are filed in the SCI originate from a litigation that commenced in some part of the country where the 'clients' are located. It is therefore, the 'local advocate' who is likely to have direct contact with such client and will probably collect their signatures on the *vakalatnama* and pleadings. Because the SCI is a melting pot of filings from across the country, not every client is going to travel to the SCI for the filing. He will be happier to go to his local advocate, drop the papers and have them sent here. So, I would agree with you. With the AoR not likely to have direct contact with the client, the pleadings must be accompanied by a certificate on the lines as suggested.

Editor: *Over the years, the filings in the SCI have shown a marked increase with many a lawyer advising – and perhaps not wisely – the client to 'take a chance' and challenge any conceivable order of a HC or Tribunal (even if it an order granting or refusing an adjournment) before the SCI by an SLP. As a result, every Monday and Friday, the thirty-four judges of the SCI, in about fifteen Benches, are spending a substantial amount of time deciding which among the huge influx of fresh cases will go past the first post of 'admission'. With each Bench of a minimum of two judges, having a caseload of around sixty-five cases on such 'miscellaneous days',[17] the average time spent on a case could be as little as two to three minutes, thus leaving many a litigant and lawyer disillusioned. It's a heartbreak for many a client, knowing that this is the last court. And the costs incurred up to this point are substantial.*

There has been a suggestion that a group of five SCI judges sitting in chambers can screen out the 'deserving' cases, at the threshold and list for hearing only such cases. In other words, no oral hearing will precede such a screening.

Ms Arora: I think to reach that standard, first of all, your quality of drafting has to improve substantially. You also need highly competent and experienced law graduates assisting each judge. Not the fresher law clerks who have just graduated.[18]

---

[17] The term 'miscellaneous' connotes, in legal jargon, cases that are yet to be 'admitted' to the Court's docket. The formal admission happens when 'leave' is granted by the SCI. This means that the cases would then get to join a long, unending queue of 'already leave granted' cases (also known as 'appeals') waiting for their turn for five years and more. To avoid this consequence, lawyers persuade the Court to hear such cases at the 'after notice' stage on a non-miscellaneous day ('NMD'). However, this, too, has not solved the problem of delays.

[18] There is an annual rigorous exam conducted for the intake of Law Clerk/Research Associate. Every judge can have upto four law clerk/research associates. See Abhinav Chandrachud, 'From Hyderabad to

Till that happens, it may not be advisable to go in for a system of screening as you suggest with three out of five votes of judges in chambers deciding if a case makes the cut. We have to evolve much more for such a system. I do believe, however, that the Bar will improve in due course.

Editor: *What if we had all admission hearings only online, so that the chaotic running between courts on Mondays and Fridays by the lawyers could be avoided?*

Ms Arora: That's quite doable I think, and I completely agree with you. It worked very well during COVID-19 and the SCI is one of the best-equipped courts for online hearings. Not all the HCs can handle this but the SCI, fortunately, has a system where sitting in your room, you can hear and see your other party and you can see the judges. There is a scope for improving the technology to streamline the hearings, both at the SCI and the HCs. With many lawyers switching to the 'paperless mode', the virtual hearings combined with online filings being made mandatory in the SCI will undoubtedly increase the efficiency. It would also free up the physical space in the Court premises which is taken up in large measure with the storage of paper records.

Editor: *Apart from admission hearings, there is also the backlog of the cases already admitted, which the Court does not seem to find the time to clear out. How did this come about and is there a way out?*

Ms Arora: The problem, according to me, is largely owed to the inconsistency in the SCI's approach to the admission of cases. While one would expect a hands-off approach in cases where an interlocutory order is under challenge, there are no clear guidelines laid down with a view to encouraging a consistent approach by the fifteen-plus Benches of the SCI. The comment that we have fifteen SCIs and not just one is not wholly unjustified. Another factor contributing to the increasing caseload is a Bench of the SCI at the 'drop of a hat' questioning a settled precedent and reopening it. The more precedents you unsettle, the more litigation you generate. There is a crying

Harvard: How US Law Schools Make It Worthwhile to Clerk on India's Supreme Court' (2014) *IJLP*, 21(1), 73–101, as well as the 'Scheme of Engaging Law Clerk-cum-Research Associates on Short-Term Contractual Assignment in the Supreme Court of India – January, 2024' <https://cdnbbsr.s3waas.gov.in/s3ec0490f1f4972d133619a60c30f3559e/uploads/2024/02/2024021281.pdf> accessed 21 April 2025. Interestingly, an earlier version of the rules for law clerks/researchers was struck down by the Delhi HC as being unconstitutional in *Phaguni Nilesh Lal v. Supreme Court of India* (2014) 206 DLT 674.

need to evolve, through a process of consensus, a clear set of guidelines or principles that will be consistently followed. It could also be in the form of a judicial order by a large enough Bench that will not get easily overturned. Judges will also have to adhere to a 'judicial discipline' at all levels in the judicial hierarchy if this has to be properly worked out. And if that happens, there may be no need to resort to the 'curative' jurisdiction or powers under Article 142 in order to do 'complete justice'. An increasing resort to such methods perhaps undermines the legitimacy of the legal system generally and the expectation that the decisions of the SCI as a court of last resort will be both clear and conclusive.

Editor: *Talking about Article 142, we have this phenomenon of the SCI using that one provision to pass orders that would otherwise be impermissible in law. Typically, the Hindu Marriage Act does not permit divorce on the ground of 'irretrievable breakdown' of marriage and yet, day in and day out, the SCI does that, and that too in petitions by one spouse seeking transfer of the matrimonial proceedings from the Court where it is instituted to a court which the Petitioner finds convenient.*

Ms Arora: Absolutely. If a HC dissolves a marriage on the ground that it has irretrievably broken down, the SCI will set it aside. Instead of driving everyone to the SCI, the law itself should be changed or the HC should be given similar powers. The same goes for the modification of an arbitral award, of course that is now pending before a larger Bench.[19] In my view, Article 142 has been used far too much. The Ayodhya temple judgment is a classic example of the Court doing something clearly impermissible in law and the only legal basis for the ultimate directions issued, if at all, is that it was the SCI and it alone has powers to do so under Article 142 of the Constitution.

Editor: *Given the scale of fees charged these days, most Senior Advocates are unaffordable for the average (non-State/non-corporate) litigant. Although there are mid-level competent lawyers who charge affordable fees, the system appears to favour the Senior Advocates because they have a better audience before the Court. The Bar, which appears to operate on the supply/demand rules of the marketplace,*

---

[19] The reference was answered in *Gayatri Balasamy v. M/S ISG Novasoft Technologies Ltd* 2025 INSC 605. It has been held by a 4:1 majority that courts under Sections 34 and 37 of the Act can modify arbitral awards in four limited circumstances: (i) where the award is severable (ii) to correct clerical/computational errors (iii) to vary post-award interest and (iv) under Article 142 for complete justice.

starkly depicts the inequalities in terms of both the availability of work and the corresponding earnings of lawyers. Is any course correction possible?

Ms Arora: Having been part of the Bar for over four decades, I can safely state that not all Senior Advocates are necessarily well-prepared or effective in the Court. A Senior could charge even Rs 3–5 lakhs for a hearing and still end up being a non-performer. On the other hand, I know for a fact that there are some competent AoRs, capable of arguing themselves. It is a good sign that in every batch of newly designated Senior Advocates, there is a sizable number of AoRs. This is a sure way of ensuring that the Bar does not come to be dominated by a clutch of high-charging Senior Advocates.

Editor: *Moving on to Law Officers,*[20] *there is a criticism that over the years, they are less the 'officers of the Court' that they are expected to be and have increasingly been lawyers for the government that appoints them. Would you agree?*

Ms Arora: Absolutely. When you come to occupy such offices, you also stand for the values, for the law, and for what is right. You have to have the independence to do what is right, rather than just being a mouthpiece and wanting to please your masters. Now that, unfortunately, I don't see anymore.

Editor: *And then you haven't had a single woman AG.*

Ms Arora: I think that will take some time. It is not going to happen very soon. We have not had even that much representation on the Bench as yet. But I must say, I'm still happy to be here. This is a country that still accepts women in some of these positions.

Editor: *At the same time, it is still true, isn't it, that women professionals do not have the same freedom of choice as their male counterparts? Women who opt to get married and have children invariably have to leave the profession for a number of years and it is certainly not the same when they return.*

Ms Arora: Yes, I am afraid that is never going to go away. In law firms, both abroad as well as at home, if a woman lawyer announces that she is expecting, she is assigned non-significant areas of work. When she returns, she finds

[20] The collective term 'law officers' refers to the Attorney General for India (AG), the Solicitor General of India (SG) and the Additional Solicitors General of India.

it impossible to get into the same groove. Her juniors would likely have superseded her. That's a very big issue.

Editor: *The legislature has persisted with creating more and more Tribunals under the pretext of lessening the load of the regular courts, but from experience, it has been counterproductive. Apart from the quality of the decisions handed down by most Tribunals being not of acceptable standard, it has increased the workload of the regular courts that are tasked with reviewing such orders. It has also added to the delays, costs and uncertainties suffered by the litigant. Would you agree?*

Ms Arora: The Tribunals are a mess. Some are just completely defunct and not functioning. You have had problems with 'National Company Law Tribunal (NCLT) also, recently.[21] Don't forget one thing – NCLT is only and only doing insolvency. The Companies Act matters are not being heard at all. I have a case from 2006 which has not been heard yet. So, the Tribunals have, according to me, failed. I think the system of having the courts was frankly much better. You could have, in the HCs and maybe even in the SCI, special Benches for particular areas such as Intellectual Property Rights, etc. However, you are going to have the same set of 'in-demand' lawyers appear in these cases as well. It is going to take some years of specialist training to have a dedicated Bar in niche areas of practice.

Editor: *I would like to talk about the quality of free legal services available in the SCI. It has certainly improved over the years. What has been your experience and is there scope for improvement?*

Ms Arora: You know, in the SCI, some of the lawyers who want to take up legal aid matters are extremely good. Judges would do well to encourage them. One way is to make it count for the purpose of designation as Senior Advocates. That will also assure the recipients of legal aid of the quality of the representation in Court.

---

[21] In *State Bank of India v. The Consortium of Mr. Murari Lal Jalan and Mr. Florian Fritsch* 2024 INSC 852, certain critical remarks regarding the functioning of the NCLT were made by the SCI, including the political nature of appointments, its tendency to not adhere to orders of the SCI as well as the lack of domain knowledge of its members.

Recollections and Reflections

GOPAL SUBRAMANIUM

I

The journey of the legal profession is a fascinating one, where different personalities enter and exit the train. It can be somewhat discursive too. I hope to acknowledge those who have left an indelible mark, conducting themselves in accord with the highest standards of the legal profession.

Lawyers played a prominent role in India's struggle for freedom. Mahatma Gandhi, after nearly two decades of law practice in South Africa, returned to India in 1915. In his travels across the country, he was able to inspire Indians (and lawyers, in particular) to resist oppression, even encouraging a social audit in villages. In the Champaran satyagraha, Gandhiji was joined by several young lawyers, including one who would become the first President of free India – Dr Rajendra Prasad. Other prominent figures in the freedom struggle like Motilal Nehru, Jawaharlal Nehru, Sardar Patel, Dr BR Ambedkar and C Rajagopalachari were all lawyers by training, and combined their political and professional lives with remarkable skill. KM Munshi and Alladi Krishnaswami Iyer, who were leading legal practitioners and played an active part in the Constituent Assembly, were tasked with drafting the Constitution of India. A leading light of the Bombay Bar, Bhulabhai Desai, brilliantly defended the three Indian National Army-accused in the Red Fort trials of 1945.[22]

The Indian Constitution was adopted on 26 November 1949. It came into force on 26 January 1950. The first Attorney General for India (AG) was Motilal Chimanlal Setalvad, who by then had already established himself as the leader of the Bombay Bar. In fact, from May to September 1949, Setalvad had acted as Advocate General of India. He was present at the inaugural sitting of the SCI on 28 January 1950. In his opening speech, he exhorted the Court to attain judicial eminence, reminding it that epoch-making judgments will illuminate its records. He said, 'that like all human institutions, the Supreme Court, we hope, will earn reverence through truth.'[23] CJI Kania looked forward to a Bar which would set a high

[22] AG Noorani, *Indian Political Trials* 1775-1947 (Oxford University Press 2005).

[23] Motilal C Setalvad, *My Life – Law and Other Things* (Universal, reprint 2000) 149.

standard. He further said that the legal profession would naturally resist encroachments attempted in the name of law and order on the liberty of the subject and fundamental human rights.[24] Setalvad, throughout his long and distinguished career, maintained near absolute standards of independence and integrity, matched by great ability and a flair for precision.[25]

Alongside Setalvad, there was CK Daphtary, a former Advocate General of Bombay, who was the first Solicitor General of India (SG). His arguments were marked by humour, wit and legal craftsmanship. He was, famously, the public prosecutor in the trial of the accused in Gandhi's assassination case. He was a versatile lawyer.[26] SV Gupte, who was an acclaimed author on Hindu law, was appointed as Additional Solicitor General and later, as Solicitor General.[27] He was a very sharp, forceful lawyer. He could handle many branches of law. Following him was HN Sanyal, who was a brilliant legal mind, conversant with textbooks and cases.

The well-known case of *AK Gopalan v. State of Madras*[28] was argued before a six-judge Constitution Bench of the SCI by MK Nambyar, a doyen of the Madras Bar. His arguments in the case reflected his deep knowledge of comparative constitutional law and the developing international law on civil liberties. Other prominent legal luminaries who were his contemporaries included NC Chatterjee, GS Pathak and Barrister Ashoke Kumar Sen, who went on to serve as a Member of Parliament (MP) and was a Law Minister in both Prime Ministers (PMs) Jawaharlal Nehru and Indira Gandhi's cabinets. The titanic constitutional scholar, HM Seervai, travelled to Delhi often to address the Court in some of our nation's most famous constitutional cases. He served for several years as Advocate General of Maharashtra. His reverence for the Courts was best described by former CJI RS Pathak, who acknowledged that Seervai 'was extremely jealous of protecting their public reputation,

---

[24] Ibid 150–51.

[25] The late RK Garg, who was inspired by Setalvad's analytical thinking, told this writer how he analysed judgments based on logic, reason and an openness to a change of views. He referred to a young barrister – B Sen – who later become a distinguished Senior Advocate of the SCI, following Setalvad's etiquette and code of conduct in examining and preparing cases.

[26] Daphtary had a great sense of humour which has been admirably captured in the book – Fali S Nariman and Vinoo Bhagat, *The Delightful Mr. Daphtary* (Law and Justice Publishing Co Pvt Ltd 2023).

[27] Interestingly, Setalvad had recommended Gupte to be a Judge of the SCI. Gupte declined, and a former Advocate General, SM Sikri, was appointed as Judge of the SCI. Years later, a law officer who followed the course of SM Sikri was Kuldip Singh.

[28] AIR 1950 SC 27. KK Venugopal, *M.K. Nambyar: A Constitutional Visionary* (Ebury Press 2024)

anxious to see that the stream of justice flowed unpolluted, and ensured that no deviation, which came to his knowledge, remained uncorrected.'[29]

Dominating the SC Bar between the decades of the 1960s and 1990s were three leading lights of the Bombay Bar. The first was Nani Palkhivala, the second, Fali Nariman, and the third, Soli Sorabjee. Each one had a distinct style of advocacy.

Palkhivala was the most voracious reader and would not spend a moment in chatter or idle conversation. His fascination for spirituality and knowledge of the many works of Shri Aurobindo left an indelible impression.[30] He entered the courtroom slowly and graciously. Not in one moment did he lose his self-control or raise his voice. Out of the many great moments I witnessed him in Court, two come to my mind. The first was his appearance on behalf of Mrs Indira Gandhi, whose election had been set aside by the Allahabad HC. In a vacation hearing presided over by the legendary VR Krishna Iyer, he argued with restraint, calmness and gentleness, which must have persuaded the Court to pass a conditional order of stay.[31] The second moment was when the CJI (the late AN Ray) attempted a review of the judgment in the *Kesavananda Bharti* case[32]. The arguments of Palkhivala were brilliant, and many of his submissions, handwritten, were so persuasive that the Judges persuaded the CJI to dissolve the reference.[33]

Fali Nariman, a brilliant lawyer who traced his routes to Burma, was meticulous in every detail. He used his walking time for transcendence and thinking. He was adept in most branches of the law, was used to severe critical enquiry and placed institutional reputation at a very high level. His masterly performance in the *Escorts* case[34] in the Bombay HC (in Tilak's Hall before Reddy and Rege JJ) was a treat, so much so that his opponents admired him all the way. He argued good points, dropped bad ones and could weave a narrative where

---

[29] RS Pathak, 'H.M. Seervai – A Tribute' in Feroza H Seervai (ed), *Evoking H.M. Seervai* (Universal 2005) 14; Seervai set for himself the highest moral standards, and had an unwavering commitment to discipline, candour and commitment to the administration of justice.

[30] Nani A Palkhivala, *We, the People: India: The Largest Democracy* (UBS Publishers & Distributors Ltd 1999); Soli J Sorabjee and Arvind P Datar, *Nani Palkhivala: The Courtroom Genius* (LexisNexis 2012).

[31] (1973) 4 SCC 225.

[32] TR Andhyarujina, *Kesavananda Bharati Case – The Untold Story of Struggle for Supremacy by Supreme Court and Parliament* (Lexis Nexis 2014)

[33] See also, Fali S Nariman, *Before Memory Fades: An Autobiography* (Hay House Publishers India 2010).

[34] *Escorts Ltd. v. Union of India* (1985) 57 Comp Cas 241.

only a few pieces existed. He was a great reader, a consummate writer and an advocate for freedom, liberty and the protection of minorities.[35]

Soli Sorabjee was yet another advocate of admirable skill and ability. He had a prodigious memory, and a child-like sense of innocence and trust. He was a lover of books and music. In the Court, he was ready from start to finish. An early riser like Fali, incredibly industrious, he had the power of quick reading and identification of facts.[36] His arguments in the famous *St. Xavier's* case[37] were enthralling and held the Court spellbound.

A special mention must also be made of GS Pathak, who returned to the Bar after demitting office as Vice President of India. He was very persuasive and industrious. Likewise, Sachin Chaudhri, the son of the eminent JN Chaudhri of the Allahabad HC, would argue with dignity, elegance and immense courtesy.

There were retired judges, too, who contributed to the Court and its precincts. One was ST Desai, an authority on Hindu law, whose skill in tax matters was amazing to witness. He would wake up at 2 a.m. to read his briefs and would arrive at the court at 10 every morning. The other was Vishwanatha Sastri, who impressed both the Bar and the Bench with his brilliance and disarming simplicity.

There are a few more lawyers whose names deserve a tribute. Foremost among them is KK Venugopal, whose manners, etiquette and analytical presentation has led to many successes from his stables. Two of his juniors rose to be judges of the SCI as direct appointees.[38] He is very courteous to the Court and his opponents. His heart is full of compassion. In matters of the Constitution, he is an acclaimed authority. His father, the late MK Nambyar was one of the foremost thinkers of constitutional law.

K Parasaran, son of Kesava Iyengar, a legendary lawyer from Madras, was himself an extraordinary lawyer.[39] He began as a civil law expert, but like

---

[35] Fali S Nariman, *India's Legal System: Can it be Saved?* (Penguin Random House India 2006); Fali S Nariman, *You Must Know Your Constitution* (Hay House Publishers India 2023); Fali S Nariman, *Beyond the Courtroom: Reflections on Law, Constitution, and Nationhood* (Hay House Publishers India 2024).

[36] Abhinav Chandrachud, *Soli Sorabjee: Life and Times: An Authorized Biography* (Penguin Random House India 2022).

[37] *Ahmedabad St.Xavier's College Society v. State of Gujarat* (1974) 1 SCC 717.

[38] RF Nariman and KV Viswanathan JJ.

[39] SASTRA University, *Law and Dharma: A Tribute to the Pitamaha of the Indian Bar* (2016).

Setalvad, in no time, mastered constitutional law. He held the office of AG with distinction. He was preceded by Lal Narayan Sinha, a doyen of the Patna Bar whose deep understanding of constitutional law was complemented by his dignified and understated presentation of a case.[40] Succeeding Parasaran as AG was another leading light of the Madras Bar, G Ramaswamy. His wit and repartee in Court livened the court proceedings.[41]

In the field of criminal law, Ram Jethmalani stood out as an exceptional lawyer and played a long and successful innings, dabbling in politics as well.[42] A lawyer from Allahabad who rose to national prominence was Shanti Bhushan, who conducted the trial of the election case that unseated the sitting PM Indira Gandhi in 1975.[43] He served as a Law Minister in the cabinet of PM Morarji Desai.

Another distinguished criminal lawyer in India was Frank Anthony. He always carried multiple coloured pens. His memory and description of evidence and facts were mesmerizing. He was a leader of the Anglo-Indian community, the founder of a school, amazingly punctual and had a specially designed Ambassador car that could house his books when he travelled for various trials. His junior, Sushil Kumar, has carried the mantle in criminal law. KK Luthra was another great criminal lawyer who appeared in all Courts, always prepared and dressed to perfection.

In the field of civil liberties, two lawyers require special mention. VM Tarkunde, a former judge of the Bombay HC and a keen follower of MN Roy, was progressive in his outlook and during the inglorious Emergency, was

---

40 His son, LM Sharma, would become the CJI.

41 Justice S Muralidhar, *'GR: The Client's Lawyer, The Lawyer's Envy, The Legal World's Pride'* High Court of Madras Sesquicentennial: 1862–2012 Madras High Court A Saga (High Court, Madras) 185.

42 He served as a Law Minister in the cabinet of PM Atal Bihari Vajpayee; He commenced his practice in Sindh at the unbelievably early age of nineteen and shifted his practice to Bombay on the country's partition. Although his expertise was in criminal law and preventive detention, he also had strong command of constitutional law. His masterly performance for the defense in the *Parliament Attack* case was a lesson worthy of emulation. *State (NCT of Delhi) v. Navjot Sandhu* (2005) 11 SCC 600. See also Ram Jethmalani, *Maverick Unchanged, Unrepentant* (Rupa Publications 2014); Ram Jethmalani, *Big Egos Small Men* (1st edn, Har-Anand Publication Pvt Ltd 2017); Ram Jethmalani and DS Chopra, *Parliamentary Privileges - Law and Practice* (Thomson Reuters 2015).

43 Shanti Bhushan appeared for Raj Narrain. This verdict delivered by JN Sinha J of the Allahabad HC precipitated the declaration of the infamous Emergency that lasted from 26 June 1975 till 21 March 1977; Shanti Bhushan was a fiercely independent professional. He was fond of science, mathematics and was a positivist logician. His thorough reading and analysis of every brief, and his determination to get justice for his client, will be always remembered.

fearless, calm and determined. He was one of the prominent co-founders of the People's Union of Civil Liberties. Gobinda Mukhoty, another leading light from the Calcutta Bar, helped establish the Peoples Union for Democratic Rights. He was a hardworking, people-oriented, sharing and caring lawyer, protective of the junior members of the Bar and their well-being.

Dr LM Singhvi, an eminent jurist and parliamentarian, was the founder of the Institute of Constitutional and Parliamentary Studies. A scholar of depth, profundity and eloquence, he spoke with intelligence, craftsmanship and thoroughness.[44]

Anil B Divan's work as *amicus curiae* in the *Vineet Narain* case[45] made notable contributions to the independence of investigating agencies.[46] Ashok K Desai, a successful senior lawyer from the Bombay Bar, was admired for the manner in which he conducted himself with dignity and objectivity while holding the office of the AG. Likewise, Dipankar Datta embellished the office of the SG with his pleasant demeanour and understated depth of learning.[47]

GL Sanghi and PP Rao were the epitome of scholarship and industry. Among the prominent lawyers from Assam, who made a mark in the SCI, was Prasanta Kumar Goswami, whose fidelity to the record of a case stood out as an iconic feature of his professionalism. From the Orissa Bar came Gobind Das, who had earlier served as the Advocate General of Orissa. He was one of the most prodigiously well-read lawyers of his time.[48] His interests went beyond law, into art, philosophy and multiple areas of intellectual questioning. Dr YS Chitale distinguished himself as a lawyer of great eminence. He will be remembered for assisting the SCI as *amicus curiae* in the *Sunil Batra*[49] and *Bachan Singh*[50] cases. One of his juniors is Raju Ramachandran, a Senior Advocate, whose self-definition of standard and professional rectitude is a

---

[44] His able son, Dr AM Singhvi, is a leading practitioner today.

[45] *Vineet Narain v. Union of India* (1998) 1 SCC 226.

[46] Anil Divan, *On the Front Foot: Writings of Anil Divan on Courts, Press and Personalities* (2nd edn, Universal Law Publishing – An Imprint of Lexis Nexis 2016).

[47] He pupiled in the chambers of Barrister Siddharth Shankar Ray, who rose to great prominence in the Calcutta Bar and was a leading politician in the Congress party. He went onto become the CM of West Bengal in the early 1970s. Later, in the 1990s, he was the Governor of Punjab.

[48] Govind Das, *Supreme Court in Quest of Identity* (2nd edn, Eastern Book Co 2000) and Gobind Das, *Justice in India: A Study of Last Two Decades* (Shangon and Shangon 1967).

[49] *Sunil Batra v. Delhi Administration* (1978) 4 SCC 494.

[50] *Bachan Singh v. State of Punjab* (1980) 2 SCC 684.

role model for young lawyers and young Seniors.[51] From the Punjab Bar came HL Sibal, who commenced his practice in Lahore prior to Partition and then moved to Chandigarh where he established a flourishing practice.[52] His son Kapil Sibal has been on top of the legal profession for several decades now and in 2024, was the President of the SCBA.[53]

JM Thakore, who remained an Advocate General of Gujarat for over four decades, would argue with calm and composure. The other Advocate Generals of the states who made a mark in the SCI included VKT. Chari, Govind Swaminadhan, Narasa Reddy, AS Bobde and Tehmtan R Andhyarujina. Each of them contributed immensely to building a high degree of professional and ethical standards.

While the former Advocate General of Punjab SM Sikri was the first among the lawyers to be directly elevated as an SCI judge,[54] after a long gap, he was followed by other successful practitioners – Kuldip Singh, Santosh Hegde, Rohinton Nariman, L Nageswara Rao, UU Lalit and Indu Malhotra.[55]

The SCI has lost an opportunity in failing to nominate some of the most outstanding jurists of their time as its judges. Three names come to mind – Professor PK Tripathi,[56] Professor Upendra Baxi and Professor Lotika Sarkar.[57] They were distinguished but deeply distinctive from each other's way of teaching and thinking.

Shyamalha Pappu was among the earliest of the women lawyers to be designated as Senior Advocate and actively practiced in the SCI.[58] Indira Jaising, coming from the Bombay Bar, distinguished herself with her thoroughness of

---

[51] Raju was also an Additional Solicitor General of India. Another of Chitale's juniors, Mukul Mudgal became a judge of the High Court of Delhi and retired as Chief Justice of the Punjab and Haryana High Court.

[52] He served a very long term as Advocate General for the States of Punjab and Haryana for two terms each.

[53] Kapil Sibal is a parliamentarian and has served as a Union Minister in the cabinets of Manmohan Singh for two terms. Both his sons Amit Sibal and Akhil Sibal are Senior Advocates as well.

[54] Sikri went on to become a CJI and headed the Bench that decided the *Kesavananda* case.

[55] The most recent elevations are of PS Narasimha and KV Viswanathan.

[56] Pankaj Kumar Tripathi, *Constitution of India: A Comprehensive Premie*r (PVP Pvt Ltd 2021); Pankaj Kumar Tripathi and Pramod Kumar Upadhyay, *Emerging Social, Economical, Legal & Challenges in Developing India* (Edwin Incorporation 2017).

[57] Amita Dhanda and Archana Parashar (eds), *Engendering Law: Essays in Honour of Lotika Sarkar* (Eastern Book Company 1999).

[58] She was the first woman lawyer to be designated Senior Advocate by the Delhi High Court in 1971.

preparation and admirable presentation of cases, contributing significantly to the development of labour and human rights jurisprudence.[59]

Today, the Bar has amongst its seniors Harish Salve, CS Vaidyanathan, Rakesh Dwivedi and Dushyant Dave – a set of eminent, illuminating and forceful advocates for their clients and the positions they believe in. Further, the pioneering work of mediation by Sriram Panchu and the late Sadhana Ramachandran is inspirational.

Each of these lawyers have helped develop the law and strengthen the independence of the judiciary. It is possible that in this recapitulation, this writer may have omitted the names of many a worthy individual. This is inadvertent and may be forgiven.

II

Today, the profession is blessed with extraordinary talent in its many young Seniors. They will require reflection over the values, the traditions and the nature of the judicial exercise. It is on their shoulders that the responsibility of maintaining the traditions of the profession now rests.

Several traditions, which many of the eminent counsel I mentioned before would have taken for granted, now slowly wither away. The tradition followed in all hearings – namely, that the Respondent waited to speak until he was called upon by the Court – has yielded to a simultaneous opportunity for all Counsel to speak, even argue at the same time. The Respondents are meant to respond, but increasingly, they choose instead to open a case. One of the reasons for this tradition, this basic rule, was that the rule against interruption existed in aid of judges so they may be able to apply themselves with a degree of comfort and clarity. There is much to be done.

Another area in which the Courts have become increasingly liberal is to enable counsel to make statements that are not supported by the record. The practice was seriously frowned upon in the first forty-five to fifty years of the SCI's history. It enabled caution and care to weigh on a lawyer's mind when they made a statement about the facts in a case.

In the SCI, the tradition was always that irrespective of clients' interests, the lawyer was first and last an officer of the Court. This tradition, too, if not

[59] An interview with Indira Jaising is separately carried in this book.

passionately protected, may face a quick death. One must hope that the new generations of Seniors and Law Officers bring these traditions back to the SCI and to Courts across India.

As Bernhard Schlink wrote, 'once parties, unions and associations, churches and clubs, universities, schools and courts have been forced into line, there comes a point when the ethics of opposition survive only in quixotic heroic gestures.'[60]

III

The Rule of Law in India has its roots in the freedom struggle, in the writing of the Constitution, and most importantly, in its practice by institutions and individuals. The Rule of Law is the legal constraint on the authority of a state in matters of person, life and liberty. Lawyers, like judges, are guardians of the Rule of Law.

As intermediaries between individuals and the legal system, they ensure fairness in the application of the laws. They are protectors, burdened with a loyalty to their clients, but with a higher loyalty to justice. More than the executive and the legislature, it is the Bar that truly checks transgressions by the judicial branch. An ethical, independent and unaligned Bar preserves public trust, leading to the long-term stability of the State. Thus, a lot depends upon the lawyers in the profession.

---

60 Bernhard Schlink, *Guilt About the Past* (House of Anansi Press 2010) 32–33.

Legal Education and the Supreme Court

KAMALA SANKARAN

'The more things change, the more they remain the same.'[1] The aphorism captures the sentiment aptly when reading the Report of the Indian Universities Commission, 1902 today, particularly its section on legal education. It raises the question of how much has changed these past hundred years and more, and how much further we need to go in order to build a suitably relevant legal education environment suitable for India today. A look at the past also brings out why and how the role of the judges of the Supreme Court of India (SCI) as distinct from the role of the SCI became fairly central in legal education, and the important role judges and the Court continue to play in determining the future of legal education.[2]

Judges and Governance of Universities

The 1902 Report chronicles that the first (modern) universities were set up in 1857 in Calcutta, Bombay and Madras. The university at Calcutta had the Governor General as the Chancellor, whereas the other two universities had the Governor as Chancellor. This began a tradition of the head of the Executive serving as the Chancellor of a university, which, in large measure (excluding the national law schools that mark a departure from this tradition) continues until today. Such a structure was not surprising since the Committee set up to examine the structure and prepare regulations for these future universities was appointed by the Government of India.

What is also noteworthy is that the modern university system beginning in 1857 established an important role for the judiciary too. The Committee

[1] This aphorism is attributed to the French writer Jean-Baptiste Alphonso Karr.

[2] There is a rich body of literature examining reforms and changes in legal education. This essay focuses solely on the role of judges and the SCI as important stakeholders in this process.

constituted to draft the Bill of Incorporation of these universities was headed by the Honourable Sir James William Colvile, Chief Justice (CJ) of the SC in Bengal. Sir James Colvile went on immediately thereafter to become the first Vice-Chancellor (VC) of the University of Calcutta.

The 1902 Report reviewed these developments in the governing structures of these multi-disciplinary universities that arose after 1857 and noted that these included the appointment of Fellows in these universities who were 'persons who have acquired proficiency in different branches of Literature, Science and Art'.[3] The Fellows included judges and representatives of the Bar, who together with the Chancellor and the VC constituted the Senate of these universities. The presence of Fellows reflected the view that the university is a microcosm of a larger universe; having a cross-section of stakeholders represented in its highest decision-making body served this purpose well. The Report draws one's attention to the growing role played by the judiciary in legal education in contrast to other disciplines taught in colleges and universities, and where the end user played a more indirect role in shaping the content of education imparted by such institutions.

The 1902 Report also endorsed the idea of Fellows being not only appointed, but also elected by the graduates of the university. This shift initiated the tradition of electing persons to other decision-making bodies in the country. It is interesting to observe that the mode of electing representatives to the universities' decision-making bodies (introduced by the Indian Universities Act, 1904), consequent upon the recommendations of the 1902 Report, was prescient. Similar changes were to follow in the political realm too; the process of directly electing (not merely nominating) persons to representative bodies began with the Indian Councils Act, 1909.

In the particular context of legal education in colleges and universities, the 1902 Report went on to recommend that 'in the council or governing body it is desirable that the Bench and Bar of the local High Court (HC) should be *strongly represented*' (emphasis supplied).[4] Such an approach of including members of the Bench and the Bar in the crucial decision-making bodies of legal educational institutions continues till today and has ensured the fairly

[3] Thomas Raleigh, *Report of the Indian Universities Commission, 1902* (Government Central Printing Office 1902) 4.

[4] ibid 35; Ministry of Education, Government of India, *Report of the University Education Commission, December 1948–August 1949*, 1st reprint edn (Manager, Government of India Press 1962).

dominant voice of the judiciary, and the Bar, in the development and growth of legal education.[5] The presence of judges in the governing bodies of the central universities became commonplace following the recommendation of the 1902 Report.

The relationship *inter se* between the executive and the judiciary, however, changed somewhat as universities continued to be established.[6] The University of Calcutta had a CJ of the (then) SC in Bengal as its founding VC; that trend continued for some years with other judges occupying that position but gradually shifting in favour of, first, civil servants, and later, academics.[7] A notable exception to this shift was Sir Maurice Gwyer, CJ of the Federal Court, who went on to become a distinguished VC of the University of Delhi. He was not the only judge to become a VC. CJI SR Das was a member of the University Grants Commission from 1962 to 1965 and also the VC of Visva-Bharati University from 1959 to 1965.[8] CJI PB Gajendragadkar, who took a deep interest in legal education (and chaired several key committees as we note below), was appointed the Honorary VC of the University of Bombay for five years in 1967 following his retirement from the Bench.

With the advent of the National Law School of India University (NLSIU), the CJI, where he consents, becomes its Chancellor, whereas the President of India its Visitor.[9] In some subsequently established National Law

---

[5] It must be noted that sites of legal education are located outside universities and colleges too. Prof. Baxi notes that sites, such as worker education/people's education programmes, could be sites on 'non-certificatory' legal learning modes. See, Upendra Baxi, 'Enculturing Law? Some Unphilosophic Remarks' in Mathew John and Sitharamam Kakarala (eds), *Enculturing Law: New Agendas for Legal Pedagogy* (Tulika Books 2007); However, this essay is confined to legal education in formal universities and colleges.

[6] For instance, in the case of the University of Delhi set up in 1922, while the President of India is its Visitor, the Vice President is its Chancellor and the CJI its Pro Chancellor. Further, members from the legal profession are also to be elected as members of the University Court, which is the highest governing body of that university. Judges have been members of its Faculty of Law, which permits the appointment of external members.

[7] For instance, Claudius James Erskine was a Judge of the Bombay HC before he was appointed as the VC of the University of Calcutta in 1862. Sir Gooroodas Banerjee was the first Indian judge of the Calcutta HC and later became the first Indian VC of the University of Calcutta in 1890. Notable among the early academic VCs of the University was Sir Henry Sumner Maine, comparative jurist and historian. Sir Ashutosh Mookerjee is perhaps the most well-known of the VCs, educationist and mathematician who served the University twice in that capacity.

[8] See, 'Late Justice S.R. Das (Condolence)' (1977) 4 SCC (Jour) 1.

[9] For a background to the establishment of the NLSIU and its early years, see V Vijayakumar, 'Legal Education in India and the National Law School Experiment—Achievements and Challenges' in Lokendra Malik and Manish Arora (eds), Legal Education in India: Essays in Honour of Professor

Universities (NLUs), while variations exist, the Chancellor is often the CJ of the relevant HC and the Visitor (where such a position exists) could be the CJI or his nominee, or a Judge of the SCI. Judges of the SCI and HCs, including CJs of the HCs, are members of the governing bodies of these NLUs. The initiative taken by the Bar Council of India (BCI) in setting up NLSIU, and the subsequent setting up of other NLUs, has ensured a strong presence of members of the BCI, including its Chairperson, in several of these universities with the presence of the Bench and Bar predominating these bodies.

The unique position of the first NLU, viz. the NLSIU, has been recognized by the Karnataka HC speaking through BV Nagarathna J when the Division Bench held that the legislation setting it up 'conceptualizes it as an autonomous and independent entity free from state control. It is in this background that the State has not reserved any power unto itself regarding the management and administration of the respondent/Law School.' The Bench also highlighted the 'deep and pervasive role' of the BCI in the NLSIU as compared to other NLUs, and noted further that 'that the respondent/Law School cannot be on par, nor is it in the same league with the National Law Schools in other States.'[10]

Speaking generally of all NLUs, though these are set up as state universities, they are termed, and viewed, as 'national' law universities for good reasons. Unlike other state universities that normally have the Governor of the relevant state as the Chancellor, as noted earlier, in the case of the NLUs, the Chancellor is often the CJ of the relevant HC. The intake of students is also consciously all-India based, including in the NLUs where there is state-level domicile reservation. The national-level presence of students is ensured through the conduct of all-India entrance examinations for admission of students.[11] By and large, many of the NLUs recruit their teaching faculty from across India with no particular domicile requirements. Locating suitable students and

---

Ranbir Singh (Universal Law Publishing Co 2014). Also see Deepa Badrinarayan, 'India's State of Legal Education: The Road from NLSIU to Jindal' (2014) 63(3) *Journal of Legal Education* 521–23. For an overview of the challenges facing the national law universities and a survey of literature pertaining to these universities and also for a survey of scholarly literature on legal education see, F Mustafa, JS Sohi, S Chauhan, S Kumar and V Ganjiwale, *Suggestions for Reforms at the National Law Universities Set Up Through State Legislations* (National Academy of Legal Studies and Research 2018).

10 *Master Balachandar Krishnan v. State of Karnataka* ILR 2021 Kar 1245.

11 The Common Law Admission Test (CLAT), the All-India Law Entrance Test and the National Law School's Admission Test (NLSAT) are examples.

faculty from across India has allowed them to claim a national status. Yet, it must be noted that despite this, they are not treated as institutions of national importance by the central government, neither are they listed as such by any central law. Yet there is no doubt that the presence of the judges in particular has enhanced the prestige of the NLUs leading to a broad acceptance of these universities as ones of a national level.

There are also specialist law universities outside the NLU fold. The Indian Law Institute has now become a 'deemed' university even though it was established as a society. The Tamil Nadu Ambedkar Law University is another specialist umbrella law university for government law colleges across the state – which is not an NLU, unlike the Tamil Nadu National Law University. Judges are present in the governing bodies of not only these NLUs but other legal institutions too. The BCI had earlier created a charitable trust called the Bar Council of India Trust, which, in turn, registered a Society known as the National Law School of India Society. It led directly to the setting up of the NLSIU under National Law School of India Act, 1986 in Karnataka. Some decades later, the BCI set up yet another legal entity, the BCI Trust–Pearl First, in order to set up the India International University of Legal Education and Research (IIULER) at Goa with two judges as member-trustees.

How has the presence of members of the judiciary in university structures impacted the functioning of the universities? While the impact on the legal education, its content and quality, is examined later in this essay, here we focus on the impact it has had on the governance and style of functioning of the universities, particularly law universities.

The presence of SCI or HC judges at the helm of affairs of the NLUs has certainly reduced the kind of political pressure faced by administrators that is the fate of many state-level universities. Their presence in the Executive Council (which is the body most closely linked to the administration of the university, the management of its revenue and property, the appointment of faculty and staff, sanctioning of the budget and disciplinary decisions) has strengthened the capacity of the university to function freely without undue regard for the political fall-out of 'difficult' decisions pertaining to academic standards or attendance or discipline.[12] This may also account for the growing

---

[12] This has been my personal experience too as a VC of one of the NLUs – the Tamil Nadu National Law University at Tiruchirappalli, Tamil Nadu (TNNLU).

importance of such law universities as compared to law colleges in other state universities across various metrics and rankings.[13]

Having a judge in a position of responsibility in a university serves to strengthen the robustness of the decision-making and administrative processes. Quite apart from the domain knowledge that a judge brings to bear on the various decisions taken by a university, the legal acumen and acuity with which statutory processes are followed by virtue of the presence of judges in various offices and bodies of a university that are fortunate enough to have them in their governance structures has contributed in no small measure to the strengthening of the governance of the law universities as compared to other universities.

The presence of judges in the governing structures of a law university can also be used for strengthening the academic experience of law students and deepening their understanding of court processes. If law students can be provided with opportunities to clerk, not only with SCI and HC judges, but also with the district judiciary, it would greatly widen their understanding of the judicial system.

There are reportedly over 1,500 law colleges in India at present and many of them are private colleges affiliated with various universities. Students of these private colleges do not get the benefit of regular interaction with judges or with the National Legal Services Authority, a facility that is currently available to students studying in NLUs or other leading public and private universities. Students in these private colleges would greatly benefit from having opportunities to intern/clerk with different levels of the judiciary, work in district/state-level legal aid programmes, participate in Lok Adalats, and have regular interactions with judges (serving and retired) who can also provide guidance to such colleges. Putting in place such institutional initiatives and mechanisms is essential to addressing the unmet legal and justice needs of our society.

Judges and the Direction of Legal Education

The 1902 Report, which was the first to examine the role of universities and colleges offering (legal) education, had an interesting insight to offer on the

[13] For instance, under the National Institutional Ranking Framework conducted by the Ministry of Education, the NLUs occupy many of the top slots in the ranking.

purpose of education. The oldest Sanskrit College in Benaras (now Varanasi) founded in 1791 (long before the Wood's Despatch of 1854) was set up 'for the preservation and cultivation of the Laws, Literature and Religions of the nation, to accomplish the same purpose for the Hindus as the Madrasah for the Mohamedans and specially to supply qualified Hindu Assistants to European Judges.'[14] The role of such institutions was to assist judges in the performance of their duties and not to train advocates or legal professionals that seems commonplace today. What is noteworthy is how far we have come from such a narrow conception of education – in particular legal education.

Yet in many ways, the 1902 Report appeared to be way ahead of its times. It bemoaned the poor quality of legal education. It notes that the pleaders who were frequently found to be teaching in various law colleges 'lack the power to apply their knowledge to the case before them'. It therefore recommended that 'the best corrective of this defect would be supplied by the practice of teaching from cases, the system now followed by many of the best teachers of Law in England and America' and called for the 'preparation of books of cases for students'.[15]

What is surprising however, is that it took half a century longer for the introduction of the case method approach in legal education in India. The role of the Ford Foundation and the initiative taken by Prof. Anandjee at the Benaras Hindu University and Prof PK Tripathi in Delhi University, both Deans, to introduce the case method in Indian universities has been well-documented.[16] The emphasis on a case method–based legal learning, no doubt, contributed to 'weaning studies of law from a treatise-based, doctrinal understanding of law', but led, as Prof. Upendra Baxi notes, to a form of 'case madness'.[17] Such a case-centric focus does not adequately permit the impact of social movements or events happening in society to inform legal education and the curriculum.

---

14 '*Report of the University Education Commission*' (n 3) 8.

15 The 1902 Report, without naming him, draws upon the approach of Christopher Columbus Langdell and his powerful impact on legal education in Harvard Law School and, later, elsewhere.

16 See, Rajeev Dhavan, 'Legal Research in India: The Role of Indian Law Institute' (1985) 27 (2) *Journal of the Indian Law Institute* 223; Jayanth K Krishnan, 'Professor Kingsfield Goes to Delhi: American Academics, the Ford Foundation, and the Development of Legal Education in India' (2004) 46 *American Journal of Legal History* 447. Also see, Jayanth K Krishnan, 'From the ALI to the ILI: The Efforts to Export an American Legal Institution' (2005) 38 *Vanderbilt Journal of Transnational Law* 1255; Arthur Taylor von Mehren, 'Law and Legal Education in India: Some Observations' (1965) 78 *Harvard Law Review* 1180.

17 Baxi, 'Enculturing Law?' in *Enculturing Law* (n 5) 9.

Surprisingly, the debates in the Constituent Assembly a decade earlier did not focus much on legal education, or whether the legal system needed a thorough overhaul to go back to its 'indigenous' roots. Marc Galanter noted that 'The Constituent Assembly (1947–49) contained no spokesmen for a restoration of dharmasatra [sic], nor for a revival of local customary law as such.'[18] One of the rare occasions where a Speaker in the Constituent Assembly addressed the matter of legal education, though indirectly, was Mr K Santhanam. Speaking on the need of the SCI, on occasion, to interact with the Parliament and the Executive without repercussions on its independence, Santhanam pointed out that matters such as who was entitled to practise before the Court, and what kind of legal education would entitle a person to do so, were eminently matters that required that sort of coordination between the three arms of the State.[19]

In a contemporaneous development, the Government of India had appointed the University Education Commission, which worked between 1948 to 1949, headed by Dr S Radhakrishnan and comprising members drawn from academia. The Commission had very little to say about legal education except to note, bleakly, that 'The law has also given us great leaders and men consecrated to public service. Most conspicuous of these is Gandhiji. Here the comparison ends. We have no internationally known expounders of jurisprudence and legal studies.'[20] Yet this very first Commission on education reporting in independent India went on to state that 'The volume of evidence and experience indicates that a broad general education followed by thorough training in scientific legal study and techniques offers the best hope of success,' and further observed, 'We do not think that a set curriculum of studies can be offered throughout India for the degree course in Law.'[21] Clearly the thrust was on ensuring quality, rather than ensuring uniformity.

The late 1950s and 1960s were a period of ferment in legal education, and the judges of the SCI played a major role in the changes that were introduced. The political stage was well set for introduction of modern methods of reforming legal education and to address the gaps that a modern, independent India required. And the judges of the SCI were one of the first to take up the issue of improving legal education as well as legal research. They did so not

[18] Marc Galanter, 'The Aborted Restoration of "Indigenous" Law in India' (1972) 14(1) *Comparative Studies in Society and History* 53.

[19] *Constituent Assembly Debates*, 6 June 1949, vol 8, para. 8.99.186, speech by K Santhanam.

[20] '*Report of the University Education Commission*' (n 3) 224.

[21] ibid 227.

just in terms of providing recommendations or guidance but in creating an institutional structure that could serve as a vehicle to systematically address and provide answers to the challenges confronting the legal system.[22]

The judges of the SCI led by CJI SR Das played a key role in the setting up of the Indian Law Institute, a society and an institution, one which was provided space at a prime location adjacent to the SCI to carry out its activities. Speaking at the inauguration of the Indian Law Institute (ILI) in the Central Hall of the Parliament on 12 December 1957, CJI SR Das stated, 'We are, thus, launching the Institute on its career of usefulness, full of hope that it will take its rightful place as one of the great centres of legal research.'

The emergence of the ILI with its close connections to the SCI is along lines similar to what had taken place in Germany over fifty years earlier at the turn of the twentieth century. Wilhelm von Humboldt, who had been rediscovered in the early 1900s around the time of publication of the 1902 Report, encouraged the establishment of 'research institutes outside the university – in other words, a separation of knowledge production and knowledge dissemination.'[23]

The idea of setting up the ILI – in 1956 – was the first step in creating such a specialized institution.[24] Its governing committee included the CJI as ILI's President and the Attorney General for India as its Vice President. Rajeev Dhavan notes that MC Setalvad, Attorney General for India, after a visit to several American law schools 'was convinced that an American style programme was better than an English one'.[25] The subsequent research programme set up in coordination with the Americans had the presence of 'an Indian academic (PK Tripathi), two HC judges (CB Agarwala of Allahabad

---

[22] This essay, in its limited capacity, cannot possibly contain the role of various judges of the SCI over its seventy-five-year period and is confined to the role of few select judges. For a more comprehensive review, see, in particular, George H Gadbois Jr., *Judges of the Supreme Court: 1950–1989* (OUP 2011).

[23] Johan Östling, *Humboldt and the Modern German University: An Intellectual History* (Lund University Press 2018) 56.

[24] Rajeev Dhavan notes, 'It is significant that its founders were a future Chief Justice of India, three other judges of the Supreme Court of India, two civil servants (one of whom worked in the Ministry of Law and the other was a legal adviser to the Ministry of External Affairs), two administrator-academics from Delhi University (namely its VC and the dean of its faculty of law) and a lawyer-member of Parliament.'; Rajeev Dhavan 'Legal Research in India: The Role of Indian Law Institute' (1985) 27(2) *Journal of the Indian Law Institute.*

[25] Dhavan, 'Legal Research in India' (n 24) 223.

and PB Mukharji of Calcutta) and two Indian lawyers (GN Joshi of Bombay and Advocate-General SM Sikri of Punjab).'[26]

The broader task of examining the content and delivery of legal education and to consider how well it aligned with the requirements of an independent India was also one that was taken up by various stakeholders including the SCI. Yet the immediate impetus for this to happen once again involved judges of the SCI – CJI SR Das and CJI PB Gajendragadkar, who were to have an enormous impact on legal education through the 1950s and 1960s. SR Das former CJI while he was VC of the Visva-Bharati University became a member of the Kothari Commission to draft a Model Act for Universities.[27]

Another report to have far-reaching impact on universities was the *Report of the Committee on Governance of Universities and Colleges* headed by former CJI PB Gajendragadkar who was the VC of the University of Bombay.[28] While acknowledging that the Committee did not have within its purview the 'problems of the contents of education', the Report did deal with the growth of universities and the need to link it to the Indian society, which it noted was in 'ferment', and that '[b]ossism of "senior members" must be eradicated, and that deliberations and debates . . . must be free, fearless and objective'.[29]

The (First) Report of the Curriculum Development Centre (CDC) in Law commissioned by the University Grants Commission (UGC) and chaired by Prof. Upendra Baxi, laid out a periodization, noting that 'The principal "moments" or trends in this complex discourse may be outlined as follows. In the first phase (roughly 1950–65) , the principal theme was how best to transform legal education away from the colonial heritage, and in a way to Indianize it, in the second phase (roughly 1965–75) the emphasis was on sound reorganization of curricula and pedagogy towards professional legal education; in the third phase (1976-88), the focus shifted to "modernization" of law curricula so as to make these increasingly relevant to the problems of a

[26] Rajeev Dhavan details the significant role played by PB Gajendragadkar CJI in pushing forward the research agenda of the ILI as well as the inputs of later CJIs such as K Subba Rao, M Hidayatullah and SM Sikri CJJ. And later still that of Krishna Iyer J and his colleagues, colleagues including YV Chandrachud CJ, PN Bhagwati, O Chinnappa Reddy and DA Desai JJ in evolving a research agenda.

[27] DS Kothari, *Report of the Committee on 'Model Act for Universities'* (Ministry of Education, Government of India, 1964). This Committee was chaired by Dr DS Kothari, chairperson, UGC.

[28] PB Gajendragadkar, *Report of the Committee on Governance of Universities and Colleges* (New Delhi: University Grants Commission 1971).

[29] ibid 7, 10.

society and state in deep throes of transition.'[30] Prof. NR Madhava Menon had a different periodization of legal education in mind. He stated that the 'first generation reforms' in legal education commenced soon after the enactment of the Indian Advocates Act, 1962. Subsequently, to cope with the expansion of law colleges, he described the 'second generation law reforms' as led by the setting up of the NLSIU focusing on academic excellence, social relevance and professional competence.[31] While Prof. Menon's approach focused more on institutional structures, the first CDC, headed by Prof. Baxi, focused more on the content of legal education, and importantly, on the de-colonization of legal education, discussed later in this essay.

The institutional inclusion of the law teacher as a significant voice in determining the direction of legal education got a fillip when, in 1993, the CJI set up a Committee titled 'Committee on Reforms in Legal Education and Regarding Entry into Legal Profession' consisting of AM Ahmadi J as its Chairperson and M Jagannadha Rao J (CJ of Kerala) and BN Kirpal J (CJ of Gujarat) as its members. Among its several recommendations was one that pertained to a revamped Legal Education Committee.[32] Some of these recommendations were taken forward by the BCI immediately thereafter. M Jagannadha Rao J was subsequently appointed the Chairperson of the Law Commission of India (LCI). The 184th Report of the LCI made a recommendation to strengthen the presence of the judiciary, BCI and academicians in the Legal Education Committee of the UGC[33]. This Report reiterated a trend that had begun well over a hundred years ago. The LCI Report also had a great deal to say about developing the professional skills of the law student and, as in the earlier period of the 1950s and 1960s, drew upon *The MacCrate Report* (1992) prepared by the American Bar Association alongside other initiatives in the USA and the UK to develop a set of recommendations pertaining to legal education and training of law students.

Acknowledging the separate responsibilities of the various stakeholders in legal education will ensure that the content of legal education moves meaningfully

---

30 University Grants Commission, *Report of the Curriculum Development Centre in Law* (UGC 1990) 1.

31 NR Madhava Menon, 'Transformation of Indian Legal Education' in *An Idea of a Law School, Ideas from the Law School,* ed. NR Madhava Menon, Murali Neelakantan, and Sumeet Malik (EBC 2019).

32 The Law Commission of India in its 14th Report (1958) drew attention to the need for law academics to have a presence in such a committee dealing with legal education in decision-making.

33 See, PP Rao, 'Legal Education under the Advocates Act, 1961' in *Legal Education in India: Essays in Honour of Professor Ranbir Singh*, ed. Dr Lokendra Malik and Dr Manish Arora (Universal Law Publishing Co. 2014).

with the times and serves multiple societal requirements. The 142nd *Report on the subject 'Strengthening Legal Education in View of Emerging Challenges before the Legal Profession'* submitted in 2024 by the Parliamentary Standing Committee on Personnel, Public Grievances, Law and Justice observed:

> So, the Legal curriculum in education institutions needs to be designed in a manner that enables the development of skills required for pursuing diverse legal professions and not just courtroom practice. Thus, there is no sense in the BCI having regulatory powers over the entire spectrum of legal education. Further, the BCI has neither power not expertise to meet the challenges of the ever-changing globalized world… Accordingly, the Committee recommends that the BCI's powers to regulate legal education should be limited to the extent of acquiring basic eligibility for practicing at the Bar.[34]

The Committee recommended the setting up of an independent authority for regulating higher education in law. Evidently, how the courts, universities, the BCI, other stakeholders in the legal system, as well as those deprived of legal rights and access to justice, obtain a voice in the shaping of legal education requires broad-based consultation and building a consensus regarding the direction of legal education.

The Supreme Court and Legal Education

The enormous number of cases dealing with educational matters, whether relating to admissions, affiliation of institutions, admission of students, appointment of teachers and staff, disciplinary matters, appointment of authorities under the relevant enactments, among others, are testament to how often those aspiring to be admitted to various educational institutions and those within them resort to litigation. Some years ago, Prof. Upendra Baxi wrote an article titled 'Mass Copying: Should Courts Act as Controllers of Examination?' that captured this increased litigation as well as the varied matters that require the Court's attention.[35] Yet, given the nature of our legal

---

[34] Parliamentary Standing Committee on Personnel, Public Grievances, Law and Justice, *142nd on the Subject 'Strengthening Legal Education in View of Emerging Challenges before the Legal Profession'* (Rajya Sabha Secretariat, Parliament of India, February 2024).

[35] Upendra Baxi, 'Mass Copying: Should Courts Act as Controllers of Examination?' *Delhi Law Review* 6 (1977) 248.

system and the breadth of judicial review, such an oversight seems inevitable, given that the judiciary is often the last resort for anyone with a grievance. Necessarily therefore, a large number of cases dealing with different aspects of the governance or functioning of legal educational institutions come before the courts. One of the cases argued before the SCI in recent times that has far-reaching implications for legal education has arisen from a Special Leave Petition filed in 2008.

In *Bar Council of India v. Bonnie Foi Law College*, the SCI had occasion to deal with the issue of falling standards of legal education and the regulatory role of the BCI. Speaking for the Constitution Bench, Sanjay Kishan Kaul J stated that '[h]alf baked lawyers serve no purpose' and that 'quality control of entry into the Bar is the need of the hour'. The Court also noted the wide-ranging powers granted to the BCI to introduce a pre-enrolment training course or examination.[36]

The focus of the courts has necessarily been on maintaining the quality of the Bar, since that is an important source for appointments to the Bench. Training students to become future lawyers, to 'think' like a lawyer, increasing professional skills has been the focus of the BCI, academicians and even the LCI, as evidenced in their 184th Report. Training a law student to become a judge of course has considerable overlaps with the skill needs of a lawyer, yet it also requires a different approach. Problem-solving, an ability to see both points of view, seeking a consensus are also aspects that need to be included in the curriculum. Measures to deepen such efforts that are already in place need to be strengthened, as legal education is a feeder channel for both the Bar and the Bench.

While considering the scheme of the Advocates Act, 1961, the SCI had earlier held: 'The scheme of the Act thus lays down a complete code for regulating the legal education and professional equipments of an aspirant seeking entry to legal profession from the grassroot level where he is student of law till he equips himself with essential legal knowledge and seeks enrollment and even thereafter till he practices law and completes his professional career as advocate.'[37]

---

[36] *Bar Council of India v. Bonnie Foi Law College* (2023) 7 SCC 756, holding that *V Sudeer v. Bar Council of India* (1999) 3 SCC 176 does not lay down the correct position of law in this regard.

[37] *(Dr) Haniraj L Chulani v. Bar Council of Maharashtra & Goa,* (1996) 3 SCC 342.

The Constitution Bench in *Bonnie Foi* made a significant clarification regarding the powers of universities vis-a-vis the BCI in this case after examining the provisions of the Advocates Act, 1961, by stating, 'These provisions do not entrust the Bar Council of India with direct control of legal education, as primarily legal education is within the province of the universities. Yet, the Bar Council of India, being the apex professional body of the advocates, is concerned with the standards of legal profession and the equipment of those who seek entry into that.'[38] While there is no doubt that there is some overlap, this decision is significant as it delineates the separate responsibilities of universities and the BCI (a view partly echoed by the 142nd Report Parliamentary Standing Committee on Personnel, Public Grievances, Law and Justice noted above).

The limited remit of the petition in *Bonnie Foi* did not allow the Court's focus to be on the lack of diversity amongst the student body of legal educational institutions, along with the financial, linguistic and other obstacles that students from marginalized communities continue to face in obtaining admission, and later, studying in such institutions. SCI judges, in their individual capacity, have often raised these matters. For instance, CJI DY Chandrachud has alluded to the 'elitism' of the NLUs and called for a culture of empathy and inclusion.[39] The lack of diversity within NLUs has been dealt with at length in academic writing.[40] Shamnad Basheer who campaigned for greater inclusivity within the NLUs, and was the founder of Increasing Diversity by Increasing Access (IDIA), filed a petition before the SCI that sought, *inter alia*, a rationalization of the entrance test fees, and for the common entrance test in law to be conducted in 'a scientific, competent and consistent manner'.[41] The rapid, uneven growth and privatization of legal education are surely matters that will be raised before the Court in future. The Court as a public institution

---

38 *Bonnie Foi Law College* (n 36) [29].

39 '"This Elitism Must Be Condemned" Justice Chandrachud on Discrimination by Few Law Firms Against Graduates from Ordinary Law Colleges [Read the Full Text of Speech]' (*LiveLaw*, 17 December 2017) <https://www.livelaw.in/elitism-must-condemned-justice-chandrachud-discrimination-law-firms-graduates-ordinary-law-colleges-read-full-text-speech/> accessed 17 November 2024.

40 See, for instance, Shamnad Basheer, KV Krishnaprasad, Sree Mitra and Prajna Mohapatra, 'The Making of Legal Elites and the IDIA of Justice' in David B Wilkins, Vikramaditya S Khanna and David M Trubek (eds), *The Indian Legal Profession in the Age of Globalization: The Rise of the Corporate Legal Sector and Its Impact on Lawyers and Society* (Cambridge University Press 2017) 578–605; see also F Mustafa et al., *Suggestions for Reforms at the National Law Universities Set Up Through State Legislations* (National Academy of Legal Studies and Research 2018).

41 *Shamnad Basheer v. Union of India*, Writ Petition (Civil) 600/2015. This petition is pending.

is in a position to engage in such a dialogue among various stakeholders of legal education following a 'bounded deliberative' approach that it has taken in other matters of great public interest.[42]

Looking Back, Going Forward

Much of the focus of reform measures in legal education has been on the manner law universities and colleges have been structured. Where the content of legal education has been the focus, attention has centred around the ability of law graduates to become better professionals who fulfil the demands of social justice and a changing society.

The future will likely see changes in the content of legal education; and therefore, the curriculum offered to law students needs to respond to a changing India along with addressing the need for law to be an instrument of relevant social change. The demand for decolonization of theory and knowledge that has become the focus of attention in many other post-colonial societies has neither found an equivalent echo amongst the academia nor among students in India. The reasons are many, including the emphasis on professionalization along with a relative 'de-politicization' of legal education and universities.

The effect of what some commentators have termed as 'colonial continuity' has had an effect on determining the direction of reform in legal education. As some scholars have noted, in a post-colonial society, 'it may not be an exaggeration to say that it is really the State (and the Law) that is the peculiarly modern invention that comes to colonize our imagination in this period.'[43] The attempts to reject colonial continuities and reworking a legal education relevant to our present times has been and continues to be an important aspect of the reform of legal education. Yet, the matter of the content or changes in the curriculum of legal education has received less attention from the courts, because such matters are considered as best left to the academic bodies of the universities.

---

[42] See, for instance, *In Re: Distribution of Essential Supplies and Services During Pandemic*, order dated 30 April 2021, Suo Motu Writ Petition (Civil) No. 3 of 2021, where DY Chandrachud J speaking for the Bench was mindful of the separation of powers principle and indicated the limited role of the Court in facilitating such a dialogue among stakeholders within the constitutional scheme.

[43] Aditya Nigam, *Decolonizing Theory: Thinking Across Traditions* (Bloomsbury 2020) 30.

One aspect that has remained unexamined but is likely to grow in significance is the question of the language in which legal education is imparted. The pervasive medium of instruction is in English due to several factors: the availability of books and resources in English, English being designated as the language of the HCs and the SCI, among others. Our laws, and the Constitution itself, remains largely unavailable in all the 8th Schedule languages, let alone all the other Indian languages. With the emergence of quicker translation of materials, including SCI judgments using technology, the possibility of broadening access to legal education and, therefore, of improving the access (and delivery) of justice has improved. The near future may well witness a paradigm shift in legal education, as technology deepens access to the law and the judicial system.

The aspiration for justice, as well as the need to align the law with justice, continues to be a strong motive force in society. Respect for the law is in a great measure dependent on the legal institutions performing their role in sensitizing students to the larger context within which India operates. The subject of making education, particularly legal education, more socially relevant has been a running theme over the decades. The role of legal educational institutions and individual faculty within it are also critical to a reform agenda.[44]

Writing more than three decades ago, the (First) Report of the Curriculum Development Centre in Law set up by the UGC noted, 'What makes legal education somewhat (and also the law teacher) distinct is that its signal contribution to societal and national integration by offering techniques, arenas, and platforms for rational, orderly and non-violent settlement of disputes and handling of conflicts.'[45] The scaffolding within which such a transformation

---

[44] Amita Dhanda, 'The Power of One: The Teacher in the Legal Academy' in *Decolonisation of Legal Knowledge,* ed. Amita Dhanda and Archana Parashar (Routledge 2009).

[45] The CDC Report acknowledges, '1.6 The concern to make legal education more "modern" and "contemporary" to make it "socially relevant" and humanistic for the teacher and taught has always guided discourse on law teaching and research in India. The concern is articulated in innumerable seminars, symposia, papers and reports. We here identify only a few landmarks: the 1964 Rasauli seminar on legal education (convened by Prof. GS Sharma), the 1972 Pune international seminar on Indian legal education (convened by Prof. SR Agarwala), the Dharwad workshop on teaching of jurisprudence (convened by Professors GV Ajjappa and Upendra Baxi) were major efforts at rearticulation of legal learning and research in India. To these must be added: the 1975–76 UGC convened workshops on socially relevant legal education (leading to a report by Professor Upendra Baxi published in 1979) and the UGC 1981 Report on the status of Teaching and Research in the Discipline of Law (prepared by

can happen requires the support of the courts and professional bodies. The challenge in the coming period is whether that sense of idealism and the sense of justice can continue to be inculcated and nurtured by institutions training future legal professionals and judges in the country.

Professors SR Agarwala and Mohammed Ghouse).'; UGC, *Report of the Curriculum Development Centre in Law* 1 (UGC, 1990), 1–2.

Part VI

The Court and the Future

Cartoon © Pencilashan.

Digitalizing the Judiciary: Technology and Courts

S MURALIDHAR

Prologue

On 23 March 2020, in a televised address, the Prime Minister of India announced a complete lockdown throughout the country on account of the COVID-19 pandemic.[1] Only essential services were, to a limited extent and subject to precautions, permitted. This meant that although courts would not cease to function, there was a certain anxiety that access to justice may be severely hampered, filings in courts may drop dramatically, hearings in the various accounts across the judicial hierarchy would be adversely impacted and the overall disposal of cases interminably delayed.

Faced with having to keep the courts functional, the judiciary had to find ways to facilitate both online hearings and e-filing of cases on a large scale and at all levels of the courts. A series of directives were issued by the Supreme Court (SCI),[2] and adopted by the High Courts (HCs), on which types of urgent matters would be heard by the courts in virtual mode, and how filing of fresh cases could take place in an online mode either using the special filing software or by e-mail. While the overall filing in the district courts did drop during the pandemic,[3] there was, notwithstanding the digital divide,[4] a clear

---

1 Abantika Ghosh, 'PM Modi Declares Lockdown: "Crossing Your Home's Lakshmanrekha Will Invite COVID-19 Inside"' (*The Indian Express*, 25 March 2020).

2 For the complete set of directives in the first phase of COVID-19 till May 2021, reference may be made to 'Covid Coverage: Court's Functioning' (*Supreme Court Observer*, 1 May 2021) <https://www.scobserver.in/journal/covid-coverage-courts-functioning/> accessed 8 May 2025.

3 The report titled 'Data Speak: A Look At the District Courts' Performance During the Pandemic', brought out by the Vidhi Centre for Legal Policy, analysed the data for 642 district courts during the pandemic years 2020 and 2021, and found that filings decreased by 32 per cent and disposals by 42.33 per cent. Bail petitions were prioritized across all the courts in the districts.

4 The lack of a uniform and unhindered network connectivity across the country was a challenge during

shift in the manner of filing and presentation of cases by lawyers – online or in hybrid mode, a feature that has come to stay even after the pandemic.[5] Where network connectivity was problematic, judges and lawyers communicated through mobile phones, on speaker mode. Signed orders were transmitted online.[6] Lawyers and judges adapted to the new work from home regime. Judicial orders were issued by the SCI extending the limitation for filing cases at all levels;[7] prisons were decongested in a regulated manner closely supervised by High Power Committees of the HCs.[8]

In a speech in July 2022, DY Chandrachud J, then the Chairperson of the SCI's e-Committee, disclosed that 19.2 million cases had been heard virtually by the end of April 2022 and 17.8 million cases had been disposed of.[9] There was a preparedness to adapt technology to aid the working of the courts. It was almost as if it was waiting to happen, and the pandemic gave it the final push.

The Beginnings

The essential framework of the Indian judiciary, with its hierarchy of courts, was a continuation of the system that existed for at least a hundred years prior to the country gaining independence. The 14th Report of the Law Commission of India (LCI), chaired by the then Attorney General for India (AG) MC Setalvad and submitted on 26 November 1958, disagreed that the complexity of the procedural laws were the primary cause of judicial delays but 'a host of extraneous and personal factors' like 'an inefficient and inexperienced judiciary, insufficient number of judicial officers, and incompetent and corrupt ministerial and process serving agency, the diverse delaying tactics adopted

COVID-19 and continues even thereafter. Given that not all lawyers could afford smart devices, many district courts and HCs set up e-kiosks within their premises to facilitate online filings and hearings.

5 See generally, Rahela Khorakiwala, 'The Majesty and Dignity of Courts: Changes in Court Dynamics with the Onset of the Covid-19 Pandemic in India' (2022) 18(1) *Socio-Legal Review* 51.

6 In 2021, the SCI approved the Fast and Secured Transmission of Electronic Records (FASTER), which helps in the transmission of electronically authenticated copy of interim orders, stay orders, bail orders, record of proceedings through a secured electronic communication channel, Indian Judiciary Annual Report 2021-22, 125.

7 *In Re: Cognizance for Extension of Limitation* Suo Motu WP (C) No 3/2020, order dated 23 March 2020.

8 *In Re: Contagion of Covid-19 Virus in Prisons* Suo Motu WP (C) No 1/2021, order dated 7 May 2021.

9 Joanne Harris, 'Access To Justice: India Leads Post-Covid Shift in Courts' Use of Technology', (International Bar Association, 12 October 2022) <https://www.ibanet.org/Access-to-justice-India-virtual-courts> accessed 8 May 2025. These include a large number of smaller cases such as traffic offences and contractual disputes, as well as more significant matters.

by the litigants and their lawyers, the un-methodical arrangement of work by the presiding judge and the heavy file of arrears.'[10] There was, however, no improvement even two decades later, as noted by the LCI in its 77th Report and even in 1992, with Krishna Iyer J lamenting that for the lay person, the judicial process was a 'riddle wrapped in a mystery inside an enigma, with its baffling legalese, lottery techniques, habitual somnolence, expensive proclivities, multi-deck inconsistencies, tyranny of technicalities and interference in everything with a touch of authoritarian incompetence.'[11] He suggested the constitution of a high-powered 'Judicial Planning Commission' which would undertake research and development of better judicial processes and management.[12]

The preparation for transforming the functioning of the judiciary through use of technology had its beginnings in 1989, when computers were deployed in the SCI for caveat matching.[13] This was perhaps the launch of the digitalization[14] of the courts. By the time AM Ahmadi J took over as CJI in 1996, computers were being used not just for their word processing functions, but for generation of daily cause lists and allocation of cases to different Benches, category-wise.

From the inception, the judiciary did not seek to establish an IT wing that would cater exclusively to its needs. Instead, it was the National Informatics Centre (NIC)[15] functioning under the control of the Ministry of Electronics and Information Technology (MeitY), Government of India, that undertook

---

[10] Law Commission of India, 14th Report vol 1 (Government of India, 26 September 1958). <https://cdnbbsr.s3waas.gov.in/s3ca0daec69b5adc880fb464895726dbdf/uploads/2022/08/2022080514.pdf> accessed 18 January 2025.

[11] VK Krishna Iyer, *Justice at Crossroads* (Deep & Deep Publications 1992) 138. At 150, he added: 'Management incompetence is writ so large in the system that a grocer's shop is better managed than a munsiff's court and a business house has infinitely superior management skills than High Courts and Supreme Court. Of course, judges, wise in other ways, are infants in judicial business management.'

[12] ibid 145, 150.

[13] Caveat matching is a legal process introduced in India in 1989, primarily utilized in appellate courts. When one party anticipates litigation against them, they can lodge a caveat in the court, notifying the court not to pass any order without hearing them if the opposing party appeals. This ensures that both parties are given an opportunity to present their arguments before a decision is made.

[14] The terms 'digitalization' and 'digitization' are often used interchangeably, but they have slightly different meanings. Digitization is the conversion of analogue information into digital format, like scanning paper documents into PDFs, enabling electronic processing, storage and transmission. Whereas Digitalization is a broader concept involving the use of digital technologies to transform business models, operations and customer interactions, leveraging tools like cloud computing, big data analytics, AI and Internet of Things (IoT).

[15] The NIC functions under the control of the Ministry of Electronics and Information Technology (MeitY) and is the technology partner of the Government of India. Established in 1976, NIC provides technology-driven solutions to Central and State Governments.

the streamlining of the court registry operations in 430 district courts in 1997. In 1998, the work of complete computerization of twenty-seven district courts commenced in Nanded district, Maharashtra.

Phase I

In the early 2000s, focused efforts were directed towards comprehensive computerization. A centrally sponsored scheme aimed at computerizing 700 city courts across Delhi, Kolkata, Mumbai and Chennai was initiated between 2003 and 2004.[16] The focus at this stage was primarily on back-office tasks. The first ever e-Committee to formulate a National Policy on the computerization of the Indian Judiciary[17] was constituted by the CJI in July 2004. This was chaired by Dr GC Bharuka J.[18]

A strategic plan was presented to the then CJI RC Lahoti J in May 2005. This laid the foundation for a national policy and action plan, emphasizing judicial autonomy in technology adoption. The Department of Justice (DoJ) of the Union Government identified 14,938 courts in the districts across the country for computerization in three stages, emphasizing citizen-centric services, software development models and the migration to cloud infrastructure. The project was launched in October 2005 as one of the centrally sponsored schemes, and in June 2006, was declared as one of the Mission Mode Projects under the National e-governance Plan.[19] After financial sanction was accorded in February 2007, Phase I of the e-Courts Project was formally launched in July 2007. A Vision Statement and Action Plan was announced in 2009 as a result of the deliberations at the Conference of Chief Ministers and Chief

---

16 J Rattan and V Rattan, 'Role of Information and Communication Technologies in the Metamorphosis of Justice Administration in India: A Legal Study' (2023) 69 (1) *Indian Journal of Public Administration* 72–86. In addition, 900 courts in capitals of the States or cities where a HC was situated were chosen for computerization.

17 Official website of e-Committee, Supreme Court of India <https://ecommitteesci.gov.in/> accessed 15 February 2024.

18 After his transfer from the Patna HC in 1994 to the Karnataka HC, in 1998, Bharuka J helped in the setting up of the latter Court's website, on which, apart from the cause list, information about case status, judgments and orders and the status of certified copy applications were made available. For ICT enablement in all the 600 courts in the districts in Karnataka, a user-friendly software named 'Litigation Management System (LMS)' was created: See generally, Dr GC Bharuka, *Rejuvenating Judicial System Through E-Governance & Attitudinal Change* (1st edn Wadhwa & Co. 2003); Dr GC Bharuka, 'Technology and Timely Justice: Intelligent Use of ICT Can Revamp the Indian Justice Delivery System' (2016) 35 (1) *Common Cause* 12.

19 The project was soon delinked from the centrally sponsored schemes and converted to a central sector scheme with 100% central government funding.

Justices (CJs) held that year.[20] It also set out elaborate measures for the digitalizing of courts.[21]

As regards the deployment of software, NIC decided in 1997 itself to opt for Free and Open Source Software (FOSS), specifically the Linux system. The push to have a common Case Information System (CIS) software application for the e-Courts Project came from the e-Committee in May 2008. This was done by the Open Technology Centre of the NIC using Linux-based platform with the Ubuntu operating system. Following the success of the pilot run at Ernakulam, the CIS was implemented across all the courts in the districts in Maharashtra, Kerala, Andhra Pradesh and Karnataka by 2012, with a uniform code and database. There were still issues as there were specific requirements of courts in the different states. To address this, it was decided to develop a National Core (NC) version and allow the HCs to develop a 'peripheral' version to address specific needs.[22]

Some of the HCs decided to take things forward by having a separate unit of skilled technical manpower and adopt innovations faster than others. For instance, the Delhi HC oversaw the conceptualization and design of India's first electronic court launched in July 2009 in the Karkardooma District Court complex in East Delhi.[23] The court which functioned in a paperless mode[24] had an array of high resolution cameras through which the court would be

---

[20] It also drew on the recommendations in the 230th Report of Law Commission of India (Government of India, 2009) <https://cdnbbsr.s3waas.gov.in/s3ca0daec69b5adc880fb464895726dbdf/uploads/2022/08/2022081063-2.pdf> accessed 18 January 2025.

[21] This Action Plan of 2009 led to the creation of the National Arrears Grid for a scientific study of arrears. Another similar conference held in 2011 resulted in the establishment of the National Mission for Justice Delivery and Legal Reforms in the DoJ and the National Court Management System (NCMS) in the SCI. For a detailed discussion, see, Atul Kaushik, 'Bringing the "E" to Judicial Efficiency: Implementing the e-Courts System in India' in *State of the Indian Judiciary* (DAKSH 2016) 25 <https://dakshindia.org/wp-content/uploads/2023/02/State-of-the-Judiciary.pdf> accessed 27 January 2025.

[22] Since the legacy systems were on structured query language (SQL) server/visual basic (VB), migration script was written to enable migration of all legacy data on NC. The CIS 2.0 and 3.0 versions were rolled out in the second phase and implemented across the country as far the courts in the districts were concerned. Another CIS model for the data of the HCs was implemented during the third phase of the e-Courts Project.

[23] A video prepared on the occasion, explaining the various features of the Court is available at <https://youtu.be/LlCXdP0n0r0?si=GvxQR9OnIXNpZFnm> accessed 8 May 2025. The IT Committee of the HC of Delhi at this time comprised Babar Durrez Ahmed, Anil Kumar, RS Endlaw JJ and the author.

[24] A computer monitor was on the dais, on which the judge would read the case papers that were scanned at a special unit set up for that purpose in the court premises. There was an exclusive server room adjoining the chamber of the judge. The video recordings of the proceedings were stored in the servers and could be edited for future reference under the supervision of the judge.

connected to the jail (where the prisoner was located and could view the proceedings), the forensic science laboratory (from where the scientific expert could depose online), the government hospital (from where the doctor who examined a victim or conducted an autopsy might be able to depose about a report prepared, which would be shared with them on a computer screen through a document visualizer) and the police station (where the investigating officer might be located, and could access the proceedings and reports through a broadband IP or an ISDN network. It meant that these official witnesses did not necessarily have to wait in the court premises and could be allocated definite time slots for their depositions; they could even be cross-examined online by the defence lawyer present in the court. The ultimate control over the video interface software was with the presiding judge. The implementing agency of this 'pilot project' was The Centre for Development of Advanced Computing (C-DAC), Pune.[25] Many years later, this helped launch virtual courts in 2021 in the districts in Odisha when the author was the CJ.[26]

The country's first ever paperless court in a HC was launched in the Delhi HC in December 2009 and was presided over by S Ravindra Bhat J.[27] This was preceded by a systematic digitization of current records, e-filing of fresh cases,[28] launching the system of e-court fees, book-marking of the scanned files, selection of a suitable touch-screen monitor on which – using proprietary software – the judge would be able to make notes with a digital pen while the hearing was in progress, training of the staff and lawyers and drawing up detailed practice directions.[29] A dedicated technical team of expert technical personnel, complemented by the NIC team, prepared the software in-house and implemented all these measures.

---

[25] For a detailed account of how the project was conceived and implemented, see, T Rishi Prakash and others, 'ICT in Indian Court: Challenges and Solution' (2011) 1 (2) *IJIC* 21.

[26] For a somewhat detailed description, see, Annual Report of the High Court of Orissa (2021) 52.

[27] In February 2010, the author presided over the second paperless court.

[28] This was different from online filing, which would happen much later. To facilitate e-filing, kiosks were set up in the HC premises, where lawyers or the clerks could use a desktop PC to upload a soft copy of the petition and documents directly onto the HC's servers. The checking of such petitions by court staff for defects also happened online. Lawyers who did not have the facility of scanning their petitions could hand over the hard copies to the staff at the filing counters, along with a scanning fee. The documents would then be scanned by the court staff using scanners available at the filing counters, and the soft copy would be handed over to the lawyer in a pen drive. To encourage lawyers to shift to the paperless mode, the Delhi HC provided them soft copies free of charge.

[29] Initially, only a few judges shifted to the paperless mode. The COVID-19 pandemic compelled each of them to make the shift.

Phase I of the e-Courts Project, which commenced in 2007 and ended on 31 March 2015, saw the efforts of the e-Committee at standardizing procedures and devising uniform formats for legal documents in the various courts encounter several hurdles. For effective implementation, each court complex having e-courts had to have a Judicial Service Centre to facilitate the e-registration of cases, a server room with uninterrupted supply of electricity and the creation of ducts for fibres for local area network (LAN) installation. Sufficient bandwidth for connectivity of courts with data centres through leased lines and virtual private network (VPN) over broadband procured from the Bharat Sanchar Nigam Limited (BSNL), the availability of trained technical personnel in the court premises for installing and regular maintenance of the systems, and the provision of continuous training of trial court judges and staff were also imperative.

While the adoption of Linux was advantageous from the point of costs, there were issues of compatibility with licensed software that were sold pre-bundled with most hardware like desktop computers and laptops. Even the hardware that was purchased, including laptops provided to judicial officers, were either not used to their full potential or worse still, not at all.[30] During Phase I, some of the district courts, the HCs and the SCI had their own websites, digital display boards and digitally published cause lists and orders, however, this was not yet universal across all courts. Likewise, video conference facilities between jails and courts to facilitate online remand proceedings, the automation of case workflows, the establishment of virtual courts, and the introduction of mobile-based services were not uniformly available across the country. Issues of network connectivity and availability of uninterrupted power supply remained.[31] The push for transformation of the courts using technology came from either the judiciary itself or the State and not from the users themselves. Therefore, at a broad level, there was resistance to change

[30] At a national conference held in Vijayawada in 2018, which the author attended, one judicial officer mentioned that the desktop computers supplied to some of the district courts remained unopened for several years since there was no technical personnel to activate them, much less provide for their maintenance.

[31] Courts had to rely on the state-owned agencies like the BSNL for broadband, which was neither reliable nor widespread. Also, although provision was made in the budgets for purchase of diesel generators for each court complex, in the absence of advisories regarding the brands that worked best, and with the process of purchase through tenders or through the Government Electronic Market (GeM) being cumbersome and time-consuming, a large percentage of these budgets remained unutilized and money returned unspent to the government concerned.

from the legal fraternity, including lawyers and their clerks. The progress of digitalization across courts thus remained uneven.

Writing in 2014, Dr Bharuka, J was critical of the decision to entrust the task of digitalizing the judiciary to the NIC, whose capabilities, according to him, were 'inadequate to run such a project, as established by the failure of earlier three similar projects.'[32] He pointed out that by not accepting the e-Committee's request to have a public private partnership (PPP) model for implementation of the project,[33] there was 'sluggishness' in its execution with the result that 'despite lapse of more than fifteen years and spending of hundreds of crores on technology upgradation in the Indian courts, litigants have not been provided an Information and Communication Technology environment as is available in many parts of the world.'[34]

Phase II

The Policy and Action Plan for Phase II of the e-Courts Project was brought out by the e-Committee in 2014 for implementation over a period of three years. One important change was as follows: In Phase I, the e-Committee as a user would place its needs before the DoJ, which apart from managing the finances, was responsible for strategic direction and guidance; the NIC was the implementing agency for the project responsible for the procurement and supply of hardware and the preparation and installation of software applications. In Phase II, however, the e-Committee took over the task of policy planning, strategic direction and guidance. The DoJ would provide the financial approvals, monitoring the budgetary aspects and the allocation/reallocation of funds. Also, it was not the NIC but the HCs that were to be the implementing agencies.

As a result, every HC had a Central Project Co-ordinator (CPC), a judicial officer with an aptitude for ICT. Invariably, such CPCs had to be the bridge

---

[32] Bharuka, 'Technology and Timely Justice: Intelligent Use of ICT Can Revamp the Indian Justice Delivery System' (n 18); The three projects were the computerization of the district courts (1997), of the metro cities courts (2001), and of the capital cities courts (2002).

[33] This model was adopted successfully in other sectors like railways, passport department, company affairs, aviation and banking.

[34] Bharuka, 'Technology and Timely Justice: Intelligent Use of ICT Can Revamp the Indian Justice Delivery System' (n 18); Dr Bharuka caustically remarked: 'Independent enquiries will show that in the past, the only interest of the NIC had been to buy and flood the court halls with hardware and some nominal software which has failed to deliver the desired result.'

between both the HC and the e-Committee on the one hand and also between the HC and the NIC on the other. The e-Committee organized the training of judicial officers from the different states as 'master trainers' who would in turn impart training to the other judicial officers within the states. There were IT Committees set up at each HC and also in the district courts.

The Phase II Action Plan[35] was approved by the Government of India on 4 August 2015. What was meant to be a three-year phase got extended till 2023. The ambitions of this Action Plan were to host case data on cloud computing environments, thereby optimizing server requirements and facilitating big data computing.[36] The focus was to be on citizen-centric services.

A significant development took place in September 2015, towards the end of Phase I of the e-Courts Project, when the CJI made the National Judicial Data Grid (NJDG) open to public access. This grid contains the complete information regarding case details, listings and orders in each of the cases pending in the courts in various districts across the country. It allows the user to 'drill down' from the aggregate statistics at the national and state level to the district level and even further below in the judicial hierarchy. The e-Committee published on its website a series of tutorial videos to enable lawyers, litigants and even judicial officers to access and collate data for their own purposes. Nevertheless, problems remained, with a lack of uniformity in case types,[37] case categories,[38] the absence of timely uploading of orders and so on. It was still a work in progress.

In a reply to a question raised in the Parliament in August 2023, the Union Law Minister claimed that in Phase II of the e-Courts project '7 platforms have been created to provide real time information on case status, cause lists, judgements etc. to lawyers/Litigants through SMS Push and Pull (2,00,000 SMS sent daily), Email (2,50,000 sent daily), multilingual and tactile e-Courts services Portal (35 lakh hits daily), Judicial Service centres and Info Kiosks. In addition, Electronic Case Management Tools (ECMT) have been created

[35] *Policy and Action Plan Document Phase II of the e-Courts Project* (E-Committee of the Supreme Court of India, 2014) <https://cdnbbsr.s3waas.gov.in/s388ef51f0bf911e452e8dbb1d807a81ab/uploads/2020/05/2020053169.pdf> accessed 8 May 2025.

[36] For improving connectivity, it sought to utilize a combination of options: national knowledge network (NKN), state-wide area network (SWAN), national informatics centre network (NICNET), broadband, etc.

[37] Similar kinds of petitions could be referred to with different terms across courts.

[38] Cases of a similar type could be categorized differently across courts as either civil or criminal, based on the contents.

with Mobile App for lawyers (total 1.88 cr. downloads till 30th June 2023) and JustIS app for judges (19,164 downloads till 30th June 2023).'[39]

The onset of COVID-19 accelerated the pace of adaptation of ICT tools. Live-streaming of court proceedings had commenced in the HCs of Gujarat, Gauhati, Orissa, Karnataka, Jharkhand, Patna, Madhya Pradesh and the SCI. Courts at all levels were equipped with the capability of conducting hearings online or in hybrid mode.[40] Online payment of court fees was now available in at least twenty-two HCs, the e-filing version 3.0 had been rolled out, and 819 e-Seva Kendras were set up to facilitate litigants and lawyers to use the ICT facilities notwithstanding the digital divide.[41] What was not known, however, was the extent of the use of these facilities during and after COVID-19. Also, not all courts simplified their processes or dispensed with the need to file hard copies of petitions in addition to the soft copies.[42] Even in Kerala, where an indigenous system was developed for e-filing with the help of the Digital University, there was severe resistance to the changed system by the lawyers' clerks who saw it as a threat to their livelihoods.[43]

---

[39] 'Answer to Unstarred Question No 425 on Judicial Vacancies in High Courts' (Rajya Sabha, 8 February 2024) <https://sansad.in/getFile/annex/265/AU425_7NFYpw.pdf?source=pqars> accessed 24 February 2025.

[40] The official information was that the 'District & Subordinate courts heard 1,98,67,081 cases while the High Courts heard 78,69,708 cases (totalling 2.77 cr) till 30.06.2023 using video conferencing system.' The SCI 'held 4,82,941 hearings through video conferencing till 15.05.2023.' VC facilities were enabled between 3,240 court complexes and corresponding 1,272 jails.

[41] It was claimed that 'in addition to eSewaKendras, as part of the DISHA (Designing Innovative Solutions for Holistic Access to Justice) scheme the Government of India has launched Tele Law program since 2017, which provides an effective and reliable e-interface platform connecting the needy and disadvantaged sections seeking legal advice and consultation with panel lawyers via video conferencing, telephone and chat facilities available at the Common Service Centres (CSCs) situated in Gram Panchayat and through Tele-Law mobile App.'

[42] The SCI noted that the e-filing in the National Consumer Disputes Redressal Commission must be made fully operational, and orally remarked that asking advocates to file physical copies in addition to e-filing would defeat the purpose of e-filing in *Usha Garg v. Union of India* WP (C) No 313/2024 (SCI, 20 August 2024); Anmol Kumar Bawa, 'Why Ask Lawyers to File Physical Copies in Addition to E-Filed Copies? Supreme Court Asks NCDRC' (*LiveLaw*, 21 August 2024) <https://www.livelaw.in/top-stories/why-ask-lawyers-to-file-physical-copies-in-addition-to-e-filed-appeals-supreme-court-asks-ncdrc-267233> accessed 18 January 2025.

[43] Hannah M Varghese, 'Advocate Clerks Reduced to Marginal Players in Legal System: Plea Before Kerala High Court Seeks Their Involvement in E-Filing Procedure' (*LiveLaw*, 19 February 2022) <https://www.livelaw.in/news-updates/advocate-clerks-reduced-to-marginal-players-in-legal-system-plea-before-kerala-high-court-seeks-their-involvement-in-e-filing-procedure-192303> accessed 18 January 2025; Giti Pratap, 'E-Filing and Loss of Livelihood: Kerala Advocate Clerks Association Writes to CJI NV Ramana with Concerns' (*BarandBench*, 4 June 2022) <https://www.barandbench.com/news/e-filing-and-loss-of-livelihood-kerala-advocate-clerks-association-writes-to-cji-nv-ramana-with-concerns> accessed 18 January 2025.

Traffic challan cases were sought to be dealt with through Virtual Courts where 'non-contesting' defendants could pay fines and penalties without having to attend courts in person. Twenty-two of these 'virtual courts' were established in eighteen states/UTs. It was claimed that more than 3.26 crore cases had been handled by these virtual courts and 'in more than 39 lakhs (39,16,405) cases online fine of more than Rs. 419.89 crores has been realized till 30.06.2023.'[44] The National Service and Tracking of Electronic Processes (NSTEP) was launched in 28 states/UTs for ICT-enabled process serving and issuing of summons. The government's press release in August 2024 claimed that a third-party evaluation of Phase II of the e-Courts Project by the National Council of Applied Economic Research (NCAER) had reported great deal of user satisfaction and further that 'the pendency of cases over 5 years have displayed slow but steady decline over the years.' However, a study undertaken by a private research body revealed mixed feelings among lawyers and litigants towards these changes.[45]

In November 2022, an online Right to Information (RTI) portal was launched by the SCI through which RTI applications as well as appeals could be filed online, and related payments could also be made online. This portal has also been replicated by various HCs.[46] In order to increase the free-of-cost access to judgments delivered by the SCI, it has launched the e-SCR (Supreme Court Reporter) in January 2023. This is an online record of all reported judgments of the SCI since 1950. The portal, built on a free and open-source software, was also developed keeping in mind functionality and convenience.[47] Digital Supreme Court Reports (Digi SCR), an online fortnightly law reporter of the SCI, was also launched.[48]

---

[44] 'Answer to Unstarred Question No 1439 on Pending Cases in Courts' (Government of India, Ministry of Law and Justice, Lok Sabha, 4 August 2023) <https://sansad.in/getFile/loksabhaquestions/annex/1712/AU1439.pdf?source=pqals> accessed 24 February 2025.

[45] 'Answer to Unstarred Question No 1174 on Pendency of Cases in Courts' (Government of India, Ministry of Law and Justice, Lok Sabha, 8 August 2023) <https://sansad.in/getFile/loksabhaquestions/annex/1715/AU1174.pdf?source=pqals> accessed 24 February 2025.

[46] 'Empowering Citizens – SC's Online RTI Portal', *Indian Judiciary Annual Report 2023-24* (2024) 100 <https://cdnbbsr.s3waas.gov.in/s3ec0490f1f4972d133619a60c30f3559e/uploads/2024/11/2024112991.pdf> accessed 24 February 2025.

[47] 'e-SCR: Easing Access to Judgments', *Indian Judiciary Annual Report* (n 46) 128 <https://cdnbbsr.s3waas.gov.in/s3ec0490f1f4972d133619a60c30f3559e/uploads/2024/11/2024112991.pdf> accessed 24 February 2025.

[48] 'Digi SCR', *Indian Judiciary Annual Report* (n 46) 128 <https://cdnbbsr.s3waas.gov.in/s3ec0490f1f4972d133619a60c30f3559e/uploads/2024/11/2024112991.pdf> accessed 24 February 2025. Digi-SCR can be viewed at https://digiscr.sci.gov.in/.

Artificial Intelligence (AI) was deployed by the e-Committee for the translation of SCI judgments into regional languages[49] and for transcribing oral arguments in cases before the Constitution Benches of the SCI from February 2023 onwards.[50] The SCI also launched a Neutral Citation System on 6 July 2023 for 'a uniform, reliable, and secure methodology for identifying and citing judgments and orders of the SC in a phased manner.'[51]

Phase III

Phase III of the e-Courts Vision Plan[52] was approved by the Union Cabinet on 13 September 2023. It was declared as a Central Sector Scheme for a period of four years, with a financial outlay of Rs. 7,210 crores.[53] The document was prepared by a sub-committee of experts from three private bodies,[54] and claimed to be guided by the principles of 'access and inclusion'. Its avowed focus is on creating digital courts, simplifying procedures and establishing a robust digital infrastructure. The major premise that forms the thematic core of the document is spelt out thus:[55]

---

[49] 'Supreme Court Vidhik Anuvaad Software' in *Indian Judiciary Annual Report 2019–20* (2020) 114; A press release of the PIB dated 9 August 2024 claimed that 'as on 05.08.2024, 36,271 Supreme Court Judgments have been translated in Hindi language and 17,142 Judgments of Supreme Court have been translated in other 16 regional languages and the same are available on the e-SCR portal.' Further, '8 High Courts have already started e-High Court Reports (e-HCR) and other High Courts are in the process of launching e-HCR.'

[50] 'AI-Powered Transcripts: Enhancing Accessibility and Transparency' in *Indian Judiciary Annual Report 2023–24* (2024) 130 <https://cdnbbsr.s3waas.gov.in/s3ec0490f1f4972d133619a60c30f3559e/uploads/2024/11/2024112991.pdf> accessed 24 February 2025.

[51] 'Neutral Citations' in *Indian Judiciary Annual Report (n 46)* 133 https://cdnbbsr.s3waas.gov.in/s3ec0490f1f4972d133619a60c30f3559e/uploads/2024/11/2024112991.pdf> accessed 24 February 2024.

[52] 'Digital Courts Vision & Roadmap e-Courts Project Phase III' (E-Committee of the Supreme Court of India 2022) <https://cdnbbsr.s3waas.gov.in/s388ef51f0bf911e452e8dbb1d807a81ab/uploads/2023/04/2023042088.pdf> accessed 15 February 2025.

[53] Just like in Phase II, the system of DoJ providing financial support, with implementation agencies being the HCs under the overall supervision of the e-Committee, continues.

[54] These were DAKSH, Agami and Vidhi Centre for Legal Policy. This is perhaps for the first time that the Plan document itself acknowledged 'outsourcing' of this significant activity. It is not insignificant that each of these bodies receives substantial funding from private corporate philanthropies involving possible conflict of interests.

[55] DAKSH in collaboration with Vidhi Centre for Legal Policy, 'Report on the Vision Document for Phase III of eCourts Project' (2022). <https://cdnbbsr.s3waas.gov.in/s35d6646aad9bcc0be55b2c82f69750387/uploads/2024/07/20240716162080 4267.pdf> accessed 18 January 2025.

'Given the large, diverse and constantly evolving needs of different users and the constant evolution of technology, dispute resolution must not just remain as a sovereign function, but evolve as a service: to mitigate, contain and resolve disputes by the courts (in discharge of their sovereign function of justice administration) and a range of public, private and citizen sector actors (alongside courts).'

Advocating an 'ecosystem approach', the document states that instead of 'developing all the solutions itself, Phase III will curate the right environment and infrastructure for solutions to emerge rapidly from the ecosystem to create a multiplier effect for change. It can achieve greater adoption and impact by leveraging the collective strength of the ecosystem.'[56]

To deconstruct this jargon, what the thrust appears to be is to provide private players with the access to the data gathered and thus enable them to develop solutions. This becomes clearer when the document speaks of the creation of 'Digital Infrastructure and Capabilities',[57] of 'Open APIs to enable co-creation of services by different eco-system of actors'[58] and opening up the avenues for an 'infinite number of additional services/solutions.'[59] It talks of setting 'standards, specifications and certifications: guardrails for different actors to build solutions across space and time.'[60] Among other recommendations is the creation of a Digital Courts Technology Office and a National Judicial Technology Council.[61] Thus, the document seeks to relieve NIC of these tasks and entrust it to private actors under an overall supervision of the special bodies created. The document hopes that through decentralized implementation and leveraging emerging technologies like AI and Machine Learning (ML), Phase III will bridge the digital divide, streamline processes, reduce case backlogs, and make the justice delivery system more accessible, cost-effective and citizen-centric.

---

[56] ibid 2.

[57] ibid 3.

[58] ibid 4.

[59] ibid 3.

[60] ibid 4.

[61] ibid 90.

The Orissa Story

Even before the commencement of the implementation of Phase III of the e-Courts Project, some measures suggested by it were rolled out by some of the HCs. The HC of Orissa undertook a large-scale digitization project of not just digitizing the disposed of and current records in a state-of-the-art Record Room Digitization Centre,[62] but also replicating this exercise for the district courts through the creation of ten digitization hubs.[63] One offshoot of this exercise was the creation of the Centre for Judicial Archives, where 200-year-old judgments and orders of the HC as well as other courts in the districts were restored through chemical treatment in a scientific manner and carefully digitized using overhead scanners.[64] This was the precursor to establishing paperless courts not only in the HC[65] but also in the district courts.[66] Digitization was extended to the administrative files of the HC of Orissa by getting Tata Consulting Services (TCS), a private entity, to customize an exclusive Judicial Workflow Automation System, which included transforming the office of the CJ to be entirely paperless.[67]

The demand by the Bar – in as many as six districts – to have separate Benches of the HC was effectively neutralized during Phase I by launching virtual Benches in ten districts where district court lawyers could e-file their petitions in the HC, cure the defects, mention the case for listing in virtual mode, argue before the HC and also receive certified copies of the orders/judgments without having to physically travel to the HC in Cuttack.[68] This

---

[62] Annual Report of the High Court of Orissa 2021 (n 26) 41.

[63] The District Court Digitization Centres (DCDCs), aimed at extending the principles of storage, scanning, preservation and retrieval of legacy records to district and taluka courts, commenced with a pilot phase encompassing four major district courts of Cuttack, Ganjam, Sambalpur and Balasore.

[64] This was a separate project sanctioned by the state government and the first of its kind anywhere in the country.

[65] 'e-Filing User Manual for District Courts', (High Court of Orissa, 2021) <https://www.orissahighcourt.nic.in/uploads/rules/efiling/eFiling_District_Courts.pdf> accessed 24 February 2025.

[66] '50 More Paperless Courts Opened in Odisha Taking Total Tally to 84; Ganjam Becomes First District to Have All Paperless Courts' (*LiveLaw*, 4 July 2023) <https://www.livelaw.in/news-updates/orissa-high-court-paperless-courts-inauguration-chief-justice-muralidhar-digital-judiciary-initiative-231790> accessed 18 January 2025.

[67] Again, a first of its kind in the country; it reduced the time for the CJ to clear a file in as little as two to five minutes, and resulted in expediting the process of decision-making and implementation.

[68] These Virtual Centres are equipped with video conferencing facilities and include a vital 'Back Office' to support lawyers in e-filing their cases, facilitating the transition to digital operations. Additionally, for individuals less proficient with computers, the Back Office employs dedicated staff to assist in tasks such as scanning, preparing and e-filing petitions and documents.

was simultaneous with extensive sessions of 'hands on' training of lawyers, court staff and the judicial officers.[69] Two Model Virtual Courtrooms in the District Court complexes of Angul and Nayagarh were launched in November 2021, and were operational in twenty-four districts by November 2022.[70] These Model Virtual Courtrooms were equipped with advanced audio and visual equipment, allowing the accused or litigant (whether in a criminal or civil case) to attend court virtually. Remote point co-ordinators were appointed for each of these courts.[71] Each District Court complex was separately provided with a Vulnerable Witness Deposition Centre to provide a safe space for victims of sexual violence, including children, to depose.[72] Paucity of space does not permit a further detailing of the various steps taken in Odisha adapting the latest in technology to improve the efficiency of the courts.[73]

The Kerala HC rolled out a separate system of e-filing for lawyers practising before it and then extended this system to the district courts.[74] This was an effort aided by expertise provided by the Digital University in Kerala. While there was resistance to some extent from the legal fraternity, the clerks of lawyers and even judges,[75] the IT committee of that HC has persisted with their plans. Most recently, Kerala was among the first to introduce the 24x7 Online Court, in keeping with one of the goals of Phase III of the e-Courts Project.[76] It is still too early to assess whether the Phase II targets are capable of being achieved within the four-year period as envisaged in the Vision 3.0 document.[77]

---

69 Master trainer judicial officers were deployed to provide such training.

70 'Annual Report 2022' (High Court of Orissa) 46.

71 This was later replicated throughout the State.

72 'Annual Report 2022' (n 70) 46; They were operationalized by The High Court of Orissa Vulnerable Witnesses Deposition Centres (VWDC) Scheme 2022.

73 These are listed out in detail in the Annual Reports of the HC of Orissa for the years 2021, 2022 and 2023, which are available on its website. Among the other measures were the provision of e-libraries in district courts for the benefit of lawyers, e-inspection of records and a separate PIL portal on which the details of the pending PILs, the orders passed in them and the important affidavits and reports filed have been made available.

74 Leah Varghese and Anandita Pattanayak, 'The Technological Transformation of the Kerala High Court' (DAKSH, October 2023).

75 Lydia Suzanne Thomas, 'Kerala High Court Bar Expresses Concerns About E-Filing Rules; KHCAA Resolves to Abstain from E-Filing' (*LiveLaw*, 17 May 2021) <https://www.livelaw.in/news-updates/kerala-high-court-bar-expresses-concerns-about-e-filing-rules-174233> accessed 18 January 2025.

76 'First in India: 24-Hour Online Court Opens in Kerala's Kollam District' (*The New Indian Express*, 21 November 2024).

77 The target is the digitization of 3,108 crore pages of legacy, records and cloud infrastructure, setting up 4,400 fully functional eSewa Kendras in all court complexes, and the use of emerging technologies like AI/ ML.

Challenges

We now turn to the challenges to the judiciary posed by technology. First is the problem of reception, preservation and the retrieval of electronic records. This is an aspect not dealt with adequately even by the Vision 3.0 document, although there is already a report submitted on this very aspect by a Committee of HC judges to the SCI way back in November 2018.[78] Our courts (and perhaps even the tribunals) have vast repositories of electronic records submitted in a variety of media – floppy disks, CDs, pen drives, data cards, SIM cards, mobile phones, recorders, cameras and video footage – and for the preservation of which no standard operating protocols have been formulated. As a result, there is a real possibility of crucial electronic evidence that is required to be produced and proven during trials becoming unavailable. Redundancy of the software used to create the electronic record and the non-availability of hardware devices to read such documents is another possibility. These require to be urgently addressed; the report referred to, which is itself six-years-old, does offer some solutions. Unfortunately, it has found no takers yet.

There is much to be done in the area of collection and sharing of data on the functioning of the courts. For the NJDG and eCourts services to become a reliable repository of the statistics regarding pendency and disposal of cases, it will have to be 'cleaned up' on a regular basis to make it up-to-date and consistent with other statistical information available on the websites of the SCI, the HCs and the district courts. A recent critical study points out that the NJDG data could be grossly inflated both as regards the disposal and pendency of cases, one major reason being that cases are being 'double-or-triple counted'.[79] There is also a problem with how data is entered onto the

[78] On 23 April 2016, the CJ's Conference resolved to create uniform guidelines for electronic evidence. The CJs of Punjab & Haryana and Delhi were tasked with forming a committee to draft model rules for HCs. A five-judge committee was constituted on 28 July 2018, comprising Rajesh Bindal, S Muralidhar, Rajiv Sahai Endlaw, Rajiv Narain Raina and RK Gauba JJ. After extensive consultations with law enforcement and investigative agencies, the Committee finalized its report in November 2018, proposing comprehensive guidelines and Draft Rules for the Reception, Retrieval, Authentication and Preservation of Electronic Records. The SCI referred to these draft rules in 2020 and asked for them to be given statutory force by authorities concerned, *Arjun Panditrao Khotkar v. Kailash Kushanrao Gorantyal* (2020) 7 SCC 1, 65.

[79] Prashant Reddy T, Chitrakshi Jain, *Tareekh pe Justice* (Simon and Schuster 2025) 98. The authors further explain that while in civil cases, the various motions or applications are logged as part of the same case number, in criminal cases, each application is logged as a separate case and therefore, counted separately by the NJDG.

system, particularly, when cases pending for several years in a court are 're-numbered' to hide the actual age of the case.[80] The numbers will have to be cross-checked by each court by undertaking a periodic physical inventory of the files in the court premises.

Then there is the serious issue of ensuring the security and confidentiality of large volumes of personal information forming part of the case record which is available in the servers used by the judiciary.[81] For instance, a significant shift took place in 2013 during the gathering and disclosure of data by the police with a pilot of the Crime and Criminal Tracking Networks and Systems (CCTNS) launched by the Union Home Ministry. Its purpose was to interconnect about 15,000 police stations and an additional 5,000 offices of supervisory police officers across the country, and to also digitize data related to FIR registrations, investigations and charge sheets in all police stations, with a view to help in developing a national database of crime and criminals.[82] In 2017, the Union Government decided to launch an interoperable criminal justice system through integrating CCTNS with e-Courts, e-Prisons, Forensics and Prosecution.[83] A further development was the decision undertaken by the SCI in 2016 to mandate the uploading of all FIRs that had been registered across the country onto the police website, barring those in sensitive cases involving sexual offences.[84] This meant that

---

80 Devendra Damle and Tushar Anand, Problems with the e-Courts data (National Institute of Public Finance and Policy 29 July 2020) <https://www.nipfp.org.in/media/medialibrary/2020/07/WP_314_2020.pdf> accessed 16 April 2025; Kshitiz Verma, 'Analyzing HC-NJDG Data to Understand the Pendency in High Courts in India' Research Gate (2023) <https://www.researchgate.net/publication/327646919_Analyzing_HC-NJDG_Data_to_Understand_the_Pendency_in_High_Courts_in_India> accessed 17 April 2025; Enfold Proactive Health Trust, *The Possibilities of eCourts Data for Advancing Research on Law Implementation* (2025); Bibrek Debroy and Aditya Sinha, 'Data in the Dock: A Little-Noted Flaw in the Judicial System Is the Recording of Incomplete & Wrong Information' (*The Times of India* blog, 27 May 2023) <https://timesofindia.indiatimes.com/blogs/voices/data-in-the-dock-a-little-noted-flaw-in-the-judicial-system-is-the-recording-of-incomplete-wrong-information-this-skews-calculations-of-disposal-rates-especially-for-old-cases/> accessed 17 April 2025; Tushar Anand and Karan Gulati, 'The Unrealised Potential of Judicial Data' (*The Indian Express*, 18 December 2020).

81 In India, the judiciary, at all levels, does not have an exclusive data centre and is entirely dependent on the NIC to provide data hosting facilities.

82 'Govt Launches Crime Tracking Pilot Project' (*The Hindu*, 17 November 2021) <https://www.thehindu.com/news/national/Govt-launches-crime-tracking-pilot-project/article12289850.ece> accessed 18 January 2025.

83 'Inter-Operable Criminal Justice System (ICJS)' (Ministry of Home Affairs, Government of India) <https://www.mha.gov.in/en/commoncontent/inter-operable-criminal-justice-system-icjs> accessed 18 January 2025.

84 *Youth Bar Assn of India v. Union of India* (2016) 9 SCC 473 [11.4].

a large volume of personal information, including unverified allegations concerning individuals and entities, was available online. These measures were mandated at a time when the historic judgment of the SCI recognizing the fundamental right to privacy had not been pronounced.[85]

With the much-promised data security legislation not made operational,[86] there are no statutory safeguards for the litigants whose information is vulnerable to theft, misuse or distortion, and no corresponding statutory responsibility on the judiciary yet.[87] And then there is the issue of litigants approaching the court to request the deletion of references to their names and/or personal information forming part of an order or judgment that already stands uploaded on the internet and which is available readily on any of the search engines.[88] The Court is yet to find an answer to their seeking to enforce their 'right to be forgotten' or right to 'remain hidden'.[89] The rules on live-streaming of proceedings of the SCI is still in the making. Meanwhile, some of the HCs have their own set of rules.[90] This, apart from rendering enforcement weak, makes it possible for unscrupulous users of the net to selectively pick out bits of the video-recordings and sensationalize them in order to attract viewership and consequently monetize the 'hits'.[91]

---

85 The SCI recognized the right to privacy as a fundamental right in *KS Puttaswamy (Privacy-9J) v. Union of India* (2017) 10 SCC 1. This decision was pronounced on 24 July 2017, a year after the judgment in *Youth Bar Assn. of India* (n 84).

86 The Digital Personal Data Protection Act 2023 has not been operationalized yet.

87 The digitization of court proceedings and records brings the risk of unauthorized access and potential exposure of sensitive information. The Data Protection and Privacy (DPDP) Act plays a crucial role in regulating the collection, storage, processing and sharing of personal data. Compliance with these regulations involves implementing robust encryption, access controls and secure storage methods. Regular security audits and assessments are to be essential to identify and rectify vulnerabilities.

88 The Madras HC in *Karthick Theodore v. Registrar General* WAMD No 1901/2021 vide order dated 27 February 2023 ordered Indian Kanoon to take down the judgment. The Delhi HC in *Jorawer Singh Mundy v. Union of India* WP(C) No 3918/2021 (vide order dated 12 April 2021) granted interim relief to the petitioner and directed Indian Kanoon to block the judgment from being accessed.

89 The SCI in *Ikanoon Software Development Pvt Ltd v. Karthick Theodore* SLP(C) No 15311/2024 (vide order dated 24 July 2024) has stayed the Madras HC judgment in *Karthick Theodore v. Registrar General* (n 88), and has kept the question of law open for adjudication.

90 The Gujarat High Court (Live Streaming of Court Proceedings) Rules 2021; The High Court of Orissa Live Stream Proceeding Rules 2021; Live Steaming and Recording of Court Proceedings Rules of the High Court of Delhi 2022. See also, SCI Model Rules, 2022.

91 Siddhi Nigam, 'Madhya Pradesh High Court Frowns Upon Reels, Memes of Live-Streamed Court Proceedings, Orders to Take Them Down' (*LiveLaw*, 5 November 2024) <https://www.livelaw.in/high-court/madhya-pradesh-high-court/madhya-pradesh-high-court-live-streaming-court-proceedings-videos-sharing-social-media-misuse-274265> accessed 18 January 2025. During the hearing of the Kolkata rape and murder case, Senior Advocate Kapil Sibal requested the Court to stop the live

There have been, not infrequently, instances of the courts' websites being hacked,[92] rendering vulnerable the court-controlled digital data repositories. This would require periodic security audits, but as of now, there appears to be no clear set of binding advisories issued by the e-Committee.[93] The e-Committee is also yet to find out how the success in the 'islands of excellence' in some HCs can be scaled up for replication across the courts in the country.[94] It will need to issue advisories on both the appropriate software and hardware that can be relied upon to cater to the particular needs of the judiciary. This will have to be on a regular basis considering the speed at which technology becomes outdated.[95] There is also a genuine concern regarding these measures that extensively use technology for enhancing the 'efficiency' of courts possibly hampering access to justice in the real sense. Only a thorough review, in an introspective mode, can address these concerns.

To effectively utilize the full potential of the proposed measures, the e-Committee will have to devise intensive hands-on training for judges and court staff and even lawyers at all levels. Having video tutorials or online training does not seem to have worked thus far. The e-Committee itself will have to broad-base itself; it will have to bring in judges of both the HCs and the SCI with sufficiently long tenures and with an aptitude for technology to devise the plans and ensure continuity in their execution. There is also a

---

proceeding after disturbing comments were made against the advocates appearing for West Bengal. See, Sunil Prabhu, 'Kapil Sibal's "No Livestream" Request, Chief Justice's "Open Court" Reply' (*NDTV*, 17 September 2024) <https://www.ndtv.com/india-news/kapil-sibals-no-livestream-request-chief-justices-open-court-reply-6584394> accessed 18 January 2025.

92 'Supreme Court's YouTube Channel Hacked to Promote XRP Cryptocurrency' (*The Hindu*, September 20, 2024); Subrata Chattoraj, 'Calcutta High Court Live-Stream Hacked, Investigation Launched by Cyber Crime Department' (*The Times of India*, 29 October 2024).

93 Judges of constitutional courts, judicial officers and the staff have been provided individual email IDs by the NIC but these are not user-friendly. As a result, Gmail is still the most preferred mode of communication, even for official business undertaken by the judiciary as a whole. It might surprise the lay reader to know that many a draft judgment is prepared and stored on digital devices on files that are not password-protected.

94 Although the Kerala High Court developed an in-house e-filing system and was willing to share the source-code, it was not possible to customize that system for other HCs as was realized when the author was the CJ of the Orissa HC. This has delayed the transition to the next stage of e-filing in these HCs, particularly since the e-Committee is yet to formally launch the e-filing 4.0 version that it claims to have developed.

95 Chris Cancialosi, 'Outdated Tech Is Costing You More Than You Think' (*Forbes*, 16 August 2017) <https://www.forbes.com/sites/chriscancialosi/2017/08/16/outdated-tech-is-costing-you-more-than-you-think/> accessed 18 January 2025.

need to issue a checklist of do's and don'ts – for example, eschewing the lazy temptation of 'cut and paste' that can cause embarrassment to both lawyers and judges,[96] and to properly acknowledge the sources of texts to avoid the charge of plagiarism.[97]

Artificial Intelligence in judicial functions can introduce bias and lack transparency, raising ethical concerns.[98] There are already instances of ChatGPT generated fictitious cases being cited in Indian courts.[99] Addressing this issue involves establishing ethical guidelines for AI use, ensuring transparency in algorithmic decision-making, and regularly auditing AI systems for bias. Striking a balance between automation and human supervision is crucial to maintaining fairness and justice.

Clear protocols and governance frameworks are essential for controlling the use of technological tools. Establishing accountability mechanisms for errors or misuse ensures responsible implementation. Transparency in processes, decisions and the functioning of technology is vital for maintaining public trust and confidence in the judicial system's integrity. At the end of the day, the user of the judicial system has to have a satisfactory answer to the following question: Will these measures improve both access to justice as well as the quality of justice?

---

[96] In the case of *UPSC v. Bibhu Prasad Sarangi* (2021) 4 SCC 516, the SCI observed that the cut-copy-paste practice followed by courts had become common and noted that the National Judicial Academy may take up the issue; Recently, The Court of Appeal of the Singapore Supreme Court affirmed the setting aside of an arbitral award rendered by a three-member tribunal comprising a former CJI and two former CJs after finding that nearly half of the award from 'copy-pasted' from two other awards passed by the same presiding arbitrator, Aaratrika Bhaumik, 'Singapore's top court sets aside 'copied and pasted' arbitral award passed by former CJI Dipak Misra-led tribunal'(*The Hindu*, 9 April, 2025).

[97] 'Delhi HC Bench apologises after law intern copies tracts from foreign journal into its judgment' (The News Minute, 9 December 2015) <https://www.thenewsminute.com/news/delhi-hc-bench-apologises-after-law-intern-copies-tracts-foreign-journal-its-judgment-36667> accessed 17 April 2025; The software 'IThenticate' was deployed to check each of the essays in this book to ensure their originality.

[98] 'Artificial Intelligence: Examples of Ethical Dilemmas' (UNESCO, 21 April 2023) <https://www.unesco.org/en/artificial-intelligence/recommendation-ethics/cases> accessed 18 January 2025.

[99] The Karnataka HC recently called for action to be taken against a civil court judge for citing non-existent Supreme Court and Delhi HC judgments in an order, which probably were due to the use of a resource lke ChatGPT, Ayesha Arvind, 'Karnataka HC proposes action against judge for citing non-existent rulings' (*The Hindustan Times*, 27 May 2025); A judge in the Punjab and Haryana High Court openly acknowledged the use of ChatGPT in collating research while deciding a bail application, Manjeet Sehgal, 'Punjab and Haryana HC asks ChatGPT about bail when assault is laced with cruelty. Here's what it said' (*India Today*, 28 March 2023); 'Relying On AI For Legal Research Risky, Platforms Like ChatGPT Have Generated Fake Case Citations:Justice Gavai' (*LiveLaw*, New Delhi, 11 March 2025) <https://www.livelaw.in/top-stories/relying-on-ai-for-legal-research-risky-platforms-like-chatgpt-have-generated-fake-case-citations-justice-gavai-286190> accessed 17 April 2025.

Epilogue

28 January 2025 in the SCI is a court working day, not easily comparable with the day of its inauguration seventy-five years earlier. There are, of course, some permanent features like judges, lawyers, their forms of dress, address and language, of paper books, records and files, of costs, uncertainties and delays, of there being too many cases for proportionately far too fewer judges.[100] What is markedly different though are the ubiquitous 'display boards', not just in the crowded corridors of the SCI but also on the handheld digital devices and computers of lawyers, litigants and just about anyone anywhere in the world! Lawyers can both watch and participate in the proceedings in any of the courtrooms in the SCI and in the HCs in virtual mode, and to a large extent, even before the district courts, irrespective of their geographical location or distance from anywhere in the world – the only requirement being that they must be 'properly' attired and remain in a fixed place (judges rightly frown on lawyers appearing in court hearings/proceedings while being present in moving vehicles).[101] Lawyers practising in the SCI can download from the Court's website the 'bookmarked' digital record of the case in which they have been engaged and hence operate in a totally 'paperless' mode, as can, of course, the judges who have before them, on the dais, appropriate digital devices. Visible additions to the courtroom are microphones on the sides of both judges and lawyers, large display screens for online appearances and of course, the grumbles, groans and disapprovals when the network is poor, rendering the arguing lawyer invisible or inaudible. And yet, some lawyers know, and some judges make it obvious, that it is preferable to be physically present in court to present arguments. That might take some time to change.

But the times have indeed changed. At the traffic signal outside the SCI premises at the junction of Tilak Marg and Bhagwan Das Road, there is a large digital display board, the Justice Clock, where on the changing screens are statistics on the pendency of cases in the SCI and for how long.[102] A daily

---

[100] Soutik Biswas, 'Supreme Court: Why India's Powerful Top Court Is in a "Crisis"' (BBC, 30 July 2023) <https://www.bbc.com/news/world-asia-india-66292895> accessed 18 January 2025.

[101] A lawyer appearing online simultaneously before the SCI, HCs and Tribunals is now passé. It is also true that a majority of lawyers in India may still not be able to afford smart digital devices.

[102] On 31 May 2025, at 10.00 a.m., the total pendency figure in the SCI, according to this Justice Clock, was 81,801. Among these, cases that were more than twenty years old were 492 and those between ten and twenty years were 9,960.

reminder of the tasks that lay ahead not just for the institution but everyone concerned about its future.

These transformations are seemingly irreversible but must address the concerns of the users if they have to gain acceptance. Few would disagree that the Indian litigant of 2025 is not in a 'better' place than their counterpart in 1950. The SCI of 28 January 2050 will undoubtedly be different, but in a positive sense only if it is still not grappling with finding solutions to the same problems faced by 'We the people of India' when it began its journey seventy-five years ago.

The Supreme Court and the Next 25 Years

AN INTERVIEW WITH SRIRAM PANCHU

The Editor interviewed Sriram Panchu in October 2024 on his views on the issues and challenges faced by the justice system. Panchu has been a close observer of the courts and has contributed to public opinion-making through his writings in the print and social media. He played a foundational role in shaping the mediation movement in India.

The Editor's remarks and questions are in italics.

Judicial Delays

Editor: *You have been in the legal profession for nearly five decades and nearly three of them as a Senior Advocate. At close quarters, you have been a participant observer of the entire judicial process, including the Supreme Court of India [SCI]. The issue of growing pendency of cases, not just in the district courts and the High Courts (HCs) but also in the SCI, has been a cause for concern for many decades now. What in your view has led to this situation?*

Panchu: Since this book is about the SCI, I will focus on the SCI. It is the highest court in the land and the last resort for conventional litigation. It also has original jurisdiction, which means it is the court of first instance when the disputes are between states, or between states and the union. We have Article 131 of the Constitution for that purpose. Many of the river-water disputes are subject matter of such suits, involving the states. Under Article 143, the SCI, in its advisory jurisdiction, renders opinions on questions specifically referred to it by the President of India. Then there are the routine writ petitions (under Article 32), special leave petitions (SLPs) both civil and criminal, tax and revenue cases and an overarching public interest (PIL) jurisdiction. As of today, there are well over 85,000 cases pending in the SCI alone.[1]

[1] There are over 5,400,000 pending cases in HCs and over 45,000,000 pending cases in district courts.

The SCI has thirty-four judges and at least fifteen Benches (of either two or three judges) on any given day. There are larger Benches of five or more judges, specially constituted from among these thirty-four judges to hear questions of constitutional importance. Here again, the workload is considerable.[2] Managing this workload well requires a careful pruning of the cases that the Court is going to hear.

The constitutional scheme envisaged HCs to be the last point for litigation. If the case involved a 'substantial question of law', the HC would grant a certificate of leave to appeal to the SCI.[3] Over the years, this was given a go-by, and Article 136, which was the 'SLP jurisdiction' to be exercised sparingly, has constituted the bulk of the work of the SCI.

Week in and week out, hundreds of such SLPs are filed[4] against any conceivable order of an HC, including interim orders, procedural matters and decisions on bail petitions. On at least two days of the week, Mondays and Fridays (known as SLP days), the thirty-four judges sitting in Benches deal with a few hundred fresh SLPs.[5] It is not unusual for a SCI judge of an average age of sixty years to have to deal with at least sixty to sixty-five cases on a single day! This means that judges have no choice but to read the papers in advance[6] of the hearing. Nowhere else in the world does a judge of a Supreme Court have to deal with this kind of work pressure.[7]

Not surprisingly, given the backlog, there is an enormous compulsion on the

---

Data obtained from National Judicial Data Grid (NJDG), HCs of India, <https://njdg.ecourts.gov.in/hcnjdg_v2/?app_token=> accessed 24 February 2025.

[2] As of December 2024, there are seventeen, five and three cases pending before Benches of five, seven and nine judges respectively. Data obtained from the National Judicial Data Grid (NJDG), Supreme Court of India <https://scdg.sci.gov.in/scnjdg/?p=home&app_token=> accessed 24 February 2025.

[3] The Constitution of India 1950, arts 132–34.

[4] In 2023, 33,484 SLPs were filed and 25,379 were disposed of. In 2024, 28,252 SLPs were filed and 25,610 were disposed of, meaning that the Court virtually runs hard to stay in the same place as far as overall pendency is concerned. National Judicial Data Grid (NJDG), Supreme Court of India <https://scdg.sci.gov.in/scnjdg/?p=home&app_token=> accessed 24 February 2025.

[5] An average Monday and Friday of 2024 had between 450–500 fresh SLPs listed.

[6] Nick Robinson, 'The Structure and Functioning of the Supreme Court of India' in Gerald Rosenberg, Sudhir Krishnaswamy and Shishir Bail (eds), *A Qualified Hope: The Indian Supreme Court and Progressive Social Change* (CUP 2019) <https://ssrn.com/abstract=3483275> accessed 24 February 2025.

[7] The US Supreme Court, for instance, admits only 100–150, and of these, only 70–80 are set down for oral hearings. See, Supreme Court of the United States, 'Oral Arguments', <https://www.supremecourt.gov/oral_arguments/oral_arguments.aspx> accessed 24 February 2025.

SCI judges to have to decide 'how many cases to dismiss at the threshold' rather than 'how many cases to admit'. Even if one goes by the general rule of thumb that only one in ten fresh cases gets past the first door,[8] it could easily translate to many a 'good case' (involving a substantial question of law) being dismissed at the threshold, apart from the possibility of an unmcritorious case making the cut, leading to general dissatisfaction, if not disillusionment, among litigants and lawyers. There is no time for a long hearing on admission. This is monumental work. With this goes the best part of the week. Imagine a gardener spending half his time not tending to the flowers in his garden but deciding which not to tend to.

The above phenomenon leads to an entire army of Advocates-on-Record and Senior Counsel at the SCI, attempting to get their cases past the first post, week after week, no matter how slim the 'chance' might be. One could say that this is a problem created to a large extent by the SCI itself.

The SCI does not sit together (*en banc*) to decide cases. Naturally therefore the 'polyvocality' of the judges leads to conflicting viewpoints often leading to irreconcilable decisions of Benches of equal strength. This then leads to further rounds of 'course correction' – therefore, more work. Typically, Benches comprise a senior judge and a junior judge, the latter often content to be led by the senior, which results in important questions of law basically being determined by one judge.

Editor: *How do you see a way out of this?*

Panchu: There is an urgent need for a larger strength of judges in Benches of the SCI that deal with the most important issues, and this can be done only by lessening the burden of the SCI and ensuring that the original scheme under the Constitution is implemented as intended. However, there is a lamentable decline in the quality of the HC judgments in the last seven decades. Some cases in the HC stop with single-judge Benches. Even in Division Benches, there are cases where the Bench is, for all practical purposes, a single-judge Bench. When a very junior judge sits with a senior judge, it is not really a

8 Robinson, 'The Structure and Functioning of the Supreme Court of India' (n 7).

Bench of two, it is one judge and one yes-man who says nothing even when he should. The HCs do go wrong quite a bit.

While it is true that HC decisions may require reconsideration and that the doors of the judiciary cannot be shut to those seeking justice, it is possible to envisage a new mechanism that would address both – reducing the workload of the SCI and the need to have a relook at HC judgments. An intermediate Court of Appeal between the HCs and the SCI is an answer that comes to my mind.

A Court of Appeal, with four to five circuit Benches – one in each region of the country – could hear appeals from the HCs. The hearing on admission could take place in online or physical mode; once a case has been admitted, the Court of Appeal should function online in the normal course. This will require all appeals to be filed in digital form and for the courts to be paperless. That this is a possibility was demonstrated when, during the COVID-19 period, our courts continued to function in online mode. However, the entire judicial infrastructure will have to be upgraded and maintained with professional expertise for this purpose.

It is important to ensure that while there would not be any need for a certificate of appeal from the HC to take matters to the Court of Appeal, it must be made mandatory for litigants to obtain a certificate from the Court of Appeal if they wish to approach the SCI. Thus, as a matter of routine, the Court of Appeal becomes the final arbiter of disputes. The discretionary and extraordinary nature of the SCI's jurisdiction under Article 32 and Article 142 must be preserved by the judges to prevent the top court from being overburdened and flooded with matters indiscriminately filed from all over the country. While the SCI may be petitioned, this must be by written submissions demonstrating that the law needs to be clarified or precedents overturned, not just that the case has been wrongly decided on facts.

If this suggestion works, the SCI could well function with a reduced strength of twenty-five judges, sitting as five Benches of five judges each. Their workload would be restricted to Article 32 petitions, matters under the original jurisdiction of the Court, references made to it by the President, cases that reach the Court through an appeal from the Court of Appeal, and a very sparing use of petitions by special leave.

Editor: *This suggestion of an intermediate Court of Appeal has been made earlier*[9] *but, did not find favour either with the SCI itself*[10] *or the SCI lawyers. One of the issues that might arise is an increased burden on the Court of Appeals because of the proximity of its regional Bench to the prospective litigant. Secondly, with the governments and government bodies (both Centre and state) being the major litigators, this would hardly deter them from challenging every adverse order from the HC to the Court of Appeals. Thirdly, a move that introduces one more tier of litigation, with concomitant increase in costs and delays, can hardly be said to be litigant-friendly. How best can one respond to these concerns?*

Panchu: As I see it, it will cost a lot less to take a matter to the Court of Appeal than to the SCI as at present. The emphasis on online arguments will lessen costs. Proximity to the litigant is another plus factor.

The idea is that litigation stops with the Court of Appeal, and only those matters that are scrutinized as needing the corrective or clarificatory eye of the SCI should go further, as far as conventional litigation is concerned.

On the issue of costs to the litigant, let us start getting realistic in recognizing that there must be deterrents for non-meritorious cases or frivolous matters. Governments and corporate litigants especially should cough up the entire cost of litigation borne by the successful other side.

The Court of Appeal Benches will have the time to examine matters coming up before them, and if they exercise discretion and discrimination well, I don't see that this additional tier presents a problem. The emphasis in the Court of Appeal should be on written submissions with time-controlled minimal oral arguments, with judges having both the time and the inclination to read the papers in advance.

Similarly, this would also require a relook at the position of the CJI as the master of the roster. Deciding the roster cannot be left solely at the hands

---

9 KK Venugopal, 'Towards a Holistic Restructuring of the Supreme Court of India' (RK Jain Memorial Lecture, 30 January 2010) <https://www.jeywin.com/wp-content/uploads/2009/12/Towards-Holistic-Restructuring-of-the-Supreme-Court-of-India.pdf> accessed 24 February 2025; See also, Law Commission of India, 229th Report on Need for Division of the Supreme Court into a Constitution Bench at Delhi and Cassation Benches in Four Regions at Delhi, Chennai/Hyderabad, Kolkata, and Mumbai (Ministry of Law and Justice, Government of India, 5 August 2009) <https://cdnbbsr.s3waas.gov.in/s3ca0daec69b5adc880fb464895726dbdf/uploads/2022/08/2022081088-2.pdf> accessed 24 February 2025.

10 Union Minister for Law and Justice, 'Answer to Starred Question No 291 on 17 December 2021 in the Lok Sabha regarding "Regional Benches of Supreme Court"' (Lok Sabha, 17 December 2021) <https://sansad.in/getFile/loksabhaquestions/annex/177/AS291.pdf?source=pqals> accessed 24 February 2025.

of the CJI. This is too much power considering the way the Court functions. Considering that the new system would have only five Benches and the variety of cases that reach the Court would be severely limited, a simple system that provides definiteness and clarity to litigants regarding the way cases would be allotted to the Benches is the need of the hour. Such a clear, concise system with exceptions carved out only for special cases would streamline the way the Court functions and prevent the practice of Bench-hunting. The power to constitute the Bench can often enough determine the result. It cannot be left to one person even if he or she is the CJI. If appointments to the Court cannot be left solely to the CJI, then neither should the power to constitute Benches. It would be far better to have a systemic clear and well-understood method for Bench composition, paying attention to éxpertise and seniority and achieving the best balance possible. Sensitive matters may demand special allocation, but that too should be a group decision.

Judicial Appointments

Editor: *You have been critical of the present Collegium system for the appointment of judges to the HCs and the SCI. Going forward, what according to you might work best?*

Panchu: In my view, the Collegium system suffers from a severe lack of transparency and is terribly insular. This is a serious problem considering the power that judges of the SCI hold.

Among the alternatives suggested, one is by the National Commission to Review the Working of the Constitution in 2002. Their suggestion was to have a National Judicial Commission composed of five members – the CJI, two senior-most judges of the SCI, the Union Minister for Law and Justice, and an eminent person nominated by the President of India after consulting with the CJI. This would be a great improvement. It gives the judges primacy but not exclusivity, and brings in other voices to ask crucial questions. If the SCI in the National Judicial Appointments Commissions case had just limited the number of eminent persons to one instead of two and upheld the Act, it would have arrived at this result, sorted out the issue once and for all and we would not be seeing delays and obstructive tactics. we could have then insisted that decisions taken at the table are forthwith implemented. Recently, Rohinton Nariman J has made a case for a Permanent Commission consisting of the CJI and four retired judges who would be chosen by judges of the SCI excluding the CJI based on recommendations by select practising lawyers of the SCI and HC Bars.[11] This Commission would recommend names for elevation to the Court and their recommendations must be followed unless the National Commission objects for reasons to be recorded in writing. The benefit of this arrangement would be that retired judges will have the time to properly scrutinize the background and suitability of candidates, something which sitting judges do not possess.

The Permanent Commission must function in an honest, transparent and ethical manner. In the United Kingdom, applications are accepted for judicial positions; the benefit of that needs to be weighed. What is more important is that the Committee must meet people, study candidate records, meet the candidates and conduct an extensive review before recommending a name for appointment of judges. In appointments to the SCI, seniority must not be the binding factor, nor should the field be limited to only HC judges; it is time we had an academic voice in the Court. In such a system, it will be possible to get the best candidates – independent judges who go by the Constitution and are honest, capable and good judges.

It is also necessary then, to set a uniform age of retirement for judges of the HCs, Courts of Appeal and the SCI, say sixty-five, sixty-seven or even seventy. This would take care of the problem of a clamour for moving up the judicial ladder. A senior HC judge may well decide to continue in the HC as CJ rather than become a junior SCI judge with barely three years to go.

Editor: *On the one hand we have a multitude of tribunals created by statute that require to be filled up with former judges and on the other it encourages an unhealthy practice of expectations by those close to retirement of being considered for such appointments, which would be under the overall control of the Central or state governments. Is there a way out of this paradox?*

Panchu: I think we should seriously relook the need for Tribunals. Their composition, functioning and output make out a good case for dismantling them. We have denuded the HCs of significant portions of their traditional

11 'Former SC Judge Rohinton Nariman Moots a Permanent Commission to Appoint Judges' (*The Hindu*, 22 April 2024) <https://www.thehindu.com/News/Cities/Chennai/Former-Sc-Judge-Rohinton-Nariman-Moots-a-Permanent-Commission-to-Appoint-Judges/article68090719.ece> accessed 24 February 2025.

jurisdiction by creating these tribunals – company matters, service matters for a start – and that has had deleterious effects on the justice system in several ways.

The benefit or 'carrot' of executive discretionary post-retirement appointments as Governors, Chairpersons of Commissions, etc., has a severe impact on the perception of the judiciary's independence and is something that must be rectified post-haste.

An interesting idea here could be the creation of a cadre of public service. On retirement, judges could be given the option to enter such a cadre. Appointments to commissions, tribunals and even governorship should be made from this cadre, which could include non-judges too. Appointments must be vetted and even Court referred arbitrations must go to members of this cadre. Appointments as Governors must go by rotation. Members of this cadre must be taken care of with post-retirement benefits for life. Their workload/burden can be reduced post the age of seventy. Judges who want to do private arbitrations post-retirement may do so independently outside the envisaged system but would not receive court-referred matters.

This system will also have the much-needed effect of promoting arbitrations and alternate dispute resolution (ADR) by making it simpler. Through this system, arbitrations can be made time-bound and reasonable costs/fees can be fixed.

Arbitration

Editor: *That brings us to the issues currently plaguing both major forms of ADR, namely arbitration and mediation. Let us begin with arbitration. Haven't we brought into arbitration all the bad practices of formal court-based litigation, thus making it an inefficacious and expensive remedy? What are your thoughts on this?*

Panchu: I believe that one way to deal with the problem is to insist on a fixed fee for the entire arbitration and adhere uncompromisingly to the time schedules fixed in advance. In addition, witness action could be discouraged by requiring parties to argue on the basis of pleadings and documents on record; if that cannot be avoided then shorten the cross-examination of witnesses and limit oral arguments again within strict timelines. I see no option but to adopt the best practices of international arbitration, particularly in awarding of costs and quality and timeliness of awards.

My personal experience has been that where parties had reached the point of 'litigation fatigue', they were willing to go in for mediation, which could often end in a mutually acceptable settlement.

Mediation

Editor: *You have been an earnest promoter of mediation as an effective ADR mechanism. However, it cannot work for a large chunk of pending criminal cases. Also, even in civil disputes, where one of the contesting parties is the government, it does not seem to work. Any thoughts on this?*

Panchu: While I agree that the government is a major litigant, I do not see why they should not be encouraged to participate in mediation, particularly in the area of commercial and property litigation and arbitration, which involve a large number of awards, claims, several rounds of litigation and huge delays. Interestingly, when I recently broached the topic with the Union Minister for Transport, he appeared to respond favourably but with a caveat – that the bureaucrats may be reluctant as they apprehend vigilance inquiries or proceedings down the line. So, I said, create some high-level committee, staff it by a SCI judge, ex-Central Bureau of Investigation, Central Vigilance Commission, whoever. Let your officers negotiate and bring the draft settlement to this committee. The committee either says 'yes', or it says 'no', or it says 'go and modify'. But once the committee gives its approval, there should be no going back on the settlement and there should be immunity for the negotiating officers. If this happens, you will find a large number of cases being settled.

There is some forward movement on these lines in the Mediation Act, 2023, however not to the extent I mentioned above.

A recent government memorandum has gone to the extent of dampening arbitration and encouraging mediation, and that is a welcome step.[12]

There is a lot that the court – including the SCI – can do at every level to utilize mediation, which yields practical solutions with far less cost and time, and respects relationships. Courts should pay mediators well. They should send

12 Procurement Policy Division, Department of Expenditure, Ministry of Finance, Government of India, 'Office Memorandum: Vivad se Vishwas II (Contractual Disputes)' (No F1/7/2022-PPD, 29 December 2023) <https://doe.gov.in/files/circulars_document/Vivad_se_Vishwas_II_Contractual_Disputes_2.pdf> accessed 24 February 2025.

cases to mediation; and these can even be drawn from the backlog of arrears (the backlog is a nightmare for judges, a treasure trove for mediators). There is no need to ask the government for funds to pay mediators in the court system; simply post successful mediations where the stakes are substantial before a judge, and you will see parties willingly making payment. Apart from this, courts should encourage the growth of private mediation by asking parties to find their own mediator before accessing the court-annexed mediation system. Four simple steps. Just see the difference it will make.

I must add that not every judge or lawyer, however brilliant, can be a good mediator. It requires training. I have been arguing for a dedicated mediation service, Indian Mediation Service (permanent or short service), where we would have trained mediators drawn from a variety of disciplines of which law is but one. Building strong and independent systems of ADR would go a long way in increasing the efficiency of the courts, and mediation would play a key role in this process.

The newly minted Mediation Act, which could have encouraged this, is – as you know – yet to be fully operationalized.[13]

Editor: *Given the main areas of practice where mediation is likely to work such as family law, property law, contracts between private parties, controlled by a niche set of lawyers in the civil courts, there is a discernible trend of lawyers discouraging their clients to settle during a mediation process. Would you agree?*

Panchu: In mediation, the parties become the chief drivers to settlement once they see the possibilities. Secondly, there are ways to incentivize lawyers to settle. All that is needed is to adopt the concept of 'mediation settlement fee' and get over the difficulty caused by a per-hearing fee, which is what can discourage a lawyer representing a client in mediation. This does not offend our rule against champerty – the fee being based on the result. That was to discourage litigation. Here, we have a result-based fee to bring litigation to an end.

---

[13] The Mediation Act, 2023. Some provisions of the Act were notified on 9 October 2023. <https://legalaffairs.gov.in/sites/default/files/4.Notification_of_enforcement_dated_09.10.2023.pdf> accessed 12 January 2025.

Court Administration

Editor: *If we could move on to the topic of enhancing the efficiency of court administration through technology. Recently, both in Kerala and Orissa, there has been considerable success in the digitization of records and the introduction of paperless courts. Do you think that this could happen across the country?*

Panchu: I believe so. The use of technology in the court system must be made pervasive with the use of satellite bandwidth. Online hearings and disposal of cases must become the norm, but that is not enough. There must be a complete digitization of all records of the courts, and courts must truly become paperless. All filings, petitions, orders, etc., can be streamlined through a digital system, and each judge can be given a technical assistant to help them navigate the new system. This would make justice more accessible and the maintenance of records more secure. Steps have already been taken in this direction as a way of adapting to the pandemic, but intentional efforts must be made to take this system further and ensure the digitization of the judicial system.

I also believe that, once it becomes clear that all these moves really benefit the litigant and not just the courts, the resistance of one section of the Bar to these changes will die down. Take, for instance, the live-streaming of proceedings. The initial doubts of the sceptics have obviously been overcome, and we find more and more courts prepared to live-stream their proceedings. This can surely be regulated further by giving the lawyers and litigants the option of objecting to live-streaming a particular case where it might involve questions of privacy and confidentiality.

Judicial Education and Training

Editor: *So, let us finally talk about judicial education and training. You have been a resource person for the judicial academies, both the NJA (National Judicial Academy) at Bhopal and the state judicial academies at the locations of various HCs. Do you have suggestions on how the programmes offered at the academies can be tailored and executed to serve the judicial officers and judges better?*

Panchu: Judges at all levels require being constantly reminded of their role and the expectations that people have of them. They need to be fully oriented in the constitutional values, as much as in ground realities. I am personally of the view that most judges function behind a type of wall. I think fresh learning comes only when something is hugely exciting. Unless the resource person commands a lot of respect for her or his learning and experience, lectures in academies cannot be expected to bring about by themselves any change in judicial attitudes. We have to remember that judges rarely swim against the stream. Also, they are interested in what is immediately relevant for their functioning in the court, at a practical level.

In my view, both mentoring and peer-learning have a huge part to play in shaping a good judge. I believe the CJ of an HC, for instance, can play a significant role in pairing junior judges with senior ones in a way that facilitates this type of learning.

Editor: *Any concluding remarks?*

Panchu: The task of reformation of the system as a whole is indeed daunting. It consists of several parts, each in a different stage of transition and needing specific attention to detail. It may be difficult to find a single broad overarching principle to guide the transformation. It is bound to be a work in progress. What I do hope for, however, is that twenty-five years from now, we would have far less congested courts and less dissatisfied litigants.

Acknowledgements

A book that brings together essays from a diverse range of contributors could not have been possible without each of them willing to take on the challenging task of critically examining the evolution of the law through more than seven decades of the SCI. The Editor would like to thank each of them for their commitment and patience through the execution of this project.

For encouraging the idea of this book, believing in its possibility and then staying the course, the Editor would like to thank Devangshu Datta, Commissioning Editor at Juggernaut Books. A big thank you to the copyediting team, and in particular, Nishtha Kapil, Rhea Gupta and Krishna Sawant, for considerably enhancing the readability of the final product.

The efforts of Maitreya Subramaniam and Ninni Susan Thomas have ensured that each of the essays and the interviews were carefully checked for factual accuracy and consistency.

Thank you to Rupali Samuel and Sumedha Sarkar for the initial reading of some of the essays and comments. MA Karthik and Pallak Bhagat were of great assistance in the final reads for some of the essays.

The Editor is grateful to Rachita Taneja, Satish Acharya, Manjul, Sandeep Adhwaryu, Pencilashan and Rohan Chakravarthy for readily agreeing to contribute their cartoons to the book, and working within tight timelines. The book has been enriched by their insightful work.

For the book's cover design, a sincere thank you to Antra K for her patience in incorporating various inputs and for bringing a personal touch by visiting the Supreme Court premises to capture the essence of the project.

The generous contribution of AdalatAI, who offered to transcribe the interviews, is greatly appreciated.

Thanks also to the dedicated staff in the Editor's chambers and the many interns who contributed their time and efforts. Thank you, Zain Bhana for all the help in the final lap.

Finally, the Editor would like to express his gratitude to the many unnamed individuals who believed in and supported this project along the way.

Topic Index

Page Numbers with *fn* indicate foot note.